THE LAW OF IN

MW01181521

For decades, Martti Koskenniemi has not just been an influential writer in international law; his work has caused a significant shift in the direction of the field. This book engages with some of the core questions that have animated Koskenniemi's scholarship so far. Its chapters attest to the breadth and depth of Koskenniemi's oeuvre and the different ways in which he has explored these questions. Koskenniemi's work is applied to a wide range of functional areas in international law and is discussed in relation to an even broader range of theoretical perspectives, including history, political theory, sociology and international relations theory. These invaluable insights have been expertly brought together by the volume editors, who identify the key and common themes of many of the book's contributions. This volume demonstrates the importance of critical legal scholarship in the ways international law is enacted, shaped and reshaped over time.

WOUTER WERNER is Professor of Public International Law at the Centre for the Politics of Transnational Law at Vrije Universiteit, Amsterdam.

MARIEKE DE HOON is Assistant Professor of International Law at the Centre for the Politics of Transnational Law at Vrije Universiteit, Amsterdam.

ALEXIS GALÁN is a post-doctoral researcher at the Angelo Sraffa Department of Legal Studies at Bocconi University, Milan.

THE LAW OF INTERNATIONAL LAWYERS

Reading Martti Koskenniemi

WOUTER WERNER

Vrije Universiteit, Amsterdam

MARIEKE DE HOON

Vrije Universiteit, Amsterdam

ALEXIS GALÁN

Università Commerciale Luigi Bocconi, Milan

CAMBRIDGE
UNIVERSITY PRESS

CAMBRIDGE
UNIVERSITY PRESS

University Printing House, Cambridge CB2 8BS, United Kingdom

One Liberty Plaza, 20th Floor, New York, NY 10006, USA

477 Williamstown Road, Port Melbourne, VIC 3207, Australia

314-321, 3rd Floor, Plot 3, Splendor Forum, Jasola District Centre, New Delhi - 110025, India

79 Anson Road, #06-04/06, Singapore 079906

Cambridge University Press is part of the University of Cambridge.

It furthers the University's mission by disseminating knowledge in the pursuit of education, learning and research at the highest international levels of excellence.

www.cambridge.org
Information on this title: www.cambridge.org/9781316643983
DOI: 10.1017/9781108147620

First published 2017
First paperback edition 2018

A catalogue record for this publication is available from the British Library

ISBN 978-1-107-19318-5 Hardback
ISBN 978-1-316-64398-3 Paperback

CONTENTS

v

CONTRIBUTORS

Editors

ALEXIS GALÁN is a post-doctoral researcher at the Angelo Sraffa Department of Legal Studies at Bocconi University. Prior to that, he did his PhD at the European University Institute, wherein he critically analysed the importance of legitimacy in international law. His recent research has delved into the geographical imagination of international constitutional law and the plural character of authority within European private law.

MARIEKE DE HOON is Assistant Professor at Vrije Universiteit, Amsterdam. Her research focusses on the law and politics of international criminal justice, use of force and human rights. Her PhD dissertation was on the law and politics of the crime of aggression. Moreover, she is Director of the Netherlands Office and Senior Counsel at the Public International Law and Policy Group (PILPG), where she provides legal assistance to clients in conflict and post-conflict situations with regard to international criminal law, transitional justice, peace negotiations, post-conflict rule of law development and human rights redress.

WOUTER WERNER is Professor of Public International Law at the Free University, Amsterdam. His recent work has focussed on imaginaries of the future in international law as well as on cinematic representations of international criminal law. Wouter Werner is co-director of the Centre for the Politics of Transnational Law, www.ceptl.org.

Chapter Contributors

JUTTA BRUNNÉE is Professor of Law and Metcalf Chair in Environmental Law, University of Toronto, where she previously served as Associate Dean of Law, Graduate (2010–14) and Interim Dean (2014). She has published widely in the areas of public international law and international environmental law. She is co-author of *Legitimacy and Legality in International Law: An Interactional Account* (Cambridge, 2010), which was awarded the American Society of International Law's 2011 Certificate of Merit for preeminent contribution to creative scholarship. She served on the Board of Editors of the *American Journal of International Law* (2006–16) and was elected Fellow of the Royal Society of Canada in 2013.

DAVID DYZENHAUS is Professor of Law and Philosophy at the University of Toronto and a Fellow of the Royal Society of Canada. He holds the Alfred Abel Chair of Law and was appointed in 2015 to the rank of University Professor. He is the author of *Hard Cases in Wicked Legal Systems: South African Law in the Perspective of Legal Philosophy* (1991/2010), *Legality and Legitimacy: Carl Schmitt, Hans Kelsen, and Hermann Heller in Weimar* (1997) and *Judging the Judges, Judging Ourselves: Truth, Reconciliation and the Apartheid Legal Order* (1998). In 2004 he gave the JC Smuts Memorial Lectures to the Faculty of Law, Cambridge University. These were published by Cambridge University Press in 2006 as *The Constitution of Law: Legality in a Time of Emergency*.

JAYE ELLIS is Associate Professor in the Faculty of Law and School of Environment and Acting Director of the School of Environment, McGill University. She chairs the Coordinating Committee of the International Environmental Law Interest Group, European Society of International Law, and teaches public international law, international environmental law and environmental epistemology and ethics. Current research projects focus on transnational law, intersections between law and science and rule of law in transnational and international spheres. Recent publications include 'Political Economy and Environmental Law: A Cost-Benefit Analysis' in Ugo Mattei and John D. Haskell, eds, *Research Handbook on Political Economy and Law* (2015); 'Stateless Law: From Legitimacy to Validity' in Helge Dedek and Shauna Van Praagh, eds, *Stateless Law: Evolving Boundaries of a Discipline* (2015); and 'Constitutionalisation of Nongovernmental Certification Programmes' in *Indiana Journal of Global Legal Studies* 20, no. 2 (2013).

MARTTI KOSKENNIEMI (b. 1953) is Academy Professor of International Law at the University of Helsinki and Director of the Erik Castrén Institute of International Law and Human Rights. He was a member of the Finnish diplomatic service in 1978–94 and of the International Law

Commission (UN) in 2002–6. He has held visiting professorships in, among other places, New York University, Columbia University, University of Cambridge, London School of Economics and Universities of Brussels, Melbourne, Paris, Sao Paulo and Utrecht. He is a Corresponding Fellow of the British Academy and has a doctorate hc. from the Universities of Uppsala, Frankfurt and McGill. His main publications include *From Apology to Utopia: The Structure of International Legal Argument* (1989/2005), *The Gentle Civilizer of Nations: The Rise and Fall of International Law 1870–1960* (2001) and *The Politics of International Law* (2011). He is currently working on a history of international legal thought from the late medieval period to the nineteenth century.

FRIEDRICH KRATOCHWIL studied philosophy, politics and classics at Munich and went as a Fulbright grantee to the US, where he received a MA from Georgetown University in international relations and a PhD in political science from Princeton University. He has published widely on international relations, social and political theory and international law and organization. From 2000 to 2004, he was the editor of the *European Journal of International Relations*, and he has served since the 1980s on editorial boards of political science, law and sociology journals in the US, Europe and Asia. He taught at the universities of Maryland, Columbia, Denver and Pennsylvania in the US before returning to Europe in 1995 and becoming chair of international relations at the LMU in Munich and at the European University Institute in Florence (2003–11). After his retirement, he has been Visiting Professor at Kyung Hee University at Seoul, the Central European University in Budapest and the PUC–Minas Gerais (Papal University) at Belo Horizonte, Brazil. His latest books were titled *The Puzzles of Politics* (2011) and *The Status of Law in World Society* (Cambridge, 2014). Presently he is finishing a book titled *Praxis: On Acting and Knowing.*

ANDREW LANG is Professor of Law at the London School of Economics, teaching public international law, with a specialty in international economic law. He has a combined BA/LLB from the University of Sydney, and his PhD is from the University of Cambridge. From 2004 to 2006, Lang was Junior Research Fellow at Trinity Hall, University of Cambridge. His research focusses on the relationship between law and expert knowledge, law and economic theory and sociological approaches to the study of international economic law.

SUSAN MARKS is Professor of International Law at the London School of Economics. She previously taught at the University of Cambridge and King's College London. Her research seeks to bring insights from critical social theory to the study of international law and human rights. She is the author of *The Riddle of All Constitutions* (2000) and, with Andrew Clapham, *International Human Rights Lexicon* (2000), and she edited *International Law on the Left* (Cambridge, 2008).

FRÉDÉRIC MÉGRET, PHD, is Associate Professor and Dawson Scholar at the Centre for Human Rights and Legal Pluralism, Faculty of Law, McGill University. He holds an LlB from King's College London, a DEA from the Université de Paris I and a PhD from the Graduate Institute of International Studies (Geneva) as well as a diploma from Sciences Po Paris. He publishes on international law, international human rights law, international criminal justice and the laws of war.

SAMUEL MOYN is Jeremiah Smith Jr. Professor of Law and Professor of History at Harvard University. His most recent books include *The Last Utopia: Human Rights in History* (2010) and *Christian Human Rights* (2015).

GREGOR NOLL is the Chair of International Law at the Faculty of Law, Lund University. His main areas of research are international refugee and migration law, human rights law, the theory of international law and international humanitarian law. Currently he is working on how neurotechnology, robotics and artificial intelligence impact international humanitarian law and human rights law, and he considers how our ontological history affects our way of operationalizing international law.

LILIANA OBREGÓN is Associate Professor of Law at the Universidad de los Andes in Bogotá, Colombia. She holds a law degree from the same university; an MA from the School of Advanced International Studies, Johns Hopkins University; and a doctoral degree (SJD) from Harvard University. She was a research scholar at the University of Helsinki from 2009 to 2012 under the direction of professors Martti Koskenniemi and Bo Strath. Obregón has been a visiting scholar or visiting professor at several universities in the Americas and Europe and has published broadly on international legal history. During 2016–17, she will be a David Rockefeller Center for Latin American Studies Fellow (Fall) and a Weatherhead Institute for Global History Fellow (Spring) at Harvard University to finish a book manuscript provisionally titled *Writing International Legal History during the Long Nineteenth Century: Lawyers as Global Historians (1750–1914)*.

ANNE ORFORD is ARC Kathleen Fitzpatrick Laureate Fellow, Redmond Barry Distinguished Professor and Michael D. Kirby Chair of International Law at Melbourne Law School, where she directs the Laureate Program in International Law. She holds the Raoul Wallenberg Visiting Chair in International Human Rights and Humanitarian Law at Lund University and has held numerous other visiting positions, including as Hedda Andersson Visiting Research Chair at Lund University, Visiting Professor at University Paris 1 Panthéon-Sorbonne, Torgny Segerstedt Visiting Professor at the University of Gothenburg and Senior Emile Noël Research Fellow at NYU Law School. Her publications include *International Authority and the Responsibility to Protect* (Cambridge, 2011), *Reading Humanitarian Intervention: Human Rights and the Use of Force in International Law* (Cambridge, 2003), the edited collection *International Law and Its Others* (Cambridge, 2006) and, as co-editor, *The Oxford Handbook of the Theory of International Law* (2016).

ERIC A. POSNER is Kirkland and Ellis Distinguished Service Professor of Law, University of Chicago. His books include *The Twilight of International Human Rights* (2014), *Economic Foundations of International Law* (with Alan Sykes, 2013), *Contract Law and Theory* (2011), *The Executive Unbound: After the Madisonian Republic* (with Adrian Vermeule, 2011), *Climate Change Justice* (with David Weisbach, 2010), *The Perils of Global Legalism* (2009), *Terror in the Balance: Security, Liberty and the Courts* (with Adrian Vermeule, 2007), *New Foundations of Cost-Benefit Analysis* (with Matthew Adler, 2006), *The Limits of International Law* (with Jack Goldsmith, 2005) and *Law and Social Norms* (2000). He is a Fellow of the American Academy of Arts and Sciences and a member of the American Law Institute.

NIKOLAS M. RAJKOVIC is Professor and Chair of International Law at Tilburg University (Netherlands), Adjunct Professor in International Law and International Relations at Kyung Hee University (South Korea) and a senior faculty member of Harvard Law School's Institute for Global Law and Policy (IGLP).

SAHIB SINGH is a post-doctoral researcher at the University of Helsinki. He is currently completing his PhD, titled 'Critique in Times of Crisis', at the University of Cambridge, under the supervision of Judge James Crawford. His publications have appeared in the *Leiden Journal of International Law* and the *British Yearbook of International Law*.

STEPHEN J. TOOPE is Director of the Munk School of Global Affairs at the University of Toronto. He was President and Vice-Chancellor of the University of British Columbia from 2006 to 2014. A former President of the Pierre Elliott Trudeau Foundation, and Dean of Law, McGill University, Toope also served as Law Clerk to the Rt. Hon. Brian Dickson of the Supreme Court of Canada. He was President of the Canadian Council on International Law and a member of the Executive Council of the American Society of International Law. Toope also served as Chair of the United Nations Working Group on Enforced and Involuntary Disappearances. He was made an Officer of the Order of Canada in 2015.

NIGEL D. WHITE is Professor of Public International Law at the University of Nottingham, formerly Professor of International Law at the University of Sheffield. He has held a full-time academic post since 1988 and a chair since 2000. He is currently Head of the School of Law at Nottingham and was previously Dean of the Faculty of Law at the University of Sheffield. As well as a number of co-authored and co-edited books, he is author of *Keeping the Peace* (2nd edn, 1997), *The UN System: Toward International Justice* (2002), *The Law of International Organisations* (3rd edn, 2016), *Democracy Goes to War: British Military Deployments under International Law* (2009), *Advanced Introduction to Conflict and Security Law* (2014) and *The Cuban Embargo under International Law: El Bloqueo* (2015).

ACKNOWLEDGEMENTS

This book began to take shape on a somewhat sunny day in September 2012 at the central station of Amersfoort, a small and lovely Dutch city east of Amsterdam. Although we had been discussing the idea of editing a volume that would critically engage with the writings of Martti Koskenniemi for a while by then, it was during our meeting in the 'glocal' Starbucks of Amersfoort that we decided to go ahead. We thought, and we still think, that despite all the attention given to Martti's oeuvre, including special issues in a variety of journals, there was still sufficient space to engage with his ideas from different angles, which is a testament to how varied and rich Martti's work is. Moreover, we aimed at going beyond previous contributions not only by focussing on Martti's texts and the particular claims raised in them but also by connecting the issues his oeuvre raises to broader trends that take place in international law and exploring what this means for the current state of international law and the role of the international lawyer that works with it. This double objective aimed to capture and follow Martti's 'spirit'. Anyone who has read even one of Martti's extensive scholarly contributions can attest to how he not only writes towards the 'profession' but is also equally preoccupied with pressing issues affecting international law. This book in your hands is the result of such intuition/feeling/sensation/hunch.

As with any type of collective endeavour, this book would not have arrived to its final destination without the help and support of many individuals and institutions. First and foremost, this volume would not have become the collection it has become without the extraordinary scholarship of its authors: we thank them for the exceptional chapters they delivered, for wanting to push the boundaries and for coming up with some really inventive ways to consider Martti's work and the law of international lawyers more generally. We are furthermore grateful to Jan Klabbers for thinking along with us in the early stages on how to give shape and form to this project. Midway through the development of this book, we had a most thought-provoking and inspiring authors' meeting in Amsterdam, 'Koskenniemi and His Critics: Reflections on the Past and Future of International Law' (10–12 April 2014). We are grateful to the Vrije Universiteit Amsterdam and COST (Cooperation in Science and Technology) for generously facilitating this meeting. We are particularly indebted to Tanja Aalberts, Juan Amaya-Castro, Geoffrey Gordon and Bas Schotel for providing extensive and insightful commentaries on the chapters that helped not only push the various chapters but also the book as a whole to the next level. And we thank all participants in this meeting for enthusiastic and exhilarating discussions and for pushing each other's work forward. Last, but certainly not least, we would like to thank Martti Koskenniemi. It cannot have been easy to trust others with probing and pushing one's oeuvre in the many directions that we could come up with, and we thank him for the confidence and trust he put in us to do this conscientiously. Moreover, we are grateful for his willingness to take the vulnerable position to participate in the authors' meeting and, in particular, for taking up the incredible challenge that the authors posed with their chapters to write the epilogue, pushing his own reflection on his writings yet again to another level, thereby accepting vulnerability in order to open up to critique and engage in the discussion on what this all means for international law and lawyers.

We hope you will get as much enjoyment from reading this book as we had making it.

Introduction

The Law of International Lawyers

WOUTER WERNER, MARIEKE DE HOON AND ALEXIS GALÁN

'Words are politics. When vocabularies change, things that previously could not be said, are now spoken by everyone; while what yesterday seemed obvious, can no longer be said at all. With a change of vocabularies, new speakers become authoritative'.[1] A few years ago, this is how Koskenniemi introduced his readers to an incisive critique of multi-disciplinary scholarship. Koskenniemi's emphasis on the political nature of words served a specific purpose, to warn international lawyers against the siren song of objectivity and neutrality that can be found in some schools in international relations today. However, the insight that speaking a language is a political act through which worlds are created or foreclosed transcends the specific context of current debates on multi-disciplinarity. For one, it also applies to the words of Martti Koskenniemi himself.

For decades, Martti Koskenniemi has not just been an influential writer in international law; together with a handful of other scholars[2] he has been nothing less than a game changer. After the publication of *From Apology to Utopia*, it became possible to speak of international law's indeterminacy in ways that did not exist before. Another game-changing act was performed with *The Gentle Civilizer of Nations*. The book transformed the self-image of the discipline, pointing at the nineteenth century, elitist-cosmopolitan roots of the profession and giving rise to a large number of studies dedicated to the history of international law as a professional and colonial enterprise. A third game-changing move occurred when Koskenniemi turned his attention to the problem of functional differentiation, expert rule and managerialism in international law. In a relatively short period of time, the politics of fragmentation, the perils of managerialism and the pitfalls of instrumentalism moved centre stage in debates on international law. With, at the time of the publication of this volume, a new upcoming

1

book, it is likely that the world of international law will be redirected again, this time towards a study of the close connections between sovereignty and property, international and domestic law as well as law between the fields of law, politics, diplomacy and morality.[3] Also the method chosen for the new book is likely to set an agenda for future research: a study of how, since the late middle ages up to the 1870s, individual jurists, theologians, philosophers, politicians and political scientists have used vocabularies of law to advance particular projects.

And indeed, with a change of vocabulary, new speakers became authoritative. While critical legal scholarship used to be a marginal enterprise in international law, it is now pretty much established as one of the ways in which international law can be studied. An illustration of the growing 'mainstreaming' of critical perspectives is the publication of a widely used textbook that adopts Koskenniemi's critical approach as a starting point.[4] Another indication is the slight unease within critical legal circles about their own success, which has spurred renewed reflections on the relation between power and critique.[5] However, it is not just the critical stream that has become authoritative; it is also (and even more) specific persons that came to enjoy authority to speak. By now, Martti Koskenniemi has been established as an authority in international law, as evidenced by countless invitations to act as keynote speaker, his role in the United Nations, special issues being dedicated to his work[6] and numerous references to his work in academic publications, almost as if an article on international law is incomplete without the invocation of the voice from Helsinki.

At first sight, the current popularity of Koskenniemi's work may come as a surprise. After all, his work poses fundamental challenges to what Judith Shklar has called the 'ethos of legalism'; an ethos that is still predominant among (international) lawyers today, including many of whom enthusiastically quote Koskenniemi's work.[7] Legalism, in Shklar's account, is an attitude made up of four interrelated elements:[8] (1) it views social relationships in terms of rights and duties as determined by more general rules; (2) it treats law as something 'out there', something that can be grasped through legal training and education; (3) it believes in the possibility to separate law from non-law (morality, politics, aesthetics etc.); and (4) it fears and fights arbitrariness. To underscore the latter point, Shklar affirmatively quotes De Tocqueville's observation that lawyers, 'if they prize freedom much, they generally value legality still more: they are less afraid of tyranny than of arbitrary power'.[9] Koskenniemi's work puts many of these elements into question. The idea that social relations would be governed by objective and non-arbitrary rules that substitute power for reason is fundamentally challenged by his indeterminacy thesis of legal argumentation. Moreover, for Koskenniemi law is not 'out there' but rather 'between us'. While his work knows many ruptures in topics, tones and arguments, there is one theme that runs through his oeuvre from the late 1980s until the present day, 'without international lawyers, there would have been no international law'.[10] Or, put differently, 'there is no access to legal rules or the legal meaning of international behaviour that is independent from the way competent lawyers see those things'.[11] Instead of treating law as something to be discovered through its sources or through naturally given categories, Koskenniemi refocuses attention to the ways in which argumentative structures, sensibilities, taboos, authorities etc. are constructed and contested in the professional field. Paradoxically, the focus away from international law as being 'out there' may also explain why Koskenniemi's work (eventually) resonated within such a wide audience. After all, international lawyers recognize his world as their own. Koskenniemi's work is about the things that international lawyers do, the grammar they use, the social worlds they inhibit, about the anxieties and hopes that drive the field, about the ways in which international lawyers reflect (or refuse to reflect) upon themselves as the ones that 'think and make international law'.

The insight that international law is (also) the product of the imagination of international lawyers constitutes the starting point of this volume. The chapters in this book reflect the breadth of Koskenniemi's oeuvre and thus vary widely in terms of substance, approach and political program. Yet, they all engage with the question what it means to make sense of the world through international law, and what it is to be an international lawyer. The chapters thereby also immediately speak to the work and person of Martti Koskenniemi, who has never set himself (totally) apart from the field he studies, critiques and defends. As a consequence, many of the oppositions, tensions and paradoxes that characterize the (international) legal profession somehow reappear in Koskenniemi's reflections upon international law and his ideas about legal scholarship. Without making any claim to be exhaustive, we have identified three (overlapping) oppositions or tensions that run through different parts of Koskenniemi's work from the late 1980s until the present day. None of the three are mere intellectual propositions; they reflect what international lawyers experience when they make interventions in the name of international law and they relate to some of the anxieties of contemporary international legal scholarship. Another way of considering them is as indicative of the different 'styles' that are available to international lawyers. The relevance, force and meaning of these styles are different in different contexts and how they are put to use depends on the 'politics, fears and passions' of the individual lawyer.[12]

The *first* pertains to the complicated relation between the indeterminacy of international law and the 'culture of formalism'. As Koskenniemi sets out in the epilogue to *From Apology*, international law is indeterminate because 'it is based on contradictory premises and seeks to regulate a future in regard to which even single actors' preferences remain unsettled'.[13] As a result, any conceivable position can be defended in terms of international law.[14] And yet, when Koskenniemi expresses sympathy for Wolfgang Friedmann's stance in the 1966 debates on the US intervention in the Dominican Republic, it is precisely because Friedmann defends a legal mind-set, the reality of international law and the integrity of the legal profession. In this way, Friedmann expresses the anti-formalist style of legal argumentation that is at the heart of Koskenniemi's culture of formalism. Moreover, when international law is under threat of liberal universalism, managerialism or certain forms of interdisciplinary scholarship, Koskenniemi defends it as the vocabulary to express injustices on a global scale, while characterizing the (international) rule of law as another 'name for the external institutions that administer what is a moral-political project'.[15] Here again, he links the culture of formalism to an anti-instrumentalist understanding of international law. Of course, there is no necessary contradiction between the indeterminacy thesis and the culture of formalism. In some important respects, lack of determinacy is rather a precondition for the idea of international law as a moral-political project that cannot be reduced to merely an instrument for higher purposes.[16] Nevertheless, arguing about international law in terms of the indeterminacy thesis comes with quite different styles, anxieties and purposes than arguing about international law in terms of a culture of formalism. This is evidenced in the different chapters in part one of this volume, which take up different relationships between indeterminacy and formalism. Building on different intellectual traditions and adopting quite different styles of reasoning, formalism and indeterminacy are discussed by Gregor Noll, David Dyzenhaus, Nigel White, Jaye Ellis, Eric Posner and Jutta Brunnée & Stephen Toope.

The *second* is about the relation between structure and freedom; between the lawyer as construction and as constructor of the discipline. One of the aims of Koskenniemi's work has been to lay bare the structural conditions under which international law is practiced. In *From Apology* this took the form of an analysis of the linguistic deep structure or grammar of international legal language as the 'condition of possibility' of international legal argumentation. Any 'competent' international lawyer has to follow certain formal argumentative patterns in order to be heard. In later publications (including the epilogue to the reissued *From Apology*), this was extended to the economic, socio-political and professional structures that determine how international law is practiced and to explain why certain biases distort its application. Being an international lawyer is not only about obtaining a competence in formal reasoning, but also about being able to operate in a social environment that determines what can be said and how things can be said. At the same time, however, Koskenniemi's work can be read as a continuous attempt to explicate where international lawyers appear as active subjects that make and remake the field of international law and legal decision making. None of the different styles available to international lawyers, Koskenniemi argues, provides 'the comfort of allowing the lawyer to set aside his or her 'politics', his or her subjective fears and passions'.[17] Despite the fact that international law is structured in terms of grammar, professional positions and power relations, it is the individual subject who has to perform her politics. In addition, the critical subject emerges as the one who bears responsibility for her choices and carries the burden of guarding international law's 'horizon of universality, ... culture of restraint (and) commitment to listening to others'.[18] This interplay between structure and individual agency, between the discipline and the disciples of international law is taken up in part two of this volume, in the chapters by Nicholas Rajkovic, Sahib Singh, Friedrich Kratochwil and Frédéric Mégret.

The *third* tension in Koskenniemi's work pertains to the use of history in international legal argumentation and the self-understanding of international lawyers. As may be recalled, one of the driving forces behind Koskenniemi's turn to history was the acknowledgement that the structuralism of *From Apology* rendered a rather static picture of international law.[19] While the reader learned that international legal argument left room for radically different substantive arguments, she found little that helped her understand why individual lawyers came to adopt certain positions. Koskenniemi's answer was a reconstruction of the history of the discipline through a study of the sentiments, anxieties and political struggles of individual international lawyers. The publication of *Gentle Civilizer* spurred renewed attention for the history of international law and the legal profession, both in the discipline as a whole and in the work of Koskenniemi himself. The turn to history also functioned as a corrective to established accounts of international law, for example when it comes to the importance of the profession's self-awareness in the late nineteenth century. In this context, 'history' refers to what happened in the past, and one of the tasks of critical scholarship consists of deconstructing flattened, biased or simply mistaken accounts of the development of the course of international law. However, 'history' is never just a matter of recording past events. Invoking history is a political act that involves selection, storytelling and making interventions that could have implications for the present and the future. This is certainly true for Koskenniemi's use of history. *Gentle Civilizer* is not a neutral report of what drove international lawyers since the late nineteenth century; it is also an intervention in current debates on managerialism, multi-disciplinarity and the role of law in international politics. In similar fashion, the culture of formalism is not just a set of principles to live by in the future; it is also the articulation of a sensibility that Koskenniemi brought to life through his stories of international lawyers from the past. The use of history in international law will thus always be judged by both the past and the future; something that is reflected in part three of this book, in the chapters by Anne Orford, Samuel Moyn, Andrew Lang and Susan Marks and Liliana Obregón.

The three topics identified above are all rooted in Koskenniemi's personal (professional) experiences with international law. The impressive amount of literature, the various intellectual traditions and disciplines upon which his work is built;[20] all are mobilized to articulate intellectually what he experienced as lawyer, as advisor and as academic. His career has been formed by his time as diplomat for Finland in its International Law Division and UN Permanent Mission in New York (1978–94), the various Finnish International Court of Justice cases he was involved in, as member of the Administrative Tribunal of the Asian Development Bank (1997–2002), and as member of the International Law Commission (2002–6), where he led the drafting of the report on the fragmentation of international law. Informed by his experiences in practice, Koskenniemi tried to articulate and critically examine his concerns with the state of international law as a professional practice and an academic discipline. In David Kennedy, Koskenniemi found an intellectual sparring mate and ally to develop and articulate this critique. Meeting at a diplomatic cocktail party in Geneva in 1985, the practising lawyer that yearned for the academy (Koskenniemi) and the academic that was considering a career in practice (Kennedy) recognized in each other a similar sense that the international law field had lost a sense of professional self-awareness and intellectual spirit. Moreover, rather than leaving international law behind they both decided to endeavour in making intellectual sense of 'the con-sciousness of the establishment'[21] and of the question why in their effort to settle doctrinal and theoretical dilemmas, international lawyers appeared to reproduce these dilemmas rather than resolve them. In the years after, Kennedy published his seminal *International Legal Structures* (1987) and Koskenniemi *From Apology to Utopia* (1989). Looking back on his semi-nal work after more than fifteen years, Koskenniemi explains one of the main reasons that informed the book as follows: 'existing reflection on the field had failed to capture the experience I had gained from it through practice within Finland's Ministry of Foreign Affairs, especially in United Nations contexts'.[22] The self-proclaimed aim of the book at the time was to articulate, at a general level, the deep structure of the production of international legal arguments by professional lawyers. The 'indeterminacy thesis' that made the book so famous (and notorious) is thus no mere intellectual proposition about the nature of law. Rather, it is an explication of what it takes to engage in the practice of international law today.

This also explains why it would be mistake to reduce *From Apology to Utopia* only to the thesis that international legal arguments cannot be sustained on their own terms. After all, professional practices are many things at the same time. A crucial aspect of the professional practice of international law is to stabilize the meaning of legal provisions, notwith-standing the lack of solid foundations in law. What is more, the legal profession tends to make international law appear as maybe not the only, but certainly the most civilized game in town. Problems that can easily be translated into the language of international law thus come with a com-parative advantage to problems that are mostly perceived as belonging to the institutionally less well-developed fields such as ethics.[23] Illustrative in this respect is the difference between the enthusiasm of international lawyers for the newly developed field of international criminal law com-pared to the number of international law chairs, articles, master programs and PhD positions dedicated to world poverty. The professional practice of international law, in other words, is not just characterized by indeter-minacy; it is also characterized by structural biases coming from different sources. The existence of such structural biases is what gives *From Apology to Utopia* its critical bite. The book not only articulates what it is to think international law, but also opens the professionals' eyes to what it is to engage with international law:

> Although logically speaking, all positions remain open ... in practice
> it is easy to identify ... moments where mainstream has consolidated
> or is only marginally threatened by critique. Professional competence in

international law is precisely about being able to identify the moment's hegemonic and counter-hegemonic narratives and to list one's service in favour of one or the other.[24]

Enthusiasm about international law and the academy had not always been a driving force in Koskenniemi's life. In an interview Koskenniemi conveyed that he went to law school with the idea that this would allow him to 'rule the world' rather than for a real interest in international law as such, because he thought that lawyers rule the world.[25] After discovering that they did not, he went on to diplomatic school, with the same hopes and disappointments for the diplomatic profession. It was only in the multilateral treaty negotiations context that the real zeal for the practice of law emerged; a zeal that he later sought to articulate in his idea of 'the culture of formalism'. In *The Place of Law in Collective Security*, Koskenniemi narrates his own surprise that during the events of Iraq's invasion of Kuwait, all those diplomats with whom he worked at the UN and didn't appear to have much interest for the legal aspects of their practice before, suddenly became greatly enthusiastic about the legal status of various courses of actions that could be taken.[26] In his experience, this enthusiasm of his diplomat colleagues was not out of formalist naivety that law would bring the 'one right answer' nor realist cynicism that using legal language would camouflage the play of ideologies, power and interests behind a legalistic façade. Rather, during the Kuwait crisis, Koskenniemi felt a spirit of law as a working culture of the 'gentle civilizer'. Law's contribution does not lie in the substantive solutions it gives, but in the process of justification that it brings to the practice of diplomacy and in its assumption of responsibility for the policies that are chosen. Yet at the same time came a realization that the legal profession and multilateral diplomacy was little concerned with whether their professional successes also contributed to changing the lives of human beings. While skewing away from any grand theory of justice, Koskenniemi does press the point that lawyers should take responsibility for their substantive choices, as well as for the styles or methods of argumentation they adopt.[27] Central in his work is the view that law is not just about managing bureaucratic processes or deciding cases, but also 'to reflect upon ideal futures that contrast with present practices'.[28] He therefore directs his attention to lawyers to take the responsibility to understand law as a project directed at human flourishing; in the sense that 'law is meant to realize the happiness of human beings as social animals', law as the science of the flourishing of the human and cosmopolitan community.[29]

Especially in *Gentle Civilizer* this universalizing promise of international law is not only *argued*, but also *illustrated* through the life and times of examples such as Lauterpacht and Friedmann. Their stories are told also as a source of inspiration, to show how individuals have tried to spell out international law's promise of justice. Where *From Apology* almost exclusively used intellectual, cognitive argument, *Gentle Civilizer* also mobilizes the emotions of the reader, with rich, almost novel-like accounts of the lives, times and anxieties of its main characters. In this way, *Gentle Civilizer* calls upon international lawyers to retain this aspiration to justice in the face of managerial mind-sets, depoliticized legal pragmatism and imperial policy agendas. The culture of formalism, introduced at the end of the book, is a combination of example-setting, mobilization of professional pride, appeal to justice and a sense of reality, all to cultivate 'a culture of resistance to power, a social practice of accountability, openness, and equality whose status cannot be reduced to the political positions of any one of the parties whose claims are treated within it'.[30] Rather than fixing the universal in a particular, positive space, such as a law, procedural rule or an institution, a *culture* of formalism would resist such fixation and instead is aimed at a *horizon* of universality: a space beyond the mere particular, where what is lacking in each particularity is sought in universal terms, in a horizon of possibility, unattainable but still necessary.[31] Where Koskenniemi's structural analysis points at the conditions of possibility for speaking international law, the culture of formalism seeks to articulate why we should speak international law in the first place.

As we stated above, Koskenniemi has by now grown into one of the icons of the discipline. And yet, as David Kennedy has pointed out in relation to *From Apology to Utopia*, 'although often cited, Martti's book is rarely challenged or deeply engaged'.[32] Unfortunately, the same goes for many other references to Koskenniemi's work. Often references to Koskenniemi's work are nothing more than signals that the author knows the hierarchies in the professional field and wants to assure the reader that she is aware of the critical turn in international legal scholarship. Happily, there are also several examples of the opposite, including three relatively recent special issues that were devoted to discussing Koskenniemi's work. Marking the re-issue of *From Apology to Utopia*, the *German Law Journal* organized a symposium and published a special issue in 2006 in which the book was both celebrated and questioned on what makes it so influential for the study and profession of international law. In 2013, the *Temple International & Comparative Law Journal* built on this further by holding a symposium and publishing a special issue in which the contributions develop a number of important issues that Koskenniemi has raised in his writings. While we are writing this introduction, the *Leiden Journal of International Law* prepares a symposium on the re-issue of *From Apology*, to be published in 2016.

This volume further builds on these special issues, in an attempt to contextualize, challenge and engage with Koskenniemi's work. In this context, 'engagement' or 'challenge' is not necessarily the same as setting out why Koskenniemi was right or where he went wrong. Of course, assessing the correctness of the arguments of one of the authoritative figures in the profession is a valuable exercise in and of itself. However, what we aim for is a critical engagement that opens up fresh perspectives on how one can read and contextualize Koskenniemi's work, and thereby how we can obtain novel understandings of what it is to study and practice international law. To that end, the contributors have applied Koskenniemi's work to a wide range of functional areas in international law, and discussed it from an even broader range of theoretical perspectives, including anthropological studies of the workings of magic, the philosophy of Sartre, Catholic theology, geography, systems theory, history, political theory, sociology and international relations theory – quite something for a book dedicated to the work of one the main advocates of counterdisciplinarity! The contributions do justice to the critical intent that has been driving Koskenniemi's oeuvre throughout; an intent that makes his work stand 'apart from the prevailing order of the world and ask(s) how that order came about'.[33] In similar fashion, contributions to this book pose the question how Koskenniemi's own work came about, what its (hidden) assumptions and politics are, where it has taken us so far, how we can think differently about law and the legal profession and where his work leaves room for critique and adaptation.

As we have explained in more detail above, the chapters are organized around three overlapping and by no means exhaustive topics or oppositions that have run though Koskenniemi's work so far.

1

The first tension is the complicated relation between the indeterminacy thesis and the culture of formalism.

This tension structures the chapter by **Gregor Noll**, which focuses on two forms of movement in Koskenniemi's work. The first is circular movement, as is present in the oscillation between descending and ascending arguments. Noll sets out the metaphysical assumptions informing this circularity through a comparison between *From Apology to Utopia* and the influential work of the Catholic theologian Erich Przywara, *Analogia Ente*. Just like the creator in Przywara's theology escapes human cognition, authority in international law can only be known indirectly, incompletely and in paradoxical ways. The second movement is progress, as exemplified by, inter alia, Koskenniemi's culture of formalism. This culture is characterized by an orientation upon the future, through the idea of a promise of justice and the belief in a universal, inclusive community. The invocation of otherworldly ideals for a worldly practice – law – that are always yet to come places Koskenniemi's work in the Pauline tradition, as it is 'in hope alone that international lawyers participate in the coming community'.

The same relation also occupies a central place in **David Dyzenhaus'** contribution, which argues that Koskenniemi's indeterminacy thesis is incompatible with his culture of formalism. Although the claim that law is indeterminate may look like a statement of fact, he contends, in reality it is a political, anti-formalist position. Through a discussion of the history of legal positivism, Dyzenhaus shows that the core question is not whether legal rules need interpretation (obviously they do) but rather how one should characterize the controversies that unavoidably surround the application of rules. Answering this question takes us back to normative political theory. Claiming that law is indeterminate then is one among different possible answers to this question, and one that would take us closer to decisionism than Koskenniemi is willing to accept. The culture of formalism is another possible answer. However, this answer pushes us in the other direction, towards further reflection on the rule of law as the reign of non-instrumental rules, Dyzenhaus submits.

An opposite position is adopted by **Nigel White**, whose chapter invokes both the indeterminacy thesis and the culture of formalism to highlight international law's potential in conflict resolution and collective security. For White, there is no tension between indeterminacy and the culture of formalism. On the contrary, he treats both aspects as mutually reinforcing and beneficial aspects of international legal rules. White takes the indeterminacy of international law as an essential condition for its acceptability, as it allows contesting parties to develop common understandings based on international standards. At the same time, he sees the spirit of Koskenniemi's culture of formalism embodied in the rules of state responsibility, based as they are on the idea of restoring normalcy and friendly relations. Through its combination of indeterminacy and formalism, White argues, international legal rules create space for a politics based on mutual respect, peaceful co-existence and reciprocity.

Jaye Ellis discusses one of the contexts in which the culture of formalism obtains specific meaning: international environmental law, a field characterized by highly specialized, technical regimes on the one hand, and broad, largely uninfluential procedural rules on the other. Within this context, the dangers of instrumentalism, colonization of law by science and managerialism loom large. In order to face these challenges, Ellis links insights from systems theory to Koskenniemi's culture of formalism. The point of her analysis is to safeguard both the necessary openness of law to science *and* to protect the specific function of law in society, in particular the intermediary potential of legal rules and procedures. She evokes Koskenniemi's work on fragmentation and links it to Teubner's plea for a legal pluralism that does justice to law's specific functions in society. Instead of providing solutions to the problems that come with the increasing functional specialization of society, Ellis propagates a form of law that enables interaction between different regimes, as well as between law and knowledge claims coming from science. Legal rules then operate as *moda vivendi*, not as instruments in a system driven solely by its own rationality.

The chapter by **Eric Posner** builds on the tension between law's openness and attempts to mobilize it for the promotion of global justice. He makes a (somewhat ironical) attempt to provide empirical, rational choice informed evidence for Koskenniemi's critique of human rights. He starts out from the observation that the proliferation of international human rights law has hardly affected the actual behaviour of states. According to Posner, widespread human rights violations still occur frequently, and where human rights are respected there is little to suggest that this has to do with their protection in international law. Posner argues that it is the very proliferation of human rights itself that has contributed to their marginal importance in domestic and world politics. It is attractive for states to sign up to many human rights treaties, because they can enhance their standing in the international community, while at the same time leaving much discretion to balance and prioritize the long list of rights. In this way, Posner not only seeks to ground Koskenniemi's human rights critique in empirical research, but also attempts to show that the anxieties about social science incursions into the field of law are unfounded.

Finally, the chapter by **Jutta Brunnée and Stephen Toope** argues that Koskenniemi's recourse to a culture of formalism leaves international law too vulnerable to the twin dangers of abstract morality and power politics.

They propose the 'culture of legality' as an alternative way of making sense of legal practice. Brunnée and Toope read the culture of formalism as a rather narrow notion that revolves around the formal opportunity to be heard, a promise of justice and the ever-looming possibility that, in the end, material power decides the law. The culture of legality, they argue, is thicker as it involves the use of principles, processes and techniques rooted in shared understandings, meeting a set of (Fullerian) criteria of legality and giving rise to a congruent social practice. Through a discussion of the Syrian crisis and the Responsibility to Protect they illustrate what it means to view law through the prism of a culture of legality and assert that law has a disciplining force that goes beyond formal equality and the anxiety that law collapses into an apology for those in power.

2

The second relation under study is that between structure and freedom; between the subject as construction and constructor of international law; between individual international lawyers and their moral autonomy on the one hand and the professional field that makes them into lawyers on the other.

Nikolas Rajkovic mobilizes this tension in his critique of Koskenniemi's plea for counterdisciplinarity; his attempt to safeguard a special place for the international lawyer and her profession. According to Rajkovic, the call for 'counterdisciplinarity' stands for a broader trend in international legal scholarship that seeks to defend the discipline of international law in spatial terms; as a 'distinctive (European) space' that should be protected against possible interventions from (American) international relations scholarship. Treating the discipline as if it were a separate space, however, provides a false sense of geographical security and runs the risk of ending up in new forms of Orientalism. Rajkovic witnesses this in the combined attempts to link international law to a civilizing mission and to fix its identity vis-à-vis adjacent disciplines through the invocation of the Aristotelian distinction between practical judgement and theoretical science. In this way, Rajkovic holds, Koskenniemi obscures how disciplines have been formed and transformed through abstraction, specialization and differentiation. Rather than viewing inter-disciplinarity in spatial, othering terms, Rajkovic advocates an understanding of inter-disciplinarity as the result of the abstract, overlapping and migratory characteristics of knowledge production. This, he asserts, is the proper context in which the moral agency of international lawyers should be discussed.

The chapter by **Sahib Singh** explores a notion that has been crucial yet understudied in critical scholarship, the critical subject. What is this subject that it supposed to do all the critical and emancipatory work? Singh sets out that there are two subject types at work in Koskenniemi's work, as well as in critical legal studies more generally. The first subject is socialized, constituted by the historical, professional and social conditions in which she operates. The second is a subject that stands apart from these conditions and is able to overcome them. This latter subject stands in opposition to an outside that it seeks to transcend through reflective consciousness. In this way, as Singh puts it 'Sartre is the dirty little secret at the heart of *From Apology to Utopia*'. The critical subject thus comes with inherent tensions and antinomies. It strives for inter-subjectivity and community, yet seeks to impose its own, supposedly superior consciousness over others. It invokes freedom as absence from constraint, yet also as impossible without enabling social conditions. It critiques liberalism but grounds this critique in an idea of freedom that dovetails with that very same ideology.

Friedrich Kratochwil discusses the limits of relying on Kant's moral politician as a way to safeguard inclusiveness and the promise of justice. For Koskenniemi, the moral politician constitutes an antidote to managerial tendencies that seek to do away with the formality and politics of law. However, as Kratochwil argues, the professional, organizational and societal contexts in which lawyers operate hardly leave room for such cultivation of judgement. What counts as virtuous action (or, for that matter, what counts as independent expert knowledge) is highly context-dependent. It can only be discovered through a more context-specific study that takes into account professional and organizational environments as well as changing links between the profession and society at large. Through a historical exploration of the organizational forms which have shaped and framed the legal profession and its *praxis*, Kratochwil sketches new ways of thinking about what it is to be an (international) lawyer.

Frédéric Mégret's chapter departs from Koskenniemi's observation that the opposition between apology and utopia constitutes the 'condition of possibility of there being something like a distinct experience of international law in the first place'. However, he does not treat the opposition as a matter of epistemology, legal logic or psychology. Instead, Mégret uses it as the starting point for an inquiry into the social field of international law. Using the laws of armed conflict as an illustration, Mégret shows how the opposition between apology and utopia structures professional practices and competition in international law. Apology and utopia, as Mégret puts it 'are also constituencies, embodied positions and specific sites'. Combining *From Apology to Utopia* with Bourdieu's theorizing on the social field allows for a fresh look at the practice of international (humanitarian) law, showing how the humanitarian project became legalized, how core and periphery are constructed, how symbolic capital is accumulated and how the practice of law is grounded in a 'habitus'; a 'feel for the game'. What it means to be an international lawyer cannot be answered by pointing at argumentative patterns only; it is about how one should perform in a social field.

<h1 style="text-align:center">3</h1>

The final part of the book explores the dual function of history in international legal scholarship: as a recount of what happened in the past as well as an intervention in contemporary debates to explore what should happen in the future.

This tension is at the heart of the chapter by **Anne Orford**. For Orford, *The Gentle Civilizer* stands out as a critical and emancipatory book, because it keeps together the history of international law, its sociology and international legal practice. However, the unity of these three elements has been threatened by the reception of the book by historians as providing an account of how things 'really were', coupled with some of Koskenniemi's own warnings against anachronisms and conceptual imperialism. Orford asserts that while it is of course important to do justice to the context of historical works and concepts, the more relevant question is what counts as the 'proper context' in the first place. For international lawyers this will involve the reception and narration of works and concepts over time and the potential political uses that come with them. Losing sight of the different knowledge-interests when it comes to doing history forecloses rather than opens up critical potential, Orford submits. She argues that international lawyers should thus resist colonization of their field by historians and retain the vital connection between the history, theory and practice of their field.

Andrew Lang and Susan Marks analyse how Koskenniemi invokes history to recover the idea of moral agency in international law. More specifically, Lang and Marks focus on the means through which Koskenniemi performs the past of international law. They read *Gentle Civilizer* as a nostalgic book, which seeks to re-enact a moral sensibility that inspired Lauterpacht and the men of 1873. Building on insights from semiotics, anthropology and the study of 'magic', they show how *Gentle Civilizer* works through (1) the law of similarity (Lauterpacht and the men of 1873 as role models); (2) the law of contact (the re-enactment of the past through contagion; bringing our ancestors into our world); and (3) the production of artefacts (the text that puts us into contact with earlier generations). They hold that history then becomes a 'secret sympathy to be sensed'; a force that could inspire the readers to act as morally responsible international lawyers.

Samuel Moyn shares the argument made by Lang & Marks: Koskenniemi performs history in order to carve out models for responsible political action. At the same time, however, he questions whether the approach adopted in *Gentle Civilizer* actually helps to achieve that. According to Moyn, the publication of *Gentle Civilizer* has inspired readings of history that tend to exaggerate the role of international law in world politics. Treating law as an important force in decision making may be justified today, but this does not mean it is always accurate when it comes to historical events. The net result, Moyn contends, is not just an anachronistic reading of history – something that may not be problematic in and of itself. More importantly, it portrays formalism and recourse to law as the only – or at least the best – ways to civilize politics. In this way, historical studies push aside the role of law as comforter of power, as well as the different non-legal ways of bettering politics that were available to our ancestors.

Liliana Obregón takes up a theme that Koskenniemi described as 'the alien that was inside and had to come out', international law and Eurocentrism. While it is impossible to speak the language of international law without buying into some form of Eurocentrism, it still matters a great deal how one relates to the colonial heritage of the field. Obregón explores different manifestations and critiques of Eurocentrism, ranging from the rise of Eurocentric thought in eighteenth-century Europe to the critiques that have been voiced by thinkers from the Americas, the Soviet Union, Africa, Asia and Muslim countries. The overview of Eurocentrism and its critics is followed by an interview on the topic that Obregón had with Koskenniemi. The interview explores how the topic of Eurocentrism entered Koskenniemi's work, how it affected his understanding of international law and how international lawyers can (and cannot) deal with Eurocentrism in order to mobilize the emancipatory potential of international law.

The book concludes with an epilogue by **Martti Koskenniemi**, in which he relates the different chapters in this volume to ongoing struggles over the Transpacific and Transatlantic Partnership Treaties (TTP and TTIP). This move is a performance in and of itself, as it directly shows the central message of the epilogue: the point of theorizing international law is not to develop abstract categories that absorb the particularities of concrete situations. On the contrary, the purpose is to critically reflect on the role of international lawyers in those situations. In this context, Koskenniemi invites international lawyers to be aware of the *enchanting* power they often exercise. Through the use of legal vocabularies, lawyers have the power to make others believe in the existence of institutional legal facts, the legal powers of authorities as well as in the rightness or wrongness of certain forms of behaviour. Lawyers, in other words, are trained to let others (and themselves) suspend their disbeliefs. Koskenniemi illustrates how the enchanting power of law can be solicited in the service of abstract ideologies, just like social science vocabularies of 'objectivity' or universalistic moral programs. By way of resistance, Koskenniemi refers to Adam Smith's theory of moral sentiments, where law's virtue 'is recognizable in individual instances and 'feelings' more than in the day's rational discourses'. Critique then, is a way of escaping the enchanting power of abstract discourses, be it in law, science or morality.

Notes

1. M. Koskenniemi, 'Miserable Comforters, International Relations as New Natural Law', *European Journal of International Relations* 15 (2009): 395.
2. The one that stands out in this context is, of course, David Kennedy. We will come back on the influence of Kennedy on Koskenniemi's work and career later.
3. M. Koskenniemi, '*The Sanction of All the World': Legal Imagination and International Power 1300–1870* (Cambridge: Cambridge University Press, forthcoming).
4. J. Klabbers, *International Law* (Cambridge: Cambridge University Press, 2013).
5. A. Orford, ed, *International Law and Its Others* (Cambridge: Cambridge University Press, 2009).
6. See the special issue of the *German Law Journal* 7, no. 12 (2006), entitled 'From Apology to Utopia: A Symposium', and the special issue of the *Temple International and Comparative Law Journal* (Fall 2013), entitled 'Engaging the Writings of Martti Koskenniemi'. At the time of writing of this introduction, the *Leiden Journal of International Law* is preparing a special issue on *From Apology to Utopia*.
7. For an analysis of legalism in international legal scholarship, see W. Werner, 'Security and International Law; between Securitization and Legalism', in P. Bourbeau (ed.), *Security – Dialogue across Disciplines* (Cambridge: Cambridge University Press, 2015), 196.
8. These four elements are reconstructed from Shklar's account of legalism in J. Shklar, *Legalism Law, Morals and Political Trials* (1964; repr., Cambridge, MA: Harvard University Press, 1986), 1–28.

9. Ibid., 15. The quote is taken from Alexis de Tocqueville, *Democracy in America*, P. Bradley (ed.) (New York: Vintage Books, 1952), 275.
10. Martti Koskenniemi, *International Lawyers*, www.helsinki.fi/eci/Publications/Koskenniemi/MKINTERNATIONAL%20LAWYERS-07b.pdf.
11. Martti Koskenniemi, *From Apology to Utopia – The Structure of International Legal Argument*, reissue with new epilogue (Cambridge: Cambridge University Press, 2005), 569.
12. M. Koskenniemi, 'Style as Method: Letter to the Editors of the Symposium', in *The Politics of International Law* (Oxford: Hart, 2011), 300.
13. Koskenneimi, *From Apology to Utopia*, 590.
14. Ibid., 564.
15. Martti Koskenniemi, 'Constitutionalism as a Mindset: Reflections on Kantian Themes about Law and Globalization', *Theoretical Inquiries in Law* 8 (2007): 27.
16. For this argument, see A. Leander and W. Werner, 'Tainted Love: the Struggle over Legality in International Relations and International Law', in T. Aalberts, T. Gammeltoft-Hansen and N. M. Rajkovic (eds), *The Power of Legality* (Cambridge: Cambridge University Press, 2016).
17. Koskenniemi, *Politics of International Law*, 300.
18. Ibid., 128.
19. M. Koskenniemi, *The Gentle Civilizer of Nations: the Rise and Fall of International Law 1870–1960* (Cambridge: Cambridge University Press, 2001), 1.
20. For a more elaborate discussion of the different intellectual sources of Koskenniemi's work, see E. Jouannet, 'Koskenniemi: a Critical Introduction', in Koskenniemi, *Politics of International Law*, 1.
21. D. Kennedy, 'The Last Treatise: Project and Person (Reflections on Martti Koskenniemi's *From Apology to Utopia*)', *German Law Journal* 7 (2006): 984.
22. Koskenniemi, *From Apology to Utopia*, 562.
23. For an illustration of this point in the context of the ICC, see S. Nouwen and W. Werner, 'Monopolizing Global Justice: International Criminal Law as Challenge to Human Diversity', *Journal of International Criminal Justice* 13 (2014): 157–76.
24. Koskenniemi, *From Apology to Utopia*, 607.
25. Dana Schmalz, 'On Kitsch, Zombies and True Love – an Interview with Martti Koskenniemi', http://voelkerrechtsblog.com/2014/05/21/on-kitsch-zombies-and-true-love-an-interview-with-martti-koskenniemi/.
26. M. Koskenniemi, 'The Place of Law in Collective Security', in *Politics of International Law*, 79.
27. See, for his attack on liberal legal theory as failing to recognize the structural bias that it represents and the inclusions and exclusions that it produces, Koskenniemi, 'Style as Method'.
28. Speech in acceptance of the honorary doctoral degree at McGill on 28 May 2015, www.youtube.com/watch?v=P57LPBiy70Q.
29. Ibid.
30. Koskenniemi, *Gentle Civilizer*, 500.
31. Ibid., 506–7.
32. Kennedy, 'Last Treatise', 991.
33. Robert W. Cox, 'Social Forces, States and World Orders: beyond International Relations Theory', *Millennium* 10 (1981): 129.

Bibliography

Cox, Robert W. 'Social Forces, States and World Orders: beyond International Relations Theory'. *Millennium* 10 (1981): 126–55.

Jouannet, Emmanuelle. 'Koskenniemi: a Critical Introduction'. In Martti Koskenniemi (ed.), *The Politics of International Law* (Oxford: Hart, 2011).

Kennedy, D. 'The Last Treatise: Project and Person (Reflections on Martti Koskenniemi's From Apology to Utopia)'. *German Law Journal* 7 (2006): 982–92.

Klabbers, J. *International Law* (Cambridge: Cambridge University Press, 2013).

Koskenniemi, Martti. 'Constitutionalism as a Mindset: Reflections on Kantian Themes about Law and Globalization'. *Theoretical Inquiries in Law* 8 (2007): 27.

From Apology to Utopia: The Structure of International Legal Argument. Reissue with a new epilogue (Cambridge: Cambridge University Press, 2005).

The Gentle Civilizer of Nations: The Rise and Fall of International Law 1870–1960 (Cambridge: Cambridge University Press, 2001).

'Miserable Comforters: International Relations as New Natural Law'. *European Journal of International Relations* 15 (2009): 395–422.

The Politics of International Law (Oxford: Hart, 2011).

'*The Sanction of All the World*': Legal Imagination and International Power 1300–1870 (Cambridge: Cambridge University Press, forthcoming).

Leander, Anne, and Wouter Werner. 'Tainted Love: the Struggle over Legality in International Relations and International Law'. In T. Aalberts, T. Gammeltoft-Hansen and N. M. Rajkovic (eds), *The Power of Legality* (Cambridge: Cambridge University Press, 2016).

Nouwen, Sarah, and Wouter Werner. 'Monopolizing Global Justice: International Criminal Law as Challenge to Human Diversity'. *Journal of International Criminal Justice* 13 (2014): 157–76.

Orford, Anne (ed.). *International Law and Its Others* (Cambridge: Cambridge University Press, 2009).

Shklar, Judith. *Legalism: Law, Morals and Political Trials* (1964; repr., Cambridge, MA: Harvard University Press, 1986).

Werner, Wouter. 'Security and International Law; between Securitization and Legalism'. In Philippe Bourbeau (ed.), *Security – Dialogue across Disciplines* (Cambridge: Cambridge University Press, 2015).

1

What Moves Law?

Martti Koskenniemi and Transcendence in International Law

GREGOR NOLL*

1.1 Why Is Koskenniemi Read?

Martti Koskenniemi's work is widely quoted. To the extent this impression needs confirmation, a quantitative analysis of his name's occurrence in a corpus of English-language books does just that. The quotes and references are so frequent as to place him into the upper segment of international law scholars of his generation.[1] The relatively narrow circle of scholars interested in international legal theory can but account for a minor fraction of these occurrences, I would think. Then again, Koskenniemi's work does not exactly offer itself to those seeking confirmation of valid law. So why the frequent references?

Is it that Koskenniemi's texts confirm that the idea of progress is the sole unifying factor left to international law? After all, they seem to be so open to international lawyers of different ideological convictions, methodological schools and formative experiences. Perhaps all these writers referencing Koskenniemi share a metaphysical dilemma with him, whose importance is confirmed by each footnote. Here it is: explicit reference to divinity is socially impossible in a contemporary international law claiming to be secular, and so is an explicit reference to redemption. Then again, the structures provided by Christian metaphysics continue to shape and precondition the practice of international law, and international lawyers need the idea of 'hope' and 'progress' to retain a sense, or sentiment, of purpose.

Take the sceptical reactions to Martti Koskenniemi's 1999 'Letter to the Editors'[2] by exponents of positivism or law and economics. Simma and Paulus call for legal interpretation to be 'operational'[3], and Dunoff and Trachtman search for 'better law'[4], all four seeking to promote the suppression of atrocities through law. The stark methodological differences between these authors and Koskenniemi apart, their contributions smack of an agnostic, yet progressivist framework. Koskenniemi and these four sceptics might express their agnosticism and imply their progressivism in different ways and degrees. Nonetheless, in referencing his work, sceptics and supporters unwittingly refer to the idea of progress as a common point of reference and, indeed, a common aspiration. If 'progress' is indeed what makes international law into a coherent whole today, I wonder whether it can be supported by an agnostic framework. More particularly, is the framework offered in Martti Koskenniemi's work indeed as agnostic as the panoply of references seem to suggest?

1.2 A Way of Reading Koskenniemi

If international law is all about progress, it makes sense to think about quite literally what movement is supposed to bring about progress. In my reading of certain works by Martti Koskenniemi, I will focus on movement. As we will see, movement might help us advance towards an end, but movement might also take the form of oscillation, a kind of flicker that largely keeps us in the same place. So movement as progress and movement as oscillation need to be distinguished in Koskenniemi's work.

In *From Apology to Utopia*, movement between two poles is a central feature of international law.[5] First, international law is structurally indeterminate; law and politics are mutually dependent in their practice. It follows, second, that liberalism as the privileging of law over politics must be resisted within international law. Koskenniemi's point is certainly not to counter the advance of liberalism by a reverse privileging of politics over law. Making that into a kind of ideological prescription would arrest movement all the same and exchange a particular one-sidedness for another. Perhaps the point is simply that the mutuality in the dependence of law and politics, once set in motion, *is* international law.

Koskenniemi has described the way in which the work of international lawyers makes the structure of international law move and come alive. A major point in his contribution was that the movements taking place across dichotomies were not necessarily acknowledged by international lawyers themselves. Very likely, these movements are the product of tacit assumptions. So an important question raised by his work is, *what movements follow from our metaphysical assumptions?*[6]

For the better part of this text, I attempt to understand the relation between metaphysical assumption and argumentative movement in Martti Koskenniemi's work. I try to elaborate the particular form they take and think about the implications of those forms along the way.

For a start, and to let the particular form of Koskenniemi's dynamism appear in relief, I shall contrast it with a particular form of Roman Catholic dynamism. When reading the work of the German Jesuit theologian and philosopher Erich Przywara (1889–1972), its considerable parallels with the way that Koskenniemi casts dynamism struck me. In the present text, I explore if that sense of likeness can be borne out in a more thorough comparison as well as where the Catholic philosopher and the international legal scholar part ways.

Why Przywara, why Roman Catholicism? Would not an exploration of, say, the dynamism expressed by structuralist and post-structuralist thinkers be more appropriate, given that Koskenniemi's work invokes these traditions? Przywara's Catholic thought should work like a contrast agent: ideally, we will be able to make out the metaphysical choice enabling Koskenniemi's contestation of international legal liberalism.

I should point out what all this is not: outing a scholar of secular international law as a closet Catholic thinker.

So who was Erich Przywara? Born in 1889 in Katowice as the son of a Polish businessman and his German wife, he entered the Society of Jesus at the Dutch Exaten College in 1908.[7] The Society being prohibited in Germany since 1872, his geographical move beyond German borders illustrates well that the tension between spiritual and worldly normativity was something of a leitmotif in his biography.[8] In the following years, Przywara pursued studies of philosophy and theology; he acquired a doctorate in 1921. Phenomenology left a significant mark on his work; Edmund Husserl and his circle, Martin Heidegger and Edith Stein, were among his interlocutors, as were Martin Buber and, not least, Karl Barth, his great Protestant adversary.

Przywara's main work, *Analogia Entis*,[9] continues to have considerable impact on Catholic theology and the teachings of the Roman Catholic Church.[10] Recently, John Betz and David Bentley Hart published an English translation,[11] which makes Przywara's analogical thought accessible to a broader audience beyond the linguistic boundaries of its original German language. *Analogia Entis* lives entirely off Przywara's ability to foreground and detail the rhythmical, dynamical structure of the analogy of being,[12] which he roots in the traditions of Thomism and negative theology.

How do I go about this? I first perform a few comparisons between Koskenniemi's work and that of Przywara on the theme of authority (Section 1.3). This comparison will provide me with the opportunity to introduce key elements of Przywara's *Analogia Entis* to those international legal scholars unacquainted with his work. Second, I try to track which movements take place between the normative and the concrete and how they relate to analogous movements in the work of Walter Ullmann, the Austro-Jewish historian, to then fold this back into the discussion on Przywara and Koskenniemi (Section 1.4). In Section 1.5, I consider whether Koskenniemi may be understood to eliminate creation while retaining redemption as a transcendent source of normativity. Przywara will no longer be his sparring partner then: I shall also read Koskenniemi as part of a Pauline tradition. In the final section, Section 1.6, I project my reading of Koskenniemi back onto the enthusiastic and sceptical responses his work has met and end where I started.

1.3 Authority and the Limits of Human Cognition

In Martti Koskenniemi's earlier work, ultimate authority appears to be beyond human reach. '*From Apology to Utopia* assumes that there is no access to legal rules or the legal meaning of international behaviour that is independent from the way competent lawyers see such things'.[13] International lawyers are left with complex opposites that always presuppose each other. There is no breaking through to a higher harmony of the one right answer that dissolves the opposites and decides the legal argument. Take the consideration of sovereignty and sources of law in the epilogue of the 2006 re-edition of *From Apology to Utopia*. The temporal relationship between the sovereign and the source of law does not allow for any conclusion on which of it 'is first' in terms of hierarchy: law or fact, idealism or realism, descending arguments or ascending arguments. The approach from sovereignty and the approach from sources, Koskenniemi concludes, are

> [b]oth ... correct; each has resources to ground and explain [*sic*] the law. Yet each is vulnerable to criticisms from its opposite: sovereignty seems too servile to power to become a reliable basis for a normative system, while sources fail to give a good account of where the law emerges if not from concrete State power and policy.[14]

From the level of ultimate authority, Koskenniemi shifts focus to a level just below it. God may be non-committal, absent or even dead; international lawyers are alive and intent. Making sense of their practice is as good as it can get. And here is a book on the *grammar* of international law (Koskenniemi's own term), which lets its opposites interact. *From Apology to Utopia* invites its readers to study not so much what authority *is* as *how* it is in the world. For legal authority, the point is to understand *how it is spelt out as knowledge.* Surely, authority is not banned from Koskenniemi's apologetic-utopian 'machine'.[15] It just happens to be never fully knowable and always channelled through humans. So is legal argument: never fully subjective, always channelled through authority. The beauty of his book lives off this chiasmus.

And so does the beauty of Przywara's *Analogia Entis.* First, what we know about authority is always limited by what we do not know. And our ignorance is always greater than our knowledge. This is so, because God (here in his capacity as authority) is so radically different from us humans. Przywara recurs throughout his work to the formula of the Fourth Lateran Council of 1215. Its Second Canon reads as follows in English: 'between the creator and the creature there cannot be a likeness so great that the unlikeness is not greater'.[16]

So if the creator is present in creation, and international law is part of creation, our knowledge about that law will be relativized by our ignorance of its creator. Reading Koskenniemi through Przywara, there seem to be good reasons why international legal argument ultimately remains unstable and indecisive to humans. To the extent other international legal scholars imply the possibility of 'one right answer', they presuppose a fully knowable authority that endorses this answer.[17] This authority might be divine, but it cannot be a divinity of the type thought by Przywara. Now, Koskenniemi's emphasis on oscillation might be read in two ways. Oscillation suggests that the creator is present in the being of international law, and that it is our inability to fully understand the creator that makes international law ultimately unstable.[18] If this is a correct reading, Koskenniemi would really move away from the widely held idea of secular law. Indeed, justice would be no less metaphysical in Martti Koskenniemi than the divine in Erich Przywara. Or, in the alternative, Koskenniemi's oscillation is fully worldly and caused by our inability to comprehend humans.[19]

Second, Przywara's thought is grounded in a Thomistic differentiation between essence (*essentia*) and existence (*esse*).[20] Both are separated in creatures but coincide in God. To some extent, God has made himself real in the world by creating it. Divine power is the author of the world. In creation, this divine potency continues to push towards actuality, thereby revealing itself. Seen as such, it is clear that essence seeks to realize itself in secular existence. Likewise, authority needs a human being to incarnate it in the world, to embrace it with knowledge and to argue it towards a point of actuality and concreteness.

Przywara's *Analogia Entis* does not start with divine authority but with the search for a philosophical foundation of sorts. But the tension between divine potency and actual creation runs through this search as well. Essence takes on the form of knowledge, a knowledge that is but revealed essence. Existence, on the other hand, is the object of that knowledge, the things of the world that actually are. Should metaphysics first deal with the act of knowledge itself, before studying that which is? Or should it proceed first to the being that it wants to know about, before contemplating on its ways of gathering knowledge? 'The neutral duality between knowledge-act and knowledge-object . . . cannot be interpreted away and does not allow for locking oneself up into that which is "pure"'.[21] Now, let the knowledge-act refer to the *sources* of international law and the knowledge-object to the *sovereign*. Or let *knowledge* assume the position of idealism in international law and *being* take that of realism: the Catholic philosopher and the international lawyer are barking up the same tree. The question is whether they are doing it in the same manner.

1.4 Movement

So being, including the being of international law, is always a little too elusive to be known in a firm, 'substantive' way. *From Apology to Utopia* devotes much of its argument to convince the reader that the law is actually and inevitably unstable, and that this is a problem for the liberal position that the rule of law provides a frame for a lawful politics.[22] Something that is not stable moves. The question is what movements this particular instability entails, and what significance to attach to it. On these points, its author is less pronounced. International legal argument remains 'in constant flux'.[23] Repeatedly, Koskenniemi exposes its *circularity* (e.g. in the construction of custom, or in the concept of the state), a circularity that he once labels as 'hopeless'.[24] Argumentative movement is also described in terms of *oscillation*, a swinging to and fro. In his elaboration of schools of thought in international law, the impression prevails that their movement is also confined to an all too narrow space. So any movement taking place in the descriptive parts of *From Apology to Utopia* is movement made in a trap.

Then again, Martti Koskenniemi also makes a second, normative argument, and critiques a liberal over-reliance on the possibility of a rule of law. This counter-position is labelled as 'progressive'.[25] This cannot be the progress I am making when pacing through my prison cell. And I cannot fail to note that the title of the book making both arguments is *From Apology to Utopia*, indicating that there might be a linear progress beyond the mere reproduction of yet another circle. If this is indicative of anything more than the need to give any book some title, and I think it always is, the movement to utopia is circular perhaps, but linear, too. The question is what it means to move to utopia, to *ou topos*, to a non-place, or, quite simply, towards eternity.

A decisive distinction for Koskenniemi is that between descending and ascending patterns of argumentation. He links it to he opposition of normative and concrete patterns, and it runs through the whole of *From Apology to Utopia*, if not his work at large. Both oppositions seem to operate in parallel throughout his work. When introducing the first, he refers to the Walter Ullmann, who coined the opposition in his *Law and Politics in the Middle Ages*, published in 1975.[26]

I note however, that the couplet of descending and ascending argument is not a straightforward and congruent loan from Ullmann. Koskenniemi explains it as follows:

> There are two ways of arguing about order and obligation in international affairs. One argument traces them down to justice, common interests, progress, nature of the world community or other similar ideas to which it is common that they are anterior, or superior, to State behaviour, will or interest. They are taken as a given normative code which precedes the State and effectively dictates how a State is allowed to behave, what it may will and what its legitimate interests can be. Another argument bases order and obligation on State behaviour, will or interest. It takes as given the existence of States and attempts to construct a normative order on the basis of the "factual" State behaviour, will and interest.[27]

In Ullmann's original formulation, however, the couplet marks a wider span and juxtaposes popular with divine government.

> [T]he main point [of the ascending theme, GN] is that lawcreative power is located in the people itself (who belongs or does not belong to it, is of no concern in this context): the populace at large is considered to be the bearer of the power that creates law either in a popular assembly or diet, or, more usually, in a council or other organ which contains the representatives chosen by the people.[28]

It is not difficult to see that Ullmann's 'populace' corresponds to Koskenniemi's states, and that behaviour of these entities is characteristic for a form of government (Ullmann) and a form of argument (Koskenniemi).

For the descending theme, however, Ullman offers a distinctly political-theological account:

> Opposed to this ascending theme is the descending one according to which original power is located not in the broad base of the people, but in an otherworldly being, in divinity itself which is held to be the source of all power, public and private. The totality of original power being located in one supreme being was distributed downward – or 'descended from above' – so that the mental picture of a pyramid emerges: at its apex there was the Ruler who had received power from divinity and who distributed it downwards, so that whatever power was found at the base of the pyramid was eventually traceable to the supreme head.[29]

Observe that Ullmann is conceptualizing medieval history; coordination and conflict between secular and ecclesiastical law being a key aspect of its study. Koskenniemi secularizes this terminology by moving it from the Middle Ages into Modernity. More importantly, he flattens out the pyramid, and Ullmann's explicit reference to divinity is lost in the process. Yet he says himself to prefer the couple of ascending and descending to the alternative couplet of deductive and inductive, which he finds too scientific.[30] If science is a notch too far towards the secular-logical and the concrete, Ullmann's couplet seems to attract him with its explicit otherworldliness. But Koskenniemi beheads Ullmann's couplet in a significant way by obliterating the divine.

This alteration might explain the difference in movement between Koskenniemi's circulation-oscillation and Przywara's movement which is circular but simultaneously progressing. If arguments from justice are disconnected from divinity, are they not just a different manifestation of worldly being, of the concrete? Will this not confine humans to self-referentiality, performed as oscillation? In the alternative, there would be a divine authority disinterested in progress: a presumedly evil god who confines humanity to meaningless commotion.

Then again, *From Apology to Utopia* is not only about oscillation, it is also about the resurrection of the political in law, about progress. While Ullmann thinks that the ascending form of government took historical precedence, Koskenniemi's very point is that neither form takes precedence in law. I cannot avoid noticing, however, that he reverses Ullmann's presentational order. Ullmann, true to his chronology, sets out the ascending form first, to then explain the descending form in its differences. Koskenniemi does the opposite, perhaps because this is the order a liberal understanding of international law would subscribe to. The introductory section on the couplet in *From Apology to Utopia* is entitled 'The

descending and ascending patterns of justification'.[31] If the law descends
from creation to creaturely existence and ascends again to redemption,
this is a striking parallel to Christian eschatology, however simplified.
Setting the ascending move last means to put the question of a non-place
once more as the culmination point.

So far, I note a certain tension between the oscillating features of
Koskenniemi's work and its progressive-redemptive features. The grammar of international law is also a grammar of international legal scholarship. But what movement is there between them – one of sheer oscillation,
or one of oscillation *and* progression?

Consider the metamorphosis of the descending that is marked out from
Ullmann to Koskenniemi. With the divine being gradually evacuated from
justice, there is no ground for oscillating arguments: that which is ever
more worldly, secular and concrete, will be ever more self-referential and
knowable, and ever less contentious. An ever more positive law will impose
its rule on us.[32] This is the process of unification that the political Catholic
Carl Schmitt conjures up: the end of the nomotic world, and end that he
feared, and that his millennial Spanish colleague Alvaro D'Ors asked him
to welcome, because it was a precondition for the parousia.[33]

What exactly is positive about this ever more positive law? It is its
complete worldliness, its diametrical opposition to that which is knowable, measurable and manageable for humans. But did not Koskenniemi's
decision to rescind the divine from the descending actually contribute
to this positivation and secularization? I would think so. This is all the
more remarkable, as Koskenniemi speaks out ever more strongly against
managerialism and instrumentalism in his later writings. Perhaps this
polemics may also be read as his attempt to correct the consequences
flowing from a secularized concept of the descending.

Then again, Koskenniemi himself operates with a descending argument
that is clearly otherworldly. A quote from 'What is international law for?'
suggests as much:

> [I]nternational law exists as a promise of justice. The agnosticism of politi-
> cal modernity has made the articulation of this teleological view extremely
> difficult. The justice towards which international law points cannot be
> enumerated in substantive values, interests, or objectives. It has no prede-
> termined institutional form. All such languages and suggestions express
> inadequate and reified images (partial) points of view.[34]

So there are, I conclude, two types of descending arguments in Koskenniemi's work. One is at work in oscillation, described in the first argument

of From Apology and Utopia. The second type of descending argument is moving international law along a trajectory of progress. As Koskenniemi shares, or seems to share the 'agnosticism of political modernity', the second type is more hinted at than explained. It is the second type, and the conceptions of justice and law coming along with it, that interests me.

'If there is law', Koskenniemi writes, 'there is no justice, there is only a (more or less well-founded) *expectation* of justice'. In the same paragraph, there is another sentence that merits consideration: 'There is a Messianic structure to international law, the announcement of something that remains eternally postponed'.[35] Both statements are captivating. Law is related to justice only as its promise. Justice is temporally separated from the law promising it. It is, indeed, anathematic to law, as much as the secular is anathematic to the eternal. The expression 'eternally postponed' might be read as equivalent to 'postponed into eternity', which suggests that eternity exists normatively for international law. Koskenniemi depleted the descending pattern in *From Apology to Utopia* from spirituality only to reinvest it into a redemptive justice, whose role would be more prominent in his later writings.

This particular separation of law and justice across the divide between the secular and the eternal is a trope quite familiar to theologians. In Paul's Letter to the Romans, the salvation of Israel plays a decisive role in the structure of the text.[36] In explaining Israel's apostasy, Paul marshals two types of justice. Israel, which had been given the law, hoped for justice from works, and did not receive it. The Gentiles, by contrast, have received a justice from faith, without works and without law. Acknowledging that the people of Israel have a zeal for God, Paul nonetheless suggests that they remained too focussed on worldly justice:

> For they being ignorant of God's righteousness, and going about to establish their own righteousness, have not submitted themselves unto the righteousness of God.
>
> For Christ is the end of the law for righteousness to every one that believeth.[37]

Koskenniemi denounces the 'homo economicus' in international law who 'projects external objectives upon the law'[38] and whose concern is 'compliance'. Why are the objectives of the instrumentalists that Koskenniemi targets 'external' to the law? One explanation I see is because these objectives are now fully worldly ones, and no longer bear any relation to the eternal justice which international law is tasked to point to. This reverberates of Paul's analysis that the focus on 'works' led Israel away from faith. Without denying its normative importance for worldly life, neither Paul's Letter to the Romans nor Koskenniemi's text makes the law into a precondition for justice. Paul:

> Therefore we conclude that a man is justified by faith without the deeds of the law ... Do we then make void the law through faith? God forbid: yea, we establish the law.[39]

Read through this quote, an international law without faith is not 'established'. Law's worldly 'objectives' are but an empty shell. In a Pauline sense, such law is, indeed, less than law. Is this law of faith something that makes international law move, that liberates it from the oscillation between worldly law and worldly justice? I am not sure. Is the task of worldly law just to signpost eternal justice? Or is it to prepare for international justice in an additional sense? If law were a mere signpost, we would have to conclude that oscillation is a mere worldly movement, and progress a mere spiritual movement. The two would remain separate: one seemingly mobile, but translating any movement into the inertia of the circular, the other linear and truly mobile. The difference to Przywara's essential potency pushing towards existential actuality in slowly progressing peristaltic movements could not be starker. But why signpost something, unless it is to guide the behaviour of humans here and now?

It is here that Koskenniemi's promotion of a 'culture of formalism' needs to be considered. While acknowledging that formalism may serve the weak as much as the strong, Koskenniemi points out that 'the political significance of formal law ... is that it expresses the universalistic principle of inclusion at the outset, making possible the regulative ideal of a pluralistic international world'.[40] Engaging in a culture of formalism means to endorse this universalistic principle, which seems to be related in some way to the ideal of universality in community.

In 'The Fate of International Law', Koskenniemi writes:

> [T]he tradition of international law has often acted as a carrier of what is perhaps best described as the regulative idea of universal community, independent of particular interests or desires. This is Kant's cosmopolitan project rightly understood: not an end-state or party programme but a project of critical reason that measures today's state of affairs from the perspective of an ideal of universality that cannot be reformulated into an institution, a technique of rule, without destroying it. The fate of international law is not a matter of re-employing a limited number of professionals for more cost-effective tasks but of re-establishing hope for the human species.[41]

International law is more than a signpost. An international lawyer engaging in the culture of formalism actually engages with a transcendent nucleus of the law, grooms it and thereby 're-establish[es] hope for the human species'. So it is the faith in a universal community to come that is cultivated in formalism. The dynamic of the law is not provided by divine creation in the past, but by its inspiration from the future. It is only through *this* faith in *this* law that progress is possible. The parallel to Paul's letter to the Romans strikes me: 'Do we, then, nullify the law by this faith? Not at all! Rather, we uphold the law'.[42]

I think that a comment on universality needs to be added here. In his Letter to the Romans, Paul claims that the Jews will not be saved until all Gentiles have 'come in'.[43] Adding all Gentiles to the Jews makes no less than a universal community. Redemption for *anyone* is conditioned on the community embracing *everyone*. This Pauline criterion for redemption is repeated in Koskenniemi's culture of formalism.

Reading Koskenniemi through Paul, I see him suggesting, or perhaps merely implying, that redemption presupposes humans exercising a form of redemptive universality in worldly law. This makes me think that there are two movements described in (and by) Koskenniemi's work. First, legal argument oscillates around two poles of law and justice that are placed completely within the secular world. The second movement seems to be very similar to that which Przywara sets out. A worldly practice – law – implies a universality claim that relates it to an otherworldly ideal – that of a redemptive community. Just as in Przywara's work, the driver of the movement between these two poles is the potency of universality pushing to actuality. As in Paul, redemption presupposes the fullness of universality and therewith the gathering of every single person. Once the existence of secular universality in law has become congruent with its essence of eternal universality, there will be redemption. Why? Przywara would respond that it is only in the divine that essence and existence are identical.

1.5   Redemption without Creation?

Przywara's analogy of being tells a story stretching from divine creation of the world to its divine redemption. Koskenniemi's story first seems to limit itself to connect secular modernity with the contours of redemption. With creation having no significant role in Koskenniemi's work, little wonder that law seems a worldly thing given over to oscillation.

Eliminating otherworldly creation is to part ways with a Thomistic analogy of being. While Thomists as Przywara place divine normativity at the beginning (creation), the end (redemption) and the life of humans in between, an account solely working backwards from redemption is less stable and answers fewer questions. What is so tempting about Przywara and Catholicism is that it offers a totality of divine authority and its movements in the world, while Koskenniemi's account can only ever be partial. Christianity's promise of redemption seems to be so much stronger, as its divinity control so much more than the redemptive force in Koskenniemi's account. So why mess things up?

One answer is because messing things up has always been part of the Christian tradition. Marcion, one of the first declared heresiarchs of the Early Christian Church, taught that the God of the Scriptures was different from the father of Christ, the God of the Gospel. Structurally, this severs the line between a god of creation and a god of redemption, between law and faith, between justice and love, and between an imperfect world and the perfection of the Saviour. As Jacob Taubes has pointed out, this lineage continues over Deism well into modernity, citing the example of Adolf Harnack.[44] Yet Taubes also stresses that these movements of thought possess a foundation in the text of the Gospel, and, in particular, in Paul.[45]

The gesture performed in this tradition is that of a radical rejection of divine wrath in the world. To the extent the law is part of it, it also forms part of this rejection.[46] So another answer would be that existing laws and structures are easier denounced as unjustified, the less they participate in a benign transcendent normativity. If the present world is altogether corrupt, including its laws, I will reject the normative significance of any transcendence that created it. Conversely, I will embrace any transcendence that redeems me from the world and its law. No paradox resides in the fact that law is a condition for this embrace. It is the worldly law that Paul advises the Romans to adhere to. Or, in a different terminology, it is the 'culture of formalism' of Koskenniemi's later writings.

1.6   Conclusion

Koskenniemi rejects, as we saw, the translation of universal justice into the concrete practice of norms and institutions. I start to realize that he works in a radically Pauline tradition of thought. The Pauline tradition explains why he is so popular, while the radical spin explains the scepticism he meets. Karl Barth, the Swiss theologian, once set out an analogy of faith (*analogia fidei*) as a counter-position to the Catholic analogy of being. It is in hope alone that international lawyers participate in the coming community. Barth thought theology without religion; Kosken-niemi thinks redemption without creation.

Why would an international lawyer like the work of Martti Kosken-niemi? Because, first, it can be read simply as confirming the secularity of international law. All the while, it benefits from the appeal of well-rehearsed theological structures that are transposed into a worldly set-ting. The language is familiar; yet the content seems to be more within human reach. This kind of lawyer might also be attracted to something like a fleeting sensation of transcendent normativity. Obviously, he or she would avoid pursuing the causes of that comfortable sensation.

Or, second, Koskenniemi's work is liked because it can be read to con-firm the hopelessness of secular international law, unless a transcendence of sorts is worked into it. Here, the reasons for liking Koskenniemi are the reverse. This lawyer would appreciate transcendent normativity and insist on a place for progress, transformation and hope in international law. Some in this group of readers would regret that our language is still contaminated with theological overtones. They would prepare for a transcendent politics. Others, surely a minority, would realize that the transcendence cannot be had without otherworldly redemption, and like his work for exactly that reason. They would prepare for grace.

Why would an international lawyer dislike the work of Martti Kosken-niemi? Obviously, both sets of sympathetic reasons can be reverted into their opposites. But obliterating the particular normative power of cre-ation also alienates quite a few international law scholars and practi-tioners, I believe. Why would an international lawyer want to retain transcendence in creation? Because it infuses concepts such as *jus cogens*, obligations *erga omnes*, non-derogable human rights and the unity of international law with transcendent normative strength from their origin as well as from their end.[47] Koskenniemi's law, by contrast, would receive transcendent normative power by its end alone. Locating transcendence solely in redemption also raises the difficult question of how a redemp-tive future may affect a worldly present. The question implies a form of retroactivity and would leave most international lawyers perplexed.

On this particular point, much will depend on how we imagine our work with this retroactive normative power as international lawyers. Is it a strictly individual task, sending us into introversion and conscientious objection, or a collective one, making us eliminate a set of 'false con-sciousnesses'? There is a striking analogy between the work of the Apostle Paul and that of the international lawyer treading the path sketched up by Koskenniemi: both are universalizing communities, and both use the language of law for that end. There is an elitist element in the transcendent designation coming with an apostolic role that would be deeply worrying to any international lawyer seeking transformation, I would think.

Notes

* The author owes thanks to the editors of this volume, to Janne Nyman and other participants of the Amsterdam Authors' Workshop for their helpful comments. He is particularly indebted to Matilda Arvidsson, Leila Brännström, Ulf Linderfalk and Thomas Spijkerboer for commenting on drafts and thoughts related to this text. Library assistance by Gunilla Wiklund and research assistance by Cecilia K. Andersson is gratefully acknowledged. The author would also like to acknowledge the support by the Torsten and Ragnar Söderberg Foundations for this project.

1. I used the Google Books NGram Viewer and performed a search on his name and such names of international law scholars born in the 1950s that I deemed sufficiently unique to avoid the problem of multiple persons generating occurrences under one and the same name. I chose the corpus 'English' and searched from 1989 onwards. The software set an outer limit to my search in 2008. Any reader repeating my search would be able to verify that Koskenniemi's curve is indeed among the more prominent ones from the mid 1990s onwards.

2. M. Koskenniemi, 'Letter to the Editors of the Symposium', *American Journal of International Law* 93 (1999): 351–61.

3. B. Simma and A. L. Paulus, 'The Responsibility of Individuals for Human Rights Abuses in Internal Conflicts: A Positivist View', *American Journal of International Law* 93 (1999): 302–16.

4. J. L. Dunoff and J. P. Trachtman, 'The Law and Economics of Humanitarian Law Violations in Internal Conflict', *American Journal of International Law* 93 (1999): 394–409.

5. 'Existing academic works seemed to me too focused on either the formal or the substantive without suggesting a plausible account of the relations between the two'. M. Koskenniemi, 'Epilogue to the Reedition of From Apology to Utopia', in *From Apology to Utopia – the Structure of International Legal Argument*, reissue with new epilogue (Cambridge: Cambridge University Press, 2006), 564 (hereinafter referred to as FATU). As will emerge in the following, the various polar opposites used by Koskenniemi (law and politics, apology and utopia, form and substance, the normative and the concrete, ascending and descending, etc.) are marked by a family resemblance without being congruent.

6. This is a question that is individual for each lawyer. Yet it may also be raised on assumptions common to the discipline of international law.

7. M. Zechmeister, 'Przywara, Erich', *Neue Deutsche Biographie* 20 (2001): 752, www .deutsche-biographie.de/pnd118742116.html (accessed 11 February 2016).

8. This experience grew more intense during the Third Reich and culminated with the Gestapo closing down the office of the Jesuit publication *Stimmen der Zeit*, which Przywara edited, in 1941.

9. E. Przywara, *Analogia Entis. Metaphysik. I Prinzip* (Munich: Jösel und Pustet, 1932). A revised and expanded version was published as *Analogia Entis Metaphysik. Ur-Struktur und All-Rhythmus* (Einsiedeln: Johannes, 1962) (hereinafter referred to as AE). Its first part contained the revised text of 1932, and its second part consisted of

thirteen articles and contributions to edited volumes. In the following, all references to AE are to the latter publication.

10. From a Google Ngram search in the corpus 'English', it follows that Przywara's reception has reached a high point in the early 1960s, with the curve ascending again since the late 1990s. The influence of Przywara's work on the thinking of the Swiss Roman Catholic theologian Hans Urs von Balthasar (1905–88) was considerable. Von Balthasar, in turn, is one of the most important Roman Catholic theologians of the past century, whose impact on the thought of Pope Benedict XVI can be readily traced. More generally, Przywara has proven to be of interest to theologians seeking to bridge the gap between Roman Catholic theology and twentieth-century philosophy.

11. E. Przywara, *Analogia Entis: Metaphysics – Original Structure and Universal Rhythm*, J. R. Betz and D. Bentley Hart (trans.) (Grand Rapids, MI: William B. Eerdmans, 2014).

12. The being of beings can be cast as totally different, merely converging on the use of one and the same word. This is called *aequivocatis entis* – voicing the word 'being' on something similar, but ultimately different. In law, this understanding is present in the postmodern belabouring of law's indeterminacy. Or indeed, in the other extreme, beings converge substantially in being. This is *univocatis entis* – voicing the word 'being' indeed denotes something identical to us all. The universality of human rights as cast in advocacy discourses is perhaps the most straightforward example here, but some might think of 'humanity' outright. A middle way between total difference and total identity is to understand my own being as analogous to that of other beings. What I then have in common with others is a relation. This choice is termed the analogy of being – *analogia entis*.

13. FATU, 568–69. This would correspond to the concept of apostolic interpretation of the scripture within the Roman Catholic Church. The Apostles and their rightful successors form a class of persons competent to resolve issues of interpretations in the scriptures.

14. Ibid., 575.

15. Ibid., 617.

16. The Latin original reads 'inter creatorem et creaturam non potest tanta similitudo notari, quin inter eos maior sit dissimilitudo notanda'.

17. This is a matter different from the discussion of law's one right answer amongst legal philosophers. While the possibility of 'one right answer' was defended by the early Dworkin contra Hart, the later Dworkin differentiated his position to a degree where simple conceptions of one right answer no longer apply. See B. Bix, *Law Language and Legal Determinacy* (Oxford: Clarendon, 1995), 77–78.

18. In Roman Catholic theology, this conception of oscillation is perhaps best represented by Hans Urs von Balthasar's idea of *Schwebung* (literally translated as 'flotation' or 'levitation'). Von Balthasar's term describes a state in which a single element is held in suspension by surrounding forces, and that element becomes 'expressive of a surrounding mystery', representative of divine 'glory'. O. Davies, 'Von Balthasar and the Problem of Being', *New Blackfriars* 79 (1998): 11.

19. Why would we be unable to fully comprehend humans? Because they are unknowable to the extent they partake in the divine, or because our scientific cognition is so limited? The unknowability of humans is a good example of how ideas migrate from Christian metaphysics to non-Christian metaphysics in the course of secularization.

20. St. Thomas Aquinas, *On Being and Essence* [*De Ente et Essentia*], R. T. Miller (trans.) (1997), www.fordham.edu/halsall/basis/aquinas-esse.asp#f1 (accessed 11 February 2016).
21. Author's translation. 'Die unwegdeutbare neutrale Dualität zwischen Wissens-Akt und Wissens-Gegenstand ... lässt keine Möglichkeit der Selbstverschliessung in ein "rein"'. AE, 25. Compare this to Koskenniemi's recourse to the real and the ideal in metaphysics in FATU, 517: 'While idealism and realism seem opposite they still need to rely on each other. Philosophy is in a dilemma: though it explains knowledge as a relation between the knowing subject and the object (whether an idea or a fact) it seems incapable of keeping the two separate. In some way, we seem trapped in a circle in which the subject's subjectivity is constructive of the objects perceived while that subjectivity seems to possess existence only in relation to a pre-existing framework of ideas and facts'.
22. 'Concreteness and normativity are, in this sense, necessary and sufficient conditions for the law's objectivity. Now, the bulk of this work has gone to demonstrate that these conditions cannot simultaneously be met'. FATU, 513. Not if law is fully concrete, yet imagined as being the ultimate framing of any political conflict, I should add. So the liberal version of international law is particularly affected by any analogy between its own metaphysics and those of Christianity.
23. FATU, 515.
24. Ibid., 434.
25. Ibid., 605, 611, 616.
26. W. Ullmann, *Law and Politics in the Middle Ages: an Introduction to the Sources of Medieval Political Ideas* (Ithaca, NY: Cornell University Press, 1975).
27. Ibid., 59.
28. Ullmann, *Law and Politics*, 30.
29. Ibid., 31.
30. FATU, 59n141.
31. Ibid., Section 1.3.1.
32. 'But given the deep structure of positive law, the attempt to impose itself will fail, would it not?' commented Wouter Werner on this passage. It will fail, I think, but only in the perception of those who find the means to resist its imposing narrative.
33. An exchange of letters between Schmitt and D'Ors is documented in G. Maschke (ed.), *Carl Schmitt: Frieden oder Pazifismus? Arbeiten zum Völkerrecht und zur internationalen Politik 1924–1978* (Berlin: Duncker and Humblot, 2005). In his sceptical response to Schmitt's katechonic position that the Antichrist needs to be countered, D'Ors said, 'Doch die Ankunft des Antichrist ist nichts anderes als eines der Zeichen, die der Parusie Jesu Christi vorausgehen; in diesem Sinne darf jenes Ende nicht nur nicht zurückgewiesen werden, sondern es muß ersehnt werden'. (But the arrival of the Antichrist is nothing but one of the signs that precedes the parousia of Jesus Christ. In that sense, this end may not only not be refused, but it must be longed for.) Ibid., 852–53.
34. M. Koskenniemi, 'What Is International Law For?' In *The Politics of International Law* (Oxford: Hart, 2011), 266.
35. Ibid., 267 (emphasis original).
36. In Jacob Taubes's interpretation, Paul's Letters to the Romans and the Corinthians pivot on the Greek word *pan* (all). Taubes, *Die politische Theologie des Paulus* (Munich: Fink, 2003), 9 and 72.

37. Romans 10:3–4 (KJV).
38. Koskenniemi, 'What Is International Law For?', 266.
39. Romans 3:28 and 31 (KJV). Some English translations render the last words (*histemi nomos*) with 'we uphold the law' instead.
40. Koskenniemi, 'What Is International Law For?', 256–57 (footnote omitted).
41. M. Koskenniemi, 'The Fate of Public International Law: between Technique and Politics', *Modern Law Review* 70 (2007): 30.
42. Romans 3:31 (NIV).
43. 'For I would not, brethren, that ye should be ignorant of this mystery, lest ye should be wise in your own conceits; that blindness in part is happened to Israel, until the fulness of the Gentiles be come in. And so all Israel shall be saved: as it is written, There shall come out of Sion the Deliverer, and shall turn away ungodliness from Jacob: For this is my covenant unto them, when I shall take away their sins'. Romans 11:25–27 (KJV).
44. Harnack, one of the most significant German theologians of the late Wilhelminian period, polemicized against the fact that the twentieth century still saw the Old Testament being retained in the Christian canon. Taubes, *Politische Theologie des Paulus*, 84–85.
45. Taubes explains that Paul reduced Christ's 'Great Commandment' to love the Lord and to love one's neighbour to the last of its two limbs in Romans 13:9, making a double commandment into a single one. Taubes, *Politische Theologie des Paulus*, 80–83. To the extent that *agape* – love of one's neighbour, indeed, of anyone, neighbour or not – is the worldly practice of a community to come, it is indeed remarkable that Paul chooses to organize it from redemption rather than from creation.
46. In Taubes's analysis, both Judaism and Christianity grapple with the problem of God's wrath as illustrated by Jom Kippur and Paul's casting himself as a new Moses. See Taubes, *Politische Theologie des Paulus*, 43–55. When God decided to annihilate the people of Israel for its breach of the Covenant, Moses offered himself as a scapegoat, and ultimately brought God to redeem Israel. It is noteworthy that the relationship between God and his people is cast in legal form (a covenant), and it can be renegotiated by the weaker side (the people of Israel through Moses). This illustrates that the laws of wrath give way to the laws of redemption.
47. Koskenniemi has famously articulated the kitsch character of *jus cogens*. The kitschiness of *jus cogens* is that it converts the transcendent into a fully worldly product. Jean-Luc Marion holds Catholic kitsch to be a safeguard against idolatry, because nobody would actually confuse it for God. Seen such, we should perhaps add further ornament to the doctrine of *jus cogens*. See M. Koskenniemi, 'International Law in Europe: between Tradition and Renewal', *European Journal of International Law* 16 (2005): 113–24.

Bibliography

Aquinas, St. Thomas. *On Being and Essence [De Ente Et Essentia]*, Robert T. Miller (trans.) (Internet Medieval Sourcebook, 1997).
Bix, Brian. *Law, Language, and Legal Determinacy* (Oxford: Clarendon, 1995).

Davies, Oliver. 'Von Balthasar and the Problem of Being'. *New Blackfriars* 79 (1998): 11–17.

Dunoff, Jeffrey L., and Joel P. Trachtman. 'The Law and Economics of Humanitarian Law Violations in Internal Conflict'. *American Journal of International Law* 93 (1999): 394–409.

Koskenniemi, Martti. *From Apology to Utopia: The Structure of International Legal Argument.* Reissue with a new epilogue (Cambridge: Cambridge University Press, 2006).

'International Law in Europe: Between Tradition and Renewal'. *European Journal of International Law* 16 (2005): 113–24.

'Letter to the Editors of the Symposium'. *American Journal of International Law* 93 (1999): 351–61.

'What Is International Law For?' In *The Politics of International Law* (Oxford: Hart, 2011), 241.

Maschke, Günter (ed.). *Carl Schmitt: Frieden Oder Pazifismus? Arbeiten Zum Völkerrecht Und Zur Internationalen Politik 1924–1978* (Berlin: Duncker and Humblot, 2005).

Przywara, Erich. *Analogia Entis: Metaphysics – Original Structure and Universal Rhythm,* John R. Betz and David B. Hart (trans.) (Grand Rapids, MI: William B. Eerdmans, 2014).

Analogia Entis: Metaphysik. I Prinzip (Munich: Jösel und Pustet, 1932).

Analogia Entis Metaphysik. Ur-Struktur Und All-Rhythmus (Einsiedeln: Johannes, 1962).

Simma, Bruno, and Andreas L. Paulus. 'The Responsibility of Individuals for Human Rights Abuses in Internal Conflicts: a Positivist View'. *American Journal of International Law* 93 (1999): 302–16.

Taubes, Jacob. *Die Politische Theologie Des Paulus* (München: Fink, 2003).

Ulmann, Walter. *Law and Politics in the Middle Ages: an Introduction to the Sources of Medieval Political Ideas* (Ithaca, NY: Cornell University Press, 1975).

2

Formalism, Realism and the Politics of Indeterminacy

DAVID DYZENHAUS*

2.1 Introduction

In *From Apology to Utopia*, Martti Koskenniemi argued that formalism and anti-formalism or realism in international law are locked in a perpetual conflict with each other, a conflict in which neither has priority over the other and indeed the existence of each depends on the other.[1] In his much-discussed 'epilogue' to the re-issue of the book, Koskenniemi described crisply the 'descriptive concern' of the project:

> to try to articulate the rigorous formalism of international law while simultaneously accounting for its political open-endedness – the sense that competent argument in the field needed to follow strictly defined formal patterns that nevertheless allowed (even enabled) the taking of any conceivable position in regard to a dispute or problem[2].

However, Koskenniemi did not articulate with the same degree of specificity his normative concern. He spoke only of the 'political commitment' from which the 'cosmopolitan project' of international law had once arisen, one which has to do with 'meaningful international legal practice'.[3] Moreover, it seemed that for him normativity is on the one side of the set of terms associated with formalism that contrast with the set of terms that associate with anti-formalism. On the one hand, we have formalism and normativity and on the other realism and concreteness, with international law oscillating between the two sets.[4]

To the extent that there is a shift in the 'epilogue' from the book it is to understanding the opposition between formalism and anti-formalism as 'the *condition* of *possibility* of there being something like international law in the first place'. International law has to be thought of 'as a language' and 'the opposition [between formalism and anti-formalism] as a key part of its (generative) grammar'.[5] That is, rather than understanding realism as a position that seeks to undermine international law's ability to provide an arena for a kind of deliberation qualitatively different from what we might think of as the calculations of power politics, it is part of what makes such deliberation possible at all. Indeed, not only is it part of what makes such deliberation possible, but it is also part of the deliberation itself, as much of Koskenniemi's fine-grained analysis of actual reasoning processes seeks to show the oscillation between formalism and realism within legal discourse.

In this chapter, I undertake a tour of legal theory that, in my view, illuminates a deep problem in Koskenniemi's work. I should note that no particular detail of what I set out below will be news to Koskenniemi, or to his many readers, since he alludes often to much the same family of ideas. But my claim is that my reconstruction reveals a logic that is mirrored in the trajectory of Koskenniemi's thought and that this helps us to see that he yearns for formalism at the same time as supposing that anti-formalism is correct as a matter of description. And that supposition is entailed in his mistaken belief that what he calls 'the indeterminacy thesis'[6] – the claim that law is radically indeterminate – states an empirical fact about the world of law, when it is a political position that is presupposed in an anti-formalism that opposes the politics of formalism. That mistake leads him to oscillate between two positions: an external realism about the law that utterly debunks the practice of law and an internal realism, a kind of immanent critique of that practice. Moreover, as I shall show, a large part of his problem is that the formalism for which he yearns is of the wrong kind.

2.2   Formalism in Legal Theory

Formalism in law is often regarded as a nineteenth-century construct of legal order as a formal *system* of formal *rules*. The formality of the system pertains to the provenance of the rules. One knows whether a rule is a valid member of the system because there are tests for membership that are formal in that they are purely procedural, or what in the tradition of British parliamentary supremacy are called rules of 'manner and form'.

Consider the example of a monarch, Betty, who makes her laws known to her people by writing them on a notice board in the town square. This rule is purely procedural since all that Betty has to do to make a law is to write the law down on the board. In a more complex legal society, such as the UK, the rules of manner and form will be more elaborate, involving different stages in the House of Commons and the House of Lords, as well as royal assent. But by and large these rules are purely procedural in the same way as in Betty's simpler society. So the first attribute of formalism in law is the systemic one that the rules for determining what counts as law are purely procedural.

The formality of the rules has also to do with the fact that for the rules to do their work of ruling, they must have the attribute of having a content that can be identified by tests that refer to the text that appeared on the notice board and not to Betty in her personal capacity. If legal subjects – those subject to the law Betty make – asked Betty what to do instead of relying on the rules as stated by Betty on the notice board, they would be subject to Betty's say-so and not to her rules.

The distinction between Betty in her personal capacity and Betty in her official role as legislator is of immense importance. The first comprehensive philosophical treatment of it is to be found in Hobbes's *Leviathan*, in Chapter XVI 'OF PERSONS, AUTHORS, and things Personated', where Hobbes sets out the characteristics of artificial persons in order to clarify the claim with which he begins the work – that the sovereign is the artifact of the natural individuals in the state of nature, akin to God's *Fiat* at the moment of creation, '*Let us make man*'.[7] But the idea behind the distinction is of much more ancient provenance, found for example in the Talmudic stories about the human interpreters of God's written law who during their deliberations about some controversial issue of interpretation of the law reject God's offer to clarify his intentions. For the distinction between legislation and interpretation on which these stories turn entails the distinction between God in his artificial capacity as the maker of divine law and in his personal or natural capacity as an individual capable of intervening in particular ways in the world.

As we will see, there is more to the formality of rules than the attribute just discussed. For example, Lon L. Fuller set out a list of eight principles of legality, including generality and publicity, with which law has to comply if it is to accomplish the task of ruling.[8] However, it is controversial whether these or other such lists are formal or procedural or even substantive in nature, as well as the extent to which law has to comply with them.

For the moment, I want to note that the claim that the rules have to be formal faces more than the problems just sketched. It is also generally agreed that questions will arise about the application of rules, no matter how carefully they are drafted, that can only be answered by a creative act of interpretation. Rules do not, in short, determine their application. But if the creative judgement of some persons or group of persons is what determines the application of rules, it might seem that legal subjects are subject not to the rules but to the will of that person or persons. And if that is the case, they are no longer authentic legal subjects – subject to the rule of law. Rather, they are subject to the arbitrary will of the interpreters.

There is a formal device adopted in domestic legal orders to ensure that the person who determines the application of the rules is not the same person as the person who makes the rules. I mean, of course, the separation of powers between the legislature, the body with the authority to make law, the judiciary, the body with the authority to interpret the law, and the executive, which has the task of implementing the law. So here we have a third aspect of legal formalism, the formalism of institutions – of formally delineated institutional roles.

However, in the face of the problem of rule application, such institutional formalism might seem at best capable of ensuring that one is subject to the will of a different group of persons from the ones who made the rule. Indeed, while the separation of powers is committed to the principle of judicial independence, on the assumption that judges are tasked not only with interpreting the law, but also with ensuring that the executive acts within the limits set by the law as interpreted, the problem of rule application threatens to undermine the very distinction between interpretation and legislation. And it poses the same threat to the formalism of the legal system, since that property depends on the existence of purely procedural rules and these rules are no more immune to the problem of rule application than any other rules. Since the problem will have to be resolved by one or other institution within the separation of powers, there will inevitably be an explicitly political contest when such a problem arises, which is why H. L. A. Hart in *The Concept of Law* could offer only the miserable comfort that in such situations 'all that succeeds is success'.[9]

Moreover, if every act of interpretation transcends the rule that is being interpreted, and if every act of rule application involves interpretation, the separation of powers far from decreasing the occasions for arbitrariness multiplies them. Indeed, we might think it preferable to be subject to the arbitrary will of Betty alone than to be subject to the arbitrary will of a multitude of her subordinate officials. As Hobbes suggests in *Leviathan*, it is short-sighted to suppose that there is something 'obnoxious' about subjection to the 'lusts' and 'other irregular passions' of one sovereign with unlimited power, when the contrast is the 'dissolute condition of masterlesse men' or subjection to the arbitrary will of the many in the state of nature.[10]

Recall that the problem of rule application seems to arise quite apart from the other problems identified – what the criteria of form are and whether any candidate is really formal or political substance disguised as legal form. It might thus seem that there is nothing to be gained in proceeding to discuss these other problems, since the problem of rule application by itself destroys any hope for a formal theory of law. Indeed, this was the view taken by the Free Law Movement at the turn of the twentieth century, a group of sociologically minded scholars in Germany, who reacted against the formalism of the 'jurisprudence of concepts' of nineteenth-century German thought, a view of law as a 'seamless network of rules that answered all problems scientifically, and excluded all extra-neous values',[11] thus refusing to confront the problem of rule application. A similar reaction to home-grown, nineteenth-century formalism took place in the US in the anti-formalism of the early Legal Realists, a reaction that has its later manifestations in movements with quite different politics, for example, Law and Economics and Critical Legal Studies, and in the general orientation within the US legal academy towards an exclusively functionalist and policy-oriented analysis of law.

I have in this section described the problem as one of 'rule application' rather than 'indeterminacy' for a reason. As I shall start to show in the next section, 'indeterminacy' is not an objective or value neutral description of the empirical situation of law. Rather, it carries an implicit political charge.

2.3   Legal Positivism and the Indeterminacy Thesis

When used in relation to law, the term 'indeterminate' implies that the content of the law cannot be determined by legal reasoning alone, reasoning that relies exclusively on the resources that law itself makes available for determining the content of the law. While the term is usually portrayed by those who use it as a mere description of the empirical situation, their mode of description turns out to be a politically charged characterization.

I do not wish to deny that there is often controversy about how to interpret or to apply the law. Rather, my claim is that a great deal turns on how that controversy is characterized, and that the question of how best to characterize it is ultimately one that can only be addressed by normative political theory, and thus in a contest of substantive political positions. Moreover, once one finds oneself on political terrain, it becomes clear that a choice has to be made about whether to take law seriously, meaning the commitment to strive for the rule of law.

The place to start though is not with realism, but in a genealogy of legal positivism, which at least in its late-twentieth-century version, regards the indeterminacy of law as a fact of the matter and thus regards 'indeterminate' as a value neutral, descriptive term. However, as I shall now show, legal positivism was once associated with a kind of formalism and that was because of its substantive political commitments to what we can think of as democratic utilitarianism.[12]

This last claim will seems at odds with legal positivism's association since the 1950s with a purely instrumental view of law, according to which law is no more than a particular way of exercising political power in the service of whatever interests the power-holder deems fit. Hence, legal positivists have a debunking stance towards theories in the natural law tradition that seek to show that there is some necessary moral quality to the rule of law. Moreover, this debunking stance includes exposing the 'childish fiction' that judges never make law. Writing in 1958 and again in 1961, Hart indignantly rejected the association of formalism with legal positivism. His positivist predecessors, Hart asserted, had insisted that in cases where it was controversial what the law required, judges are in a 'penumbra' of unsettled law and they have to legislate an answer. Indeed, Hart pointed out, John Austin had welcomed judicial legislation.[13]

But at one point legal positivism was associated with a kind of formalism that argues that judges have to legislate an answer when it is controversial what the law requires. Since, on this view, judicial legislation is illegitimate, legal institutions should be reformed in such a way as to make as rare as possible occasions when it would be controversial what the law required and then, to the extent that one might have to rely on judges to resolve such cases, their resolutions would have no legal force beyond the parties to the controversy. In other words, we have Bentham's radical solution to what he perceived as the ills of the common law tradition – codification of statute law and the abolition of the doctrine of precedent.

The shift in attitude of positivist legal philosophers to judicial legislation from Bentham to Austin, which is not discussed by Hart or his positivist followers, comes about because of a fundamental political shift. Bentham's utilitarianism proposes that the best way to calculate utility is to have the masses elect representatives to parliament who will translate the preferences of the majority into legislation. It is thus illegitimate for judges to superimpose their moral views on law that has a content that in fact reflects the outcome of legitimately performed calculation. But Austin concluded that the experiment with democracy had by his day shown that

Bentham was wrong to trust the masses. They are still too ignorant and so elites, including judicial elites, should perform the calculations.

As I have tried to show in previous work, the positivist distinction between law and morality is not best understood as a claim that there is no necessary connection between law and morality, the so-called Separation Thesis of Hart's legal positivism.[14] Rather, it is a claim about how to determine the content of the law, one which is fully consistent with, even entailed by, a utilitarian political theory such as Bentham's, which for reasons of political morality argues that the popularly elected legislature should be the exclusive source of the rules of the legal system. For such a theory, it is essential both that there are formal tests for identifying what counts as the law of the system and formal tests for identifying the content of the law. In other words, a substantive political morality – democratic utilitarianism – lies behind the commitment to formality.

Hence, the politics of this kind of formalism is that of a polity designed on utilitarian lines. In order to ensure the greatest happiness of the greatest number, one designs a political system in which the people's representatives will, first, make a collective calculation about how to achieve that goal, second, they will translate that goal into law, and, third, law will be implemented in a way faithful to that goal.

It follows from this view that any moment when it is unclear what the law requires is a threat because it might permit an official other than a legislator to legislate. Judges were Bentham's principal concern, as he regarded the judicial elites of his day as intent on arrogating legislative power to themselves, disguised by their claim that the common law provided them with a resource of timeless, transcendent values to which they had privileged access, and in whose light they should interpret statute law. Bentham was thus intent on stripping the mask of mystery from the common law and on reducing the opportunities for judges to impose their values on the law. As a result, he was utterly opposed to bills of rights since these give to judges the authority both to interpret statutes in light of the rights and to test the validity of statutes for their compliance with the rights.

When Anglophone legal positivism took a descriptive or conceptual turn away from Bentham's political project under Hart's guidance, the problem of indeterminacy was reconceived not as a political problem, but as a problem that arises as a matter of fact about law. Indeterminacy will arise because of the constraints of language, lack of perfect foresight (there will be unanticipated situations) and in any case it is often considered desirable to build deliberately some indeterminacy into the law in order to permit judges and administrators to adapt it to a complex and changing social world. On this view, the common law and entrenched bills of rights are ways of constructing legal order that will likely create more indeterminacy than one will find in legal orders that avoid both. But legal positivism takes no position on the political question of how best to design legal order.

However, and as critics of this strange but influential version of legal positivism argued, the view that indeterminacy is something simply to be observed as a matter of fact is itself premised on a view that the content of the law is what is ascertainable as matter of fact. The claim that law is indeterminate when competent lawyers disagree about what law requires, so that judges have to legislate an answer in an extra- or at best quasi-legal space, is premised on the view that legal requirements exist if and only if there is a consensus among competent lawyers about what as a matter of fact the content of the law is.

The point here is not that competent lawyers will always agree, or that law could be transformed (as Bentham hoped) to the point where there would be such agreement nearly all the time. It is, first, that how one characterizes the disagreement matters, second, that the rival characterizations flow from different conceptions of law, and, finally, that the differences are ultimately political. This point has been articulated and elaborated over the years by Ronald Dworkin and I shall show in the next section how suitably adapted it has considerable explanatory power when it comes to Koskenniemi's position.[15]

2.4 Internal and External Realism

Dworkin's first challenge to Hart's legal positivism advanced the view that in what Hart had called penumbral cases judges are under a legal duty to decide the case by resort to principles already immanent in the law. Dworkin's own theory of interpretation holds both that in what he called 'hard cases' there is one right answer and that this answer is fully determined by the 'full' law – the positive public record and the principles that show that record in its best moral light.[16]

The change in terminology is significant. To call a case hard is meant to signal no more than competent lawyers reasonably disagree about what the law requires. And that avoids implying that the mere fact of disagreement entails that the lawyers have moved outside some 'core' of determinate law into a 'penumbral', extra-legal space.[17] Hart sought to deal with this challenge by claiming that the choice between principles could not be settled by the law but only by a legally unconstrained act of judicial choice or discretion. Put differently, he claimed that the more Dworkin showed that the adjudication of hard cases involves creative reasoning based on legal principles, the better the evidence for the positivist thesis about judicial legislation.[18]

Dworkin's second and later challenge was to Hart's assumption that a positivist view of legal order as consisting of determinate rules is not threatened by the penumbra of uncertainty. There is supposed to be no threat because the core is in fact much larger than the penumbra and this provides the certainty that makes legal order possible. Dworkin argued there is no core in the positivist sense. What appears to be the core is the product of interpretation in just the way that Hart took decisions in the penumbra to be. The core is merely an area of provisional agreement between rival political conceptions of law.[19]

Dworkin's second challenge makes the first more radical. If there is no clear boundary between core and penumbra so that the core does not so much diminish in size as disappear, then Hart's response to Dworkin's first challenge implodes legal positivism. For if, as Hart indicates, a decision on the basis of an interpretation of legal principles is always ultimately unconstrained by law, and if all questions about what law is are interpretative in this sense, then there is no such thing as law. More precisely, there is no such thing as law in the positivist sense of a set of rules whose content can be determined as a matter of fact, that is, by formal tests of the sort the tradition of legal positivism favoured. The problem that positivists acknowledged as occurring only at the margins of legal order now appears throughout.

Such a conclusion is welcome to realists who assert that it is illusory to believe that law could constrain power. With positivists, realists claim that when the law is indeterminate, legal meaning is determined by power because, again with positivists, they start from the premise that the content of the law is what is ascertainable as matter of fact. But since realists also claim that the law is never determinate – there is no core – law can never, on their view, operate as a constraint on power. In this respect, but in this respect only, they can accept Dworkin's critique of legal positivism. For them Dworkin's position is just another vain attempt by a liberal to stabilize indeterminate law by implausibly insisting that the principles that underpin the public legal record are substantive principles of a liberal political morality. Hence, realists hold that what passes for the content of the law is the product of communities powerful enough to have their preferred meaning imposed as the law.

In making these moves, realism denies the worth of legal theory altogether, seeing it as an attempt to hide the facts of power. However, in
seeking to debunk legal theory and refocus our concerns on political and
social forces, realism also gives up on the aspiration of the rule of law
to replace the arbitrary rule of men with something qualitatively better.
Realism is an account of the dynamics of power, not an account of authority and obligation. Moreover, it is an account of power that tries to cut the
ground from under an account of authority. It does not simply mount an
inquiry from a different theoretical perspective.[20]

All of these moves are to be found in Carl Schmitt's work, beginning in
his publication of 1912, *Gesetz und Urteil* – 'Law and judgement'.[21] There
Schmitt deals in some detail with Bentham and Austin on indeterminacy.
He concludes that there is no way of stabilizing law from the inside, so he
suggests as a solution the social character of the judiciary. If judges are of
the same empirical type, they can be counted on to interpret law in much
the same way.

The trajectory of Schmitt's work during the travails of Weimar can then
be seen in terms of his increasing realization of the radical implications
of the indeterminacy thesis and, correspondingly, that the only way to
stabilize both legal and political order is through a much more radical
idea than a socially homogeneous judiciary. One needs a sovereign who
can establish the substantive homogeneity of the *Volk*. Once society is
organized on the basis of a set of thick communal values, with all who do
not or cannot subscribe to such values excluded from the community, law
can successfully be used to express the concrete order of that community.
In this way, Schmitt's position is negative. He does not set out a substantive
political position, but claims only that a genuine political position has to
have the thick communal substance that liberalism cannot have. He thus
rules out liberalism but allows in any political position that expresses what
he regards as an authentic vision of the substantive homogeneity of the
people.[22]

Koskenniemi would reject utterly Schmittean talk of substantive homogeneity as the solution to the problem of indeterminacy. But there are two
respects in which his position is difficult to distinguish from Schmitt's.
The first is what he calls in the 'epilogue' to *From Apology to Utopia* 'The
nature of indeterminacy',[23] and he says that most of the book 'is devoted
to the demonstration of the indeterminacy thesis'.[24] He is anxious to
assure his audience that his position on indeterminacy is not merely the
standard legal positivist one that rules have a observable 'core' of settled meaning and an observable 'penumbra' where it is not clear what
law requires. Rather, he wishes to explain how indeterminacy arises in

international law. Interpretations of international law will vary according to how interpreters discern the reason behind the rule and here they will differ inevitably because they have 'contradictory priorities', that is, political objectives or what we can call reason of state. The 'most unambiguous rule' is thus 'infected by the disagreements that concern how that reason should be understood and how it ranks with competing ones'. From this it follows that '*any* course of action' can be defended by 'professionally impeccable legal arguments'.[25]

However, Koskenniemi hastens to assure his readers that this infection is neither a 'scandal' nor a 'structural deficiency'. Rather, it is an 'absolutely central aspect of international law's acceptability' that it is so open.[26] The only limit he contemplates is what he calls 'structural bias', and this idea – the 'main political point' of the book – tells us that, despite the radical openness of the space of international law argument, there will at any one time be a 'professional consensus or a mainstream answer to any particular problem'. Indeed, it seems that the space is radically open only 'logically' speaking, and that in practice professional competence lies in knowing what the 'hegemonic . . . narratives' are as well as their 'counter-hegemonic' ones, so that one can deploy 'one's services in favour of one or the other'.[27]

Since structural bias stabilizes the international order, though it seems in a way that will generally serve the interests of the powerful, it is not clear why Koskenniemi thinks that his 'empirical argument' about structural bias turns a 'weak' indeterminacy thesis into a 'strong' one.[28] One would expect, that is, that bias would turn any strong indeterminacy argument into a weak one, for bias seems to ensure that only those legal arguments will succeed that happen to advance the interests of the politically more powerful states.

This sociological effect could be compounded by another – the second respect in which Koskenniemi's position approaches Schmitt. For like Schmitt in 1912, Koskenniemi seems to see the answer to the problem of indeterminacy in the legal profession, in its sociological make-up. International lawyers by dint of their training and social formation are a relatively homogeneous group, a sociological type, and that has the effect that they will cluster around the same sets of results despite the radical openness of law. In combination, these two sociological effects can create a great deal of stability in what would otherwise be an international state of nature.

Koskenniemi does differ from Schmitt in a way that should in principle make a difference to his approach to such problems. He regards it as important not that the lawyers share the same political and social ideology, but that they have been socialized into accepting a professional ideology, one that values above all competence in legal argument and thus what one might think of as fidelity to law. For such lawyers will be committed to making *legal* arguments – to offering only reasons and chains of reasoning that other competent lawyers will recognize as authentically legal, even though they might disagree fundamentally on which legal reasons are relevant, as well as how the reasons that are agreed to be relevant should be weighed, interpreted, etc. It is thus in this commitment to the culture of legal formalism that Koskenniemi detects a possible antidote to what we can think of as an external realism about the law – a position that utterly debunks the practice of law. However, he also accepts a kind of internal realism about the law, and internal realism cannot maintain any stopping place between itself and Schmittean or external realism.

I call Koskenniemi's position internal realism because he sees it as a form of 'immanent critique'. On his account of the practice of argumentation in international law, 'the justifying principles of international law – the liberal doctrine of politics – in fact fail as justifying principles'.[29] Notice that his claim is that liberalism *is* the doctrine that justifies international law but that the justification fails. This claim is also made by Schmitt, as well as by later realists. It has the following form. Liberalism provides the only possibility for an immanent justification of the law, one that appeals, as it were, to law's own principles. But when we look inside of law, all we find is disagreement that cannot be resolved because it is between contradictory ideologies. Law then supplies a space for the contest of the political ideologies while not being able to discipline that contest. That Koskenniemi supposes that that '*any* course of action' can be defended by 'professionally impeccable legal arguments' is a statement of internal realism, not of formalism.

However, since he thinks that internal realism is true of any possible case, his internal realism about the law becomes external realism. For if the grammar of international law is so capacious that a competent lawyer can formulate a perfectly formed legal sentence that advances 'any conceivable position', it is not at all clear that the grammar contains resources to say more about the sentence than that one disagrees with it for reasons external to the legal discourse. If this were right, France's legal disagreement about the legality of the US-led invasion of Iraq was not one in which either side had the force of the better argument, where force means the force of being better from the perspective of international law. For there were in principle[30] competent lawyers on both sides who could produce equally well-formed legal arguments to support their countries' positions. In the result it was political force that resolved and had to resolve the disagreement, whether or not the lawyers produced well-formed legal arguments – the force that comes from having the most powerful military in the world.

Given this, one might wonder why Koskeniemmi's superiors in government would have been 'baffled' and 'disappointed' and would certainly not have consulted him again had he, when asked for a legal opinion, responded that this was a 'stupid question' and he would tell them 'where Finnish interests lay', or 'what type of State behaviour was desirable'.[31] For what was he accomplishing in giving them an opinion about the law if both he and his superiors knew that that amounted to merely finding the legal language to advance what someone in government took to be Finnish interests, given that there was no limit to the positions that could be advanced through law?

There is, to put things another way, an important difference between two ways of framing the request from one's superiors for professional legal advice. On the one hand, the request can be framed conditionally. 'X is what the government would like to do in the international arena; given our understanding of our country's interests, is X permissible under international law?' On the other hand, the request can be framed unconditionally. 'X is what the government would like to do in the international arena; given our understanding of our country's interests, find the legal argument that supports the proposition that X is permissible under international law'.

Notice that the issue is not how the request is actually framed by the government, but how lawyers frame it. For even if the government adopts the second way of framing the request, the lawyers, as long as they reframe it in the first way, have available to them the response: 'We can't find a legal justification for X. So you will have decide whether you want to act lawfully or not'. In addition, the lawyers are also entitled to say: 'We can find a legal justification, but it is so thin that to act on its basis would undermine our reputation as a nation committed to international law'. Finally, if the government decides to go ahead and act unlawfully while pretending that its advice was that it was acting lawfully, its senior law advisors would have to consider whether their commitment to professional integrity permitted them to keep silent and/or stay in office.

But if international law does not provide a basis that requires legal professionals to adopt the first frame, they are not entitled to give either of the responses just set out, and the question of their integrity simply does not arise. For if international law does not condition the range of possible responses, it cannot begin to provide criteria for saying what is a better response within the range, and the international lawyer will never find him or herself in a conflict between the pull of law and what his or her superiors are asking.

This is, of course, an extreme position, and one which (again) I am sure Koskenniemi rejects, an impression that is only strengthened by the trend in his more recent work to advocate a Kantian version of formalism as an antidote to what he seems to regard as the rampant realism of international lawyers.[32] But the question is whether he is entitled to reject this position, given his continued insistence that international law does not condition the range of possible responses. Kantian formalism, on his account, does nothing to constrain legal argument and indeed its normativity has only to do with its radical openness to argument, a quality that Koskenniemi deems democratic because no voices are excluded. As long as your country has competent lawyers, it will be able to make its voice heard on the international stage. There can, in short, be no such thing as a 'scandal' in international law.

There is, nevertheless, something to the thought that Koskenniemi and Schmitt share that the content of the law, whether domestic or international, is unlikely to match a particular substantive position, for example a substantive liberal position such as Dworkin's, as there is to Koskenniemi's hints that formalism has the potential to do more work than the liberal legalism he criticizes with Schmitt. But, as I shall argue in the final section of this chapter, he has so far not been able to do more than hint at the potential, in part because he has only glimpsed the most promising way of elaborating it.

2.5   Law's Form

A notable omission from Koskenniemi's legal scholarship is any serious discussion of the rule of law. Correspondingly, as already mentioned, there is no discussion of the body of work prompted by Fuller's claim that there are eight principles of legality with which law has to comply substantially to be law and that together ensure that law has a moral quality to it. My point is not that Koskenniemi never mentions the rule of law. Rather, when one uses the index of his books as a guide to his views on this topic, one generally finds the rule of law equated with the rule of 'neutral and objectively verifiable rules'.[33] Since for him the indeterminacy thesis utterly debunks the thought that there could be such a rule, he can proceed on the assumption the topic need not detain him further. However, here, as elsewhere, his analysis is driven by the assumption that if there is no legal content that is 'objectively verifiable', there is no law.

This neglect of Fuller is a pity because while Fuller himself called his eight principles 'procedural', they are better understood as formal, and his work on legality/the rule of law is very much dedicated to elaborating the idea of a formal legal culture. Indeed, Fuller's work had a direct influence on a political philosopher who has at least a marginal presence in some of Koskenniemi's formalist moments, Michael Oakeshott.[34] For example, when Koskenniemi suggests that the 'political significance of formal law' is that 'it expresses the universalistic principle of inclusion', thus 'making possible the regulative ideal of a pluralistic international world', he elaborates this thought with a quotation from Terry Nardin, a prominent scholar of Oakeshott, which relies on Oakeshott's idea that the rule of law is the rule of non-instrumental rules: '[O]nly a regime of noninstrumental rules, understood to be authoritative independent of particular beliefs or purposes is compatible with the freedom of its subjects to be different'.[35]

Koskenniemi continues:

> The form of law constructs political adversaries as equals, entitled to express their subjectively felt injustices in terms of breaches of rules of the community to which they belong no less than their adversaries – thus affirming both that inclusion and the principle that the conditions applying to the treatment of any member of the community must apply to every other member as well.[36]

But the point of a regulative ideal of this sort is not wholly to describe what is the case but also to bring it about that it is the case. Consider how realists describe the pockets in the law where it is not clear how the law regulates a situation so that an official has to decide. As we know, they will describe these as pockets of uncontrolled discretion. So described, the pockets can be used as building blocks for a broader argument that includes all of legal practice in its scope, and which seeks to reconstitute it in its image, that is, the image of law as exercising no constraint proposed by external realism. In contrast, those committed to a culture of formalism will not see these pockets as voids for external politics dressed in legal garb to fill. Rather, formalists will see these as opportunities for argument that must seek to show how any conclusion offered by a lawyer, or determined by a judge, is acceptable both as an interpretation of the relevant law and an exemplification of just those values that Koskenniemi alludes to as the political values of formalism.

However, these values are not the immediate bases for adjudication or legal argument. To suppose that they are is to make the mistake made by Dworkin when he claims that a particular liberal understanding of equal concern and respect will be found to ground interpretation in any hard case. Rather, the values are mediated by the principles of legality that serve those values. The claim here, unexplored in Koskenniemi's work, is, first, that attention to the form that law has to take in order to be law will show that rule by law is always rule in accordance with the rule of law. Second, it is that law's form disciplines the space of legal argument and thus the conclusions that can be reached within that space in a way that serves the values identified by Koskenniemi as the politics of formalism.

This kind of focus makes available a different understanding of the importance of the professional competence of international lawyers in maintaining formalism from the sociological conception to which Koskenniemi seems committed. International lawyers should be regarded, and should regard themselves, as a community united by what Fuller called 'fidelity to law'.[37] On Fuller's view, law has certain formal features that lawyers have a professional duty to maintain and these features condition both legal argument and legal content in a way that makes it sensible to regard law as having a moral quality to it, an inner morality of law. The thought that there is an ethics of role is in Fuller's work dependent on the claim that there is such a morality, a claim that is utterly inconsistent with the indeterminacy thesis. And only if that claim can be vindicated, is it possible to sustain the distinction between legislation and interpretation.

For only this distinction can respond to the fact that in international law states have to regard themselves as not only players bent on winning the international relations game, but also as judges, as interpreters of the rules of the international legal system. When states occupy the judicial role, they accept certain commitments: to being bound by the text of the rules; to offering reasonable interpretations of what a rule requires in cases where it is controversial how it applies; to taking into account for the sake of fairness the way in which the rule has been previously interpreted in analogous situations; to treating each participant as an equal when it comes to interpretation.

These commitments makes it possible for the players to adopt as a regulative assumption of the game that its rules make up a unified system that contains within itself an answer to all possible questions that might arise about the application of the rules. Because there is for the most part only one level of judges – there is no final or any court of appeal – these commitments have to be taken all the more seriously in order to maintain trust, in particular the requirement to offer only reasonable interpretations of the rules. That is, because those who are locked in dispute with each other are judges in their own cause, there is much more pressure on them to achieve agreement on the most reasonable interpretation of the rules than in a legal order with a separation of powers and a hierarchically organized judiciary.[38]

The politics of this kind of formalism opposes the politics of the indeterminacy thesis. How this might work in practice is well illustrated by the case study Jutta Brunnée and Stephen J. Toope undertake in their chapter in this volume.[39] They show that once actors enter the space of legality and accept the commitments of role that attend such entry, the actors will find that they are not only constrained in the kinds of arguments they can make, but also that those commitments endow both the process and its outcome with the legitimacy.

This quality of legitimacy is not, I should note, moral in the sense that it derives from some set of moral standards that are somehow prior to politics, so that politics and law are to be understood as either the means of enacting these standards or as constrained by these standards.[40] Rather, morality is the quality that accrues to law because of the formal conditions of legal politics. Once we see this, we are in a position also to see why realism amounts to a kind of negative politics.[41] That is, it is a view of politics as producing the kind of a substantive content of which law, suitably conceived, can be the instrument. Realism and Benthamite utilitarianism share both this view of politics and the understanding of law that goes with it. They differ only in that realism is agnostic or negative about the content. Realism merely stipulates that there must be such a content, while Benthamite utilitarianism stipulates how content is to be produced before it gets poured into law.

Notice that in line with my argument above both positions are also committed to a kind of formalism about law – law's form is what makes it possible for externally determined content to be transmitted unadulterated to the subjects of political power. Schmitt ultimately thought that this could be achieved only by putting in place a substantively homogeneous people. Legal realism of the late-twentieth-century kind rejects this normative aspiration and settles for the claim that law's formal existence is unattainable, so that particular sites within law will always be prone to capture by whatever elite is 'hegemonic' in that space. If such realists are cheerful Schmitteans, they believe that under the right conditions liberal democracy can be maintained despite law's inability to discipline politics.

If they are despondent Schmitteans, they think that the liberal-democratic
ship has run aground, with no hope of rescue.[42]

But realism of any sort is not a 'key part' of the '(generative) grammar'
of international law.[43] Rather, as I have argued, it is committed to a denial
that there is such a grammar and thus ultimately to denying that there
could be such a thing as international law.[44] Of course, making sense of
international law as a matter of form requires attending to the fact that
the international legal order lacks attributes that exist in domestic orders,
a state, a division of powers, etc. But whether that fact makes the project
of understanding law as formal law more or less difficult is, I think, an
open question. Formalism, says Koskenniemi, 'can no longer be blind to
its own politics'.[45] But it also should not be blind either to the features of
law's form or to the way that those features endow law's content with a
moral quality that solves what he has called the 'mystery of obligation'.[46]

Notes

* The author thanks Jutta Brunnée and Karen Knop for several discussions of the
  issues canvassed in this chapter and Joanna Langille for valuable research assistance
  and comments on a draft.
1. M. Koskenniemi, *From Apology to Utopia: The Structure of International Legal
   Argument*, reissue with new epilogue (Cambridge: Cambridge University Press,
   2006).
2. Ibid., 563–64.
3. Ibid., 562–63.
4. Ibid., 565. 'Apology' and 'utopia', though, cannot be put into these sets, as formalism
   and anti-formalism can issue in either.
5. Ibid., 565.
6. Ibid., 610.
7. T. Hobbes, *Leviathan*, Richard Tuck (ed.) (Cambridge: Cambridge University Press,
   2013), 10, emphasis original.
8. L. L. Fuller, *The Morality of Law*, rev. edn (New Haven, CT: Yale University Press,
   1969).
9. H. L. A. Hart, *The Concept of Law*, 2nd edn (Oxford: Clarendon Press, 1994), 153.
10. Hobbes, *Leviathan*, 128.
11. J. M. Kelly, *A Short History of Western Legal Theory* (Oxford: Oxford University
    Press, 1992), 360. Kelly offers a brief but illuminating account at pp. 359–69.
12. For fuller discussion, see D. Dyzenhaus, *Hard Cases in Wicked Legal Systems: Patholo-
    gies of Legality* (Oxford: Oxford University Press, 2010).
13. H. L. A. Hart, 'Positivism and the Separation of Law and Morals', *Harvard Law
    Review* 71 (1958): 609–10.
14. Dyzenhaus, *Hard Cases*, Chapter 8.
15. I have in mind here the discussion of external and internal skepticism about the
    law in R. Dworkin, *Law's Empire* (London: Fontana, 1986), 78–86, 271–75.

16. R. Dworkin, 'The Model of Rules', in *Taking Rights Seriously* (London: Duckworth, 1978), 14–45.
17. Hart, 'Positivism and the Separation of Law and Morals', 607–8.
18. H. L. A. Hart, *Essays in Jurisprudence and Philosophy* (Oxford: Oxford University Press, 1983), 7.
19. Dworkin, *Law's Empire*.
20. For a more detailed elaboration of these ideas, see D. Dyzenhaus, 'The Compulsion of Legality', in V. Ramraj (ed.), *Emergencies and the Limits of Legality* (Cambridge: Cambridge University Press, 2008), 33–59.
21. C. Schmitt, *Gesetz und Urteil. Eine Untersuchung zum Problem der Rechtspraxis* (1912; repr., Munich: C. H. Beck, 1969).
22. See D. Dyzenhaus, *Legality and Legitimacy: Carl Schmitt, Hans Kelsen and Hermann Heller in Weimar* (Oxford: Oxford University Press, 1997).
23. Koskenniemi, *From Apology to Utopia*, 590.
24. Ibid., 610.
25. Ibid., 590–91, emphasis original; see also 62–63.
26. Ibid., 591.
27. Ibid., 606.
28. Ibid., 606–7.
29. Ibid., 610.
30. The qualification 'in principle' is necessary only because of the possibility that the lawyers were not competent, which would explain international lawyers' doubts about the arguments that were in fact made on the US side. But as I understand Koskenniemi's position, those doubts cannot attach to the potential in the circumstances for a well-formed legal argument for invasion of Iraq, only to the actual argument.
31. Koskenniemi, *From Apology to Utopia*, 564.
32. For example, M. Koskenniemi, 'Constitutionalism as Mindset: Reflections on Kantian Themes about International Law and Globalization', *Theoretical Inquiries in Law* 8 (2007): 9–36.
33. Koskenniemi, *From Apology to Utopia*, 88.
34. See M. Oakeshott, *On Human Conduct* (Oxford: Clarendon Press, 1975), 153n1. I explore this theme in D. Dyzenhaus, 'Dreaming the Rule of Law', in D. Dyzenhaus and T. Poole (eds), *Law, Liberty and State: Oakeshott, Hayek and Schmitt on the Rule of Law* (Cambridge: Cambridge University Press, 2015), 234.
35. Quoted in Martti Koskenniemi, 'What Is International Law For?', in Koskenniemi, *Politics of International Law*, 256–57. And in a footnote to a recent piece, he refers to the 'still valuable distinction' proposed by Michael Oakeshott between a '"civil association" whose members relate to each other by reference to rules and institutions recognized by them as authoritative, and managerial "enterprise-association" whose members are united by shared purposes'; 'What Use for Sovereignty Today?', *Asian Journal of International Law* 1 (2011): 69n26, referring to Oakeshott, *On Human Conduct*, 108–326. See further T. Nardin, 'Theorising the International Rule of Law', *Review of International Studies* 34 (2008): 385–401, for a valuable critique of Koskenniemi's writings on formalism. Note that Kelsen is much discussed by Koskenniemi, who has a high regard for his attempt to show that the state is an artificial person and that its officials may act only on the basis of legal authorization. See M. Koskenniemi, 'The Wonderful Artificiality of States', *Proceedings of*

the American Society of International Law 88 (1994): 28–29. Indeed, Kelsenian legal positivism differs dramatically from its twentieth-century Anglophone counterpart in that Kelsen is concerned more with legality than with the problem of indeterminacy, which is why Oakeshott could remark that the conception of the rule-of-law state (which Oakeshott elaborated in a magnificent but neglected essay) 'hovers over the reflections of many so-called "positivist" modern jurists'; M. Oakeshott, 'The Rule of Law', in *On History and Other Essays* (Indianapolis, IN: Liberty Fund, 1999), 175.

36. Koskenniemi, 'What Is International Law For?', 257.
37. L. L. Fuller, 'Positivism and Fidelity to Law: A Reply to Professor Hart', *Harvard Law Review* 71 (1958): 630–72.
38. See D. Dyzenhaus, 'Hobbes on the International Rule of Law', *Ethics and International Affairs* 28 (2014): 53–64, for further exploration of this point.
39. 'The Rule of Law in an Agnostic World: The Prohibition on the Use of Force and Humanitarian Exceptions'. My argument differs from theirs only in that I think that a culture of formalism is a culture of legality and that I am perhaps more ready than they are to equate legitimacy with possession of a moral quality.
40. This is not, I should note, morality in the sense that there is some set of moral standards that are somehow prior to politics, so that politics and law are to be understood as either the means of enacting these standards or as constrained by these standards. See B. Williams, 'Realism and Moralism', in *In the Beginning Was the Deed: Realism and Moralism in Political Argument* (Princeton, NJ: Princeton University Press, 2005), 1–3. Rather, morality is the quality that accrues to law because of the formal conditions of legal politics. I develop this argument in D. Dyzenhaus, 'Process and Substance as Aspects of the Public Law Form', *Cambridge Law Journal* 74 (2015): 284–306.
41. Hence, there is a surprising difference between the politics of formalism and the politics of anti-formalism. Formalism turns out to be based on substantive political commitments, whereas anti-formalism turns out to supply merely a negative framework for politics. It is thus unclear why Koskenniemi's formalism does not amount to exactly the kind of political position that he attributes to liberalism in *From Apology to Utopia*, 5–6.
42. As I have elsewhere described Eric Posner and Adrian Vermeule in order to contrast their position with Martin Loughlin's despondent Schmitteanism. See D. Dyzenhaus, 'The End of the Road to Serfdom?', *University of Toronto Law Journal* 63 (2013): 322. In its more left-wing or progressive versions, for example, in Critical Legal Studies, realism holds out the hope that progressive groups can fill the voids of indeterminacy with their values.
43. Koskenniemi, *From Apology to Utopia*, 565.
44. Bentham, who coined the term 'international law', is often taken to have denied that there could be such a thing as international law. But his position is more complicated – see M. W. Janis, 'Jeremy Bentham and the Fashioning of "International Law"', *American Journal of International Law* 78 (1984): 405–18.
45. M. Koskenniemi, '"The Lady Doth Protest Too Much": the Turn to Ethics in International Law', in *Politics of International* Law, 129. Schmitt was very attentive to this aspect of formalism. See C. Schmitt, *Constitutional Theory*, J. Seitzer (trans.) (Durham, NC: Duke University Press, 2008), Section 16, 'Bourgeois Rechtsstaat and Political Form'.

46. M. Koskenniemi, 'The Mystery of Legal Obligation', *International Theory* 3 (2011): 319–25.

Bibliography

Dworkin, Ronald. *Law's Empire* (London: Fontana, 1986).

Taking Rights Seriously (London: Duckworth, 1978).

Dyzenhaus, David. 'The Compulsion of Legality'. In Victor V. Ramraj (ed.), *Emergencies and the Limits of Legality* (Cambridge: Cambridge University Press, 2008).

'Dreaming the Rule of Law'. In David Dyzenhaus and Thomas Poole (eds), *Law, Liberty and State: Oakeshott, Hayek and Schmitt on the Rule of Law*. (Cambridge: Cambridge University Press, 2015).

'The End of the Road to Serfdom?' *University of Toronto Law Journal* 63 (2013): 310–26.

Hard Cases in Wicked Legal Systems: Pathologies of Legality (Oxford: Oxford University Press, 2010).

'Hobbes on the International Rule of Law'. *Ethics and International Affairs* 28 (2014): 53–64.

Legality and Legitimacy: Carl Schmitt, Hans Kelsen, and Hermann Heller in Weimar (Oxford: Oxford University Press, 1997).

'Process and Substance as Aspects of the Public Law Form'. *The Cambridge Law Journal* 74 (2015): 284–306.

Fuller, Lon L. *The Morality of Law*. Rev. edn (New Haven, CT: Yale University Press, 1969).

'Positivism and Fidelity to Law: a Reply to Professor Hart'. *Harvard Law Review* 71 (1958): 630–72.

Hart, Herbert L. A. *The Concept of Law*. 2nd edn (Oxford: Oxford University Press, 1994).

Essays in Jurisprudence and Philosophy (Oxford: Oxford University Press, 1983).

'Positivism and the Separation of Law and Morals'. *Harvard Law Review* 71 (1958): 593–629.

Hobbes, Thomas. *Leviathan*. Richard Tuck (ed.) (Cambridge: Cambridge University Press, 2013).

Janis, Mark W. 'Jeremy Bentham and the Fashioning of "International Law"'. *American Journal of International Law* 78 (1984): 405–18.

Kelly, John M. *A Short History of Western Legal Theory* (Oxford: Oxford University Press, 1992).

Koskenniemi, Martti. 'Constitutionalism as Mindset: Reflections on Kantian Themes about International Law and Globalization'. *Theoretical Inquiries in Law* 8 (2007): 9–36.

From Apology to Utopia: the Structure of International Legal Argument, reissue with a new epilogue (Cambridge: Cambridge University Press, 2006).

'"The Lady Doth Protest Too Much?": the Turn to Ethics in International Law'. In *The Politics of International Law* (Oxford: Hart, 2011).

'The Mystery of Legal Obligation'. *International Theory* 3 (2011): 319–25.

The Politics of International Law (Oxford: Hart, 2011).

'What Is International Law For?' In *The Politics of International Law* (Oxford: Hart, 2011).

'What Use for Sovereignty Today?' *Asian Journal of International Law* 1 (2011): 61–70.

'The Wonderful Artificiality of States'. *Proceedings of the American Society of International Law* 88 (1994): 22–29.

Nardin, Terry. 'Theorising the International Rule of Law'. *Review of International Studies* 34 (2008): 385–401.

Oakeshott, Michael. *On Human Conduct* (Oxford: Clarendon Press, 1975).

'The Rule of Law'. In *On History and Other Essays* (Indianapolis, IN: Liberty Fund, 1985).

Schmitt, Carl. *Constitutional Theory*. Jeffrey Seitzer (trans.) (Durham, NC: Duke University Press, 2008).

Gesetz und Urteil: Eine Untersuchung Zum Problem Der Rechtspraxis (1912; repr., Munich: C. H. Beck, 1969).

Williams, Bernard. 'Realism and Moralism'. In *In the Beginning Was the Deed: Realism and Moralism in Political Argument* (Princeton, NJ: Princeton University Press, 2005).

3

Settling Disputes

A Matter of Politics and Law

3.1 Introduction

Intractable disputes are characterized by multi-layered accusations and counter-accusations and involve situations where history, politics and law conspire to render an already complicated situation impenetrable to weaker mechanisms of collective security. In addition, as a result of the various interests of the five permanent members of the Security Council, most such disputes are beyond the reach of Chapter VII of the UN Charter. Long-running disputes, for example, between Israel and Palestine over the Occupied Territories, India and Pakistan over Kashmir, Cyprus and Turkey over Northern Cyprus, the US and Cuba over unremediated confiscations of US property following the seizure of power by Fidel Castro in 1959 and the subsequent imposition of an embargo by the US, US and Iran over the latter's nuclear ambitions, the sovereignty disputes over the Falklands/Malvinas between the UK and Argentina and over Gibraltar between the UK and Spain, remain unresolved and seemingly insoluble.

This chapter attempts to explore dispute settlement in this barren landscape where it seems that the politics of opposition, in which states not only oppose each other but, after a time, often oppose a solution to the dispute, outweigh the restoration of normal relations between states based on basic principles of international law. The chapter treads a precarious path between two extremes to dispute settlement, one based more or less on politics and one based on applying legal rules, neither of which provide evidence of success. At one end we have settlement by means of power politics in its various manifestations, which may or may not involve the use of measures authorized by the Security Council under Chapter VII of the Charter, for example Iraq in 2003,[1] Dayton in relation to Bosnia in 1995,[2] or Kosovo in 1999.[3] On the other, there is a formalist approach to settlement, which fails because it does not facilitate a process of the coming together of the disputant states seen, for example, in the approach of the European Community to the disintegration of Yugoslavia in the early 1990s, exemplified by the work of the Badinter Commission, even though its legal reasoning was suspect.[4]

The approach identified in this chapter allows for political settlement within a legal framework. It does this by arguing that the primary rules of international law can provide a framework for settlement and that the secondary rules on state responsibility should, within limits, facilitate the practicalities of dispute settlement. Rather than diminish the relevance of international law, it is demonstrated that there is potential for law to play a central role in helping the parties to create an agreed framework within which they can settle their dispute. This contrasts with a more orthodox approach to rule application when law is applied, in a determinant manner, in a method under which one side loses and the other wins. International law works best, in dispute settlement at least, when the focus is less on deciding on who wins and who loses and, rather, on offering a framework for states to decide on how to resolve their differences and the issues between them.

Even if a dispute does find its way to an authoritative judicial body, such as the International Court of Justice, there is little guarantee that the losing state will accept the judgment of the Court, especially in such a complex case as would be presented by the parties to any of the disputes mentioned thus far. If dispute settlement is to work in these circumstances, it is essential that alternative understandings of the principles of international law,[5] as well as alternative mechanisms for dispute settlement, are considered by the parties, if agreement is to be achieved. There is no magic formula that will solve the dispute and, it is submitted, that it is a mistake to consider that international law works in such a manner.

This chapter places dispute settlement broadly within Martti Koskenniemi's indeterminacy thesis, and then adapts his idea of international law as the 'gentle civilizer of nations', which he posited generally in the form of a question: 'between the arrogance of universality and the indifferences of particularity, what else is there apart from the civilized manner of gentle spirits?'[6] After outlining Koskenniemi's analysis of how law can play a role in relation to collective security, this chapter applies such thinking to bilateral disputes. In so doing, it shows that such disputes are not resolved by the 'indifferences of particularity' but, drawing on Koskenniemi's idea, it argues that when the political regime encasing the dispute collapses, or radically changes, law can play a crucial role in establishing a new political regime based on the normalization of relations.

Such a normalization of relations is not only based on applicable principles of international law, but also on underpinning values of peace, justice and reconciliation. These values find current expression, for example, within modern ideas of transitional justice, a regime that has emerged most strongly within the context of post-conflict rebuilding. Transitional justice is based on the premise that without both a reckoning (as regards past abuses) as well as a reconciliation (between groups and individuals on different sides of the conflict), the underlying cycle of violence will only be broken temporarily. Clearly, there is a tension between reckoning and reconciliation so that often a peace process contains forms of compromise between the two, such as conditional amnesties and alternative forms of accountability.[7] Thus, in bilateral disputes, characterized by regular outbreaks of armed conflict (over Kashmir in 1949, 1965 and 1971; in the Middle East, principally in 1948, 1956, 1967 and 1973; against Cuba in the Bay of Pigs in 1961; over Cyprus with the Turkish intervention in 1974; and over the Falklands/Malvinas in 1982), the levels of hostility between the two countries have been such that, before normal relations can be established, a post-dispute (or post-confrontation) phase has to be navigated by the parties. Transitional justice and related arguments for a *jus post bellum*,[8] although not directly applicable to disputes between states, serve to illustrate that international law has the potential to facilitate a dynamic environment in which both peace and justice can be built. Furthermore, the chapter demonstrates that the values most prominently found in transitional justice are also actually located, but buried more deeply, in the more orthodox and traditional methods of dispute settlement between states.

The chapter is structured as follows: first it considers the place of law in the politics of settlement, drawing on Martti Koskenniemi's analysis of the indeterminacy of international law, and how, despite that, international law still has relevance, not only as a 'gentle civilizer' in times of relative stability, but as an important form of stability in times of change. The chapter then moves on to consider how this applies within a bilateral dispute where the principles of reciprocity and restoration, which are shown to be interlaced in the structures of international law, help to ensure that the bilateral situation moves from the politics of confrontation towards the politics of normalization; in other words, from a situation that violates international law and threatens international relations, towards one that is in conformity with international law and restores a condition of peaceful co-existence between states. The chapter also considers how diplomacy can lead to finding common legal ground, enabling the parties to achieve relative certainty within a system of primary and secondary rules of international law characterized by indeterminacy. The chapter goes on to demonstrate that this understanding of international law is compatible with traditional political (non-judicial) methods of dispute settlement, which are based on reciprocity and restoration, and that it is helpful, but not necessary, to use analogies with transitional justice to make this point.

3.2   Place of Law in the Politics of Settlement

Law, at any level, whether national, regional or international, is a product of politics, but law is also expected to provide a normative framework within which political discretion should be exercised so that the political system is subject to the rule of law. In international relations, however, given the continuing dominance of sovereign states, it is more difficult to maintain that there exists an international rule of law, despite UN rhetoric to that effect.[9] The deeper reason for this is clearly exposed by the critical methodology of Martti Koskenniemi, who wrote in 1990 against the backdrop of a claimed new world order emerging in the radically changed circumstances at the end of the Cold War, that:

> Our inherited ideal of a World Order based on the Rule of Law thinly hides from sight the fact that social conflict must still be solved by political means and that even though there may exist a common legal rhetoric among international lawyers, that rhetoric must, *for reasons internal to the ideal itself,* rely on essentially contested – political – principles to justify outcomes to international disputes.[10]

The internal problem faced by international law is that the law, especially custom, is generated by state practice and so can be seen either as an excuse or an apology for state behaviour. Any attempt to depart from state practice can be dismissed as utopian and, therefore, irrelevant in that it will have no impact upon state behaviour. In order to achieve universal agreements in more formal documents, treaties or resolutions, norms are crafted in abstract and indeterminate terms. Thus, in these conditions:

> Behind ritualistic references to well-known rules and principles of international law (the content of which remains a constant object of dispute), legal practice has increasingly resorted to resolving disputes by a

contextual criterion – an effort towards an equitable balance. Though this has seemed to work well, the question arises as to whether such practice can be adequately explained in terms of the Rule of Law.[11]

In this way, law forms part of the debate and discussion within which disputes can be resolved but, in the end, abstract, disputed and often indeterminate universal rules can only provide guides towards an equitable solution that is politically just.[12] The growth, since 1990, of specialist international legal regimes, with greater precision in terms of rules, does not remove political choices,[13] given that disputes refuse to neatly fit within only one legal regime. The US-Cuba dispute, for instance, involves issues of forcible and non-forcible measures, sovereignty and self-determination, democratic and socio-economic rights, as well as trade and investment. Resort to human rights norms and mechanisms will produce a different range of answers to ones sought within a trade regime. The problem is exacerbated when the disputants' participation in different regimes does not overlap significantly or even marginally (for example, by not being parties to the same multilateral treaties).

Furthermore, despite problems with indeterminacy, Koskenniemi argues that international laws can, especially at certain crucial points, have a significant role to play, even within highly politicized regimes concerning the security of states. In contrast, realism foresees security being achieved in such circumstances by states acting out of self-interest and, eventually, by achieving a balance of power.[14] Koskenniemi argues that a pure realist approach still contains within its method normative premises involving stylized and abstract understandings of concepts, such as 'interest' (as in the national 'interest'), 'security' (as in national 'security') and 'power' (as in balance of 'power'). In addition, he argues that the legal justifications invariably put forward by states for their actions, under a balance of power or similar system, are not simply excuses but meaningful justifications and explanations for action.[15] In effect, it could be argued that to act both out of self-interest and within the constraints of the law are not mutually exclusive actions given that law influences how self-interest can be pursued.

According to Koskenniemi, when the political context is stable, as it largely was during the superpower confrontation of the Cold War (at least after the period of decolonization), law primarily plays a limited role, for example, in helping shape the text of Security Council resolutions to broadly conform with the UN Charter, as well as providing states with justifications for their political actions.[16] Politics are, in effect, poured into a variety of legal vessels (treaties, resolutions and soft laws). However, when the political context radically changes and becomes unstable, the Charter, and international law more generally, take on a central role in shaping the boundary between law and politics. In these circumstances, international law acts as a constraint on discretion, not in a fully 'constitutional' sense,[17] rather in a 'political' sense. International law performs the function of being a container within which politics are confined. This signifies that within a new political context international law provides the parameters for political action, but international law is not a strong or, indeed, a rigid enough framework to fully constrain political considerations. In these conditions, the legal framework is significantly expanded and developed by interpretation and subsequent practice.[18]

In this way, at the end of the Cold War, international law was reinterpreted to apply to new circumstances, for example, in the Badinter Commission's interpretations of self-determination in the context of the break-up of Yugoslavia in the early 1990s.[19] Faced with the break-up of a federal state, the Commission, established by the European Community, extended the idea of external self-determination, which in the Cold War period occurred in relation to colonial territories, so as to cover new states emerging from the federal units within a collapsing Communist state. Essentially, decolonization (arguably another period of instability in the 1950s and 1960s) was given normative form by the General Assembly's Declaration on Decolonization of 1960,[20] which contained a principle of international law on external self-determination within colonial boundaries, and it was this norm that was adapted in the post–Cold War era to another sort of boundary within collapsing communist states.

According to Martti Koskenniemi, law also took on a shaping role in the 1990 crisis that followed the Iraqi invasion of Kuwait. The end of the Cold War meant that:

> The traditional patterns of Council decision making had become irrelevant and inapplicable. There was no anterior political agreement, no longstanding negotiation with fixed positions, and no routine language to cover events. The situation was canvassed nowhere but in the Charter itself. As the debate took on a legal style and an engaged aspect, the rest of formalism followed suit.[21]

This took place, for example, in the search for legal precedent in the management of sanctions, in which the comprehensive regime against white Rhodesia from 1965 to 1979 was clearly the template, while the mandating resolution for force in 1950 against North Korea was used as the template for Resolution 678 (1990), which authorized member states to enforce the Security Council's demand for Iraqi withdrawal from Kuwait and 'to restore international peace and security to the area'.

The move to law was evidenced in the way these precedents were put together with other legally based responses, including declaring Iraq's annexation of Kuwait as null and void, in a suite of resolutions whereby the Council used its full range of Chapter VII powers in a unique way in 1990, but one in accordance with the UN Charter of 1945. It started with a determination of a breach of the peace under Article 39 and a demand for Iraqi withdrawal under Article 40 (in Resolution 660), then the Security Council successively imposed comprehensive sanctions against Iraq under Article 41 (Resolution 661), determined that Iraq's annexation of Kuwait was null and void (Resolution 662), authorized naval forces to enforce sanctions in a limited application of Article 42 (Resolution 665) and then it authorized full-scale force to remove Iraq (Resolution 678), with many fine-tuning resolutions in between. The war was brought to an end by a unique Resolution (687 of 1991), which imposed severe conditions upon Iraq, including supervised disarmament and a mechanism for providing compensation to victims of its aggression. Resolution 687 illustrates the malleability of international law in changed political conditions, but this does not mean that the Resolution was *ultra vires*, for if the Security Council is empowered to authorize the waging of war on a state it is equally empowered to bring it to an end.

The consensus between the five permanent members enabled the Council to develop a legal framework for its post–Cold War actions (implicitly acting under Charter Article 41's open-ended list of non-forcible measures) that would have been unimaginable during the Cold War. In addition to imposing post-war conditions upon Iraq, this enabled it to create international criminal tribunals for Yugoslavia and Rwanda and post-conflict administrations for Kosovo and East Timor. However, that consensus had dissipated by 2003, with the US and the UK, bridling against Iraq's perceived lack of compliance, especially with the disarmament provisions of Resolution 687 (1991), taking unilateral military measures culminating in the full-scale invasion of Iraq in 2003.

In 2003 law once again took a back seat to politics, evidenced by the unconvincing attempts by the UK, in particular, to justify the use of force against Iraq on the basis that Resolution 678 of 1990 was somehow still a legally valid authorization to use force. The 'revival' argument, as it came to be known, only came to the fore once it became clear that a follow-up resolution, one that would have allowed for the enforcement of the weapons of mass destruction inspection regime re-established by

Resolution 1441 (2002), was not going to be achieved due to French
and Russian reticence.[22] Law was used instrumentally within the political
context that became established after 9/11 in 2001.

After the terrorist attacks on New York and Washington of 11 September 2001, in which the world's remaining superpower was significantly
wounded by a relatively small non-state terrorist group, the political context changed to a 'war on terror' or, more accurately, an age of terror.
Arguably, international law, this time on self-defence, provided a constraint on US reaction within this new political context, but at the same
time self-defence was adapted to a new form of threat. However, even
after the new self-defence paradigm seemingly became accepted following 9/11, the expansion of the right suffered from abuse in that it was used
as a justification for a continuing war of self-defence against terrorism,
specifically al-Qaida, from 2001 to the present day. From receiving broad
support for its initial use of force against Afghanistan in October 2001,
US actions changed from those of a lawman to potentially those of a bad
man, due to its ill-considered prosecution of an unending defensive global
war on terror.

Realism, relying on a 'clear differentiation between legal "rules" and
"political" interests and on the priority of the latter over the former',[23]
challenges the claim that international law has any traction in any of
these instances, irrespective of changes in political context. Indeed, realists would point to the fact that powerful states' behaviour in 1990, 2001
and 2003 was unaffected by weak rules of international law. Furthermore,
by recognizing the indeterminacy of international law, and the primacy of
politics, does the approach advocated by Koskenniemi itself open the door
to realism? Michael Glennon argues that realism (what he terms 'pragmatism') provides a better explanation and approach to international law.
For Glennon, realists 'believe that what ostensibly are background considerations inevitably affect legalist decision making; that reliance upon
formal legal categories masks the decision-making process that actually
occurs, which is situationally contingent'.[24] Glennon points out that not
only are the formal rules largely irrelevant to state behaviour, especially
in the areas of high politics concerning security and other national interests, but that, furthermore, there are no foundational principles upon
which a legal order can be constructed.[25] He rejects any notion of a moral
basis for action, any concept of hierarchy in international law embodied in notions of *jus cogens*, as well as any purportedly abstract concepts
such as 'community' or 'justice'.[26] Realists reject the 'paper rules' found
in the Charter and in other treaties and in the distillation of custom by

positivist international lawyers or judges, in favour of the 'working rules' that are observable empirically and do actually work in terms of inducing compliance.[27]

While superficially attractive because it is premised on the primacy of politics, realism effectively collapses any distinction between law and politics, between breach and compliance. Law is not simply an externally observable explanation of behaviour, but has an internal or argumentative aspect, evidenced by the use of normative language.[28] For example, while the UN failed to agree on action against Iraq in 2003, a realist analysis of the 'real' rules would describe the policies and actions of those that wanted to use force. A realist analysis will usually shed light on the complexities of politics and power that go into decision-making processes, but this does not reveal the law, at least if we ascribe any autonomous function to the 'law'. The real 'rules' of realism are not rules at all but are wholly contingent explanations of behaviour, what Koskenniemi labels the 'indifferences of particularity'.[29] The fact that the US used force in Iraq in 2003 out of self-interest and perceptions of threats to its security (and out of a sense of a job unfinished in 1991 and a vague idea that 9/11 and Iraq were related), and not out of a belief in the revival argument as a valid exception to the ban on the use of force, is not a 'rule' in any sense other than that any act of unpunished violence creates an argument that can be wielded against those that insist on a formal application of the law. According to Martti Koskenniemi, arguing that 'normative factors are either irrelevant or only marginally relevant ... undermines the degree to which any social action, including international activity, makes constant reference to normative codes, rules, or principles'.[30] Furthermore, 'political events are never simply physical acts or people behaving empirically in this way or that', rather they 'exist in relation to a shared normative code of meaning'.[31]

The only rules that emerge from a realist analysis are those as defined by the realist – that power and self-interest explain action. In effect, such an approach replaces one set of foundations (based on *jus cogens* and other basic principles and purposes of international law) with normative foundations of another kind based on power and self-interest. Real rules are so contingent as to be impossible to formulate in any meaningful sense, resulting in a case-by-case analysis where any lessons learned cannot be put forward as universal rules. Legal principles may be weak in comparison to this reality, but the formal laws remain as constraints, no matter how weak, on power. To conflate power and law is to remove law from having any independent function from power including, arguably, its key function – as a restraint on power.

It may well be very difficult to prove that most states do not use force because of a formal legal principle prohibiting force in the UN Charter,[32] but constant restatement of that principle by organs of the international community, such as the General Assembly, must indicate that the legal principle, despite problems with indeterminacy, is and will be a factor that helps shape state behaviour. Furthermore, Koskenniemi makes the point that 'Realism's causal modes were dependent upon, or could not be applied in abstraction from, normative choices regarding desirable courses of action'.[33] The alleged failure of the Security Council to fully adapt to the changed conditions of Iraq in 2003 does not mean that it has been irrelevant since its creation in 1945 when geopolitics were very different.[34] The Council did adapt in 1990. Besides which, it is equally plausible to argue that the Security Council's inability to authorize force in 2003 was because the weight of world opinion was behind the threatened vetoes of France and Russia and not behind the warlike intentions of the US and the UK. In other words, the Council, by its inability to authorize force, reflected contemporary thinking on the rules governing when force should be used, meaning that the use of force by the US and the UK was not somehow lawful, but was what most believe it to be – an illegal use of force.

The invasion of Iraq 2003 can be analysed convincingly in terms of law's survival and continued independence from politics; but the fact remains (and this is the ultimate realist argument) that the US and UK got away with it, at least in the short term. In response to this one can point to the problems both countries had in imposing their will on Iraq after the invasion, despite having Security Council approval for their occupation and state building (itself a legal contradiction since the law of occupation is antithetical to state building).[35] That initial intervention, in breach of the *jus ad bellum*, undermined the justice of their cause when trying to rebuild Iraq.

In fact, even during the Cold War the General Assembly played an important role as the conscience of the world community, regularly condemning superpower breaches of international law – for example, by the Soviet Union for its invasions of Hungary in 1956 and Afghanistan in 1979;[36] the US for its hemispheric interventions, for example, in Grenada in 1983 and Panama in 1989;[37] and, in the post–Cold War era, the punitive and vindictive US embargo of Cuba.[38] Koskenniemi describes the Assembly as a temple of justice and warns against the Security Council taking on the mantle of justice, as this would lead to the police entering the temple.[39] Unfortunately, this has not prevented the Security

Council from deciding on issues of justice, or at least setting up mechanisms to deliver justice, for example, the ad hoc criminal tribunals in Rwanda and Yugoslavia.[40] The Assembly, in contrast, has recently rediscovered its voice as the world slides once again towards great power confrontation following Russian intervention in Ukraine in 2014. The Assembly called upon states to 'desist and refrain from action aimed at the partial or total disruption of the national unity and territorial integrity of Ukraine, including any attempts to modify Ukraine's borders through the threat or use of force or other unlawful means'.[41]

What the above analysis shows is that law plays a role in the most hostile of environments concerning collective and national security, where achieving agreement to take collective action against threats to the peace is extremely difficult, even more so when seeking to achieve agreement and take action within the parameters of international law. It is largely true, as argued by Koskenniemi,[42] that in periods of political stability law is instrumental, but this perhaps misleads us into thinking that law has no controlling function. The fact that politics, to have longer-term relevance, have to be activated through legal instruments adopted in accordance with the UN Charter and broader principles of international law is a constraint, albeit a limited one. Moreover, as argued by Koskenniemi, in times of dramatic political change and instability, international law serves a much more central function in stabilizing international relations and in framing diplomacy, settlement and more coercive measures.

The period following the invasion of Iraq in 2003 raises the question of whether, in general terms, international law has settled back into being a handmaiden to politics in issues of security, or whether it plays an external role to politics, challenging and perhaps controlling politics, despite it being, in a sense, inside social practices. Within bilateral disputes we are confronted with an additional layer of politics, namely that governing the relations between the two states, in addition to the broader political context pervading in international relations. In these conditions law may be expected to have reduced prospects as a means for settling disputes. Indeed, we might expect the particularities of the dispute to push out the generalities of international law. Bearing in mind Koskenniemi's warning against viewing the weaknesses of international law's claims to universality as an argument for simply dealing with particularities, it is contended that his analysis does apply to bilateral disputes so that law, despite its indeterminacy and its general subservience to politics, has relevance. In doing this we are not guilty of reducing international law to particularities, rather we are making the claim that it is, in one sense, easier to make the universalities of international law work within a bilateral context than it is within a collective context where the achievement of inter-subjective agreement is more difficult.[43] This has to be balanced against the fact that in long-running bilateral disputes the levels of disagreement can go much deeper than at the multilateral level.

It follows that for international law to take on a significant shaping role in any process of dispute settlement there must be a significant break in the prevailing political context. The end of the Cold War created new conditions enabling the revitalization of existing (and seemingly exhausted) principles of law, such as self-determination in the context of the former Yugoslav and Soviet Republics, and self-defence in the context of the terrorist attacks of 9/11. In addition, this period saw further innovations in collective measures against international crimes (for example, the international criminal tribunals for the former Yugoslavia and Rwanda),[44] and terrorism (for example, Security Council 'legislation' prohibiting support for terrorism).[45] Arguably, the end of the Cold War should have been the context-breaking event that led to the end of a number of intractable bilateral disputes, for example, the US-Cuban confrontation, given the removal of Soviet support for Cuba and the opening of the Cuban economy to wider trade. However, the US decision was to continue the same political framework and, indeed, to re-enforce it by tightening the embargo in order to remove one of the few remaining Communist regimes.[46] In effect, in 1991 the Cold War had ended between the superpowers but continued across the Florida Straits. However, it is contended that in bilateral disputes, while the broader international political conditions remain a factor, of more importance is the political relationship between the two states – if this sees a fundamental shift, then international law can operate to stabilize and normalize the relationship.

3.3   Bilateral Disputes: Seeking Agreement Based on Reciprocity and Restoration

As has been argued, in many bilateral disputes there are instances of uses of force between the states concerned and, although a condition of war may have been relatively brief, the dispute has been one of confrontation or conflict in a broad sense and could not be said to be a state of peace, so that there is a clear need for a process that leads to a peace agreement. In the reality of dispute settlement and negotiation of peace agreements international norms jockey for influence within a politically unstable context. Indeed, peace agreements in the post–Cold War period have shown a number of similarities to the extent that it has been argued by Christine Bell that what is emerging is a form of *lex pacificatoriae*.[47] Although most of these agreements are aimed at bringing an end to intra-state conflicts, those common principles identified by Bell are, in the main, also applicable to inter-state disputes.

Common features of peace accords include agreement by the parties on methods of achieving peace and security, self-determination and human rights, transitional justice (to address wrongful acts committed), and on the provision of access to justice. Without such an agreement covering peace and justice between the two disputant states, the cycle of confrontation and conflict will not be broken. Restoration of international relations takes precedence over retribution by means of punishment for wrongdoing, although the latter will normally have to be addressed.[48]

In addition to the primary rules of international law that are applicable to dispute settlement and peace agreements, the secondary rules of international law on state responsibility are also firmly grounded in securing the restoration of normal relations between states once they have been disrupted by internationally wrongful acts. Responsibility in international law is neither clearly delictual nor criminal, rather it is reflection of the very different legal and political order applying between states in international relations. It is worth noting in this regard that the criminalization of certain aspects of state behaviour was not the route taken by the International Law Commission (ILC) in its drafting of the Articles on the Responsibility of States for Internationally Wrongful Acts in 2001.[49] Whether or not the concept of state crimes persists, it is true to say that the law on state responsibility is not primarily concerned with punishing sovereign states for their wrongdoing, but on restoring peaceful and normal relations between them. Although the rules on state responsibility seem rather abstract and formal, it will be shown that they operate within what Koskenniemi calls a 'culture of formalism' that 'builds on formal arguments that are available to all under conditions of equality'.[50] The 'culture of formalism':

> Seeks to persuade the protagonists (lawyers, decision-makers) to take a momentary distance from their preferences and to enter a terrain where these preferences should be justified, instead of taken for granted, by reference to standards that are independent from their particular positions or interests.[51]

International law, both of a primary and secondary nature, is used by protagonists in this manner – its function is rudimentary – allowing protagonists to continue the 'search for something beyond particular interests and identity politics, or the irreducibility of difference'.[52] Such a function is not predicated on notions of criminality or otherwise, although states may occasionally deploy such accusations, particularly when faced with intransigent behaviour. As stated by Kimberly Trapp in the context of approaches to terrorism, state responsibility is not focussed on retribution or punishment, it concentrates on restoration of the relations between the wronged state and the responsible state, a rationale that must be even stronger in situations where both states are wronged and wrongdoers (as if often the case in intractable long-running disputes).[53] For example, in the case of the Cuban-US dispute there is the uncompensated seizure of US property by the Cuban government in 1960 on the one hand, and the prolonged and punitive embargo imposed by the US on Cuba starting in the same year on the other.

As stated by Kimberly Trapp, the law on state responsibility 'seeks to re-establish the primary legal relationship between states as a necessary element of their peaceful co-existence'.[54] Furthermore, Trapp states that the 'possibility of punitive measures imposed on a wrongdoing state does not sit comfortably within an international legal paradigm built on the sovereign equality of states, and was rejected by the ILC in its consideration of a regime of criminal responsibility for states'.[55] Trapp points out that in the area of state-sponsored terrorism, the restoration of normal relations between two states (for example, between Libya and the UK as regards the Lockerbie bombing of 1988) can involve the acceptance of state responsibility by the state sponsoring terrorism, as well as measures taken to ascertain the criminal responsibility of individuals involved in terrorism. The latter was illustrated in the UK-Libya dispute by the agreement of the two countries to the trial of the two Libyan agents suspected of the Lockerbie bombing before a Scottish constituted court situated in the Netherlands in 2000–1.

If the restoration of friendly relations is combined with an understanding of peaceful settlement between states, one that combines peace and justice, then it is not necessary to stretch modern mechanisms of transitional justice, such as truth and reconciliation commissions, that have developed *within* post-conflict states to apply them, by analogy, to disputes *between* states. Nonetheless, it is helpful to keep in mind the development of transitional justice as its underpinnings are more immediately transparent than traditional modes of dispute settlement.[56] By delving deeper into the traditional methods, however, it will be seen that, for example, commissions of inquiry can play a similar role to truth and reconciliation commissions in the context of bilateral disputes between states. The principles of peace and justice underpinning transitional justice are revealed to be the same as those that underpin international law.

The principles of transitional justice provide inspiration for any modern peace process, whether internal or international, since they are founded upon achieving both peace and justice. While the traditional methods of dispute settlement applicable to inter-state disputes are normally characterized as being concerned with the attainment of peace, a deeper analysis of the more successful processes reveals that they have a concern for justice as well. Traditional methods of dispute settlement facilitate a reciprocal exchange of rights and duties between the parties as well as a restoration of normal relations between sovereign states based on mutual respect and cooperation. Both theories of transitional justice and state responsibility point to restoration rather than retribution as the guiding principle. This has implications for the peace process and the mechanisms established by it, in particular, that any judicial element of the peace process, which apportions blame or punishes violators, must be balanced by non-judicial means aimed at restoration and remediation. Judicial mechanisms, by themselves, will not bring peace.

Christine Gray makes the point that the International Court of Justice is an acceptable forum for the settlement of maritime and land boundary disputes, where the impact of its decision is mitigated by its tendency to rely on principles of equity and by the fact that both parties are looking for a genuine solution to a lack of clarity as to where the boundary between them lies. However, such limited conditions are absent in complex disputes, where political and legal disagreements are far too deep for a rules-based decision of the court, even one infused with equity. Gray questions the value of 'propaganda' type cases, such as the *Tehran Hostages Case* of 1980 brought by the US against Iran, and the *Nicaragua Case* 1986 brought by Nicaragua against the US,[57] in which the respondent state resists both the jurisdiction and judgment of the International Court. These cases might help to develop international law in controversial areas, but they do little to settle the dispute between the states.[58]

Similar limitations are revealed in ad hoc judicial bodies, for example, the Iran-US Claims Tribunal. Despite its successes, the underlying tensions and confrontation between the two countries have not been resolved, showing that a broader approach to dispute settlement will be necessary if success is to be achieved.[59] The Iran-US Claims Tribunal was created in a politically difficult and unfavourable environment after the revolution in Iran had 'deeply disturbed the relationship between Iran

and the US at the end of the 1970s'.[60] Parallels with the Cuban revolution and expropriations of US-owned property and assets in 1959–60 can
be seen. It is true to say that the Iran-US Claims Tribunal has become
an 'exceptional arbitration mechanism' rich in jurisprudence on state
responsibility for expropriations.[61] In many ways it was a successor to
the mixed claims commissions established at the beginning of the twentieth century, although it more clearly gave individuals access to justice
by enabling complainants to file claims directly, rather than relying on
their national states exercising diplomatic protection on their behalf.[62]
However, there is little evidence that the Iran-US Claims Tribunal has
helped with reconciliation between the US and Iran, whose relationship
has remained one of confrontation up to the level of threats of force and
limited uses of force.[63] Indeed, in 1981 the Iran-US Claims Tribunal came
to a decision (by majority) that Article II of the claims settlement declaration did not include a right for Iran to bring claims against US nationals on
the grounds that a 'clear formulation' of that provision excluded Iranian
claims from the jurisdiction of the Tribunal. Although the majority could
draw support for this interpretation from a textual reading of the Article,
the minority pointed out that this undermined any reciprocity underpinning the agreement.[64] By disregarding that reciprocity, the Tribunal has
provided only one-sided justice and, although that is some justice, it is
not one upon which to build reconciliation and restoration between the
two countries.

3.4   Towards a Peace Agreement

In the field of complex dispute settlement international law works as
part of a political process, rather than as part of a judicial-type process
based on the attempted application of rules to provide black-and-white
solutions and answers. The indeterminacy at the heart of international
law signifies that a purely formalist approach is at worse a deception, at
best a genuine, but flawed, attempt at syllogistic reasoning. In contrast,
Koskenniemi's 'culture of formalism' is based on a conception of universality that is 'neither a fixed principle nor a process but a *horizon of
possibility* that opens up the particular identities in the very process where
they make their claims of identity'.[65] Dispute settlement is driven by political interests and compromises, but it is argued that the most legitimate
agreements, and, therefore, those having the best chance of longer-term
success emerging from a peace process, are those framed by international
law and, indeed, key principles of international law provide the basis for

agreement. The International Court of Justice may be a suitable forum for specifically (and narrowly) defined disputes, but it is no match for diplomacy and associated non-judicial methods when complex disputes are being addressed. This does not mean that international law is irrelevant, but what it does mean is that we have to think about international law in terms of revealing a 'horizon of possibilities' for negotiators, in contrast with negotiations that are simply framed by politics, which will result in a 'clash of incommensurate "value systems" none of which can be rationally preferred'.[66]

The importance of diplomacy was made clear by the International Court of Justice in a 1980 case concerning US hostages being held in Iran, another facet of the confrontation between the US and Iran. The Court described diplomacy as an 'instrument essential for effective cooperation in the international community, and for enabling states, irrespective of their differing constitutional and social systems, to achieve mutual understanding and to resolve their differences by peaceful means'.[67] Bearing in mind the importance of diplomacy establishing a basis of reciprocity in order to achieve restoration of normal relations between states involved in a bilateral dispute, the chapter now turns to the methods of dispute settlement normally deployed in international law and relations. It will be seen that these methods are a practical application of what Koskenniemi has called the need to achieve an 'equitable balance' in resolving disputes.[68]

The whole process of negotiation towards an agreement with reciprocal rights and duties is premised on the obligation to settle disputes peacefully, which is a basic principle of international law as located in the UN Charter.[69] Furthermore, the purposes of the UN Charter prominently include the admonition to 'bring about by peaceful means, and *in conformity with the principles of justice and international law*, adjustment or settlement of international disputes or situations which might lead to a breach of the peace'.[70] It is that combination of justice and law that facilitates an equitable interpretation and application of legal principles within a new or emerging political context.[71]

Chapter VI of the UN Charter, which covers the peaceful settlement of disputes, obligates disputant states to 'seek a solution by negotiation, enquiry, mediation, conciliation, arbitration, judicial settlement, resort to regional agencies or arrangements, or other peaceful means of their own choice', before resorting to the Security Council.[72] These methods of settlement are not necessarily mutually exclusive. All settlement processes commence with negotiation and, in relatively confined issues, this may be sufficient to produce agreement.[73] In relation to intractable disputes, an unwillingness by the parties to meet face-to-face, or the lack of progress in 'talks about talks', might lead the parties to allow for third-party intervention in the settlement process. At one end of a spectrum third-party involvement may simply take the form of 'good offices' or a 'channel for communication', while the other end involves the 'assignment' to the third party or body 'to investigate the dispute and to present the parties with a set of formal proposals for its solution'. The latter is known as 'conciliation', whereas 'mediation' is situated somewhere between good offices and conciliation.[74] The mediator is an 'active participant authorized, and indeed expected, to advance fresh proposals and to interpret as well as transmit, each party's proposals to the other'.[75]

Given the historical animosity between the parties in the disputes mentioned at the outset of this chapter, mediation may represent a suitable method rather than to face-to-face negotiations, also bearing in mind that neither government of the disputant states would necessarily want to be faced with a concrete set of proposals for peaceful settlement coming from a conciliation commission. Mediation accords with the idea of a settlement process that operates within an equitable framework of law and justice, underpinned by reciprocity and aiming for restoration. Ultimately, it is up to both parties to agree on a mediator. John Merrills asks:

> What of the mediator's substantive contribution? The aim ... must be to satisfy both parties. In some situations it will be possible to do this by giving each state all or most of what it wants. This is because the aims of the parties in an international dispute are rarely identical and often quite different. Of course, the fact that there is a dispute indicates that the parties' aims are not entirely compatible, but unsuccessful negotiations may cause these differences to become the exclusive focus of attention. A mediator who can remind the parties of their essential objectives (or cause them to be redefined) may therefore be in a position to suggest a mutually satisfactory arrangement.[76]

Alternatively, or possibly in addition, the parties might be encouraged to agree on another traditional method of inter-state dispute settlement – inquiry. Inquiry involves bringing in a third party or body to 'provide the parties with an objective assessment'.[77] Traditional inquiries have, on occasions, gone beyond providing an independent assessment of the facts underlying or leading to the dispute and have made recommendations towards settlement of the dispute and reconciliation of the parties. For example, the Dogger Bank Inquiry of 1904–5, consisting of admirals from the UK, Russia, France, US and Austro-Hungary, was established to report on the circumstances and issues of responsibility and blame surrounding the damage done to the Hull trawler fleet by the Russian navy in the North Sea. The Inquiry's report helped to avoid conflict and normalize relations between the UK and Russia.[78]

3.5   Finding Common (Legal) Ground

Most of the disputes mentioned at the outset of this chapter involve issues of territory, sovereignty, self-determination (political and economic), and may also extend to human rights (socio-economic as well as civil-political). Disagreements on their meaning and application continue to fuel the dispute, for example, in the Cuba-US dispute, between the self-determination of the Cuban people based on independence from outside domination (as argued by the Cuban government) and self-determination based on free expression of the people in multi-party elections (as argued for by the US). For example, in the UN Human Rights Universal Periodic Review of Cuba in 2013, the Cuban representative pointed to the 'relentless attempts by the United States to impose a regime of change on the Cuban people', which was a 'serious violation of its right to self-determination'.[79] The US understanding of self-determination is made clear in the wording Helms-Burton Act of 1996, which embodied the long-standing embargo in legislation and, in so doing, stated that the purpose of continuing and tightening the embargo was 'to encourage the Cuban people to empower themselves with a government which reflects the self-determination of the Cuban people' and, further, 'to facilitate the rapid movement from such a transitional government to a democratically elected government in Cuba that results from an expression of the self-determination of the Cuban people'.[80]

Disagreements on the fundamental principles of international law represent the core of disputes and, therefore, they inevitably will form the general framework for any dispute settlement process. The aim of any peace process will be for those states involved to achieve common understandings on such principles in the context of the bilateral relationship between them. The genuine consent of the two states in achieving any such agreement will reconcile the common understanding of the two states in the concrete dispute between them with general principles of international law in their abstract form, unless any agreement is clearly in conflict with a norm of *jus cogens*.

According to the Articles on State Responsibility of 2001, consent cannot be used as an excuse for a peace agreement adopted in violation of a norm of *jus cogens*.[81] This principle is also contained in the Vienna Convention on the Law of Treaties 1969, to the effect that any peace treaty adopted in violation of a peremptory norm of international law will be seen as null and void.[82] Alexander Orakhelashvili has demonstrated that self-determination is a peremptory norm of international law accepted by the international community as allowing no derogation.[83] However, this has to be placed within the context of the indeterminacy that haunts the principle of self-determination in international law, in both its political and economic aspects, allowing states a significant degree of room to negotiate as to how it will be protected and implemented. As Rein Müllerson points out in relation to another norm of *jus cogens* – the prohibition on the use of force – while states agree that the prohibition is *jus cogens*, they are not agreed on its precise content or the content of the exceptions to it.[84] More generally, it has been accurately stated that 'one of the criticisms of *jus cogens* is that they lack sufficiently robust meaning to provide effective constraints on decision making'.[85]

Finding common legal ground involves a recognition that international laws often do not give black-and-white answers, for example, as to whether sovereignty is absolute or mediated,[86] whether non-intervention covers all forms of interference, whether self-determination is a purely external one-off event or whether it is internal ongoing process (and the meaning of this), and whether civil and political rights have priority over socio-economic rights.[87] Such uncertainty signifies that alternative choices can be made by states and a variety of contextual understandings agreed upon. It follows that while legal principles frame discussions, they cannot determine the dispute without common agreement on their meaning and application in the context of the political relationship between the two states, as well as the broader geopolitical context. Drawing upon the works of Jürgen Habermas, Steven Wheatley depicts such an approach as one of 'deliberative diplomacy',[88] where the aim is to establish a 'communicative consensus' about the parties' 'understanding of a situation as well as justifications for the principles and norms guiding their actions'.[89] Parties refer to a common system of norms and rules,[90] with international law supplying the 'rules of the game'.[91] This signifies that 'once international relations are framed in terms of law, they operate within the disciplinary constraints of an interpretive community'.[92] Legal discourse involves 'appeals to legal norms as they are understood not by each actor individually (subjectively) or in some abstract sense (objectively) but together as a collective law-interpreting body (inter-subjectively)'.[93] While powerful states have greater leverage within diplomatic relations, they 'cannot change those rules (and shift the terms of the debate) instantaneously and at will'.[94] Powerful states have to respect the 'conventions of argument, persuasion and justification associated with the particular enterprise in which the deliberations occur'.[95] However, given the problems of indeterminacy in a number of applicable principles and rules of international law, there is scope for 'divergent legal arguments'.[96]

In effect, international law operates as the common language for diplomacy, not as a system of readily applicable rules. This allows the parties to achieve understanding upon which a peaceful solution can be built, building on Koskenniemi's idea that when the political relationship governing two states comes to an end international law operates to fill in the space vacated by politics, but it does not do so by providing a ready solution or answer. Furthermore, while indeterminacy takes away the legs from a purely formalist approach to international law, Koskenniemi's critique reveals that a 'culture of formalism' whereby, 'although every (legal) decision is constitutive, and not just a reproduction of some underlying structure, each decision also acts as a kind of surface on which the horizon of universality becomes visible'.[97] Thus, while 'indeterminacy provides scope for divergent legal arguments',[98] it 'does not render discourse meaningless'.[99] International legal principles applicable to the dispute, indeed often at its heart, must be discussed, interpreted, agreed upon in formal or informal terms and, finally, implemented. If common ground has been successfully captured in that agreement, subsequent political relations can be framed by international law as encapsulated in the agreement.

The flexibility contained within the primary rules of international law, facilitating choice and agreement by the parties to an inter-state dispute, is matched by the secondary rules of international law. Although the 'rules' on state responsibility may appear to be rigid and formal, these rules are constructed in such a way that enable them to be shaped and applied by states in order to facilitate the settlement of disputes between them. All state disputes, and indeed any situation where a state is responsible for breach of the primary rules of international law, are governed by the Articles on State Responsibility of 2001, which, for instance, provide that 'full reparation for the injury caused by the internationally wrongful act shall take the form of restitution, compensation and satisfaction, either singly or in combination'.[100] The Articles also provide that the 'state responsible for an internationally wrongful act is under an obligation to give satisfaction for the injury caused by that act insofar as it cannot be made good by restitution or compensation' and that 'satisfaction may consist in an acknowledgement of the breach, an expression of regret, a formal apology or another appropriate modality'.[101] The point is that even under the apparently formal rules of state responsibility there is a range of remedies that can be adjusted as appropriate to the dispute under consideration. States involved in a complex dispute, in which both sides have violated international law, may have to concede that remedies will be available against them if settlement is to be achieved. In this way the secondary rules of responsibility fit the notion that international law provides a framework within which states can settle their disputes. As recognized by Martti Koskenniemi, in the practical world of dispute settlement the 'applicable rules come about through a complex diplomatic play that aims at freedom and constraint simultaneously'.[102]

It has to be borne in mind that the secondary rules on state responsibility, as found in the ILC's Articles of 2001, should not be seen as a form of international legislation, to be applied by courts and other bodies without regards to practice and context. They are abstract principles that require shaping and re-shaping by states within particular contexts to provide them with tools of international law with which they can normalize their international relations with other states after a rupture between them involving violations of international law. To view the Articles on State Responsibility as an inflexible set of rules would be a mistake. They are not constructed in such a way. The very fact that the ILC's Articles did not take the form of a treaty, but are left as soft laws to be developed by interpretation and application to disputes, implies that they are meant to be adapted and shaped by state practice.

3.6   Conclusion

It has been argued in this chapter that the parties to those disputes outlined in the introduction will, at a certain critical point in the future, seize the moment when there is a dramatic break in the political context that has governed their relations, thereby setting off a process of diplomacy whereby the parties, through discussion of general issues and specific mechanisms, move towards a peace agreement in which the parties agree to normalize their diplomatic, political and economic relations over a period of time. The peace process and peace agreement in inter-state disputes is primarily aimed at restoring and normalizing peaceful relations between the parties. However, it has been shown in this chapter that the concept of 'restoration' is not just embodied in modern notions of transitional justice, as applied within conflict-ridden states, but is also found within the primary and secondary rules of international law and mechanisms that are applicable to states in their inter-state relations to provide for accountability for breach of those rules.

The indeterminacy of the primary and secondary rules of international law, as unveiled by Martti Koskenniemi particularly in his earlier work,[103] enables the parties to negotiate a common understanding of them in the context of their dispute and the political conditions between them. Koskenniemi makes it clear that his characterization of indeterminacy is not that all international legal terms are 'semantically ambivalent', but is a much stronger claim that 'even where there is no semantic ambivalence whatsoever, international law remains indeterminate because it is based on contradictory premises', for example, as to whether sovereignty entails freedom or responsibility, or whether self-defence contains within it an element of anticipation and, if so, how much.[104] Nonetheless, Koskenniemi's message is a positive one – that such inherent indeterminacy is not to be seen as a 'structural deficiency', but as an 'absolutely central aspect of international law's acceptability'.[105] In this sense, the weakness of international law, so pointedly identified by Koskenniemi, can also be a strength if its role as a 'gentle civilizer', developed by Koskenniemi in his later works,[106] is properly recognized and allowed to function and flourish within political processes.

Indeed, all of Koskenniemi's work is united by a recognition that international law appears as a rigorous form of formalism while, at the same time, being simultaneously politically open-ended.[107] The key to understanding international law is to resist the 'pull of either excessive "formalism" or excessive policy-oriented "realism"',[108] and to see it primarily 'as a language of justification'.[109] This means that international law is a 'means to articulate particular preferences or positions in a formal fashion', which will reveal the 'possibilities and limits of political contestation through the adoption of a culture of formalism in a particular institutional environment'.[110] Justifications and arguments are made not in the abstract but in relation to concrete cases so that, for example, '"sovereignty" cannot be grasped by examining the "idea of sovereignty" somehow floating autonomously in conceptual space but by studying how that word is invoked in institutional contexts so as to make or oppose particular claims'.[111] For Koskenniemi, this signifies that the 'grammar of sovereignty shifts between assuming the full rights of States (concrete) and their complete submission to a binding law (normative)' and, furthermore, that 'closure is attained by balancing formulas' such as 'reasonable' or 'equitable', or 'simply by agreeing to seek agreement in a local or otherwise situation-specific context'.[112] While this chapter has argued for the profound relevance of such an approach in a bilateral inter-state dispute, it has also adopted the position that any such local agreement coming out of the process will not only embody particularities, but will contain agreement on contested terms of international law such as 'sovereignty' and 'self-determination', meaning that international law can provide the basis for a meeting of the minds. The peace agreement will also include compromises based on the equitable sharing of resources, liabilities and assets. However, those compromises flow from inter-subjective agreement between the parties on disputed legal principles and that, following Koskenniemi, those formalistic legal arguments adopted by the parties represent their political preferences.

The approach outlined in this chapter, influenced by the thinking of Martti Koskenniemi, is compatible with the process of 'deliberative diplomacy' identified by Habermas and Wheatley and, furthermore, is also resonant with the work of Christine Bell, a leading exponent of the law of peace and peace agreements. Bell examines a number of peace agreements in detail (the Oslo Accords of 1993 containing the Israel-Palestinian Declaration of Principles, the Agreement on the Constitution of South Africa of 1993, the Dayton Accords on Bosnia of 1995 and the Good Friday Agreement of 1998 for Northern Ireland). While recognizing the deficiencies of these agreements (particularly, though not exclusively, the failure to fully deliver the Palestinians' right to self-determination, the lack of accountability for past atrocities in Northern Ireland, the failure to fully address the embedded nature of inequalities in South Africa, and the paternalistic interventionist nature of Dayton), Bell's conclusion on the role of law in peace agreements is largely in line with the argument and analysis found in this chapter:

> As regards international law, while its traditional regulative function may seem particularly susceptible to political vagaries, this observation is not new. However, the facilitative impact of a broad range of soft and hard law standards indicates a greater role for international law than might have been imagined, and a need for international law to rise to the occasion. Politicians agreeing to human rights measures in the heat of negotiations often draw on international standards. Continued evolution of the facilitative function of international law does not necessarily depend upon a hardening of the law, but more on international law remaining creatively connected to notion of 'good practice' and capable of commanding a moral normativity.[113]

The argument in this chapter is a simple one: that, while acknowledging the indeterminacy of key principles of international law, it is possible to apply the approach Bell outlines to inter-state disputes, even apparently intractable ones, drawing on those strengths underpinning the primary and secondary rules of international law – of mutual respect, peaceful co-existence and reciprocity – to achieve a restoration and normalization of international relations.

This chapter has placed dispute settlement broadly within Koskenniemi's indeterminacy thesis and then adapted Koskenniemi's idea of international law as the 'gentle civilizer of nations', which he posited generally in the form of a question: 'between the arrogance of universality and the indifferences of particularity, what else is there apart from the civilized manner of gentle spirits?'[114] After showing how Koskenniemi's analysis of law can play a role in relation to collective security, this chapter applied such thinking to bilateral disputes. In so doing, the chapter has demonstrated that such disputes will not be resolved by the 'indifferences of particularity' but, drawing on Koskenniemi's ideas, it has shown that when the political regime encasing the dispute collapses, or radically changes, law can and should play a crucial role in establishing a new political regime based on the normalization of relations.

Notes

* The author would like to thank Marc Wesley and Lydia Davies-Bright for their research assistance on this chapter.

1. J. Strawson, 'Provoking International Law: War and Regime Change in Iraq', in F. Johns, R. Joyce and S. Pahuja (eds), *Events: The Force of International Law* (Abingdon, UK: Routledge, 2010), 246, 247: 'the long reach of colonialism has bequeathed doctrinal ambiguities on the use of force, occupation and regime change, the key issues at stake over Iraq'.

2. See e.g. R. Caplan, 'International Authority and State Building: The Case of Bosnia and Herzegovina', *Global Governance* 10 (2004): 58: 'can change that will allow Bosnia to function as a *self-sustaining* liberal democratic state be achieved ultimately by means of administrative fiat?'; F. Ni Aolain, 'The Fractured Sole of the Dayton Peace Agreement: A Legal Analysis', *Michigan Journal of International Law* 18 (1998): 971: 'this is a Dayton constitution not a Bosnia constitution'.

3. J. Alvarez, 'Hegemonic International Law Revisited', *American Journal of International Law* 97 (2003): 873–88: 'few appear terribly concerned about the prospect of hegemonic rule through the collective processes of international law, including the Security Council'.

4. P. Radan, 'Post-Secession International Borders: a Critical Analysis of the Opinions of the Badinter Arbitration Commission', *Melbourne University Law Review* 24 (2000): 74: 'To insist, in cases of secession from a federal state, that internal federal

borders automatically should become international borders is to establish the Badinter Borders Principle as a new rule of international law. On the analysis of the legal reasoning adopted by the Badinter Commission in *Opinion No 3* this rule has no principled foundation in international law. More fundamentally, irrespective of whether this new rule of international law is or is not soundly based in international law, it is, in political and practical terms, too simplistic and inflexible as is amply illustrated in the case of the fragmentation of the SFRY'.

5. S. Allen and E. Guntrip, 'The Kosovo Question and *Uti Possidetis*: The Potential for a Negotiated Solution', in J. Summers (ed.), *Kosovo: a Precedent? The Declaration of Independence, the Advisory Opinion and Implications for Statehood, Self-Determination and Minority Rights* (Leiden, Netherlands: Martinus Nijhoff, 2011), 303, 315.

6. M. Koskenniemi, *The Gentle Civilizer of Nations: the Rise and Fall of International Law* (Cambridge: Cambridge University Press, 2002), 515.

7. A.-M. La Rosa and X. Phillipe, 'Transitional Justice', in V. Chetail (ed.), *Post-Conflict Peacebuilding: A Lexicon* (Oxford: Oxford University Press, 2009), 368.

8. C. Stahn, J. E. Esterday and J. Iverson (eds), *Jus Post Bellum: Mapping the Normative Foundations* (Oxford: Oxford University Press, 2014), 5: 'it is still unclear whether *jus post bellum* is a construct, a strand of research, or a sub-discipline of existing paradigms'.

9. See e.g. UN Doc. A/RES/68/116 (2013): 'The rule of law at the national and international levels', which, at para. 4, '*reaffirms* the imperative of upholding and promoting the rule of law at the international level in accordance with the principles of the Charter of the United Nations'.

10. M. Koskenniemi, 'The Politics of International Law', *European Journal of International Law* 1 (1990): 7.

11. Ibid., 14.

12. Ibid., 31.

13. M. Koskenniemi, 'The Politics of International Law – 20 Years Later', *European Journal of International Law* 20 (2010): 11.

14. J. J. Mearsheimer, 'Back to the Future: Instability in Europe after the Cold War', *International Security* 15 (1990): 5–56.

15. M. Koskenniemi, 'The Place of Law in Collective Security', *Michigan Journal of International Law* 17 (1996): 465, 469, 472, 476.

16. Ibid., 473. See further R. Higgins, 'The Place of International Law in the Settlement of Disputes by the UN Security Council', *American Journal of International Law* 63 (1970): 4.

17. Koskenniemi, 'Place of Law in Collective Security', 478, 480.

18. Subsequent practice is recognized as a means of interpretation in Article 31(3)(2)(b), Vienna Convention on the Law of Treaties 1969.

19. See M. Craven, 'The European Community Arbitration Commission on Yugoslavia', *British Yearbook of International Law* 66 (1995): 333–413.

20. UN Doc. A/RES/1514 (1960), Declaration on the Granting of Independence to Colonial Countries and Peoples.

21. Koskenniemi, 'Place of Law in Collective Security', 476–77.

22. See Parliamentary Written Answer to House of Lords given by the Attorney General Lord Goldsmith, *Hansard* HL, Vol. 646, WA2–3, 17 March 2003.

23. Koskenniemi, 'Place of Law in Collective Security', 463.
24. M. J. Glennon, *The Fog of Law: Pragmatism, Security, and International Law* (Stanford, CA: Stanford University Press, 2010), 3.
25. Ibid., 5.
26. Ibid.
27. Ibid., 27.
28. H. L. A. Hart, *The Concept of Law*, 3rd edn (Oxford: Clarendon, 2012), 89–91.
29. Koskenniemi, *Gentle Civilizer of Nations*, 515.
30. Koskenniemi, 'Place of Law in Collective Security', 468.
31. Ibid.
32. Glennon, *Fog of Law*, 89.
33. Koskenniemi, 'Place of Law in Collective Security', 471.
34. But see Glennon, *Fog of Law*, 163: 'the world today is saddled with the outmoded institutions of a bygone era'.
35. UN Doc. S/RES/1483 (2003).
36. UN Doc. A/RES/1004 (1956); UN Doc. A/RES/ES-6/2 (1980).
37. UN Doc. A/RES/38/7 (1983); UN Doc. A/RES/44/240 (1989).
38. See e.g. UN Doc. A/RES/67/4 (2012).
39. M. Koskenniemi, 'The Police in the Temple Order, Justice and the UN: a Dialectical View', *European Journal of International Law* 6 (1995): 325–48.
40. UN Doc. S/RES/827 (1993); UN Doc. S/RES/955 (1994).
41. UN Doc. A/RES/68/262 (2014) adopted by 100–11 with fifty-eight abstentions.
42. Koskenniemi, 'Place of Law in Collective Security', 473, 478, 480.
43. On achieving inter-subjective agreements, see I. Johnstone, 'Legislation and Adjudication in the UN Security Council: Bringing Down the Deliberative Deficit', *American Journal of International Law* 102 (2008): 275–308. See also J. Habermas, *Between Facts and Norms: Contributions to a Discourse Theory of Law and Democracy*, W. Rehg (trans.) (Oxford: Polity, 1996), 107, where Habermas writes that 'just those action norms are valid to which all possible affected persons could agree as participants in rational discourses'.
44. UN Doc. S/RES/827 (1993); UN Doc. S/RES/955 (1994).
45. UN Doc. S/RES/1373 (2001).
46. By means of the Torricelli Act 1992 and the Helms-Burton Act 1996. For discussion, see P. J. Haney and W. Vanderbush, *The Cuban Embargo: The Domestic Politics of an American Foreign Policy* (Pittsburgh, PA: University of Pittsburgh Press, 2005), 86–89, 104–7.
47. C. Bell, 'Peace Agreements: Their Nature and Legal Status', *American Journal of International Law* 100 (2006): 373–75.
48. La Rosa and Philippe, 'Transitional Justice', 368; D. Shelton, *Remedies in International Human Rights Law*, 2nd edn (Oxford: Oxford University Press, 2005), 12–15.
49. Crawford states that 'there is little or no state practice to support "punitive" or "penal" consequences for breaches of international law'. J. Crawford, *State Responsibility: the General Part* (Cambridge: Cambridge University Press, 2013), 52.
50. Koskenniemi, *Gentle Civilizer of Nations*, 501.
51. Ibid.
52. Ibid., 500.

53. K. Trapp, *State Responsibility for International Terrorism* (Oxford: Oxford University Press, 2011), 263.
54. Ibid.
55. Ibid.
56. See e.g. R. G. Teitel, *Transitional Justice* (Oxford: Oxford University Press, 2000), 69–94; W. Lambourne, 'Tranformative Justice, Reconciliation and Peacebuilding', in S. Buckley-Zistel, T. K. Beck, C. Braun and F. Mieth (eds), *Transitional Justice Theories* (Abingdon, UK: Routledge, 2014), 19.
57. *US Diplomatic and Consular Staff in Tehran*, (1980) ICJ Rep 3; *Military and Paramilitary Activities in and Against Nicaragua*, (1986) ICJ Rep 14.
58. C. Gray, 'The Use and Abuse of the International Court of Justice in the Enforcement of International Law', in K. Koufa (ed.), *International Law Enforcement: New Tendencies* (Athens: Sakkoulas, 2010), 198, 202.
59. On the 2015 nuclear deal with Iran that has led to a thawing in Iranian-US relations, see M. Fitzpatrick, 'Iran: a Good Deal', *Survival* 57 (2015): 47–52.
60. D. Müller, 'Other Specific Regimes of Responsibility: the Iran-US Claims Tribunal', in J. Crawford, A. Pellet and S. Olleson (eds), *The Law of International Responsibility* (Cambridge: Cambridge University Press, 2010), 843.
61. Ibid.
62. Müller, 'Other Specific Regimes of Responsibility', 844–45.
63. See *Oil Platforms (Islamic Republic of Iran v United States of America)*, (2003) ICJ Rep 161. In 2010 there was an unattributed cyber-attack using Stuxnet against Iran's nuclear plants resulting in the destruction of centrifuges essential for the enrichment of uranium.
64. Iran-US Claims Tribunal, 'Interpretation of the Algerian Declaration of 19th January 1981', *International Law Reports* 62 (1982), 599–600.
65. Koskenniemi, *Gentle Civilizer of Nations*, 506.
66. Ibid., 505–6.
67. *Tehran Hostages Case*, (1980) ICJ Rep 3 at 91.
68. Koskenniemi, 'Politics of International Law', 14.
69. Article 2(3), UN Charter 1945.
70. Article 1(1), UN Charter 1945, emphasis added.
71. Koskenniemi, 'Politics of International Law', 14.
72. Article 33(1) UN Charter 1945. See also Article 25 OAS Charter.
73. J. G. Merrills, *International Dispute Settlement*, 5th edn (Cambridge: Cambridge University Press, 2011), 22–25.
74. Ibid., 26.
75. Ibid.
76. Ibid., 35.
77. Ibid., 41.
78. Ibid., 42–43.
79. Human Rights Council, Report of the Working Group on the Universal Periodic Review: Cuba, UN Doc. A/HRC/24/16 (2013), paras 5–6.
80. Cuban Liberty and Democratic Solidarity (Libertad) Act 1996, Title II, Section 201 (P.L. 104-114).
81. Articles 20 and 26, Articles on the Responsibility of States for Internationally Wrongful Acts 2001.
82. Article 53, Vienna Convention on the Law of Treaties 1969.

83. A. Orakhelashvili, *Peremptory Norms in International Law* (Oxford: Oxford University Press, 2006), 51–53.
84. R. Müllerson, 'Jus Ad Bellum: Plus Ca Change (Le Monde) Plus C'est La Meme Chose (Le Droit)?', *Journal of Conflict and Security Law* 7 (2002): 149–90.
85. M. Del Mar, 'System Values and Understanding Legal Language', *Leiden Journal of International Law* 21 (2008): 58.
86. M. Pérez-Stable, *The Cuban Revolution: Origins, Course, and Legacy*, 2nd edn (Oxford: Oxford University Press, 1999), 37.
87. M. Koskenniemi, *From Apology to Utopia* (Helsinki: Finnish Lawyers' Publishing Co., 1989), 67, where he states that 'international law is singularly useless as a means for justifying or criticising behaviour'.
88. S. Wheatley, *The Democratic Legitimacy of International Law* (Oxford: Hart, 2010), 138.
89. T. Risse, '"Let's Argue": Communicative Action in World Politics', *International Organization* 54 (2000): 9.
90. Ibid., 10.
91. J. Habermas, 'Does the Constitutionalization of International Law Still Have a Chance?', in C. Cronin (ed.), *The Divided West* (Cambridge: Polity, 2006), 115, 119.
92. Wheatley, *Democratic Legitimacy*, 143.
93. I. Johnstone, 'The Plea of "Necessity" in International Law Discourse: Humanitarian Intervention and Counter-Terrorism', *Columbia Journal of Transnational Law* 43 (2005): 381.
94. Ibid., 383.
95. Ibid.
96. Wheatley, *Democratic Legitimacy*, 149.
97. Koskenniemi, *Gentle Civilizer of Nations*, 508.
98. Wheatley, *Democratic Legitimacy*, 149.
99. S. Toope, 'Emerging Patterns of Governance and International Law', in M. Byers (ed.), *The Role of Law in International Politics* (Oxford: Oxford University Press, 2000), 91, 102.
100. Article 34, Articles on the Responsibility of States for Internationally Wrongful Acts 2001.
101. Ibid.
102. M. Koskenniemi, 'Doctrines of State Responsibility', in Crawford et al., *Law of International Responsibility*, 45, 51.
103. Koskenniemi, *From Apology to Utopia*, 67.
104. See his 2005 epilogue to his original work in M. Koskenniemi, *From Apology to Utopia: The Structure of International Legal Argument*, reissue with new epilogue (Cambridge: Cambridge University Press, 2006), 590–91.
105. Ibid., 591.
106. Koskenniemi, *Gentle Civilizer of Nations*, 515.
107. Koskenniemi, *From Apology to Utopia* (2006), 563.
108. Ibid., 564.
109. Ibid., 570.
110. Ibid., 571.
111. Ibid., 572.
112. Ibid., 583.

113. C. Bell, *Peace Agreements and Human Rights* (Oxford: Oxford University Press, 2000), 320–21.
114. Koskenniemi, *Gentle Civilizer of Nations*, 515.

Bibliography

Allen, Stephen, and Edward Guntrip. 'The Kosovo Question and Uti Possidetis: The Potential for a Negotiated Solution'. In James Summers (ed.), *Kosovo: a Precedent? The Declaration of Independence, the Advisory Opinion and Implications for Statehood, Self-Determination and Minority Rights* (Leiden, Netherlands: Martinus Nijhoff, 2011).

Álvarez, Jose E. 'Hegemonic International Law Revisited'. *The American Journal of International Law* 97 (2003): 873–88.

Aolain, Fionnuala Ni. 'The Fractured Soul of the Dayton Peace Agreement: a Legal Analysis'. *Michigan Journal of International Law* 19 (1998): 957–1004.

Bell, Christine. *Peace Agreements and Human Rights* (Oxford: Oxford University Press, 2000).

'Peace Agreements: Their Nature and Legal Status'. *American Journal of International Law* 100 (2006): 373–412.

Caplan, Richard. 'International Authority and State Building: the Case of Bosnia and Herzegovina'. *Global Governance* 10 (2004): 53–65.

Craven, Matthew C. R. 'The European Community Arbitration Commission on Yugoslavia'. *The British Year Book of International Law* 66 (1996): 333–413.

Crawford, James. *State Responsibility: the General Part* (Cambridge: Cambridge University Press, 2013).

Del Mar, Maksymilian. 'System Values and Understanding Legal Language'. *Leiden Journal of International Law* 21 (2008): 29–61.

Fitzpatrick, Mark. 'Iran: a Good Deal'. *Survival* 57 (2015): 47–52.

Glennon, Michael J. *The Fog of Law: Pragmatism, Security, and International Law* (Stanford, CA: Stanford University Press, 2010).

Gray, Christine. 'The Use and Abuse of the International Court of Justice in the Enforcement of International Law'. In Kalliop Koufa (ed.), *International Law Enforcement: New Tendencies* (Athens: Sakkoulas, 2010).

Habermas, Jürgen. *Between Facts and Norms: Contributions to a Discourse Theory of Law and Democracy*, William Rehg (trans.) (Oxford: Polity, 1996).

'Does the Constitutionalization of International Law Still Have a Chance?' In Ciaran Croning (ed. and trans.), *The Divided West* (Oxford: Polity, 2006).

Hart, Herbert L. A. *The Concept of Law.* 3rd edn (Oxford: Clarendon, 2012).

Higgins, Rosalyn. 'The Place of International Law in the Settlement of Disputes by the Security Council'. *American Journal of International Law* 64 (1970): 1–18.

Johnstone, Ian. 'Legislation and Adjudication in the UN Security Council: Bringing Down the Deliberative Deficit'. *American Journal of International Law* 102 (2008): 275–308.

'The Plea of Necessity in International Legal Discourse: Humanitarian Intervention and Counter-Terrorism'. *Columbia Journal of Transnational Law* 43 (2005): 337–88.

Koskenniemi, Martti. 'Doctrines of State Responsibility'. In James Crawford, Allain Pellet and Simon Olleson (eds.), *The Law of International Responsibility* (Oxford: Oxford University Press, 2010).

From Apology to Utopia: the Structure of International Legal Argument (Helsinki: Finnish Lawyers' Publishing Co., 1989).

From Apology to Utopia: the Structure of International Legal Argument, reissue with a new epilogue (Cambridge: Cambridge University Press, 2006).

'The Place of Law in Collective Security'. *Michigan Journal of International Law* 17 (1995): 455–90.

'The Police in the Temple Order, Justice and the UN: a Dialectical View'. *European Journal of International Law* 6 (1995): 325–48.

'The Politics of International Law'. *European Journal of International Law* 1–2 (1990): 4–32.

'The Politics of International Law – 20 Years Later'. *European Journal of International Law* 20 (2009): 7–19.

Lambourne, Wendy. 'Transformative Justice, Reconciliation, and Peacebuilding'. In Susanne Buckley-Zistel, Teresa K. Beck, Christian Braun and Frederike Mieth (eds), *Transitional Justice Theories* (Abingdon, UK: Routledge, 2014).

La Rosa, Anne-Marie, and Xavier Philippe. 'Transitional Justice'. in Vincent Chetail (ed.), *Post-Conflict Peacebuilding: a Lexicon* (Oxford: Oxford University Press, 2009).

Mearsheimer, John J. 'Back to the Future: Instability in Europe after the Cold War'. *International Security* 15 (1990): 5–56.

Merrills, John G. *International Dispute Settlement*, 5th edn (Cambridge: Cambridge University Press, 2011).

Müller, Daniel. 'Other Specific Regimes of Responsibility: the Iran-US Claims Tribunal'. In James Crawford, Allain Pellet and Simon Olleson (eds), *The Law of International Responsibility* (Oxford: Oxford University Press, 2010).

Müllerson, Rein. 'Jus Ad Bellum: Plus Ça Change (Le Monde) Plus C'est La Même Chose (Le Droit)?' *Journal of Conflict and Security Law* 7 (2002): 149–90.

Orakhelashvili, Alexander. *Peremptory Norms in International Law* (Oxford: Oxford University Press, 2006).

Pérez-Stable, Marifeli. *The Cuban Revolution: Origins, Course, and Legacy*. 2nd edn (Oxford: Oxford University Press, 1999).

Radan, Peter. 'Post-Secession International Borders: a Critical Analysis of the Opinions of the Badinter Arbitration Commission'. *Melbourne University Law Review* 24 (2000): 50–76.

Risse, Thomas. '"Let's Argue!" Communicative Action in World Politics'. *International Organization* 54 (2000): 1–39.

Shelton, Dinah. *Remedies in International Human Rights Law*, 2nd edn (Oxford: Oxford University Press, 2005).

Stahn, Carsten, Jennifer S. Easterday and Jens Iverson (eds.). *Jus Post Bellum: Mapping the Normative Foundations* (Oxford: Oxford University Press, 2014).

Strawson, John. 'Provoking International Law'. In Fleur Johns, Richard Joyce and Sundhya Pahuja (eds), *Events: the Force of International Law* (Abingdon, UK: Routledge, 2010).

Teitel, Ruti G. *Transitional Justice* (Oxford: Oxford University Press, 2000).

Toope, Stephen J. 'Emerging Patterns of Governance and International Law'. In Michael Yers (ed.), *The Role of Law in International Politics: Essays in International Relations and International Law* (Oxford: Oxford University Press, 2000).

Trapp, Kimberley N. *State Responsibility for International Terrorism* (Oxford: Oxford University Press, 2011).

Vanderbush, Walt, and Patrick Jude Haney. *The Cuban Embargo: the Domestic Politics of an American Foreign Policy* (Pittsburgh, PA: University of Pittsburgh Press, 2005).

Wheatley, Steven. *The Democratic Legitimacy of International Law* (Oxford: Hart, 2010).

4

Form Meets Function

The Culture of Formalism and International
Environmental Regimes

JAYE ELLIS[*]

4.1 Introduction

International environmental law seems to have reached an impasse. This is hardly surprising: the complexity of environmental problems, even when considered apart from underlying social, political and economic factors, is staggering. Scientific understandings of environmental degradation and its causes evolve rapidly. The underlying causes of such degradation are very often activities that bring significant social and economic benefits, with the result that political authorities have no wish to prohibit or strictly regulate them; incentive structures may often constitute a more promising avenue. The complexity of questions about human impacts on the environment and how to decrease or mitigate them calls for a high degree of specialization, while at the same time requiring coordinated action on a number of fronts. In light of these challenges, international environmental law has followed a trajectory that seems inevitable: from general rules whose vagueness often impeded their usefulness to highly specialized, technical regimes focussed on narrowly defined phenomena and interacting with each other in a rather hesitant and clumsy fashion, and more recently to the acceleration of transnational, including non-state, regime building. It becomes increasingly difficult to discern the particular contribution that law can make to environmental protection as it takes on the role of handmaiden to science, economics, politics, ethics and other social systems.

In this chapter, I examine sites of interaction between scholarship on specialized regimes viewed through the lens of systems theory, particularly as developed in the work of Andreas Fischer-Lescano and Gunther Teubner, and of Martti Koskenniemi's culture of formalism and constitutional mind-set. The two approaches are divergent in important respects: their analysis of the phenomenon of fragmentation is different, and their theoretical projects are quite distinct. Nevertheless, both approaches are preoccupied with the instrumentalization of law, and seek ways for law to transcend the confines of specialized regimes. Both are concerned with the colonization of law by other expert systems, and identify resources to bolster law's autonomy, to put it in systems theoretical terms, or the *proprium* of law, to use Koskenniemi's expression.

In the section that follows, I present a brief overview of those elements of systems theory that are essential to the argument developed below. I then provide a sketch of current developments in international environmental law. Parallel themes in the work of Koskenniemi, Fischer-Lescano and Teubner are then explored before I turn to a discussion of science in environmental regimes.

4.2   Law as Social System

The approach that I take to law is based on the systems theory of Niklas Luhmann, particularly as developed by Gunther Teubner, and may require some unpacking. A useful starting point is system theory's conception of society: as it develops increasingly complex understandings of its environment, it begins to undergo processes of fragmentation in which semi-autonomous social systems, each possessing its own manner of communicating with its environment, begin to emerge.[1] These systems possess boundaries that they themselves establish and maintain, and which, while they permit contact between system and environment, necessitate processes of translation as those communications pass across system boundaries, following a process of selection and translation by the system to which the message is directed. For example, legislation, resulting from political processes, is reconstructed by the legal system in the form of new legal norms. The impact which legislation has on the legal rules cannot, however, be determined by the legislature; on the contrary, these impacts will be contingent on a range of factors, notably the types of disputes that arise and the manner in which the rules are interpreted by lawyers and judges. The rules may lie dormant. A conflict may be found between the legislated rules and other rules within the system. This is not (necessarily) a matter of dysfunction or subversion. It is inevitable whenever systems seek to observe their environments in increasingly complex ways.

Consider the example of evidence obtained in breach of an accused's rights. Such evidence is not admissible, regardless of how useful it might be in determining what happened at a crime scene. For the purposes of the judgement, that evidence may be seen not to exist. There are political and ethical reasons for this rule, but operational closure means that political and ethical arguments for or against the exclusion of evidence in a given case do not have a direct impact on the outcome. Even if solid ethical arguments for the admission of evidence could be made, say, on consequentialist grounds, the ruling in law may well remain the same: the evidence is excluded. The exclusion of the evidence is an operation that is made by and for the legal system.

The distinctiveness of a system lies in its unique prestation (*Leistung*; often translated as performance or contribution); law's prestation is generally described by systems theorists as the stabilization of normative expectations.[2] The manner in which this prestation emerges and comes to be attributed to a particular system is a matter of contingency. For example, the emergence of separate legal, ethical, political, religious, and scientific systems seems, in certain parts of the world at least, to have a good deal to do with the rise of the secular society. One result of this is that law and justice, while in close contact with one another in various ways, must be seen to be separate: when different conceptions of the good life are in contention with one another, and different types of authority can be invoked to support a range of world views, legal disputes can no longer be settled by the light of justice, for to attempt to do so could lead to clashes between different putative authorities on the content of justice. This does not mean that law should be understood as a society-wide set of values while justice is particular and parochial. In a pluralistic society, one needs a system for the stabilization of normative expectations that operates throughout that society. Law is not seen from the vantage point of systems theory as hierarchically superior to other systems such as ethics, but rather as coexisting with it, on the same plane. The fact of legal decision does not make the underlying conflicts go away: a man may go to jail for ending the life of his seriously disabled daughter, but debates about whether he is thus treated fairly, justly or appropriately continue to rage in ethical, scientific and political arenas. The decisions are made on the basis of rules that are purported to possess independence from any particular cultural, ethical or political camp; when they are revealed to be closely aligned with one camp or another, they are subject to criticism on this basis.

The autonomy of law from other social systems such as science, ethics or politics thus may be understood as essential to law's ability to carry out its prestation. Threats to law's autonomy may be regarded as just another contingency, which will result in further evolution of law and other social systems.[3] Systems theory provides us with a vocabulary and a set of analytical frameworks that shed light on evolutionary process that could, if they continue, lead to the colonization of the legal system into one or several other social systems. For example, law may come to be colonized by science: the question of a rule's violation may cease to involve efforts to interpret and apply rules, and come to turn on scientific inquiry into the effects of certain inputs into the environment in a particular instance. Similarly, law could be colonized by economics: the question whether it is reasonable to expose a given community to an environmental risk could cease to be made in light of substantive or procedural legal rules and be turned over to cost-benefit analysis. I regard these possibilities not with the cool detachment to which a Luhmannian scholar should aspire but with concern, largely as a result of my contact with Koskenniemi's scholarship over the years. As a scholar of environmental law, I do not wish to clear away the clutter of issue-specific regimes drawing heavily on scientific expertise and attending to context; I am not particularly interested in a concept of international law as a unified, and neatly hierarchical edifice. There is a great need for political and legal decision-making processes, including the framing, interpretation and application of legal rules, to draw heavily on scientific and other forms of expertise, and for the operation of feedback loops to gather information on impacts that these regimes appear to be having on ecosystems. If law ceases to carry out its prestation of stabilizing normative expectations and comes to be treated as an instrument for the achievement of sustainable development, then, in all likelihood, a new system charged with stabilizing normative expectations will eventually emerge, but in the meantime, law will fail to make any progress towards its newly defined goal. Law cannot identify sustainable levels of resource exploitation any more than science can seek to ensure fairness in decision-making processes. But any time decisions must be made about complex phenomena in a heterogeneous society in which there is no agreement on the nature of a good life or of a substantively good outcome, law – or something like law – has a role to play.

The fragmentation, or differentiation, of society into a series of autonomous social systems evokes a different kind of fragmentation, namely fragmentation within law. These processes of fragmentation are very different from one another, but are nevertheless mutually relevant, as indicated by the work of Andreas Fischer-Lescano and Gunther Teubner. Of central importance is the Luhmannian depiction of law as one system.

Luhmann, as a sociologist, is looking at the system from without, as part of a broader set of phenomena, whereas jurists interested in the fragmentation of law are standing within the legal system and therefore seeing something quite different. One of the things which certain jurists see – notably Fischer-Lescano, Koskenniemi and Teubner, is a multi-faceted process identified by a range of terms: Fischer-Lescano and Teubner refer to functionalization, and Koskenniemi to deformalization and the managerial mind-set. There are intriguing similarities and overlaps between both the analysis of the phenomenon conducted by these authors and their approaches to addressing the phenomenon.

4.3 International Environmental Law: Culture and Counter-culture

In his discussions of the managerial mind-set and the deformalization of law, Koskenniemi frequently makes reference to environmental law, notably to the carving out of implementation and compliance procedures from the general law of state responsibility, to the increased resort to soft law, and to the heavy reliance on equitable balancing.[4] A brief sketch of the architecture of international environmental law reveals vague, general principles at one end; highly detailed and technical rules and standards articulated at the level of specialized regimes at the other end; and a series of potentially useful but underspecified – and, unfortunately, largely uninfluential – procedural rules between the two.[5] Furthermore, a large number of general principles and regime-specific standards take the form of soft law. Attempts to flesh out a series of general rights and obligations for states (and potentially for other actors, as well) have been ongoing, but those efforts seem to have faltered with the publication by the International Law Commission (ILC) of the 2001 Draft Articles on Prevention of Transboundary Harm from Hazardous Activities[6] and the 2006 Draft Principles on the Allocation of Loss in the case of Transboundary Harm arising out of Hazardous Activities.[7] A formalist approach exercised influence in international environmental law until perhaps the late 1980s or early 1990s, during which time authors relied heavily on both public international law and private law within municipal systems in their attempts to articulate potential future directions for international environmental law.[8] A trend away from such an approach and towards the construction of regulatory regimes became apparent in the late 1980s and seems to have been well established by the time of the second earth summit in Rio de Janeiro, Brazil, in 1992.[9]

The emergence of specialized environmental regimes is part of a much larger trend in international law.[10] This trend represents a certain kind of fragmentation – not in the sense of the proliferation of adjudicatory instances leading to potentially conflicting rulings, but in a different and deeper sense: Koskenniemi and Päivi Leino state that '[t]o read the debate about fragmentation as if it had to do only with coherence in the abstract is to be mistaken about what is actually at stake'.[11] Here the authors hint at what Koskenniemi makes more explicit elsewhere: the kind of fragmentation that calls for attention is of a different nature, involving the creation of regimes for specific purposes, establishing decision-making processes oriented not towards the resolution of disputes as such or the reconciling of different interests, but rather towards the pursuit of the regime's objectives.[12] This analysis applies very well to international environmental law, even to the extent that one can speak of fragmentation of the fragment, as various environmental regimes develop their own highly technical vocabulary, standards and procedures.

4.3.1   The ILC and Transboundary Harm

At first blush, the efforts of the ILC to develop general rules of universal application to address environmental harm may have been meant as a counterweight to the trend towards fragmentation and managerialism, but if so, it is likely that they have failed.[13] The Draft Articles were initially intended to complement the Articles on State Responsibility by creating a strict liability regime.[14] In the end, however, the ILC produced a dramatically more modest document.[15] The central obligation, obtained through a combined meaning of arts 3 (Duty of prevention), 9 (Consultations on preventive measures), and 10 (Factors involved in an equitable balancing of interests), can be read as an obligation to conduct, in collaboration with affected states, a cost-benefit analysis regarding an existing or proposed activity and possible mitigation measures or alternatives.

One concrete result of this gradual hollowing out of the obligation of prevention is to leave lawyers – and the legal system more generally – with little to do. The matter will be settled, not by the application of legal rules, but through political negotiation with heavy reliance on a range of experts, notably ecologists, engineers and economists. The relevance of inputs from such experts is not in doubt. Indeed, it is difficult to see how general rules on state responsibility and liability for environmental harm could function, given the peculiarities of such harm: its production through activities that are lawful, as well as being largely beneficial and useful;

the overwhelming role of private actors; and the heavy dependence on science to understand the harm itself and potentially available mitigation measures. Yet the most obvious alternative – the colonization of law by science, economics and other cognate social systems – is hardly attractive.

The dangers presented by materialization and deformalization of this nature are well captured by Jürgen Habermas's comments on similar phenomena in the domestic sphere. Habermas points to social welfare laws, policies and programmes intended to pursue substantive, not simply formal, equality by, among other things, putting resources into the hands of people who appear to need them in order to overcome a disadvantage.[16] Lying behind such laws is a fairly detailed portrait of what a good, worthy person's life path would look like.[17] Habermas describes the process of materialization of law in the following terms:

> The classical scheme for separate branches of government becomes less tenable the more laws lose the form of conditional programs and assume instead the shape of goal-oriented programs. As a rule, these 'materialized' laws, too, appear as general norms formulated without proper nouns and directed to an indeterminate number of addressees. However, they contain general clauses and vague statutory language, or set concrete policies (analogous to special legislation) that leave the administration considerable room for discretion. Due to the developments leading to state interventionism, more and more areas of law have been materialized, with the result that an administration geared for planning, services, and policymaking is increasingly unable to limit itself to simply implementing general and sufficiently determinate norms in a technical manner unburdened of normative questions.[18]

At first glance, these critiques are hard to distinguish from those of scholars generally associated with the political right, notably Hayek.[19] However, Habermas notes with interest the contributions to these arguments by feminist theory, stating that '[i]t is no accident that this critique arises in the context of a *feminist theory of law* that rejects the welfare paradigm'.[20] He quotes Iris Marion Young:

> Domination consists in institutional conditions which inhibit or prevent people from participation in determining their actions or the conditions of their actions. Welfare capitalist society creates specifically new forms of domination. Increasingly the activities of everyday work and life come under rationalized bureaucratic control, subjecting people to the discipline of authorities and experts in many areas of life.[21]

This deformalization results from a desire to instrumentalize law, that is, conceiving of it simply as a tool for achieving particular social outcomes.

The vague, general standards allow scope for decision makers to refer to experts in various relevant domains to help them to craft context-specific responses to legal claims. In some cases – this is often true in environmental regimes – the general principles will be complemented by technical, regime-specific standards. Through these moves, legal rules lose their general character, and instances of rule-interpretation and -application need not be carried out with a view to consistency and coherence, except as respects the pursuit of the material objectives inscribed in a given regime.

One of the features of deformalization and materialization is the weakening of law's autonomy vis-à-vis science. Law's capacity to (purport to) operate in a pluralistic environment in which arise deep-seated disagreements about ultimate ends is threatened as a result. Scientists can and do provide essential input into decision-making processes about responsibility for environmental harm, or about the extent to which a proposed project respects existing norms. However, *qua* scientists, they cannot make decisions on the specific topics of responsibility and legality. Environmental regimes need scientists to identify potential risks, but cannot rely on them to make decisions about the acceptability of such risks or whether a defendant acted unreasonably in creating a risk.

4.4   Deformalization and the Culture of Formalism

If deformalization is a threat to law, then we are faced with the question whether a return to formalism is in order. This hardly seems wise, particularly following the trenchant critique of formalism conducted by the Critical Legal Studies movement. One of the signature observations of that movement is that the indeterminacy of legal rules makes them highly malleable and subject to manipulation; they are as vessels into which can be poured any number of interests or ideological commitments.[22] The place to look for the lawyer's identity, argues Koskenniemi, is between sociological description and moral speculation,[23] 'not because lawyers would have dismissed sociology or ethics as unworthy enterprises but because neither one nor the other is able to answer the question that lawyers are called upon to answer: namely the question about (valid) law'.[24] Koskenniemi anchors his discussion of a culture of formalism in a debate between Wolfgang Friedmann, on one hand, and A. J. Thomas and Adolph A. Berle on the other, regarding the US invasion of the Dominican Republic in 1965. Thomas and Berle, Koskenniemi recounts, expressed frustration with the lawyerly obsession with correct terminology and the parsing of words in the face of matters of life and death, freedom and oppression. One can hardly help sympathizing with Friedmann and feeling that he is right to resist the instrumentalization of legal rules and concepts to justify an imperial act, while at the same time observing how difficult it is to articulate Friedmann's position in a manner that does not seem hollow. Articles 2(4) and 51 do not constitute an adequate bulwark against aggression and imperialism, yet one is ill at ease with the use of these provisions to serve the aims of aggression and imperialism. Koskenniemi asserts that 'nothing has undermined formalism as a culture of resistance to power, a social practice of accountability, openness, and equality whose status cannot be reduced to the political positions of any one of the parties whose claims are treated within it'.[25] Formalism, then, as culture, as practice, as contributing to the constitutional mind-set. Law may have the capacity to transcend the specialized regimes in which so many contemporary legal developments are taking place, by way of 'continuing the search for something beyond particular interests and identity politics, or the irreducibility of difference'.[26]

What would law accomplish that these other expert systems could not? A lawyer is faced with a number of intersecting problems or phenomena, all of which must be attended to: the dispute at hand, and the actors, interests and priorities at stake; the truth of the matter – will the risk materialize? A third is the law, which does not contain and cannot provide a decision in the instant case. The culture of formalism seems to suggest an attitude of fidelity to the law: that is, a starting assumption that the law contains, or can be used to construct, meaning in the form of arguments that seek, at one and the same time, to make sense of the dispute that one is considering *and* to make sense of and contribute to the enterprise of law.[27] The terms 'culture' and 'mind-set' suggest an attentiveness to the subject rather than the object: that is, to the lawyer and not merely to the law. Law is indeterminate; it does not answer our questions for us. In interacting with legal rules, we must take responsibility for our own interpretations and be prepared to justify them. A parallel position can be identified in systems theory: it is not the legal *rules* which can serve to stabilize normative expectations, but rather legal *operations*, that is, arguments and decisions using legal rules, that are carried out within the system.

4.4.1 Fragmentation: Two Perspectives

Up to a point, Koskenniemi and autopoietic scholars such as Teubner present similar analyses of the phenomenon of specialized, expert-driven regimes, citing each other with approval. Fischer-Lescano and Teubner note the awareness of Koskenniemi and Leino that the 'problem' of fragmentation lies not at the level of an absence of hierarchy among international courts and tribunals but at a deeper, political level.[28] They then state that Koskenniemi and Leino have not gone far enough in their analysis, pointing instead to 'deep contradictions between colliding sectors of a global society',[29] about which relatively little might be done:

> [H]igh expectations of our ability to deal adequately with legal fragmentation must be curbed since its origins lie not in law, but within its social contexts. Rather than secure the unity of international law, future endeavors need to be restricted to achieve weak compatibility between the fragments. In the place of an illusory integration of a differentiated global society, law can only, at the very best, offer a kind of damage limitation.[30]

Koskenniemi picks up on Fisher-Lescano's and Teubner's modest tone: 'Luhmannians such as Teubner and Fischer-Lescano derive from this the experience of law's epiphenomenality: "a legal reproduction of collisions between the diverse rationalities within global society". A part of the problem and not its solution, law has no argument to defend its ambition to be anything but a "gentle civiliser of social systems"'.[31] He then states his concern that Fisher-Lescano's and Teubner's brand of legal pluralism 'ceases to pose demands on the world'.[32]

Interestingly, Teubner seems to have reached a similar conclusion – not in respect of his own approach to legal pluralism, of course, but rather regarding the new legal pluralism which, in the words of Sally Engle Merry, 'moves away from questions about the effect of law on society or even the effect of society on law towards conceptualizing a more complex and interactive relationship between official and unofficial forms of ordering'.[33] Teubner reacts to this development by remarking that

> [t]here is a price to be paid for progress. As a consequence of its own construction, the new legal pluralism is confronted with the disquieting question: 'Where do we stop speaking of law and find ourselves simply describing social life?' Two things have been lost in the course of progress, in the move from spatial separation to discursive interwovenness: (1) the notion of what is distinctively 'legal' in the new legal pluralism as well as (2) a clear-cut concept of the interrelations between the social and the legal.[34]

To simply describe social life is to avoid the vacillation between apology and utopia, it is true, but in a particularly unsatisfying way, one far too reminiscent of the approach taken by Goldsmith and Posner, who conclude that much of what lawyers do is to describe behaviour and call it law.[35] Teubner considers and rejects two responses to the problem of law's unresponsiveness to society: rendering the law more political, and rendering it more open to the expertise available through the social sciences, noting that this move might make law more responsive to political and scientific constructs, but questioning whether it would have any impact on law's responsiveness to society.[36] Teubner proposes instead a form of legal pluralism that does not foster the collapse of law into society, but rather seeks to protect the autonomy of law and other social systems.[37]

Those who associate legal fragmentation not with political but rather with deeper social fragmentation often express pessimism regarding law's capacity to prevent the dilution of its particular logic as it seeks to respond to the material goals pursued within societal fragments (corruption),[38] and to address conflicts between societal fragments.[39] If law is entirely encapsulated in specialized regimes pursuing their own rationality, then it loses its capacity to transcend those regimes and simply becomes another conduit through which noise for the echo chamber of regime rationality is generated. The approach adopted by Fischer-Lescano and Teubner describes law as a single system even when it manifests itself in the form of disjointed bundles of rules within issue-specific regimes. This does not mean that law forms a coherent, comprehensive whole, composed of norms arranged in neat hierarchies. Nor does this mean that the legal system is capable of accessing a greater truth than that available to a managerial regime. It simply means that a legal operation, whether carried out within a human rights or a trade or an environmental regime, remains a legal operation – part of the same social system and therefore legible elsewhere in the social system of law; part of the legal culture. These regimes may not be arrayed in a hierarchical fashion, such that one has the authority to review the decisions of another, but they nevertheless keep one another under observation, and react to one another's moves. Fischer-Lescano and Teubner illustrate this by reference to a conflict between the World Trade Organization, interpreting rules on intellectual property, and the World Health Organization and other bodies concerned with HIV/AIDS. A likely outcome of such a conflict could involve human rights organizations concluding that production of generic medications is legal because it promotes the human right to health, while the trade organization concludes that such production is illegal because in violation of intellectual property rights. Each would simply conclude that the other is wrong, but neither would have the authority to trump the other. Nor, it would appear, would there be resources available within international law to resolve the conflict: any choice between the two conclusions would simply involve a preference for one set of rules and one outcome over the other, with no legal reasoning available to render that preference non-arbitrary. But all three authors – Fischer-Lescano, Koskenniemi and Teubner – recognize that resources are available, if not to resolve the conflict, then at least to move beyond stalemate. The regime's objectives are understood from within the regime as being in the service of a further set of ends, which may be referred to as the common good. The common good that each regime aims at is made in its image, with the result that there is no consensus on its content. It nevertheless serves the important purpose of calling for the application of a rule to overshoot its context, aligning itself with a much broader array of purposes and interests than those around which the particular regime is constructed.[40] This will mean that it may not be easy for a regime to ignore norms lying outside its boundaries that may be relevant to a given dispute. These norms, because they are legal norms, can be taken up by specialized regimes even if they are external to it: the process bears some resemblance to the borrowing or transplanting of norms from one state's legal system to that of another. In the process, they become part of the regime, transformed to suit its purposes. This process can be taken one step further: rather than simply appropriating the norms of other regimes ad hoc, more general and stable understandings could develop on how to address substantive conflicts between regimes that interact often. Fischer-Lescano and Teubner refer to substantive conflict of laws norms[41] as well as the development of *ius non dispositivum*.[42] This approach involves, in short, the development of *moda vivendi* between regimes that interact frequently. The process through which this occurs does not involve the reaching of substantive agreement between regimes, based on a common purpose that transcends their individual objectives. Rather, the processes involved include mutual observation and irritation, followed by blind co-evolution: that is, the regimes observe one another's attempts to influence their environment, and react by seeking to exercise influence themselves. For example, if an environmental regime begins to take it upon itself to interpret rules respecting international trade and commerce when they have potential environmental implications may eventually provoke a reaction on the part of a trade regime, which will in turn elicit a reaction by the environmental regime. There is no reason to assume that these processes of mutual observation and irritation will result in evolution in the direction of a harmonious, mutually beneficial relationship, but Fischer-Lescano and Teubner indicate that they could lead out of impasse and stalemate.

If we switch fields and look at the systematicity of law not from a sociological but from a legal point of view, the perspective changes: we are now seeking to understand law as a body of rules that constitute a coherent, comprehensive whole, or to use the language of the Study Group on the Fragmentation of International Law, rules with meaningful relationships between them.[43] Conflicts or tensions between rules can be treated as conflicts between system rationalities, but can also be treated as problems of legal interpretation for which the legal system possesses resources. These resources can take the form of principles such as *lex specialis derogat leges generali*,[44] or as guidelines and caveats regarding the manner in which these principles are to apply.[45] The Study Group does not give explicit indications as to how conflicts between special regimes are to be addressed, but strong hints appear to be made in Section 4 of the document, which addresses systemic integration, expressed as the proposition that 'whatever their subject matter, treaties are a creation of the international legal system and their operation is predicated upon that fact'.[46] In commenting on the then-unpublished conclusions of the Study Group, Koskenniemi noted that '[l]aw has a centripetal pull ... Legal words cannot be separated from the language in which they lead their life. They operate only in the context of other legal words and of a professional grammar about how they are used in relation to one another'.[47]

Returning to Fischer-Lescano and Teubner's discussion of interactions between specialized regimes, one may detect efforts at locating processes through which that grammar comes to be constituted locally. In their analysis of the dispute over generic AIDS medication in apparent violation of the Agreement on Trade-related Aspects of Intellectual Property Rights, the authors note the presence in international trade law of exceptions to patent protections that were intended to provide for a response to epidemics, pandemics and other health emergencies, but note as well that such provisions appeared designed to fail, or at least to be overwhelmingly difficult to invoke.[48] Yet despite the apparent inadequacy of the legal rules within the World Trade Organization (WTO) regime to address conflicts, a response was crafted involving 'an internal limitation on [the WTO's] own logic through the reformulation of a principle of health protection', through reference to international human rights law which was 'reconstructed' as WTO law.[49] Fischer-Lescano and Teubner are highly sceptical of the capacity of the WTO adequately to address the demands that it was facing from the World Health Organization and from human

rights organizations in the context of the AIDS pandemic.[50] They point
to the immense political and social pressure that the trade regime came
under, particularly as the United Nations General Assembly was preparing
a special meeting on HIV/AIDS, as being instrumental in the creation
of openings for attenuation of intellectual property rights in favour of
human rights to health.[51] In short, this is not a story of the law being able to
triumph over economic and political might. It is, instead, an indication of
the ways in which, as Gralf-Peter Calliess and Peer Zumbansen describe it,
a dispute can be lifted out of its political-economic context and addressed
on the terrain of law.[52]

In the section that follows, I wish to focus squarely on the managerialism of environmental regimes. To recast this issue in system-theoretic
terms, we are here addressing problems of communication between law
and science. Politics becomes involved in these relations as well. The
quest for legitimacy causes politics to vacillate between resort to democratic principles, notably participation and representation, and resort to
scientific authority as possessing universalizable validity, in a way that
fragmented, materialized and functionalized law does not.

4.4.2 Putting Law and Science on Speaking Terms

Faced with scientific knowledge that is relevant to legal decision making, jurists may wade in and seek to address this knowledge on scientific
terms, or they may feel obliged to accept at face value any scientific evidence presented to them, making arbitrary rulings in the face of scientific
uncertainty or controversy. Both these options lead to the colonization of
law by science and the triumph of the new naturalism.[53] A judge may hope
that, when the scientific expertise of the respective parties go toe-to-toe,
only one will be left standing. If instead both experts remain on their feet,
the judge may have the option of resorting to a court-appointed expert,[54]
but this may do little to foster the necessary processes of translation from
science to law.

The response from new naturalism to law's heavy reliance on science
when seeking to address issue areas such as environmental protection is,
essentially, to invite law to take a back seat. However, this is certainly
not the only available avenue. The often excessive deference that law has
paid to science in fields such as environmental protection is a result of
inadequate bridges between law and science, with the result that law has
an increasingly difficult time performing legal operations on scientific
knowledge. The model of scientific knowledge that law has constructed

for itself in order better to grasp scientific inputs – that is, the heuristic device that is used in legal reasoning to reach some understanding of scientific causation and bring that concept into contact with the rough equivalent in law[55] – is far too unsophisticated. This is particularly true in branches of science such as ecology that are concerned with complex systems.[56]

Karl-Heinz Ladeur argues that law requires its own decision principles to determine, for example, when there is sufficient scientific evidence to provide a basis for a ruling in a legal dispute – so-called 'stop rules' that limit deliberation regarding the presence and nature of risks.[57] Prominent examples of such stop rules include standards and burdens of proof and rules on the admissibility of evidence. However, these rules depend for their functioning on an awareness of the different prestations of law and science, and the very different ends to which scientific evidence is put in the two systems. When law begins to defer too much to science, it cannot put stop rules into effect, since ongoing scientific uncertainty, or controversy, or even the probabilistic rather than binary nature of many scientific conclusions regarding complex systems, will prevent the making of a decision.[58] What is needed are legal concepts and mechanisms that are more attuned to the manner in which scientific conclusions are arrived at and eventually accepted within scientific communities. However, at the same time, legal decision-making processes that mimic scientific ones are not to be wished for. Scientific conclusions are of a different nature than legal conclusions; the scientific enterprise pursues a different range of objectives than does the legal enterprise; science and law perform, in our society at least, significantly different roles[59] or, to put it in Luhmannian terms, the nature of their prestation differs.[60]

As Teubner has argued, law cannot simply take up scientific knowledge and transpose it into legal normativity; what it can do, however, is to 'misunderstand' scientific insights, for example into the probability of a given scenario for sea-level rise assuming global warming of 2° C, as thresholds that could then eventually be translated into legally binding carbon emission limits.[61] This insight can be applied not only to attempts to translate the content of scientific knowledge into legal normativity, but also to the procedural, methodological, judgemental and argumentative aspects of the generation of scientific knowledge. This is captured in William Rehg's discussion of the cogency of scientific judgements. Rehg's objective is to identify ways in which scientists can communicate with other scientists within their discipline, scientists from other disciplines and non-scientists the reasons why they judge a particular scientific conclusion to be cogent.[62] In each setting, the reasons that can be communicated to other actors are different, ranging from detailed analyses of the scientific argument through to much more general discussions of the manner in which the integrity of the scientific process was respected.[63] When scientists seek to communicate with the general public – or more specifically to political or legal authorities – they can usefully focus on features such as the disinterestedness and independence of the members of the scientific team, the ability of all members of the team to voice their opinions about choices regarding such things as methodology or cut-off points for statistical significance, and the peer review process.[64] Rehg further indicates the need for common understandings of cogency and for institutional structures that foster the development of such understandings and the analysis of scientific knowledge in light of them.[65] In a similar vein, Ladeur notes the role of stop rules in building trust in processes of knowledge construction: they function to reassure observers that rules or decisions stand on an adequate evidentiary foundation.[66]

4.5   The Culture of Formalism and International Environmental Law

Teubner's systemic approach to law allows us to see how law could avoid instrumentalization at the hands of a multitude of fragmented regimes. In this section, the focus will be narrowed to the interaction of law and science within these regimes. The concern here is how the legal system can perform operations on scientific knowledge, translating that knowledge into terms that are legible to law. Both Rehg and Ladeur gesture in the direction of proceduralism, Rehg implicitly and Ladeur explicitly. Rehg points to ways in which scientific knowledge production and argumentation can be structured so as to generate confidence on the part of decision makers and members of the public. For his part, Ladeur argues that wherever decision making must proceed under conditions of uncertainty, law should take a decidedly procedural turn, focussing in the first place on the creation of linkages among institutions and organizations and on the creation of incentive structures for the generation of knowledge and in the second place on the development of stop rules that help political and legal authorities to determine that the time is ripe for a decision.[67]

The approach sketched here leaves a good deal of scope for scientific expertise in international environmental regimes. Opinion will differ as to whether this is a good thing, either for the regimes or for the legal system. Certainly, the implications for democratic forms of government are potentially enormous, as Ladeur readily acknowledges.[68] He sees this not as the result of the colonization of law and politics by science, but rather as indicative of the failure of the paradigm that held nature to be subject to mastery and instrumentalization:[69] environmental degradation, interpreted as an incursion of chaos into order, calls for law to restore order through damage awards or administrative or criminal penalties.[70] However, Ladeur argues, the avoidance of unintended and undesirable environmental impacts is not simply a matter of good will.[71] When one considers that the second great megafauna extinction is correlated to hunting and modification of the landscape by fire by our hunter-gatherer ancestors in the Pleistocene, some ten thousand years ago, one begins to discern the truth in this statement: in the Anthropocene,[72] the world is full of hybrids, and the question to ask is not whether an outcome or phenomenon is natural or not, but rather whether we can live with it or must expel it.[73]

4.6 Concluding Remarks

Among the many important contributions of Martti Koskenniemi's scholarship is his ability to make his readers understand the culture of formalism as a project worthy of our support, and not as a dogmatic, narrow-minded approach to law favoured by jurists because, and only because, of their lack of imagination – 'a worn-out form of legalism that betrays a systematic conservatism'.[74] When faced with threats of massive, global and permanent environmental degradation, it is natural to want to stop the machine that is driving us in this direction with whatever means at hand. The temptation, therefore, is to take the best framework for producing ecological knowledge available to us – science – and to combine it with a system of commands backed by sanctions – law. Faced with impending disaster, it seems impossibly churlish to respond to such efforts with the remark 'But you misunderstand law'. It is to Koskenniemi's credit that he can make us understand how very important it is to strive to understand the law and to care about its fate. King Rex's failures must not lead us to rely on psychiatrists and public relations specialists.[75]

In this chapter I have sought to identify the basis for a continued conversation between Koskenniemi and Teubner, who also wants to rescue law from instrumentalization. Systems theory provides us with a vocabulary and methodology that are extremely useful in addressing one of the great challenges of environmental protection, namely the interaction between law and science. Finally, Rehg and Ladeur provide us with frameworks for analysing legal decision making under conditions of complexity and uncertainty. They remind us how difficult of application concepts such as breach, violation, transgression or wrong are in the context of environmental protection. As Kerry Whiteside notes, one feature of environmental decision making that makes it somewhat unusual is the difficulty of relying on *phronêsis*.[76] This is so for a range of reasons, including the scales of time and place over which environmental impacts make themselves felt, the weaknesses of ordinary powers of observation when it comes to detecting links between inputs and environmental degradation, and the fact that much environmental degradation is not caused by bad people doing the wrong thing, but by people and groups pursuing their perfectly acceptable ends in good faith. We have little choice but to rely on a range of experts, if not to make our decisions for us, then at least to make us aware of a range of relevant facts, risks and uncertainties that we require in order to make those decisions. But the responsibility for the decision remains with us, and requires careful thought about our political and legal structures and processes.

Notes

* The author wishes to acknowledge the very helpful comments and suggestions provided by Marieke de Hoon, Alexis Galán, Gunther Teubner and Wouter Werner. The financial support of the Social Sciences and Humanities Research Council is also gratefully acknowledged.
1. M. King and C. Thornhill, *Niklas Luhmann's Theory of Politics and Law* (London: Palgrave Macmillan, 2006), 96–97.
2. Gralf-Peter Calliess and Moritz Renner, 'Between Law and Social Norms: the Evolution of Global Governance', *Ratio Juris* 22 (2009): 260–80.
3. Niklas Luhmann ends *Law as a Social System* (Oxford: Oxford University Press, 2004) by entertaining the possibility 'that the current prominence of the legal system and the dependence of society itself and of most of its functional systems on a functioning legal coding are nothing but a European anomaly, which might well level off with the evolution of global society' (490).
4. M. Koskenniemi, 'Breach of Treaty or Non-Compliance? Reflections on the Enforcement of the Montreal Protocol', *Yearbook of International Environmental Law* 3 (1992): 123–62; M. Koskenniemi, 'The Fate of Public International Law: between Technique and Politics', *The Modern Law Review* 70 (2007): 1–30; M. Koskenniemi, 'Peaceful Settlement of Environmental Disputes', *Nordic Journal of International Law* 60 (1991): 73–92; M. Koskenniemi, 'International Law and Hegemony: a Reconfiguration', in *The Politics of International Law* (Oxford: Hart, 2011), 219.
5. The fate of procedural rules of environmental law is well illustrated in the *Case concerning Pulp Mills on the River Uruguay (Argentina v. Uruguay)*, International Court of Justice, judgment of 20 April 2010. Despite a violation by Uruguay of the obligation to notify Argentina of planned works (para. 111) and to communicate

its environmental impact assessment to Argentina prior to authorizing the works (para. 122), the Court imposed no remedies beyond the finding of a breach, which the Court deemed provided satisfaction to Argentina (para. 269). In view of its finding that Uruguay had not breached substantive obligations, the Court declined to order restitution (para. 275).

6. *Yearbook of the International Law Commission*, 2001, vol. II, Part Two (hereinafter Draft Articles on Transboundary Harm).

7. *Yearbook of the International Law Commission*, 2006, vol. II, Part Two (hereinafter Draft Articles on the Allocation of Loss).

8. International environmental literature from the 1960s to the 1980s is replete with the articulation of rules of general application, anchored in public international law and in private municipal law. See e.g. G. Handl, 'Liability as an Obligation Established by a Primary Rule of International Law: Some Basic Reflections on the International Law Commission's Work', *Netherlands Yearbook of International Law* 16 (1985): 49–79; C. W. Jenks, 'Liability for Ultra-hazardous Activities in International Law', *Recueil de cours de l'Académie de droit international* 117 (1966): 99–198; L. F. E. Goldie, 'Liability for Damage and the Progressive Development of International Law', *International and Comparative Law Quarterly* 14 (1966): 1189–264; L. F. E. Goldie, 'Concepts of Strict and Absolute Liability and the Ranking of Liability in Terms of Relative Exposure to Risk', *Netherlands Yearbook of International Law* 16 (1985): 175–248; P.-M. Dupuy, 'Due Diligence in the International Law of Liability', in OECD (ed.), *Legal Aspects of Transfrontier Pollution* (Paris: OECD Publications, 1977), 369. Most academics lost interest in these questions around the time of the 1992 Summit on Environment and Development; fortunately, there are some important exceptions, including A. Boyle, 'State Responsibility and International Liability for Injurious Consequences of Acts Not Prohibited by International Law: a Necessary Distinction?', *International and Comparative Law Quarterly* 39 (1990): 1–26; J. Barboza, *The Environment, Risk and Liability in International Law* (Leiden, Netherlands: Martinus Nijhoff, 2011); X. Hanqin, *Transboundary Damage in International Law* (Cambridge: Cambridge University Press, 2003). This literature is canvassed in J. Ellis, 'Liability for International Environmental Harm', *Oxford Bibliographies Online – International Law* (2013).

9. This trend can be illustrated by the trajectory of the regime to regulate ozone-depleting substances: the framework Vienna Convention for the Protection of the Ozone Layer was adopted in 1985 and entered into force in 1988. The Montréal Protocol on Substances that deplete the Ozone Layer was adopted in 1987 and entered into force in 1989. The Montréal Protocol was an innovative instrument, featuring schedules for the elimination of ozone-depleting substances (Arts 2A-I) and a flexible amendment procedure that permitted both the expansion of lists of substances subject to regulation and the acceleration of phase-out schedules (Art. 11 and Rules of Procedure for Meetings of the Parties to the Montréal Protocol, Decision I/1 of the Meeting of the Parties to the Montréal Protocol (MOP), contained in Annex I to the Report of the First Meeting of the Parties, Helsinki 1989). The famous and highly innovative Non-compliance Procedure was adopted by II/5 of the MOP, contained in Annex III of the Report of the Second Meeting of the Parties, London, 1990. The ozone-depleting regime contains many features that came routinely to be incorporated in other multilateral environmental agreements, including robust reporting requirements, panels tasked with researching and reporting on various

technical, technological, and scientific issues, and financial mechanisms for the provision of assistance to states, notably developing states, that required assistance in meeting their obligations under the regime. Not all of these features were innovations at the time of the adoption of the Montréal Protocol, of course, but this regime was a pioneer in the manner in which it brought together a wide range of mechanisms and procedures in a complex regulatory regime.

10. M. Koskenniemi and P. Leino, 'Fragmentation of International Law? Postmodern Anxieties', *Leiden Journal of International Law* 15 (2002): 578.
11. Ibid.
12. Ibid.
13. Koskenniemi, 'Fate of Public International Law', 11ff.
14. Barboza, *Environment, Risk and Liability*; Boyle, 'State Responsibility'; A. Boyle, 'Codification of International Environmental Law and the International Law Commission: Injurious Consequences Revisited', in A. Boyle and D. Freestone (eds), *International Law and Sustainable Development: Past Achievements and Future Challenges* (Oxford: Oxford University Press, 1999), 61–85. Special Rapporteur Quentin Baxter's schematic outline established an obligation of result, or strict liability, for transboundary harm caused by an activity in the territory or under the control of the source state, but the obligation to make reparation was, in this outline, subject to negotiation. R. Q. Quentin-Baxter, *International Liability for Injurious Consequences Arising out of Acts Not Prohibited by International Law* (A/CN.4/360), 23 June 1982, Sections 4 and 5. Alan Boyle describes the schematic outline in seeking 'a world in which nothing was either prohibited or made obligatory and everything was negotiable' in 'State Responsibility', 5. The obligation was tightened up to some extent in the hands of Julio Barboza. Where an activity on the territory or otherwise under the jurisdiction of a state causes transboundary harm or creates a risk of such harm (Art. 1), the state is presumed to have knowledge of the activity and its harmful nature (Art. 3) and, unless that presumption is refuted, 'shall make reparation for appreciable harm caused by [such] an activity' (Art. 9). The scope of the obligation to make reparation would remain subject to negotiation, but in the course of such negotiations the states concerned are to '[bear] in mind ... that reparation should seek to restore the balance of interests affected by the harm' (Art. 9). J. Barboza, *Sixth Report on International Liability for Injurious Consequences Arising out of Acts Not Prohibited by International Law* (A/CN.4/428), 15 March 1990.
15. The 2001 Draft Articles on Transboundary Harm present no obligation to make reparation. The closest they come is an obligation to 'enter into consultations ... with a view to achieving acceptable solutions regarding measures to be adopted in order to prevent significant transboundary harm or at any event to minimize the risk thereof (art. 9(1))'. The objective of these consultations is to 'seek solutions based on an equitable balancing of interests (art. 9(2))', whose contours are outlined in Art. 10.
16. J. Habermas, *Between Facts and Norms: Contributions to a Discourse Theory of Law and Democracy*, W. Rehg (trans.) (Cambridge, MA: MIT Press, 1998), 416. See also W. Rehg, 'Translator's Introduction', ibid., xxxii–xxxiii.
17. Habermas, *Between Facts and Norms*.
18. Ibid., 190.
19. F. A. Hayek, "Planning and the Rule of Law', in *The Road to Serfdom* (1944; repr., Chicago: University of Chicago Press, 2007), Chapter 6. See also B. Z. Tamanaha,

On the Rule of Law: History, Politics, Theory (Cambridge: Cambridge University Press, 2004), 67ff.

20. Habermas, *Between Facts and Norms*, 419.
21. I. M. Young, *Justice and the Politics of Difference* (Princeton, NJ: Princeton University Press, 2011), 76, quoted in Habermas, *Between Facts and Norms*, 420. Deformalization and materialization are not unique to the welfare state, as early observers of these processes noted. Deformalization may serve commercial interests extremely well. Franz Neumann, for example, noted the extent to which commercial interests under the Weimar Republic embraced open-ended principles such as unconscionableness or good faith. W. E. Scheuerman, *Frankfurt School Perspectives on Globalization, Democracy, and the Law* (New York: Routledge, 2008), 24ff. Kathryn Sikkink takes note of the same trend today in the context of international or transnational codes of conduct for corporate entities. K. Sikkink, 'Codes of Conduct for Transnational Corporations: The Case of the WHO/UNICEF Code', *International Organization* 40 (1986): 815–40.
22. See e.g. D. Kennedy, 'Legal Formality', *Journal of Legal Studies* (1973): 351–98. Koskenniemi notes that the groundwork, at least, for this observation had been laid by Kant. M. Koskenniemi, 'Formalism, Fragmentation, Freedom: Kantian Themes in Today's International Law', *No Foundations* 4 (2007): 7–28. Koskenniemi refers to Kant's *Critique of Pure Reason* where he notes that rules do not lay out the conditions of their application (9), as well as by Schmitt and Kelsen. M. Koskenniemi, *The Gentle Civilizer of Nations: The Rise and Fall of International Law 1870–1960* (Cambridge: Cambridge University Press, 2001), 496: 'Kelsen and Schmitt agreed that no decision could be automatically inferred from a pre-existing norm, but that each decision set down a new individual norm, an obligation that did not exist before'. Footnote omitted. The references are to H. Kelsen, *Introduction to the Problems of Legal Theory* (Oxford: Clarendon Press, 1992), and C. Schmitt, *Gesetz und Urteil. Eine Untersuchung Zum Problem Der Rechtspraxis* (München: Beck, 1969), respectively.
23. Koskenniemi, *Gentle Civilizer of Nations*, 494. The question I seek to address is slightly different, namely the law's (contingent) identity.
24. Ibid., 494–95.
25. Ibid., 500.
26. Ibid.
27. Koskenniemi, 'Formalism, Fragmentation, Freedom', 10. Lon Fuller describes the enterprise of law as 'subjecting human conduct to the governance of rules'. L. L. Fuller, *The Morality of Law*, 2nd edn (New Haven, CT: Yale University Press, 1964), 74.
28. A. Fischer-Lescano and G. Teubner, 'Regime-Collisions: The Vain Search for Legal Unity in the Fragmentation of Global Law', *Michigan Journal of International Law* 25 (2004): 1003, citing Koskenniemi and Leino, 'Fragmentation of International Law?'.
29. Fischer-Lescano and Teubner, 'Regime-Collisions', 1004.
30. Ibid., 1045; see also A. Fischer-Lescano and G. Teubner, *Regime-Kollisionen. Zur Fragmentierung Des Globalen Rechts* (Frankfurt am Main, Germany: Suhrkamp, 2006), 170.
31. Koskenniemi, 'Fate of Public International Law', 23. The quotations are both from Fischer-Lescano and Teubner, *Regime-Kollisionen*. Fischer-Lescano and Teubner do

not in fact describe law as epiphenomenal; it is legal fragmentation that is described as an epiphenomenon (in the sense of secondary effect or by-product) of underlying societal fragmentation. Ibid., 24.

32. Koskenniemi, 'Fate of Public International Law', 23.
33. S. Engle Merry, 'Legal Pluralism', *Law and Society Review* 22 (1988): 873.
34. G. Teubner, 'The Two Faces of Janus: Rethinking Legal Pluralism', *Cardozo Law Review* 13 (1991–92): 1449.
35. J. L. Goldsmith and E. A. Posner, *The Limits of International Law* (Oxford: Oxford University Press, 2005). See also Koskenniemi, 'Formalism, Fragmentation, Freedom', 17.
36. Teubner, 'Two Faces of Janus', 1461.
37. Ibid., 1461–62; G. Teubner, 'Rechtswissenschaft und -praxis im Kontext der Sozialtheorie', in Stefan Grundmann and Jan Thiessen (eds), *Interdisziplinäres Denken in Rechtswissenschaft und -praxis* (Tübingen: Mohr Siebeck, 2015), 154ff.
38. G. Teubner, '"Global Bukowina": Legal Pluralism in the World Society', in *Global Law without a State* (Aldershot, UK: Dartmouth, 1997), 19.
39. Fischer-Lescano and Teubner, 'Regime-Collisions'.
40. Fischer-Lescano and Teubner, *Regime-Kollisionen*, 64; Fischer-Lescano and Teubner, 'Regime-Collisions', 1033.
41. Fischer-Lescano and Teubner, 'Regime-Collisions', 1021.
42. Ibid., 1033.
43. *Conclusions of the Work of the Study Group on the Fragmentation of International Law: Difficulties Arising from the Diversification and Expansion of International Law*, adopted by the International Law Commission at its 58th Session, A/61/10, para. 251, 2006, para. 1(1) (hereinafter Study Group on Fragmentation).
44. Ibid., para. 2(5).
45. See e.g. the caveat regarding conflicts between interpretive principles that arise in a given instance and that must be resolved in light of the context. Ibid., para. 2(6).
46. Ibid., para. 4(17).
47. M. Koskenniemi, 'Constitutionalism as Mindset: Reflections on Kantian Themes about International Law and Globalization', *Theoretical Inquiries in Law* 8 (2007): 20–21. Elsewhere, Koskenniemi refers to the then unpublished report of the Study Group on Fragmentation as 'illustrat[ing] the constitutional mindset at work'. Ibid., 18.
48. Fischer-Lescano and Teubner, 'Regime-Collisions', 1026, referring to Arts. 30 and 31 of TRIPS. This discussion is expanded upon in Fischer-Lescano and Teubner, *Regime-Kollisionen*, 81ff., with reference to the failure of the Doha Declaration on the TRIPS Agreement and Public Health adequately to address the problem faced by developing states.
49. Fischer-Lescano and Teubner, 'Regime-Collisions', 1030.
50. Fischer-Lescano and Teubner, *Regime-Kollisionen*, 82.
51. Fischer-Lescano and Teubner, 'Regime-Collisions', 1027–28.
52. G.-P. Calliess and P. Zumbansen, *Rough Consensus and Running Code: a Theory of Transnational Private Law* (Oxford: Hart, 2010), 44.
53. M. Koskenniemi, 'Declaratory Legislation: towards a Genealogy of Neoliberal Legalism', in R. Livoja and J. Petman (eds), *International Law-Making: Essays in Honour of Jan Klabbers* (London: Routledge, 2014), 17–38.
54. See the criticism of the International Court of Justice regarding its failure to do just that in D. K. Anton, 'Case Comment: *Case Concerning Pulp Mills on the River*

Uruguay (Argentina v. Uruguay) (Judgment) [2010] ICJ Rep (20 April 2010)', *Australian International Law Journal* 17 (2010): 213–23; P. Merkouris, '*Case Concerning Pulp Mills on the River Uruguay (Argentina v. Uruguay)*: of Environmental Impact Assessments and "Phantom Experts"', *The Hague Justice Portal* (2010); J. G. Sandoval Coustasse and E. Sweeney-Samuelson, 'Adjudicating Conflicts over Resources: the ICJ's Treatment of Technical Evidence in the Pulp Mills Case', *Goettingen Journal of International Law* 3 (2011): 447–71. See also the dissenting opinion of Justices Al-Kasawneh and Simma, paras 2ff. The Court, in its wisdom, chose to bypass the experts and interrogate the scientific data directly. In addressing the claim that the pulp mills resulted in water pollution, the Court noted that 'it has before it interpretations of the data provided by experts appointed by the Parties, and provided by the Parties themselves and their counsel. However, in assessing the probative value of the evidence placed before it, the Court will principally weigh and evaluate the data, rather than the conflicting interpretations given to it by the Parties or their experts and consultants, in order to determine whether Uruguay breached its obligations under Articles 36 and 41 of the 1975 Statute in authorizing the construction and operation of the Orion (Botnia) mill'. (para. 236)

55. G. Teubner, *Recht als autopoietisches System* (Frankfurt am Main, Germany: Suhrkamp, 1989), 75. Teubner describes a process of reconstruction within law of the logics and languages of other social systems, such reconstructions making it possible for analyses carried out within those other social systems to be translated into the language of law. Such translations inevitably involve misunderstandings, notes Teubner, but these misunderstandings can be productive when they lead to the development of concepts, and eventually legal norms, that map onto the analyses carried out in other social systems. It is through the reconstruction of other social systems using the conceptual architecture of law that law can be made receptive to other social systems. Teubner, 'Rechtswissenschaft', 156–57.

56. Karl-Heinz Ladeur makes reference to the concept of causation, once a boundary object (not his term) that existed within a range of social systems, including science and law. While scientific and legal causation were never identical, they bore a sufficient resemblance to one another to act as a bridge between scientific and legal rationalities. As science moves away from linear causal explanations in order better to address complexity and chaos, the construction of new bridges between science and law becomes necessary. K. H. Ladeur, *Das Umweltrecht der Wissensgesellschaft: von der Gefahrenabwehr zum Risikomanagement* (Berlin: Duncker and Humblot, 1995), 120ff. C. S. Holling describes a model that is relied on by laypersons in general and by political and legal authorities most in particular, namely the 'equilibrium-centered "Nature Constant"' model which assumes constancy, homogeneity, linear causation, and a single point of equilibrium. Holling describes this model as 'represent[ing] a policy world of a benign Nature where trials and mistakes of any scale can be made with recovery assured once the disturbance is removed'. C. S. Holling, 'Simplifying the Complex: The Paradigms of Ecological Function and Structure', *European Journal of Operational Research* 30 (1987): 140. Holling goes on to review a series of policy decisions that were made on the basis of this model, and to describe and analyse their short-term success and long-term failure, concluding 'that the equilibrium-centered concepts and methods inherent in the view of "Nature Constant" is false'. Ibid., 144.

57. Ladeur, *Das Umweltrecht der Wissensgesellschaft*, 121.

58. An example of a problematic conflation of law and science is found in the *Pulp Mills* case, specifically in the decision of the bench to bypass the conclusions presented by scientists incorporated into the legal teams of the two parties and instead seek to interpret the data themselves and draw appropriate conclusions. The fact that the scientific evidence was presented as part of the legal submissions of the parties and not as expert evidence is also problematic. Lying behind both these moves can be detected a series of questionable assumptions about the legibility of scientific data and argumentation to laypersons. See *Pulp Mills*, particularly para. 167.

59. See the discussion on the different objectives pursued by law and science in S. Jasanoff, 'Just Evidence: the Limits of Science in the Legal Process', *Journal of Law, Medicine and Ethics* 34 (2006): 328–41.

60. For a particularly limpid discussion of the prestation (here translated as 'performance') of law, see Calliess and Renner, 'Between Law and Social Norms'.

61. G. Teubner, 'Idiosyncratic Production Regimes: Co-Evolution of Economic and Legal Institutions in the Varieties of Capitalism', in M. Wheeler, J. Ziman and M. A. Boden (eds), *The Evolution of Cultural Entities* (Oxford: Oxford University Press, 2002), 171.

62. W. Rehg, *Cogent Science in Context: the Science Wars, Argumentation Theory, and Habermas* (Cambridge, MA: MIT Press, 2009), 250.

63. Among scientists working in the same sub-discipline, the cogency of a scientific argument's content is evaluated. Among scientists in different sub-disciplines, the focus is on 'the quality of the transactions that produced the argument', including, for example, the means that were used for allowing dissent to be aired and for fostering consensus within a scientific team. Ibid., 184ff.

64. Ibid., 254ff.

65. Ibid., 252. Rehg states, 'The capacity [of a scientific argument] to travel is not a sufficient condition for public merits. The macrosocial space through which the argument travels – the networks and aggregates of transactional contexts – must also be one that sustains collective reasonableness'.

66. Ladeur, *Das Umweltrecht der Wissensgesellschaft*, 270. Trust is a key concept in Rehg's writing on science at the interface with policy as well. Since scientific conclusions can be understood on their merits to a decreasing extent the farther one travels from the lab in which they were initially reached, successive circles of interlocutors need different kinds of indicators or proxies that permit them to conclude that the processes that produced the scientific conclusion under examination were sound. See Rehg, *Cogent Science in Context*.

67. Ladeur, *Das Umweltrecht der Wissensgesellschaft*, 270.

68. Ibid., 20, 270.

69. Ibid., 19.

70. Ibid., 22ff.

71. Ibid., 269.

72. W. Steffen, P. J. Crutzen and J. R. McNeill, 'The Anthropocene: Are Humans Now Overwhelming the Great Forces of Nature?', *Ambio: A Journal of the Human Environment* 36 (2007): 614–21.

73. B. Latour, *Nous n'avons jamais été modernes* (Paris: La Découverte, 2006), Chapter 1.

74. Koskenniemi, *Gentle Civilizer of Nations*, 503.

75. Fuller, *Morality of Law*, 38.

76. K. H. Whiteside, *Precautionary Politics: Principle and Practice in Confronting Environmental Risk* (Cambridge, MA: MIT Press, 2006), 30ff.

Bibliography

Anton, Don K. 'Case Comment: Case Concerning Pulp Mills on the River Uruguay (Argentina V. Uruguay)(Judgment) [2010]ICJ Rep (20 April 2010)'. *Australian International Law Journal* 17 (2010): 10–84.

Barboza, Julio. *The Environment, Risk and Liability in International Law* (Leiden, Netherlands: Martinus Nijhoff, 2011).

Sixth Report on International Liability for Injurious Consequences Arising out of Acts Not Prohibited by International Law (A/CN.4/428). 15 March 1990.

Boyle, Alan. 'Codification of International Environmental Law and the International Law Commission: Injurious Consequences Revisited'. In Alan Boyle and David Freestone (eds), *International Law and Sustainable Development: Past Achievements and Future Challenges* (Oxford: Oxford University Press, 1999).

'State Responsibility and International Liability for Injurious Consequences of Acts Not Prohibited by International Law: a Necessary Distinction?' *International and Comparative Law Quarterly* 39 (1990): 1–26.

Calliess, Gralf-Peter, and Moritz Renner. 'Between Law and Social Norms: the Evolution of Global Governance'. *Ratio Juris* 22 (2009): 260–80.

Calliess, Gralf-Peter, and Peer Zumbansen. *Rough Consensus and Running Code: a Theory of Transnational Private Law* (Oxford: Hart, 2010).

Dupuy, Pierre-Marie. 'Due Diligence in the International Law of Liability'. In OECD (ed.), *Legal Aspects of Transfrontier Pollution* (Paris: OECD Publications Centre, 1977).

Ellis, Jaye. 'Liability for International Environmental Harm'. In *Oxford Bibliographies Online – International Law* (2013).

Engle Merry, Sally. 'Legal Pluralism'. *Law and Society Review* 22 (1988): 869–96.

Fischer-Lescano, Andreas, and Gunther Teubner. 'Regime-Collisions: the Vain Search for Legal Unity in the Fragmentation of Global Law'. *Michigan Journal of International Law* 25 (2004): 999–1046.

Regime-Kollisionen: Zur Fragmentierung des globalen Rechts (Frankfurt am Main, Germany: Suhrkamp, 2006).

Fuller, Lon L. *The Morality of Law*. 2nd edn (New Haven, CT: Yale University Press, 1964).

Goldie, L. Frederick E. 'Concepts of Strict and Absolute Liability and the Ranking of Liability in Terms of Relative Exposure to Risk'. *Netherlands Yearbook of International Law* 16 (1985): 175–248.

'Liability for Damage and the Progressive Development of International Law'. *International and Comparative Law Quarterly* 14 (1966): 1189–264.

Goldsmith, Jack L., and Eric A. Posner. *The Limits of International Law* (Oxford: Oxford University Press, 2005).

Habermas, Jürgen. *Between Facts and Norms: Contributions to a Discourse Theory of Law and Democracy*, William Rehg (trans.) (Cambridge, MA: MIT Press, 1996).

Handl, Günther. 'Liability as an Obligation Established by a Primary Rule of International Law: Some Basic Reflections on the International Law Commission's Work'. *Netherlands Yearbook of International Law* 16 (1985): 49–79.

Hayek, Friedrich A. *The Road to Serfdom* (1944; repr., Chicago: University of Chicago Press, 2007).

Holling, Crawford S. 'Simplifying the Complex: the Paradigms of Ecological Function and Structure'. *European Journal of Operational Research* 30 (1987): 139–46.

Jasanoff, Sheila. 'Just Evidence: the Limits of Science in the Legal Process'. *The Journal of Law, Medicine and Ethics* 34 (2006): 328–41.

Jenks, C. Wilfred. 'Liability for Ultra-Hazardous Activities in International Law'. *Recueil des Cours de l'Académie de droit international* 117 (1966): 99–200.

Kelsen, Hans. *Introduction to the Problems of Legal Theory*, Bonnie L. Paulson and Stanley L. Paulson (trans.) (Oxford: Clarendon, 1992).

Kennedy, Duncan. 'Legal Formality'. *The Journal of Legal Studies* 2 (1973): 351–98.

King, Michael, and Christopher Thornhill. *Niklas Luhmann's Theory of Politics and Law* (London: Palgrave Macmillan, 2006).

Koskenniemi, Martti. 'Breach of Treaty or Non-Compliance? Reflections on the Enforcement of the Montreal Protocol'. *Yearbook of International Environmental Law* 3 (1993): 123–62.

'Declaratory Legislation: towards a Genealogy of Neoliberal Legalism'. In Rain Liivoja and Jarna Petman (eds), *International Law-Making: Essays in Honour of Jan Klabbers* (London: Routledge, 2014).

'The Fate of Public International Law: between Technique and Politics'. *Modern Law Review* 70 (2007): 1–30.

'Formalism, Fragmentation, Freedom: Kantian Themes in Today's International Law'. *No Foundations* 4 (2007): 7–28.

The Gentle Civilizer of Nations: the Rise and Fall of International Law 1870–1960 (Cambridge: Cambridge University Press, 2001).

'International Law and Hegemony: a Reconfiguration'. In *The Politics of International Law* (Oxford: Hart, 2011).

'Peaceful Settlement of Environmental Disputes'. *Nordic Journal of International Law* 60 (1991): 73–92.

Koskenniemi, Martti, and Päivi Leino. 'Fragmentation of International Law? Postmodern Anxieties'. *Leiden Journal of International Law* 15 (2002): 553–79.

Ladeur, Karl-Heinz. *Das Umweltrecht der Wissensgesellschaft: von der Gefahrenabwehr zum Risikomanagement* (Berlin: Duncker and Humblot, 1995).

Latour, Bruno. *Nous n'avons jamais été modernes* (Paris: La Découverte, 2006).

Merkouris, Panos. 'Case Concerning Pulp Mills on the River Uruguay (Argentina V. Uruguay): of Environmental Impact Assessments and "Phantom Experts"'. *The Hague Justice Portal* (2010).

Quentin-Baxter, Robert Q. *International Liability for Injurious Consequences Arising out of Acts Not Prohibited by International Law* (A/CN.4/360). 23 June 1982.

Rehg, William. *Cogent Science in Context: the Science Wars, Argumentation Theory, and Habermas* (Cambridge, MA: MIT Press, 2009).

'Translator's Introduction'. In Jürgen Habermas, *Between Facts and Norms: Contributions to a Discourse Theory of Law and Democracy*, William Rehg (trans.) (Cambridge, MA: MIT Press, 1998).

Sandoval Coustasse, Juan Guillermo, and Emily Sweeney-Samuelson. 'Adjudicating Conflicts over Resources: the ICJ's Treatment of Technical Evidence in the Pulp Mills Case'. *Goettingen Journal of International Law* 3 (2011): 447–71.

Scheuerman, William E. *Frankfurt School Perspectives on Globalization, Democracy, and the Law* (New York: Routledge, 2008).

Schmitt, Carl. *Gesetz und Urteil: Eine Untersuchung Zum Problem Der Rechtspraxis* (1912; repr., Munich: C. H. Beck, 1969).

Sikkink, Kathryn. 'Codes of Conduct for Transnational Corporations: the Case of the WHO'. *International Organization* 40 (1986): 815–40.

Steffen, Will, Paul J. Crutzen and John R. McNeill. 'The Anthropocene: Are Humans Now Overwhelming the Great Forces of Nature?' *AMBIO: A Journal of the Human Environment* 36 (2007): 614–21.

Tamanaha, Brian Z. *On the Rule of Law: History, Politics, Theory* (Cambridge: Cambridge University Press, 2004).

Teubner, Gunther. '"Global Bukowina": Legal Pluralism in the World Society'. In Gunther Teubner (ed.), *Global Law without a State* (Aldershot, UK: Dartmouth, 1997).

'Idiosyncratic Production Regimes: Co-Evolution of Economic and Legal Institutions in the Varieties of Capitalism'. In Michael Wheeler, John Ziman and Margaret A. Boden (eds), *The Evolution of Cultural Entities* (Oxford: Oxford University Press, 2002).

Recht als autopoietisches System (Frankfurt am Main, Germany: Suhrkamp, 1989).

'Rechtswissenschaft und -Praxis im Kontext der Sozialtheorie'. In Stefan Grundmann and Jan Thiessen (eds), *Interdisziplinäres Denken in Rechtswissenschaft und -Praxis* (Tübingen: Mohr Siebeck, 2015).

'The Two Faces of Janus: Rethinking Legal Pluralism'. *Cardozo Law Review* 13 (1991–92): 1443–62.

Whiteside, Kerry H. *Precautionary Politics: Principle and Practice in Confronting Environmental Risk* (Cambridge, MA: MIT Press, 2006).

Xue, Hanqin. *Transboundary Damage in International Law* (Cambridge: Cambridge University Press, 2003).

Young, Iris M. *Justice and the Politics of Difference* (Princeton, NJ: Princeton University Press, 2011).

Martti Koskenniemi on Human Rights

An Empirical Perspective

ERIC A. POSNER*

International law is a vast field governing countless relationships between states, yet a very small part of it receives most of the attention – human rights. This may seem puzzling. The treaties that created the human rights regime are no different from the treaties that created the law of the sea and international trade law. Yet people think about human rights law differently from the rest of international law. Lawyers who discuss the law of the sea or international trade law are likely, sooner or later, to ask whether the rules in those areas are consistent with human rights norms, while human rights lawyers can discuss human rights law without thinking about the law of the sea or the WTO. Many people insist that states are bound to respect human rights even if they have not ratified the relevant treaties, or have ratified them subject to reservations – while countries that do not belong to the WTO are not bound by its rules. Some people believe that human rights law binds states even when states explicitly repudiate it; human rights law is said to have a 'constitutional' dimension.

An enormous infrastructure has grown up around human rights. Countless NGOs monitor compliance with human rights in various countries. Governments routinely criticize each other for violating human rights. An endless array of commissions, councils, committees, courts and offices attempt to administer the human rights treaties. While other treaty regimes also are governed by international organizations (the WTO, the Law of the Sea Authority), no other area of international law has thrown up quite so many institutions, with complex, overlapping jurisdictions. It is also hard to think of another area of international law where there is so much activity: so many proposals for additional treaties, for expanding the scope of existing treaties, for strengthening and constructing new institutions.

And yet the accomplishments of international human rights law seem rather slim. Countries rarely try to enforce the treaties against each other – at least, in a systematic way. They do not 'retaliate' against each other for violating the treaties the way they often retaliate against countries that violate trade law. Countries do threaten human rights violators with sanctions from time to time, but they do not do so in a systematic way, and usually human rights violations are offered as an excuse or redundant justification for sanctions when the real basis for concern is a country's militarism or aggression. And most human rights violators are left alone. The international institutions that monitor human rights lack adequate staffing and funds, and with few exceptions are deprived of formal legal authority. There is not much evidence that human rights law has caused governments to improve respect for human rights.

What are we to make of this phenomenon? I will examine this question through the lens of Martti Koskenniemi's writings on human rights. His most focussed writing on this topic can be found in two chapters of The Politics of International Law.[1] He is interested in the tension between human rights discourse and the institutionalization of human rights. The discourse is fluid and indeterminate. The institutions, by contrast, are rigid. As he argues:

> [W]hile the rhetoric of human rights has historically had a positive and lib-
> erating effect on societies, once rights become institutionalized as a central
> part of political and administrative culture, they lose their transformative
> effect and are petrified into a legalistic paradigm that marginalises values
> and interests that resist translation into rights-language.[2]

The reasons are complex. Human rights discourse is frequently indeterminate and, when it isn't, it privileges certain moral relations over others in an arbitrary fashion. Indeterminacy can be seen in the ubiquitous problem of trade-offs. When a person criticizes the government, his human right to expression must be weighed against interference with the government's legitimate activities, like providing security. These tensions can be characterized as conflicts between rights – in this case, a conflict between one person's right to freedom of expression and other people's right to security – and the human rights treaties provide no method for resolving such conflicts. The larger problem is that governments have numerous responsibilities and limited resources. If they use some of their resources to advance certain human rights, there will be fewer resources left over for advancing other human rights or other legitimate interests of the public. There is no 'recipe' for making these trade-offs and judgements. The morally correct result depends on context.[3]

Worse, human rights law privileges certain moral values at the expense of others. So even if a government properly respects human rights, it could end up causing other moral harms. For example, in families moral claims are not based on rights but on relationships; there are pervasive worries that conceptualizing family relationships in terms of rights (for example, children have rights to love and support) mischaracterizes and damages them. In the US, a recent lawsuit by a teenager against her parents claiming that they were legally required to pay her expensive high school tuition sparked widespread outrage. Although the plaintiff had a weak case, the concern is that she would not have even brought the case but for a culture in which everyone thinks about everything in terms of rights. A government that sought to protect human rights in the family context may end up harming family relationships.

When human rights are institutionalized – and here Koskenniemi seems to have in mind domestic legal and constitutional structures – the moral trade-offs (the first problem) are put in the hands of courts and administrators who may make them improperly, reflecting self-interest, the values of the elites, institutional self-preservation, or error. The bureaucratic enforcement of rights then leads to denigration of moral values that cannot be put into the language of rights (the second problem).

The upshot is that although people who are treated unjustly often can advance their cause by using the language of rights, once those rights are recognized, legalized and institutionalized, they become just one of a large number of rights that must be traded off against each other, often with disregard to moral values not (yet) recognized as rights. This seems to be the petrification that Koskenniemi alludes to. One might add that the problem is not just that other moral values are not recognized, but that the institutions may, while recognizing many rights, not make the right trade-offs and thus effectively violate some or many of them.

Koskenniemi's discussion is abstract; as I mentioned, he seems to have in mind a vaguely defined human rights discourse that is partially legalized. In this essay, I bring down the level of abstraction, and examine how his argument plays out in international law. My starting point is evidence compiled over the last decade that suggests that international human rights law has been ineffective. I will argue that the problem is not petrification of human rights but the difficulty of eliminating discretion and trade-offs. Countries try to promote the interests of the domestic public or specific domestic constituencies, and resist the straitjacket of a rights regime that would interfere with this agenda. As a result, states have deliberately ensured that international human rights law is vague, and that international legal institutions are too weak to give it content. I argue that the failure can be traced to a basic conceptual problem with rights. Because any effort to reduce the public good to a short list of rights unavoidably skirts things that people care about, there will always be constant pressure to increase the number of rights. This pressure comes from the public, NGOs, political activists and many other persons and organizations. But as the number of rights increases (a phenomenon I call the 'hypertrophy' of human rights), and it becomes more and more necessary to make trade-offs between them, it becomes harder to criticize countries for failing to advance some rights rather than others. Paradoxically, the huge quantity of human rights gives states immunity to criticism for violating them.

This theory, and the evidence that supports it, supports Koskenniemi's critique of human rights law. Yet in his recent writing, Koskenniemi argues that social science research is just as empty and indeterminate as the formalism of human rights law. After discussing the evidence, I provide some thoughts about this conundrum.

5.1   Some Evidence

Until recently, it was taken for granted among international lawyers that human rights treaties advanced the cause of human rights. How could they not? Governments, NGOs and other institutions put a huge amount of effort into negotiating these treaties. They set up committees, commissions, and courts to monitor compliance, interpret terms and pester governments that fail to live up to their obligations. Leaders of virtually all governments regularly declare their devotion to human rights, and criticize other governments for violating human rights. Thousands of NGOs have been formed by people who hope to hold their governments and foreign governments to those governments' human rights obligations. Aid may be conditioned on human rights. Routine human rights violators may be isolated. The International Criminal Court was created to ensure that government officials responsible for the worst human rights violations are held criminally accountable.

Over the decades, international human rights law has deeply penetrated domestic political and legal institutions. Many governments have drafted new constitutions, and every new constitution contains rights that can be traced to international documents. Domestic courts are often empowered to enforce those rights. The European Court of Human Rights has taken the lead in deepening and advancing the human rights regime.

Roughly contemporaneous with the rise of international human rights law, democracy spread from country to country, in a series of waves that took place after World War II, during the 1970s and during the 1990s. Today, most countries are democracies, and even non-democracies must pay tribute to democratic ideals by holding (fake) elections.

One of the most interesting features of the human rights regime is the rapid increase in the number of human rights treaties, and the rapid increase in the number of internationally recognized human rights (most but not all of them created by the treaties). Major treaties entered into force in 1969, 1976 (two), 1981, 1987, 1990, 2003, 2008 and 2010. The number of rights that came into existence expanded from 20 or so in the first treaty (depending on how one counts them), to over 100 in 1976, more than 150 in the 1990s, to around 300 today. Or to put the point differently, the range of human activities that are governed by international human rights law has expanded greatly, so that today, nearly everything one might think of is formally governed by human rights law – the family, the workplace, political institutions, religious organizations, education, health, indigenous groups, disability, and on and on.

This might seem like a triumph for human rights, but the picture, like an impressionist painting, becomes murkier as one looks more closely at it. Human rights monitors churn out dismal reports at an ever-greater rate, and these reports show that human rights violations remain common in most countries. Torture is used routinely to extract confessions or intimidate dissidents. Police use extrajudicial killings to keep order or extract bribes. Women are treated extremely badly in all but the most advanced western countries. In poor countries, children are forced to work and denied adequate education. Health care is miserable. Religious freedom is limited. Press freedom varies greatly even in democracies, as does the ability of the public to exercise its will through political institutions.

The various international institutions charged with monitoring and enforcing the treaties are starved for funds and routinely ignored by states. The treaty committees are marginal institutions. The UN Human Rights Council is tainted by its human rights violating members who protect themselves from criticism. The European Court of Human Rights has presided over the return of authoritarianism to Russia, Poland, and Hungary. And the effectiveness of domestic human rights institutions is questionable. Outside the West, most countries have weak and frequently corrupt legal institutions.

And while democracy has indeed spread, and so has the incorporation of rights into national constitutions, it seems hardly accurate to say that human rights – at least, in the conventional western sense – play a dominant ideological or political role around the world. Consider the ten most populous states, which in aggregate contain well over half the population of the world. Of them, only the US and (to a lesser extent) Japan could be considered a liberal democracy where rights are widely respected. Russia and China are authoritarian countries. India is a democracy and enjoys a free press, but culturally – with its lingering caste system and mistreatment of women, especially in vast rural areas – it is about as far from liberal as one can imagine. Indonesia, Pakistan, Bangladesh and Nigeria also would be well down on the list of leading rights-respecting nations. Brazil, the best of the remaining lot, has enormous problems like rampant extrajudicial killing.

Nor is there much evidence that the progress that has been achieved is related to international law per se. The leading liberal democracies – including the UK, the US, France, Germany, the Netherlands, Canada, Australia – respected human rights long before the international treaty regime was put into place in the 1970s. Some of these countries can trace their commitment to human rights back to the Enlightenment. The causes of recent conversions to human rights lie outside the law. The failure of numerous authoritarian regimes – after World War I, World War II and the Cold War – immensely bolstered the prestige of democracy and human rights. Democracy and respect for human rights appear to be correlated with economic growth – and there may well be a causal relationship running from wealth to rights. Thus, the factors that cause countries to respect human rights appear to be unrelated to international law.

Over the last fifteen years, law professors and political scientists have attempted to test rigorously the hypothesis that international human rights law improves respect for human rights. This hypothesis implies that if a country enters into a human rights treaty, its human rights performance will improve at the same time or in the years afterwards. In fact, there is hardly any evidence for this pattern, as Figure 5.1 illustrates.

The graph shows four types of human rights-related outcomes – freedom of speech, extrajudicial killings, freedom of religion and independence of the judiciary, where 0 is worst and 2 is best.[4] When a country ratifies the ICCPR, it binds itself to recognize rights to freedom of expression and freedom of religion – and so measures of respect for those rights should increase. In addition, the country binds itself to recognize the right to due process, and accordingly one would expect the country's avoidance of extrajudicial killings and the independence of its judiciary would improve. Yet the graph shows that performance along these dimensions

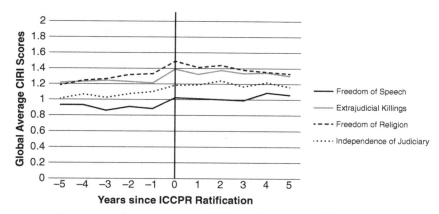

Figure 5.1 Effect of International Covenant on Civil and Political Rights on four types of rights.

hardly budges. There is perhaps a small improvement in the year leading up to ratification, but this improvement erodes over the next several years. Statistical studies that control for other factors like changes in the country's wealth confirm that treaty ratification does not affect a country's human rights performance at a statistically significant level.[5]

The pattern for other treaties is roughly the same, though there is some variation. Scholars have found some evidence that literacy rates for women improved in countries that ratified the Convention on the Elimination of All Forms of Discrimination against Women, for example. But respect for other rights go *down* after ratification. When there are dozens or even hundreds of rights, random variation will ensure that some coefficients are statistically significant. But the overall pattern is clear: treaty ratification either has no effect on human rights, or a very small effect that is greatly at variance with all the attention given to human rights.

5.2   Explanations

Why haven't human rights treaties increased respect for human rights? There are a number of familiar explanations. One is that countries do not really care about human rights, and the treaties are a hypocritical exercise in propaganda. And the advanced liberal countries made sure to design the treaties so that they ratified rights that those countries already recognized, so no change in behaviour was necessary. Another is that countries do care about human rights, but not very much, so while countries enter into human rights treaties in good faith, it turns out to be too difficult to comply with them because of problems of entrenched interests, civil disorder and so forth. Wealthy and powerful countries that might be expected to enforce human rights in other countries must contend with competing interests like security and geopolitical stability.

I want to explore a third possibility, one more closely in line with Koskenniemi's claims. Koskenniemi argues that rights become oppressive when they are institutionalized because they marginalize certain interests that are not protected by these rights. Part of the explanation is that certain human values do not lend themselves to embodiment in rights. He mentions nationalistic aspirations: many people feel that they have a duty to make sacrifices for the good of the nation, but they do not believe that anyone else has a corresponding right to those sacrifices. Another example perhaps is embodied in the idea of virtue. A person may feel that she has an obligation to improve her talents without thinking that she has a right to do so. Family relations are notoriously difficult to describe in the language of rights: does one spouse have a right to care and support from the other spouse?

Yet while these familiar objections to 'rights-talk' carry some force, it is not clear that they apply to the international human rights regime. After all, that regime has never demanded that government disregard morality that is not embodied in rights. The idea from the start was to create a set of minimum or basic rights, not to dictate the entire moral system. Governments can pursue their own (or their population's) vision of the good if they like without running afoul of the human rights regime.

Another theory for the failure or weakness of human rights treaties is 'rights hypertrophy' – the proliferation of human rights to the point that any specific human right loses its normative content.[6] All countries have limited resources, whereas most rights – at least, if understood naively – require a large expenditure for vindication. A country can stop torture and guarantee due process only by investing resources in training police and judges, paying them adequately and investigating corruption. It is very hard to know what fraction of the country's GDP must be spent on these activities in order to vindicate the rights of criminal suspects. Everyone understands that rights violations cannot be brought down to zero, and so the question becomes how many rights violations can be tolerated for a country to be deemed in compliance with the human rights treaties.

Meanwhile, this same hypothetical country must vindicate numerous other rights. It must respect the right to free speech – which means providing security and crowd control for demonstrations. It must respect the right to freedom of religion – which may mean providing legal exemptions as well as protection for religious minorities. It must respect rights to education and health – which means investing substantial resources in schools and medical clinics. It must reduce discrimination against women – which again will require, especially in a traditional society, massive investments in education, training and protection. If, as is normally the case, respect for rights requires a modern, well-funded legal system, then resources must go in that direction as well. And while doing all of this, the government must maintain political support among traditional groups and conservative citizens who object to these policies. And yet if resources are limited – and they always are – then the country must make trade-offs, and invest less in vindicating rights than might seem appropriate in the abstract.

Anxieties based on these sorts of considerations have led many commentators to argue that human rights should be arranged hierarchically, so countries are encouraged to address the most important rights, like rights related to bodily integrity. But there has been no movement in this direction. The reason for this is that most governments see their role as that of advancing the general public good. Even cynical, corrupt and authoritarian governments put some effort into providing benefits to the public – even if they are more concerned with helping themselves and their cronies – if only to prevent a revolution. The public good is typically understood as some mixture of economic prosperity, security and protection of values. Governments do best by allocating resources to these goals in proportion to the marginal benefits that are available. If torture exists because it is a deeply entrenched practice among local police, and no amount of money spent on retraining will eliminate it, then it is better to use money to build schools and medical clinics than throw it away on investigations and training programs that will not make a dent in the torture problem. If spending more money on schools does not turn out to improve educational outcomes by very much, then at the margin money may be better spent on parks, or better streets, or higher salaries for civil servants, or a stronger military.

Philosophers dislike rights hypotrophy because the proliferation of rights (including rights to leisure and vacation) seems to trivialize the human rights project.[7] But it is reasonable for a government to spend resources on apparently trivial goods (vacation, leisure) if those resources cannot on the margin purchase goods that might seem more significant or otherwise more deeply connected to human well-being (bodily integrity, religious freedom). It is probably for this reason that the list of rights continues to grow rather than contract. To rationalize spending on parks when many people receive inadequate schooling or medical care, someone will advocate a 'right to parks', or claim that park-building advances some other rights to leisure or environmental well-being or some such thing. The flexibility of language combines with the needs of policy to ensure that rights are indeterminate in practice. Governance is complicated; good governance cannot be reduced to a list of well-defined obligations.

If all this is so, one can see why human rights treaties seem to be as entrenched as ever, and indeed continue to be proposed and ratified, with the number of recognized rights increasing all the time – while at the same time the treaties do not have measurable effect on the behaviour of countries. Countries add new treaties and new rights to make clear that they are not bound to a short list of basic rights, including the liberal or negative rights touted by the US in particular, and can instead act with the flexibility that they believe necessary to meet public needs. Commentators and scholars abet this activity by discovering new human interests that the rights regime should protect. But the upshot is the treaties become unenforceable. It becomes difficult to argue that a country violated a treaty X because it violated right Y, when the country can reply that it cannot afford to respect right Y while also ensuring the vindication of rights W and Z. These arguments are familiar. Many poor countries claim that they can exercise a right to development in order to excuse their failure to comply with political rights. We may (or may not) criticize these arguments on moral grounds, but the treaties themselves provide no resources for criticism. If the treaties were (implausibly) interpreted to require countries to reduce all rights violations to zero, then they would require the impossible, and countries can't be asked to do the impossible. But if, more plausibly, the treaties require countries to use 'best efforts' or 'good faith' to reduce violations, and to make reasonable trade-offs, then they provide no basis for distinguishing countries that are in compliance and those that are not – putting aside extreme cases like countries that commit genocide or (like North Korea) sustain totalitarian systems that exploit and impoverish their populations.

One might respond to this argument by pointing out that many advanced countries respect the human rights of their citizens, and the trade-off problem does not render this promise indeterminate, even when many rights can be bound in the constitution. In these countries, people can tell when the government violates their rights, and can obtain redress in the courts. But the difference between the domestic case and international law is that in the domestic case countries use institutions to resolve conflicts about rights, to make whatever trade-offs that are necessary. Those institutions draw on their understanding of the public good and popular opinion in order to make these trade-offs, which are then embodied in law that is often (although not always) predictable in application. The difficulty with international human rights is that no comparable institutions exist. International human rights institutions are feeble and lacking in legitimacy. The reason for that is that legal institutions can operate only when they are trusted or at least accepted by the public, and while populations in advanced states generally trust their domestic institutions, they do not trust international institutions. And for that reason, governments cannot give international institutions the resources and respect that would enable them to operate effectively.

5.3 From International Law to the Sociology of the International Law Profession

Readers might notice a significant irony in the argument that social-scientific scholarship provides evidence for Koskenniemi's arguments about the indeterminacy of human rights law. In recent years, Koskenniemi has criticized international legal scholarship influenced by social science in terms not much different from his criticisms of the empty formalism of traditional international legal doctrinalism.[8] If I understand his arguments correctly, he thinks that the scholars, whom he calls 'managerialists', are merely replacing one vocabulary with another, privileging new power relationships, and serving as 'miserable comforters' (to quote Kant) for the ruling elites.

Koskenniemi overstates the collapse of progressive thinking in international law and the rise of 'managerialism'. In the US, at least, the progressive thinking he criticizes continues to dominate international law scholarship. For every paper written about trade, the law of the sea, or state responsibility, dozens are written about human rights. The human rights papers typically seek to expand the reach of the human rights regimes – by defining existing rights broadly or proposing new rights. I know European scholarship less well, but it seems clear that human rights is also a central feature of that scholarship, indeed, where there is a commonly asserted view (still rare in the US) that international human rights have become 'constitutionalized'.

Figure 5.2 shows the rapid increase in the frequency of law review articles in the US that mention the term 'human rights'. It is a crude

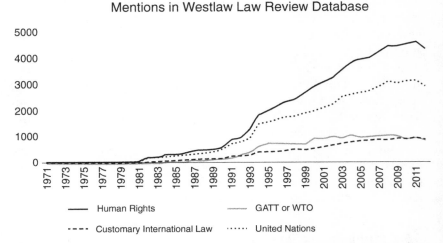

Figure 5.2 Frequency of mention of 'human rights' and other terms in legal articles. Compiled from Thomson Reuters, *Westlaw JLR Database* (2016). Available at www .westlaw.com (accessed 15 February 2016).

measure – since not all of these articles are focussed on human rights – but it seems intuitively right. Writing about human rights received two boosts. The first was the Carter administration's promotion of human rights in the late 1970s, which was surprisingly adopted by the Reagan administration. The second was the end of the Cold War, which suddenly seemed to make a cosmopolitan order based on western human right principles possible.

What is true is that this type of scholarship is not taken very seriously by scholars outside of international law, appears to have little influence on governments, and has been challenged in recent years by empirically oriented legal scholars and political scientists, who have, as I explained above, provided evidence that human rights treaties have had little effect on the behaviour of states. The normative proposals to expand human rights and to strengthen human rights institutions have become increasingly difficult to sustain in the face of state intransigence – much as Koskenniemi has documented and predicted.

Moreover, Koskenniemi is right that social science methods have made significant inroads in international law. Indeed, as Koskenniemi notes, there has always been a strand of 'realist', that is, anti-formalist, thinking in US international legal scholarship, going back at least to Morgenthau, who introduced modern 'realism' to international relations theory. After a significant hiatus, the success of social science methods in domestic law scholarship finally began to exert influence on international law scholars in the 1990s. Initially, they drew on theories from the international relations field in political science, then from economics. A search was on for useful models. In the last decade, a major development has been rigorous empirical scholarship using statistical methods drawn from economics and political science.[9]

Much of this scholarship is oriented towards empirical investigation in the (legal) realist tradition. When do countries comply with treaties? When don't they? Do international courts exert influence over the law? And so on. This turn to empiricism, with it complex vocabulary ('r-squared', 'instrumental variable'), has been unwelcome to scholars who have not been trained in it, but it is in fact a natural development for international law. International lawyers were traditionally empiricists, who derived the norms of international law in part from the practices of states. When most international law was customary, a major task for international jurists was to discover how states around the world regarded putative norms. It is hardly surprising that the ad hoc methods of empiricism that they used and that became entrenched in the profession would eventually be challenged by those who had been trained in more sophisticated empirical methods.

One would think that Koskenniemi, after a long and distinguished career as a critic of formalism, would welcome this development. But, no, it turns out that social-scientific international law scholarship is just as tainted as traditional doctrinal scholarship – just as tainted by indeterminacy that allows for the play of hidden normative agendas and careerist imperatives. But Koskenniemi's criticisms of this new style of scholarship are not as deeply informed as his criticisms of formalism. He very rarely has addressed any of the scholarship in any detail. He is never clear about the mechanism: whether, for example, scholars act opportunistically, hoping to be rewarded with offices and prestige; or perhaps they conform to certain social and cultural expectations, or absorb the prevailing ideological Zeitgeist in the countries in which they live. Clarity on this score would be helpful since different theories suggest different empirical tests. And here Koskenniemi would benefit from close study rather than dismissal of the new literature. His ad hoc empiricism, so common among the formalists that he criticizes, is vulnerable to numerous criticisms; above all, that he selected a handful examples to illustrate his claims rather than performing rigorous analysis of the data. Yet the data and the methods are available. It would be a simple matter to see whether the arguments of law professors correlate with the interests of their governments, or if scholars who make certain types of arguments are rewarded with offices and prestige. Koskenniemi makes empirical claims; as a scholar, he has an obligation to use the most rigorous methods to validate them.[10]

As Koskenniemi would be the first to tell us, empirical research is not value-free. Scholars need to decide what to investigate, and empirical results will always be interpreted by reference to Bayesian priors. Scholars must make certain simplifying assumptions. Should countries be regarded as billiard balls, or as groups of interests? If the latter, which interests should be singled out? Do we expect treaties to affect behaviour immediately or only after a lag? Back-and-forth between data analysis and theorizing should help people refine their assumptions and improve their theories. Values, normative agendas and political biases can never be fully eliminated, but they are brought to the surface, where they can be debated. There is nothing about this process that should comfort those in power, since the outcome will be based on empirical facts over which they have no control. Nor is it intrinsically oriented towards the status quo since scholars can make whatever normative arguments they want to.[11]

The effort to claim that formalism – traditional doctrinal legal scholarship – and the new social-scientific literature on international law 'inhabit the same conceptual space' founders because the two modes of argument are oriented towards different ends. Formalism attempts to make predictions about how legal actors will decide disputes or tries to persuade them to decide disputes in certain ways.[12] Once the indeterminacy of legal materials is recognized, formalism loses its self-respect, and possibly its legitimacy, and can only be seen as a cover for pursuing a hidden political agenda. By contrast, social science attempts to establish the truth. Like any method, it can be abused, but because the rules of social science are relatively clear, people who abuse it can be criticized and often consensus can be reached that transcends political disagreement. Grudgingly, Koskenniemi admits this. 'Of course, empirical and technical knowledges have their uses', says Koskenniemi. 'They sharpen analysis and give a clearer sense of the available alternatives for action' – [13] which is quite unlike formalism, which conceals the available alternatives for action by ruling them out on supposed legal grounds. It is for this reason, and this reason alone, that social science scholarship has a greater claim to legitimacy than formalism does.

Notes

* Thanks to the editors and Adam Chilton for helpful comments and to Hannah Waldman for research assistance.
1. For a useful overview of Koskenniemi's writings on human rights law, see F. Mégret, 'The Apology of Utopia: Some Thoughts on Koskenniemian Themes, with Particular Emphasis on Massively Institutionalized International Human Rights Law', *Temple International and Comparative Law Journal* 27 (2013): 455–97.
2. M. Koskenniemi, *The Politics of International Law* (Oxford: Hart, 2011), 133.
3. Ibid., 143.
4. D. L. Cingranelli, D. L. Richards and K. C. Clay, *The CIRI Human Rights Dataset* (2013), www.humanrightsdata.com (accessed 22 February 2016).
5. I discuss the evidence in E. A. Posner, *The Twilight of Human Rights Law* (Oxford: Oxford University Press, 2014).
6. Ibid.
7. J. Griffin, *On Human Rights* (Oxford: Oxford University Press, 2009), 186.
8. See e.g. M. Koskenniemi, 'Miserable Comforters: International Relations as New Natural Law', *European Journal of International Relations* 15 (2009): 395–422, and 'The Politics of International Law – 20 Years Later', *European Journal of International Relations* 20 (2009): 7–19.
9. J. L. Goldsmith and E. A. Posner, 'The New International Law Scholarship', *Georgia Journal of International and Comparative Law* 34 (2006): 463–84.
10. For an example of an effort to use statistical methods to link the claims of scholars and their ideologies, see A. S. Chilton and E. A. Posner, 'An Empirical Study of Political Bias in Legal Scholarship', *Coase-Sander Institute for Law and Economics Research Paper No. 696*, University of Chicago (2016).
11. For a general critique of Koskenniemi's arguments about international relations scholarship, see M. Pollack, 'Is International Relations Corrosive of International Law? A Reply to Martti Koskenniemi', *Temple International and Comparative Law Journal* 27 (2013): 339–75. As Pollack points out, Koskenniemi conflates many different strands of scholarship.
12. Koskenniemi, 'Politics of International Law – 20 Years Later', 16.
13. Ibid.

Bibliography

Chilton, A. S., and E. A. Posner. 'An Empirical Study of Political Bias in Legal Scholarship'. University of Chicago Coase-Sander Institute for Law and Economics Research Paper No. 696 (2016).

Cingranelli, D. L., D. L. Richards, and K. C. Clay. *The CIRI Human Rights Dataset* (2013). www.humanrightsdata.org (accessed 2 February 2016).

Goldsmith, J. L., and E. A. Posner. 'The New International Law Scholarship'. *Georgia Journal of International and Comparative Law* 34 (2016): 463–84.

Griffin, J. *On Human Rights.* 1st edn (Oxford: Oxford University Press, 2009).

Koskenniemi, M. 'Miserable Comforters: International Relations as New Natural Law'. *European Journal of International Relations* 15 (2009): 395–422.

The Politics of International Law. 1st edn (Oxford: Hart, 2011).

'The Politics of International Law – 20 Years Later'. *European Journal of International Relations* 20 (2009): 7–19.

Mégret, F. 'The Apology of Utopia: Some Thoughts on Koskenniemian Themes, with Particular Emphasis on Massively Institutionalized International Human Rights Law'. *Temple International and Comparative Law Journal* 27 (2013): 455–97.

Posner, E. A. *The Twilight of Human Rights Law.* 1st edn (Oxford: Oxford University Press, 2014).

The Rule of Law in an Agnostic World

The Prohibition on the Use of Force and Humanitarian Exceptions

JUTTA BRUNNÉE AND STEPHEN J. TOOPE*

Dying of malaria when the available technical and economic resources are sufficient to prevent this, or suffering torture in a hidden detention camp, are not just unfortunate historical events touching only the physical persons concerned. In a secular society, it is the political business of constitutionalism to endow such events with sacredness or with a symbolic meaning that lifts them beyond their individuality. They work as archetypes, or normative moorings for political identity.

– Martti Koskenniemi[1]

The virtue of constitutionalism in the international world follows from a . . . universalizing focus, allowing extreme inequality in the world to be not only shown but also condemned. This inequality may be explained by historical causes and described in economic or sociological terms. But something like a constitutional vocabulary is needed to articulate it as a scandal insofar as it violates the equal dignity and autonomy of human beings.

– Martti Koskenniemi[2]

In the most recent writings of a productive career, Martti Koskenniemi has shifted his emphasis. Starting as a straight-on 'crit' whose primary message was that all law is indeterminate and that all law is inevitably controlled by materially powerful elites, his recent work has softened the edges of critique. Now Koskenniemi is interested in 'constitutionalism as mindset', an expression of a culture of formalism.[3] Today, Koskenniemi looks for the 'sacredness' in law,[4] describing the 'faith' and 'commitment' that sit at the heart of legal practice, at the heart of those of us who still seek to understand the 'mystery of obligation'.[5] One might conclude from the use of such language that Koskenniemi's law had taken on moralistic or naturalistic overtones, but one would be wrong.

Despite the intensity of feeling revealed in language such as 'extreme inequality' and its condemnation, 'equal dignity' and the 'scandal' of its violation, the heart of law remains, for Koskenniemi, irredeemably cold. There is no promise of political consensus through legal interaction, no ability to learn through social intercourse.[6] Even the invocation of love itself is nothing but a subtle expression of power relations.[7] International law should be understood, Koskenniemi suggests, as a 'promise of justice', but it is a promise that remains eternally unfulfilled.[8]

In Koskenniemi's view, contemporary international law is descending down three inter-twining paths that lead to impotence for most of the world's peoples: 'deformalization', 'fragmentation' and 'empire'.[9] While international law can provide a space or 'surface' for argument to resist these trends, at the moment of decision, any seeming rhetorical victory slips away, as the contestation simply slides into the realm of politics, at which point power will win. In any event, even within the frame of legal argument, any decision will have been determined not by the persuasiveness of argument but by the structure into which the argument inserts itself – and legal structures are also direct expressions of power.[10]

In such a structurally determined world, where legal interaction is merely an opportunity to be heard – to experience a formal equality – but not actually to effect change, is there anything that international lawyers can do to give concrete expression to the 'mystery of obligation'?[11] In recent work, Koskenniemi's language has tended to suggest a positive answer, through the formality of constitutionalism. But despite his yearnings for 'faith' in and 'commitment' to international law Koskenniemi remains seduced by the siren calls of radical indeterminacy,[12] and trapped by a rigid belief in the immutability of power in the absence of revolution.[13] One senses a desire to sail away from these shoals, to escape into hope, but consistency with his past writings precludes any such move.

We argue, in contrast, that contemporary international law is not so fixed in a downward spiral, that social learning is possible through law, and that this learning has the potential to drive limited shared understandings across cultures and nations. An admittedly modest Rule of Law is achievable in an agnostic world. Koskenniemi's recent insights actually help to point us in this direction; we in turn hope to show him that international law's 'promise of justice' can sometimes, and with admitted fragility, be fulfilled.

We will focus upon the ways in which our interactional understanding of international law,[14] especially in its reliance upon 'the practice of legality', helps us to construct a contemporary understanding of the Rule of Law in international society. In so doing, we will focus upon two of the themes proposed by the editors of this volume: the culture of formalism, attending especially to Koskenniemi's description of 'structural biases' in law and institutions, and the politics of international law, where we will show that Koskenniemi unduly discounts agency in international law.

Our understanding of the Rule of Law involves practices of actors within international society that are shaped and sometimes even controlled by 'criteria of legality' that allow actors to pursue their purposes and organize their interactions. The instantiation of these criteria in continuing practice generates a distinctive form of legal legitimacy, thereby building a sense of commitment among those to whom law is addressed, helping to explain legal obligation. One might call this a 'culture of legality' that is thicker in its content and its ability to shape behaviour than Koskenniemi's 'culture of formalism'. However, this 'culture of legality' does not require commitments to strong substantive ends or goods, so it cannot be dismissed as an exclusionary and value-laden liberal internationalism.

We will argue that the Rule of Law is not rooted primarily in any specific legal institutions, be it parliaments or courts. The Rule of Law can therefore operate in international society, where these types of institutions are less developed. This is not to say that institutions are unhelpful in promoting or strengthening practices of legality, only that such practices can emerge in diverse ways even in the absence of formal institutions. The Rule of Law project is not only about constraining power in hierarchical settings (i.e. limiting governmental power within states), although it can perform this function. The Rule of Law also manages and shapes power within 'horizontal' systems like international law. In both settings, it is practices shaped by criteria of legality that limit and channel power, although they may manifest themselves in different ways through the efforts of various actors.

Finally, using a case study on attempts to create 'humanitarian' exceptions to the prohibition on the use of force, we show how our emphasis upon the practice of legality reveals that building and maintaining the Rule of Law is a collective enterprise. Empowered agents (actors in international society) are therefore central, yet international law is not simply what states and others 'want it to be'. All actors are constrained by the requirements of legality, providing a relative autonomy of law from politics. Like Koskenniemi, who also seeks to insulate the structures of law from raw material power, but whose 'culture of formality' – even when paired with 'constitutionalism as a mindset' – ultimately fails in that objective, we stress that law's autonomy is only relative. We recognize that particular norms may be promoted for political reasons and that material resources affect the ability of actors to participate in law's construction. But we show that power does not strictly condition or control law. Our 'culture of legality' explains how legal actors can resist power and constrain the influence of even the most powerful social actors, as has happened with both the responsibility to protect doctrine and the claimed right of humanitarian intervention.

6.1   Interactional International Law

Over the last ten years, we have developed a comprehensive interactional understanding of international law that connects insights from international relations constructivism to the legal theory of Lon Fuller.[15] We were drawn to Fuller because, among twentieth-century legal theorists, he was the most clear in recognizing and explaining the essential 'horizontality' of law, which is of particular interest to international lawyers. Fuller's approach to domestic law helps confront head-on the persistent critique that international law cannot be true law because it lacks many of the hierarchical structures of authority that are commonly seen to define law. Fuller illustrated that what is often assumed to be a vertical relationship of authority and subordination is better understood as a reciprocal relationship in which citizens 'accept as law and generally observe' the promulgated body of rules and, in turn, are able to expect that the government will abide by and apply these rules. Constructivism provides useful insight into the emergence, maintenance and operation of social norms, and to the role of agency and structures in the evolution of those norms.

Drawing on these two influences, our framework has three interrelated elements. First, building on constructivist insights, we posit that legal norms can only arise in the context of social norms built upon shared understandings that are themselves socially constructed and subject to social learning. Second, what distinguishes law from other types of social ordering is not simply provenance from a particular 'source', but adherence to a series of criteria of legality most comprehensively posited by Fuller: generality, promulgation, non-retroactivity, clarity, non-contradiction, not asking the impossible, constancy and congruence between rules and official action. When norm creation meets these criteria and when, third, there exists what we call a 'practice of legality' (norm application and interpretation that also satisfy the legality requirements), actors can pursue their purposes and organize their interactions through law. These features and practices of legality are crucial to generating a distinctive legal legitimacy and a sense of commitment among those to whom law is addressed. Together, they demystify what Koskenniemi has called the 'mystery' of legal obligation.[16]

On this reading of international law, it is the instantiation of the practice of legality through principles, processes and techniques that creates a continuing possibility of the Rule of Law. These principles, processes and techniques are in turn disciplined by the requirements of legality. In other words, practices of legality can operate in a range of settings, whether relatively more horizontal or hierarchical in nature. For example, customary international law is made, maintained and changed through relatively diffuse processes, framed by certain principles that govern the assessment of whether or not a norm exists at custom. The principles that govern the making and operation of treaties are more explicit and detailed, and the processes through which treaties are made and applied are more structured than those that shape customary law.

There also exist a range of international processes and techniques that are centralized or hierarchical in nature, such as various decision-making processes within intergovernmental organizations or treaty regimes, or judicial and other dispute settlement processes across a wide range of fields. Equally, some processes and techniques of norm use are horizontal, such as consensus decisions of Conferences of the Parties or 'standards' that emerge from quasi-regulatory voluntary agencies in international society.

The image of the constant interaction of practice and legality (Figure 6.1), and of the agents who pursue their goals through legality and the structures in which they act, helps us understand that the relative autonomy of law is a collectively built phenomenon. In other words, in legal interaction, agents are not fully autonomous to pursue any argument or any end because what 'counts' in law is shaped by the criteria of legality. Within this interactional framework, then, material power is relevant but not necessarily determinative of legal outcomes. Attempts to shape law even by the most powerful actors will fail if they do not meet the criteria of legality.

6.2   Structural Biases and Shared Understandings

It is important to emphasize that the criteria of legality do not contain strong substantive values, beyond a commitment to the relative autonomy of actors in society and communication on the basis of formal equality. In this sense, our description of the fundamental purposes of international law begins at a similar point to that of Koskenniemi, and allows for value-based diversity – or value-agnosticism – in international society.[17]

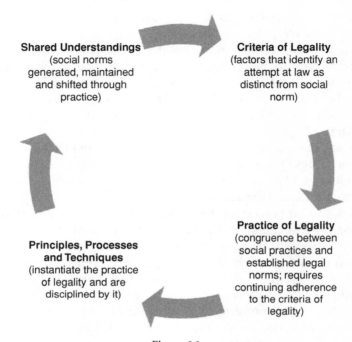

Shared Understandings
(social norms
generated, maintained
and shifted through
practice)

Criteria of Legality
(factors that identify an
attempt at law as
distinct from social
norm)

Practice of Legality
(congruence between
social practices and
established legal
norms; requires
continuing adherence
to the criteria of
legality)

**Principles, Processes
and Techniques**
(instantiate the practice
of legality and are
disciplined by it)

Figure 6.1

However, unlike Koskenniemi, we argue that this diversity can actually be promoted and upheld through law. That is because we describe processes through which social norms are generated through social learning in interaction. In turn, these norms can form a basis upon which legal norms are built. Consensus in international society is difficult to achieve, but is not impossible.

Some norms in international law are genuinely the product of shared understandings, though we have always argued that these norms are limited and often 'procedural' in nature. The idea that parties are bound by their agreements (*pacta sunt servanda*) is a core procedural norm. We argue below that the commitment to strict limits on the use of force in international affairs is a robust substantive norm supported by a practice of legality. Other norms that look like law may turn out to be empty vessels because they are not based on any actual consensus, with the Kyoto Protocol commitments to reduce greenhouse gases being a powerful recent example.[18]

Koskenniemi suggests that true consensus in international society is impossible because seeming agreement is only produced by a structure of power politics.[19] '[C]onsensus-seeking', he observes, 'may often hide a subtle authoritarianism'.[20] Hence, to the extent that international norms and institutions emerge, they are not genuinely shared understandings, but merely 'structural biases' imposed through the exercise of power within specific institutions. Legal institutions may have different structural biases.[21] In this argument Koskenniemi shows himself to be a self-conscious 'realist'. But, as David Dyzenhaus argues, realism is not a descriptive account of practice; it is simply one normative theory. Practice can be made to correspond to this theory, but it can equally be constructed in terms of legality. There is a normative choice to be made about making the world more or less subject to the Rule of Law.[22] Koskenniemi *chooses* to see human interaction as a struggle for position and power, and simply asserts that no other construction is possible.

Yet, processes that engage actors in interaction though formal negotiation and informal discussion are not inevitably empty scaffolding. Even in Koskenniemi's terms, discourse that places all actors on a 'shared surface' can help to create or reinforce formal equality. We go a step further to argue that discourse and active engagement among actors can produce social learning and shared understandings. We *choose* to see evidence of human interaction that is based upon a desire to pursue admittedly limited common ends through social engagement.

For Koskenniemi, structures of power determine all social outcomes. Material conditions dictate results. Koskenniemi believes that the possibility of formal legal argument is the only frame in which agents can be heard, and that is why he is so committed to the 'culture of formalism' as a limited form of international constitutionalism. Yet, he admits that the culture of formalism proves to be decidedly weak: the 'hearing' that states are afforded cannot result in any social or legal change because of law's indeterminacy and its structural biases. For good lawyers 'any' argument is possible and holds equal validity, so no argument can persuade. Indeed, any 'rule' created in institutions of law will be equally opposable by a contrary rule – all rules are fundamentally indeterminate. (We will come back to this important point when we discuss an alternative view, our 'culture of legality'.) Moreover, at the moment of 'decision' the biases of structure come into play and the result is determined not by argument at all, but by power as exercised in a given institutional setting.[23]

In short, the culture of formalism in law is, for Koskenniemi, the only way that adversaries can be constructed as legally equal. At the same time, Koskenniemi's chosen realism means that law can do nothing more. There is a promise of justice, eternally unfulfilled.

6.3   The Power of Agency

Koskenniemi argues that the structures of law cannot impose a discipline on the structures of material power.[24] Agents may be granted a voice through formal legal argument, but they will win or lose at the point of decision depending upon the institutional structure in which they are arguing, what Koskenniemi calls 'structural biases'. There is a tiny hint of hope in that formal equality will mean that a more powerful agent will not be able to directly dictate a legal result to a less powerful agent. However, the very institutional structures in which the arguments are being made will have been shaped by existing distributions of power – the resulting determinism is only slightly less direct. Such an insipid hope!

Oddly, the only truly empowered agents in Koskenniemi's legal universe are international lawyers. They are not constrained in any way by law except that they must make arguments that state the concrete in seemingly universal terms; they must adhere to what Koskenniemi sees as the structure of legal argument – a culture of formalism. But 'universalism' is itself false and rules are indeterminate, so every argument is equally possible. There is no real distinction between good and bad legal argument. Decisions will be political, an 'anti-formal choice':[25]

> The argumentative architecture allows *any* decision, and thus also the critique of any decision without the question of the professional competence of the decision-maker ever arising.[26]

The implication is that 'competent practice' in international law is nothing more than an ability to argue; 'competence is the ability to use grammar in order to generate meaning by doing things in argument'.[27] Arguments merely 'justify' outcomes, because legal argument is rooted simply in an ability to manipulate the antimonies of fact and law, consent and justice and form and substance.[28] International lawyers seem to be the ultimate 'free agents' whose only responsibility is to make an argument of whatever sort, grounded in an asserted universalism that is admittedly false. Oddly, the agents (states, for example) represented by those same lawyers are absolutely unfree, because all they can do is see arguments made that will never persuade and then be subjected to the rules imposed through institutions purely on the basis of power.

We share Koskenniemi's focus on 'practice' as the best explanatory vehicle to understand the operation of law, and of its effects in the world. However, we understand 'practice' very differently, in the light of constructivist international relations scholarship that highlights the mutually constitutive nature of agency and structure. On the one hand, agents generate and promote particular understandings, whether through norm entrepreneurship or through the work of epistemic communities. As we have detailed above, shared understandings then emerge, evolve or fade through processes of social learning.[29] On the other hand, once in existence, shared understandings become 'structures' that shape how actors perceive themselves and the world, how they form interests and set priorities, and how they make arguments or evaluate others' arguments.[30]

For us, agents (or what we also call 'actors') matter as much as structures and they are connected through practice. On our interactional account, legal practice is a distinctive type of social practice, framed and deeply shaped by the criteria of legality. Whereas Koskenniemi sees law's formalism constraining only to the extent that lawyers must argue in a certain way, we see the 'practice' of law as containing structural elements that more strongly affect what can be argued as 'law'. For Koskenniemi, to make a formally valid legal argument one must only make a particular claim in terms that are universally applicable (even though the invocation of the universal is essentially 'false'). What is more, given Koskenniemi's fundamental commitment to dialectical argument, there is no boundary to what can be argued: everything and its opposite is equally valid.

We agree that making arguments that are not openly self-serving is a core element of competent practice. That is why legal claims must be, in Fuller's terms, 'general'. We suggest that all legal interaction must be open to diverse participants and interests, so that resulting norms are applicable to all. But to insist upon 'universal' international law, as does Koskenniemi,[31] is to ask much more of international law. By asserting international law's universalism, Koskenniemi sets up the inevitable sense of failure that he wants to project upon law, making it seem obvious that the promise of justice can never be fulfilled.

All international lawyers are aware of the aspiration towards 'universalism', but equally aware that it is often merely asserted or falsely projected as a pretext for self-interested claims. In this sense, Koskenniemi's argument may seem banal. But it carries import: simply calling for generality – that a prohibition, requirement or permission be generally applicable, a rule rather than an ad hoc standard – is less extravagant than calling for universalism.[32] The latter is unattainable; the former may be attained even when interests differ. At the same time, the requirement of generality can also make it harder for actors to invoke universalism, precisely because it will tend to highlight false invocations of universalism, as it did when senior US officials argued for new norms on 'pre-emptive' force that they would not have accepted if claimed by other states.[33] In other words, the requirement of generality helps law provide a middle ground between the specific and the universal – between 'apology and utopia'.[34]

In any event, generality is only one of the requirements of legality. Although it plays a significant role, it cannot bear the full load of creating an authentic sense of obligation (Koskenniemi's 'mystery'). As we have detailed above, what one can argue as a matter of competent practice is disciplined by a range of what we call 'criteria of legality', internal requirements that must be met if law is to generate fidelity and produce obligation. At times Koskenniemi acknowledges the importance of process values such as accountability, transparency, neutrality and reciprocity that are close to the criteria of legality. He does this in the context of framing particular claims in universal terms. Koskenniemi argues that his culture of formalism 'constitutes a horizon of universality, embedded in a culture of restraint, a commitment to listening to others' claims and taking them into account'.[35] But these values turn out to be unable to do any useful work because of the ultimate indeterminacy of rules. Whatever the process, however much certain process values might aspire to project justice and produce the mystery of obligation, at the moment of decision, the legal result is radically indeterminate: any given rule is matched by an opposite, or at least by an exception that destroys any meaning in the rule. In other words, and fundamentally for Koskenniemi, law has no purchase whatsoever on power.

Although we accept and indeed agree with Koskenniemi's critique of the false universalism of legal claims that are either self-centred or frank assertions of power, we part company with him in a fundamental way. Our interactional understanding of international law treats the criteria of legality as constitutive of law when matched with continuing practices that uphold the criteria. Importantly, these criteria exert constraints upon power, while obviously not excluding its relevance in legal analysis. The criteria and practice of legality also enable agents to communicate their claims in a grammar that is understood by other agents as being disciplined; as meeting requirements that generate a sense of reciprocity in submitting to a shared Rule of Law. Without that sense of reciprocity, law cannot generate fidelity or 'mystery' and power will act without legal constraint.

6.4   Syria as a 'Lawmaking Moment': Agency and Structure in the Prohibition on the Use of Force

As we suggested earlier, international legal norms are produced and maintained through practice. When interactions among international actors generate shared understandings that meet requirements of legality and are upheld by practices of legality, international law governs actors' relations. In this section, we illustrate our argument through a concrete example, involving the crisis in Syria triggered by atrocities perpetrated against local populations, including use of chemical weapons in 2013, and the attendant efforts to reshape the prohibition on the use of force by asserting exceptions based on the responsibility to protect and the doctrine of humanitarian intervention, respectively.

We aim to show that the requirements and practices of a 'culture of legality' have considerably more 'bite' than Martti Koskenniemi's 'culture of formalism'. Our Syrian example reveals that some norms in international law are grounded in genuinely 'shared' understandings; they are more than just 'structural biases' rooted in material power. What is more, precisely because the creation and maintenance of shared understandings are collective processes, individual actors, even powerful ones, cannot dictate the content of international law. In a 'culture of legality', it is not possible for international lawyers to argue 'anything' or for influential states to shift the law to suit their preferences. Actors may well invoke the law and assert legal claims in self-interested ways. But those arguments will only prevail as legal arguments if they are grounded in shared understandings that meet the requirements of legality. Legal argumentation is constrained by the requirements of legality as well as by other actors' reassertion of those requirements through sustained practices of legality. Furthermore, because legal norms must meet the criteria of legality, not all normative claims will be effective in generating new legal norms.

Debates over the crisis in Syria may, at first glance, appear to bear out Koskenniemi's fear that international law enables universalism to be falsely invoked to overcome constraints imposed by law. Whereas in Kosovo in the late 1990s,[36] the debate swirled around the uneasy relationship between 'legitimacy' and 'legality' in the justifications offered by NATO members for intervention, the atrocities perpetrated in Syria, culminating in vicious chemical weapons attacks in 2013, prompted various 'universalist' arguments in support of intervention. For US President Obama, the chemical weapons attacks were 'an assault on human dignity' and risked 'making a mockery of the global prohibition on the use of chemical weapons'.[37] Former US State Department Legal Advisor Harold Koh opined that 'under certain highly constrained circumstances' international law allowed states to 'use or threaten force for genuinely humanitarian purposes'.[38] Perhaps acknowledging the difficulties of this argument, Koh called on the US and its allies to 'treat Syria as a lawmaking moment' to reframe international law.[39]

The UK did attempt to do just that, asserting that 'intervention may be permitted ... in exceptional circumstances where the Security Council is unwilling or unable to act in order to avert a humanitarian catastrophe'.[40] Meanwhile, the former UK Foreign Office Legal Advisor, Sir Daniel Bethlehem, appeared to admit that international law does not in fact permit humanitarian intervention.[41] But he asserted that 'there is room for a different view', and that 'an analysis that simply relies on ... Article 2(4), and its related principles of non-intervention and sovereignty, is overly simplistic'.

6.4.1 Shared Understandings versus Structural Bias

Contemporary international law does at times strain under the tension between its foundational norms concerning the protection of fundamental human rights and those concerning the prohibition on the use of force. A set of basic human rights norms exists the violation of which can be said to be the common concern of all states. This proposition is reflected, for example, in the rise of international criminal law, most obviously through the notions of war crimes, crimes against humanity and genocide. Pursuant to the rules on state responsibility, breaches of these norms legally entitle all states to hold violators accountable, and also require them not to facilitate the violations and, arguably, to help bring them to an end through appropriate action in response.[42] But, leaving aside the question how strongly shared these latter propositions actually are among international actors, the scheme provides that third states can take only 'lawful measures', measures *not* involving the use of force.[43] That is because the prohibition on the threat or use of force is also a foundational legal norm. As we shall see, for good or ill, it may even be a stronger norm than those protecting human rights.

In earlier work, we have demonstrated that Article 2(4) of the UN Charter, along with the other principles highlighted by Bethlehem, remains one of the most widely and deeply shared understandings in international society.[44] The opening paragraph of the preamble to the UN Charter expresses members' determination to 'save succeeding generations from the scourge of war, which twice in our lifetime has brought untold sorrow to mankind'. Accordingly, the Charter enshrines an absolute prohibition on the inter-state use of force, modified by only two exceptions: self-defence, and UN Security Council authorization under Chapter VII of the Charter. It does not envisage humanitarian intervention.

Even the proposition that the Security Council could authorize such an intervention within a state was initially controversial, given that the Council's original Chapter VII mandate revolved around the maintenance of *international* peace and security. Although states came to accept that the Security Council could intervene in humanitarian crises, its actual capacity to do so was severely constrained by the veto power of the Council's five permanent member states.[45] Indeed, its inability to act in Kosovo in 1999, due to the prospect of a Russian veto, as well as the lack of solid legal foundation for the subsequent NATO intervention, provided the immediate impetus for the elaboration of the concept of the responsibility to protect.[46]

The responsibility to protect, as later endorsed by the UN General Assembly in the 2005 UN World Summit Outcome,[47] builds on the basic legal framework sketched out above. It constitutes an attempt to square the normative circle, outlining three 'pillars' that are used to build a structure that supports both human rights protection and the rules on the use of force. We will see below that the stability of that structure is doubtful. On the one hand, while emphasizing the primary responsibility of all states to protect their own populations against genocide, war crimes, ethnic cleansing, and crimes against humanity (first pillar), the Outcome document also confirms that such abuses give rise to a common responsibility of all states to help protect vulnerable populations through 'appropriate diplomatic, humanitarian and other peaceful means' (second pillar). On the other hand, when it comes to the use of force, the Outcome document confirms that the authorization of the Security Council is needed for collective action (third pillar).[48]

The responsibility to protect quickly gathered adherents,[49] perhaps because it attempts to resolve the long-standing tension between international law's humanitarian and anti-war norms, and perhaps because, as cast in the Outcome document, it did not actually purport to change international law.[50] The Security Council began to invoke the responsibility to protect shortly after its endorsement in the Outcome document, first in April 2006, in Resolution 1674 on the protection of civilians in armed conflict and next in August 2006, in Resolution 1706, which authorized a peacekeeping mission for Darfur.[51]

In February 2011, in what many observers at the time saw as a coming of age for the responsibility to protect norm,[52] the Council unanimously adopted Resolution 1970 on Libya. The Council recalled 'the Libyan authorities' responsibility to protect its population',[53] and, acting under Chapter VII, referred the situation in Libya, involving 'widespread and

systematic attacks ... against the civilian population [that] may amount
to crimes against humanity' to the International Criminal Court (ICC).[54]
Less than a month later, the Council reiterated this assessment in Resolution 1973 and authorized member states to take military action. Specifically, it authorized member states to take 'all necessary measures ...
to protect civilians and civilian populated areas ... while excluding a
foreign occupation force of any form on any part of Libyan territory'.[55]

Russia and China did not block the adoption of the resolution at the
time, but allowed its adoption by abstaining, along with Brazil, Germany
and India. These abstentions signalled that the shared understanding
supporting the responsibility to protect norm was less than robust. Each
of these states had significant reservations, with Brazil and Germany
questioning the efficacy of forcible intervention, India considering it to
be premature, China reiterating its categorical rejection of the use of
force for humanitarian reasons, and Russia concerned about slippage
into a large-scale intervention.[56]

The apparent high point for the responsibility to protect norm quickly
turned into a low point as the NATO intervention proceeded. NATO not
only established no-fly zones, but also provided general support to rebel
forces, attacked Libyan military assets and ultimately precipitated regime
change in the country. Libya's ruler, Muammar Gaddafi, was deposed
and eventually killed and a new government was installed. The reaction by other states was swift. Then-Russian Prime Minister Vladimir
Putin compared the operation to the 2003 intervention in Iraq and to a
'medieval call for a crusade'. China emphasized its opposition to an 'abuse
of force causing more civilian casualties'. Brazil, Germany and India each
expressed their misgivings, and the African Union demanded an immediate halt to the NATO attacks.[57] These reactions buttressed other states'
temporarily suppressed reservations concerning the responsibility to protect. Although a majority of states had nominally supported the norm as
captured in the Outcome document, many states, especially members of
the Non-Aligned Movement, had serious concerns about its third pillar
concerning the authorization of the use of force through the Security
Council.[58]

To be sure, after Libya, the Security Council adopted a number of other
resolutions that invoked the responsibility to protect.[59] But the disagreements surrounding the intervention in Libya carried over to the Security Council's handling of the continuing humanitarian crisis in Syria.
Notwithstanding the mounting evidence of atrocities and urgent calls for
action,[60] the Council was slow to confront Syrian human rights abuses.

China and Russia, although condemning the killing of innocent civilians, vetoed three resolutions intended to increase the pressure on the Syrian regime. In so doing, they emphasized Syria's sovereignty, political independence and right to non-interference.[61] China underscored its opposition to 'military intervention under the pretext of humanitarianism' and 'externally imposed solution[s] aimed at forcing regime change'.[62] Russia noted that 'the situation in Syria cannot be considered in the Council separately from the Libyan experience'. Indeed, according to Russia, the international community was 'alarmed' by the notion that Libya might be 'a model for future actions of NATO in implementing the responsibility to protect'.[63]

In the face of the rapidly mounting death toll in Syria and the government's ruthless disregard for its population, the members of the Security Council became increasingly frustrated with what they perceived to be China and Russia's intransigence. Some members expressed their displeasure in strong terms, with Morocco voicing 'great regret and disappointment',[64] Pakistan asserting that the situation recalled 'two thousand years ago Pontius Pilate, washing his hands and saying, I have nothing to do with this',[65] Germany labelling the Council's failure to act a 'scandal',[66] the US expressing its 'disgust',[67] and the UK going so far as to name China and Russia directly, stating it was 'appalled by the[ir] decision ... to veto'.[68]

The use of chemical weapons in Syria in August 2013, and possibly also assertions by the US and the UK governments that they could take military action against Syria without Security Council authorization, finally changed the dynamics such that the Security Council was able to pass two resolutions in response to the escalating crisis. In September 2013, after the US and Russia reached agreement to allow for the destruction of Syrian chemical weapons,[69] the Council adopted Resolution 2118, which set out a destruction regime. The Council also decided 'in the event of non-compliance with this resolution, ... to impose measures under Chapter VII of the United Nations Charter'.[70] In Resolution 2139, adopted in February 2014, the Council focussed on the 'significant and rapid deterioration of the humanitarian situation in Syria' and demanded 'that all parties, in particular the Syrian authorities, promptly allow rapid, safe and unhindered humanitarian access for UN humanitarian agencies and their implementing partners'.[71] The Council also expressed its intent to take further steps in the case of non-compliance, but a reference to Chapter VII was notably absent.

The most important feature of these two resolutions, for present purposes, is that neither makes any reference whatsoever to the responsibility to protect, not even to its first pillar (the primary responsibility of each state to protect its own population). The same is true for a French draft resolution concerning the referral of the Syrian situation to the ICC.[72] Still, when the Security Council finally voted on the proposed resolution, its adoption was vetoed by China and Russia.[73]

However, bringing the international debate back full circle to the Kosovo crisis, two major Western powers renewed their claims that protective force could be used without Security Council authorization. Yet, the US and UK justificatory approaches were different. As we have seen, the US President, in explaining why the US considered a military intervention to be warranted, at least in theory, invoked neither the responsibility to protect nor the concept of humanitarian intervention. The UK, by contrast, argued that in exceptional circumstances, such as those it considered to be present in Syria, individual states would be permitted to act under the doctrine of humanitarian intervention. Perhaps most importantly, according to the UK, 'the legal basis of humanitarian intervention and the concept of the responsibility to protect are not the same thing'.[74]

These developments had significant implications for the responsibility to protect norm, as well as for the rules governing the use of force for humanitarian purposes more generally. Although the responsibility to protect emerged because the underlying idea seemed to be supported by widely shared understandings,[75] the shared ground concerning the collective use of force pillar of the norm was fragile, and seemed to be decaying. The failure of the Security Council to invoke the responsibility to protect in relation to the crisis in Syria underscored this point, with China and Russia pulling back their tentative support for the collective use of force and retrenching into a stance of categorical rejection of intervention on humanitarian grounds.

It is certainly true that a wide range of states expressed outrage with the Chinese and Russian stance concerning Syria. But the responsibility to protect norm remained strongly contested. Its development appeared to have stalled, at least as far as the collective use of force pillar was concerned. The resurgence of debates on the legality of unilateral intervention highlights dissatisfaction with the Security Council process. But the overwhelming majority of states continued to sidestep the question of the legality of unilateral intervention, or rejected it outright. The UK and US found themselves virtually alone in their effort to revive arguments for unilateral intervention, Belgium being the only other state that explicitly claimed a right to intervene in Kosovo in 1999.[76] A large number of states and commentators forcefully rejected the notion at the time, and continue to do so.[77] Indeed, the Libyan experience seems to have strengthened the resolve of many states to resist any use of force justified on humanitarian grounds.

In other words, the prohibition on the use of force proved to be remarkably resilient, with a multitude of actors working to maintain it in the face of renewed arguments for an humanitarian exception. We suggest that the norm prohibiting the use of force is not merely a 'structural bias', but a shared understanding. Interestingly, it was the strongest military power, and one of its closest and relatively most powerful allies, that argued for a unilateral exception to the prohibition. If the 'structure' of decision making always dictated results, as Koskenniemi argues, one would have expected the US and its allies to 'win' this argument. They had a 'universal' claim of human rights protection on their side, and the material power to act. Yet, it would seem as if, in the clash between human rights norms and the norms on the use of force, the latter were more strongly and widely held. Neither the norm entrepreneurs promoting the responsibility to protect nor the powerful actors asserting the legality of unilateral humanitarian intervention were able to shift the normative framework.

We do not argue here that this normative result is either positive or negative for global society, merely that the practice of legality surrounding the prohibition on the use of force remains vital. This effect contradicts Koskenniemi's claims that structural biases dictate results and that agency is weak in the international arena.

6.4.2 Agency and the Culture of Legality

As we argued above, legal norms are rooted in shared social understandings. Yet, many social norms exist that never reach the threshold of legal normativity, a threshold marked by adherence to specific criteria of legality and the presence of a continuing practice of legality. We argue that these requirements of what might be called a 'culture of legality' impose real discipline on actors as they invoke legal norms or seek to build new law. We suggest that this discipline is far stronger than the 'formal equality' provided by Koskenniemi's 'culture of formalism'. An analysis through the lens of the 'culture of legality' provides additional insights into why efforts to anchor the responsibility to protect in international law or advance a legal doctrine of humanitarian intervention may face an uphill battle. We begin by focussing upon the responsibility to protect norm, followed by observations on the implications for the prohibition on the use of force generally and the concept of humanitarian intervention.

Looking first at the criteria of legality, it is clear that the inclusion of the responsibility to protect in the Outcome document served some aspects of the promulgation requirement. It did not promulgate the norm into law, of course. But it did publicize the parameters of the norm, parameters around which the legal debate has revolved since. The fact that the Outcome document tied the responsibility to protect to a set of established international crimes significantly enhanced the clarity of the triggering events and scope of the norm. This framing also helps ensure the norm's consistency with existing international law, thereby addressing the requirements of non-contradiction and constancy over time. In limiting the responsibility to protect to 'genocide, war crimes, ethnic cleansing and crimes against humanity', the Outcome document tied the responsibility to protect to norms that are often considered to have both *erga omnes* effect and *jus cogens* status.[78] The first and second pillars of the responsibility to protect could be seen as specific articulations of the general consequences that international law attaches to the violation of *jus cogens* and *erga omnes* norms. However, as is well known, international practice invoking these consequences remains scarce.[79]

The norm's third pillar maps onto the existing law on the use of force, keeping recourse to force firmly tied to Security Council action under Chapter VII. However, the Outcome document left open whether collective action presupposes that a situation involving the triggering crimes must first be determined to constitute a threat to international peace and security, whether all such situations would constitute threats to peace and security, or whether the Security Council can intervene whenever a state is 'manifestly failing' to protect its population. The Council's sole Chapter VII resolution on the responsibility to protect, Resolution 1973 on Libya, suggests that the determination of a threat to peace and security does remain a threshold requirement. As a result, the third pillar of the responsibility to protect remains tied to a deliberately fluid and broadly political decision-making criterion. This assessment is reinforced by the Outcome document's reference to 'case-by-case' decisions on the use of force. This terminology suggests there is no obligation on the part of the Council to intervene under Chapter VII even when the triggering events are manifestly present. Rather, the framing of the third pillar maintains space for political assessments and tends to weaken the legality of the responsibility to protect as regards the requirements of generality, clarity and constancy over time. Concerns regarding the generality of the norm are heightened by the limited membership of the Security Council, and the role of the five permanent members in its decision making, notably through their veto power.

In light of these features of the responsibility to protect as articulated in the Outcome document, it is not surprising that many of the interventions in the 2009 General Assembly debate raised concerns about its third pillar.[80] Furthermore, the main proposals for further development of the norm could be seen as aimed at strengthening the legality of the norm. For example, calls for a more representative Security Council addressed the concern about generality. Questions as to who would decide whether a crisis situation involved a triggering crime and requests for clarification of the circumstances in which the Security Council could resort to collective action addressed the clarity requirement, as well as the delineation between legal and political space.[81]

In turn, the call by many states for guidelines on the use of force underscores the importance of generality, clarity and constancy. Such guidelines would enhance the legality of the norm by subjecting case-by-case decisions to overarching criteria that identify the extreme and exceptional cases to which military intervention should be restricted. They would also help highlight cases in which force should in fact be used, and demand a reasoned justification of inaction.[82] Finally, the call for non-use of the veto in cases involving one of the listed crimes[83] is also related to legality considerations. The veto power for the five permanent members undercuts the generality of the protective force option, and weakens the potential for consistent decision making by the Council.[84] However, there are no indications that a sufficient number of states, let alone key states such as China, Russia, the UK and the US have any appetite for the development of guidelines on the use of force or the use of the veto. In many ways, then, the criteria of legality are not met by the existing responsibility to protect framework, and efforts to promote the criteria have proven to be ineffective.

We now turn to the proposition that robust practices of legality (norm application that also satisfies the requirements of legality) are necessary for a norm to emerge, and to be maintained, as law. As noted above, Fuller, whose work focussed on domestic law, captured this idea in the requirement that official action be congruent with existing rules. He emphasized the need for 'reciprocity' between officials and citizens in the creation and sustenance of all law. Reciprocity, in Fuller's conception, means that officials must be able to expect that citizens will 'accept as law and generally observe' the promulgated body of rules. However, in order for these rules to be able to guide their actions, they must meet the criteria of legality. Therefore, conversely, citizens must be able to expect that the government will abide by and apply these rules, that the actions of officials will be congruent with posited law, and consonant with the requirements of legality.[85]

In international society, this deep sense of reciprocity (not the mere coordination of material interests) is even more salient because states are both subjects and lawmakers. To the extent that international law is created without congruence with shared norms and the criteria of legality, neither commitment to law nor a sense of obligation among states will be generated.[86] The central insight is that international legality is created and maintained collectively. To be sure, not all members of international society must be engaged in this effort. International law can withstand individual defiance so long as a solid majority of actors works to uphold legality. But when explicit norms are unrelated to how states and other international actors actually behave, law cannot arise or is eventually destroyed.

The considerations inherent in the congruence requirement shed further light on the trajectory of the third pillar of the responsibility to protect framework. Simply put, past practice falls far short on the need for congruence. Indeed, it has been notoriously uneven. So far, the Council has only once invoked the responsibility to protect in a resolution that authorized collective recourse to force. But, in the eyes of many observers, the ensuing NATO intervention in Libya demonstrated the potential for abuse of the responsibility to protect to effect regime change and other purposes beyond its immediate protective goals. And, as we have seen, the Council's resolutions relating to the humanitarian crisis in Syria, adopted in 2013 and 2014, did not mention the responsibility at all, let alone its third pillar.

As has been rightly pointed out, the strength of the responsibility to protect norm should not be measured simply against whether or not the Council authorizes protective force in all salient cases.[87] The key question is whether it consistently considers and debates its actions within the responsibility to protect framework. But the Council's approach to Syria strongly suggests that the responsibility to protect did not meet even this less stringent test. Although a wide range of states expressed outrage at the Council's blockage on Syria, and in unusually strong terms, assertions of a need for action were not usually tied to invocations of the responsibility to protect. According to a recent analysis, only seven Security Council members made explicit references to the norm during the twelve publicly recorded sessions between October 2011 and April 2013 during which the Council discussed the situation in Syria. None of these states, however, commented on third pillar responsibilities – all remarks were focussed on Syria's primary responsibility towards its population.[88]

It would appear that most states and other observers do not expect the Security Council to apply the responsibility to protect norm with any consistency. Rather, the expectation appears to be that a body in which powerful states hold veto rights will always produce politically and strategically motivated action and inaction. Indeed, the requirement of a practice of legality instructs that it would not be enough to adopt guidelines on the use of force or an undertaking by the permanent members not to exercise their veto. Even if the norm's legality were to be further developed along these lines, the responsibility to protect will not emerge as a global legal norm unless there also emerges a practice that consistently upholds the norm and adheres to the requirements of legality.

The emergence of the responsibility to protect norm illustrates both the potential and the challenges of concerted norm-building efforts. The responsibility to protect norm seemed to be on a steady rise in the early to mid 2000s. The 2011 intervention in Libya may not have destroyed the norm, as some observers suggested,[89] but it certainly dampened the hopes invested in its third pillar. The patterns that we have surveyed, including the scant invocations of the norm in relation to Syria, suggest that its consolidation, let alone further elaboration, stalled or even slipped.

The Security Council remains hobbled by divisions over collective action on humanitarian grounds. Furthermore, and perhaps as a result of these factors, the third pillar of the responsibility to protect, to the extent that it was intended to promote collective action, remains handicapped by the limited extent to which it meets the requirements of legality that we outlined.[90]

As for Harold Koh's suggestion that the 'U.S. and its allies could treat Syria as a lawmaking moment', not for the responsibility to protect, but rather 'to crystallize a limited concept of humanitarian intervention',[91] our interactional law analysis suggests that these efforts ran up against three obstacles. The first was the strongly held understandings concerning the prohibition on the use of force and a concomitant lack of support for any unilateral right to use force on humanitarian grounds. The second rested in the weakly developed legality of the asserted right, illustrated, inter alia, by the divergent criteria advocated by various proponents for identifying conditions under which the intervention would be lawful.[92]

As in the Kosovo situation, the US did not offer any specific basis for the asserted legality of an intervention in Syria.[93] Only the UK decided to seize the moment. It joined Belgium in positing a concrete legal justification for unilateral humanitarian intervention.[94] This justificatory pattern also points to a third obstacle to success in promoting normative change: the absence of congruence or any discernible practice of legality. It is difficult to see how the justificatory moves of two major Western powers and their former advisors on international law could overcome the almost total rejection of unilateral intervention by a majority of states around the world. Again, the agency of states has been asserted in the face of materially powerful actors. That agency was buttressed by the lack of any shared understanding supporting unilateral humanitarian intervention, and by its failure both in meeting the criteria of legality and in even the prospect of generating any continuing practice of legality.

The examples of the interventions in Kosovo, Iraq, and Libya and the ongoing debates around Syria also suggest that individual states' failures to meet the requirements of legality, be it through actions or argumentation, have the potential to reinforce otherwise widely shared norms, prompting other states to push back so as to maintain collective practices of legality. Conversely, arguments that strain the requirements of legality, including in particular the congruence requirement, face an uphill battle, precisely because more is at stake than whether a particular course of action is legal or not. Failure to resist a given argument, if widespread and repeated over time can lead to the erosion of the collective practice of legality that is required to maintain the underlying norm. For better or for worse, the prohibition on the use of force is among the most widely and strongly shared international legal norms. Violations do occur with frequency, but when states assert new or more expansive rights to resort to force, such as an expanded right of self-defence or a unilateral right to humanitarian intervention, the response has tended to be swift and strong. States may be prepared to tolerate the violation of the existing rules, but they seem to have little inclination to widen the scope of exceptions to the prohibition.

6.5   Conclusion

Our short case study on the rule prohibiting the use of force and attempts to extend exceptions on humanitarian grounds, either through the responsibility to protect or humanitarian intervention, shows that international law can provide more than Koskenniemi's shared surface for falsely universal arguments that are decided only on the basis of material power. Attempts by even the most powerful actors to alter the law to provide more freedom for unilateral action did not succeed, even though claims to protect human rights are the most 'universal' imaginable.

Whereas Koskenniemi's 'culture of formality' would allow any argument to be made, with a structurally determined outcome imposed at the moment of decision, a 'culture of legality' allows for analysis of the quality of an argument that is purportedly legal. The quality is evaluated first on the question whether or not a candidate rule is rooted in shared understandings; it is further evaluated on the grounds of its compatibility with the criteria of legality. Finally it is evaluated on the continuing practice of legality that either supports or undercuts the rule. This disciplined set of evaluations undermines the ability of the strong simply to impose their will and it arms weaker members of international society to challenge attempts to project false universalism or purely self-interested politics masking as law. In such evaluation there is a promise of justice, not a guarantee, but a hope that is stronger than the ever-receding hope that flickers in the culture of formality.

The argument supporting an international 'culture of legality' helps to explain how the Rule of Law is possible in an 'agnostic' international society where shared values are limited and where law is only relatively autonomous from power. When agents have the capacity to learn through their social interactions, and where their claims of lawful action must meet criteria of legality and be further supported by a continuing practice based in those criteria, the mystery of obligation is explained. Obligation is internal, created through the legitimacy generated by interactional processes where law-givers and law-takers are reciprocally bound by the same criteria and practices of legality. Agents matter in international law and politics as much as do structures.

Notes

* The authors thank David Dyzenhaus for his incisive comments on an earlier draft and Robert Hersch, JD (2016), for his excellent assistance in the finalization of this chapter. The manuscript was completed in 2014 and the case study presented in section 6.4 of the paper deals with legal debates revolving around an international response to atrocities, including use of chemical weapons, perpetrated against local populations in Syria in 2013. The case study does not address the more recent debates regarding the use of force against terrorist actors operating from Syrian territory.

1. M. Koskenniemi, 'Constitutionalism as Mindset: Reflections on Kantian Themes about International Law and Globalization', *Theoretical Inquiries in Law* 8 (2007): 9–36.
2. Ibid.
3. Ibid., 12.
4. Note that Koskenniemi invoked the theme of 'sacredness' in earlier work. See e.g. M. Koskenniemi, 'The Police in the Temple Order, Justice and the UN: a Dialectical View', *European Journal of International Law* 6 (1995): 325–48 (focusing not on prescribing an attitude, however, but on critiquing the tendency to reduce justice ("temple") to order ("police")).

5. See M. Koskenniemi, 'Law, Teleology and International Relations: an Essay in Counterdisciplinarity', *International Relations* 26 (2011): 12. See also J. L. Dunoff, 'From Interdisciplinarity to Counterdisciplinarity: Is There Madness in Martti's Method?', *Temple International and Comparative Law Journal* 27 (2013): 335–36.

6. M. Koskenniemi, *From Apology to Utopia: The Structure of International Legal Argument*, reissue with a new epilogue (Cambridge: Cambridge University Press, 2006), 597–98 (arguing that 'we know virtually nothing of "understandings" or "beliefs": the insides of social agents remain irreducibly opaque. In fact, consensus-seeking (like appeals to love) may often hide a subtle authoritiarianism').

7. M. Koskenniemi, 'Human Rights, Politics, and Love', *Finnish Year Book of International Law* 79 (2002): 79 (suggesting that '[h]uman rights are like love, both necessary and impossible. We cannot live without them, but we cannot have them, either. As soon as we are safely installed in a social order that promises to guarantee our rights, that order starts to appear oppressively totalitarian').

8. See M. Koskenniemi, 'What is International Law For?', in *The Politics of International Law* (Oxford: Hart, 2011), 266–67 (concluding that 'the justice that animates political community is not one that may be fully attained. Not only is law never justice itself, the two cannot exist side by side. If there is justice, then no law is needed – and if there is law, then there is only a (more or less well-founded) *expectation* of justice').

9. See e.g. Koskenniemi, 'Constitutionalism as Mindset', 13.

10. See e.g. Koskenniemi, *From Apology to Utopia*, 569–70.

11. M. Koskenniemi, 'The Mystery of Legal Obligation', *International Theory* 3 (2011): 319.

12. See Koskenniemi, *From Apology to Utopia*, 590 (arguing that 'the claim of indeterminacy ... is not at all that international legal words are semantically ambivalent [footnote omitted]. It is much stronger ... and states that even where there is no semantic ambivalence whatsoever, international law remains indeterminate because it is based on contradictory premises and seeks to regulate a future in regard to which even single actors' preference remain unsettled').

13. See Koskenniemi, 'Constitutionalism as Mindset', 35 (discussing the transformative political effect of the French Revolution that was 'brought about by the language of constitutionalism'). See also Martti Koskenniemi, 'What Should International Lawyers Learn from Karl Marx?', *Leiden Journal of International Law* 17 (2004): 246 (similarly arguing for the transformative potential of the 'myth' of universalism, but observing that 'an aspect of the difficulty that any fundamental challenge to the iron laws of power must imply' is that this potential 'appears only occasionally, and even then in connection with events of exceptional magnitude, even scandal').

14. J. Brunnée and S. J. Toope, *Legitimacy and Legality in International Law: an Interactional Account* (Cambridge: Cambridge University Press, 2010), 271–349.

15. See generally Brunnée and Toope, *Legitimacy and Legality*, 1–55; J. Brunnée and S. J. Toope, 'Interactional International Law: an Introduction', *International Theory* 3 (2011): 307–18.

16. See Koskenniemi, 'Mystery of Legal Obligation'.

17. Koskenniemi, 'What Is International Law For?', 256–57 (arguing that 'the political significance of formal law – that is, of law irrespective of what interests or preferences particular legislation might seek to advance – is that it expresses the

universalistic principle of inclusion at the outset, making possible the regulative
ideal of a pluralistic international world'. See also J. d'Aspremont, 'The Politics of
Deformalization in International Law', *Goettingen Journal of International Law* 3
(2011): 546.

18. See detailed assessment in Brunnée and Toope, *Legitimacy and Legality*, 126–219.
19. Koskenniemi, *From Apology to Utopia*, 584 (arguing that 'social meaning is generated by individual psychologies, while what those psychologies produce is conditioned by the material conditions in which they are formed').
20. Ibid., 598.
21. See M. Koskenniemi, 'The Politics of International Law – 20 Years Later', *The
European Journal of International Law* 20 (2009): 10.
22. D. Dyzenhaus, 'Hobbes on the International Rule of Law', *Ethics & International
Affairs* 28 (2014): 54.
23. Koskenniemi, *From Apology to Utopia*, 589, 607.
24. Ibid., 598, 607. See also Koskenniemi, 'Law, Teleology and IR', 22.
25. Koskenniemi, *From Apology to Utopia*, 588.
26. Ibid., 589.
27. Ibid., 571, emphasis removed.
28. Ibid., 570, 589.
29. A. Wendt, *Social Theory of International Politics* (Cambridge: Cambridge University
Press, 1999).
30. E. Adler and S. Bernstein, 'Knowledge in Power: the Epistemic Construction of
Global Governance', in M. N. Barnett and R. Duvall (eds), *Power and Global Governance* (Cambridge: Cambridge University Press, 2005), 294.
31. Koskenniemi, 'Law, Teleology and IR', 5. (Surprisingly, given the structural bias of
actual legal decisions, to 'do international law' is to work for the 'good of humanity
itself'.)
32. Ibid., 22 (asserting that '"Rules" by definition universalize single situations').
33. Brunnée and Toope, *Legitimacy and Legality*, 271–349.
34. We thank Robert Hersch for sharpening this point.
35. M. Koskenniemi, '"The Lady Doth Protest Too Much": Kosovo, and the Turn to
Ethics in International Law', *The Modern Law Review* 65 (2002): 174.
36. See Koskenniemi, 'Lady Doth Protest'.
37. B. Obama, 'Statement by the President on Syria', 31 August 2013, www.whitehouse
.gov/the-press-office/2013/08/31/statement-president-syria.
38. H. H. Koh, 'Syria and the Law of Humanitarian Intervention (Part II: International
Law and the Way Forward)', *Just Security*, 2 October 2013, justsecurity.org/2013/
10/02/Koh-Syria-part2.
39. Ibid.
40. See UK Foreign and Commonwealth Office, 'Letter Responding to a Question
from the House of Commons Foreign Affairs Select Committee', 14 January 2014,
justsecurity.org/wp-content/uploads/2014/01/Letter-from-UK-Foreign-Common-
wealth-Office-to-the-House-of-Commons-Foreign-Affairs-Committee-on
-Humanitarian-Intervention-and-the-Responsibility-to-Protect.pdf. See also UK
Prime Minister's Office, 'Chemical Weapon Use by Syrian Regime: UK Government Legal Position', 29 August 2013, www.gov.uk/government/publications/
chemical-weapon-use-by-syrian-regime-uk-government-legal-position/chemical-
weapon-use-by-syrian-regime-uk-government-legal-position-html-version.

41. D. Bethlehem, 'Stepping Back a Moment – the Legal Basis in Favour of a Principle of Humanitarian Intervention', *EJIL: Talk!*, 12 September 2013, www.ejiltalk.org/stepping-back-a-moment-the-legal-basis-in-favour-of-a-principle-of-humanitarian-intervention/.
42. International Law Commission, 'Draft Articles on Responsibility of States for Internationally Wrongful Acts', *Report of the International Law Commission on the Work of Its Fifty-third Session*, UN General Assembly Official Records, 56th Sess., Supplement No. 10, 43, UN Doc. A/56/10 (2001), Draft Article 41.
43. Ibid., Draft Article 50.
44. Brunnée and Toope, *Legitimacy and Legality*, 271–349.
45. M. P. Scharf, *Customary International Law in Times of Fundamental Change: Recognizing Grotian Moments* (New York: Cambridge University Press, 2013), 157–81.
46. Independent International Commission on Kosovo, *The Kosovo Report: Conflict, International Response, Lessons Learned* (Oxford: Oxford University Press, 2000), and International Commission on Intervention and State Sovereignty, *The Responsibility to Protect* (Ottawa, ON: International Development Research Centre, 2001).
47. UN General Assembly, *2005 World Summit Outcome*, UN Doc. A/RES/60/1 (24 October 2005), paras 138–39, www.un.org/summit2005/documents.html.
48. Ibid.
49. For a detailed assessment, see J. Brunnée and S. J. Toope, 'The Responsibility to Protect and the Use of Force: Building Legality?', *Global Responsibility to Protect* 2 (2010): 191–212.
50. J. M. Welch, 'Norm Contestation and the Responsibility to Protect', *Global Responsibility to Protect* 5 (2013): 375–77.
51. UN Security Council (UNSC), *Resolution 1674*, 28 April 2006, UN Doc. S/Res/1674, www.un.org/en/sc/documents/resolutions/2006.shtml. UNSC, *Resolution 1706*, 31 August 2006, www.un.org/en/sc/documents/resolutions/2006.shtml.
52. See J. Morris, 'Libya and Syria: R2P and the Spectre of the Swinging Pendulum', *International Affairs* 89 (2013): 1271. See also A. J. Bellamy, 'Libya and the Responsibility to Protect: the Exception and the Norm', *Ethics & International Affairs* 25 (2011): 263–69.
53. UNSC, *Resolution 1970*, 26 February 2011, UN Doc. S/Res/1970, preamble, www.un.org/en/sc/documents/resolutions/2011.shtml.
54. Ibid., para. 4.
55. UNSC, *Resolution 1973*, 17 March 2011, UN Doc. S/Res/1973, para. 4, www.un.org/en/sc/documents/resolutions/2011.shtml.
56. Morris, 'Libya and Syria', 1272.
57. See B. Smith, V. Miller and A. Lang, 'Military Interventions: Some Comparisons', *UK House of Commons Library Standard Note SNIA 6715*, 29 August 2013, www.parliament.uk/business/publications/research/briefing-papers/SN06715/military-interventions-some-comparisons.
58. See Brunnée and Toope, 'Responsibility to Protect and the Use of Force'.
59. Resolution 1975 (2011) on the situation in Côte d'Ivoire, Resolution 1996 (2011) establishing a peacekeeping mission in South Sudan, and Resolution 2014 (2011) on human rights violations in Yemen.
60. The UN General Assembly and the Human Rights Council condemned the 'widespread and systematic' human rights violations and demanded that the Syrian

government cease all violence and protect its people. The UN High Commissioner for Human Rights recommended that the situation in Syria be referred to the ICC and called upon the Security Council to act upon its responsibility to protect the Syrian population. The UN Secretary-General stressed the need for an urgent solution and his then Special Adviser on the Prevention of Genocide, Adama Dieng, declared in December 2012 that the 'Government of Syria is manifestly failing to protect its population'. See United Nations, 'Background Note: The Responsibility to Protect', April 2013, www.un.org/en/preventgenocide/rwanda/pdf/Backgrounder %20R2P%202013.pdf.

61. See UNSC, *Sixty-Sixth Year, 6627th Meeting*, UN Doc. S/PV.6627, 4 October 2011, www.securitycouncilreport.org/atf/cf/%7B65BFCF9B-6D27-4E9C-8CD3-CF6E4F-F96FF9%7D/Golan%20Heights%20S%20PV%206627.pdf, and UNSC, *Sixty-Seventh Year, 6711th Meeting*, UN Doc. S/PV.6711, 4 February 2012, www.securitycouncilreport.org/atf/cf/%7B65BFCF9B-6D27-4E9C-8CD3-CF6E4FF96FF9 %7D/Syria%20SPV%206711.pdf.

62. See UNSC, *Sixty-Seventh Year, 6826th Meeting*, UN Doc. S/PV.6826, 30 August 2012, 33, www.securitycouncilreport.org/atf/cf/%7B65BFCF9B-6D27-4E9C-8CD3 -CF6E4FF96FF9%7D/s˙pv˙6826.pdf.

63. UNSC, *6627th Meeting*, 2011, 4.

64. UNSC, *6711th Meeting*, 2.

65. Ibid., 10.

66. Ibid., 4.

67. Ibid., 5.

68. Ibid., 6.

69. A. Gearan and S. Wilson, 'U.S., Russia Reach Agreement on Seizure of Syrian Chemical Weapons Arsenal', *Washington Post*, 14 September 2013, www.washingtonpost.com/world/us-russia-reach-agreement-on-seizure-of-syrian -chemical-weapons-arsenal/2013/09/14/69e39b5c-1d36-11e3-8685-5021e0c41964 ˙story.html?utm˙term=.5e00bf3a8a15.

70. UNSC, *Resolution 2118*, 27 September 2013, www.un.org/News/Press/docs/2013/ sc11135.doc.htm.

71. UNSC, *Resolution 2139*, 22 February 2014, www.un.org/News/Press/docs/2014/ sc11292.doc.htm.

72. Text available at N. Abi Saab, 'French Draft Resolution Refers Syria to the ICC', 12 May 2014, un-report.blogspot.ca/2014/05/french-draft-resolution-on-icc-syria .html?spref=tw.

73. UN News Centre, 'Russia, China Block Security Council Referral of Syria to International Criminal Court', 22 May 2014, www.un.org/apps/news/story.asp? NewsID=47860#.U4XwX2dOUeg.

74. UK Foreign and Commonwealth Office, 'Letter Responding to Foreign Affairs Select Committee'.

75. Brunnée and Toope, 'Responsibility to Protect and the Use of Force'.

76. D. Akande, 'The Legality of Military Action in Syria: Humanitarian Intervention and the Responsibility to Protect', *EJIL: Talk!*, 28 August 2013, www.ejiltalk.org/ humanitarian-intervention-responsibility-to-protect-and-the-legality-of-military-action-in-syria/.

77. G-77, 'Declaration of the South Summit', 10–14 April 2000, www.g77.org/ summit/Declaration_G77Summit.htm; see also D. Kaye, 'Harold Koh's Case for

Humanitarian Intervention', *Just Security*, 7 October 2013, justsecurity.org/2013/
10/07/kaye-kohs-case/.

78. E. Strauss, 'A Bird in the Hand Is Worth Two in the Bush – on the Assumed Legal
Nature of the Responsibility to Protect', *Global Responsibility to Protect* 1 (2009):
291–323.

79. J. Brunnée, 'International Legal Accountability through the Lens of the Law
of State Responsibility', *Netherlands Yearbook of International Law* 36 (2005):
21–56.

80. P. Quinton-Brown, 'Mapping Dissent: the Responsibility to Protect and Its State
Critics', *Global Responsibility to Protect* 5 (2013): 260–82.

81. Brunnée and Toope, 'Responsibility to Protect and the Use of Force'.

82. Ibid.

83. A. Blätter and P. D. Williams, 'The Responsibility Not to Veto', *Global Responsibility
to Protect* 3 (2011): 301–22.

84. Brunnée and Toope, 'Responsibility to Protect and the Use of Force', 209.

85. Lon L. Fuller, 'Human Interaction and the Law', *American Journal of Jurisprudence*
14 (1969): 1–36, reprinted in Kenneth I. Winston (ed.), *The Principles of Social
Order: Selected Essays of Lon L. Fuller*, rev. ed. (Oxford: Hart, 2001), 235.

86. Brunnée and Toope, *Legitimacy and Legality*, 53–54.

87. Welch, 'Norm Contestation and the Responsibility to Protect', 368.

88. Morris, 'Libya and Syria'.

89. D. Rieff, 'R2P, RIP', *New York Times*, 7 November 2011, www.nytimes.com/2011/
11/08/opinion/r2p-rip.html?pagewanted=all&_r=0.

90. The same, of course, is true for all Security Council action under Chapter VII, which
serves to highlight the importance of political rather than legal considerations in
the Council's decision-making.

91. Koh, 'Syria and the Law of Humanitarian Intervention'.

92. A. Nollkaemper, 'Intervention in Syria and International Law: Inside or Out?',
Opinio Juris, 1 September 2013, opiniojuris.org/2013/09/01/syria-insta-symposium
-andre-nollkaemper-intervention-syria-international-law-inside/.

93. See Obama, 'Statement by the President on Syria'. This failure to articulate a clear
legal argument was precisely what prompted Harold Koh, the former US State
Department Legal Advisor, to call on the Administration to treat Syria as a law-
making moment.

94. UK Prime Minister's Office, 'Chemical Weapon Use by Syrian Regime'; UK Foreign and Commonwealth Office, 'Letter Responding to Foreign Affairs Select
Committee'.

Bibliography

Adler, Emanuel, and Steven Bernstein. 'Knowledge in Power: The Epistemic Construction of Global Governance'. In Michael N. Barnett and Raymond Duvall
(eds), *Power in Global Governance* (Cambridge: Cambridge University Press,
2005).

Akande, Dapo. 'The Legality of Military Action in Syria: Humanitarian Intervention
and the Responsibility to Protect'. *EJIL: Talk!*, 28 August 2013.

Bellamy, Alex J. 'Libya and the Responsibility to Protect: the Exception and the Norm'. *Ethics & International Affairs* 25 (2011): 263–69.

Bethlehem, Daniel. 'Stepping Back a Moment – the Legal Basis in Favour of a Principle of Humanitarian Intervention'. *EJIL: Talk!*, 12 September 2013.

Blätter, Ariela, and Paul D. Williams. 'The Responsibility Not to Veto'. *Global Responsibility to Protect* 3 (2011): 301–22.

Brunnée, Jutta. 'International Legal Accountability through the Lens of the Law of State Responsibility'. *Netherlands Yearbook of International Law* 36 (2005): 21–56.

Brunnée, Jutta, and Stephen J. Toope. 'Interactional International Law: an Introduction'. *International Theory* 3 (2011): 307–18.

   Legitimacy and Legality in International Law: An Interactional Account (Cambridge: Cambridge University Press, 2010).

   'The Responsibility to Protect and the Use of Force: Building Legality?' *Global Responsibility to Protect* 2 (2010): 191–212.

d'Aspremont, Jean. 'The Politics of Deformalization in International Law'. *Goettingen Journal of International Law* 3 (2011): 503–50.

Dunoff, Jeffrey L. 'From Interdisciplinarity to Counterdisciplinarity: Is There Madness in Martti's Method'. *Temple International and Comparative Law Journal* 27 (2013): 309–37.

Dyzenhaus, David. 'Hobbes on the International Rule of Law'. *Ethics & International Affairs* 28 (2014): 53–64.

Fuller, Lon L. 'Human Interaction and the Law'. *The American Journal of Jurisprudence* 14 (1969): 1–36.

Gearan, Anne, and Scott Wilson. 'U.S., Russia Reach Agreement on Seizure of Syrian Chemical Weapons Arsenal'. *Washington Post*, 14 September 2013.

Independent International Commission on Kosovo. *The Kosovo Report: Conflict, International Response, Lessons Learned* (Oxford: Oxford University Press, 2000).

International Commission on Intervention and State Sovereignty. *The Responsibility to Protect* (Ottawa, ON: International Development Research Centre, 2001).

Kaye, David. 'Harold Koh's Case for Humanitarian Intervention'. *Just Security*, 7 October 2013.

Koh, Harold H. 'Syria and the Law of Humanitarian Intervention (Part II: International Law and the Way Forward)'. *Just Security*, 2 October 2013.

Koskenniemi, Martti. 'Constitutionalism as Mindset: Reflections on Kantian Themes about International Law and Globalization'. *Theoretical Inquiries in Law* 8 (2007): 9–36.

   From Apology to Utopia: the Structure of International Legal Argument, reissue with a new epilogue (Cambridge: Cambridge University Press, 2006).

'Human Rights, Politics, and Love'. *Finnish Yearbook of International Law* 13 (2004): 79–94.

'"The Lady Doth Protest Too Much": Kosovo, and the Turn to Ethics in International Law'. *Modern Law Review* 65 (2002): 159–75.

'Law, Teleology and International Relations: an Essay in Counterdisciplinarity'. *International Relations* 26 (2012): 3–34.

'The Mystery of Legal Obligation'. *International Theory* 3 (2011): 319–25.

'The Police in the Temple Order, Justice and the UN: a Dialectical View'. *European Journal of International Law* 6 (1995): 325–48.

'The Politics of International Law – 20 Years Later'. *European Journal of International Law* 20 (2009): 7–19.

'What Is International Law For?' In *The Politics of International Law* (Oxford: Hart, 2011).

'What Should International Lawyers Learn from Karl Marx?' *Leiden Journal of International Law* 17 (2004): 229–46.

Morris, Justin. 'Libya and Syria: R2p and the Spectre of the Swinging Pendulum'. *International Affairs* 89 (2013): 1265–83.

Nollkaemper, André. 'Intervention in Syria and International Law: Inside or Out?' *Opinio Juris*, 1 September 2013.

Obama, Barack H. 'Statement by the President on Syria'. 31 August 2013.

Quinton-Brown, Patrick. 'Mapping Dissent: the Responsibility to Protect and Its State Critics'. *Global Responsibility to Protect* 5 (2013): 260–82.

Rieff, David. 'R2P, RIP'. *New York Times*, 7 November 2011.

Scharf, Michael P. *Customary International Law in Times of Fundamental Change: Recognizing Grotian Moments* (New York: Cambridge University Press, 2013).

Smith, Ben, Vaughne Miller and Arabella Lang. 'Military Interventions: Some Comparisons'. *UK House of Commons Library Standard Note SNIA 6715*, 29 August 2013.

Strauss, Ekkehard. 'A Bird in the Hand Is Worth Two in the Bush – on the Assumed Legal Nature of the Responsibility to Protect'. *Global Responsibility to Protect* 1 (2009): 291–323.

Welsh, Jennifer M. 'Norm Contestation and the Responsibility to Protect'. *Global Responsibility to Protect* 5 (2013): 365–96.

Wendt, Alexander. *Social Theory of International Politics* (Cambridge: Cambridge University Press, 1999).

Winston, Kenneth I. (ed.). *The Principles of Social Order: Selected Essays of Lon L. Fuller* (Oxford: Hart, 2001).

The Space between Us

Law, Teleology and the New Orientalism of Counterdisciplinarity

NIKOLAS M. RAJKOVIC*

STREPSIADES: *What in god's name [is this instrument], then? Tell me.*
PUPIL: *This one here is for . . . geometry.*
STREPSIADES: *So what's that good for?*
PUPIL: *For measuring land.*
STREPSIADES: *You mean land for settlers?*
PUPIL: *No, land in general.*
STREPSIADES: *Talk about sophisticated! That device is democratic, and useful too.*
PUPIL: *And look, this is a map of the entire world. See? That's Athens right here.*
STREPSIADES: *What do you mean? I don't believe it; I don't see any juries in session . . . but where's Sparta?*
PUPIL: *Let me see; right here.*
STREPSIADES: *So close to us! Do change your minds and move it very far away from us.*
PUPIL: *That's impossible.*
STREPSIADES: *By Zeus, you'll be sorry if you don't!*
– Aristophanes, *The Clouds*[1]

This scene from Aristophanes' comedy plays with perceptions of space, and the full extent might escape even the critical legal eye. What stands in the foreground is an apparently daft and childish Strepsiades who suggests not simply a failure to grasp his physical surroundings but, also, a view of maps as human artefacts drawn to reflect objects among other purposes. On the surface there is an alleged blurring of normativity, symbolism and fact, and the immediate comedy is one of a person who evidently has not grasped what is commonly thought as geographic reality. Yet, when one digs deeper into the performance of this script, appreciating that our reading brings together an Ancient dialogue with a (post)modern mindset, it becomes plausible that the broader comedy might be less about Strepsiades' presumed naivety and more to do with our contemporary failure to seize what 'scientific' mapping has subtly taught us to forget:[2]

every map or geographic representation remains a symbolized image of reality and no less an asset of epistemic, social[3] and economic[4] power. Strepsiades in effect was not naïve but bait serving to lure out spatial fetishisms constituted by the geographical imagination of our scholarly present.[5]

The significance of spatial representation, mapping and geography rings with newfound urgency for disciplinary International Law (IL).[6] This pertains to a growing jurisdictional challenge[7] from disciplinary international relations (IR) which has seen resurgent research on law and politics across a number of theoretical cleavages[8] and hybrid research problems,[9] ranging from international criminal justice, food product safety to climate change. However, the mention of geography might seem odd for international lawyers since it grinds against a 'common sense' division of labour tied to what historical sociology calls perceived 'objective qualities' of professions.[10] In this vein, treaties and cases belong 'objectively' to international lawyers much in the way the notion of space seems the natural stuff of geographers (terrestrial distribution), physicists (matter) or even astronomers (outer space or cosmology). Yet, this functional map misleads since, as historical sociology further notes, the academic and professional division of labour continually changes because, first, objective qualities can materially transform and, second, cultural or subjective interpretation crucially influence the epistemic placement of presumed 'objective qualities'; and this in turn (re)constitutes disciplines and the scale of their tasks.[11]

What does this all have to do with geography and its relevance for the discipline and profession of IL? Strepsiades re-emerges with a familiar intervention: it is about marking one's perceived turf and being well advised to move potential competitors further away when mapping *our place* in any world. To translate this by reworking Martti Koskenniemi's famous opening from his first critique of IR as *the new natural law*: '[Maps] are *politics*; When [disciplinary maps] change, things that previously could not be said are now spoken by [others] ... With a change of [the disciplinary map], new speakers become authoritative'.[12] In this light, the perceived map of the disciplines, and IL's position on that map, gains a crucial and new imperative. Research on international law from IR raises the prospect that the perceived 'objective quality' of international law is now appropriable beyond the discipline,[13] and this elevates the spectre of an evolutionary teleology via IL's potential *marginalization* or even *de-specialization* on the epistemic map of disciplines.[14]

These spatial stakes are not trivial since leading IL scholars and practitioners, such as Philip Allott, James Crawford, Jan Klabbers and Martti Koskenniemi, have each jumped to intervene, and often repeatedly, invoking spatial frames of encroaching deformalization, compromised autonomy and the defence of IL's rightful domain. Collectively, the interventions reveal a European elite resorting to spatial discourses to counteract how particular liberal segments of IR,[15] combined with 'law and economics' scholarship,[16] seem to be challenging the jurisdictional hold of IL over international law as its perceived exclusive domain.[17] What is more, this race to space reveals different representational strategies of asserting IL's *distinctive place* in that interdisciplinary world. For example, Crawford portrays IL as the metaphorical 'home' and discusses interdisciplinarity with the feel of an obscure neighbourhood where threats, promises and frauds lurk.[18] Klabbers deploys more welcoming metaphors, i.e. music and Mozart, to associate but no less hierarchize the relationship between IL and IR: 'the two disciplines have as much in common as the musicologist studying Mozart's string quartets, and the gentleman at the ticket counter trying to sell tickets to next month's performance of *Die Zauberflote*'.[19] Allott appeals directly to physical and trans-Atlantic geography: IR's encroachment relates to an American imperial mind-set which is chronically unreflective, anti-philosophical and infiltrated by foreign policy imperatives.[20]

Yet, it is Koskenniemi's intervention that engages in a more elaborate representational strategy of epistemic mapping and locational geography. With his unveiling of *counterdisciplinarity* to an IR audience,[21] he produces a lucid narrative that attempts to establish, in virtual terms, a continental distinction between what IL and IR *do*. This locational mapping bears affinity to Kant's 'geography of reason'[22] as Koskenniemi provides the (meta)theoretical basis for a geography of disciplinarity between law and the social sciences using Aristotle's distinction between practical judgement (*phronêsis*) and theoretical science (*epistêmê*). Yet, as Koskenniemi illustrates, the power of locational mapping is not merely used to discursively mark IL's place on the nomadic plain of interdisciplinary knowledge, it also grants IL elevated topography vis-à-vis potential challenger(s):

> Interdisciplinary vocabularies of 'scholarship' and 'science' miss what for most international lawyers is the most obvious aspect of our trade: namely, its craft-likeness, its being above all a practice. International law is not a social science. It is not a (theoretical) science at all – that is to say, it does

not operate on the basis of demonstrable, even less empirical truths, nor
with ideas about moral goodness. Legal 'truth' or 'goodness' is concerned
with ... the *correctness* of the legal decision. Even as lawyers may use
empirical arguments from 'theory' and sometimes invoke moral sentiments, the practical reasoning – *phronêsis* – that best characterizes what
lawyers do cannot be reduced to either one or the other ... Above all,
discussing [international law] through a methodological vocabulary borrowed from the social sciences – such as a choice between realism, liberalism, constructivism, for example – while perhaps useful in a political
science context, conveys no sense of the eclectic and pragmatic character
of *legal praxis* ... Law is an argumentative practice that operates in institutional contexts characterized by adversity. Its point is to persuade but
also to 'win' against polemic adversaries.[23]

In this way, Koskenniemi reveals that the disciplinary map assumes a
strategic and geographic imperative, identified by a lawyerly and adversarial awareness that the stakes pertain to *positional superiority* and, crucially,
disciplinary propriety. Hence, it is with this voice of geographic distinction
and topographical elevation that this chapter engages, both analytically
and critically. The aim is to raise awareness among international lawyers
that the geographic move of Koskenniemi's *Counterdisciplinarity* is less
constituted by epistemic facts as it is propelled by an adversarial mind-set
and, pivotally, a cultural geography concerned with imposing the superiority of one place over another.

With this notion of spatial domination, I argue that Edward Said's
Orientalism[24] becomes insightful vis-à-vis his assertion that a 'distribution of geopolitical awareness' has historically informed 'Occidental', or
specifically European, perceptions of alternate places as manifestly different and lesser.[25] This cultural impulse to *orientalize*, and correspondingly
assert a positional superiority,[26] I argue resonates when one probes how
Counterdisciplinarity diminishes a perceived jurisdictional challenge from
IR via an implied locational and topographical geography. Yet, I argue, this
orientalizing move undermines the constant need to assert disciplinary
relevance since its geographic mind-set fails to grasp how all disciplinary
space is profoundly abstract, overlapping and non-terrestrial and thus
unable to sustain positional absolutes and locational reification. Ironically, as this chapter will explain, *Counterdisciplinarity* in effect cultivates
a false sense of geographic security for a doctrinally centred and often
court-fetishizing scholarship in a funding context where disciplines are
no longer central to the definition of subject matter and research problems, which makes IL more vulnerable to losing increasingly heterodox
research on law and politics.

7.1 Knowing *One's* Place: Edward Said and the Geography of Us and Them

Edward Said was a scholar of English and Comparative Literature by occupation, but he considered himself foremost to be a critical 'humanist'[27] concerned with how a spatial discourse had naturalized a profound asymmetry of geo-social relations. *Orientalism*, Said's acclaimed monograph first published in 1978, traces the emergence of Orientalism as a complex representation and discourse which constituted the socio-political notion of 'the Orient', and how this Eurocentric idiom assumed an epistemic authority to personify, manage and subversively rule over non-European peoples, societies and lands.[28] In part, Orientalism was an inquiry into the 'dynamics of contemporaneous history' in the Middle East; yet Said underlined how his critique was most crucially concerned with how a 'protocol of pretended suprapolitical objectivity'[29] imposed an essentialized geography capable of engendering two unequal halves of a known world.

In his monograph, Said traced a series of moments through the history of Britain and France's imperial encounters with peoples that – based on the sunrise – fell to the east of post-Enlightenment Europe. However, Said emphasized that the making of 'the Orient' was not related to fact or navigational reference but rather the elaboration of a cultural and social fiction which arbitrated the 'particular closeness experienced' by Britain and France vis-à-vis the Orient.[30] As such, Orientalism, as it emerged, had a distinct epistemic constitution characterized by both the will to understand others and also the will to dominate them. Therefore, as Said pointed out, these imperial encounters were guided not by 'an inert fact of nature' but rather produced the Orient as a complex 'social fact' through a cultural vocabulary, imagery and, ultimately, geography which gave 'reality and presence' to the man-made frame for asserting systematic difference and superiority:

> We must take seriously Vico's great observation that men make their own history, that what they can know is what they have made, and extend it to geography: as both geographical and cultural entities ... The Orient was Orientalized not only because it was discovered to be 'Oriental' in all those ways considered common-place ... but also because it *could be* – that is, submitted to being – *made* Oriental.[31]

Thus, as Said underscores, the making of the Orient was tied to a discourse and methodology directed at disciplining the perception and cognition of other worlds. Everything imperial Europe came to know about distant 'others' derived from the information mostly provided and ordered by scholars, officials, linguistics, priests and, sometimes, travellers originating from colonizing states. Their letters, dispatches and books constituted the emergent academic discipline of Orientalism; and, as Said notes, this formative field became crucial not merely because it supplied information for the governing of the empire but, more so, it represented the extension of disciplinary and productive power in the most Foucauldian sense: the attempt to intellectually master, via an authoritative ordering of scientific, normative and imaginative knowledge, an object of study for the purpose of asserting political domination.[32]

In this way, Said's analytical framework of Orientalism represents more than an inquiry into a period of imperial history, but rather an exploration into the quiet power of discourses and how their ordering and presenting of knowledge could configure a portion of the human world into a subject of discipline and control.[33] This led Said to assert, in the preface of the 2003 re-publication, how modern imperialism commanded perpetuity owing to the 'epistemological mutation'[34] derived from generations of Orientalist vision which sought to order and present the world through the dualism of 'the self' and 'the other' in a way that naturalized a structured pattern of superiority and domination.[35] A profound dualism distinguished by Orientalism' disciplining ambition and seemingly objective hierarchy: establishing a difference *through nature* to sustain a claim of essential difference vis-à-vis a specific group in a particular place, and thus justify a narrative of organization and distribution of possibilities which *by nature* leads – figuratively – to *their* exclusion and *our* entitlement. As Said explains:

> Indeed, my real argument is that Orientalism is – and does not simply represent – a considerable dimension of modern political-intellectual culture, and as such has less to do with the Orient than it does with 'our' world. Because Orientalism is a cultural and a political fact, then, it does not exist in some archival vacuum; quite the contrary, I think it can be shown that what is thought, said, or even done about the Orient follows (perhaps occurs within) certain distinct and intellectually knowable lines ... Most humanistic scholars are, I think, perfectly happy with the notion that texts exist in contexts, that there is such a thing as intertextuality ... Yet, there is a reluctance to allow that political, institutional and ideological constraints act in the same manner on the individual author ... [P]hilosophers will conduct their discussions of Locke, Hume, and empiricism without ever taking into account that there is an explicit connection in these classic writers between their 'philosophic' doctrines and racial theory, justifications of slavery, or arguments for colonial exploitation. These are

common enough ways by which contemporary scholarship keeps itself pure.[36]

This last point on the common ways scholarship 'keeps' in apparent purity, and thus free from more overt political motive, I argue becomes of central relevance for international lawyers vis-à-vis *Counterdisciplinarity*'s spatial move to ward off jurisdictional challenge. While IR's asserted encroachment may not rise from an actual geographic east, 'the style of thought'[37] that is Orientalism provides a potent modality in how it seeks out essentialized difference in relations of 'particular closeness', and then naturalizes positional imperative. As such, the most geographic iteration of the *Counterdisciplinarity* move, produced by Koskenniemi, with its painstaking narratives that discursively map an essential duality between what IL and IR scholars *are* and *do*, I claim echoes of a new Orientalizing discourse subtly at work in the evolving encounters between IL and IR scholarship.

However, my argument that Koskenniemi's Counterdisciplinarity resembles an Orientalizing project does not mean Counterdisciplinarity is the successor of a racially inspired project which became the cultural foundation for imperial subordination. Rather, the reference here to a *new Orientalism* points to how an engrained strategy of structuring social relations, through a naturalizing discourse on 'the self' and 'the other', becomes reconstituted and redeployed to address a different epistemic but no less social struggle for control over the way wider intellectual audiences see the constitution of the disciplinary world. Indeed, power, superiority and domination remain all in play; yet while the disciplining objective is similar, the field of contest, its players and stakes have a different – more (meta)theoretical – scope of consequence. This is about discursively mastering one's metaphorical neighbourhood in an intellectual world, not imperial domination over the world at large.

Accordingly, we now work with the term 'discipline' in two profound ways: as a referential noun relating to a community portending specialized knowledge, and in the Foucauldian manner pertaining to the construction or constitution of a subject. The interplay between these two meanings of discipline become central vis-à-vis Koskenniemi's Counterdisciplinarity because, I argue, his powerful normative and historical discourse on the essential intellectual difference between IL and IR manifests a narrative display of orientalizing. Foremost, in compositional terms, Koskenniemi places his narrative voice at a high level of theoretical abstraction and thus positions himself as an authoritative surveyor and orderer of both fields.

This enables Koskenniemi to cast an alleged unruly expanse of IR 'legal' scholarship as *his* subject to discipline, and thus, with prosaic confidence, reduces IR's jurisdictional challenge to a misguided jurisdictional conflation which fails to appreciate the normative (occidental) heights upon which IL's epistemic practice is stationed.

Yet, the alleged orientalizing character of Koskenniemi's discourse is not sustained because he merely identifies epistemic differences between what IL and IR do – which is just taxonomy. In fact, Koskenniemi's emphasis, in both the *Miserable Comforters*[38] and *Counterdisciplinarity*,[39] that international law involves an 'argumentative practice'[40] becomes a valuable critique that addresses how a liberal and influential IR research agenda on 'legalization' largely disregarded the linguistic and interpretive core constitutive of much legal work and application.[41] Therefore, I argue, what makes the divide Koskenniemi draws between IL and IR *orientalizing in quality* is in fact its absolute and categorical weight used to justify a profound intellectual separation; and he makes this contrast pronounced and disciplining through two reifying moves.

First, Koskenniemi uses a teleological argument to elevate international lawyers, and consequently IL, as a fundamentally different kind of scholar/practitioner and, by implication, *other* the legal research IR scholars may perform as something which stands outside the eminent *mission civilizatrice*[42] which international lawyers uniquely possess. As Koskenniemi explains:

> For Cassesse and countless other international lawyers, the field in which we have made our professional careers is more than just another technical discipline. It possesses an inbuilt moral direction to make human rights, justice and peace universal. To 'do' international law is to operate with a teleology that points from humankind's separation to unity ... Whatever differences may exist between international lawyers, we tend to be united in our understanding that legal modernity is moving towards what an influential Latin American jurist labelled in 2005 a new *jus gentium* uniting individuals (and not states) across the globe ... It seems impossible, or at least very difficult, to do international law without some such teleology, some sense that one is working not only to coordinate the activities of states but for the good of humanity itself.[43]

His second move buttresses this *mission essentielle* by drawing upon Aristotle's distinction between practical judgement (*phronêsis*) versus theoretical science (*epistêmê*). Here, Koskenniemi projects an *essentialized division of labour* where IR scholars wear the lab coats of behavioural scientists monolithically concerned with 'demonstrable truths', while IL

scholars are cloaked as rhetorical craftsmen concerned with the normative resonance and audience aesthetics of their adversarial arguments.[44]
One need not be familiar with social anthropology and the ethnographic
method,[45] the 'empirical turn' in international law,[46] or have even read
Bruno Latour's work on science as a rhetorical practice[47] to get a sense
that the stylized dichotomy Koskenniemi tries to impose between what
social scientists and lawyers quintessentially *do* strains the bounds of ideal-
typical analysis[48] and overstates the extent to which practical judgement
is exclusively within the lawyerly arts. Furthermore, a concern arises that
Koskenniemi provides an oversimplified reading of Book VI of Aristotle's *Nicomachean Ethics*, the place where Aristotle engages in a complex
discussion of how the human mind produces not two but five interrelated categories of knowledge: technical (*technê*), scientific (*epistêmê*),
practical (*phronêsis*), wisdom (*sophia*) and understanding (*nous,
dianoia*).[49]

However, the central problem with Koskenniemi's use of Aristotelian
epistemology is its presentation as a trans-historical and enduring
essence,[50] brushing over discontinuities and variation which have developed since that Ancient categorical scheme. From a macro-historical
perspective, and as will be expanded upon in the next section, the constitution of contemporary disciplines owes less to the categorical structure
of Ancient Greek epistemology and more to the principles of abstraction,
specialization and internal differentiation which transformed disciplinarity along with much of social thought in the nineteenth century.[51] Hence,
Koskenniemi's use of Aristotle's categorical framing, while lending an
apparent pedigree to his Counterdisciplinary argument, overstates the
actual impact of Aristotelian categorization in the constitution of the
(post)modern (inter)disciplinary world. Aristotle's epistemic geometry
has since mutated many times over into a self-referential, overlapping
and loosely networked assemblage of disciplinary fields, with each working to promote their disciplinary abstractions into broader epistemic
application and relevance.[52]

Thus, if there is a teleology behind contemporary disciplinary differentiation: it is not categorical demarcation but rather competitive
abstraction, which breeds a propensity for spatial extension and correspondingly disciplinary insecurity.[53] Such dynamics yield to imperial
trajectories resembling what historians of international law and colonialism are familiar with through the story of Francisco de Vitoria and how
the abstraction of human space became integral to the 'discovery' and
conquest of the 'new world', with its consequent *epistemic dispossession*

of indigenous populations.[54] Similarly, when disciplinary space is understood as ordered by academic disciplines with competing abstractions, this propels adversarial drive and the impulse for positional imperative of the kind Counterdisciplinarity manifests. What is more, orientalizing discourses become potent in this context because they appeal to the quaintness of physical space, geography and, pivotally, the strategic importance of mapping an inherent order of jurisdiction between 'Us' and 'them'. We now reflect on that predicament in the ensuing section, and the existential pressures it creates to not merely press Aristotle's metaphysics into service but, vitally, project a geographic representation of (inter)disciplinary space which naturalizes the boundaries of IL as an allegedly pre-given jurisdictional domain.

7.2   The Nature of *Things*: Disciplinary Space and Competitive Abstraction

To this point we have dealt with two meanings of 'discipline', but now a third needs to enter our field of view: the notion of 'disciple' and the influence that intellectual followings have over perceptions of a given epistemic order. This notion becomes pertinent less for its religious connotation and more to express how each discipline is constituted by students, scholars and practitioners which each engage and reproduce disciplinary identities, doctrines, theories and methods to construct *their own world* of study.[55] In this process, each discipline develops a cognitive form and collective belief – a discipline effect[56] – among those within and beyond the intellectual assemblage that the discipline has a social reality,[57] thingness and even pre-given spatial quality upon which the boundaries of disciplinarity are traced.

This mode of reifying constitutes an epistemic legacy under-examined not merely by international lawyers but, specifically, by Koskenniemi with his teleological call for Counterdisciplinarity to assert the jurisdictional endurance of IL as a discipline. In a manner, one might note, resembling how IL Positivists and IR Realists assert the endurance of sovereignty.[58] Thus, what sits at the epistemic and social core of Counterdisciplinarity, and behind all disciplines as intellectual constructions, is the symbolic influence of the physical body.[59] As such, all modern social entities, like disciplines, have revolved around the imagination of some internal constitution or bodily thingness which marks a natural self/other boundary.[60] Based on this bodily presumption there emerges, subsequently, the expectation of unitary space or even, in Marxist terms of analogy, a kind of disciplinary fetishism which generates its own form of reifying consciousness.[61]

This section engages this will to reify the discipline, this sense of absoluteness, as something both generated by intellectual practices within an institutionalized community and also as a productive strategy intended, as Counterdisciplinarity exhibits, to project an imaginary of disciplinary space as an inborn intellectual entity or even territory. Yet, taking a page from Andrew Abbott's influential work on professional boundaries, I argue, this presentation of a modern discipline as an essential jurisdiction overlooks how the perceived boundaries of disciplinary and professional labour have been shaped and reshaped through processes and strategies of (re)abstraction by often competing scholarships and professions.[62] Thus, the image of a discipline as self-evident, while ultimately the aim and effect of an invested following, masks how modern disciplines are better understood as evolving histories rather than as absolute categories; the outcome of ongoing jurisdictional transformations, strategies and struggles which require a more systematic excavation, historicization and, crucially, spatial theorization.[63]

This brings us to the omission Koskenniemi makes in his reflexive attempt to critique the jurisdictional encroachment by IR upon legal research: he does not interrogate systematically the notion of the discipline, and only examines it indirectly through the proxy of his teleological argument on legal practice. In this way, while Counterdisciplinarity amounts to reflexive theorization on the nature of IL as a discipline, Koskenniemi takes for granted the very dimension of epistemic space upon which he asserts IL's rightful place in the disciplinary world; shifting attention to preferred foundational questions involving normative, political and legal theory. The notion of 'discipline' as a constitutive concept of epistemic space is thus only partially addressed, since Koskenniemi pursues a strategy of narrative framing where disciplinarity concerns comparative positioning across an absolute field of reified competitors.

Yet, in light of the centrality of the notion vis-à-vis the perceived structure of epistemic reality, it becomes essential to appreciate the discipline in three interrelated senses as: a historically specific jurisdiction, a modality of modern knowledge production, and a strategic dimension of academic and professional politics. In other words, we need to theorize this constitutive space as integral to the politics of epistemic ordering through which a modern discipline is configured spatially, reproduced socially and assumes its imagined thingness. From this critical perspective, Koskenniemi's Counterdisciplinarity, while historiographical and philosophically excavating in its tactics, actually attempts to circumvent that more spatial and political interrogation through strategic use of a civilizing mission and an Ancient aura to essentialize IL's epistemic place.

This means that a fully reflexive discussion of inter-disciplinarity, or Counterdisciplinarity, requires an account of the notion of discipline not as a fixed and trans-historical container, but rather as a medium for the spatial politics of epistemic ordering concerned with perceived relevance, intellectual position and, lest we forget, social influence. Further, it requires awareness that the ultimate goal of this spatial politics is the production and expansion of disciplinary space through techniques of argument and representation asserting bodily permanence and even terrestrial scope. What becomes valuable, therefore, is a spatial interrogation of disciplines which engages them as jurisdictions that compete to homogenize vast problems and institutions using their distinct knowledge and techniques. It is a spatial dynamic and politics intensified when jurisdictions are generically proximate, such as IL and IR, and manifest overlap onto institutions or problems of identified social significance and endowed funding. As Andrew Abbott explains:

> Academic knowledge excels at invention precisely because it is organized along abstract lines ... It can make connections that seem nonsensical within practical professional knowledge, but that may reveal underlying regularities that can ultimately reshape practical knowledge altogether ... The academic, abstract knowledge system is thus universally important ... [and] it is therefore not surprising that jurisdictional assaults are often directed at the academic level ... Under some conditions, clarity [of jurisdictional borders] is a good defence. Certainly it has served lawyers well against psychiatry's attacks on the notion of responsibility. A similarly sharp border has generally been effective in defending American medicine from the invasions of faith healers. At the same time, clarity does give an easy target for attempts at 'seizure by absorption'. Thus, hydrologists in the United States have been very clear about what exactly is their area of expertise. But they lost jurisdiction over many of the country's water problems because their clear claims were made subordinate to the foresters' much more vague conception of 'good resources management'. For many years foresters dictated the entire jurisdiction, with hydrologists essentially as subordinates.[64]

Thus, Abbott underscores how the thingness of a discipline is tied to the productive representation of its jurisdictional boundaries over time and, even more so, the way those within the discipline engage in the bounding, or even the bordering, of the disciplinary project relative to other proximate and potentially competing groups. In this way, a discipline is revealed to possess a constitutional character like most jurisdictional projects: perceived thingness depends on the forcefulness and resonance of its spatial narrative across a number of intended internal and external audiences. Further still, this narration becomes an exercise in the constitution of intellectual difference, the locating of such asserted difference, and projecting a cartography of that difference through what Abbott calls an imagined 'metric of propinquity' or, in more common terms, choosing whether to 'yoke', bound, border or wall intellectual others.[65] Ultimately, the resonance of the narrative and symbolism through which that storytelling is conveyed affects projection of the intended spatial arrangement and ruling imaginary.

Koskenniemi's Counterdisciplinary provides a vivid example of this propinquity exercise not merely because it is openly concerned with reinforcing a boundary between the disciplines of IL and IR, but also because it provides a very elaborate and deeply teleological story to sustain what Abbott refers to above as a clear border of jurisdictional demarcation. As noted earlier, Koskenniemi buttresses that spatial move with the use of Greek philosophy and particularly Aristotle's distinction between *phronêsis* and *epistêmê*. It provides a powerful rhetorical argument that uses an ancient scheme of knowledge classification, often seen as hereditary for modern western thought, to convey an almost geological representation of epistemic order, much in the way fault lines would appear on a terrestrial surface.[66]

However, the question emerges on the extent to which Koskenniemi is fetishizing[67] rather than historicizing the significance of Aristotelian categorization? Since, in part, Koskenniemi does valuably remind us that the ordering of human knowledge originates from epistemic principles and debates stretching back to Aristotle and Plato;[68] a poignant intervention considering some 'empiricist' scholars within IR seem to dig no further than Popper.[69] Nonetheless, Counterdisciplinarity has a problem both in terms of the narrowness of what it tells us in relation to Aristotelian categorization and, further, its failure to connect Ancient Greece to ensuing layers of epistemic history which made and consolidated the modern discipline(s).[70] The limits of this chapter restrict the analysis of those historical layers in any detail, nonetheless there are two fundamental points to take note of and appreciate as crucial relative to the spatial strategy that Koskenniemi imparts via Counterdisciplinarity.

First, while Koskenniemi's use of Aristotelian phronêsis imparts what seems a horizontal partition between what IL and IR *are* and *do*. We need to be conscious that Aristotle's distinctions did not merely attempt to distinguish between kinds of knowledge but were also concerned with ordering and, specifically, the question of hierarchy between different types of perceived higher and lower forms of knowledge.[71] It is a polemic that has seen much iteration over the centuries via the perennial question of whether one type of knowledge is more useful than another. In this way, Koskenniemi's use of Aristotelian epistemology needs a disclaimer: it is a classificatory scheme concerned with ordering and the potential imposition of superiority; an epistemological legacy that no doubt feeds impulse for an orientalizing strategy of distinction as discussed in the prior section.

Second, Counterdisciplinarity's strategic use of Aristotelian epistemology has a mystifying effect in how it sculpts our historical understanding of the constitution of modern disciplinary space. In particular, it invokes Aristotle's phronêsis in a trans-historical manner to establish the perceived clarity and enduring essence of IL's jurisdiction[72] but, in the process, occults historical developments that have substantially mutated and even undercut Aristotelian principles of epistemic ordering over time. Here, a number of epochal developments require brief excavation to breathe the transformative effects of knowledge abstraction into our comprehension of modern disciplinary space.

For starters, the nominal birth of the discipline arises not in Ancient Greece but in the late Middle Ages, when universities in Bologna, Paris and Salerno began to displace the holist approach of the *artes liberales* or *studia generalia* with the term 'discipline' to facilitate the more specific and vocational needs of medicine, law and theology.[73] This nominal shift was later built upon with epistemological transformations precipitated by the Scientific Revolutions' overthrow of the classical natural order and the subsequent Enlightenment drive to collect, classify and systematize of all discernible information and knowledge.[74] That immense collecting and classification catalysed the emergence of modern disciplinarity since it led to an ever-expanding and complex accumulation of 'data', and, in parallel, increasingly delineated and inward looking patterns of disciplinary communication and exchange.[75]

What ensued from that conjuncture was no less than an epochal reordering of epistemic space relative to the classificatory demarcation which had endured in varying degrees since Ancient times. Foremost, information about the world underwent growing abstraction since it was constructed through specialized concepts, criteria, theories and methods, and this meant that knowledge production was less reliant on direct contact with the immediate world of experience and also increasingly differentiated from one discipline to another.[76] During the eighteenth and nineteenth centuries, these dynamics reached a socio-epistemic tipping point when the overwhelming mass and diversity of knowledge abstraction became consolidated by the closure of disciplinary communications.[77] Consequently, the disciplines were no longer seen as organized with reference to a 'natural object' or an Ancient schema, but instead through the social bounding of scholarly communities yoked by shared concepts, theories and methods which defined research problems according to an exclusive disciplinary agenda. The centuries-old classification system of *hierarchical differentiation* morphed into an *internally differentiated* system of knowledge production, where each discipline became understood as a knowledge production system in its own right breaking down the teleological coherence presumed of all knowledge creation since antiquity.[78]

In this way, modern knowledge production gained a profoundly revised and fragmented teleology: its constitutive mission was *specialization*, with each discipline assuming the spatial character of an epistemic regime capable of producing and projecting knowledge as far as its succession of abstractions could socially travel across intellectual and endowment giving audiences. At the end of the nineteenth century, when the disciplines moved out of the holistic organization of the Academies of Sciences and into the autonomous departments of universities, this transformation became consolidated and the categorical schema of knowledge ordering displaced by the abstract, overlapping and expansive qualities of knowledge specialization.[79] The modern discipline as an internally differentiated, self-referential and self-amplifying social entity assumed the epistemic realization which continues to a considerable extent into the present; ruptured from the categorical classification system of premodern epistemology which one can now observe Koskenniemi tries to reify as pedigreed support in counter-attack against asserted jurisdictional encroachment by an 'interdisciplinary IR'.

7.3 The 'Same Conceptual Space'? Supra-disciplinarity and the Politics of Disciplinary Migration

The significance of rupture and reification now takes centre stage as we head figuratively back to the future to scrutinize interdisciplinary anxieties, and appreciate how Koskenniemi's use of Aristotle is in fact symptomatic of a larger game of knowledge abstraction that provokes competition between disciplines over epistemic turf and perceived social ownership. Put another way: the abstract quality that characterizes modern disciplinary space suggests that Koskenniemi's appeal to Aristotelian epistemology is historically and spatially tenuous. As such, we need to situate Aristotle's mobilization as part of a broader discursive strategy to *other* IR's re-abstraction of problems and institutions which IL scholars have asserted as within their given knowledge specialization – and here the relationship between the terms 'given' and 'specialization' harbour a distinct tension in a modern knowledge context.

Thus, Aristotle's invocation represents a metaphorical ringing of the bells in existential alarm,[80] calling out to a disciplinary following for vigilance on what makes the knowledge of international lawyers manifestly different relative to a migration of IR scholarship which potentially re-appropriates, in whole or in part, the seeming preserve of juridical research. To set this out in clearer spatial terms, the abstract incursion of IR into the study of international law forebodes not simply the loss of jurisdictional monopoly for IL but, more radically, the potential for IR to discursively flatten the historical, social and normative conditions of international law that then facilitates IL's homogenization and subordination to an imagined *supra-disciplinarity* for IR knowledge. In this sense, the root cause for disciplinary anxiety derives from how knowledge abstraction represents a qualitatively new matrix of socio-epistemic organization with the conceptual capacity to pulverize epistemic distinctions of the kind pre-modern knowledge classification had taken for granted, and to which Koskenniemi seemingly finds strategic salvation.

At this point, your mind should start drawing parallels to Abbott's earlier cited story on the history between hydrologists and foresters, where the foresters' vaguer and more pliable boundary of 'good resources management' eventually facilitated the subordination of hydrology's presumably 'natural' but no less reducible domain. It is a story that pushes us towards a pivotal and comparative question: if the hydrologists could not shield their knowledge jurisdiction with the storied naturalness and material quality of water, how is it that international lawyers expect to fare much better in shielding their jurisdiction with reference to an even greater social construction such as law? When water has no pre-given jurisdictional encompassment in the context of knowledge abstraction, the same rules also apply to law of any variety – including international.

This is more than a hypothetical concern in an ecological context of the burgeoning 'knowledge society' where universities and disciplines seem to be losing their monopoly over the terms of knowledge production,[81] and need to increasingly interact and compete with a network of public/private 'think-tanks' and cross-disciplinary research institutes. What is more, the significance of 'external' funding agencies for the formulation of subject matters and research problems, combined with the rise of such hybridizing notions as policy-relevance, global governance, counter-terrorism or climate change, all work to alter the scholarly and institutional horizon of endowed research agendas. It is an epistemic and evolutionary trajectory which, as Anne-Marie Slaughter illustrates, a community of liberal IR scholarship grasped some two decades ago and have since attempted to harness with their diplomatic but no less strategic pronouncement of a shared 'conceptual space' between IL and IR:

> International law and international politics cohabit the same conceptual space. Together they comprise the rules and the reality of 'the international system', an intellectual construct that lawyers, political scientists, and policymakers use to describe the world they study and seek to manipulate. As a distinguished group of international lawyers and a growing number of political scientists have recognized, it makes little sense to study one without the other.[82]

Thus, with the lens of knowledge abstraction one can appreciate how a seeming 'interdisciplinary' overture amounts to a discursive move by liberal IR scholars into a knowledge jurisdiction traditionally settled by international lawyers. It is important to understand that that migration, like all migrations, has not been haphazard but rather grounded in existential circumstances and motivations.[83] Specifically, this interdisciplinary projection became instigated at a time when disciplinary IR, then dominated by Neo-Realism and rationalist theory, faced decline in traditional avenues of research after it could not foresee or analyse the peaceful collapse of the Soviet Empire and the Cold War.[84] It was an epistemic crisis that prompted reconfiguration and the need to seek out new avenues of productive research by migrating concepts, theories and methods, i.e. regime theory, liberal institutionalism and rational choice modelling,[85] into areas of international research that appeared open to fruitful extension, i.e. legalization and compliance studies. As such, Slaughter's declaration of a shared 'conceptual space' represented a pulverizing move of knowledge abstraction *par excellence*, which shrewdly proposed the transformation of an external disciplinary boundary into an overlapping proto-boundary[86] between 'lawyers, political scientists and policymakers'; forwarding a narrative whereby fragments of once distinct scholarships reintegrate and innovate across disciplinary lines to address new worldly complexities (i.e. a post–Cold War World) and hence a hybridizing imperative for new knowledge production.

In doing so, Slaughter's 'inter-disciplinarity' tried to seize upon what was ultimately the overlapping character of modern disciplinary and professional boundaries or, to use a terrestrial imaginary, how the modern disciplinary division of labour possessed no inherent borders and instead amounted to a variable and interactive geography captured less by the metaphor of landed jurisdiction (i.e. scholarly title) and more by the historical dynamics and politics of intellectual migration.[87] With this light, it becomes possible to grasp how spatial discourses which have emerged from IL to deflect that jurisdictional challenge with an orientalizing vernacular, the vanguard led by Koskenniemi's Counterdisciplinarity, appear to have acutely misread the abstract and malleable terrain which is modern disciplinary space. In particular, by hypostatizing IL and simultaneously othering juridical research by IR scholarship, Counterdisciplinarity propagates, via an eloquent teleological prose, what is more accurately an ideology of intellectual superiority buttressed with a topographic and geographic reification of epistemic space.

Yet, this narrative and geographic posturing manifests a strategic and spatial oversight in that it overlooks how the jurisdictional crossing which liberal IR scholars have pursued under 'inter-disciplinarity' is endemic of migratory and hybridizing trajectories that are reconstituting contemporary knowledge production;[88] something disciplinary economics has manipulated with particular flare in recent decades alongside other prominent convergences ranging from astrophysics, artificial intelligence, biological anthropology, child development, feminist theory, historical sociology, materials science, medical anthropology, molecular biology, political economy to radio astronomy.[89] As a result, Counterdisciplinarity's strategic vision of storied reification, while rallying confidence in IL's apparent (occidental) elevation relative to potential challengers, actually occults how the struggle for epistemic prominence and supra-disciplinary positioning is determined by those within disciplines that exhibit the strategic agility to fox migrations and recombinations of disciplinary fragments; so that *their* jurisdiction gets steering influence over any interdisciplinary hyphen, which in turn shapes the future path and development of potentially multiple disciplines.

This all leads, therefore, to some key spatial and normative questions that international lawyers now become confronted with in the face of the orientalizing and topographic imaginary Counterdisciplinarity prescribes for IL's disciplinary future. Foremost, is the furtherance of a topographic and oriental geography between IR and IL a truly reflexive strategy in light of the abstract and flattening qualities of modern disciplinary space?

Further, is a discourse of teleological supremacy and innate scholarly distinctions consistent with critical international law's concern over the way the legal world provides the linguistic, social and institutional resources for political domination and inequality? Moreover, does Counterdisciplinarity as a strategic doctrine blind critical international lawyers to what is ultimately the spatial lesson imparted by neo-liberal 'interdisciplinarity' between IR and IL scholars: the struggle for disciplinary position, or even superiority, is determined by a dynamic and penetrating strategy that seeks to yoke disciplinary overlaps and pull together – rather than repel – cross-disciplinary fragments amenable to a critical scholarly, political and social agenda.[90]

Curiously, when one looks back to Koskenniemi's ground breaking critique in *From Apology to Utopia* one sees that hybridizing acumen and stress on the significance of looking beyond one's own discipline to address the character of the social world, and how it could be changed. Yet, Koskenniemi's recent attempt to recover an imagined purity and piety of lawyerly jurisdiction suggests angst over losing a coveted domain, which engendered professional exclusivity and disciplinary superiority for a privileged class of international supra-lawyers.[91] As such, Counterdisciplinarity might be better understood as a professional postscript written by Koskenniemi *the supra-lawyer*, suggesting that his initial and shattering call for trans-disciplinary critique of international legal rule was perhaps of the kind scholars of philosophy categorize as an 'early' work. Counterdisciplinarity, in this manner, represents the cold shower which the privilege of professionalization performs to forsake transformative possibilities, consigning a critical inter-disciplinarity, of the kind Koskenniemi once boldly contemplated, to the archive of oriental indulgences:

> [T]he whole of international legal 'talk' is an extended effort to solve problems created by a particular way of understanding the relationship between descriptions and prescription, facts and norms in international life. My argument is that the persisting disputes within the realms of theory and doctrine result from the fact that these disputes bear a close relationship to controversial topics encountered beyond specifically 'legal' discourses. The ideas of statehood, authority, legitimacy, obligation, consent, and so on which stand at the heart of international law are also hotly debated issues of social and political theory. In each of these realms the problems turn on the justifiability of assumptions about what the character of the present social world is and how it should be changed. It would be futile to assume that the assumptions which characterize modern social and political discourse are different, or separable from those which control legal discourse on these same matters.[92]

7.4   Conclusion: Counterdisciplinarity as the Geography of Class and Professional Privilege

Ultimately, what this chapter has endeavoured to do is prompt critical reflection on the presumptions Counterdisciplinarity makes about disciplinary space and knowledge production. Specifically, it has sought to develop an alternate critical discourse vis-à-vis 'inter-disciplinarity' that is concerned less with reifying a monumental and monolithic history of IL's inherent teleology and more with furthering the 'methodology use of critical reason'[93] through disciplinary migrations and overlaps that shape and reshape how law's rule is understood. As such, the chapter has sought to explain to critical international lawyers that inter-disciplinarity is neither a choice nor a label exclusive to liberal IR scholarship, but rather a practical and strategic reality of the abstract, overlapping and migratory characteristics of knowledge production. As the National Research Council of the US unmasked with its scrutiny of Physics and Chemistry, inter-disciplinarity happens, whether formally recognized or not, across the everyday research practices of disciplines which may even appear impermeable:

> The interface between physics and chemistry has been crossed so often in both directions that its exact location is obscure; its passage is signalled more by gradual changes in language and approach than by any sharp demarcation in content. It has been a source of continual advances in concept and application all across the science of molecules and atoms, surfaces and interfaces, and fluids and solids. Yet, in spite of this, the degree of direct, collaborative interaction between physicists and chemists in the United States, especially at universities, has remained surprisingly limited.[94]

Flowing from this, the chapter relates how such informal and formal practices of inter-disciplinarity provoke politics between disciplines over spatial jurisdiction, and of the kind the earlier discussed Strepsiades knew all too well: the perennial sanctity of perceived turf. While the abstract quality of modern knowledge production has precipitated migration and hybridization between fragments of disciplines, this has no less irritated a locational and topographical mind-set bred by centuries of the categorical and jurisdictional ordering of knowledge production and even social life. As such, Counterdisciplinarity is symptomatic of that territorial mind-set, and illustrative of the discursive lengths possible to establish geographic place and pre-eminence upon the perceived map of disciplinary labour. This is where the work of Edward Said became insightful for an analysis of how Counterdisciplinarity can be situated within a historical tradition and cultural practice of discursive othering for the purpose of establishing positional superiority. In our knowledge context, Said's Orientalism was of pivotal importance for uncovering how an asserted colonial past, and its technique of cultural disciplining, could be reinvented and find informal extension in a disciplinary struggle over appropriate jurisdictional bounds and, ultimately, the perceived distribution of epistemic and academic turf.

Yet, peril remains that critical international lawyers will still buy into Counterdisciplinarity as a doctrine of self-proclaimed resistance against a liberal brand of IR 'inter-disciplinarity', wrongly conflating normative cleavages of IR scholarship into a stylized nemesis[95] and failing to see how Counterdisciplinarity actually promotes descent into a pantheon mentality. Where critical international lawyers are encouraged to extoll the virtues of a glorious and teleological tradition, while forsaking how the transformative purpose of critical social theory, of which critical international law is a part, demands quite the opposite. Specifically, a scrutiny of this teleological past and mission as being intimately tied, through the naturalization of social, geographic and political hierarchies, to the institutionalization of systematic and profound imbalances of power and wealth on a global scale – past, present and future. In this way, the thrust of Counterdisciplinarity appears less concerned about resisting the vast penetration of neo-liberal thought across the humanities and social sciences – yes law is included – and more with establishing a gated community which preserves class and professional privilege in the face of that encroachment, masked with an aesthetic use of Aristotelian epistemology to give a flavouring of natural order.

Notes

* I extend my gratitude to the editors for providing the space and encouragement to pursue this piece, as well as appreciation to Martti Koskenniemi for his gracious reception and engagement with my critique. My thanks for the helpful comments received from Tanja Aalberts, Yutaka Arai, Mike Buenger, Juan Maya Castro, Cyra Choudhury, Jeffrey Dunoff, Jaye Ellis, John Haskell, John Heieck, Friedrich Kratochwil, Nicholas Onuf, Zoran Oklopcic, Harm Schepel, Bas Schotel, Sahib Singh and Anna Sobczak.

1. Aristophanes, 'The Clouds', in J. Henderson (ed. and trans.), *Aristophanes: Clouds; Wasps; Peace* (Cambridge, MA: Harvard University Press, 2005), 33–37.
2. See G. Bateson, 'Form, Substance, and Difference', in *Steps to an Ecology of Mind: Collected Essays in Anthropology, Psychiatry, Evolution, and Epistemology* (San Francisco: Chandler, 1972), 460.

3. J. B. Harley, 'Historical Geography and the Cartographic Illusion', *Journal of Historical Geography* 15 (1989): 85.
4. T. Mitchell, 'Principles True in Every Country', in *Rule of Experts: Egypt, Techno-Politics, Modernity* (Berkeley: University of California Press, 2002), 54.
5. See D. Gregory, *Geographical Imaginations* (Cambridge, MA: Blackwell, 1998).
6. 'Maps are graphic representations that facilitate a spatial understanding of things, concepts, conditions, processes, or events in the human world'. J. B. Harley and D. Woodward, *History of Cartography*, vol. 1 (Chicago: University of Chicago Press, 1987), xvi.
7. K. W. Abbott and D. Snidal, 'Law, Legalization, and Politics: an Agenda for the Next Generation of IL/IR Scholars', in J. L. Dunoff and M. Pollack (eds), *Interdisciplinary Perspectives on International Law and International Relations* (Cambridge: Cambridge University Press, 2013), 33; K. W. Abbott, 'Modern International Relations Theory: a Prospectus for International Lawyers', *Yale Journal of International Law* 14 (1989): 335–411; R. O. Keohane, 'International Relations and International Law: Two Optics', *Harvard Journal of International Law* 38 (1997): 487–502; M. Koskenniemi, *The Gentle Civilizer of Nations: the Rise and Fall of International Law 1870–1960* (Cambridge: Cambridge University Press, 2001), 483–84.
8. Frequently overlooked are the liberal versus critical cleavages not merely within IR theory generally, but crucially within Constructivist IR as well. This, for instance, has led IL scholars to focus on the more liberal work of Jeffrey Checkel, Peter Katzenstein, Kathryn Sikkink and Alexander Wendt as being typical of Constructivist IR, while ignoring the original and more critical body of Constructivist scholarship following from scholars such as Nicholas Onuf, Friedrich Kratochwil and Jens Bartelson; see N. G. Onuf, *World of Our Making: Rules and Rule in Social Theory and International Relations* (Columbia: University of South Carolina Press, 1989); F. Kratochwil, *Rules, Norms and Decisions: on the Conditions of Practical and Legal Reasoning in International Relations and Domestic Affairs* (Cambridge: Cambridge University Press, 1991); and Jens Bartelson, *A Genealogy of Sovereignty* (Cambridge: Cambridge University Press, 1995).
9. O. Kessler, "So Close Yet So Far Away? International Law in International Political Sociology", *International Political Sociology* 4 (2010): 303–4.
10. A. Abbott, *The System of Professions: an Essay on the Division of Expert Labour* (Chicago: University of Chicago Press, 1988), 36.
11. Ibid.
12. M. Koskenniemi, 'Miserable Comforters: International Relations as the New Natural Law', *European Journal of International Relations* 15 (2009): 395. For an excellent introduction to critical cartography, see J. B. Harley, 'Deconstructing the Map', *Cartographica* 26 (1989): 1–20.
13. See A.-M. Slaughter Burley, 'International Law and International Relations Theory: a Dual Agenda', *American Journal of International Law* 87 (1993): 205–39.
14. See M. A. Pollack, 'Is International Relations Corrosive of International Law? A Reply to Martti Koskenniemi', *Temple International and Comparative Law Journal* 27 (2013): 339–75.
15. Foremost encapsulated with the launch of the 2000 special issue in *International Organization* on 'legalization'; see K. W. Abbott, R. Keohane, A. Moravcsik, A.-M. Slaughter and D. Snidal, 'The Concept of Legalization', *International Organization* 54 (2000): 401–19.

16. See Jack L. Goldsmith and Eric A. Posner, *The Limits of International Law* (Oxford: Oxford University Press, 2005).

17. See A.-M. Slaughter, 'International Law and International Relations Theory: Twenty Years Later', in Dunoff and Pollack, *Interdisciplinary Perspectives*, 613.

18. J. Crawford, 'International Law as a Discipline and Profession', *Proceedings of the American Society of International Law* 106 (2012): 473.

19. J. Klabbers, 'The Bridge Crack'd: A Critical Look at Interdisciplinary Relations', *International Relations* 23 (2009): 120.

20. P. Allott, 'Review of Books', *British Yearbook of International Law* 80 (2010): 416–22.

21. M. Koskenniemi, 'Law, Teleology and International Relations: an Essay in Counterdisciplinarity', *International Relations* 26 (2012): 3–34.

22. See J. Malpas and K. Thiel, 'Kant's Geography of Reason', in S. Elden and E. Mendieta (eds), *Reading Kant's Geography* (Albany: State University of New York Press, 2011), 195; I. Kant, 'On the Impossibility of a Sceptical Satisfaction of Pure Reason That Is Divided against Itself', in *Critique of Pure Reason*, P. Guyer and A. Wood (trans.) (1998), A760/B788.

23. Koskenniemi, 'Law, Teleology and International Relations', 19.

24. E. W. Said, *Orientalism* (New York: Vintage, 2003).

25. Ibid., 12.

26. Ibid., 7.

27. See E. W. Said, *Humanism and Democratic Criticism* (New York: Columbia University Press, 2004).

28. Said, *Orientalism*, 1–3.

29. Ibid., 10.

30. Ibid., 4.

31. Ibid., 5–6.

32. See M. Foucault, 'The Subject and Power', in J. D. Faubion (ed.), *Power: Essential Works of Michel Foucault*, vol. 3, R. Hurley (trans.) (New York: New Press, 2000), 326.

33. E. W. Said, "The Scope of Orientalism", in M. Bayoumi and A. Rubin (eds), *The Edward Said Reader* (New York: Vintage, 2000), 93–94.

34. Said, *Orientalism*, xvi.

35. M. Samiei, 'Neo-Orientalism? The Relationship between the West and Islam in Our Globalised World', *Third World Quarterly* 31 (2010): 1146.

36. Said, *Orientalism*, 12–13.

37. Ibid., at 2.

38. Koskenniemi, 'Miserable Comforters'.

39. Koskenniemi, 'Law, Teleology and International Relations'.

40. Ibid., 19.

41. See Koskenniemi, 'Miserable Comforters', 405–11.

42. Said notes in particular how the notion of *mission civilizatrice* is an integral part of orientalism which has been reinvented over time. See Said, *Orientalism*, xvi.

43. Koskenniemi, 'Law, Teleology and International Relations', 4.

44. Ibid., 19.

45. L. J. Seligman, 'Ethnographic Methods', in D. Druckman (ed.), *Doing Research: Methods of Inquiry for Conflict Analysis* (Thousand Oaks, CA: Sage, 2005), 229.

46. G. Shaffer and T. Ginsburg, 'The Empirical Turn in International Legal Scholarship', *American Journal of International Law* 106 (2012): 1–46.

47. B. Latour, *Science in Action: How to Follow Scientists and Engineers through Society* (Cambridge, MA: Harvard University Press, 1987).
48. See D. Della Porta and M. Keating (eds), *Approaches and Methodologies in the Social Sciences: A Pluralist Perspective* (Cambridge: Cambridge University Press, 2008).
49. It is worth further mentioning that the way Koskenniemi describes international law in *Counterdisciplinarity*, with simultaneous reference to 'craft-likeness', 'correctness' and 'practice', in fact blends three Aristotelian types of knowledge: *epistêmê*, *technê* and *phronêsis*. See Aristotle, *Nicomachean Ethics*, R. Crisp (ed. and trans.) (Cambridge: Cambridge University Press, 2000), 1139b/1144b1.
50. See D. Vigneswaran and J. Quirk, 'Past Masters and Modern Inventions: Intellectual History as Critical Theory', *International Relations* 24 (2010): 107–31.
51. S. Turner, 'What Are Disciplines? And How Is Interdisciplinarity Different?', in P. Weingart and N. Stehr (eds), *Practicing Interdisciplinarity* (Toronto, ON: University of Toronto Press, 2000), 46–51.
52. See S. Fuller, 'Disciplinary Boundaries and the Rhetoric of the Social Sciences', in E. Messer-Davidow, D. R. Shumway and D. J. Sylvan (eds), *Knowledges: Historical and Critical Studies in Disciplinarity* (Charlottesville: University Press of Virginia, 1993), 125.
53. J. Thompson Klein, 'Blurring, Cracking, and Crossing: Permeation and the Fracturing of Discipline', in Messer-Davidow et al., *Knowledges*, 185.
54. See A. Anghie, *Imperialism, Sovereignty, and the Making of International Law* (Cambridge: Cambridge University Press, 2005), 3–4; M. Koskenniemi, 'Empire and International Law: the Real Spanish Contribution', *University of Toronto Law Journal* 61 (2011): 3.
55. For more on world-making, see N. G. Onuf, 'Worlds of Our Making', in *Making Sense, Making Worlds: Constructivism in Social Theory and International Relations* (London: Routledge, 2013), 21.
56. Which is very much related to what John Agnew discusses relative to the 'territorial trap' and Timothy Mitchell refers to as the 'state effect', see J. Agnew, 'The Territorial Trap: the Geographical Assumptions of International Relations Theory', *Review of International Political Economy* 1 (1994): 53–84; T. Mitchell, 'Society, Economy and the State Effect', in A. Sharma and A. Gupta (eds), *The Anthropology of the State: a Reader* (Oxford: Blackwell, 2006), 169.
57. See M. Lamont, *How Professors Think: Inside the Curious World of Academic Judgment* (Cambridge, MA: Harvard University Press, 2009), 53–57.
58. See J. Havercroft, *Captives of Sovereignty* (Cambridge: Cambridge University Press, 2011), 15–52.
59. M. Foucault, 'Docile Bodies', in P. Rabinow (ed.), *The Foucault Reader* (New York: Pantheon Books, 1984), 179.
60. A. Abbott, 'Things of Boundaries', *Social Research* 62 (1995): 860.
61. See H. Lefebvre, *The Production of Space*, D. Nicholson-Smith (trans.) (Oxford: Blackwell, 1991), 82–83.
62. Abbott, *System of Professions*, 8–9, 35–38.
63. This follows from Lefebvre's emphasis on scrutinizing the 'politics of space' in representations of the state and social relations generally; see H. Lefebvre, 'Space: Social Product and Use Value', in N. Brenner and S. Elden (eds), *State, Space, World: Selected Essays of Henri Lefebvre*, G. Moore, N. Brenner and S. Elden (trans.) (Minneapolis: University of Minnesota Press, 2009), 185.

64. Abbott, *System of Professions*, 55–56.
65. Abbott, 'Things of Boundaries', 867–69
66. Metaphors of geology and topography are used prominently in the recent international legal theorizing of Hans Lindahl; see H. Lindahl, *Fault Lines of Globalization: Legal Order and the Politics of A-Legality* (Oxford: Oxford University Press, 2013).
67. For a useful discussion of historical fetishizing, see J. Hobson, 'What's at Stake in Bringing Historical Sociology Back into International Relations? Transcending "Chronofetishism" and "Tempocentricism" in International Relations', in S. Hobden and J. Hobson (eds), *Historical Sociology of International Relations* (Cambridge: Cambridge University Press, 2002), 9.
68. J. Thompson Klein, *Interdisciplinarity: History, Theory and Practice* (Detroit, MI: Wayne State University Press, 1990), 19–20.
69. See G. King, R. O. Keohane and S. Verba, *Designing Social Inquiry: Scientific Inference in Qualitative Research* (Princeton, NJ: Princeton University Press, 1994), 19.
70. R. Frodeman, *Sustainable Knowledge: a Theory of Interdisciplinarity* (2014), 18–22.
71. J. Moran, *Interdisciplinarity* (London: Routledge, 2010), 3–4.
72. Vigneswaran and Quirk, 'Past Masters and Modern Inventions', 118.
73. Klein, *Interdisciplinarity*, 20.
74. M. Foucault, *The Order of Things: an Archaeology of the Human Sciences* (New York: Vintage, 1994), 130–35.
75. R. Stichweh, *Zur Entstehung des modernen Systems wissenschaftlicher Disziplinen: Physik in Deutschland 1740–1890* (Frankfurt am Main, Germany: Suhrkamp, 1984), 42.
76. P. Weingart, 'A Short History of Knowledge Formations', in R. Frodeman, J. T. Klein and C. Mitcham (eds), *The Oxford Handbook of Interdisciplinarity* (Oxford: Oxford University Press, 2010), 3, 5–6.
77. Klein, *Interdisciplinarity*, 21–22.
78. Weingart, 'A Short History of Knowledge Formations', 6–8.
79. Ibid., 7.
80. See Sahib Singh, 'Identifying Threats to the Identity of International Law', paper for the 5th Research Forum of the European Society of International Law, May 2013. Text on file with author.
81. Frodeman, *Sustainable Knowledge*, 26–27.
82. A.-M. Slaughter, 'International Law in a World of Liberal States', *European Journal of International Law* 6 (1995): 503.
83. For insightful discussion of disciplinary migrations, see J. Thompson Klein, *Crossing Boundaries: Knowledge, Disciplinarities, and Interdisciplinarities* (Charlottesville: University Press of Virginia, 1996), 42–45.
84. N. G. Onuf, 'Worlds of Our Making', 31; J. W. Legro and A. Moravcsik, 'Is Anybody Still a Realist?', *International Security* 24 (1999): 5–55; R. Koslowski and F. V. Kratochwil, 'Understanding Change in International Politics: the Soviet Empire's Demise and the International System', *International Organization* 48 (1994): 215–47.
85. P. M. Haas, 'Epistemic Communities and the Dynamics of International Environmental Co-operation', in V. Rittberger and P. Mayer (eds), *Regime Theory and International Relations* (Oxford: Oxford University Press, 1993), 168; B. Koremenos, C. Lipson and D. Snidal, 'The Rational Design of International Institutions', *International Organization* 55 (2001): 761–99.

86. Regarding the distinction between boundaries and proto-boundaries, see Abbott, 'Things of Boundaries', 867–68.
87. Klein, *Interdisciplinarity*, 43.
88. L. Apostel, *Interdisciplinarity: Problems of Teaching and Research in Universities* (Paris: OECD, 1972); M. Gibbons, C. Limoges, H. Nowotny, Simon Schwartzman, P. Scott and M. Trow, *The New Production of Knowledge: the Dynamics of Science and Research in Contemporary Societies* (Thousand Oaks, CA: Sage, 1994).
89. Ibid., 44–45.
90. See J. Amariglio, S. Resnick and Richard D. Wolff, 'Division and Difference in the "Discipline" of Economics', in Messer-Davidow et al., *Knowledges*, 150.
91. On the class power of international law, see S. Marks, 'Human Rights in Disastrous Times', in J. Crawford and M. Koskenniemi (eds), *The Cambridge Companion to International Law* (Cambridge: Cambridge University Press, 2011), 309.
92. M. Koskenniemi, *From Apology to Utopia: The Structure of International Legal Argument*, reissue with new epilogue (Cambridge: Cambridge University Press, 2007), 4–5.
93. Koskenniemi, 'Miserable Comforters', 415.
94. National Research Council, *Physics through the 1990s: Scientific Interfaces and Technological Applications* (Washington, DC: National Academy Press, 1997), 53.
95. See Koskenniemi's reductionist summary of Constructivism provided in *Counterdisciplinarity*: Koskenniemi, 'Law, Teleology, and International Relations', 16.

Bibliography

Abbott, Andrew. *The System of Professions: an Essay on the Division of Expert Labor* (Chicago: University of Chicago Press, 1988).

'Things of Boundaries'. *Social Research* 62 (1995): 857–82.

Abbott, Kenneth W. 'Modern International Relations Theory: a Prospectus for International Lawyers'. *Yale Journal of International Law* 14 (1989): 335–411.

Abbott, Kenneth W., and Duncan Snidal. 'Law, Legalization, and Politics: an Agenda for the Next Generation of IL/IR Scholars'. In Jeffrey L. Dunoff and Mark A. Pollack (eds), *Interdisciplinary Perspectives on International Law and International Relations: the State of the Art* (Cambridge: Cambridge University Press, 2013).

Abbott, Kenneth W., Robert O. Keohane, Andrew Moravcsik, Anne-Marie Slaughter and Duncan Snidal, 'The Concept of Legalization', *International Organization* 54 (2000): 401–19.

Agnew, John. 'The Territorial Trap: the Geographical Assumptions of International Relations Theory'. *Review of International Political Economy* 1 (1994): 53–80.

Allott, Philip. 'Review of Books'. *British Yearbook of International Law* 80 (2010): 409–22.

Amariglio, Jack, Stephen Resnick and Richard Wolff. 'Division and Difference in the "Discipline" of Economics'. In Ellen Messer-Davidow, David R. Shumway and David J. Sylvan (eds), *Knowledges: Historical and Critical Studies in Disciplinarity* (Charlottesville: University Press of Virginia, 1993).

Anghie, Antony. *Imperialism, Sovereignty and the Making of International Law* (Cambridge: Cambridge University Press, 2007).

Apostel, Leo. *Interdisciplinarity Problems of Teaching and Research in Universities* (Paris: OECD, 1972).

Aristophanes. *Clouds; Wasps; Peace,* Jeffrey Henderson (ed. and trans.) (Cambridge, MA: Harvard University Press, 2005).

Aristotle. *Nicomachean Ethics,* Roger Crisp (ed. and trans.) (Cambridge: Cambridge University Press, 2000).

Bartelson, Jens. *A Genealogy of Sovereignty* (Cambridge: Cambridge University Press, 1995).

Bateson, Gregory. *Steps to an Ecology of Mind: Collected Essays in Anthropology, Psychiatry, Evolution, and Epistemology* (San Francisco: Chandler, 1972).

Crawford, James. 'International Law as Discipline and Profession'. *Proceedings of the American Society of International Law* 106 (2012): 471–86.

Della Porta, Donatella, and Michael Keating. *Approaches and Methodologies in the Social Sciences: a Pluralist Perspective* (Cambridge: Cambridge University Press, 2008).

Foucault, Michel. 'Docile Bodies'. In Paul Rabinow (ed.), *The Foucault Reader* (New York: Pantheon Books, 1984).

   The Order of Things: an Archaeology of the Human Sciences (New York: Vintage, 1994).

   Power: the Essential Works of Foucault 1954–1984, vol. 3, James D. Faubion (ed.), Robert Hurley (trans.) (New York: New Press, 2000).

Frodeman, Robert. *Sustainable Knowledge: a Theory of Interdisciplinarity* (Basingstoke, UK: Palgrave Macmillan, 2014).

Fuller, Steve. 'Disciplinary Boundaries and the Rhetoric of the Social Sciences'. In Ellen Messer-Davidow, David R. Shumway and David J. Sylvan (eds), *Knowledges: Historical and Critical Studies in Disciplinarity* (Charlottesville: University Press of Virginia, 1993).

Gibbons, Michael, Camille Limoges, Helga Nowotny, Simon Schwartzman, Peter Scott and Martin Trow. *The New Production of Knowledge: the Dynamics of Science and Research in Contemporary Societies* (Thousand Oaks, CA: Sage, 1994).

Goldsmith, Jack L., and Eric A. Posner. *The Limits of International Law* (Oxford: Oxford University Press, 2005).

Gregory, Derek. *Geographical Imaginations* (Cambridge, MA: Blackwell, 1994).

Haas, Peter M. 'Epistemic Communities and the Dynamics of International Environmental Cooperation'. In Volker Rittberger and Peter Mayer (eds), *Regime Theory and International Relations* (Oxford: Oxford University Press, 1993).

Harley, John B. 'Deconstructing the Map'. *Cartographica* 26 (1989): 1–20.

'Historical Geography and the Cartographic Illusion'. *Journal of Historical Geography* 15 (1989): 80–91.

Harley, John B., and David Woodward. *History of Cartography*, vol. 1 (Chicago: University of Chicago Press, 1987).

Havercroft, Jonathan. *Captives of Sovereignty* (Cambridge: Cambridge University Press, 2011).

Hobson, John M. 'What's at Stake in "Bringing Historical Sociology Back into International Relations?" Transcending "Chronofetishism" and "Tempocentrism" in International Relations'. In Stephen Hobden and John M. Hobson (eds), *Historical Sociology of International Relations* (Cambridge: Cambridge University Press, 2002).

Kant, Immanuel. *Critique of Pure Reason*, Paul Guyer and Allen W. Wood (eds. and trans.) (Cambridge: Cambridge University Press, 1998).

Keohane, Robert O. 'International Relations and International Law: Two Optics'. *Harvard International Law Journal* 38 (1997): 487–502.

Kessler, Oliver. 'So Close yet So Far Away? International Law in International Political Sociology'. *International Political Sociology* 4 (2010): 303–4.

King, Gary, Robert O. Keohane and Sidney Verba. *Designing Social Inquiry: Scientific Inference in Qualitative Research* (Princeton, NJ: Princeton University Press, 1994).

Klabbers, Jan. 'The Bridge Crack'd: a Critical Look at Interdisciplinary Relations'. *International Relations* 23 (2009): 119–25.

Koremenos, Barbara, Charles Lipson and Duncan Snidal. 'The Rational Design of International Institutions'. *International Organization* 55 (2001): 761–99.

Koskenniemi, Martti. 'Empire and International Law: the Real Spanish Contribution'. *University of Toronto Law Journal* 61 (2011): 1–36.

  From Apology to Utopia: The Structure of International Legal Argument, reissue with a new epilogue (Cambridge: Cambridge University Press, 2006).

  The Gentle Civilizer of Nations: The Rise and Fall of International Law 1870–1960 (Cambridge: Cambridge University Press, 2001).

  'Miserable Comforters: International Relations as New Natural Law'. *European Journal of International Relations* 15 (2009): 395–422.

  'Law, Teleology and International Relations: an Essay in Counterdisciplinarity'. *International Relations* 26 (2012): 3–34.

Koslowski, Rey, and Friedrich V. Kratochwil. 'Understanding Change in International Politics: the Soviet Empire's Demise and the International System'. *International Organization* 48 (1994): 215–47.

Kratochwil, Friedrich V. *Rules, Norms, and Decisions: on the Conditions of Practical and Legal Reasoning in International Relations and Domestic Affairs* (Cambridge: Cambridge University Press, 1989).

Lamont, Michèle. *How Professors Think inside the Curious World of Academic Judgment* (Cambridge, MA: Harvard University Press, 2009).

Latour, Bruno. *Science in Action: How to Follow Scientists and Engineers through Society* (Cambridge, MA: Harvard University Press, 1987).

Lefebvre, Henri. *The Production of Space*, Donald Nicholson-Smith (trans.) (Oxford: Blackwell, 1991).

'Space: Social Product and Use Value'. In Neil Brenner and Stuart Elden (eds), *State, Space, World: Selected Essays on Henry Lefebvre* (Minneapolis: University of Minnesota Press, 2009).

Legro, Jeffrey W., and Andrew Moravcsik. 'Is Anybody Still a Realist?' *International Security* 24 (1999): 5–55.

Lindahl, Hans. *Fault Lines of Globalization: Legal Order and the Politics of A-Legality* (Oxford: Oxford University Press, 2013).

Malpas, Jeff, and Karsten Thiel. 'Reading Kant's Geography'. In Stuart Elden and Eduardo Mendieta (eds), *Reading Kant's Geography* (Albany: State University of New York Press, 2011).

Marks, Susan. 'Human Rights in Disastrous Times'. In James Crawford and Martti Koskenniemi (eds), *The Cambridge Companion to International Law* (Cambridge: Cambridge University Press, 2011).

Mitchell, Timothy. *Rule of Experts: Egypt, Techno-Politics, Modernity* (Berkeley: University of California Press, 2002).

'Society, Economy, and the State Effect'. In Aradhana Sharma and Akhil Gupta (eds), *The Anthropology of the State: a Reader* (Oxford: Blackwell, 2006).

Moran, Joe. *Interdisciplinarity* (London: Routledge, 2002).

National Research Council. *Physics through the 1990s: Scientific Interfaces and Technological Applications* (Washington, DC: National Academy Press, 1997).

Onuf, Nicholas G. *World of Our Making: Rules and Rule in Social Theory and International Relations* (Columbia: University of South Carolina Press, 1989).

'Worlds of Our Making'. In *Making Sense, Making Worlds: Constructivism in Social Theory and International Relations* (London: Routledge, 2012).

Pollack, Mark A. 'Is International Relations Corrosive of International Law? A Reply to Martti Koskenniemi'. *Temple International and Comparative Law Journal* 27 (2013): 339–75.

Said, Edward W. *Humanism and Democratic Criticism* (New York: Columbia University Press, 2004).

Orientalism (New York: Vintage, 2003).

'The Scope of Orientalism'. In Moustafa Bayoumi and Andrew Rubin (eds), *The Edward Said Reader* (New York: Vintage, 2000).

Samiei, Mohammad. 'Neo-Orientalism? The Relationship between the West and Islam in Our Globalised World'. *Third World Quarterly* 31 (2010): 1145–60.

Seligman, Linda J. 'Ethnographic Method'. In Daniel Druckman (ed.), *Doing Research: Methods of Inquiry for Conflict Analysis* (Thousand Oaks, CA: Sage, 2005).

Shaffer, Gregory, and Tom Ginsburg. 'The Empirical Turn in International Legal Scholarship'. *American Journal of International Law* 106 (2012): 1–46.

Singh, Sahib. 'Identifying Threats to the Identity of International Law'. Paper presented at the 5th Research Forum of the European Society of International law, May 2013.

Slaughter, Anne-Marie. 'International Law and International Relations Theory: Twenty Years Later'. In Jeffrey L. Dunoff and Mark A. Pollack (eds), *Interdisciplinary Perspectives on International Law and International Relations: the State of the Art* (Cambridge: Cambridge University Press, 2013).

'International Law in a World of Liberal States'. *European Journal of International Law* 6 (1995): 503–38.

Slaughter Burley, Anne-Marie. 'International Law and International Relations Theory: a Dual Agenda'. *American Journal of International Law* 87 (1993): 205–39.

Stichweh, Rudolf. *Zur Entstehung Des Modernen Systems Wissenschaftlicher Disziplinen: Physik in Deutschland, 1740–1890* (Frankfurt am Main, Germany: Suhrkamp, 1984).

Thompson Klein, Julie. 'Blurring, Cracking, and Crossing: Permeation and the Fracturing of Discipline'. In Ellen Messer-Davidow, David R. Shumway and David J. Sylvan (eds), *Knowledges: Historical and Critical Studies in Disciplinarity* (Charlottesville: University Press of Virginia, 1993).

Crossing Boundaries: Knowledge, Disciplinarities, and Interdisciplinarities (Charlottesville: University Press of Virginia, 1996).

Interdisciplinarity: History, Theory, and Practice (Detroit, MI: Wayne State University Press, 1990).

Turner, Stephen. 'What Are Disciplines? And How Is Interdisciplinarity Different'. In Nico Steher and Peter Weingart (eds), *Practising Interdisciplinarity* (Toronto, ON: University of Toronto Press, 2000).

Vigneswaran, Darshan, and Joel Quirk. 'Past Masters and Modern Inventions: Intellectual History as Critical Theory'. *International Relations* 24 (2010): 107–31.

Weingart, Peter. 'A Short History of Knowledge Formations'. In Robert Frodeman, Julie Thompson Klein and Carl Mitcham (eds), *The Oxford Handbook of Interdisciplinarity* (Oxford: Oxford University Press, 2010).

The Critic(-al Subject)

SAHIB SINGH*

8.1 Introduction

Experiencing Martti Koskenniemi's texts is akin to what I imagine Gregor Samsa felt at the beginning of Franz Kafka's *The Metamorphosis*. Samsa, a travelling salesman, awoke one morning thinking he was human, only to discover his body was now that of an insect.[1] In this moment you know you are not what you understand yourself to be. The displacement and discomfort that accompany this experience is precisely what has allowed Koskenniemi to reinvigorate the discipline. It has been for the most part a tortuous journey through apathy, marginalization, engagement, misunderstanding, trenchant resistance, polemics, and perhaps finally acceptance through subsumption. Possibly in spite of this journey, or even because of it, Koskenniemi's texts have firmly arrived into the canon of international legal thought.

At the heart of this lies *From Apology to Utopia*. A text that changed what it is possible to say within the discipline and how it is possible to say it. No small feat. Critical thought has, in part, founded its success upon its relentless willingness to intertwine epistemological concerns with ethical ones. Readers are reminded that international law is made, and re-made, through the commitments and choices of its participants. It is *we* who are responsible for the choices we make amidst the anxieties and uncertainties of living in a conflictual world.[2] But like all forms of knowledge and politics, critical thought also inscribes certain images of the characteristics and attitudes of this 'we'.[3] In short, it presumes, shapes and imposes certain images of the international lawyer; some hidden, others put front and centre and others sutured through its texts. In this chapter I excavate, flesh out and critique the images of the international lawyer that underpin *From Apology to Utopia*.

This endeavour has been guided by three questions. What images of the subject (read: international lawyer) are required by, but not always made explicit within, the text?[4] What characteristics, attitudes, or subjectivities are rhetorically assumed, created and perpetuated by the text in its making of these images? And are the images of the subject(s) that emerge capable of realizing the politics of critical thought? These questions help me to explore several understandings of the (critical) international lawyer that have become central to the discipline's imagination in recent decades.

The dominant image that emerges is the critical subject, and as we shall see, this is also a projection of the critic. Hence the designation critic(-al subject). The type of international lawyers required and sought by *From Apology to Utopia* are not always in easy view. They emerge after I excavate the assumed and presupposed subject behind the intellectual vehicles that drive Koskenniemi's text (Section 8.2).[5] Certain understandings of the critic and the critical subject are repressed and enabled by these intellectual vehicles.

The first image of the subject in *From Apology to Utopia* is a reproduction of its author's self-image (Section 8.3). This is the text's *presupposed* subject, namely, the image of an individual that the text requires in order to perform as it does. This is, to put it clearly, the *critic as an intellectual*. But Koskenniemi's text also produces another subject-type: that which is necessary to carry out its normative demands. The potential of any given (political) project depends upon and is invested in the realisation of such a subject. This critical subject is the *critical professional international lawyer*. The characteristics, attitudes and subjectivities of these two subject-types not only reflect each other but also sit in uncomfortable tension. I demonstrate how Koskenniemi's images of the critic and the critical subject are deeply rooted in a Sartrean metaphysic; they are governed by both elitism and unhappiness, for whom freedom is both a constant and overarching possibility, and yet is always embodied in a fleeting moment.

I then, finally, question whether this critic(-al subject) may not unwittingly embed the very aspects of liberal legal thought that it seeks to challenge (Section 8.4). This subject is produced, sustained and tormented by balancing certain antinomies that in many key respects reflect the characteristics and attitudes of the subject at the heart of liberal legal-political thought. And yet this is, in part, not seen because of the functioning of certain myths.

But permit me to make two clarifications before proceeding to these arguments.

To speak of a 'subject' is not to speak of a natural individual, but rather one that is created and sustained by a certain discourse upon which she is dependent. It preserves her whilst initiating and sustaining her desires and agency.[6] A form of power constitutes her and her capacities. Critical international legal thought, or more specifically the discourse and practices that it comprises, is such a form of power. Its eclecticism often produces various, and at times conflicting, images of the international lawyer.[7] It is by better grasping the dominant images within critical thought, as well as the possibilities created by contrasting or conflicting images, that we may be able re-envision our own role within the discipline. It is for this reason that it is useful to look to Koskenniemi's texts, some of which have become influential – even part of what is unconsciously presupposed or assumed, rather than what is questioned – in certain corners of the discipline.[8] But it ought also to be noted that the subject exposed here is presupposed by the text; it is produced by the text only to the extent that it is latent in the text's methods. If this image of the subject is recycled into the discipline, in any way, it is not through method, but rather in the non-reflective way in which Koskenniemi's text has circulated through the discipline.

There is also a second reason for this article. In contemporary legal thought there is a tendency to consider the subject as part of the solution. It is shared by traditional liberal and critical theories alike. In the rhetorical form that tends to structure most texts, as well as the psychology of normative legal thought – the 'problem → solution' split – the subject nearly always ends up occupying the latter position. Problems are cast outside the subject, often in specific practices structures or processes, or in certain modes of thinking. It is a rhetorical trope that removes our motivation to explore the possibility that the problem lies within specific images of ourselves as subjects of a disciplinary discourse.[9] Where critical scholarship has breached this threshold and does indeed consider the way we think of ourselves and our subjectivity, it still (1) points this analysis outwards, to modes of thought, practices and discourses other than its own; and (2) it still ultimately ends up investing the potential of its emancipatory politics within specific images of the subject. These patterns of thought deserve attention.

My hope in this chapter is to shake, and perhaps even reinvigorate, the faith that critical international legal thought invests in its subject(s).

8.2 Critical Knowledge: Methods and Theories

It is a rare breed of book that causes consternation in the ranks whilst also inspiring a generation. James Crawford, then holder of the Whewell Chair,

introduced Koskenniemi's work at the annual meeting of the American
Society of International Law by saying that the latter had shown 'with
overwhelming erudition the impossibility of our discipline'.[10] But hadn't
Koskenniemi sought to expose the discipline's 'conditions of possibility'
in *From Apology to Utopia*, rather than render it to the mercy of nihilism?
Hadn't he sought to shake the complacent intellectual foundations of
the discipline, seeking to preserve it whilst transforming the way its participants thought of it? Interpretations vary, though perhaps part of the
problem was the text's form.[11]

The sheer volume and complexity of the linguistic, social, political
and even smatterings of psychoanalytic, theories that undergird *From
Apology to Utopia* may alienate the text from its intended audience. Even
if the text is enriched in equal measure. But these intellectual vehicles
are important; an appreciation of their role in the text guards against
misunderstanding and misappropriation. It may even prevent misplaced
accusations of nihilism or other categorizations that go a long way towards
disempowering critique.[12]

Critical international legal thought has no allegiance to specific methods or theories. Early in the New Approaches to International Law
('NAIL') movement, allegiance to *a* method or theory was seen as a
form of reification.[13] Indeed, Koskenniemi has argued that the merit of
any method or theory (or style as he would prefer) lies in the strategic use
it is put to.[14] For this reason we see considerable eclecticism in his use of
theories and methods, as well as shifts in theoretical posturings across his
oeuvre.[15] This diversity has allowed him to enrich what has traditionally
been a theory-averse discipline. But there is almost certainly a common
commitment to methodological anti-formalism and what is known as the
broad church of 'critical knowledge'.[16] This form of knowledge seeks to
bring about change in a given social system by bringing an awareness of
one's concrete social reality. This in turn enables forms of transformative
action. The point, after all, is to try and change the world. And the kernel
of emancipatory politics that lies at the heart of this form of knowledge
is intimately tied to how the subject may come to see her own freedom.

And so, despite the aversion of NAIL to theoretical commitment, *From
Apology to Utopia* commits to a number of methods and theoretical predispositions in pursuit of its emancipatory politics. The majority of the text
is the demonstration of a formal structuralist method (Step 1). Koskenniemi attempts to show that professional international legal discourse
and liberal politics is constructed around binary opposites.[17] Whilst these
opposites are mutually exclusive, they can also only gain their meaning

by relying on each other. They are irredeemably interdependent.[18] International legal argument interminably oscillates between these poles and this structural indeterminacy means that a given legal question cannot be answered by reference to *only* international law. If a given argument is to prevail it has to be infused with, or motored by, political, moral, social (etc.) contexts.

This structuralism is deployed as a form of critical knowledge, whose task it is 'to undo the naturalness of conventional ways of thinking about the law'.[19] Step 1 is employed to unmask and undo the 'false consciousness' of then existing international legal thought (Step 2).[20] Clearly influenced by the critical theory of the Frankfurt School, Koskenniemi attempts to subvert the 'truth' claims of liberal political and international legal thought. Liberalism's attachment to law's objectivity and its primacy over politics is cast aside as a form of false consciousness; as a naturalized, given way of thinking that is anything but. The indeterminacy thesis, demonstrated by the text's application of structuralism, seeks to unravel international law's claim to objectivity and undoes its false consciousness, so that this claim will now 'appear as contingent and contestable, [so that] the actual will manifest itself in a new light'.[21]

Both Koskenniemi's structuralism and his ideology critique are in some ways inherently polemical. This adversarial approach is softened by what is an 'indissociable' aspect of his text: the ideals of community and inter-subjectivity (Step 3).[22] The indeterminacy thesis leads us to the conclusion that any international legal argument must find its justification in a contestable political choice. In this way the conflictual and paradoxical nature of liberal politics finds its way into international legal argument. However, critical practice 'attempts to reach those conflictual views, bring them out into the open and suggest practical arrangements for dealing with conflict without denying its reality'.[23] This normative practice urges us to 'slowly proceed towards (instead of promising to realize at once) decreasing domination and increasing a sense of an authentic community between disagreeing social agents'.[24] In Section 8.4, I will explore the nature of this this normative practice given the negative moment of Koskenniemi's critique, and whether it leads us to a deepening of liberal ideals through an arrested critique.

Finally, Koskenniemi argues for a critical identity for the international lawyer. She must be capable of acting in a conflictual world. Here, international lawyers are socialized agents, performing specific roles within specific routines, shaped by specific contexts (Step 4). But these both constrain and enable the international lawyer. She is a situated agent for whom it must be 'possible to live in the present without losing the sense of the beyond'.[25] Critical normative practice requires this particular subject. And whilst he only briefly elaborates this subject, it seems necessary for Koskenniemi to 'outline for the lawyer an existence in routine which constantly aims at transforming the context which shape it and an intellectual directedness towards context-transformation without losing touch of its embeddedness in routine'.[26]

As we follow these methodological and theoretical steps through the text, it becomes apparent that *From Apology to Utopia* is defined by a specific paradox. *Its entire critical project depends on the potential of the subject and yet it furnishes us with no analytical knowledge of her.* As we move from structuralism to ideology critique, inter-subjectivity and socialization, the subject rises to a certain prominence within the narrative. We become aware that Koskenniemi's emancipatory politics cannot do without her. She is capable of transcending her own situation by recognizing herself as reified individual, thereby changing how she may act in the world, and of constantly realizing her freedom; of bringing a sense of community and authentic commitment to the lives of actors who are constantly in conflict and disagreement; and of acting within but being able to constantly transform one's context in a given social role. The hitherto invisible subject is *doing all the work.* And yet we know nothing about her. Nonetheless, Koskenniemi's text seduces us to simply invest in her potential.

8.3   The Critic (-al Subject)

Let me begin by recalling that there are two subject-types at play in *From Apology to Utopia*. On the one hand, there is the socialized professional international lawyer who is tasked with carrying out critique's normative practice (see Step 4 above). Then there is the subject who can realize and overcome the thought-structures that have so far defined her existence. This image is presupposed by Koskenniemi's critique; and she is also the *result* of his critique. She is a projection of the critic as an intellectual. Images of this subject are repressed, composing the text's unconscious: a driving force that refuses articulation.[27] But perhaps most importantly, she is also recursively played out in other parts of critical international legal thought. She emerges from Koskenniemi's structuralism and ideology critique. In these steps we experience the reproduction of the subject found in Jean-Paul Sartre's existentialist philosophy.[28] In Sartre, as in Koskenniemi's text, we see an individual who can always transcend her situation *in reality*, rather than only as some ontological condition. The critical international lawyer may find absolute freedom in the sphere of critical rational consciousness rather than a freedom conditioned by material reality. Let me explain.

Koskenniemi, like Sartre, begins by developing an unbridgeable separation between the world and the individual. That is, between object and subject or between doctrine and lawyer. *From Apology to Utopia* dedicates most of its pages to a structural analysis that focuses on the 'object' side of the analysis (doctrine, cases, arguments). Unsurprisingly its scientific method suspends nearly all references to the subject, whose activity may constitute such objects, or whom in turn such objects may constitute.[29] The purpose of this is not to render the subject irrelevant, but to expose the varied and contradictory positions that an international lawyer can take within the diversity of international legal discourse.[30] The analytical structure of the book *reinforces a splitting between subject and object* (whilst normatively denying the impossibility of this, see Step 4 above). This 'splitting' is then recursively solidified in Koskenniemi's images of the critical subject.

In *From Apology to Utopia* this subject is able to stand *above* and *separate* from, albeit momentarily, her object. She is defined by an attitude of reflection upon her own situation, as well as upon herself. She is able to reflect on her own and her field's reified situation (because critique has done its work). She is able to see herself as a managing technician in a thingified system of rules. And she is able to transcend this understanding of herself, moving towards her own possibilities. She is able to discern all this because she can detach herself from the (international legal) world she finds herself in. Critique promises her the capacity to capture and see her 'real' situation, through the momentary distance that critique gives her from her false understanding of the world. She is able to see all this because there is a brief 'moment' and 'space' that is immune from context (from structure, from her technical role, from her beliefs etc.).

Now notice how this image of the subject is almost identical to the critic. Except the critic's operation is performed before this subject comes into view. The critic is able to stand *above* and *separate* from his object of analysis.[31] With his interrogative attitude, he is able to discern that international law works according to a determinable structure of argument, at a given historical moment. He is able to discern the patterns of structure without having to be constituted by this structure. He is able to reflect upon his own and his field's reified situation as a mere collection of managing technician working in a thingified system of rules. He is able to transcend this understanding, moving towards its possibilities. He is able to discern all of this because he is able to detach himself from the world he finds himself in and *able to conduct his diagnosis in a space that is not occupied by the very objects he wishes to analyse.* So, these very objects do not constitute him and he is able to master them. The critical theorist, here, is an individual that can know in ways that a reified individual cannot; he is capable of highlighting as contingent that which may have been falsely thought of as universally necessary. It is the knowledge acquired and given by his interrogative attitude and distance from his objects that allows him to escape the conditions of his existence:

> The critical argument's critical potential lies in showing that it is possible to escape from the frustratingly weak character of legal discourse by extending the range of permissible argumentative styles beyond the points in which it is usually held that legal argument must stop in order to remain 'legal'.[32]

> [I seek to] provide the possibility for reformed routine; a routine which allows *the lawyer to escape from the limitations of the role* and help create a better society while enabling him to live a conscious and meaningful life as a lawyer in the midst of the actuality of social and political conflict.[33]

> We have felt that extending upon imagination we must renounce the security which our legal roles offered us. Yet, remaining within roles seemed to require unreflective assimilation or engaging in phantasy. We were not relieved from the painful task of living and choosing in the midst of political conflict. Instead of impartial umpires or spectators, we were cast as players in the game, members in somebody's team. It is not that we need to play the game better, or more self-consciously. We need to re-imagine the game, reconstruct its rules, redistribute the prizes.[34]

Where the non-critical or reified lawyer is imprisoned within constraints or structures, the critical theorist in Koskenniemi's text is able to promise freedom, through choice and transformation, from these very constraints. The admittedly vague politics of this form of critical theory is one of setting the reified subject free. Within this narrative there is always something that can be done despite the structured character of one's situation.[35] And what we see, given this image of the critical subject and its projection of the critic, is the Sartrean subject.

Sartre's *Being and Nothingness* is an account of what it means for a human to be in the world. At the book's centre lies a distinction between things in the world (being-in-itself, or roughly, the object) and the human being (being-for-itself, consciousness, cogito or, roughly, the subject).

These are distinct parts of the world that compose concrete human reality only in a synthetic relationship with each other.[36] Whilst an object is a non-conscious thing that always coincides with itself, the *subject is a consciousness that is conscious of itself and always reaches beyond what it is, all the while continually creating itself.*[37] Sartre's task is 'to penetrate into the profound meaning of the relation 'man-world''.[38] This, at first blush, seems to be an ontological question concerned with the nature and relations of being. On the other hand, Koskenniemi's work offers a historical grounding for his critical international lawyer. Sartre remains relevant precisely because his analysis is not merely ontological. It *becomes historical* to the extent that he argues that it seeks to exist in concrete reality and is an attitude of living *in* the world. As a consequence, his historical stance presupposes and imports the conclusions of his ontological analysis.[39]

In Sartre's writings the individual possesses the specifically human 'attitude of interrogation'.[40] To be able to reflect upon and question oneself and one's situation is at the core of being human. A question of course does not guarantee an answer. It may also furnish an answer in the negative. Or it may even limit an affirmative answer ('It is thus and not otherwise'.)[41] For Sartre, the constant possibility of these negations constitutes the heart of what it is to be a human, a subject or a consciousness. It is this possibility of negation that conditions every process of questioning, and this process in turn is the very condition of a reflective consciousness.[42] Negations define the subject, leading to certain forms of anxiety, frustration and anguish. At the heart of the critical subject's being is a kernel of nothingness, for it is this that affords him such a role. But it is in seeking detachment from the world, *transcending its objects*, that this subject finds the possibility of freedom:

> *Anguish then is the reflective apprehension of freedom by itself. In this sense it is mediation, for although it is immediate consciousness of itself, it arises from the negation of the appeals of the world where I had been engaged –* in order to apprehend myself as consciousness which possesses a preontological comprehension of its essence and a pre-judicative sense of its possibilities. Anguish is opposed to the mind of the serious man who apprehends values in terms of the world and who resides in the reassuring, materialistic substantiation of values. In the serious mood I define myself in terms of the object by pushing aside *a priori* as impossible all enterprises in which I am not engaged at the moment; the meaning which my freedom has given to the world, I apprehend as coming from the world and constituting my obligations. *In anguish I apprehend myself at once as totally free and as not being able to derive the meaning of the world except as coming from myself.*[43]

In this passage we see why Sartre's metaphysic may lie at the heart of Koskenniemi's image of the critic and critical subject. The relationship between the individual and the world operates through splitting them and establishing a hierarchy. In Sartre, the subject can master the world without the world constituting it in turn.[44] The subject can gain a specific distance from his object of analysis. A reflective consciousness (or knowing consciousness)[45] may suffer frustration and anguish, but it is this that secures him space away from the world and its objects. And just as Koskenniemi's critic can transcend international law's reified objects and its structure, Sartre's subject is able to master and transcend the world.[46]

Sartre also accepts that an individual always finds himself in a given circumstances, not of his own making. Similarly, Koskenniemi asserts an image of the international lawyer as a social agent who occupies given social roles, through which he helps produce the structure of international legal language. But Sartre's subject, just as Koskenniemi's critical international lawyer, is able to also (momentarily) transcend the given 'situation' that so degrades her possibilities and potential. This transcendence is achieved because the *individual subject alone is able to able to determine the limits of her situation*. It is she that determines the meaning of any given adversity by choosing to see the situation in light of the goal she chooses.[47] In short: *the real limits of a given situation depend on how we exercise our absolute and free choice to see the situation and its limits.*[48] A pre-given situation is hence made the subjects own. He masters its meaning – its limits and its relevance to her own condition – all through her act of choice.

This is an imposing metaphysical logic and the one that sustains the emancipatory politics of critical legal thought. For Koskenniemi, '[conscious agents] must participate in social routine and yet, *do this from a distance*. To be a conscious actor requires relatedness to the social world in a way which it is possible to live in the present without losing a sense of the beyond'.[49] The social role does not constitute the individual lawyer, but is rather appropriated by him. The critical subject is able to make the situation his own and realize his freedom in choosing to transform it. Importantly, notice that this logic *requires* a subject that can take a specific distance from a given world – an irreconcilable and always maintained subject / object split. It requires a consciousness that can transcend the world because it is reflective and not shaped by the world's belief and social structures.[50] It requires the elementals of an *empty* subject whose choices can never be constructed by the world. Sartre, for example, considers that the constraints society placed on the Jewish population only exist (in a concrete historical sense) and have meaning to the extent that a Jew choses to see them as constraints. A Jewish person can transcend the anti-Semitic signs ('No Jews allowed here') and the anti-Semitic structures, if he choses to view these as purely external objects that do not constitute him, his freedom to choose or his beliefs and consciousness.[51]

It seems reasonable to argue that this existential notion of freedom, if it asked to live in concrete reality, borders on absurdity.[52] Sartre's philosophy, and to the extent it undergirds Koskenniemi's text, delivers the subject into a tyrannical idealism. The critic premised on a Sartrean metaphysic bears a constant and unrelenting responsibility for the world and for himself.[53] Everything rests on his *absolutely free* choices; the burden of the world is his to master.

But even as the critic has exposed the objectifying structures within international legal thought, and the critical subject realizes her 'true' situation, their *freedom is only momentary*. Or, in the words of Koskenniemi, there is 'little support for the belief that revolution or happiness could survive the first moments of enthusiastic bliss. The morning after is cold, and certain to come'.[54] This is both a historical lesson and one that emerges from Sartre's analysis. His subject can never fully coincide with the world (for then it would be an object) and it can never coincide with its actual situation. Just as the critic creates a new world, and the critical subject is re-made in the critic's image, they cannot coincide with the world their critique, or realizations, have produced. The critical subject must, at every new historical juncture, renounce the knowledge her critique has produced. And because there is no human existence without the 'situation', or no 'non-human situation', the responsibility to realize my freedom occurs in making the situation mine – to constantly make a choice on the same and new ground 'again and again without a break'.[55] Critique for this subject, like existence, knows no bounds of time except mortal death. The image of the critic that emerges from Koskenniemi's *From Apology to Utopia* is an individual who lives an essentially unhappy and constantly burdened existence, who can always realize his absolutely free choice, all the whilst knowing that any freedom achieved can only ever be fleeting. And must be fought for, over and over, each time anew, till one is no longer capable.

8.4 Productive Tensions, Limits and Myths

I have tried to make explicit the implicit. Doing so by reading Sartre alongside reading Koskenniemi. I have argued that we see the Sartrean subject at the heart of *From Apology to Utopia.* The subject, her attitudes and characteristics, her worldview may now be better understood. She ought, at the least, to be graspable. This is a subject that splits herself from and transcends the world (her object), possesses a reflective and constantly transcendent image of rational consciousness, and who believes that concrete freedom lies in absolute choice. In this final substantive section the question becomes whether this subject is capable of realizing the politics of the critical international legal thought.

In the subsections that follow, I show how the critical subject (and hence also the critic) is structured by certain productive antinomies and our image of her are sustained by certain myths. The first contradiction that constitutes this subject is the search for a politics of community, whilst simultaneously trying to dominate a part of the polity (Section 8.4.1). The second is between competing and opposite understandings of freedom; imminent and transcendant (Section 8.4.2). Third, I argue that the image of the subject that we see in *From Apology to Utopia* may, ironically, perpetuate and reproduce the very ideology of liberalism that it seeks to challenge (Section 8.4.3). And finally, I argue how we may not see these tensions and limits, because the identity of the critical subject is entrenched and reproduced by the functioning of specific myths (Section 8.4.4).

8.4.1   Between Community and Domination

The first tension arises as *From Apology to Utopia*'s critique moves from its negative to its positive moment. Or from undoing false consciousness through structuralism, towards inter-subjectivity (see earlier discussion). Koskenniemi's is a critique with the ideal of community. I argue that the performed ideology critique sits in irresolvable tension with the idealized move towards community. For no other reason than that Koskenniemi's ideology critique effects, at a subjective level, a commitment to annihilate an opponent.

To understand the nature of this 'annihilation', it must first be understood that the critic (and then the critical subject this the critic's critique engenders) abhors the situation where an individual is alienated from his freedom. Rather, to 'have identity as conscious agents they must fight constantly against alienation and assimilation'.[56] Koskenniemi sees the field of international law populated by those lawyers whose 'identity [lies] in his skill as a managing technician of [an] invisible international "system"'.[57] The form of critique that we see in *From Apology to Utopia* functions *upon* and *for* such individuals. It is critique built on a war of consciousness.[58] The task is to do away with a consciousness that does not realize itself and its potential as consciousness. It is to do away with the individual who views herself as a 'thing' that is subordinated to the standardized techniques of a given social system (i.e. as a managing technician in a system of laws). This individual cannot realize the potential of herself as a consciousness, precisely because she considers herself to fully coincide with her situation. This type of individual can only ever be an object in a Sartrean metaphysic, for she does not realize that she is always more than the possibilities of her given situation. She possesses a form of consciousness that alienates her from her freedom, her choices and her responsibilities.

Critique seeks to 'annihilate' this form of subjectivity or consciousness. It wishes to demonstrate its falsity, and replace it with its own 'truth'.[59] Ideology critique, in the particular sense we see in *From Apology to Utopia*, must begin with the undoing of a specific form of consciousness. It does this through an act of domination: the (claimed) exercise of a superior form of reason. The critic and the critical subject does what she does with all objects; she harnesses a specific distance from them and then masters them.[60] And this act of domination precedes the act of annihilation: the consciousness that does not realize itself cannot be an acceptable part of the polity where ideology critique has done its work.

We may now perhaps see how a kernel of irony lies at the heart of Koskenniemi's critique. The will to lessen domination is premised upon an act of domination. In the positive moment of his text, even if inter-subjective conflict remains in the world, we 'can slowly proceed towards ... decreasing domination and increasing the sense of authentic community between disagreeing social agents'.[61] The ideal of community presupposes an understanding of the political. It is not premised on the erasure of conflict, or the move to consensus. It does not deny dissensus, but rather provides a hermeneutic footing for disagreement. But this notion of community *does not* presuppose exclusion, or the undoing of a part of the polity. Critique, in its idealized image, has enabled this open, conversant and conflictual community. Yet in this very act of constitution lies a founding act of annihilation. One part of the community is afflicted with falsity of thought and *must* be replaced by a 'truer' form of thought. False consciousness must be undone in this war of consciousness. The subjectivity of a specific individual must be undone and replaced with another subjectivity that will bring her in closer relation to the group in which the critic resides. And so at the heart of an idealized

community where dominance is constantly lessened, is an act of domination *par excellence.*

Matters may get worse for the critic. This act of domination may be constantly re-inscribed into the fabric of the international legal community.
Can the critic we have seen emerge surrender this initial act of dominance?
The Sartrean metaphysic almost ensures that the war of consciousness is
relentless; a Sartrean subject can never let her consciousness coincide with
itself without lapsing into an object that needs to be mastered. And just
as a certain falsity is replaced by a 'truth', this 'truth' be shown to be its
own form of falsity. The anxious responsibility attached to always having
to transcend a given way of being is the recurring narrative at the heart
of both the Sartrean metaphysic and the nature of false consciousness
critique.[62] And so, the critic, and the critical subject that follows him,
will nearly always be torn between the antinomy that lies at the heart of
the negative and positive moments of his critique. The image we see in
From Apology to Utopia is that of a critic who aspires to less domination
as his ideal, all the while constantly perpetuating a form of domination
himself.

8.4.2   Emancipatory Politics between Freedoms

The critical subject's identity and Koskenniemi's text is structured by a
second antinomy. Two incompatible notions of freedom are produced
by the text: (a) freedom *from* a situation, and (b) freedom *through* a
situation. On the one hand, the Sartrean subject delivers us into the first
understanding by positing a subject who can constantly appropriate and
transcend her situation. This is the text's *presupposed* subject. But on
the other hand, Koskenniemi's structuralism delivers us into the second.
A position reinforced by the text's *normative* subject (i.e. the idealized
socialized subject we see at the end of *From Apology to Utopia*). But let
me elaborate on this antinomy.

The empty subject that we saw emerge from Sartre is one who believes
that freedom is always possible. This is the freedom of choice and it is
absolute. The subject's ontological freedom conditions and obtains her
practical freedom.[63] The critic, building on this Sartrean metaphysic,
requires a space for reflection that is not occupied by the objects of his
analysis (beliefs, structures, discourses etc.). And the critical subject is
endowed with this same 'space'. By freezing the subject-object dichotomy,
critique can maintain an image of this 'space' or momentary distance
from externalities. Not only is this necessary for the critic's and critical

subject's performance, but it is foundational to her promises. The fantasy he sells his reader depends upon the latter being able to finally occupy this same space or distance from the world (once his false consciousness is undone). But both the performance and the promise deliver us into identical ideas of freedom. Critique in *From Apology to Utopia*'s casts freedom as the absence of constraint, as freedom *from* a situation.

And yet, Koskenniemi's structuralism and his normative, socialized, subject advocates for a different understanding of freedom. 'True, the lawyer is constrained. But inasmuch as he experiences the conflicting pull of the criticisms of apology and utopia, he is not fully so'.[64] Koskenniemi's structuralism enables the lawyer to see the play of language he can enact so as to be professionally competent. It is anti-humanist to the extent that it reminds us that social structures exist and often proceed without any regard for the individual *and* always through her. But it also seeks to rescue a form of humanism as it leads the lawyer away from the stark rationalism that required the Sartrean subject to think of freedom as the absence of constraint. The logic enabled by Koskenniemi's normative text is that constraints, whether a linguistic structures, social roles, beliefs or other conditioning circumstances, *provide the enabling conditions of possibility*.[65] Freedom becomes dependent on constraint. And constraint becomes the very means by which we can enter into a given world and can realize our concrete possibilities.[66] Maurice Merleau-Ponty put it so: that 'I am a psychological and historical structure does not limit my access to the world, but on the contrary is my means of entering into communication with it'.[67] Freedom is achieved *through* one's situation.

The result is a text structured by, and oscillating between, certain antinomies. Not only do we have competing and incompatible understandings of freedom but we also have incompatible understandings of the subject. On the one hand there is the image of the individual who is always able to transcend his situation, and on the other hand, one who seeks to transform his given situation by working within and opening up its concrete possibilities. The first presupposes a bare or empty consciousness that can always master his situation and the second understands the subject as always constituted, who acts in the world through this constitution. One is presupposed by the text, the other demanded by it. Each *produced* in its own way.

These antinomies are not idle intellectual musings. Rather, they go to the very core of critical international legal thought for no other project is so driven by the politics of emancipation. The stakes are considerable. How do the critic and critical subject speak? From a disembodied, unsituated position within a momentarily separated space, or from an embodied, historical situated and produced spaces? Not only does this antinomy go the heart of the individual's sense of self and his capacity in the world, but it also goes to the heart of how we may seek to address the problems of this world. And we find it recursively being played out in critical international legal thought.[68] To say little of what is ultimately at stake: whether we may unwittingly exacerbate the hostile conditions which constitute us, or whether we are capable of understanding them in a new light and possibly bringing small amounts of welcome relief.

8.4.3   The 'Stunningly Liberal Subject'

The philosopher Jacques Rancière once stated that 'revolutionaries invented a 'people' before inventing its future'.[69] This is to say that not only does all politics require a subject but the framing of the future happens in the moment of political intervention. The critical subject is not merely the condition of possibility of Koskenniemi's text. Rather, her image frames the potential of his intervention, for the realization of his politics. It is not enough, however, that this subject is capable of realizing the politics of Koskenniemi's critical thought. More importantly, we must be seduced and manipulated in believing that this subject has this capacity. Readers, consumers, students and co-conspirators of Koskenniemi's text must come to believe that the conception of the self they see in his work is an accurate account of the nature of their being.[70] But what if the critical subject is neither capable of realizing the politics of critical thought and we as readers realize that we have been seduced by particular myths?

If you accept the argument made in Section 8.3 of this chapter, the absolute free and empty subject is presupposed by Koskenniemi's critique. Sartre is the dirty little secret at the heart of *From Apology to Utopia*. For this critical subject, no matter her conditions or situation, she is able to determine, appropriate and master it. She is always responsible for her own freedom, and indeed, freedom can only appear as a result of exercised responsibility. This freedom from constraint comes into sight as she empties herself, as she separates from and transcends her object. The problem of course is that we already live within such a cultural narrative of ourselves. It is strikingly familiar precisely because it is the narrative of political liberalism. And the image of the critical subject is, as Pierre Schlag notes in another context, that of the 'stunningly liberal subject'.[71] Liberalism has established, sustained and rejuvenated itself by constantly furnishing us with an image of the individual who is always self-determining and always capable of making any choice she wishes to. Not only is freedom equated with choice, but this choice is an ever-present possibility and always absolute. The liberal subject is seduced (and often, ironically shamed) into believing that she is the alpha and omega in her relations with the world.

So at the precise historical juncture that Koskenniemi's text seeks to challenge the main tenets of liberalism,[72] his text offers a subject who sees her emancipation on the same foundations as that of the liberal subject. The Sartrean kernel at the core of *From Apology to Utopia* is no longer innocent or dormant. One is left to question the extent to which Koskenniemi's critique is capable of realizing its politics of liberating the individual. But perhaps more damningly, Koskenniemi's critique and its view of the subject may *perpetuate the very ideology of its, of our, time*. The point is not merely that the critical subject is promised freedom through the operation of critical thought. It is that the *grounds* of this freedom are precisely the same as those embedded within the liberal subject. With this realization comes another: freedom, and its constant promise, is a mode and method through which we are managed. Sartre was all too aware of this. In 1946 he remarked:

> The revolutionary . . . distrusts freedom. And rightly so. There has never been a lack of prophets to proclaim to him that he was free, and each time in order to cheat him.[73]

Koskenniemi, many years after he wrote *From Apology to Utopia*, would state much the same: 'freedom is also a way to govern human beings'.[74] The irony should be quite apparent; critical thought sought to empower, liberate and enable the individual may then very well deliver her into the very tyranny she sought to escape. And in doing so, help sustain the very political ideology that she and her politics sought to challenge.

8.4.4   Myth and Identity

To realize that the potential of the critical subject is considerably curbed by the aforementioned antinomies and limits *should* matter. Our faith in this subject's capacity ought to be shaken. But interestingly enough, they may not matter and the reader's faith in this subject may remain intact. I suggest that this is in part because of *how* the text's readers are seduced and manipulated into believing a certain image of the critical subject, and in part, because belief cannot be so easily displaced by epistemological knowledge. A significant portion of this chapter demonstrated how *From Apology to Utopia* presumed into existence the type of psychological and social subject that was desired and required by its author's politics. And that it did so without being seen to do so. How it did so, and how it may continue to do so, is what interests me.

The starting point for this inquiry is the notion of myth. Roland Barthes wrote:

> In passing from history to nature, myth acts economically: it abolishes the complexity of human acts, it gives them the simplicity of essences, it does away with all dialectics, with any going back beyond what is immediately visible, it organizes a world which is without contradictions because it is without depth, a world wide open and walling in the evident, it establishes a blissful clarity: things appear to mean something by themselves.[75]

The economy of a myth allows it to create and sustain belief structures in society. It enables us to internally cope with the complexity of external realities – that whilst often situated outside of us, may work through us. Myths stabilize and entrench identities precisely because they have the capacity to repress any identity's internal clamour – its splits, its inconsistencies and its antinomies. This is just so with the critical subject.

A few observations ought to be quite apparent if you have followed my argument to this point. First, the kernel of *From Apology to Utopia* is a presupposed Sartrean subject. Second, this critical subject constantly tries to empty herself of content (of context, the situation, etc.); her being is in part constituted by nothingness. Third, this critical subject is none other than a projection of the critic himself. Fourth, both the critical subject and the critic are able to take a specific distance from a given object of analysis. Fifth, both images are torn between certain antinomies and limits, which question their capacity to fulfil their politics; and that each of these antinomies and limits are repressed from view. Whilst these observations give rise to a number of paradoxes, their relative coherence is sustained by the workings of a particular myth.

It is this: the *empty* subject has come to represent the work that a constituted, or fuller, subject carries out. We see this thought repressed in a number of ways. If the critical subject is a projection of the critic, then we see at the heart of *From Apology to Utopia* a subject who was part of a certain project. We see a fuller, situated individual who attended Dighton weekends, who wrote and read with other intellectuals in the field and beyond it, and who's self-image could not be divorced from a privileged, counter-cultural background. The critical subject cannot be both empty and a projection of a fuller subject that is the critic. And then note, the movement in *From Apology to Utopia* from the presupposed, empty, critical subject to Koskenniemi's socialized international lawyer that is normatively demanded by his critical thought. This movement is inevitable because neither image is sustainable on its own ground. The constituted subject must account for her agency and the empty individual must account for limits to her agency. The operation of myth has ensured that this interminable oscillation is never full inscribed *within* the critical subject or critic. These representations will *always* self-identify with the bare consciousness, all the while knowing that it is a situated critical subject that must do all the work. And they will do so, having being seduced and manipulated into believing this is possible.

But myths are useful. They are not only capable of establishing a group identity, but they may do so through 'metaphoric identities'.[76] Those, that in the act of internalizing, we can aspire and grow towards. The myths that sustain the critical subject enable it to remain an identity to which many young scholars are drawn; its aspiration nature ensures this. Our discipline, through texts such as Koskenniemi's, produces myth and then, imitates it.

8.5 Conclusion

Michel Foucault famously spoke of the 'author', describing him as not merely the author of his own work, but one that has 'produced something else: the possibilities and rules for the formation of other texts'.[77] The significance of *From Apology to Utopia* lies not in the intricacies of its text or the status of its author, but rather in its intertextuality. Namely, how it enables and shapes other texts within our discipline. In undertaking an inquiry into the subject produced by critical international legal thought, I have sought to take an approach that differs from Koskenniemi, Kennedy or Orford;[78] it is one enmeshed in the intellectual vehicles of a given text, the text's strategies of containment (i.e. exposing what it does not let us see, but depends upon) and reading generously with certain philosophical texts.

In *From Apology to Utopia* we find a recursive belief in a textually absent international lawyer. It is not a belief of pure dogma, even if it remains a constant. But just as his text takes up a disciplining role that helps to 'make' professional international lawyers and helps constitute a critical community, it offers liberating and debilitating possibilities. The images of the international lawyer that we see through his seminal text not only straddles conflicting ways of thinking about the world (community/domination; transcendent/imminent freedom; critical reason and science/imagination), but this subject is also always struggling with certain tensions that inevitably define her. Faith in our capacity as critical intellectuals or critical professionals of international law comes with a required humility.

An important point remains: Koskenniemi's text is an offer of a subject position. The images of the subject that you see in this chapter only appear as complete *within* Koskenniemi's text. To identify, consciously or unconsciously, with these images of the subject occurs, in normal legal education, through interaction with multiple other images of the international lawyer. That some images and positions (the pragmatic professional, the humanitarian saviour, the critic who speaks truth to power and offers liberating possibilities etc.) become appealing is in part a result of how they seduce us and in part, how they interact with other images. To identify as an international lawyer, to be a subject of the discipline and profession, is a process of becoming. We are constantly adjusting to rethink our place, our role and our capabilities. To be aware that we do so, and how this may be so, when we read Koskenniemi's texts, is an important first step towards re-imagining our (critical) role within today's international legal order. The uncertainties, conflicts and tensions found in our social world are not only found there; they ought to be an integral part of how we think of ourselves and our projects. The small contribution of this chapter is to suggest that we need to be willing to shake our own (critical) foundations, no matter how deep they run. Even if, and perhaps especially because, it is our identity and our politics at stake.

Notes

* Drafts of this chapter were presented at Vrije Universiteit Amsterdam in April 2014 and Boston College Law School in November 2014. In addition to the participants I would like to thank Pamela Slotte, Walter Rech, James Crawford, Juan Amaya-Castro, Geoff Gordon, Claire Vergerio, Wouter Werner, Ukri Soirila, Barrie Sander, John Haskell, Jean d'Aspremont, Jan Klabbers, Gleider Hernandez and Anne van Mulligen. Their comments, helpful criticisms and general willingness to bear with me shaped much of this chapter (and another longer paper, see S. Singh, 'Koskenniemi's Images of the International Lawyer' *Leiden Journal of International Law* 29 (2016): 699). It would not have been completed at all but for the timely aid of Saara Idelbi, to whom grovelling thanks are wholly insufficient. Final thanks go to the incomparably helpful Maria Jose Belmonte Sanchez. All mistakes remain my own.
1. F. Kafka, *The Metamorphosis* (New York: Bantam, 1972).

2. M. Koskenniemi, *From Apology to Utopia: The Structure of International Legal Argument*, reissue with new epilogue (Cambridge: Cambridge University Press, 2005), 542–48, 614–17. In this chapter, I will not be concerned with the epilogue; I explore this elsewhere, see Singh, 'Koskenniemi: Images of the International Lawyer'.

3. S. Critchley, *Infinitely Demanding: Ethics of Commitment, Politics of Resistance* (London: Verso, 2008), 103 (defining politics as being the nomination of subjectivities; in this sense of the term politics, all knowledge is political or at the very least implies a politics).

4. U. Eco, *The Role of the Reader: Explorations in the Semiotics of Texts* (Bloomington: Indiana University Press, 1979), 10–11 (distinguishing between the [model] reader and author as textual strategies seen throughout a text).

5. P. Allott, *Eunomia: New Order for a New World* (Oxford: Oxford University Press, 2001), 24–26 (paras 2.26–2.30) (speaking of the 'genetic material' of ideas).

6. J. Butler, *The Psychic Life of Power: Theories in Subjection* (Stanford, CA: Stanford University Press, 1997), 2; M. Foucault, 'The Order of Discourse', in R. Young (ed.), *Untying the Text: a Post-Structuralist Reader* (London: Routledge and Kegan Paul, 1981), 51.

7. The symbolic significance of *From Apology to Utopia* means that it is now an embedded part of international law's disciplining mechanisms. Here it competes for influence with other meanings, beliefs and ritualized behaviours. And its influence may not always be a conscious, reflective or reasoned process. Just as quickly as Koskenniemi's concepts and strategies opened upon new spaces for thought within the discipline, some have since become part of its sedimented background.

8. D. Kennedy, 'The Last Treatise: Project and Person (Reflections on Martti Koskenniemi's *From Apology to Utopia*)', *German Law Journal* 7 (2006): 991.

9. P. Schlag, 'The Problem of the Subject', *Texas Law Review* 69 (1991): 1702 (noting this problem within the American critical legal studies tradition).

10. J. Crawford, 'Introductory Remarks to Martti Koskenniemi's, "The Wonderful Artificiality of States"', *Proceedings of the American Society of International Law* 88 (1994): 22.

11. See the comments of Robert Jennings in A. Cassese, *Five Masters of International Law* (Oxford: Hart, 2011), 145–46 ('When he gets into the more sort of jurisprudential and abstract field, I get the same reaction that I think you do from Philipp [Allott]. It may be laziness of mind on my part, but I don't really follow it easily, and I don't easily understand quite what he's saying. It's partly a matter of language, certainly also with Kennedy. It leaves me cold').

12. S. Singh, 'International Legal Positivism and New Approaches to International Law', in J. d'Aspremont and J. Kammerhofer (eds), *International Legal Positivism in a Post-Modern World* (Cambridge: Cambridge University Press, 2014), 291–313 (exploring various techniques of disempowerment under the guise of discussion).

13. D. Kennedy, 'Spring Break', *Texas Law Review* 63 (1985): 1377; M. Koskenniemi, 'Letter to the Editors of the Symposium', *American Journal of International Law* 93 (1999): 351.

14. Koskenniemi, 'Letter to the Editors', 356.

15. S. Singh, 'Martti Koskenniemi: Theories and Images of the International Lawyer', *Leiden Journal of International Law* (forthcoming) (exploring the variety of theoretical and non-theoretical stances that have influenced his oeuvre).

16. M. Horkheimer, 'Traditional and Critical Theory', in *Critical Theory: Selected Essays*, M. O'Connell et al. (trans.) (New York: Continuum, 2002), 188–243.

17. It is not a deconstructionist method as some authors assumed (before critiquing the book on this basis); see e.g. I. Scobbie, 'Towards the Elimination of International Law: Some Radical Scepticism about Sceptical Radicalism', *British Yearbook of International Law* 61 (1990): 339. Koskenniemi has often referred to adding a 'deconstructive' technique to his structuralism (not to mention that these referrals always use inverted commas) but was all too aware that many would not classify it as such. Koskenniemi, *From Apology to Utopia*, 10 and note 8. See also Singh, 'International Legal Positivism and New Approaches to International Law', 296–99.

18. Koskenniemi, 'Letter to the Editors', 355.

19. Koskenniemi, *From Apology to Utopia*, 541.

20. Ibid., 537–41.

21. Ibid., 540.

22. Ibid., 541–48.

23. Ibid., 544–45. It continues: 'Some of the conflictual views have to be overridden. Others are provided with only partial satisfaction ... The legitimacy of critical solutions does not lie in the intrinsic character of the solution but in the openness of the process of conversation and evaluation through which it is chosen and in the way it accepts the possibility or revision – in the authenticity of the participants' will to agree' [footnote omitted]'.

24. Ibid., 547.

25. Ibid., 548.

26. Ibid., 549.

27. In terms of method, I apply the insights of Frederic Jameson and Pierre Macherey in the course of this argument. See F. Jameson, *The Political Unconscious: Narrative as a Socially Symbolic Act* (Abingdon, UK: Routledge, 2002), and P. Macherey, *A Theory of Literary Production*, G. Wall (trans.) (London: Routledge and Kegan Paul, 1978).

28. I rely upon, but go beyond, Pierre Schlag's argument regarding American critical legal thought; see generally Schlag, 'Problem of the Subject', 1679–705.

29. A. Supiot, *Homo Juridicus: On the Anthropological Function of the Law*, Saskia Brown (trans.) (London: Verso, 2007), 6 ('A truly scientific method aims to efface the subject in favour of the object and cannot therefore explain what founds the subject').

30. Michel Foucault's early structuralist work influenced parts of Koskenniemi's text. But importantly, Koskenniemi appears to reject Foucault's wish to do away with those discourses that place the consciousness as sovereign. The relevant remarks of Foucault: 'If I suspended all reference to the speaking subject, it was not to discover laws of construction or forms that could be applied in the same way by all speaking subjects, nor was it to give voice to the great universal discourse that is common to all men at a particular period. On the contrary, my aim was to show what the differences consisted of, how it was possible for men, within the same discursive practice, to speak of different objects, to have contrary opinions, and to make contradictory choices; my aim was also to show in what way discursive practices were distinguished from one another; in short, I wanted not to exclude the problem of the subject, but to define the positions and functions that the subject could occupy in the diversity of discourse'. See M. Foucault, *The Archaeology of*

Knowledge, A. Sheridan Smith (trans.) (New York: Pantheon, 1972), 200. For the influence of Foucault on Koskenniemi, see Koskenniemi, *From Apology to Utopia*, 7 and notes 2, 73 and 6.

31. I use the masculine because the critic's image in this text is that of the author, Martti Koskenniemi.

32. Ibid., 542.

33. Ibid., 553 (emphasis added).

34. Ibid., 561.

35. For an exploration of the connection between structuralism/ideology critique and emancipatory politics in American critical legal studies, see J. Boyle, 'The Politics of Reason: Critical Legal Theory and Local Social Thought', *University of Pennsylvania Law Review* 133 (1985): 685, 743–45; P. Gabel and D. Kennedy, 'Roll over Beethoven', *Stanford Law Review* 36 (1984): 53–54.

36. 'The concrete can be only the synthetic totality of which consciousness, like the phenomenon, constitutes only moments. The concrete is man within the world in that specific union of man with world which Heidegger, for example, calls "being-in-the-world"'. J-P. Sartre, *Being and Nothingness: An Essay on Phenomenological Ontology*, with an introduction by M. Warnock, H. Barnes (trans.) (Abingdon, UK: Routledge, 2003), 27.

37. On the object: 'Being-in-itself (*être-en-soi*): Non-conscious Being. It is the Being of the phenomenon and overflows the knowledge which we have of it. It is a plenitude, and strictly speaking we can say of it only that it is'. Sartre, *Being and Nothingness*, 650, and see also 18–21. On the subject: 'But it would be necessary to complete the definition and formulate it more like this: *consciousness is a being such that in its being, its being is in question in so far as this being implies a being other than itself*. Ibid., 18.

38. Ibid., 28.

39. H. Marcuse, 'Sartre's Existentialism', in *Studies in Critical Philosophy*, J. de Bres (trans.) (Boston: Beacon Press, 1972), 171–77 (expanding on this argument and remarking, 'This is the fallacious identification of the ontological and historical subject' [175]).

40. Sartre, *Being and Nothingness*, 28.

41. Ibid., 29.

42. Ibid. (see also 53–55).

43. Ibid., 63 (emphasis added).

44. 'The first procedure of a philosophy ought to expel things from consciousness and to reestablish its true connection with the world, to know that consciousness is a positional consciousness *of* the world'. Ibid., 7 (emphasis original).

45. Sartre considers this *the only* mode by which to become conscious of an object: 'The self-consciousness we ought to consider not as a new consciousness, but as *the only mode of existence which is possible for a consciousness of something*'. Ibid., 10 (emphasis original).

46. T. Adorno, 'Subject and Object', in A. Arato and E. Gebhart (eds), *The Essential Frankfurt Reader* (New York: Continuum, 1985), 498–99 ('The separation [of subject and object] is no sooner established directly, without mediation, than it becomes an ideology, which is indeed its normal form. The mind will then usurp the place of something absolutely independent – which it is not; its claim of independence heralds the claim of dominance. Once radically parted from the object, the subject

reproduces it to its own measure; the subject swallows the object, forgetting how much it is an object itself').

47. 'In particular the coefficient of adversity in things can not be an argument against our freedom, for it is *by us* – i.e. by the preliminary positing of an end – that this coefficient of adversity arises ... Thus although brute things (what Heidegger calls "brute existents") can from the start limit our freedom of action, it is our freedom itself which must first constitute the framework, the technique, and the ends in relation to which they will manifest themselves as limits'. Ibid., 503–4.

48. 'The technical and philosophical concept of freedom, the only one which we are considering here, means only the autonomy of choice ... Thus we shall not say that a prisoner is always free to go out of prison, which would be absurd, nor that he is always free to long for release, which we an irrelevant truism, but that he is always free to try and escape (or get himself liberated); that is, that whatever his condition may be, he can project his escape and learn the value of his project by undertaking some action'. Ibid., 505.

49. Koskenniemi, *From Apology to Utopia*, 548 (emphasis added).

50. 'In occupying and fulfilling roles which are open to us *we reproduce* those imaginative and institutional constraints through which any particular society establishes its identity ... Simultaneously, roles are a constant threat to consciousness to identity. There is this dilemma: to participate in routine, one needs to do this through a role. But the more one immerses oneself in one's role, the less one is actually participating as a conscious agent at all ... For the international lawyer, *social existence means participation in legal routine and yet doing this so as not to be wholly submerged in it*'. Ibid., 549–50 (emphasis added) (you will notice that the subject remains in control of the constraints, but is never constituted by them; constraints are rather *produced by* the individual).

51. Sartre, *Being and Nothingness*, 545–48.

52. See generally Marcuse, 'Sartre's Existentialism'.

53. Sartre, *Being and Nothingness*, 574–77.

54. M. Koskenniemi, 'Between Commitment and Cynicism: Outline for a Theory of International Law as Practice', in *The Politics of International Law* (London: Hart, 2011), 293.

55. Sartre, *Being and Nothingness*, 574–75.

56. Koskenniemi, *From Apology to Utopia*, 548.

57. Ibid., 554.

58. See generally Sloterdijk, *Critique of Cynical Reason*, M. Eldred (trans.) (Minneapolis: University of Minnesota Press, 1987) (on critique as a form of a war on consciousness).

59. I bracket any questions of the viability of this form of critique, but false consciousness critique has had a number of detractors. See M. Heidegger, *What Is Called Thinking*, F. Wieck and S. Gray (trans.) (London: Harper and Row, 1968), 34; P. Sloterdijk, *Critique of Cynical Reason*, 3–137; M. Foucault, 'Two Lectures', in C. Gordon (ed.), *Power/Knowledge: Selected Interviews and Other Writings 1972–1977*, C. Gordon et al. (trans.) (New York: Pantheon, 1980), 78. Koskenniemi has briefly intimated at the possible 'naivety' of his critical method, but whether this is his position or that of his critics is unclear. See M. Koskenniemi, 'The Politics of International Law – 20 Years Later', *European Journal of International Law* 20 (2009): 8.

60. This is also a natural consequence of Sartre's metaphysic and rationalism. Specifically, it is the consequence of the definitions of the object and subject, the subject-object hierarchy and in particular the rule of the Master-Slave dialectic in the relationship between self and Other – which is a thoroughgoing of Sartre's philosophy. On the relationship between ego and Other, see Sartre, *Being and Nothingness*, 383–452.

61. Koskenniemi, *From Apology to Utopia*, 547.

62. For a recollection on the relentless pattern of the Sartrean metaphysic, see the earlier discussion.

63. There is an argument that we see two ideas of freedom in Sartre: ontological freedom and what he calls 'freedom of obtaining'. The first conditions the second, and the second presupposes the functioning of the first. At the heart of my analysis is the understanding that Sartre collapses his ontological inquiry into the realm of the real, i.e. the concrete, historical context. Some authors may reasonably disagree with this. Marcuse and Merleau-Ponty supported my reading, but Simone de Beauvoir famously defended Sartre against these readings. See Sartre, *Being and Nothingness*, 483–84 (on 'freedom of obtaining'); Marcuse, 'Sartre's Existentialism'; J. Stewart (ed.), *The Debate between Sartre and Merleau-Ponty* (Evanston, IL: Northwestern University Press, 1998); S. de Beauvoir, 'Merleau-Ponty and Pseudo-Sartreanism', *International Studies in Philosophy* 21 (1989): 3.

64. Koskenniemi, *From Apology to Utopia*, 549.

65. See note 31 and accompanying text for a better understanding of how this may play out. Koskenniemi's structuralism does not seek to efface the subject.

66. This is, in part, why it has been so easy for people like Stanley Fish to deconstruct the very form of critique we see in Koskenniemi's *From Apology to Utopia* (although he applied it to American critical legal studies). See S. Fish, *Doing What Comes Naturally: Change, Rhetoric, and the Practice of Theory in Literary and Legal Studies* (Oxford: Clarendon, 1989), 457–67. But Maurice Merleau-Ponty believed that this type of philosophy and Fish's critique both fell into what he called the 'rationalist's dilemma: either the free act is possible, or it is not – either the event originates in me or is imposed on me from the outside'. M. Merleau-Ponty, *Signs*, R. McCleary (trans.) (Evanston, IL: Northwestern University Press, 1964), 227.

67. M. Merleau-Ponty, *Phenomenology of Perception*, C. Smith (trans.) (London: Routledge, 1962), 455.

68. See e.g. that which is implied colonial and postcolonial projects within Third World Approaches to International Law and in S. Marks, 'False Contingency', *Current Legal Problems* 62 (2009): 1.

69. J. Rancière, 'The Thinking of Dissensus: Politics and Aesthetics', in P. Bowman and R. Stamp (eds), *Reading Rancière* (London: Continuum, 2011), 13.

70. F. Michelman, 'The Subject of Liberalism', *Stanford Law Review* 46 (1994): 1831 (making the point in regard to the liberal subject).

71. Schlag, 'Problem of the Subject', 1697.

72. See generally Koskenniemi, *From Apology to Utopia*, 71–157.

73. J.-P. Sartre, 'Matérialisme et Révolution', *Les Temps Modernes* 1 (1946): 14.

74. M. Koskenniemi, 'International Law between Fragmentation and Constitutionalism', speech, 18 May 2003 (Recife, Brazil), 15 (para. 31).

75. R. Barthes, *Mythologies*, A. Lavers (trans.) (New York: Hill and Wang, 1972), 143.

76. J. Bruner, *On Knowing* (Cambridge, MA: Harvard University Press, 1997), 36.

77. Following in terms of method, M. Foucault, 'What Is an Author?', in J. Faubion (ed.), *Aesthetics, Method and Epistemology*, R. Hurley et al. (trans.) (New York: New Press, 1998), 217.
78. Kennedy takes an ethnographic approach; see D. Kennedy, 'When Renewal Repeats: Thinking Against the Box' *New York University Journal of Law and Politics* 32 (2000): 335; Koskenniemi a neo-phenomenological approach; see M. Koskenniemi, *The Gentle Civilizer of Nations: The Rise and Fall of International Law 1870–1960* (Cambridge: Cambridge University Press, 2001). Orford takes a Foucauldian approach through the constitutive role of narratives; see A. Orford, 'Embodying Internationalism: The Making of International Lawyers' *Australian Year Book of International Law* 19 (1998): 1.

Bibliography

Adorno, Theodor. 'Subject and Object'. In Andrew Arato and Eike Gebhart (eds), *The Essential Frankfurt Reader* (New York: Continuum, 1985).

Allott, Philip. *Eunomia: New Order for a New World* (Oxford: Oxford University Press, 2001).

Barthes, Roland. *Mythologies*, Annette Lavers (trans.) (New York: Hill and Wang, 1972).

Boyle, James. 'The Politics of Reason: Critical Legal Theory and Local Social Thought'. *University of Pennsylvania Law Review* 133 (1985).

Bruner, Jerome. *On Knowing* (Cambridge, MA: Harvard University Press, 1997).

Butler, Judith. *The Psychic Life of Power: Theories in Subjection* (Stanford, CA: Stanford University Press, 1997).

Cassese, Antonio. *Five Masters of International Law* (Oxford: Hart, 2011).

Crawford, James. 'Introductory Remarks to Martti Koskenniemi's, "The Wonderful Artificiality of States"'. *Proceedings of the American Society of International Law* 88 (1994).

Critchley, Simon. *Infinitely Demanding: Ethics of Commitment, Politics of Resistance* (London: Verso, 2008).

de Beauvoir, Simone. 'Merleau-Ponty and Pseudo-Sartreanism'. *International Studies in Philosophy* 21 (1989).

Eco, Umberto. *The Role of the Reader: Explorations in the Semiotics of Texts* (Bloomington: Indiana University Press, 1979).

Fish, Stanley. *Doing What Comes Naturally: Change, Rhetoric, and the Practice of Theory in Literary and Legal Studies* (Oxford: Clarendon, 1989).

Foucault, Michel. *The Archaeology of Knowledge*, Alan Mark Sheridan Smith (trans.) (New York: Pantheon, 1972).

'The Order of Discourse'. In Robert J. C. Young (ed.), *Untying the Text: a Post-Structuralist Reader* (London: Routledge and Kegan Paul, 1981).

'Polemics, Politics and Problematizations: an Interview with Michel Foucault'. In Paul Rabinow (ed.), *Ethics: Subjectivity and Truth*, R. Hurley (trans.) (New York: New Press, 1997).

'Two Lectures'. In Colin Gordon (ed.), *Power/Knowledge: Selected Interviews and Other Writings 1972–1977*, Colin Gordon et al. (trans.) (New York: Pantheon, 1980).

'What Is an Author?' In James Faubion (ed.), *Aesthetics, Method and Epistemology*, Robert Hurley et al. (trans.) (New York: New Press, 1998).

Gabel, Peter, and Duncan Kennedy. 'Roll over Beethoven'. *Stanford Law Review* 36 (1984).

Heidegger, Martin. *What Is Called Thinking*, Fred D. Wieck and Jesse G. Gray (trans.) (London: Harper and Row, 1968).

Horkheimer, Max. 'Traditional and Critical Theory'. In *Critical Theory: Selected Essays*, Matthew J. O'Connell et al. (trans.) (New York: Continuum, 2002).

Jameson, Fredric. *The Political Unconscious: Narrative as a Socially Symbolic Act* (Abingdon, UK: Routledge, 2002).

Kafka, Franz. *The Metamorphosis* (New York: Bantam, 1972).

Kennedy, David. 'When Renewal Repeats: Thinking against the Box', *New York University Journal of Law and Politics* 32 (2000).

'The Last Treatise: Project and Person (Reflections on Martti Koskenniemi's *From Apology to Utopia*)', *German Law Journal* 7 (2006).

Kennedy, Duncan. 'Spring Break'. *Texas Law Review* 63 (1985).

Koskenniemi, Martti. 'Between Commitment and Cynicism: Outline for a Theory of International Law as Practice'. In *The Politics of International Law* (London: Hart, 2011).

From Apology to Utopia: the Structure of International Legal Argument, reissue with new epilogue (Cambridge: Cambridge University Press, 2005).

The Gentle Civilizer of Nations: The Rise and Fall of International Law 1870–1960 (Cambridge: Cambridge University Press, 2001).

'International Law between Fragmentation and Constitutionalism'. *Speech*, 18 May 2003.

'Letter to the Editors of the Symposium'. *American Journal of International Law* 93 (1999).

'The Politics of International Law – 20 Years Later'. *European Journal of International Law* 20 (2009).

Macherey, Pierre. *A Theory of Literary Production*, Geoffrey Wall (trans.) (London: Routledge and Kegan Paul, 1978).

Marcuse, Herbert. 'Sartre's Existentialism'. In *Studies in Critical Philosophy*, Joris de Bres (trans.) (Boston: Beacon Press, 1972).

Marks, Susan. 'False Contingency'. *Current Legal Problems* 62 (2009).

Merleau-Ponty, Maurice. *Phenomenology of Perception*, Colin Smith (trans.) (London: Routledge, 1962).

Signs, Richard McCleary (trans.) (Evanston, IL: Northwestern University Press, 1964).

Michelman, Frank. 'The Subject of Liberalism'. *Stanford Law Review* 46 (1994).

Orford, A. 'Embodying Internationalism: The Making of International Lawyers', *Australian Year Book of International Law* 19 (1998).

Rancière, Jacques. 'The Thinking of Dissensus: Politics and Aesthetics'. In P. Bowman and R. Stamp (eds), *Reading Rancière* (London: Continuum, 2011).

Sartre, Jean-Paul. *Being and Nothingness: an Essay on Phenomenological Ontology*, with n introduction by Mary Warnock, Hazel E. Barnes (trans.) (Abingdon, UK: Routledge, 2003).

'Matérialisme et Révolution'. *Les Temps Modernes* 1 (1946).

Schlag, Pierre. 'The Problem of the Subject'. *Texas Law Review* 69 (1991).

Scobbie, Iain. 'Towards the Elimination of International Law: Some Radical Scepticism about Sceptical Radicalism'. *British Yearbook of International Law* 61 (1990).

Singh, Sahib. 'International Legal Positivism and New Approaches to International Law'. In Jean d'Aspremont and Jorg Kammerhofer (eds), *International Legal Positivism in a Post-Modern World* (Cambridge: Cambridge University Press, 2014).

'Martti Koskenniemi: Images of the International Lawyer'. *Leiden Journal of International Law* 29 (2016).

Sloterdijk, Peter. *Critique of Cynical Reason*, Michael Eldred (trans.) (Minneapolis: University of Minnesota Press, 1987).

Stewart, Jon (ed.). *The Debate between Sartre and Merleau-Ponty* (Evanston, IL: Northwestern University Press, 1998).

Supiot, Alain. *Homo Juridicus: on the Anthropological Function of the Law*, Saskia Brown (trans.) (London: Verso, 2007).

Whiteside, Kerry H. *Merleau-Ponty and the Foundations of Existential Politics* (Princeton, NJ: Princeton University Press, 1988).

9

Practising Law

Spoudaios, Professional, Expert or 'Macher'? Reflections on the Changing Nature of an Occupation

FRIEDRICH KRATOCHWIL

9.1 Introduction

The debate in legal theory over the last two generations has gravitated from a concern with the nature of legal norms via a concern with their 'systemic' character (as in this way the problem of their validity could be solved), to a theory of 'adjudication'. With the last move the issue of norm application took centre stage. Here Dworkin with his theory of one right answer (and its later reformulations) provided the sparring partner[1] for the critical legal studies movement and some post-modern critics who focussed on the strategic choice a judge wittingly or unwittingly makes among principles and rules, or by including /excluding 'facts' from the 'narrative' when deciding a case.[2] Thus different from the notion of one right answer or the 'followability' of the chain-novel – which appellate courts and even more so members of supreme courts have to keep in mind – in those latter criticisms a type of realism raises again its ugly head even though it now focuses more on intellectual hegemonies than on personal preferences or idiosyncrasies of the judges. Consequently only some 'deconstruction' utilizing new methodological tools can get at those silent assumptions, which are 'productive' of the normal practice of law.

By choosing this thumb nail sketch of the history of the legal debates I do not want to imply that this is the only story that could be told. Other narratives come easily to mind. A particularly attractive one to international legal scholars addresses the emergence of a cosmopolitan legal order or even a 'humanity's law'. In this way law has become a powerful force for calling attention to our common predicament and issues of humanitarian intervention, of making other societies to live up to the 'rule of law', had left their imprint not only on US policy making, as well as on international institutions, such as the World Bank and the International Monetary Fund, or the European Union.

All these developments are, of course, the subject to an optimistic and a pessimistic reading. While on the one hand enhanced 'transparency' and the rule of law (largely defined as functioning markets and structural reform of political and social institutions) can be interpreted as progressive moves, other observers might see them as attempts of establishing an informal or non-territorial form of empire, in which at best a 'benign despot' – whom Kant so abhorred – rather than an autonomous will determining itself is the *spiritus rector* of those moves.

A third narrative could focus on the international legal process and the increasingly 'managerial' tasks, which law, domestically as well as internationally, has taken on. Thus the administrative revolution has meanwhile reached the international arena, leading to the emergence of a global administrative law.[3] The latter is supposed to safeguard the integrity and legitimacy of decision making in the labyrinths of global governance, since these concerns might get easily lost when we too eagerly embrace a pure 'process' approach and leave decision making to the 'experts' who are operating beyond and above the state.

As different as these storylines are, there is a rather strange intersection, on which I want to focus in this chapter. It is the changing role of the legal 'professional' to which David Kennedy[4] and Martti Koskenniemi[5] in international law, and Bruce Ackerman[6] in constitutional law have called attention. Although they have addressed the issue in different ways and have come to differing conclusions, all of them agree that the former near exclusive focus on the 'system of rules' or the 'judge' needs to be supplemented by either more detailed historical studies on the development of international law,[7] or the 'constitutional moments',[8] but also with a particular attention to a prevailing 'mind-set' that is neither indebted to some form of natural law thinking nor to a purely managerial understanding of law. Here two interacting issues become relevant: one concerns the 'indeterminacy' of rules and principles; the other, closely connected with it, is how the decisions ought to be made in the face of the fact that no logically compelling argumentation is possible. Here appeals to the professional ethic and the 'character' of the rule-handlers (rather than their skills) are made.

Kant seemed to have realized these dilemmas, when he rejected the classical international lawyers -calling them pathetic comforters and suggested the need for a 'moral politician' (rather than political moralist or administrator). Thus something more seems required since the solutions to political dilemmas are not – at least not predominantly so – a cognitive issue, Kant's 'reason', Habermas's 'transcendental pragmatics', or Rawls's 'reasonableness' notwithstanding. Here history and logic show in tandem that some of the assumptions upon which these arguments rest, are indeed heroic. That something more than logical skill is involved can be seen from the fact that principles and rules do not apply themselves but require a judgement in the light of the circumstances of the case. This practical judgement is no longer determinative in the Kantian sense but can only be 'reflective', i.e. it is not apodictic but persuasive at best. Given this double indeterminacy, any judgement has therefore, to involve considerable 'discretion' granted to the rule-handlers which has to be justifiable both in abstract terms, i.e. by a 'theory' as well as by showing that the particular decision was arrived at *arte legis*, the problem on which 'professionalism' focuses.

The close connection of these two problems can be seen when we examine Aristotle's attempts of distinguishing different forms of knowledge (productive, practical, theoretical) while giving the pride of place to 'theory' because of its subject matter (the universal and necessary), while the 'particular and contingent' – which characterize *praxis*[9] – is the realm of prudence and has to rely on processes of 'deliberation', techniques of gaining assent (persuasion), and finally on the character of the actor making this choice (the *spoudaios*, or person of character).[10] The latter then gives rise to a 'virtue ethics', which uneasily sits with a Kantian deontology and the emphasis on rules. But perhaps Kant's hope for a 'moral politician'[11] suggests that the differences are not as pronounced as is usually assumed.[12]

Starting from the other end, i.e. not with a 'theory' but with particular decisions we can see why the 'bag of tricks' which lawyers have learned in order to deal with particular cases by applying rules, which are in conflict, becomes important. Here Koskenniemi, when writing the report of the ILC Study Group on the *Fragmentation of the International Legal Order*[13] put his trust. The 'solutions' provided by some form of 'professionalism' seem equally distanced from the technocratic/administrative perspective, which takes goals/means rationality or general utility as its metric, as they are from the natural law perspective. Significantly, Koskenniemi, in his 'Epilogue' contained in the second edition of *From Apology to Utopia*,[14] relies on the 'competent speaker of a language' as a model which circumvents the *aporia* created by the Humean fork as it mediates between the 'apology', concerned with the 'is' part of political praxis, while the 'utopia' points to the realm of 'ought'. The recent turn to praxis and the competence model of using language as a template for understanding the 'law' seems to me on the right track.

In this chapter I want to follow up on this turn to practice, but want to take it a step further and see how a focus on 'professions' and their practices can deal with the problem of discretion in a new and hopefully interesting way, going beyond the traditional prudential approaches. Thus the scholastic tradition mentions aside from intelligence (insights into principles) also memory (*memoria*), circumspection (*circumspectio*), open-mindedness (*docilitas*), foresight (*providentia*), shrewdness (*sollertia*), discrimination (*ratio*) but also caution (*cautela*) – which has survived in English as a characteristic of the prudent person. While such an expanded list of considerations for making choices is quite useful, it complicates matters even further. What we need is a coherent way of linking these concerns systematically to the way in which we act and reflect on our actions.

From what was said so far it should be clear that a new take on the link between knowledge and praxis could only arise after the 'theoretical' ideal, which had given the pride of place to field-independent *epistemological* criteria, was replaced by a new approach to meaning and validation. If meaning is no longer produced by 'reference' (bringing an object under some concept), but by the way of *how we use* concepts, then validation (providing the 'warrant' for our assertions) becomes more complicated since no absolute standpoint could claim to represent to us the world as it 'is'. Instead, now even 'theorizing' is understood as a practice and no longer a simple demonstration or proof of how things really 'are'. This realization has further implications. Four are of particular importance for the understanding of the social world.

One is that validation does not simply occur via reference (the 'world out there') or through a derivation from axioms, but through the use of concepts in accordance with certain criteria. This realization makes it necessary to investigate the semantic fields in which our concepts are embedded and to relate these fields to the practices and actions, which are thereby authorized, demanded or enjoined. Such a perspective will necessarily also turn our attention away from the static immutable concepts, conceived as natural kinds, to capturing their history in the process of social reproduction.

Second, since there is no absolute point from where everything can be seen, and 'truth' cannot be attained by a matching operation or a coherency test, we have now to be aware of the framing conditions (institutional facts), in which the processes of validation occur. This not only explodes the notion that there is only one true explanation, it also problematizes attempts of establishing a hierarchy of contexts.[15] Thus it would indeed be odd to claim that the explanation offered e.g. by the coroner in a murder trial would be 'truer' because it used physiological data than that that of the district attorney who employs motives and relies on circumstantial evidence.

This leads me to the third point in which the organization of knowledge for legitimizing purposes and the role of the community of practitioners become important. In ascertaining what the case is and attaching a warrant to our assertion, criteria of relevance (rather than 'truth') determine what is germane and what is out of bounds. These boundaries might be contested or become colonized by other occupations, which try to advance to professional status, but these boundary-maintaining or boundary re-drawing conflicts are taking place within a particular profession or among competing occupational groups and are not decided by philosophers of science or 'theorists' who apply their allegedly free standing criteria of true (scientific) knowledge.

Fourth, such closer look at the changes in occupational roles and of the 'knowledge' justifying their professional character involves us then in the analysis of professions as systems of occupations vying for legitimization on the basis of some knowledge and for protection from 'quacks' or 'irresponsible' elements. But it also brings into focus the links between knowledge production and the wider social process in which knowledge is disseminated and used. While these dynamics of fields, of *habitus, doxa* and '*symbolic capital*' have been explored by Bourdieu, something more needs to be said about the influence of different forms of organization on scientific or professional practices in general. In this context the emergence of e.g. the large firm both in industry and in law is of particular significance.

Despite the differences in the environment in which they operate, 'firms' rely on managerial control, rather than on fiduciary contracts between client and professionals, safeguarded by a code (of ethics). Thus the organizational settings might not only impair the chances for developing 'good judgement' and retaining a modicum of independence necessary for preserving the integrity of the law, they are also conducive to certain pathologies. This becomes obvious when even technical expertise is undermined by administrative fiat, as the post mortems of the two Challenger and Columbia space shuttle disasters suggested. Similarly, given this organizational form in which the legal profession is increasingly pressed, we might in the end neither get the Aristotelian *spoudaios* nor the independent expert which functionalism extolled

From these initial remarks my argument will take the following steps. In the next section I shall address the problem of knowledge in more detail starting from the characterization of different forms of knowledge, linking them to certain 'disciplines', and finally to occupations and their interactions within wider social contexts (labour markets). This discussion, in turn, sets the stage for Section 9.3, in which I take up the problem of professionalization, which led to attacks on some of the older professions – which had emphasized the link between knowledge, judgement and ethics – and the rise of the technical professions relying on 'expertise'. I examine how these changes in the knowledge base affected the self-conception of various professions, whereby I use Durkheim, Tawney, Weber and Parsons as my foils. In Section 9.4 I try to draw out some of the implications by looking at the managerial revolution and how it impacted on the 'older' professions and on the newer ones, based on scientific expertise, whereby space engineering serves as my case. In the conclusion I use some of the insights for an admittedly largely speculative assessment of the status of the legal profession, particularly in the context of recent controversies concerning the torture-memoranda and the growth of the legal offices within the executive branch in the US

9.2   Knowledge, Occupations, Disciplines and Markets

The upshot of the above argument was that for analysing changes in the conception of a profession it was not sensible to begin with a stipulative definition which then is applied to this particular occupation. Instead, I argued that we have to begin with 'knowledge' (or rather what counts as knowledge) and focus then on the way of how this knowledge is organized, since it is the type of knowledge that justifies the autonomy of a profession. This organization occurs first in terms of distinctions (subject matter), legitimizing thereby certain activities and practices by tying them to certain occupations. But this internal organization takes place within the larger field of other 'occupations', which frequently contest the privileging move of ascribing to one profession a particular activity (such as pleading before a court to barristers, or prescribing medicines to doctors).

Looking at the problem through the prism of 'knowledge' is by no means the only, or even the natural way of dealing with this linkage operation and the 'boundaries' which are thereby created, since we know from historical experience that such occupational ascriptions can occur via largely racial characteristics, as e.g. in the traditional India cast system, or by some crude form of functionalism, as exemplified by the *three orders* conception of early medieval times.[16] Thus what is 'knowledge' and how it gets connected to and is protected by society through a privileging move, is subject to great variation, as certain activities, bundled into occupations are either attributed to, or reserved for certain classes of people.

These few remarks linking knowledge, discipline and occupation raised several issues that need unpacking. For one, something more needs to be said on each of these concepts and their interrelations.

As to knowledge itself: the examples show that knowledge is not of one cloth: it comprises the common sense knowledge of how to go about things, but also the special skills one acquires through doing, i.e. learning a trade. It means learning a 'how to' knowledge, which consist in habituation until the techniques become one's second nature, This *know-how* or skill has then to be handed down within guilds and artisan shops and does usually not command much respect – unless artistic refinements emerge, such as in weaving whose patterns are the often 'transferred' to other trades, such as the working of precious metals, building or painting, as was the case in Florence. On the other hand, the disdain for the simple manual labourer or peasant, the *banausos*, is well documented since antiquity.

On the opposite end is the 'knowledge' of things divine – and here not only doctrinal elaborations of received revelations, but speculations about the *kosmos* and observations of nature occur together and are often monopolized by a priestly class (astronomy, cycle of seasons, hydraulic empires or Mesoamerican astrological empires). In this context it is significant that neither in Greece nor Rome such a monopolization occurred, since here religion primarily engendered 'cults' (rites, indebted more to magic, such as reading entrails or casting spells) than mythical explanations, or it spawned 'mysteries' (Greece). This allowed for the emergence of alternative unorthodox explanations of the existential puzzles. 'Sages', such as the pre-Socratic philosophers (Heraclitus) appeared, speculating about the nature of universe and man's place in it. Their particularly intensive search for wisdom relying on reflection on the 'nature of things' rather than on revelation, was continued by the Socratic turn, away from the fixation on the 'heavens' (*ta meteora*) to questions of how we should live.

Although the Socratic turn was initially legitimized by the oracle at Delphi (*gnothi sauton*) its execution soon conflicted with traditional religiosity – introducing new gods was, after all, one of the points which led to Socrates' condemnation. Furthermore, this search for self-knowledge was not guided by a withdrawal into the self or by some participation in orgiastic mysteries, but critically applied the model of occupational knowledge to wider contexts, such as questioning what the particular knowledge for the occupation of the statesman consists of, or for the pious, or the expert (sophist), who offered his services by moving from town to town.

Both Plato and his disciple Aristotle recognized, however, that this model provided a too narrow conception of knowledge, as the warrants attached to skills were quite different from those based on rational insights. Besides, a new conception of 'knowledge' had also to answer to the challenges of the sceptics, who had shaken traditional confidence in the foundational nature of sense perception – as demonstrated by the example of the broken oar in water and certain fallacies of logical inference – which the sophists had used in order to win debates.

This brief sketch raises several questions. The first one concerns the equivocal use of the term 'knowledge' in regard to a variety of matters. Whether they can be considered as instantiations of knowledge or just as equivocations is indeed an issue. Of course, no one who believes that there can only be 'one Truth' will be convinced by this exercise. S/he probably thinks in terms of essences, or properties, that allow then the determination of whether something is part of something or not, and that these distinctions are given, as they mirror reality, and that truth must also be unchanging. But when one tries to show what counts as knowledge (providing warrants for our assertions) one has not only to demonstrate that some warrants do not involve 'truth' questions at all, such as is the case in aesthetic judgements, or in law, and thus that question of validity can be assessed by different and also changing criteria. Then the issue of validity involves truth-questions in a subsidiary manner at best, such as whether a statute was actually enacted. But even here the question is about the truth of a historical fact, which is not answerable by reference to a universal or necessary cause or ontological given, even though at least some strands of natural law thinking attempt to reduce validity questions to ontology and thus to a particular theory of truth.

The upshot of this argument is that the changing connection between what constitutes knowledge and how it gives rise to disciplinary understandings and particular practices – which are, in turn, tied to certain occupations – cannot operate with concepts as if they were only unequivocal, a-temporal and unproblematic deictic instruments. Here the shift from reference to *use* is helpful as the notion of family resemblance or forms of life developed in the later works of Wittgenstein provides us with better heuristic tools for analysing change than the traditional, static taxonomies. Nevertheless, Aristotle's 'mapping' of different forms of knowledge, provides us with a starting point for placing the issue of professionalization -defining an occupation by the public recognition of a certain know-how necessary for its exercise- in the wider context of social differentiation and change.

Aristotle's classification of knowledge that is useful for production (*poiesis*) comprises both the *technai* (skill or techniques) involved in the fabrication of artefacts, and the making of more 'artistic' products, by embedding them in certain genres and styles (treated in his *Poetics*). This productive *know-how* is contrasted with *theoretical knowledge*, which is concerned with the examination of first principles and characterized by universality and necessity. But both productive and theoretical knowledge are distinguished from *praxis*, which deals with the particular and contingent. It addresses issues of action, which always take place in a particular configuration of circumstances, and occurs in time. Finally, there remains some area, which deals with understanding the processes of 'genesis and decay', a topic which is oddly enough for us taken up in his *Physics*, involving teleological reasoning. Of course, within his scheme the pride of place is given to *theoria* as it concerns the unchanging and universal and allows for inferences which are necessarily true. Thus, despite the various differences with Plato, Aristotle reproduces in the rank-ordering of different forms of knowledge the basic Platonic distinction of an unchanging being (*to ontos on*) as opposed to its different manifestations which we encounter (*ta onta*).

Consequently, the primacy is then accorded to theory as addressed in his *Metaphysics*, (also called *first philosophy*) concerned with first principle. On the other hand, practical wisdom cannot quite have the same dignity as theoretical knowledge, as it deals with the contingent and temporal.[17] Aristotle thus never as explicitly elaborates on the standards appropriate for this type of knowledge, as he does for 'theory' in his *Organon*. The *Rhetoric* and the *Topics* could perhaps be read as such an attempt since Aristotle explicitly suggests that the former treatise is not about appeals to emotions, i.e. psychological factors, but about how a speaker can convince an audience, via commonly accepted truths (*topoi*) even though he cannot rely on the 'given and universal nature' of the first principles, or on logical necessity buttressing his arguments.

Aristotle has little to say about the *technai*, i.e. techniques in making things (knowledge of production) as he considers them to represent a lower form of knowledge (since he does not know of technology, i.e. applied 'theoretical' science, which then would have to be placed at least on the same level as practical knowledge). When dealing with *poetic* production, he thinks that e.g. poetry imparts better knowledge than history because it deals with the 'general' rather than the specific, using again as a criterion the distinction between *to on* (universal) versus *ta onta* (particular instantiations).[18]

This map provides a first cut for understanding some 'functionalist' speculations, such as the Three Orders and the emergence of the high status occupations in the middle ages: the ministry, teaching at university (as philosophy became the handmaiden for theology), and 'law' – although the latter was sometimes taught and transmitted more as a skill than a 'prudential' discipline, as in the 'bars' of England. On the Continent, however, the revival of Roman law emplaced jurisprudence as a discipline – based on a distinct mode of reasoning - firmly within the university.

Medicine occupies here a curious position as it was taught at universities, but it certainly was neither a pure skill (as the letting blood, or extracting teeth), nor did it have a secure knowledge base, since the natural sciences on which it nowadays relies were all but non-existent. Again, however, the variability of what counted for knowledge comes to the fore. Medicine seems to have developed a certain 'tradition' ensconced in certain texts, which ranged from Hippocrates to Aristotle, Galen, Avicenna and the writings of the *Scuola Medica Salentiana*. The latter provided a 'primer' of medical sources, which served as a study guide for generations of medicine students.[19] These sources had attained canonical status and were studied and memorized, but many of the actual medical practices were carried out by midwives, barbers, itinerant dentists, surgeons and apothecaries and by the helpers in hospitals who tended to the sick and dying. Thus the 'discipline' was constantly challenged by healers, religious and otherwise, quacks, folklore-herbalists, etc. while seeking authority in the 'canonical books' for the most abstruse practices, or calling for spiritual intervention by priests, or making the use of 'mediums' in order to get in touch with the 'beyond'. As Peter Dobkin-Hall points out in his study of the social foundations of professional credibility of medicine, taking New England as his case study:

> The authority of the profession as gauged by the willingness of legislatures, philanthropists and the general public to support and patronize medical institutions, was established long before the content of medical practice could justify it.[20]

The last remark is a useful reminder on focussing only on knowledge as the basis for legitimizing particular occupations would be problematic on logical as well as on organizational grounds. Logically some of the distinctions establishing the asserted hierarchy can easily be undermined because the terms of 'special' and 'general' are not free standing but attain their meaning not solely by their semiotic function but from the context. Aristotle's own examples show – when he e.g. values the poet more than the historian because the latter allegedly deals only with the particular – assigning these characterizations depends then on a 'point of view'. Thus showing the failings of a hero like Orestes in a tragedy is focussing on the fate of an individual in his predicament, the historian arguably deals with the more 'general' problem of war and peace or with the fate of whole cities (Thucydides), or even 'civilizations' (Herodotus of the Europe/Asia interaction through time). Thus in both cases exemplarity rather than generality are at issue.

While 'exemplarity' shows that the presumably exhaustive dichotomy of general and particular might be highly misleading in deciding knowledge- (or validity claims), there is still another more substantive reason for being cautious. In conjunction with his study of professions Eliot Freidson has pointed out that the use the term 'generalist' and 'specialist' can be identified in no

> other than empirical terms. The same may be said of the idea of the 'whole task'. One persons 'whole task' is another person's specialty. Specialization can be delineated only by reference to some imagined or historically real other task that is considered to be the whole from which it came. It is not in practice a stable or an absolute concept. And since it is intrinsically relative, its invocation is likely to be subject to strong ideological winds.[21]

This makes it necessary to study professions as a *system of professions*, i.e. as a interaction of groups laying claims to a special knowledge and authority to judge performances in certain occupations, as Abbott did in his magisterial study.[22] It also suggests that we have to study the position of these professions within the larger division of labour and of the organization of 'markets' by public authority, since only the latter can settle turf wars between competing occupations and grant 'autonomy'. It is therefore no accident that the works of Adam Smith focussing on the beneficial aspects of a division of labour[23] and a free market and Durkheim's studies on professional ethics[24] emerged from their studies of the division of labour.[25] And it is also not accidental that they were written at the time of the professionalization push for recognition by technical occupations. Similarly, Weber's analysis of the new form of organizing work through bureaucratic administrations resulted from the analysis of the rationalization of law emphasizing the emergence of a new organizational form where power is exercised through a hierarchical arrangement of offices, which in turn is linked to a certain knowledge (rules and their application) and tied to the wider society through specific training, examinations and careers of the office holders.

In this context two interconnected topics dominate the discussion: the issue of the efficiency gains (stressed by Weber) and of the increasing predominance of economic thinking (self-interest), which threatens other ways of acting, by undermining solidarity.[26] Here the professions and, in particular, those stressing the old virtues of the *artes liberales*, instead of technical expertise, are supposed to provide a counterweight and save society from its own excesses. These writers provide us thus with a more optimistic picture of the things to come than Weber conjured up when he wrote on the last pages his *Protestant Ethic and the Spirit of Capitalism*, ruminating about the loss of a 'calling':

> Where the fulfillment of the calling cannot directly be related to the highest spiritual and cultural values, or when, on the other hand, it need not be felt simply as economic compulsion, the individual generally abandons the attempt to justify it at all. In the field of its highest development, in the US the pursuit of wealth, stripped of its religious and ethical meaning, tends to become associated with purely mundane passions, which actually give it the character of sport ... For of the last stage of this cultural development, it might truly be said: Specialists without spirit, sensualists without heart; this nullity imagines that he has attained a level of civilization never before achieved.[27]

There might have been in many of those analyses of the traditional profession some self- congratulatory myopia concerning the virtues of a traditional society when the latter was not understood, as in modernity, as an aggregation of exchange relations and where the political order was mainly concerned with protecting these exchanges among possessive individualist. Nevertheless, these studies drew our attention to the importance of systems of meaning and loyalties that were now being displaced by self-interest and calculation. Furthermore, the celebration of the professions was not a romantic or nostalgic paean to the former estate society. It insisted that access to this new 'aristocracy of talent', as Coleridge once called it,[28] was to be gained by being 'formed' through mastering a type of *savoir* that obliged, as formerly the *noblesse* (of status by birth) had obliged (*noblesse oblige*). Tawney put his criticism of modern society, where industry as a mode of production instantiates the absence of social purpose in the following way:

The difference between industry as it exists today and a profession is, then, simple and unmistakable. The essence of the former is that its only criterion is the financial return, which it offers to the shareholders. The essence of the latter is that, though men enter it for the sake of livelihood, the measure of their success is the service, which they perform, not the gains they amass. They may, as in the case of a successful doctor grow rich; but the meaning of their profession, both for themselves and for the public, is not that they make money but that they make health, or safety, or knowledge, or good government or good law. So if they are doctors, they recognize that there are certain kinds of conduct which cannot be practiced, however large the fee for them, because they unprofessional ... if judges or public servants, that they must not increase their income by selling justice for money ... To idealize the professional spirit would be absurd; it has its sordid side, and, if it to be fostered in industry, safeguards will be needed to check its excesses. But there is all the difference between maintaining a standard, which is occasionally abandoned, and affirming as the central truth of the existence that there is no standard to maintain[29].

While the above quote provides the classical definition and justification for professionalism, several things need further clarification. One concerns the issue of ethics and abuse, i.e. of the self-disciplining character of the profession which is connected to issue of the changing basis for valuing a particular type of knowledge. The second issue is whether a broadly humanist and prudential type of knowledge serves as the proper justification of autonomy, or whether expertise invoking the authority of science can better justify the claim. This discussion leads me then to the third connected problem of how actual occupational work is organized and thus generates conflict with, or reinforces the 'ideology' of professionalism. Fourth, not only do the newer professions, such as engineering, city planning, nursing, social work, hospital or public administration etc., invoke different types of knowledge – one based more on technical expertise than the notion of trusteeship of a cultural tradition – many of the older, recognized professions such as law, have been broken up into new professions (such as accounting) or 'specializations' which rely on expertise (tax law, securities law, etc.). Fifth, virtually all professions are now practiced in organizational settings, which are increasingly more managerial (such as law firms) and hierarchical than was the case in the former partnerships or the collegial structures of e.g. traditional universities. Finally, virtually all occupations, such as advertising or real estate brokerage, have in the meantime developed 'codes' of ethics – probably attempting to signal to the rest of society that they are well on their way to becoming a profession- without necessarily being recognized as such.

9.3   Aristotelian Spoudaios[30] or Expert?

If the above thumbnail sketch is correct, then clarifying the moral and
the expertise aspect of professionalism is the key for understanding both
the important social changes and the changes in the 'disciplines', both in
terms of knowledge production and in shaping occupational roles and
forms of association. A quick historical overview is instructive.

The new disciplines were originally incorporated into the 'learned professions' in the US[31] by the mid nineteenth century, while on the Continent
the form of incorporation took quite different paths, where usually 'technical universities' emerged. But over time the indifference of some applied
sciences to issues of societal trustee professionalism and the increasing
belief in science as providing the necessary expertise undermined the
predominance of societal trustee professionalism even in the US. The last
spirited defence of professionalism exemplified by the legal profession
came in Talcott Parson's address to the 50th Anniversary Celebration of
the University of Chicago Law School in 1952. There, he attempted once
more to connect professionalism to an action theory without falling into
the trap of explaining the occupational dynamics and the organizational
form it took as simple moral decay or the ascendancy of self-interested
action. Instead, he attempted to relate professional activities systematically to a more comprehensive theory of social action.

Thus the doctor who is serving her patient is not necessarily acting out
of 'altruistic' motives, but has as her interests making the patient well,
and thus gaining recognition by her peers and society in general, and
allowing her to make a living. As Parsons surmised it was the emphasis on
self-interest in our action theory that prevented us from seeing that it is
not the motive, but rather *the setting in which motive plays out* that these
differences become visible. Thus while social recognition is mediated by
peers and the society at large, and the authority granted to e.g. judges,
attorneys and doctors is mediated by understandings of specific powers
and privileges, the 'earning of a living' in modernity is also mediated by
a universal medium of exchange.

> Money is significant in what it can buy as well as in the role of a direct
> symbol of recognition. Hence in so far as ways of earning money present
> themselves in the situations, which are not strictly in line of institutionally
> approved achievement, there might be strong pressure to resort them so
> long as the risk of loss of occupational status is not too great
>
> This leads to a second consideration ... In so far as the actual state of
> affairs deviates from this type the two main elements of success, objective

achievement, which is institutionally valued, and acquisition of the various recognition symbols may not be well articulated. Actual achievement may fail to bring recognition in due proportion and vice versa achievements either of low quality or in unapproved lines by bring disproportionate recognition. Such lack of integration inevitably places great strains on the individual placed in such a situation and behavior deviant from the institutional pattern results on a large scale.[32]

Whatever the merits of this argument might have been, it was the swan song of the social trusteeship professionalism. By 1960 the notion had came under increasing attack both for the indiscriminate manner in which the term had been applied to all types of occupations,[33] and for the self-serving nature of some claims to professionalism which simply camouflaged the protection of privileged positions. Here Freidson's study of the medical profession documented many cases of self-interested practice of medicine which contradicted the claims of the doctors as being dedicated to clients and embracing the professional standards, which were, however, hardly administered by the peers in question.[34] Sometimes the analysis took a more strident Marxist tone, which saw in professions little more than market-dominating organization (monopoly) declaring everything else more or less a myth.[35] But since little attention was originally paid,[36] e.g. by Larson of the role of the state in both the 'licensing' of the professions, and in the production and imparting of the necessary knowledge, the relationship might be more complicated as the traditional Marxist approach of capture purports.

On the continent the production and dissemination of knowledge were never as independent of the state, as in the Anglo Saxon world and thus a rather different picture of the organizational matrix emerged there. This we see not only in the technical, i.e. 'late' professions – but even in law. It is especially true of France, where courts have sometimes completely reorganized their bars, and the 'magistrates' are a separate group from the avocats with different educational requirements. This pattern is obviously quite different from the English career, where barristers have a monopoly for filing the positions at higher courts.[37] In Germany the picture is again different. Although the state traditionally employed most of the lawyers trained by its universities, it also delegated to the universities the near exclusive control of the licensing and of the careers of these professionals through examinations. Thus, the first small tranche is being selected for the sometimes strange profession of notaries, who hold a public/private office, the second tranche is eligible for the appointment as judges, the third as public officials in administration, and the rest can become free professionals and practice law or become employees of firms or associations.

Despite these differences some common trends emerged over the last few decades. The issue of the social contribution of the profession is increasingly answered by the market and the by the necessary services provided by the professions and universities to business enterprises or agencies. In universities various outreach- and continuing-education programs have been institutionalized. The internal curriculum debates and the quest for practical relevance of the transmitted knowledge, are supplemented by score-keeping of what students (and the market) want and of how satisfied the customers are with teaching performances. Even the concept of 'lifelong learning' has been transformed into a continuing process of acquiring, or fine-tuning specific skills, in order to stay competitive, perhaps even of changing careers in an increasingly volatile labour market. This is rather different from the ideal of a well-rounded person with life plans, who is good at what s/he is doing and who is enjoying life rather than having 'no life' as s/he has a profession. Budgetary pressures – even in still largely publicly financed educational systems – push universities in the direction of becoming more like business enterprises by applying for grants (public or private) and providing training rather than serving as trustees of general cultural knowledge concerned with education.

Thus the old notion of trustee professionalism gets more and more associated with the non-profit sector[38] or perhaps public administration. Strangely enough, public agencies still ask for the 'virtuous' administrator, or the public oriented servant[39] but again the discrepancy between the actual practice, which relies largely on management tools (hierarchical controls), and the old professional ideal of stressing discretion, the observance of an ethical code, and relying on collegial approval, is glaring. In administrative law these tensions and contradictions between the old notions of discretion and the new managerial perspective become perhaps most visible in the detailed procedural measures relying on control through specialized 'expertise' rather than on judgement. The apparent tensions have obvious implications for both the individual and for the skills or knowledge which link individuals via organizations to the larger society. As Steven Brint (in following the work of Gerhard Lenski on stratification) has remarked

> Contemporary professionals differ from other strata in so far as they are simultaneously 'retainers', 'merchants' and 'priests'. They are 'priest-like' in their authority over secular knowledge bases. But not less importantly, they

are also merchants of the cultural and human capital that is their major source of mobility across and up organizational hierarchies; and within major organizations, they typically occupy positions of relatively high-ranking officials. Together these elements define a distinctive employment situation for the majority of professionals. These elements of the employment situation condition which is shared by professionals, and also define the main lines along which political and cultural differentiation occurs.[40]

These observations have three implications. One is that it corrects the naïve version of functionalism and expertise, in which formerly humanist ideology is finally displaced by 'true' scientific knowledge. This story line nicely fits the narrative of progress but little else, since judgement about prioritization and casing (what is this a 'case of') cannot be reduced to demonstration or the simple application of theoretical propositions to the 'real world'. This is why modern professionals mostly wear 'three hats' as Brint in the quote above suggests. The second, and more difficult one, is to conceptualize the changing role of professions – i.e. link knowledge to action, as suggested by Parsons- and show how institutionalized settings and organizational forms influence decision making. This would involve, third, an analysis of how the 'appropriate' way of coming to a decision is selected whereby not only different types of expertise might be required, but different trade-offs between conflicting values (safety first, vs. acceptable risks, vs. liability considerations and economic, or design feasibility) interact in complex ways.

Thus if the functionalist argument is unsustainable, it also makes one wonder about the prudential argument, especially since already Aristotle himself fell back on character, i.e. on the exemplary *spoudaios*, the man of virtue and good judgement.[41] Aside from the issue that here knowledge and attitude (*hexis*) interact, a further problem arises in that the necessary dispositions are *acquired*, as Aristotle himself says, rather than being simple manifestations of a given 'character'. This raises then another version of the chicken and egg problem, even if we assume – what empirically has become quite doubtful – that dispositions are good predictors or guides for action,[42] as still something more is required. All virtues in a well-ordered person have to be in harmony so that e.g. the 'bravery' exhibited by an action is not just the result of intemperance, or battling for a cause is not just the result of stupidity rather than instantiating a sense of justice. Precisely because this 'gentlemanliness' has to be developed, and this training in turn presupposes resources and leisure, most of us are not likely to develop the virtues of the Aristotelian *spoudaios*, a person of seriousness, ethical excellence and good judgement.[43] How exacting this ideal is can be seen that we can e.g. be 'good' at something, even be or become a *good* thief (when we have learned the tricks of the trade) but that we cannot be a virtuous thief.

Thus any virtuous action must to be assessed in terms of these background conditions, as already the Stoics suggested, and not against some extraordinary chance offering the opportunity for heroic action (acts of super-rogation). Actually, we might fear such opportunities as our limitations might become visible to all, and thus we focus on 'going on' with our daily lives, failing to look left or right, often exhibiting an extraordinary lack of circumspection and compassion by leaving the problems we see to others, or intimate that in this situation the normal rules do not apply.[44] Nevertheless, even though our conduct consists mostly of routinized practices they can be performed not only well but in a virtuous fashion, i.e. they can be done badly either because they are performed incompetently, or corruptly, even if this corruption does not entail malicious intent or ill-will towards specific others.

In this context the issue of the normalcy and of the banality of evil action attains its importance. As Hannah Arendt has pointed out: 'The trouble with Eichmann was precisely that so many were like him, and that many were neither perverted nor sadistic, that they were and still are, terribly and terrifyingly normal'.[45] Her controversial assessment seems however, (frighteningly enough) to be born out by the extensive psychiatric evaluations of some of the doctors at Auschwitz.[46] While a few like Mengele seemed to have a 'double personality', others, such as the head of the team of doctors selecting the victims arriving at Auschwitz, showed no psychotic traits and some of them, such as Dr. Wirth, was no rabid anti-Semite or a simple inhuman monster as he, before taking up his 'duties' at Auschwitz, had treated Jewish patients when it already was forbidden by law.[47]

Thus normalcy and pathology seem to lie much closer together than the character- and traits arguments, make it appear. This does not mean that everything can be explained by situational variables but it does point us to the importance of framing situations and of scripts by which we attempt to manage value conflicts. Here the invocation of war or exceptional circumstances serve as an important cues so as to avoid taking responsibility for actions which we consider 'otherwise' inappropriate. Similarly, as the Milgram- and the Stanford Prison experiments show, framing something as an experiment, or as an institutional problem, dramatically influences the responses of a random (or even highly selective) set of people, none of whom showed sadistic tendencies in the diagnostics before. Thus, 'science' seems to be powerful trigger for dispensing with any further question. In the first set of the often repeated Milgram experiment a person in lab-coat divides the candidates who had signed up for a 'learning' experiment, in which 'teachers' -observed by the lab-coated experimenter – and the observed persons (learners) which are seated in a separate room. The teachers were told that they had to administer increasingly painful electroshocks to the learners when the latter respond incorrectly to a word association test. After a level of 330 volt has been reached, the script of the experiment provided that there were no longer learners' responses, but the experimenter instructed the teachers to classify this as a 'non-response' (rather than checking what happened to the learner) and continue with further increases in voltage until the bitter end. Actually two-thirds of the teachers did so, and did so in virtually all repeat performances of the experiment, which varied locations, types of people, etc. but left the basic design in tact.

In the Stanford study undergraduates participated in a prison-experiment in which a group of twenty-one male college students with no history of crime, anti-social behaviour, or emotional or physical disabilities was randomly assigned to play either 'guards' or 'prisoners'. The experiment was conducted in a Stanford University basement, fitted to resemble the real thing by having cells, even a 'hole' for solitary confinement. After two days there was an insurrection and the guards, forbidden to use physical violence, were hosing down the prisoners with fire-extinguishers and used sadistic forms of punishment (like forcing prisoners to clean their toilets with their bare hands, or force feeding them). Five prisoners had to be released prematurely because of extreme disturbances such as depression, rage, acute anxiety or psychosomatic rashes. On the other hands the guards seemed to enjoy their job although being ambivalent about it and hating the prisoners for not obeying and 'making them do things' they never believed they would do to others. After 6 days the experiment, originally scheduled for two weeks, had to be cancelled.

These cases show two things. One is the importance of the definition of the situation, but even more so of the script 'requiring' certain performances when one moves within institutionalized contexts. Not only are thereby the usual ascriptions of positive values to the in-group (and negative ones to the out-group) pre-programmed, but repertoires of practices are evoked that show the potentially dark side of professionalism (and not only the callousness or indifference to others as when we lack compassion or the ability to extend ourselves to others). Two, in institutionalized contexts this downside is however accepted even though it frequently imposes considerable stress on the role occupants. After all, being involved in 'scientific research' means accepting certain costs, in the hope that these actions will yield ultimately more knowledge and thus a better life for all of us. But this means that being a guard means behaving like a guard, even if this entails unease or blind obedience to abnegating any personal engagement.

What are then the hopes for professionals in either their expert-role, or as the virtuous administrators, or representative of a trustee professionalism for upholding the professional ideal? As mentioned above this question might be difficult to answer as the professional environment has dramatically changed and individuals have had to negotiate their way by being combining and mixing traditional roles. Nevertheless, a closer look at different organizational environments analysed in terms of ideal types might be useful. I shall do this in the next section before I address more specifically what this means for the expert validated by 'science' – for which I take space engineers as my case- before I attempt to draw some conclusions for the legal professional. Nevertheless, a few general remarks 'organizational pathologies' and their alleged remedies are still in order.

While we all notice that the traditional image of the professional lawyer or doctor is no longer adequate since more than half have become simple employees in organizations (government and the service sector), the implications for the actual practice of the profession are less obvious. Furthermore, while we are clear about obvious pathologies, which certain organizational environments apparently foster, we are less certain about their correction, especially when the usual remedies, such as introducing more competition and transparency, lead to perverse effects. Thus many of the alleged remedies intended to counteract e.g. the monopolistic or corrupt tendencies do not *deliver* on their promises but are frequently counterproductive giving us two poxes for the price of one.

Examples abound when market- elements are introduced and agencies 'contract out' for services. It is indeed cold comfort that these problems cut across all professions not only the old and humanist ones, such as law and the 'helping professions', but also for engineering, where scientific expertise seemed to provide much stronger motivation of paying heed to expert advice. In the case of humanitarian organizations this has led to aggravate multiple principle-agents problems familiar from IGO and NGO/IO partnerships. It has also engendered 'feeding frenzy' among the NGOs as they have to constantly compete for the short-term contracts with the perverse effect of making the NGO as service- provider dependent on local lords who provide (and 'guarantee') the necessary information for the evaluators at contract renewal times. It also diverted the NGOs' time and attention from their actual mission.[48]

Similar problems arose in domestic governmental contracting out for which the exorbitant sum for toilet seats ordered by the Department of Defense became the symbol. When NASA introduced incentives for contractors to meet deadlines, or deliver the product even earlier, contractors cut corners, delivered shoddy work (which increased costs for costly checks and repairs) and cut down on safety precautions. The outcome were not only two nearly identical disasters in the space shuttle program (the Challenger explosion after lift-off on 28 January 1986, and the re-entry explosion of the Columbia shuttle in on 1 February 2003), but also several near misses, which subsequent investigation squarely attributed to NASA 'organizational culture', its internal resistance to learning and paying heed to sound engineering standards.

Finally, most observers agree that advertising and the introduction of transparency of fees for legal services have not lowered, but *substantially increased* the legal costs to customers in the US when compared to traditional retainers or – when exceptional circumstances prevailed-negotiated lump sums. Still worse, the resulting pre-occupation with 'bill-ables' creates, or at least significantly exacerbates, the conflict of interest between the client and his lawyer. It will be task of the next section to analyse these puzzles more extensively in order to assess chances and limits for professionalism in the form of bringing to bear particular knowledge on practical problems, preventing abusive practices and maintaining professional standards in the face of organizational pressures for conformity.

9.4   The Managerial Revolution and the Professions

This then leads to a number of observations on the contemporary professions: first, while it is quite common to distinguish between markets (supposedly based on exchange relations and self-help) and hierarchies (where pyramidal structures obtain and regulate relations through authority [and enforcement]), this distinction is far too crude and historically practically useless to provide us with an adequate map of the division of labour and their coordination mechanisms. After all, the labour markets where labour has been entirely commodified and industrial production has become nearly completely standardized, actual labour markets have always shown signs of authoritative direction. For one, guilds fought for public recognition to have the exclusive privilege to supply certain goods or services, granted by royal patents and privileges. Second, under modern conditions the development of firms based on an 'incomplete contract' involved not only an exchange of labour for wages, but also the authority to direct the contracted labour power either by the owner or by manager. In any case it established a hierarchical form of organization.

Second, professions remain here an oddity as they share with the guilds the exclusive jurisdiction over certain activities whereby this privilege is justified by the character of the task and the necessary knowledge for it. Since the tasks involve complex problems, which do not lead themselves to standardized procedures or whose quality is not readily ascertainable by the customer, this problem is taken care of by the certification a practitioner has to obtain. In this way also the quality of the practice according to certain yardsticks can be guaranteed what otherwise could lead to severe problems when customers would have to rely on trial and error and expose themselves to excessive risks.

Third, different from the authority exercised by an owner which is monocratic and derivative of 'property', the authority to practice a profession is based on being a member of a group which retains the authority to determine qualifications of its members and which negotiates the with other professions the terms of collaboration, if various tasks are required.

Fourth, still out of sight remains however the most important invention of modern organizational forms, brought about by the corporation and the managerial revolution. In that case no longer ownership but control is entrusted to persons who organize ranks and occupational hierarchies in terms of the rational legal paradigm, by assigning powers and duties to certain offices on the basis of impersonal functions and universal rules. Here of course the panoply of measures having been developed in the administration of the state was (partially) transferred to the economic sphere. There is no need to go over these developments save to recall that the new agencies were no longer functions of the royal household and their exercise is no longer 'prebendal', as Weber would have called it, (or based) on familial ties or favours, but obtaining an office was now based on qualifications, it functioned according to hierarchical controls, and promised a potentially lifelong employment and career. To insure the integrity of the service, the office holder however often was also protected from the arbitrariness of superior but had to justify his acts in terms of the specified rules which circumscribed and constituted his powers. Of course there is not a one to one transfer between these spheres: discretion granted to 'managers' is more ample, less bureaucratic and lifelong employment has been (with some exceptions such as in Japan at certain times and industries in Germany) generally unknown in the private sector.

Furthermore, the market- and profit-constraints lead to different organizational manifestations, such as different forms of 'slack', and the rather cumbersome reclassification of jobs through legislation versus redefinitions of jobs by managerial fiat, which insures greater mobility in the case of corporations. But the really interesting issue arises what happens to professionals when they work no longer as self-employed practitioners, but find themselves in complex hierarchical organizations. In a way, they still enjoy the privilege of 'sheltered jobs' as e.g. the lawyer working 'in-house' in a corporation still needs his credentials and only those having them can compete for it, and so do the doctors, and or scientists working for a hospital which is owned by a corporation and managed by a hospital administrator. This led to some subtle, and not so subtle changes, in both the autonomy- and the service- part of professionalism. As Wilenski has pointed out a long time ago:

> These organizations develop their own controls; bosses, not colleagues, rule – or at a minimum, power is split among managers, professional experts, and lay boards of directors. The salaried professional often has neither exclusive nor final responsibility for his work; he must accept the ultimate authority of non-professionals in the assessment of both process and product. For instance, compare the fee taking doctor in general practice with the salaried industrial scientist in product development. The scientist can be by-passed if his company chooses to buy up licenses or subcontract the work to outside laboratories; his work can be terminated, expanded, cut back, or disposed according to the judgment of laboratory directors responding to outside units or higher-ups; his power and status, reflected salaries and tables of organization, are lower than those of the men he serves.[49]

Of course the result need not be that grim, she actually might have a boss interested in protecting autonomy and since the professional might also have specific marketable skills she probably is able to trade them for concessions at the workplace. After all autonomy is always under pressure when demand for services is lagging and which affects self-employed or salaried professionals. On the other hand, the ability of preserving one's autonomy might perversely affect the service ideal, since the administrators might re-write the rules to satisfy their most valuable staff, but might do so at the expense of the patients, such as those with hopeless chronic illness that needs extraordinary care.

Actually it might be the care of a good administrator to keep his staff happy and together, working in a team, that might encourage some of the most problematic organizational pathologies. Not only might the administrators trade or expect favours, the experts themselves might develop in 'anticipated reaction' conformist behaviour in violation of their professional duties. The rigid separation between functionally specific authority and universal standards and 'getting along' places conflicting demands on individuals, particularly since expertise – even when based on scientific standards of knowledge- has hardly ever a clear and unequivocal solution for complex problems where different values compete (costs, efficiency, effectiveness, saliency to the public at large etc.). Knowing that dissent is not really appreciated in smoothly functioning organizations, and that sanctions might range from shunning to loss of the job, there is a strong tendency for 'group think'[50] to establish itself as the *modus operandi*. This leads to decisional pathologies in which individual failure and organizational culture mutually reinforce rather than correct each other. The value of the group and their decision based on expertise are overestimated, the search for alternatives is aborted, and self-appointed 'mind-guards' frequently appear who want to protect the group by discounting disconfirming evidence and selectively reporting and focussing on supportive information. The result is that no outside advice is sought and little time is spent on considering alternatives, contingency plans or fall-back positions.

Irving Janice developed this argument in conjunction with policy failures, such as the Bay of Pigs invasion, the escalation in the Vietnam War and Watergate. But the most classical cases are actually provided by two catastrophic accidents in the US Space flight program involving the loss of the Challenger and the Columbia shuttles and their crews. Ironically both the extensive post mortem of Challenger (Rogers Commission Report[51]) and the extensive study by Diane Vaughan[52] both had already pointed out, that there had been a clear but muted conflict between engineers and NASA administrators for quite some time, concerning the 'O rings' that insulated the hot gas from the rocket boosters strapped on each side of a external fuel tank to which the reusable 'shuttle' was tied. The seals (O rings) were supposed to prevent the hot gases from reaching the outside as such a leak could damage the attachment of the shuttle. The problem of the seals was well known since 1977, and it had led to some redesign in 1985, but the material of the seals still was demonstrably sensitive to cold temperatures. On the day of launch the temperatures had been unusually cold and engineers, in particular Roger Boisjoly had counselled a postponement. But NASA managers overrode his suggestions and the engineers were excluded from the final decision. When the management of Thiokol (the contractor) made the decision recommending or aborting launch, the one hesitant member of the team was told 'to take off the "engineering hat" and put on the "management hat"'.[53] When the mission was launched at 11:38 on 28 January it led to the break-up of the vehicle within seventy-three seconds, having reached an altitude of fifteen km.

Ironically the Columbia disaster on 1 February 2003 – this time happening at re-entry – was the result of uncannily similar failures. Part of the foam insulation had broken off at the start from the external tank and damaged the thermal protection system that shields the vehicle from the heat generated by its re-entry into the atmosphere. This time it led to a melt-down and break-up of the shuttle. Again some concern had been voiced by an engineer Rodney Rocha immediately after lift-off a flying debris (parts of the insulation) was recorded on video. Rocha assembled a Debris Assessment Team, which asked for further data on the damage sustained at launch. He also had asked for cooperation from the Department of Defense in providing satellite images of the shuttle meanwhile in orbit, but had not requested an official authorization by the Chair of the mission management team of NASA (Linda Ham). Since a formal request for help from the Department of Defense required evidence of a 'mandatory need' the NASA administrator terminated the procedures as she could not find out who had initiated the proceeding and because on the information she had received from some engineers in NASA and the Johnson Space Center, the available data did not represent a serious safety risk.[54] This left the Debris assessment in a quandary: without further data they could not make a convincing risk assessment of the actual damage, while in order to get this information 'they needed to prove' – in the words of the Columbia Accident investigation Board – 'to their program managers that there was a need for images in the first place'.[55]

Concerned with the situation Rocha wrote an e-mail to the management in which he stated that: 'In my humble technical opinion ... this is wrong, and bordering on irresponsible',[56] but then he never sent it. Instead, he shared it with some colleagues and when later asked by the Board why he acted in this way he said that he 'did not want to jump the chain of command or to be challenging the management decisions'. Concerned, another member of the Debris Assessment Team, consulted one of his engineering friends, Bob Daugherty, at Langley Research Center, to run a simulation of the possible damage to the landing gear of the craft. After completion Daugherty 'sent the most unfavourable simulation result to his peers, selected Johnson Space Center engineers, and the most favourable ones to a wider NASA audience, including Debris Asessment Team'.[57]

The flight director sent an e-mail to the Columbia crew informing the commander of the shuttle of the foam damage, but unequivocally dismissed any concerns in regard to the safety of the craft at re-entry. Losses of foam had been common but had only occasioned limited technical analysis so that even the much larger foam piece lost during lift-off of the Columbia the Space Shuttle managers rejected the foam as a probable case and stuck with their previous risk assessment. To that extent they repeated only what over the 113 missions had become a routine and maintenance concern only, as 'foam shedding' and debris impacts. Hoping for the best was at that point virtually the only hope as any rescue mission that could have been considered and which would have, in the word of a member Space flight management team 'made Apollo 13 look like a cakewalk'.[58] It would have involved a docking up with another existing shuttle still on the ground, but getting it to the Columbia would have been possible only during the first couple of days.

The point here is that with time and increasing budgetary pressures NASA had become complacent. Prior safety studies had listed 5396 critical hazards of which 4222 were considered critical (Criticality 1/1R) allowing for no compromises since they could lead to the loss of the crew and the orbiter. With the subsequent success of the missions, over the years 3233 were downgraded and 36 per cent of the waivers had – despite of contrary evidence but no loss of a craft – not been reviewed in the ten years antedating the Challenger disaster.[59] Consequently, critical voices in organizations were mostly unwelcome, as we see from the way in which 'whistle-blowers'[60] are usually treated. In short, over the years the organizational culture of NASA had degenerated (when missions were no longer considered 'developmental' but 'operational').[61] Safety concerns were subject to rubber-stamping rituals, which provided no independent assessment of the actual risks.[62] Failures in maintenance hardly evoked a response. The loss of qualified personnel did not ring any alarms, as budgets were cut while goals were ambitiously expanded – from the International Space Station, to doing experiments in space[63] – as NASA needed the publicity. All these factors worked together in order to jeopardize the integrity of the programs.

Thus while the management style had certainly degenerated into a 'kill the messenger type', as Charles Harlan,[64] a former head of safety at the Johnson Space Center in Houston remarked. Some individual actions, such as of not pressing the point or giving different advice to different groups, as did Dougherty (apparently in order to 'buy insurance') did not help either. The latter example shows perhaps most vividly how individuals tried to navigate in the shifting winds that had enmeshed the organization. However, it is quite clear that something more is required than just having more outspoken or 'better intentioned' engineers in place. For one, any organization depends on a division of labour and thus much of the professional responsibility is to get one's work done, but not to be a *praeceptor mundi*. Furthermore, evidence even in the world of science and technology is hardly ever unequivocal. Boisjoly thought the correlation between temperature and the resiliency of the O-ring was suggestive, but knew that he did not have a tight argument. Rocha knew that his fears were not shared by others as experience had shown that 'shedding' was within the limits of acceptable risks.

'It is not my job' or 'it is his job, not mine' are the usual excuses, and giving up when one has made one's point might, with hindsight, sound like a cop-out, since here not direct 'task responsibility', which professional ethics requires of the particular agent, is expected. The problem is rather one of no one taking overall responsibility (or only insufficiently so). While it is management that has to shoulder this responsibility, complex systems nearly inevitably create through interaction effects and tight coupling 'normal accidents', as Perrow[65] suggested. This makes redundancy an absolute imperative but even after that the question remains what is "enough" in the real world. Here the interface between the technical or scientific purist, the problems of production, time pressures and of costs are interacting in complex ways, especially since certain 'solutions' to identified problems might now increase risks in other unanticipated areas. To that extent imagination (what could possibly go wrong) and, in the words of the CAIB, 'a healthy fear of failure' – operations must be proved safe rather than the other way around[66] – are probably the only guidelines we have. Despite their generality they are not meaningless but of decisive importance for linking micro-decision making with organizational hierarchies and institutional cultures to the inter-organizational structures and to the wider social processes. In this way, knowledge is created and disseminated, and informs our world view, which in turn is feeding back again via classification schemes, expertise, scripts, risk assessments and organizational procedures, shaping actual choices in the realization of our common projects. As Diane Vaughn suggested – and whose findings were again born out by the Columbia accident:

[The] case (Challenger) supplies the agency missing from the new institutionalism.

It affirms a theory of practical action that links institutional forces, social location and individual thought and action. For as its essence, the case is a picture of individual rationality irretrievably intertwined with position in a structure. Position in the engineering profession, the aerospace industry and the various organizations made up the labyrinthine NASA contractor network, was a key determinant of individual and collective determinations of risk. Position determined social mission. Position determined access to information. Position determined responsibility for acting on information and the actions that legitimately could be taken. Position contributed to ability to interpret information and to the world view brought to that interpretation. Perhaps, most important, position determined power to shape opinions and outcomes in one's own and other organizations.[67]

9.5   Conclusion

Our discussion of the changing nature of the professions led to some unexpected results. It exploded several myths, such as that there is a direct link between knowledge or skill to the occupation, and that the change from trustee professionalism to the expert amounts to greater latitude for the expert than the former professional. As I have tried to show in the case study of engineering, none of these plausible possibilities seems to accord with the facts. It also exploded the myth that changes and pathologies can be reduced to a lack of ethics, brought about by the ascendance of the profit motive, drowning out other concerns. While there are certainly noticeable changes in the behaviour of occupational groups when compared to the old reference points of independence and peer acceptance, the links of the profession to the wider society are changing as well. This is a development which is reflected in different careers patterns, in the demand for different services which lead to a greater commodification of knowledge, and in the organizational form by which professions respond to such changes and try to maintain their privileged position.

One point though also emerged clearly is that such deep-seated changes cannot be explained in terms of individual failings, or be cured by personal virtue. The point here is not that ethics, even a more focussed professional ethics, does not matter. The point is rather that we need a different type of ethics if we become aware that the chances for virtuous action are powerfully shaped, evoked, supported and prevented by organizations. The latter are not just persons 'written large' but creatures of a different kind. They require different modes of analysis and different remedies since the problems exceed the opportunistic type of deviance we consider paradigmatic for all social ills and from which we extrapolate in order to 'design' the remedies.[68] Reducing the problem then to one of getting the incentives right when unintended perverse effects abound and multiple competing values interact, seems quaint indeed. Here neither the classical humanist teachings nor the extreme individualism of liberalism together with a restricted notion of instrumental rationality, are much of a help. And neither is our preoccupation with simple causality for both the explanations and the attribution of responsibility. These seemingly 'neutral' methodological orientations are more likely to misdiagnose the problem of complex systems, as Perrow has suggested.

What does this mean for the practice of law and the legal professional? Obviously no global answer is possible considering the different institutional structures and organizational cultures in the various 'systems of professions'. All we can do is to 'think through' some of the implications of the observed changes and see what we get. While it would be preposterous to assume that a couple of probes will then unite to an integrated picture that amounts to a new theory, or even theoretical sketch, they can provide at least some kaleidoscopic configurations which are informative and non-trivial in that they correct some common misconceptions.

So let us begin with the universities and the supply side of the problem. As we have seen universities too had to reposition themselves in the changing environment of the communications revolution and the needs of an information society. Thus expanding professional programs was one way of providing this service. In law such programs are cheap – in comparison to medical or high tech-programs- and promise good returns from alumni, corporations and law firms.

Law firms profit from this expansion by having access to an increasing number of possible employees who can be remunerated at lower rates than the top echelon of partners charge their clients. Since few associates can hope to advance after their apprenticeship to 'full partner' they have an incentive to specialize early, and 'reinvent themselves' during their career reacting to the signals of the market. This development encourages rent-seeking behaviour on the part of the individual, who has become an employee. The appropriation of the surplus by the firm, which is now more and more a business enterprise – with changing personnel even at the higher echelons – than a life -long partnership among professionals, has also implications. Having some 'rain makers' on board, i.e. people with good connections who could bring in lucrative contracts, becomes a virtual necessity, but has as a down side that mutual raiding also leads to the practice that partners that leave the firm frequently take 'their clients' with them to their new job.

Of course such changes were possible only after services were treated like goods with prices rather than fiduciary arrangements, which formerly regulated some important parts of the client-lawyer relationship. Here the calls for greater transparency of legal fees and the revocation of the prohibition to use advertising (because of its incompatibility with professional ethics), powerfully reinforced this trend. Although calls for greater transparency were often buttressed by claims that more competition would be a good thing, since it would reduce prices, the record seems fairly clear that this is not what happened. As in the case of the market for health care, prices are not lowered when more professionals compete, as prices prove to be not only sticky, but they tend to explode. This development, in turn, leads to a much larger spread of incomes within the occupational group, as was the case before. The ethical issue of exacerbating the potential conflict of interest between lawyer and client has already been mentioned.

Similarly the reform of the discovery proceedings has not led to the shortening of trial time but to a significant increase, as whole new slew of strategies became possible, such as hiding requested information in a lot of chaff, pursuing a 'scorched earth' strategy, exhausting the resources of the opponent (and the client), and asking for delays in order to get new evidence or expert opinion. If one adds to this the regulatory revolution in the wake of the fact that more and more risks have to be managed in a modern society using complex technologies, one has to face some mind-boggling prospects. Thus, BP's legal gamble to go to court in order to devolve some of its liabilities from the oil spills in the Mexican Gulf onto its sub-contractors created about '70 million' pages of 'evidence'.[69] (This does not include the further law-suits by the states and private individuals for damages which were filed.)

If the lawyer woks as 'in-house lawyer' his relationship to his client will not only be a privileged one, but the client will be also his 'boss'. Thus being part of the chain of command will in all likelihood further diminish the lawyer's autonomy, by becoming now subject to more direct control. S/he might enjoy the work more than in a law firm as it might be more varied and s/he has perhaps more control over their work both in terms of the schedule and the final 'product'. But s/he is now the 'hired gun' who has to advise the superiors of how 'to walk the line', like Holmes's famous bad man. S/he cannot advise them to do anything patently illegal, such as to perjure themselves but there are enough grey zones (such as 'when you do not remember with certainty, just say you do not recall the incidence or utterance' – and who has a crystal clear memory?) In these cases 'justice' is served only indirectly (by being the result of an adversarial process).

If lawyers work 'for the state', as civil servants, their client is in a way the public at large or the constitutional order. But this is a fiction, even if the tension between bureaucratic control by superiors (the government) and their exercise of power might be protected by special laws (*Beamtenrecht*) or civil service provisions. The experiences with whistle-blower have not been encouraging, as counteracting the boss and not being part of "the team" might incur significant sanctions. Things might seem better when the lawyers are not in permanent positions but hold jobs as special counsels on termed assignment, as no long-term consequences for the career seem to follow since one will be back at the university law form or corporation after the stint in government. But, depending on circumstances, matters might be even worse as one is a 'political appointment', i.e. if one comes to the job with the understanding that one has to serve the president. Disappointing this expectation and becoming disloyal might be the kiss of death at least in those professional circles and coteries, which are identified with a particular administration and a political party. Networking might have got you the job but it might also be dubious blessing when the 'word is out'. Thus having no independent political power- base, which would have to be taken into account by the decision maker, and bringing to the table only some expertise, being disloyal to the 'hand that feeds you' seems anathema and Weber's 'prebendal' logic of office-holding seems to apply in full force. Thus the lawyer on assignment might face the same fate as the professional in business. When one of the leading risks-analysts at the Royal Bank of Scotland warned his CEO that the trading patterns at the bank were exceedingly risky, he was not only fired on the spot, he never received a call from any head-hunter after that![70]

Besides, for the lawyer on special assignment, there are some enticing incentives to become a good team player. Considerable power can be wielded when one has become part of the constitutional process. Although we think that the exercise of powers has been definitely settled by the constitution and, in the case of the US, by constitutional review, actual practice shows that while judicial review might be the most significant part of a constitutional government – the old *topos* of a "government of laws and not of men" comes to mind – political practice is more varied. There are certainly "constitutional moments" where fundamental shifts occur outside the usual amendment process or judicial review (Civil Rights Act, Freedom of Information Act). But there are some new practices, such as 'providing' interpretations at the signing of a bill, which wield power although they are of debatable legality. Because these interpretations are binding on agencies until overruled by the courts their effect on policy is considerable. As Bruce Ackerman has shown, the growth of the two legal offices in the American executive branch (Office of the White House Counsel) and the Office of Legal Counsel in the Justice Department, have significantly transformed the presidency cutting it loose from its constitutional moorings by using legal expertise for the purposes of their client.

In the light of this discussion, the fate of the public international lawyer has become doubly tragic. Not only might he be reduced to one of the 'pathetic comforters' whom Kant slighted, but he may even as lawyer/diplomat see that his standing as a representative of the sovereign or a definite public has been eroded by the trans-governmental networks of the disaggregated state[71] where 'specialists' are at work. Thus he has become, in a way, a remnant of a time gone by, somewhat a bit of a master-less man who perhaps finds comfort in associating with diplomats from other countries who share the same fate, but whose role as a 'public servant' has been drastically diminished.

Meanwhile various policy-wonks, claiming special expertise, ranging from bookkeeping to peacekeeping or owing their position to personal ties to the decision maker, or to an 'inner circle', are carrying out policy. They seem equally distanced from the ideal of the 'moral politician' for whom Kant had rooted, as they are from the professional or the *spoudaios* who was the ideal of the social trusteeship professionalism. As the new expertocratic professionals are caught up in an interminable slew of meetings and deadlines, they have little time left for reflection and critical assessment. But one cannot simply withdraw, as being 'there' is all what counts. Thus comfort and confidence comes from frantic activity (being busy), being part of 'the team', and from reliance on routinized and deeply ingrained techniques. Props like graphs, PowerPoints and best practices have then increasingly to substitute for reflective judgement, as work becomes more and more reified and subject to 'scientific' (mostly quantitative) assessment, even if the quality of output is usually in doubt. Thus the modern professional becomes a *Macher* (both in the sense of the *homo faber* and the Yiddish 'fixer' who gets things done), since even in 'third sector' organizations s/he has to be a 'go-getter' and mission junkie rather than the helper of yore who lived his 'calling'.

Notes

1. R. Dworkin, *Taking Rights Seriously* (Cambridge, MA: Harvard University Press, 1978).
2. For a good discussion of the issues involved in judicial 'discretion', see Matthias Klatt, 'Taking Rights Less Seriously: A Structural Analysis of Judicial Discretion', *Ratio Juris* 20 (2007): 506–29.
3. See e.g. B. Kingsbury, N. Krisch and R. Stewart, 'The Emergence of Global Administrative Law', *Law and Contemporary Problems* 68 (2005): 14–62.
4. D. Kennedy, *The Dark Side of Virtue: Reassessing International Humanitarism* (Princeton, NJ: Princeton University Press, 2004), particularly Chapter 4. See also his 'Reassessing International Humanitarianism', in A. Orford (ed.), *International Law and Its Others* (Cambridge: Cambridge University Press, 2006), 131.
5. For two different versions of 'professional problematique', see M. Koskenniemi, 'Constitutionalization as a Mindset: Reflections on Kantian Themes about International Law and Globalization', *Theoretical Inquiries in Law* 8 (2007): 9–36, and *Fragmentation of International Law: Difficulties Arising from the Diversification and Expansion of International Law* (Helsinki: Erik Castren Institute, 2007), focusing here largely on the 'techniques' which practicing lawyers use.
6. B. Ackerman, *The Decline and Fall of the American Republic* (Cambridge, MA: Harvard University Press, 2010).
7. M. Koskenniemi, *The Gentle Civilizer of Nations: The Rise and Fall of International Law* (Cambridge: Cambridge University Press, 2001).
8. B. Ackerman, 'The Storrs Lectures: Discovering the Constitution', *Yale Law Journal* 93 (1984): 1013–72.
9. See Aristotle, *Nichomachean Ethics*, Book VI, in J. Barnes (ed.), *The Complete Works of Aristotle*, vol. 2 (Princeton, NJ: Princeton University Press, 1984), 1797–808.
10. To that extent, the issue is reduced to an argument that if persons possess a personal trait, their decisions or behavior will show trait relevant features in trait relevant eliciting conditions well beyond chance probability.
11. I. Kant, *Perpetual Peace*, in H. S. Reiss (ed.), *Kant Political Writings*, H. B. Nisbet (trans.) (Cambridge: Cambridge University Press, 1970), 93–130.
12. See e.g. R. B. Louden, 'Kant's Virtue Ethics', *Philosophy* 61 (1986): 473–89.
13. See M. Koskenniemi and P. Leino, 'Fragmentation of International Law? Postmodern Anxieties', *Leiden Journal of International Law* 15 (2002): 553–79.
14. M. Koskenniemi, *From Apology to Utopia: The Structure of International Legal Argument*, reissue with new epilogue (Cambridge: Cambridge University Press, 2005).
15. See e.g. M. Williams, 'Skepticism', in J. Greco and E. Sosa (eds), *The Blackwell Guide to Epistemology* (Malden, MA: Blackwell, 1999), 35.
16. See G. Duby, *The Three Orders: Feudal Society Imagined*, A. Goldhammer (trans.) (Chicago: University of Chicago Press, 1980).
17. See also Aristotle's remark in the *Nichomachean Ethics*, Book VI, 4 (1140a1), in Barnes, *Complete Works of Aristotle*, 1799: 'Among things that can be otherwise are included both things made and things done; makings and acting are different ... so that the reasoned state of capacity to act is different from the reasoned state of capacity to make'.
18. See Aristotle, *Poetics*, IX 1-liv, in Barnes, *Complete Works of Aristotle*.

19. See F. Wallis, *Medieval Medicine: A Reader* (Toronto, ON: University of Toronto Press, 2010).
20. P. Dobkin-Hall, 'The Social Foundations of Professional Credibility: Linking the Medical Profession to Higher Education in Connecticut and Massachusetts', in T. Haskell (ed.), *The Authority of Experts: Studies in History and Theory* (Bloomington: Indiana University Press, 1984), 107.
21. E. Freidson, *Professionalism: The Third Logic* (Chicago: University of Chicago Press, 2001).
22. A. Abbott, *The System of Professions: an Essay on the Division of Expert Labor* (Chicago: University of Chicago Press, 1988).
23. A. Smith, *An Inquiry into the Nature and Causes of the Wealth of Nations*, E. Cannan (ed.) (1838; repr., Chicago: University of Chicago Press, 1976).
24. E. Durkheim, *Professional Ethics and Civic Morals* (London: Routledge, 1957).
25. E. Durkheim, *The Division of Labor in Society* (Glencoe, IL: Free Press, 1964).
26. For a general discussion of this problem, see T. Haskell, 'Professionalism vs Capitalism: R. H. Tawney, Emile Durkheim, and C. S. Pierce on the Disinterestedness of Professional Communities', in Haskell, *Authority of Experts*, 180.
27. M. Weber, *The Protestant Ethic and the Spirit of Capitalism* (London: Routledge, 1992), 182.
28. See the interesting discussion of the English debate in H. Perkin, *The Origins of Modern English Society 1780–1880* (Toronto, ON: University of Toronto Press, 1972), 265ff.
29. R. H. Tawney, *The Acquisitive Society* (New York: Harcourt, Brace, 1921), 94ff.
30. Aristotle, *Nicomachean Ethics*, Book I, 9 (1099a23), in Barnes, *Complete Works of Aristotle*.
31. Here the creation of 'land grant colleges' and its emphasis on 'practical' disciplines provided a different environment from the high 'status' occupation of 'learning' that had prevailed in Europe and had shaped the 'professions' there.
32. T. Parsons, 'The Professions and Social Structure', *Social Forces* 17 (1939): 464.
33. This is the thrust of Harold L. Wilenski's criticism in his 'The Professionalization of Everyone?', *The American Journal of Sociology* 70 (1964): 137–58.
34. E. Freidson, *Profession of Medicine: a Study of the Sociology of Applied Knowledge* (Chicago: University of Chicago Press, 1988).
35. See e.g. M. Sarfatti Larson, *The Rise of Professionalism* (Berkeley: University of California Press, 1977).
36. She corrected this problem in a later seminal article in which Bourdieus's notion of 'symbolic capital' played a decisive role. See M. Sarfatti Larson, 'The Production of Expertise and the Constitution of Expert Power', in Haskell, *Authority of Experts*, 29.
37. See Abbott, *System of Professions*, 26–29.
38. An interesting case are the 'arts', which are perhaps 'trustees' of a cultural tradition – although here the fit is quite lose as the *avant garde* phenomenon shows – are part of a 'credentialist system' of training – although no strict licensing is involved – have some notion of a collective identity but are not directly tenuously linked to labor markets and able to safeguard their specific domain, partially also because the dynamics is crucially influenced by the possibilities of rent seeking behavior. To that extent they exhibit patterns of some former Renaissance 'artists' who emerged from guilds but became 'universal' geniuses and entrepreneurs.

39. See e.g. T. L. Cooper, 'Big Questions in Administrative Ethics: a Need for Focused, Collaborative Effort', *Public Administration Review* 64 (2004): 395–407; see also G. Adams, 'Administrative Ethics and the Chimera of Professionalism', in T. L. Cooper (ed.), *Handbook of Administrative Ethics*, 2nd ed. (New York: Marcel Dekker, 2001), 291; and J. Rohr, *Ethics for Bureaucrats* (New York: Marcel Dekker, 1988).

40. S. Brint, *In an Age of Experts: the Changing Role of Professionals in Politics and Public Life* (Princeton, NJ: Princeton University Press, 1994).

41. Aristotle, *Nicomachean Ethics*, 1106 a11–12, in Barnes, *Complete Works of Aristotle*.

42. See e.g. L. Ross and R. Nisbett, *The Person and the Situation* (Philadelphia: Temple University Press, 1991).

43. For a further discussion, see R. Schottlaender, 'Die Aristotelische *spoudaios*', *Zeitschrift fuer Philosophische Forschung* 34 (1980): 385–95.

44. As an example of the former problem, there are the widely reported incidents in which people are being assaulted and cry for help which many bystanders hear but no one calls even the police or when e.g. an expedition to the Mount Everest failed to help another two claimers suffering from exhaustion and altitude sickness but who continued their climb and returned successfully while the two others perished. As Eiuske Shikegawa justified his decision to continue with the climb instead of helping the others with oxygen: 'Above 8000 meters is not a place where people can afford morality', as quoted in J. M. Doris, *Lack of Character: Personality and Moral Behavior* (Cambridge: Cambridge University Press, 2002), 78.

45. H. Arendt, *Eichmann in Jerusalem* (New York: Viking Press, 1963).

46. See R. J. Lifton, *The Nazi Doctors: Medical Killings and the Psychology of Genocide* (New York: Basic Books, 1986).

47. Ibid., 386.

48. See A. Cooley and J. Ron, 'The NGO Scramble: Organizational Insecurity and the Political Economy of Transnational Action', *International Security* 27 (2002): 5–39.

49. Wilensky, 'Professionalization of Everyone?', 137–58.

50. See I. L. Janis, *Victims of Group Think: a Psychological Study of Foreign-Policy Decisions and Fiascoes*, 2nd ed. (Boston: Houghton Mifflin, 1982).

51. William P. Rogers et al., *Report of the Presidential Commission on the Space Shuttle Challenger Accident*, 5 vols. (Washington, DC: Government Printing Office, 1986).

52. D. Vaughan, *The Challenger Launch Decision: Risky Technology, Culture and Deviance at NASA* (Chicago: University of Chicago Press, 1997).

53. Ibid., 316.

54. See also W. Langwiesche, 'Columbia's last Flight', *Atlantic Monthly*, 292 (2003): 58–87. Langwiseche shows how on the basis of past 'experience' foam losses had become a 'normal' phenomenon considered it a 'turnaround' issue (i.e. not of the highest importance). See also Harold W. Gehman Jr. et al., *Columbia Accident Investigation Board Report*, vol. 1 (Washington, DC: Government Printing Office, 2003), 161 (hereinafter *CAIB*).

55. Gehman, *CAIB*, 157.

56. Ibid.

57. S. Marsen, 'Case Study', 3, www.tinyurl.com/marsen-case (last accessed 3 March 2016).

58. See W. Hale, 'After Ten Years: Death Never Takes a Holiday', *Wayne Hale's Blog*, 7 January 2013, www.waynehale.wordpress.com/2013/01/07/after-ten-years-death-never-takes-a-holiday/ (last accessed 3 March 2016). The Columbia Accident

Investigation Board concluded that an overlap of five days in the early part of the mission had existed in the beginning for getting Atlantis ready and safe the crew of the Columbia, de-orbiting the shuttle and sending into the Indian Ocean, see Gehman, *CAIB*, Chapter 6, 173ff.

59. American Institute of Chemical Engineers, *Self-Evaluation Tools: Key Lessons from the Columbia Shuttle Disaster (Adapted to the Process Industries)*, www.tinyurl.com/aiche-columbia (last accessed 3 March 2016).

60. While one would assume that civil servants would be much better protected against the usual organizational pressures, especially after the passage of the 1989 *Whistleblower's Protection Act* and the 1978 *Civil Service Reform Act*. A recent assessment concludes that 'those charged with interpreting and implementing the Whistleblower Protection Act are failing to meet the proper standard'. J. A. Truelson, 'Whistleblower Protection and the Judiciary', in Cooper, *Handbook of Administrative Ethics*, 407.

61. These was in the eyes of the chairman of the *CAIB*, Admiral Gehman Jr., the decisive shift which allowed for the routinization of slippage; see Gehman, *CAIB*, 2, or what Vaughn had identified as the 'normalization of deviance'.

62. Wayne Hale describes the crucial mandatory Flight Readiness review 'Mission Briefing Room' before the Challenger launch: '[t]wo large projection screens in front would show the seemingly endless power-point slides, and an oversized lectern was provided for the presenter. In the back were rows of seats, mostly with assigned name placards, the front row of seats were reserved for the NASA Administrator, Deputy Administrator and other dignitaries. Generally these seats were empty and no one was brave enough to commandeer one of them. In the very back there were a handful of unassigned seats. Most of the time the back wall was lined with folks standing. Somewhere between three and four hundred people would crow the room for the duration, generally about a day and a half.Most oppressive was the atmosphere. Presenter after presenter would lay out all the work their part of the program had completed, project pages of signatures showing that all the proper checks had been made. Rarely were questions asked, and almost always by those at the head of the table. In fact, the general impression was that people were not to question topics outside there are of concern or expertise ... In the hallway, disgruntled lower level managers would gather and complain about the opacity of particular presentations Questions would be lobbed about concerning flight rationale or engineering test results and their interpretation. But these discussions almost took place in the lobby, not the Mission Briefing Room. Nobody wanted to start a riffle in the FRR. After all, if you asked questions about their topics, they might ask questions about yours. Everybody wanted to get on the stage and off without questions'. W. Hale, 'After 10 Years: The Fateful FRR', *Hale's Blog*, 29 December 2012, www.waynehale.wordpress.com/2012/12/29/after-ten-years-the-fateful-frr/ (last accessed 3 March 2016).

63. A scientist, Matthew B. Koss, who frequently contributed to 'shuttle experiments' but doubted that most of them required experimentation in space and that experiments in orbit could be conducted safer and cheaper by remote controlled orbital spacecraft, see House of Representative Committee on Science, *Hearing on the Future of the Human Space Flight*, 16 October 2003, www.tinyurl.com/koss-hearing (last accessed 3 March 2016).

64. See James Oberg warning in 2000 predicting that '[t]he Space agency's approach, including its "faster, better cheaper" credo may be a recipe for disaster'. See

J. Oberg, 'Nasa's Not Shining Moments', *Scientific American* 282 (2000): 13–16, www.jamesoberg.com/022000nasanotshining.html (last accessed 3 March 2016).
65. C. Perrow, *Normal Accidents: Living with High Risk Technologies* (Princeton, NJ: Princeton University Press, 1999).
66. Gehman, *CAIB*, 181.
67. Vaughn, *Challenger Launch Decision*, 405.
68. For a thoughtful critique of the 'rational design' approach, see A. Wendt, 'Driving with the Rearview Mirror: On the Rational Science of Institutional Design', *International Organization* 55 (2004): 1019–49.
69. R. C. Winters, J. L. Globokar and C. Robertson, *An Introduction to Crime and Crime Causation* (Boca Raton, FL: CRC Press, 2014), 253.
70. See N. Cohen, 'Codes of Silence', *Index on Censorship* 42 (2013): 24, http://ioc.sagepub.com/content/42/1/1/22 (last accessed 25 February 2016).
71. A.-M. Slaughter, *A New World Order* (Princeton, NJ: Princeton University Press, 2004).

Bibliography

Abbott, Andrew. *The System of Professions: an Essay on the Division of Expert Labor* (Chicago: University of Chicago Press, 1988).
Ackerman, Bruce A., 'The Storrs Lectures: Discovering the Constitution'., *The Yale Law Journal*, 93 (1984):, 1013–1072.
Adams, Guy B., 'Administrative Ethics and the Chimera of Professionalism'. Iin Terry L. Cooper (ed.), *Handbook of Administrative Ethics*, 2nd ed. (New York: Marcel Dekker, 2001): 291–308.
American Institute of Chemical Engineers. *Self-Evaluation Tools: Key Lessons from the Columbia Shuttle Disaster (Adapted to the Process Industries)*. www.tinyurl.com/aiche-columbia.
Arendt, Hannah. *Eichmann in Jerusalem* (New York: Viking Press, 1963).
Barnes, Jonathan (ed.). *The Complete Works of Aristotle: the Revised Oxford Translation* (Princeton, NJ: Princeton University Press, 1984).
Brint, Steven. *In an Age of Experts: the Changing Role of Professionals in Politics and Public Life* (Princeton, NJ: Princeton University Press, 1994).
Cooley, Alexander,, Ron, James,. 'The NGO Scramble: Organizational Insecurity and the Political Economy of Transnational Action'. *International Security*, 27 (2002): 5–39.
Cooper, Terry L. 'Big Questions in Administrative Ethics: a Need for Focused, Collaborative Effort'. *Public Administration Review* 64 (2004): 395–407.
Dobkin-Hall, Peter., 'The Social Foundations of Professional Credibility: Linking the Medical Profession to Higher Education in Connecticut and Massachusetts'. Iin Thomas L. Haskell (ed.), *The Authority of Experts: Studies in History and Theory.* (Bloomington, IN: Indiana University Press, 1984): 107–41

Doris, John M. *Lack of Character: Personality and Moral Behavior* (Cambridge: Cambridge University Press, 2002).

Duby, Georges., *The Three Orders: Feudal Society Imagined*, Arthur Goldhammer (transl.), (Chicago: Chicago University Press, 1980).

Durkheim, Emile., *The Division of Labor in Society, Trans*, (Glencoe, ILll.: Free Press, 1947).

   Professional Ethics and Civic Morals (London: Routledge, 1957).

Dworkin, Ronald. *Taking Rights Seriously* (Cambridge, MA: Harvard University Press, 1978).

Freidson, Eliot. *Profession of Medicine: a Study of the Sociology of Applied Knowledge* (Chicago: University of Chicago Press, 1988).

   Professionalism: the Third Logic (Chicago: University of Chicago Press, 2001).

Gehman, Harold W., Jr., et al. *Columbia Accident Investigation Board Report*. Vol. 1 (Washington, DC: Government Printing Office, 2003).

Hale, Wayne. 'After 10 Years: the Fateful FRR'. *Wayne Hale's Blog*, 29 December 2012. www.waynehale.wordpress.com/2012/12/29/after-ten-years-the-fateful-frr/.

   'After Ten Years: Death Never Takes a Holiday', *Wayne Hale's Blog*, 7 January 2013., available at: www.wwaynehale.wordpress.com/2013/01/07/after-ten-years-death-never-takes-a-holiday/.

Haskell, Thomas L., 'Professionalism Versus Capitalism: R. H. Tawney, Emile Durkheim, and C. S. Peirce on the Disinterestedness of Professional Communities'. Iin Thomas L. Haskell (ed.), *The Authority of Experts: Studies in History and Theory*. (Bloommington, IN: Indiana University Press, 1984): 180–225.

House of Representative Committee on Science. *Hearing on the Future of the Human Space Flight*, 16 October 2003. www.tinyurl.com/koss-hearing.

Janis, Irving L. *Victims of Groupthink: a Psychological Study of Foreign-Policy Decisions and Fiascoes* (Boston, MA: Houghton Mifflin, 1982).

Kennedy, David, *The Dark Side of Virtue: International Humanitarianism Reassessed* (Princeton, NJ: Princeton University Press, 2004).

   'Reassessing International Humanitarianism'. In Anne Orford (ed.), *International Law and Its Others* (Cambridge: Cambridge University Press, 2006):131–55

Kingsbury, Benedict, Nico Krisch and Richard B. Stewart. 'The Emergence of Global Administrative Law'. *Law and Contemporary Problems* 68 (2005): 15–61.

Klatt, Matthias. 'Taking Rights Less Seriously: A Structural Analysis of Judicial Discretion'. *Ratio Juris* 20 (2007): 506–29.

Koskenniemi, Martti. *From Apology to Utopia: The Structure of International Legal Argument*, reissue with a new epilogue (Cambridge: Cambridge University Press, 2006).

'Constitutionalism as Mindset: Reflections on Kantian Themes about International Law and Globalization'. *Theoretical Inquiries in Law* 8 (2007): 9–36.

Fragmentation of International Law: Difficulties Arising from the Diversification and Expansion of International Law (Helsinki: Erik Castrén Institute, 2007).

Koskenniemi, Martti, and Päivi Leino., 'Fragmentation of International Law? Postmodern Anxieties'., *Leiden Journal of International Law*, 15 (2002):, 553–579.

Langewiesche, William., 'Columbia's Last Flight'., *The Atlantic Monthly*, 292 (2003):, 58–87.

Lifton, Robert J. *The Nazi Doctors: Medical Killing and the Psychology of Genocide* (New York: Basic Books, 1986).

Louden, Robert B. 'Kant's Virtue Ethics'. *Philosophy* 61 (1986): 473–89.

Marsen, Sky. 'Case Study', 3. www.tinyurl.com/marsen-case.

Nisbett, Richard, and Lee Ross. *The Person and the Situation* (Philadelphia: Temple University Press, 1991).

Oberg, James. 'Nasa's Not Shining Moments'. *Scientific American* 282 (2000): 13–16. www.jamesoberg.com/022000nasanotshining.html.

Parsons, Talcott. 'The Professions and Social Structure'. *Social Forces* 17 (1939): 457–67.

Perkin, Harold. *The Origins of Modern English Society 1780–1880* (Toronto, ON: University of Toronto Press, 1972).

Perrow, Charles. *Normal Accidents: Living with High Risk Technologies* (Princeton, NJ: Princeton University Press, 1999).

Reiss, Hans (ed.). *Kant's Political Writings*, H. B. Nisbet (trans.) (Cambridge: Cambridge University Press, 1970).

Rogers, William P., et al. *Report of the Presidential Commission on the Space Shuttle Challenger Accident*. 5 vols. (Washington, DC: Government Printing Office, 1986).

Rohr, John. *Ethics for Bureaucrats: an Essay on Law and Values* (New York: Marcel Dekker, 1988).

Sarfatti Larson, Magali. 'The Production of Expertise and the Constitution of Expert Power'. In Thomas L. Haskell (ed.), *The Authority of Experts: Studies in History and Theory* (Bloomington: Indiana University Press, 1984): 28–80.

The Rise of Professionalism (Berkeley, CA: University of California Press, 1977).

Schottlaender, Rudolf. 'Die Aristotelische *Spoudaios*'. *Zeitschrift für Philosophische Forschung*, 34 (1980): 385–95.

Slaughter, Anne-Marie. *A New World Order* (Princeton, NJ: Princeton University Press, 2004).

Smith, Adam. *An Inquiry into the Nature and Causes of the Wealth of Nations*, Edward Cannan (ed.) (1838; repr., Chicago: University of Chicago Press, 1976).

Tawney, Richard H. *The Acquisitive Society* (New York: Harcourt Brace, 1961).

Truelson, Judith A. 'Whistleblower Protection and the Judiciary'. In Terry L. Cooper (ed.), *Handbook of Administrative Ethics*, 2nd ed. (New York: Marcel Dekker, 2001):407-28.

Wallis, Faith. *Medieval Medicine: a Reader* (Toronto, ON: University of Toronto Press, 2010).

Weber, Max. *The Protestant Ethic and the Spirit of Capitalism* (London: Routledge, 1992).

Wendt, Alexander. 'Driving with the Rearview Mirror: on the Rational Science of Institutional Design'. *International Organization* 55 (2001): 1019–49.

Wilensky, Harold L. 'The Professionalization of Everyone?' *American Journal of Sociology* 70 (1964): 137–58.

Williams, Michael., 'Skepticism'. Iin John Greco and Ernest Sosa (eds.), *The Blackwell Guide to Epistemology*, (Oxford: Blackwell Publishing, 1999): 35–69.

Winters, Robert C., Julie L. Globokar and Cliff Robertson., *An Introduction to Crime and Crime Causation* (Boca Raton, FL.: CRC Press, 2014).

Thinking about What International Humanitarian Lawyers 'Do'

An Examination of the Laws of War as a Field of Professional Practice

FRÉDÉRIC MÉGRET

> It may be too much to say that international law is only what international lawyers do or think. But at least it is that, and examining it from the perspective of its ... practitioners might enhance the self-understanding of today's international lawyers in a manner that would not necessarily leave things as they are.
>
> — Martti Koskenniemi[1]

Perhaps no work has been more lightly cited than Martti Koskenniemi's From Apology to Utopia, to many still his masterwork. Koskenniemi's argument is often misunderstood as (simply) suggesting that international law perpetually alternates between apology and utopia. If that were all that Koskenniemi was saying, he would be saying very little indeed. The opposition between apologists and utopians (or realists and idealists, conservatives and progressivists, sovereigntists and humanitarians) is about as stale a cliché of the international order as there is. What MK is saying is evidently more complex, and has to do with the idea that international legal argument, specifically, *can only ever* alternate between apology and utopia, in ways that frustrate any attempt at definitive legal closure. Moreover, this perpetual oscillation is a result of international law being profoundly embedded in a liberal theory that is itself deeply contradictory.

Somehow, however, this revelation of the deep structure of international legal argument was not as certainty-shattering as it could have been and by and large the discipline has seemingly weathered the challenge of FATU. This is perhaps because international law was never that reliant on a theory in the first place,[2] but also perhaps because, as this chapter will argue, the need to navigate apology and utopia has always been the deep common sense of the discipline. This should perhaps not come as a surprise: after all, Koskenniemi had set out, proceeding from his frustration with existing accounts of what international lawyers (notably legal advisors) do, to provide a better and more sophisticated portrait of international legal *practice* as, essentially, deserving better than the field's ritual invocations of positivism and methodological pragmatism. If FATU has been so successful it is also because it has provided a particularly intimate and compelling portrait of the profession's argumentative word games. Although it is most commonly understood as a critique of international law, it is also a subtle apology for it, or at least for what it could become if it were not so oblivious to its limits and potentialities.

Nonetheless, it should also be clear that FATU opened a yawning gap under international lawyers' feet. If not on some sort of legal determinacy, then what is the authority of international law founded on? And how does one explain the discipline's surprising resilience even by the time some of its intellectual shallowness has been exposed? More specifically, FATU made it hard to understand why any particular international legal position would ever be more sustainable or sustained than any other *merely on the basis of the law*. Yet at the same time, Koskenniemi was well aware that international law does over time produce certain outcomes. He concedes quite willingly the point made by many following the book's publication that international law is in practice 'a constant move to reconciliation', so that 'many judgments rendered by international courts remain unchallenged' and 'many doctrinal constructions attain a solid professional consensus'.[3] For every area of international law, one is aware of broadly dominant and plausible claims.

What is the secret of international law's relative stability, then, in conditions of structural indeterminacy? The retreat to a pure concept of practice and the common sense of the international lawyer cannot, on its own, save the international legal profession from the doubts that FATU is bound to have raised. If anything, it should make them more prevalent. For that practice must seem even more unmoored and arbitrary if it is reduced to a confidential initiation devoid of grand narrative about its validity and force. International lawyers can no more do without theory than they can without courts, even though they may call theory by another name ('sources', 'doctrine', 'interpretation', etc.). The field's persistence (inflated as its actual world relevance may often be) as a social practice must result from something else than the system's self-serving theorizing about itself or the practitioner's cookbook. FATU made it sound like theorists and practitioners argued, over time, as if ping ponging across decades and centuries, but without making it clear why one would want to engage in international law's word games.

Koskenniemi's brilliant response (to himself, as it were) was to *historicize* FATU. This is obviously where the Gentle Civilizer comes in,[4] in a sense gently humanizing Koskenniemi's self-described its 'cool structuralism'[5] by delving deeply into some of biographies that have made international law what it is. The choice that MK made in the Gentle Civilizer was to re-write the history of international law as the history of the coming into being of a certain professional 'sensibility', thus acknowledging international law's debt to the formidable efforts of certain key figures to its development, and more importantly lending credence to the intuition that law cannot be understood outside the way certain lawyers at certain times chose to inhabit it. The legacy of the Gentle Civilizer was a powerful image of the international lawyer as a situated, sentient being struggling to make sense of a tradition yet ideally never entirely absorbed by it (Lauterpacht probably being the quintessential example in the sunset of that particular era).

However, the extent to which the Gentle Civilizer helped solve the riddle of FATU is open to question. The great figures of international law themselves seemed to be remarkably free of the angst of apology and utopia. Although Koskenniemi explained this away as simply an editorial choice,[6] it did suggest implicitly that something else – a vision, a form of intellectual leadership – might help break the circularity of FATU. At the same time, the Gentle Civilizer's choice to concentrate on a few grand figures evidenced a tendency towards solipsism.[7] The international lawyers in the Gentle Civilizer were solitary giants, involved in the Herculean task of fashioning compelling visions of international law. This dovetails well with FATU's own inspiration based on the experience of the relatively lone legal advisor trying to make sense of his profession. But it was not clear on what basis, given the roads cut off by FATU, these vast reconstructive exercises might arise. If not on that of charisma or pure aesthetics, then the combination of FATU and the Gentle Civilizer leaves us crucially looking for some sense of the determinants of international law. Perhaps by not providing much of an explanation, Koskenniemi even made the discipline vulnerable to the sort of crude materialist, interest-based or perhaps even technocratic takeover that he is otherwise so rightly critical of.

MK is a formidable philosopher and historian of the law, but one might say he is a less dedicated sociologist. In FATU, Koskenniemi asserts in passing that international law is in effect 'a terrain of irreducible adversity'.

Curiously however he then gives up on further characterizing that adversity, reducing it to a sort of theoretical struggle that simply grounds the need to acknowledge the irreducibly political dimension of international legal argument. What is missing, in my view, is a sense of the social reality and incidence of these struggles on the nature and reality of international law. Specifically, I want to emphasize the importance of analysing international law as a field of social and, specifically, professional practice and competition, shaped by crisscrossing strategies and interpersonal struggles that aim to sustain the discipline. I will do so by using some of the tools developed by sociologists, most notably Bourdieu and some of his followers, to understand the emergence, development and resilience of fields, including legal fields.[8] Bourdieu was notoriously not particularly interested in law as such and rather dismissive of lawyers, but he did write on the subject[9] and his thinking on the law can also be reconstructed from his more general theorizing on the notion of social fields.[10] Moreover, it has befallen some of Bourdieu's intellectual heirs to bring his analysis to new legal spheres, notably trans- and supra-national law.[11] I believe there is some potential in re-reading FATU (despite its emphasis on the legal system rather than the juridical field) and the Gentle Civilizer (despite its methodological individualism) in such a sociological vein and that in the course of doing so one may even stumble upon some deeper sense of the actual determinacy of international law despite conditions of ontological indeterminacy.

In order to do so, I propose to use the laws of war, which are the object of passing interest in Koskenniemi's larger work,[12] as an illustration. The laws of war are particularly interesting because of the way they have always stood as the epitome of the civilizing mission, a most reformist yet precarious project of humanizing war. Consequently, few failures have radicalized the anxiety of international lawyers towards the possibilities of international law than the laws of war' perceived failures. Yet the laws of war remain an enduring aspect of international law, perhaps the aspect that has the longest pedigree long after the law of neutrality or of prizes has become a distant souvenir. Indeed precisely because it is so resilient, its fortunes so tied to those of international law generally and vice versa, the field of the laws of war is a particularly interesting prism to examine the evolution of international law in general. Substantively at least, international humanitarian law is not very different in its genesis than international law *lato sensu*: a humanitarian sensitivity that seeks to graft itself onto a project of international legalization (to the point that the two become virtually indistinguishable).

10.1 The Laws of War as a Field of Professional Practice Structured by Apology and Utopia

10.1.1 The Emergence and Resilience of the Field

The notion of field is particularly interesting because it was conceived by Bourdieu as precisely a way of escaping the excessively mechanistic orientation of structuralism. To speak of the law as a field of professional practice and social interaction is to distance oneself from the view of law as only a system of norms. It is also, of course, a way of explaining law that shuns other forms of determinism, whether immanent (e.g. humanitarianism as providence) or material-dialectic (e.g. the emergence of international humanitarian law as a superstructural result of changing conditions of production). Finally, a focus on the field as such allows us to distance ourselves from various macro-explanations derived from either international legal or international relations research agendas and that foreground issues of delegation, principal and agent, functionalism, mandate, legitimacy, governance, etc. However, field analysis is also broader than simply the analysis of particular institutional dynamics[13] in that it takes seriously the notion that the field exists beyond institutional forms, often as a rather loose assortment of interests and rationalities. The notion of field is claimed by many and not always used consistently by even those authors that claim to base their theory on it. According to Bourdieu, to the extent one can reconstruct a unified definition from an extremely rich corpus spanning decades, the characteristics of the field (particularly the legal field) are that it is (1) a site of struggle or competition for control, (2) characterized by hierarchy never explicitly acknowledged as such, (3) 'engaged in a struggle with those outside the field to gain and sustain acceptance for their conception of the law's relation to the social whole and of the law's internal organization', (4) that results in the exercise of symbolic violence.[14]

The field is therefore defined by a central law (not in the legislative sense, of course), a sort of 'principle of division'.[15] In law generally, that 'law' is that the legal field is the specific field in which debates are settled by recourse to legal norms. This clearly introduces a certain circularity and in this chapter I will seek to further explore what these norms actually are, but the circularity is no doubt intended: there is no legal field independently of the social agents that populate and animate it as a result of having accepted the field's basic convention. The existence of a central law defining the field then introduces a form of specific capital: here, the capital of those who are in a position to define what the law is. This also creates space for a number of well-rehearsed struggles for domination (typically understood as *mere doctrinal debates* by their participants), as illustrated for example by the fight between orthodoxy and unorthodoxy, or the 'anciens' and the 'modernes'. In the matter at hand, this could be the struggle between those who associate with the 'laws of war' and with 'international humanitarian law', defenders of military necessity versus theorists of the 'humanization' of humanitarian law, etc.

It is here I believe that a crucial link can be made with FATU, that also provides a novel way of reading it and connecting it to some of the themes that are not far from the surface in the Gentle Civilizer. Apology and utopia, rather than the endlessly slippery theoretical slopes that they also are, can be seen as actual polarities in a field of social practice that structures what it means to be an international (humanitarian) lawyer, what it means to be successful as such, and what sort of positions we can expect over time to characterize the field. Indeed, apology and utopia, politics and morality are not just abstract points on a spectre; they are also constituencies, embodied positions, and specific sites (the 'military'/'humanitarians', states/the international community, war/peace, New York/Geneva, Big powers/small powers etc.). They serve a structuring role, but it is not so much the structuring role of pure positions on a logical spectrum as a socially structuring function for agents within the field and for the field itself. The key to the law's content or evolution, therefore, lies not in what the field typically claims to value (logical, formal reasoning) but in the social conditions of possibility of certain arguments, their changing fortunes, and how they undergird the ability of a particular form of disciplinary practice to maintain itself as socially relevant.

Over time, international humanitarian law emerges as a distinct sub-field of international law rather than a field onto itself, although it is a sub-field that maintains a certain dynamic distance from its parent field. The specificity of the laws of war as a sub-field, and indeed its specific 'force', is that it sits at the intersection of various fields between which it mediates: military rationality, a charitable inclination for civilians, and international law itself. Specifically, the genesis of the field can be traced, following the general lines of the Gentle Civilizer, to the then highly original fusion of a very lively humanitarian impulse and the ascending project of legal positivism. Where the humanitarian project can no longer be sustained by the *connivance* of chivalry, it promises to save what can still be saved from the 'ancien régime' by secularizing some of its norms and providing a new *cadre* of international lawyers specializing in the business of violence and its limitation. The crucial opening move of international humanitarian law is perhaps not so much Henry Dunant's indignation at the horrors of Solferino as his immediate intuition that was is needed to ensure the protection of the wounded in combat specifically is an *international treaty*. The move to legalization, then, ambiguous as it will remain is the fundamental opening salvo in the creation of the modern laws of war. It represents a classic Weberian shift from traditional (e.g. chivalry) or charismatic authority (e.g. Henry Dunant) to that of bureaucratic and institutional rationality (e.g. the ICRC).

In this respect, the field's very emergence relies on its ability to forge a compromise between apology and utopia. On the one hand, international humanitarian law continues to be sustained in practice by the age-old legitimacy of the humanitarian tradition. This is evident in, for example, the continued importance of the Martens clause – civilization, humanity and public conscience made law – and the fascination it continues to exercise to this day on the field.[16] International humanitarian law would have nothing to show for itself if it could not enlist the good will and cachet of humanitarian aspiration. On the one hand, even as the project is united in its foundational rejection of kriegsraison ('a doctrine above all based on contempt for the law'[17]), it seeks to endear itself to states and the military through its fundamental realism. The laws of war would lose all relevance if they effectively made war impossible and did not there-fore concede the fundamental unavoidability of war. That central tension between the field's apologetic and utopian dimensions is an intrinsic part of its appeal and therefore its social relevance. As Koskenniemi describes them, Bluntschli and von Moltke, the Prussian lawyer and the Prussian soldier, can see eye to eye when it comes to war and its increasingly civilized character.[18] Law is the key to this ambiguous deferral, 'a political compromise between irreconcilable demands, presented as the logical synthesis of antagonistic theses'.[19] The humanitarian project unites various nineteenth-century elites (business, law, the officer class) across their differences, consecrating their dominant class status around an ambition of taming the passions, gentlemanly conduct and rationality. The international humanitarian lawyer ends up 'embodying' the field's very commitment to legal humanitarianism in war, both literally and figuratively.[20]

Perhaps the most striking intuition to emerge from the study of fields such as the law is that they are both systems of intense internal competition for the definition of the law, and yet sufficiently coalescing around a core of commitment to oppose a united front to their 'exterior'. On the one hand, the compromise that results in the laws of war and is the basis for a distinct set of professional practices is fundamentally unstable. The very fragility of the compromise from which the laws of war emerge is what creates the conditions for competition within it. It creates pressures both from the outside and the inside that can collapse the precarious subfield into one of its encompassing fields.[21] Incentives appear for those within the field to identify with one of its polarities and maybe even forge alliances with or defect to its exterior (one can, needless to say, under the guise of offering 'humanitarian advice', entrust the Prince with the keys to the law's undoing). On the other hand and at the same time, international humanitarian lawyers can never risk, as it were, letting a good argument get in the way of the field's sustainability. They must, ultimately, stand together and speak with one voice, or risk the field's downfall.

10.1.2   The International Humanitarian Lawyer as Social Agent

The dynamics of the field, then, are produced by its inevitably competitive nature, but also the fundamentally cooperative aspiration that binds it together. It is on this second aspect that I want to focus here because it is the most intriguing: *how* over time do groups of individuals decide that they stand to gain more by arguing *together* as part of specialized field practices? Bourdieu's theory was not only a theory of the field as such but a theory of *individual action within fields*. This is arguably one of the most appealing aspects of his sociology, the way it makes it possible to rely on structures without granting them all causality at the expense of agency (and vice versa). The field relies on the ability of its agents to understand its basic rules and allow it to thrive. International law, in that respect, is not just a dominant superstructure speaking through international lawyers, but the particular site of power that international (humanitarian) lawyers *create for themselves*. What is it then that makes international humanitarian lawyers simultaneously competitive within the limits defined by the field and nonetheless present a united front to the field's 'outside'? The basic starting point to understand the role of agents in relation to the field is that legal professionals 'have in common their knowledge and their acceptance of the rules of the game'.[22] As it happens, MK has also spoken of the 'commitment' to international law as a psychological starting point to the trajectory of the international lawyer.[23] Commitment is understood as 'a wholesale, ultimately unreflective or sentimental "throwing-of-oneself" into one's work, a spontaneous loyalty to one's profession, its constitutive rules and traditions as well as an unwavering belief in its intrinsic goodness'.[24]

This is highly visible in international humanitarian law, a discipline in which doubts about the value of the project must be silenced and which, perhaps more than international law generally, has been characterized by a sort of crusading enthusiasm. One cannot, in a sense, be a fully *critical* international humanitarian lawyer, for *being* an international humanitarian lawyer (and no one is forced to become one) implies not being truly critical.[25] The international humanitarian lawyer, in other words, cannot be scared of inhabiting the role of the 'international humanitarian lawyer' as others have come to imagine it and as it has gradually been ratified by the field – or otherwise cease to operate within the field. As MK famously put it, 'Had I responded to my superiors at the Ministry when they wished to hear what the law was by telling them that this was a stupid question and instead given them my view of where the Finnish interest lay, or what type of State behaviour was desirable, they would have been both baffled and disappointed, and would certainly not have consulted me again'.[26] One could add that fellow international lawyers would not have thought much of such a legal advisor's tendency to jump ship. For the international humanitarian lawyer this predicament means steering at a distance from a tradition of Just war theory on the one hand, and a purely functional view of military necessity on the other in order to incarnate as closely as possible what has over time become the imagined archetypal figure of the field.

Commitment, then, is a shared legal and sociological condition of existence of the field. Legally, it delimits a horizon within which disputes are to be solved by resort to legal arguments rather than by, say, who has pled most often before international courts, has the backing of the strongest state, or has most publications. Sociologically, it delineates a community of practice united by its desire to 'make things work', and to present itself under the best auspices, as a humane and socially relevant enterprise. Politically, it promises, if not a free ride, at least a certain hope that international (humanitarian) law in and of itself has virtue. Commitment is cemented by the doxa of the field, namely that which cannot be contested and must appear as 'self-evident'. In addition to doxic elements characteristic of the international legal field (e.g. a narrative of progress and reform), the doxa includes elements specific to international humanitarian law, most notably the insistence on the canonical and foundational division between the jus in bello and the jus ad bellum.[27] Challenging the separation is perceived as risking the downfall of the entire project and will thus trigger powerful defensive reactions by the field.[28]

Nonetheless, once and at the moment the international humanitarian lawyer is constituted, we still do not know much about how he or she is to be in the world. Making that minimum commitment operational is what social actors set out to do, typically through what Bourdieu has described as the *habitus*. The space that habitus occupies in Bourdieusian sociology is a crucial one because habitus is neither norm (understood as formally binding rules) nor simply pattern (a-normative regularities). Rather it points to an intermediary set of assumptions that deeply structure a field's participants' sense of self and of praxis. To quote one of Bourdieu's own rather long definition of habitus, it is:

> un système de dispositions durables, structures structurées prédisposées à fonctionner comme structures structurantes, c'est-à-dire en tant que principe de génération et de structuration de pratiques et de représentation qui peuvent être objectivement « réglées » et « régulières » sans être en rien le produit de l'obéissance à des règles, objectivement adaptées à leur but sans supposer la visée consciente des fins et la maîtrise expresse des opérations nécessaires pour les atteindre et, étant tout cela, collectivement orchestrées sans être le produit de l'action organisatrice d'un chef d'orchestre.[29]

Bourdieu has on several occasions described habitus as the 'feel for the game'. Clearly for example chess is not only about chess *rules* but the ability to *play* within the rules and to have internalized a certain understanding of what it means to play chess. One of the striking imports of Bourdieu's notion of habitus to the study of fields is that it suggest that agents are deeply shaped by what might be understood as the 'hidden rules' of the field, rules that are not conscious yet fundamentally structuring of its practice. The habitus is, for example, what allows a field's agents to identify others who participate in it and exclude those who are seen as engaging in a different set of practices. This is a very important factor in legal fields, including international humanitarian law, whose particular monopolies rely crucially on the ability to disqualify and ostracize (as in 'this is not law', rather than simply 'this is not *the* law').

Koskenniemi's notion in the Epilogue to FATU that international law is, fundamentally, a grammar,[30] comes very close to Bourdieu's notion of habitus. My concern is nonetheless that FATU still focuses too much (if only to debunk it) on what, admittedly, international lawyers themselves tend to put at the heart of their activity, namely logos, recta ratio and the centrality of logical-deductive skills in elucidating the proper meaning of norms. Perhaps because the distinctiveness of the legal field is that it is explicitly and avowedly rule based, it is particularly difficult to envisage it as being ruled by rules other than those it conspicuously holds as defining, i.e. to see the social rules behind the legal rules. Yet as Bourdieu put it, 'même ce qu'il y a de plus codifié ... a pour principe non des principes explicites, objectivisés, donc eux-mêmes codifiés mais des schèmes pratiques'.[31] It may thus be helpful to think of international (humanitarian) law as emerging from a deeper *social* grammar dictating the conditions of the law's production and existence. The deeper sociological grammar involved, is one that involves not just speaking the language but 'living the life' as it were (or at least playing the part), a way of *being* rather than just arguing within a field. To be an international humanitarian lawyer is to learn to act like one, which involves in particular knowing 'how to be' in the field.

Here, I want to emphasize the relevance of what might be termed the 'turn to practice(s)' in the social sciences,[32] including as it might apply to international law.[33] More specifically, I want to focus on the importance of practical knowledge or, to use the richly Aristotelian term, phronêsis to the constitution of international law. Phronêsis is a form of practical judgement and intuition. It is typically opposed to tekhne (technical craftsmanship). The one scholar to have early on intuited the importance of phronêsis to understanding international lawyers' way of being in the world is Outi Korhonen, in a landmark article published in the European Journal of International Law.[34] This was a startling piece although one that failed to elicit much reaction let alone launch a program of research (perhaps because paradoxically, as Jan Klabbers has suggested, its philosophical hauteur 'was never likely to appeal to those engaged in solving practical problems'.[35]) It is true that Korhonen's concept of phronêsis is still largely the by-product of a philosophical inquiry, rather than a sociological investigation.

There is much in the notion of a phronetic practice that can help understand international humanitarian lawyers as implicated in a relatively constrained process that ends up further reifying the structure within which it operates. International (humanitarian) lawyers, in particular, are not just the 'slaves' of apology and utopia as more or less free standing structural ideational constraints; rather through their endlessly repeated legal practices they contribute to further entrench a certain image of law as only conceivable within these parameters. In playing the game (relentlessly) they reinforce its authority and appeal. Phronêsis is what makes the law 'feel right' to those who claim to articulate it because, as it were, the 'sense of the game' as if by magic always coincides with 'the game'. Whilst not minimizing the difficulties that international lawyers have to acknowledge the phronetic component of their practice (the 'hidden rules' must always in a sense remain hidden), I want to bring it to light the highly specific way in which international lawyers manage the tension between apology and utopia.

10.2   Understanding the 'Rules of the Game': Navigating Apology and Utopia

If apology and utopia are both ideas and constituencies, they are also polarities in a particular field of social practice, constraining what can be said, when and by whom. In international legal argument there are in a sense no gratuitous positions, in that every position is both constrained by the field and potentially has an impact on it. What might it mean for the field of international humanitarian law as a social field to have as its central practice the management of the tension between apology and utopia? In this section, I reflect on the 'dos' and 'don'ts' of an international humanitarian law practice structured by the twin dangers of sacrificing relevance by being too utopian and sacrificing normativity by being too apologetic. I do so by looking at the strategies deployed by actors within the field to simultaneously maximize their position within it, whilst staying true to the field's core structuring assumptions so as not to undermine it. This they try to do amidst the tumultuous waters of international politics. Borrowing heavily on a nautical metaphor I will distinguish between two roles that the international humanitarian lawyer inhabits, that of keeping the discipline 'afloat' on the one hand (A), and that of 'charting a course' on the other (B). In the process, I hope to suggest a vision of the international humanitarian lawyer as the key player in managing the dialectics of stability and change in the law.

As will be further explored, stylized positions at one end or the other of the spectrum are only possible in very limited circumstances and perhaps only in the sure knowledge that they will be offset by contrary positions more or less simultaneously held within the field. Moreover,

10.2.1   'Staying Afloat'

The existence of the field does provide a fertile ground for genuine internal controversies and a degree of *controlled heterodoxy*. The field would be nothing if it did not provide a game. At any rate, Agents can engage in the *frisson* of adopting the most apologetic or utopian positions accessible *from within the field*. Some would like to significantly humanize the laws of war (for example by requiring that civilians not even be killed collaterally), whilst others would argue for some form of much larger tolerance for violence (e.g. allowing that a great many civilians be killed collaterally as long as it was not the commander's intention). Some will seek to track a path that navigates dangerously close to what their national military would like to do, whilst others will seek to capture the moral high ground. The field offers the possibility of adopting a series of stylized identities: for example, the 'rugged realist warrior',[36] or the 'great humanitarian oracle'.[37]

There are benefits to be obtained for both sides, if they are successful. Relatively pure 'apologetic' and 'utopian' positions create niche opportunities for outliers, discreet opportunities for those on the fringe, in ways that may facilitate the forging of alliances with external constituencies and even offer opportunities for defection. For example a humanitarian apologist may find that he has the ear of the military or certain states and enjoy the benefits of *relevance* (manifested concretely in the solicitation of expertise, particular invitations, various forms of recognition); a humanitarian utopian will surely find enthusiastic audiences among other states and civil society actors. There are roles waiting to be filled along the whole spectrum of available positions, each with its particular distribution of costs and benefits. In the best of cases, the move is one that may create a new historical synthesis of apology or utopia and thus change the field's structure. For example, the early scholars who agitated for greater recognition of national liberation movements in the 1970s, built their success on the enthusiasm of a number of non-aligned capitals and their ability to sway to sway the ICRC. But most of the time the ambition is more modest and consists in the subtle search for an at least temporary ascendancy in the field, by emphasizing the (relatively) small differences that characterize one's position as opposed to others'.

There are also evident risks in swaying too far to one side or the other. One escapes the compulsive search for the safety of the middle ground at one's peril. If the international lawyer overshoots by being too utopian – for example if the ICRC were to become a humanitarian version of Amnesty International – the project might be wounded, perhaps mortally. 'Progress' would have been achieved at the cost of irrelevance, or at least at the cost of it being shrugged off by states and militaries alike. Hence the need to constantly reassure the field that one is really not innovating, that one is not introducing something that is not already there (for example the importance of the ICRC's famous study on customary international law and its insistence that it is only presenting the 'law as it is'). If the international humanitarian lawyer is too apologetic, on the contrary, then he will also lose some support, perhaps for example the field's ability to sustain a minimum sense of historical hubris and excite new vocations from aspiring humanitarian lawyers. It is only in the best of cases by targeting a sort of sweet middle spot that international humanitarian law energizes itself as a field of possibilities.

The field is constantly controlling of the positions that are taken within it. Taking too much at heart one's flight to either apology and utopia, even as it may result in opportunities at the margin, creates the conditions of one's own disciplining as other international lawyers will inevitably seek to 'put them back in their place'. One opens oneself up to disqualification ('too apologetic', 'too utopian') by those actors who, inevitably, will see an opportunity to validate their own reasonable credentials by opposition to one's wayward ways. The further from the centre, the easier it becomes for it to reaffirm its centrality: for those who stray away from the doxa, the field reserves the more brutal forms of *rappel à l'orthodoxie* in the form of accusations of incompetence, futility or naivety. Agents in the field, at least those who excel in it, know better than to open their flank to some easy criticism that they have ignored one crucial aspect (apology or utopia) of the equation. Moreover, all unorthodox strategies in the legal field are constrained by the awareness that they may end up undermining rather than renovating it. Even if individual participants do not realize that they are dangerously tilting the field in one direction or another, others will make sure to remind them. The field is always ready to compel a snapback to its preferred default position in the middle. In short, one cannot abstract oneself from the pull of the liberal mainstream that easily because in doing so one exposes oneself to one's own marginalization ('this is not law').

Indeed, one could argue that there is no habitus more central to the practice of international (humanitarian) law than, the ability to navigate apology and utopia, an ability that is internalized by necessity by every participant in the field. By navigating, I clearly mean to convey the image of a rough process of keeping a ship afloat amidst a treacherous environment in which the safeguarding of the ship is the overriding goal, above and beyond any notion of where the ship is headed, why it is at sea in the first place or who ought to command it. The ship's particular trajectory creates a community of destiny among the sailors embarked upon it, a sort of *esprit de corps* solidified by the imperative of collective survival (or at least shared interest in perpetuation). This rough image, I believe, conveys what goes at the heart of the practice of sustenance of the field.

Participants in the international legal field are constantly aware that, for all their differences, they are parts of a larger whole.

In the laws of war, this translates into the obsessive refrain that the law must, whatever else it does, strike a balance between military considerations and humanitarian elements, the local placeholders for apology and utopia. The international lawyer is, essentially and consciously, the artisan of this balance, producing normative propositions that will meet a certain degree of success or not, and on which she stakes her credibility, depending on her ability to not make the boat capsize and, ideally, to keep it moving. Of course, one man's utopia may be another's apologetics, but this matters less than the fact that the very essence of the living practice of international humanitarian law is a sort of constant effort to steer an imagined middle ground. This practice of balancing is not incompatible from more conventional techniques of legal interpretation and craftsmanship and may even occasionally appear in the form of consideration of 'policy issues', but as a commitment it is prior to such techniques (in that ultimately the international humanitarian lawyer is more invested in the survival of the historical compromise that is the basis of the field than in adhering rigidly to wherever 'positive law' might be held to push it).[38]

The point is that allowing the law to err too far towards apology or utopia does not only endanger it as a system of theoretically defensible rules within a liberal rule of law; it also and more concretely threatens the field of practice that relies on these rules for its symbolic capital. To those who follow the narrow middle path, international humanitarian law promises a life of social relevance, of being seen to speak Law to Power, of changing the world but not too much. The dynamism of the field, its creativity can be explained precisely by its density in the middle, the exciting space where two opposed gravitational pulls compete, and where indebtedness to one or the other is more easily forgiven. This for example is surely one of the keys to the ICRC's extraordinary institutional energy and creativity, its ability to lean against the established order whilst claiming humanitarian credentials, to explicitly present itself as apologetic in relation to the utopians and utopian in relation to the apologists.[39]

Because the field has emerged from the start at the very point of tension between apology and utopia, subsequent controversies tend to merely resurrect in milder form, some of its founding disputes, in ways that ensure its dynamism. That there is nonetheless a vaguely make-believe quality to the way in which energies are thrown into some of these structuring debates – as a sort of well-rehearsed *théâtre d'ombres* that makes every controversy of the day seem like a perpetual re-enactment of the very foundational tension that the field is supposed to manage – should come as no surprise and does not disqualify them. Not only is the competition real enough within its own limited terms, but it is also an inherent dimension of the field's power (if nothing else, a field that did not have internal debates would seem weak and open to challenge).

To the extent that the legal field does not implode (it has shown a remarkable ability not to) and merely buckles under the weight of various positions taken within it, it is as a result of international humanitarian lawyers' remarkable ability to keep certain debates inter se. But it is also result of a phenomenon that one can only hint at here but comes close to a form of natural inner-balancing of social fields. There is, for example, a strong element of *positionality* in all doctrinal debates. In a field such as international humanitarian law, there is in a sense no gratuitous position that would be a pure expression of legal opinion. Every legal doctrinal position takes meaning against its opposite, so that one is always being an apologist to a utopian and vice versa (Bourdieu's 'relationality'). More-over, every position is also a strategic move in relation to what is perceived as the evolution of the discipline or a particular debate within it.

Lawyers are trying if not to convince others, at least to 'weigh in' quite literally in a discussion, to reorient or tilt the field in particular way, whilst being aware of the whole gamut of existing opinions and their relative symbolic force in the field. For example, one is constantly expressing opin-ions (as scholar, advocate, advisor) in the sure knowledge that they will not miraculously be implemented as such and across the board. Rather, they will almost always coexist with contrary opinion that will simultane-ously give them salience and deflate their edge.[40] Interventions in ongoing debates, at least the most significant ones, are therefore always calculated at constituting the law's balance.[41] Success depends on the ability to 'guess' at any moment where the field is headed and to present oneself as the artisan of that change. In effect, the determination of international law is an exercise by international lawyers of 'looking at themselves', and their place within and in relation to other fields.

The image that comes to mind, to further develop the sailing metaphor, is one in which, whatever disagreements they may have about the direction the boat is taking, the sailors will at least spread their weight roughly equally on each side to prevent it from capsizing.[42] If that metaphor seems too providential, if it sounds too much like some sort of doctrinal 'invisible hand' is keeping the legal ship even keeled, it bears underling that the process of throwing doctrinal ballast is socially fraught. This general tendency to stability should of course not blind us to the fact that occasionally the sailors will get it perilously wrong and that the field will capsize with them: the laws of war may yet encounter such a fate, for example as a result of the influx of new actors not well versed in its rites or with a frank agenda to sink the boat from within (human rights lawyers, revisionist just war theorists come to mind). Indeed, how to deal with such exogenous shocks and the danger of take-overs is ultimately what requires an ability not just to sail, but to avoid major storms.

10.2.2   Charting a Course

We have been concerned in the previous section with the element of permanence and stability in legal fields, with how the field remains 'even keeled'. That element is indispensable: it is what makes the field recognizable to its practitioners and, incidentally, makes it possible for practitioners to want to invest in it as a mode of being. A legal field that did not display this fundamental character of stability over time would not be one. Yet aside from this element of stability, one might recast the central question for international (humanitarian) lawyers as how to manage *change* in international law and relations. What counts as apology and utopia changes over time, even if the need to balance them doesn't. Even if the law aims to be stable and continuous, the world around it changes.

In this context, international law cannot simply be a machine that reproduces itself. This is both because of the naturally unstable nature of the competition for the monopoly of law and the incentives created for peripheral entrepreneurs by ossification, but also simply because of what might be described as 'exogenous shocks' (e.g. war-redefining wars, new weapons, changing social attitudes, etc.) that create adaptive challenges. In effect these changes can make international law at once too apologetic or too utopian despite its best efforts by suddenly modifying its conditions of possibility. Whether it is the emergence of 'total war', the rise of national liberation struggles, or 9/11 and the 'war on terror' the field is challenged at regular interval by contenders (the jus ad bellum, anti-colonial rhetoric, human rights, law enforcement, drone warfare, etc.) to prove its continued authority. Part of the claim to relevance of the international humanitarian lawyer is his ability to generate forms of legal normativity that are attuned to the changing epoch.

The question for the international lawyer, then, is how to effect significant change in the law without simultaneously undermining its authority.

The entire post 9/11 era for example can be seen as an effort to fend off suggestions for doing away with or substantially reforming international humanitarian law, whilst stretching the paradigm from within to make the case that it can deal with the challenge. In an international context marked by severe legislative shortcomings and spasmodic adjudication, international humanitarian lawyers are called to rise up to their role as midwives of the law's change. This much is quite evident for example in the ICRC's ceaseless resort to normative initiative (proposing new treaties, new studies, new guidelines) or the way certain judges of international criminal tribunals have taken it upon themselves in a context where the law's development had been somewhat dormant to brutally update it.

Where the stability of the field is a collective endeavour, in many ways the periodic need for significant change foregrounds the role of a particular super-elite within the field, those whose opinion (by virtue of their institutional position, but also their social capital) can be decisive of macro-structural change. In ordinary circumstances, the management of the field can be left to its 'technocrats' (ICRC delegates, ordinary judges), but in exceptional circumstances some higher degree of authority is required to effect a new epochal synthesis of apology and utopia. The field's 'grand old men' or 'senior statesmen' typically combine various types of social capital (judge, academic and diplomat, such as Theodor Meron; academic and activist such as Cassese), and are the ones whose pronouncements come closest to 'speech acts' ('the law is as it is because I say it is'). Their provenance often underscores the gerontological, male and white character of this sort of decisive re-orientation of the field, although is generally preceded by a methodological effort by more peripheral players to bring attention to the need for change, until events ensure that need can no longer be ignored and the erstwhile unorthodoxy is captured by the mainstream.

This then informs a particular style of the heroic, 'landmark' decision that magically resynchronizes the law with social conditions in ways that the ordinary functioning of the discipline could not achieve. For example, if one looks at what is perhaps the key development of the laws of war in the last half-century, namely the extension of norms normally applicable to international armed conflicts to non-international ones, this change was effected not only because of the rise of the Third World or the consistent push of the ICRC, but also thanks to the opportunistic push of someone like Antonio Cassese as judge of the ICTY in the 1990s.[43] The key is that the person who stands forward to effect the change is someone 'who can pull it off' because s/he has acquired the right amount of symbolic capital that he can rally the troops can and ultimately sway the field. This is greatly facilitated by the ability to play several roles, such as being able to comment as scholar on what one decided as judge for example. There is of course no guarantee of success and the history of international humanitarian law is full of suggestions that were not taken up by the field because they failed to elicit the right support at the right time.

Historically, the challenge has repeated itself at various junctions and solicits all the energies of agents in the legal field to simultaneously cling to their capital and maintain the discipline's centrality. Needless to say there are parts of international humanitarian law that were dead on arrival or have become marginalized over the years, entire branches that have been relegated to the dustbins of history, often as a result of having turned out to be too utopian (the attempt to outlaw aerial bombardment in the 1920s), but also conceivably of being too apologetic (the law of reprisals, for example, has fallen by the wayside of IHL). Without giving up on any of the day-to-day management of the apology-utopia tension, the challenge is to help hoist the international legal project to some new normative 'plateau' that best expresses the current synthesis of apology and utopia. In this context, one may speculate that legal fields are characterized by a habitus of the every day, but that they also contain implicit practices of change in times of exception, when repetition no longer suffices and the law is at risk of deadly stagnation (a 'habitus of change', perhaps, although that seems a contradiction in terms).

Major change in the law has both a topographic and temporal element. The topographic element relates to how the field is imagined to exist in relation to competing, encompassing or subfields. Most ordinary international humanitarian reasoning presents itself as occurring within the paradigm of the laws of war. In truth, however, many of the issues that matter most occur on the fault lines of different fields and implicate, for example, the evolving relationship of the laws of war to the jus ad bellum, to human rights or to the Just War tradition. Reasoning about such issues highlights the importance of the 'architectonic mind-set' in international lawyers, and the ability to see how the 'pieces of the puzzle' fit together. Emphasizing the distinctiveness of the laws of war[44] and fending off more radical challenges to them,[45] whilst occasionally capturing the energies of neighbouring fields[46] is part of the tried and tested ways in which the field constantly renegotiates its purported centrality. Debates as to who is the lex generalis or specialis of what, for example, for all their doctrinal connotations, barely conceal very real struggles for domination of the law.

Perhaps more importantly and contrary to various homeostatic models based on the law's own plasticity (e.g. through custom), major change in the international humanitarian legal field implicates a number of *temporal* skills by the field's agents. First, the evolution of the law – its timing, its particular form – is only understandable as part of compelling and widely shared disciplinary narratives about where the law is going. The field can settle on a range of different telos, and its ability to foreground one over the other at any one time is an inherent part of the plasticity of its practices. Most likely, the telos will be some broad and hard to challenge proposition, such as the ambition of moving 'towards greater humanitarianism', to which will be harnessed some more immediate proposal for change. The international humanitarian lawyer has a goal, and that goal is imagined as gradually narrowing the gap between what is obligatory and what is moral. The vision is one in which sovereign obstacles and limitations are overcome one after the other. Although the telos is already here (in legal interpretation for example) it also exists as a receding point on the horizon that makes change in the present seem less dramatic. And of course, although the telos may be greater humanization, it can never be (from within the field of IHL) the prohibition of war through excessive humanization.

Second, beyond the commitment to telos, the international humanitarian lawyer has internalized a deep sense of the law's *rhythm*, its unfolding as a broadly regular and ordained process, even if that process can occasionally know of brusque accelerations. The law, in other words, must not go « faster than the music » (to use a French expression). Being ahead of the curve is potentially costly, at least if one is seen as being so by significant and key players who will profit from being able to point it out. The international humanitarian lawyer has been around for some time, and is in no rush. In the process, he or she is called upon to express fortitude in the light of change in ways that are characteristic of the political virtue of prudence (which I see to be part of the 'culture of formalism', a capacity for resistance to being hijacked at the first opportunity). At the same time, the field's would-be dominant agents must not miss the moment of change or risk being overrun by competitors.

For example, in the context of the 'war on terror' one argument that is sometimes heard is that changes in the underlying reality of war are now so stark as to require a complete overhaul, perhaps even an abandonment of the laws of war. Humanitarian lawyers response, has been characteristically sober. If international law were to change at the very first alert it would lose any appeal to generality. This resistance has a ritual quality:

it proves the discipline's mettle. It also has a an instrumental quality: the resistance forces those who would argue for change to up their game and foists the burden of demonstrating the need to change on them. It is thus an inbuilt mechanism of validation of change. At the same time, fortitude can quickly turn into ineptitude. The longer the field holds out, the more it incentivizes competitors to seize the opportunity to redefine it. Some holding out followed by an abrupt catching up phenomenon in which the relevance of the discipline is reasserted is thus perhaps the most characteristic pattern of change to emerge of international legal dynamics.

Third and consequently, change in international law is all about *timing*, or what in Greek rhetoric was understood as 'kairos'. The field demands that change be made at the opportune moment, what Bourdieu described as the moment of 'reasonable chance of success'.[47] This ability to 'seize the moment' requires an attention to what sort of legal arguments are likely to stick at any one point, but also a sense of changing circumstances that might make a change stick. It involves international humanitarian lawyers, fundamentally, in informed gambles about where the field can be taken, at what price and at what benefit. The vision is one of developing the law in parallel with international society in ways that both maximize the legal field's power and the law's traction. Of course, we do not know for sure where the 'international community' stands at any one point, and the attempt to 'follow' the social is just as often an attempt to 'construct' it through normative anticipation. The point is not to resuscitate a sociological jurisprudence of law that sees it as broadly representing international reality, but to suggest that international (humanitarian) lawyers have internalized a deep sense that these are the sort of calculations on which the force of the field relies.

The field of international humanitarian law is replete with references about certain changes being precocious (the abiding concern, although a contrario the sense of changes being overdue also emerges). Beginning with the Institut de droit international's early intimation in the nineteenth century that it did 'not propose an international treaty, which might perhaps be premature or at least very difficult to obtain', all the way to warnings that it is 'precocious' to consider that Protocol I has acquired customary status, the image that emerges is one of a discipline constantly edging its bets, hoping that its pronouncements will have a self-realizing reality but also, fundamentally, bidding its time before it reveals its cards. International humanitarian lawyers thus appear as crucial validators of emerging realities, even as they must resist the temptation to take their fantasies for reality.

10.3   Conclusion: 'Internalizing the External'?

As MK argues, there has always been both a descriptive and a normative ambition to FATU. How does a focus on international (humanitarian) law as a field help us understand and perhaps develop some of insights of FATU on both these levels? The model of law propounded by Bourdieu is powerfully explanatory but notoriously frustrating for lawyers themselves. It 'explains away' the law as it were as a product of social competition in ways that fail to match lawyers' own understanding of what it is they do. It is, in other word, at risk of conveying an 'external point of view' to a profession that has steadfastly committed to an 'internal point of view'. The commitment to being a lawyer entails almost ontologically that one cannot easily let go of the idea that there is a distinction worth keeping between causally explaining and justifying legal outcomes. This is not only because it is analytically significant, but because of a feeling that it is a crucial safeguard for the preservation of the law's implicit moral and political project, on the road to instrumentalization, naïve economicism and technocratic rationality.

If as lawyers we (rightly) cannot let go of the internal point of view, maybe we need to understand it in a more open way that does not defer unduly to lawyers' highly stylized understanding of it. What if, for example, we reconstructed the science of law as the science of lawyers, in ways that took seriously the particular phronetic skill set that actually makes lawyers successful as agents of the legal field? A real science of law in the Bourdieusian sense that would still be appealing to jurists would extend the study of the law beyond form and interpretative logic, to the habitus that characterizes the field yet remains largely out of sight from legal science. Habitus is not only a number of crass self-serving predispositions; rather, as an intermediary concept between pattern and norm, it also contains some of the implicit know-how and wisdom of the discipline, a wisdom that no doubt serves to elevate its holders collectively to positions of relative domination but also structures what they do in ways that contribute to making the law specifically legal. Needless to say, a political advisor or a moral counsellor would not feel the same compunction to navigate apology and utopia because they would not be specifically committed to a concept of law as binding norms.

One may think that the study of law beyond its own dominant representation as a formal-logical system will greatly wound its symbolic authority. But I wonder if exactly the opposite is not true and if this is not the secret of Koskenniemi's outsize influence. In effect, international (humanitarian) lawyers" dominant self-representation does not do justice to the richness of what legal practice is. Law and lawyers are worth better than their strategically self-serving but ultimately rather poor portrayal as servants to the Law. Including the entire mental apparatus of the habitus in the study of international law, down to structuring assumptions about the particular role of lawyers and, crucially, the ability to navigate apology and utopia in ways that maintain law as a live project of regulation can fundamentally enrich our understanding – and, one might think also, our teaching – of the law. This may even be a more faithful conclusion to FATU than the idea of a 'culture of formalism' which has in my view always stood as an odd epilogue, one that still seems to take international lawyers too much at their word.

In this respect, the one dichotomy that MK never deconstructs and that is absolutely central to the entire argument of FATU is that between the internal and the external points of view, as introduced most notably by H. L. A. Hart. I understand and sympathize with the lawyer's aspiration to retain an irreducible space of legal normativity, one for which Koskenniemi has spared no effort. But I wonder whether one could not take seriously the practices of the international legal profession that have been outlined in this article and which at some level are characteristic of an external point of view (the competition between actors) as also susceptible to an internal point of view. The ability to find the via media, to gauge what argument will stick, and when the time is ripe to take the law in new direction, is not just a game that legal actors play for symbolic power; they may well come close to delineating a truer picture of the internal practice of the law as a form of deeply socialized but nonetheless unmistakably normative practice. The field's 'feel for the game' is certainly not a rule in the conventional sense, but is a useful and complementary hermeneutic prism to understand what makes an internal point of view.

To be clear, I am not saying that we should treat the instructions of the gunman pointing a gun to our head as law; but perhaps we should consider the possibility that the lawyers themselves are the gunmen, and that their ability to compete with and outwit each other manifests a form of deep disciplinary know-how. This view, I would contend, allows us to make sense of the sort of post-FATU spleen (or rejection) that has affected many international lawyers after reading MK's book, by putting the emphasis on the lawyers as self-constituting social agents rather than on the law itself. International lawyers are the crafty artisans of a sustained social practice of international lawyering long after huge holes have been poked at its theoretical consistency perhaps precisely because as a form of practical knowledge it was never as dependent on logical consistency as it allowed itself and, crucially, others to believe. The practice, moreover, is not just one of obfuscation but a relatively sophisticated means of social engineering informed by a host of meta-legal considerations. International humanitarian law, then, might be conceived as at least that, namely a praxis that is more intellectually rich than it can afford to confess.

Of course, I am well aware that one cannot simply invoke 'practical knowledge' at the last post-ontological hour as a hope for remission for an otherwise incurably ill practice which, what is more, otherwise pays little attention to its implicit know-how. Yet at least contra international legal jurisprudence's desire to socialize the foundation of international law into something like 'international society', the sociologization proposed here is one that involves the profession. I do not think the contention needs to be that the law is thus magically made determinate but the claim to its determinacy may be less implausible if seen against the background of the structuring assumptions of the legal field. Moreover, the model offers a way of identifying the law's drift towards a via media between apology and utopia as in fact socially constrained in ways that may help better understand both its inherent conservatism and its occasional dynamism.

Second, how does attention to international law as a social field illuminate the normative possibilities of international law? Are the inner-wrangling of the 'invisible college of international humanitarian lawyers'[48] not an extraordinarily unappealing basis for the law's ambition? The study of law as a social field that informs law's production and even form certainly makes the study of the law more *interesting*, but it hardly seems to make the law more *appealing*.[49] One outcome of the field analysis of international humanitarian law may be cynicism about a group of professionals' little squabbles for domination. Bourdieu powerfully reminds us that, whatever else the field thinks it is about (humanitarianism, law, justice, reform), it is also about individual and group social advancement. Whether there was ever anything else to international law than international lawyers' project of self-aggrandizement and social domination is a question that cannot be eluded.

The attention to the way in which the field, helped in this by its most prominent and powerful articulators, constantly weighs up apology and utopia, for one thing, helps explain why it can only ever be a mild success or a mild disappointment. The ICRC owes its very success to its ability to navigate relatively closely to both state interest and humanitarian aspiration. As a result, one of the very conditions of the field's resilience is that it manage to present as 'normal' (e.g. war) what might otherwise appear as arbitrary or a manifestation of violence. Moreover, he attempt to internalize within a normative science of law the international humanitarian lawyer's phronêsis immediately brings to mind an image of international lawyers talking to themselves, mistaking their consensus or at least their carefully arrived at gambles about where the law ought to be for some universal case for the validity of certain legal outcomes. The law's precarious determinacy, in the end, may only be the certainty of a certain form of middle-of-the-road domination. It is one that requires us to at the very least invest significantly in a sense of the *noblesse oblige* that is a hard sell. Inevitably, it is also one that should lead us to question why *international humanitarian lawyers* should act as the ultimate arbiters on matters of life and death in war.

The field can be challenged but never to the point that it is no longer 'the field', and international humanitarian law no longer law. It thus becomes difficult to see the law as anything else than a way of ratifying the world as it is, of not disrupting the categories of dominance. For Bourdieu:

> il existe une correspondance entre les structures sociales et les structures mentales, entre les divisions objectives du monde social – notamment en dominants et dominés dans les différent champs – et les principes de vision et division que les agents leur appliquent.[50]

As if by 'miracle' international humanitarian law ends up being a close fit with the reality it seeks to shape, a reality deeply characterized by certain implicit hierarchies and that is, in fact, of international humanitarian law's own making. The law is the response to the problem it has defined and thus can only confirm its social relevance. At best, therefore, as Bourdieu put it, 'the communis opinion doctorum (the general opinion of professionals), rooted in the social cohesion of the body of legal interpreters, . . . tends to confer the appearance of a transcendental basis on the historical forms of legal reason and on the belief in the ordered vision of the social whole that they produce'.[51] In effect, the law ends up reproducing some of the mental predispositions of the 'dominants' in international society. This is evident for example in the insistence on the 'equality of belligerents' and the way this effectively 'launders' the behaviour of aggressors,[52] the statism and even 'big statism' of international humanitarian law, or the way it sets up an asymmetric regime of obligations for states and non-state actors, European and colonial wars, international or non-international armed conflicts, the North or the South, men or women, or even 'national liberation movements versus rebels', 'rebels versus terrorists', etc. The *dominés* of international humanitarian law may be less apparent given the law's protective solicitude, yet there is also no doubt that protection can coincide with reification, and that the laws of war were certainly never conceived as an *emancipatory* regime.

Of course, Bourdieu did set out more generally to uncover and explain domination in the first place, and he perhaps predictably found what he was looking for. Whether that social domination also provides opportunities for social contestation is something that Bourdieu would have been sceptical of (see his idea of 'méconnaissance', the process whereby the oppressed come to see power relations not for what they are but as legitimate or natural). It is however historically the case that certain dominated actors have invoked the protection of the laws of war (e.g. weaker states, national liberation movements). In doing so they have used it to their advantage even if at the cost of co-optation into international legal structures that may then further reify what war is. The competition for domination within the field, and of the field with other fields, also contains the seeds of systemic instability, of showing the social contingency of what seems immanent, and of certain groups overcoming others. No one is irreplaceable. The reflexivity of critical sociology, its ability to turn the gaze on the subject (who is the 'we' in international humanitarian law?), is a crucial part of shaking the certainty of disciplinary practices. In acknowledging the conversation as not only about the law but about the *specific* politics of law revealed in the unmasking of the habitus and doxa, finally, the sort of field analysis proposed in this chapter does contribute to re-politicize law even as it does not give up on what makes law distinct (if law were entirely political, then we might as well spare ourselves the bother and engage directly in politics). International humanitarian lawyers, it seems, are worth better descriptively than the arguably quite poor representation of their practice; but not necessarily much better normatively.

Notes

1. M. Koskenniemi, *The Gentle Civilizer of Nations: The Rise and Fall of International Law 1870–1960* (Cambridge: Cambridge University Press, 2001), 7.
2. M. Koskenniemi, *From Apology to Utopia: the Structure of International Legal Argument*, reissue with a new epilogue (Cambridge: Cambridge University Press, 2005), 600.
3. Ibid., 597.
4. Koskenniemi, *Gentle Civilizer of Nations*.
5. Koskenniemi, *From Apology to Utopia*, 607.
6. Koskenniemi, *Gentle Civilizer of Nations*, 6.

7. Because Koskenniemi's starting point is often individual, especially in the *Civilizer*, a sense of the motivations for engaging in the field clearly exists, but it often takes on a psychological and intimate connotation rather than being seen as structured by the field. Koskenniemi, *Gentle Civilizer of Nations*, 7 ('International law is a terrain of fear and ambition, fantasy and desire, conflict and utopia').

8. P. Bourdieu, 'La force du droit [Eléments pour une sociologie du champ juridique]', *Actes de la recherche en sciences sociales* 64 (1986), 3–19; P. Bourdieu, 'Les juristes, gardiens de l'hypocrisie collective', in F. Chazel and J. Comaille (eds), *Normes juridiques et régulation sociales* (Paris: Librairie Générale de Droit et de Jurisprudence, 1991), 95.

9. P. Bourdieu, 'The Force of Law: toward a Sociology of the Juridical Field', *Hastings Law Journal* 38 (1986): 805–53; Bourdieu, 'La force du droit'; Bourdieu, 'Les juristes, gardiens de l'hypocrisie collective'; P. Bourdieu, *Sur l'État. Cours au Collège de France (1989–1992)*, P. Champagne et al. (eds) (Paris: Seuil, 2012).

10. P. Bourdieu, *Règles de l'art: Genèse et structure du champ littéraire* (Paris: Seuil, 1992).

11. Y. Dezalay and B. G. Garth, *Dealing in Virtue: International Commercial Arbitration and the Construction of a Transnational Legal Order* (Chicago: University of Chicago Press, 1996); Y. Dezalay and B. Garth, 'From the Cold War to Kosovo: the Rise and Renewal of the Field of International Human Rights', *Annual Review of Law and Social Science* 2 (2006): 231–55; Y. Dezalay and M. R. Madsen, 'The Force of Law and Lawyers: Pierre Bourdieu and the Reflexive Sociology of Law', *Annual Review of Law and Social Science* 8 (2012): 433–52; A. Vauchez, 'The Force of a Weak Field: Law and Lawyers in the Government of the European Union (for a Renewed Research Agenda)', *International Political Sociology* 2 (2008): 128–44; G. Sacriste and A. Vauchez, 'Les "bons offices" du droit international: la constitution d'une autorité non politique dans le concert diplomatique des années 1920', *Critique internationale* 1 (2005): 101–17. See also, by international lawyers F. Mégret, 'Three Dangers for the International Criminal Court: a Critical Look at a Consensual Project', *Finnish Yearbook of International Law* 12 (2002): 207; M. Prost, 'International Law's Unities and the Politics of Fragmentation', *Finnish Yearbook of International Law* 17 (2006): 131; N. M. Rajkovic, 'Rules, Lawyering, and the Politics of Legality: Critical Sociology and International Law's Rule', *Leiden Journal of International Law* 27 (2014): 331–52.

12. M. Koskenniemi, 'The Pull of the Mainstream', *Michigan Law Review* 88 (1990): 1946–62; M. Koskenniemi, 'Occupied Zone: a Zone of Reasonableness?', *Israel Law Review* 41 (2008): 13–40.

13. This particular focus seems to be the one of Jens Meierhenrich's extremely rich introduction to the concept of practices, see J. Meierhenrich, 'The Practice of International Law: a Theoretical Analysis', *Law and Contemporary Problems* 76 (2013): 1–83.

14. R. Terdiman, 'Translator's Introduction to Pierre Bourdieu, Force of Law: toward a Sociology of the Juridical Field, The', *Hastings Law Journal* 38 (1987): 805–13.

15. P. Bourdieu, *La distinction: Critique sociale du jugement* (Paris: Minuit, 1979).

16. T. Meron, 'The Martens Clause, Principles of Humanity, and Dictates of Public Conscience', *American Journal of International Law* 94 (2000): 78–89; A. Cassese, 'The Martens Clause: Half a Loaf or Simply Pie in the Sky?', *European Journal of International Law* 11 (2000): 187–216.

17. C. Pilloud et al., *Commentary on the Additional Protocols: of 8 June 1977 to the Geneva Conventions of 12 August 1949* (Geneva: Martinus Nijhoff, 1987), 391.
18. Koskenniemi, *Gentle Civilizer of Nations*, 84.
19. Bourdieu, 'Force of Law', 830.
20. On this notion of the lawyer as embodiment, see A. Orford, 'Embodying Internationalism: the Making of International Lawyers', *Australian Year Book of International Law* 19 (1998): 1–35.
21. From outside international humanitarian law, the field is objectively in competition with diplomacy, military rationality or Just War theory. From within international law itself, the laws of war are under the periodic challenge of other traditions (the jus ad bellum, human rights) that could marginalize their centrality. It is this fundamental instability of the field that creates the conditions for struggles within it.
22. Bourdieu, 'Force of Law', 831.
23. M. Koskenniemi, 'Between Commitment and Cynicism: Outline for a Theory of International Law as Practice', in *The Politics of International Law* (Oxford: Hart, 2011), 277.
24. Ibid., 276.
25. Mere criticism, precisely, serves to reinforce the field and is what one might expect from competition within it. Critique, on the other hand, which seeks to truly disrupt its practice by disenchanting it can no longer really proceed *from* the field itself. On the critique/criticism distinction as it applies to the international criminal justice project, see F. Mégret, 'International Criminal Justice: a Critical Research Agenda', in C. Schwobel (ed.), *Critical Approaches to International Criminal Law* (Abingdon, UK: Routledge, 2014), 17.
26. Koskenniemi, *From Apology to Utopia*, 564.
27. Indeed, the academic article insisting on the radical distinction between the two is almost a scholarly genre in its own right. See J. Martinez and A. Bouvier, 'Assessing the Relationship between Jus in Bello and Jus ad Bellum: an" Orthodox" View', *Annual Proceedings of the American Society of International Law* 100 (2006): 109–12; J. Mertus, 'The Danger of Conflating Jus ad Bellum and Jus in Bello', *Annual Proceedings of the American Society of International Law* 100 (2006): 114–17; J. Moussa, 'Can Jus ad Bellum Override Jus in Bello? Reaffirming the Separation of the Two Bodies of Law', *International Review of the Red Cross* 90 (2008): 963–90; R. D. Sloane, 'The Cost of Conflation: Preserving the Dualism of Jus ad Bellum and Jus in Bello in the Contemporary Law of War', *Yale Journal of International Law* 34 (2009): 47–112.
28. Of course the particular doxic element involved here is underscored by the fact that it is in fact both theoretically and practically possible to conceive of asymmetrical normativity in warfare. Frédéric Mégret, 'Missions autorisées par le Conseil de sécurité à l'heure de la R2P: au-delà du jus in bello?', *The Military Law and the Law of War Review* 52 (2013): 205–40.
29. P. Bourdieu, *Le sens pratique* (Paris: Minuit, 1980), 88.
30. Koskenniemi, *From Apology to Utopia*, 566 and sq.
31. P. Bourdieu, 'Habitus, code et codification', *Actes de la recherche en sciences sociales* 64 (1986): 40.
32. E. Adler and V. Pouliot, 'International Practices', *International Theory* 3 (2011): 1–36.

33. Meierhenrich, 'Practice of International Law'.
34. O. Korhonen, 'New International Law: Silence, Defence or Deliverance', *European Journal of International Law* 7 (1996): 1–28.
35. J. Klabbers, 'Towards a Culture of Formalism; Martti Koskenniemi and the Virtues', *Temple International and Comparative Law Journal* 27 (2013): 417–35.
36. M. A. Hansen, 'Preventing the Emasculation of Warfare: Halting the Expansion of Human Rights Law into Armed Conflict', *Military Law Review* 194 (2007): 1–65.
37. T. Meron, 'The Humanization of Humanitarian Law', *The American Journal of International Law* 94 (2000): 239–78.
38. Koskenniemi, 'Pull of the Mainstream'.
39. See N. Melzer, 'Keeping the Balance between Military Necessity and Humanity: a Response to Four Critiques of the ICRC's Interpretive Guidance on the Notion of Direct Participation in Hostilities', *NYU Journal of International Law and Politics* 42 (2009): 831–916.
40. This is a phenomenon well known in litigation in which each side is naturally led to radicalize its arguments knowing that in the process of confrontation the impact of arguments will be dimmed by contrary propositions.
41. A good recent example is the controversy regarding, in some limited cases, the existence of a 'duty to capture'. Ryan Goodman wrote an excellent, history-based article making that case. R. Goodman, 'The Power to Kill or Capture Enemy Combatants', *European Journal of International Law* 24 (2013): 819–53. Regardless of the specifically historical and doctrinal discussion, one gets a sense from the very apology-oriented response that the argument was felt to tilt the law far too much in a utopian direction in ways that could disrupt the project, see M. N. Schmitt, 'Wound, Capture, or Kill: a Reply to Ryan Goodman's "The Power to Kill or Capture Enemy Combatants"', *European Journal of International Law* 24 (2013): 855–61. In vocalizing the 'reasonable', middle of the road response, those who did simultaneously burnished their credentials as reasonable legal humanitarians, on Goodman's back as it were.
42. On the idea of international law as a 'self-preserving' system and a critique of Anthony d'Amato's particular autopoietic construction of it and the need to bring in back the international lawyers, see J. d'Aspremont, 'Send Back the Lifeboats: Confronting the Project of Saving International Law', *American Journal of International Law* 108 (2014): 687–88.
43. See T. Hoffmann, 'The Gentle Humanizer of Humanitarian Law: Antonio Cassese and the Creation of the Customary Law of Non-international Armed Conflicts', in C. Stahn and L. J. van den Herik (eds), *Future Perspectives on International Criminal Justice* (The Hague: TMC Asser Press, 2010), 58.
44. Hansen, 'Preventing the Emasculation of Warfare'.
45. A. Roberts, 'The Principle of Equal Application of the Laws of War', in D. Rodin and H. Shue (eds), *Just and Unjust Warriors: the Moral and Legal Status of Soldiers* (Oxford: Oxford University Press, 2008), 226.
46. Meron, 'Humanization of Humanitarian Law'.
47. P. Bourdieu, 'Pour un savoir engagé', *Le Monde Diplomatique* 557 (2002): 3.
48. O. Schachter, 'Invisible College of International Lawyers', *Northwestern University Law Review* 72 (1977): 217–26.
49. Of course, that has largely not been the goal of sociological critique and there would be some irony if the critique were to uncover something normatively appealing

about the practice of the law that it was not particularly looking for and that even lawyers might not commonly think was there.

50. P. Bourdieu, *La noblesse d'État: grandes écoles et esprit de corps* (Paris: Minuit, 1989).
51. Bourdieu, 'Force of Law', 819.
52. F. Mégret, 'What Is the Specific Evil of Aggression?', in C. Kreß and S. Barriga (eds), *The Crime of Aggression – a Commentary* (Cambridge: Cambridge University Press, forthcoming).

Bibliography

Adler, Emanuel, and Vincent Pouliot. 'International Practices'. *International Theory* 3 (2011): 1–36.

Bourdieu, Pierre. *La Distinction: Critique Sociale Du Jugement* (Paris: Minuit, 1979).
    Le Sens Pratique (Paris: Minuit, 1980).
    'The Force of Law: toward a Sociology of the Juridical Field'. *Hastings Law Journal* 38 (1986): 805–53.
    'Habitus, code et codification'. *Actes de la recherche en sciences sociales* 64 (1986): 40–44.
    'La Force Du Droit [Eléments Pour Une Sociologie Du Champ Juridique]', *Actes de la recherche en sciences sociales* 64 (1986): 3–19.
    La Noblesse D'état: Grandes Écoles Et Esprit De Corps (Paris: Minuit, 1989).
    'Les Juristes, Gardiens De L'hypocrisie Collective'. In François Chazel and Jacques Comaille (eds), *Normes Juridiques Et Régulation Sociales* (Paris: Librairie Générale de Droit et de Jurisprudence, 1991).
    Les Règles De L'art: Genèse Et Structure Du Champ Littéraire (Paris: Seuil, 1992).
    'Pour Un Savoir Engagé'. *Le monde diplomatique* 557 (2002): 3.
    Sur L'état: Cours Au Collège De France (1989–1992), Patrick Champagne, Remi Lenoir, Franck Poupeau and Marie-Christine Rivière (eds) (Paris: Seuil, 2012).

Cassese, Antonio. 'The Martens Clause: Half a Loaf or Simply Pie in the Sky?' *European Journal of International Law* 11 (2000): 187–216.

d'Aspremont, Jean. 'Send Back the Lifeboats: Confronting the Project of Saving International Law'. *American Journal of International Law* 108 (2014): 680–89.

Dezalay, Yves, and Bryant G. Garth. *Dealing in Virtue: International Commercial Arbitration and the Construction of a Transnational Legal Order* (Chicago: University of Chicago Press, 1996).
    'From the Cold War to Kosovo: the Rise and Renewal of the Field of International Human Rights'. *Annual Review of Law and Social Science* 2 (2006): 231–55.

Dezalay, Yves, and Mikael Rask Madsen. 'The Force of Law and Lawyers: Pierre Bourdieu and the Reflexive Sociology of Law'. *Annual Review of Law and Social Science* 8 (2012): 433–52.

Goodman, Ryan. 'The Power to Kill or Capture Enemy Combatants'. *European Journal of International Law* 24 (2013): 819–53.

Hansen, Michelle A. 'Preventing the Emasculation of Warfare: Halting the Expansion of Human Rights Law into Armed Conflict'. *Military Law Review* 194 (2007): 1–65.

Hoffmann, Tamás. 'The Gentle Humanizer of Humanitarian Law: Antonio Cassese and the Creation of the Customary Law of Non-International Armed Conflicts'. In Stahn Carsten and Larissa J. van den Herik (eds), *Future Perspectives on International Criminal Justice* (The Hague: TMC Asser Press, 2010).

Klabbers, Jan. 'Towards a Culture of Formalism; Martti Koskenniemi and the Virtues'. *Temple International and Comparative Law Journal* 27 (2013): 417–35.

Korhonen, Outi. 'New International Law: Silence, Defence or Deliverance'. *European Journal of International Law* 7 (1996): 1–28.

Koskenniemi, Martti. 'Between Commitment and Cynicism: Outline for a Theory of International Law as Practice'. In *The Politics of International Law* (Oxford: Hart, 2011).

From Apology to Utopia: The Structure of International Legal Argument, reissue with a new epilogue (Cambridge: Cambridge University Press, 2005).

The Gentle Civilizer of Nations: the Rise and Fall of International Law 1870–1960 (Cambridge: Cambridge University Press, 2001).

'Occupied Zone – "a Zone of Reasonableness"?' *Israel Law Review* 41 (2008): 13–40.

'The Pull of the Mainstream'. *Michigan Law Review* 88 (1990): 1946–62.

Martinez, Jenny, and Antoine Bouvier. 'Assessing the Relationship between Jus in Bello and Jus Ad Bellum: an "Orthodox" View'. *Annual Proceedings of the American Society of International Law* 100 (2006): 109–12.

Mégret, Frédéric. 'International Criminal Justice – a Critical Research Agenda'. In Christine Schwöbel (ed.), *Critical Approaches to International Criminal Law: an Introduction* (Abingdon, UK: Routledge, 2014).

'Missions Autorisees Par Le Conseil De Securite a L'heure De La R2p: Au-Dela Du Jus in Bello'. *The Military Law and the Law of War Review* 52 (2013): 205–40.

'Three Dangers for the International Criminal Court: a Critical Look at a Consensual Project'. *Finnish Yearbook of International Law* 12 (2002): 195–247.

'What Is the Specific Evil of Aggression?' In Claus Kreß and Stefan Barriga (eds), *The Crime of Aggression – a Commentary* (Cambridge: Cambridge University Press, forthcoming).

Meierhenrich, Jens. 'The Practice of International Law: a Theoretical Analysis'. *Law and Contemporary Problems* 76 (2013): 1–83.

Melzer, Nils. 'Keeping the Balance between Military Necessity and Humanity: a Response to Four Critiques of the ICRC's Interpretive Guidance on the

Notion of Direct Participation in Hostilities'. *NYU Journal of International Law and Politics* 42 (2009): 831–916.

Meron, Theodor. 'The Humanization of Humanitarian Law'. *American Journal of International Law* 94 (2000): 239–78.

'The Martens Clause, Principles of Humanity, and Dictates of Public Conscience'. *American Journal of International Law* 94 (2000): 78–89.

Mertus, Julie. 'The Danger of Conflating Jus ad Bellum and Jus in Bello'. *Annual Proceedings of the American Society of International Law* 100 (2006): 114–17.

Moussa, Jasmine. 'Can Jus ad Bellum Override Jus in Bello? Reaffirming the Separation of the Two Bodies of Law'. *International Review of the Red Cross* 90 (2008): 963–90.

Orford, Anne. 'Embodying Internationalism: the Making of International Lawyers'. *Australian Yearbook of International Law* 19 (1998): 1–34.

Pilloud, Claude, Yves Sandoz, Christophe Swinarski and Bruno Zimmermann. *Commentary on the Additional Protocols: of 8 June 1977 to the Geneva Conventions of 12 August 1949* (Geneva: Martinus Nijhoff, 1987).

Prost, Mario. 'All Shouting the Same Slogans: International Law's Unities and the Politics of Fragmentation'. *Finnish Yearbook of International Law* 17 (2006): 131.

Rajkovic, Nikolas M. 'Rules, Lawyering, and the Politics of Legality: Critical Sociology and International Law's Rule'. *Leiden Journal of International Law* 27 (2014): 331–52.

Roberts, Adam. 'The Principle of Equal Application of the Laws of War'. In David Rodin and Henry Shue (eds), *Just and Unjust Warriors: the Moral and Legal Status of Soldiers* (Oxford: Oxford University Press, 2008).

Sacriste, Guillaume, and Antoine Vauchez. 'Les "Bons Offices" Du Droit International: La Constitution D'une Autorité Non Politique Dans Le Concert Diplomatique Des Années 1920'. *Critique Internationale* 1 (2005): 101–17.

Schachter, Oscar. 'Invisible College of International Lawyers'. *Northwestern University Law Review* 72 (1977): 217–26.

Schmitt, Michael N. 'Wound, Capture, or Kill: a Reply to Ryan Goodman's "the Power to Kill or Capture Enemy Combatants"'. *European Journal of International Law* 24 (2013): 855–61.

Sloane, Robert D. 'The Cost of Conflation: Preserving the Dualism of Jus ad Bellum and Jus in Bello in the Contemporary Law of War'. *Yale Journal of International Law* 34 (2009): 47–112.

Terdiman, Richard. 'Translator's Introduction to Pierre Bourdieu, the Force of Law: toward a Sociology of the Juridical Field'. *Hastings Law Journal* 38 (1987): 805–13.

Vauchez, Antoine. 'The Force of a Weak Field: Law and Lawyers in the Government of the European Union (for a Renewed Research Agenda)'. *International Political Sociology* 2 (2008): 128–44.

International Law and the Limits of History

ANNE ORFORD

Martti Koskenniemi's history of the international legal profession, *The Gentle Civilizer of Nations*,[1] is widely and rightly admired as a major contribution to the self-understanding of the profession of international law, as well as a landmark intellectual history of the discipline. The publication of *The Gentle Civilizer* is often presented as representing a moment at which the field of international law took a 'turn to history', or more precisely, a turn in its mode of writing history.[2] Of course, international law has always had a deep engagement with the past. Past texts and concepts are constantly retrieved and taken up as a resource in international legal argumentation and scholarship. Thus the 'turn to history' trope marks a turn to history as method, rather than a turn to history in terms of engaging with the past rather than the present. Koskenniemi himself introduced *The Gentle Civilizer* as a 'move from structure to history in the analysis of international law' and 'a kind of experimentation in the writing about the disciplinary past'.[3] In later work, however, he became much conventional in his exposition of history as method, arguing against the 'sin of anachronism' and urging critical scholars to focus on the meaning of texts for their authors' 'contemporaries'.[4] A similar turn to history as *method* more broadly begin to shape new writing about international law over the decade following *The Gentle Civilizer*'s publication.

In this chapter I suggest that the turn to history as method that followed in the wake of *The Gentle Civilizer* was an abandonment of the critical potential of that initial work. In order to explain why that is the case, this chapter begins by exploring the representation and reception of *The Gentle Civilizer* as a work of history. In the second part of the chapter, I explore the ways in which the turn to history as method began to have a conservative effect on international law scholarship. In Part 3, I consider the relation of *The Gentle Civilizer* to the scholarly field it most clearly resembles – the history of the disciplines. I suggest that *The Gentle Civilizer* shares some of the critical potential of that scholarly genre, but also some of its limitations. Part 4 returns to reflect upon what it is that marked out *The Gentle Civilizer* as a singular achievement. I argue that this lies in Koskenniemi's attempt to hold together the history of international law, the sociology of international law, and the practice of international law. If the attempt to hold together those genres is abandoned, the critical potential of *The Gentle Civilizer* is lost. I thus call for more attention to be paid to the humanist ambitions of Koskenniemi's work, as evidenced not only in *The Gentle Civilizer*, but over the course of his career as a whole.

11.1   *The Gentle Civilizer* as History: Representation, Reception, Influence

Since the 1990s, there has been an expansion of scholarly writing inter-ested in unsettling celebratory histories of international law as a pro-fession self-evidently working collectively in the interests of a common humanity and universal values. That work has taken a number of forms, some of which have been received more favourably by historians than others. One variant has sought to trace the legacies of imperial forma-tions in contemporary legal concepts, practices and institutions. This scholarship does not primarily seek to make an argument about respon-sibility for past injustices, but rather an argument about the way in which imperialism has structured the practice of international law in the present. Scholars associated with the Third World Approaches to International Law (TWAIL) movement, notably Antony Anghie, have been important players in the ongoing debate about the relevance of the history of imperialism to modern international law.[5] They have argued against the willed forgetting of international law's imperial past, and asserted that imperialism is 'ingrained in international law as we know it today'.[6]

A second critical approach sought to counter more celebratory histories of international law by providing a more complex and nuanced history of the discipline. It is here that *The Gentle Civilizer* has been seen as a milestone. It shared with other scholarly writing at the time an interest in the history of the self-understanding and sensibility of international lawyers, and the relation of the profession to a broader range of political, social and cultural developments in the late nineteenth and early twentieth centuries.[7] Where Martti Koskenniemi differed from those scholars was in squarely positioning his project as a 'history'. In a sense the methodological positioning made him more effective – *The Gentle Civilizer* has been received as a true representation of the history of the profession not only because of its erudition and elegance, but also because of its conformity with certain generic conventions of history writing.

The Gentle Civilizer aimed at developing a history of international law as a history of the profession. In that sense, it picked up where Koskenniemi's earlier book *From Apology to Utopia* had left off, with the premise that while it might be 'too much to say that international law is *only* what international lawyers do or think', it is 'at least that'.[8] Thus the subtitle of *The Gentle Civilizer* – *The Rise and Fall of International Law 1870–1960* – dramatizes the book's thesis that the history of the field can be mapped onto the invention of the profession of international law in the 1870s, and the decline and fall of that profession after 1960. The book sought to focus on the 'political and in some cases biographical context' for the work of the first generations of professionals who thought of themselves as international lawyers. The focus was on grasping the self-understanding of those lawyers, the projects they tried to advance through their professional practice, their struggles for power within the discipline, their attempts to delineate the profession from other disciplines, and their engagement in the reproduction of cultural and political hierarchies. The aim was to recount a story of the rise and fall of international law both 'because of what it might tell us of the profession as it was then', and to provide 'a historical contrast to the state of the discipline today'.[9]

In outlining his approach to writing a history of international law, Koskenniemi distanced himself from two dominant traditions. The first was the writing of epochal histories of international law that 'flatten the work of individual lawyers into superficial decorations on the surface of the silent flow of periods into one another and transformation of great ideas or legal principles'.[10] The second was the writing of biographies of key figures, as this tradition also 'reduces the field – this time to a projection of a few great minds – and fails to account for the external pressures to which the doctrines of those men sought to provide responses'.[11] Thus he presented *The Gentle Civilizer* as a set of essays that 'are neither epochal nor biographical' but which 'form a kind of experimentation in the writing about the disciplinary past in which the constraints of any rigorous "method" have been set aside in an effort to create intuitively plausible and politically engaged narratives about the emergence and gradual transformation of a profession'.[12] Koskenniemi was very clear that this was a narrative with political implications for the present:

The essays do not seek a neutral description of the past 'as it actually was' – that sort of knowledge is not open to us – but a description that hopes to make our present situation clearer to us and to sharpen our ability to act in the professional contexts that are open to us as we engage in our practices and projects. In this sense, it is also a political act.[13]

Despite that strongly presentist statement, *The Gentle Civilizer* has generally been received as a work of 'history'. And in many ways *The Gentle Civilizer* is a history – it seeks to trace the emergence of a particular professional sensibility during a narrowly delimited period in Europe, it is announced as a history by the periodization it offers, it borrows the historical rise and fall trope, and it offers a clear demarcation between 1960 and today – something died in 1960, even if, as he has suggested in his more colourful (or disconcerting) moments, it still walks, zombie-like, among us.[14] Koskenniemi described *The Gentle Civilizer* as both a 'series of essays in the history of ideas',[15] and a study of 'historical aspects of the profession' influenced in part by the inspiration that Michel Foucault had provided for many critical scholars writing new histories of the social sciences.[16] It sought to 'bring international law down from the epochal and conceptual abstractions' and to explore it as 'what international lawyers do or think' in a particular time and place, as 'actors in particular social dramas'.[17]

The Gentle Civilizer functioned as critique because it challenged standard histories of the discipline that presented an international law tradition unfolding in an unbroken line from the great European publicists of the sixteenth century through to the modern era. Koskenniemi rejected the claim that a continuous tradition of international law could be traced back to a period before the late nineteenth century, and offered an implicit challenge to the idea that international law exists as a coherent system of objective rules and principles that determine state behaviour. Instead, what international lawyers championed as either scientifically deduced rules (in the positivist version) or progressive developments in the realization of universal history with a cosmopolitan purpose (in the natural law version) were after all just human constructions – the product of struggles between people with political projects, seeking to establish the domination of their vision for the world, trying to assert power over others, and effecting the distribution of material and spiritual resources towards one group rather than another. The argument that there was a very recent history to the discipline, and that the rest was 'invented tradition',[18] *was* the critique.

11.2   The Conservative Effects of History as Method

Yet the turn to history quickly threatened to have a more conservative effect on international law scholarship. The disciplinary history approach adopted by Koskenniemi received a much warmer welcome from historians, and particularly from intellectual historians, than did the Third World approach described above. The work of international legal scholars engaged in exploring the relation of modern international legal concepts, institutions, and practices to the imperial past had an ambivalent reception among historians and legal scholars who aligned themselves with the contextualist Cambridge school of intellectual history associated with Quentin Skinner. I have discussed that critical reception more fully elsewhere,[19] but a sense of its flavour can be gained from the response of the Australian intellectual historian Ian Hunter, who argued that the critical work of international lawyers was 'dogged by debilitating anachronism and "presentism"'.[20]

The policing of anachronism was a major theme in the response to critical histories of international law among such scholars. Historians sternly cautioned international lawyers for making 'fanciful connections' between scholars of earlier periods and the modern discipline of international law, taking 'daring jumps' that destroy the 'complexity and pluralism of the discourses from various (and often very divergent) centuries',[21] and engaging in forms of '*historical revisionism*' that abandon 'some standards of historiographical analysis'.[22] Other work addressing the turn to history in international law more generally pointed to the 'deplorable' results of 'genealogic history from present to past' that 'leads to anachronistic interpretations of historical phenomena, clouds historical realities that bear no fruit in our own times and gives no information about the historical context of the phenomenon one claims to recognise'.[23]

Before going any further, I want to stress that the contextualist school of intellectual history and international lawyers find common ground in their focus on interpreting texts in 'context'. Much of the best recent work engaging with the relation between past and present in international law is in sympathy with Skinner's arguments for interpreting classic texts in that respect. For Skinner, legal, philosophical, or political texts should not be read as sources of timeless truths or authoritative statements about fundamental concepts.[24] In order to understand a particular statement, utterance or text, the historian needs to reconstruct what its author was doing in making that statement, uttering that utterance or writing that text.[25] Skinner's methodological manifestos played an important part in stressing the role of texts, including texts that made normative truth-claims, as political interventions in particular social contexts and political power struggles. In sympathy with that insight, many international lawyers seek to understand key legal texts, institutional reports, official correspondence, cases and scholarly studies from the past as interventions in political debates and innovative responses to specific problems.

But the polemical argument for 'contextualism' in the work of intellectual historians is tightly bound up with an idea about time that marks the point at which international law and contextual intellectual history part company. We can get a sense of the stakes here if we think about the weight that the Cambridge school puts on the notion of anachronism. Anachronism refers to something or someone that is not in its *correct* time. A lot of work goes on in determining the 'correct' time in which a concept or idea should be placed if we are to grasp its meaning. In his early manifestos, Skinner argued that scholars should concern themselves with studying what an author intended to do in the temporal context of 'the given occasion' when an utterance was 'performed'.[26] And in an attack on the Great Chain of Being style of reasoning that had shaped much American intellectual history, Skinner also argued that it was a mistake to study past texts in order to trace 'the morphology of a given concept over time'.[27] Contextualist intellectual historians have since focussed a great deal of attention on policing the idea that past texts must not be approached anachronistically in light of current debates, problems and linguistic usages or in a search for the development of canonical themes, fundamental concepts or contemporary doctrines. The clear demarcation between past and present, or history and politics, underpinning Skinner's conception of historical research requires that everything must be placed in the context of its time, and present-day questions must not be allowed to distort our interpretation of past events, texts or concepts.

Of course there are many historians who contest the strong separation of past and present championed by the Cambridge school. However while I am not a working historian, I am a working international lawyer. My interest is in the stakes of the methodological encounter between intellectual historians and international lawyers for critical work in international law. That encounter raises the question – what approach for engaging with past texts or concepts is proper to international law? What kind of method is appropriate to a discipline in which judges, advocates, scholars and students all look to past texts precisely to discover the meaning of present concepts?[28] As I have argued in some detail elsewhere, my concern is that to mandate historical *methods* as the only means for engaging with past texts makes it impossible to undertake a study of how legal concepts, ideas, or principles are transformed in relation to changes in the social world over time, and thus to grasp the present function of legal concepts adequately.[29] This in turn makes it difficult to reflect upon the past as a critical participant in the practice of international law in the present.

Perhaps because of his closer engagement with historians in the wake of the publication of *The Gentle Civilizer*, Koskenniemi himself began advocating a more conventional 'historical' method in subsequent work. He began lecturing on the 'sin of anachronism', and criticizing the sense given by histories of international law that it might be 'possible to carry a timeless conversation on perennial problems between the living and the dead'.[30] He joined seasoned contextualist historians in warning budding post-colonial scholars:

> The difficult step to take after the postcolonial critique has done its work is what to do next ... Most actors, contexts and events have been irredeemably lost and remaining fragments allow generalization only with the greatest difficulty. The dangers of anachronism and conceptual imperialism are constantly present.[31]

Koskenniemi provided a 'word of caution' to historians of law who seek to write 'a history of legal concepts or institutions that travel, as it were, unchanged through time' as that would be 'anachronistic'.[32] Instead, the proper context within which to write about past texts is to consider their meaning for their 'contemporaries'.[33] Histories of international law should treat 'legal vocabularies and institutions as open-ended platforms on which contrasting meanings are projected at different periods, each complete in themselves, each devised so as to react to some problem in the surrounding world'.[34]

More subtly, Koskenniemi's practice of citation reinforced the sense that critical international lawyers were not to be taken seriously. For example, in his study of the Spanish contribution to empire and international law, Koskenniemi mentioned the work of Anghie and other critical scholars of international law only in passing as examples of 'post-colonial' readings that 'neglect the complexity of the moment'.[35] While Koskenniemi did not engage in the kind of programmatic critique of Anghie's work that we saw in Hunter, he did not recognize that the work done by Anghie and other 'post-colonial scholars' had offered its own challenge to the received reading of Vitoria as a proto-humanitarian liberal by twentieth-century international lawyers. Instead, Koskenniemi's citations suggested that if his readers wanted to understand the lasting significance of Vitoria's writings for international law, they should engage either with the writings of Vitoria's contemporaries at Salamanca or those of the intellectual historians who had provided close readings of that period.[36]

The combined effects of the move by historians and legal historians to dismiss critical thinking about international law and empire became evident when I attended a seminar at which a distinguished and influential professor of international law repeatedly counselled early career scholars against trying to track the relation between legal concepts, doctrines, or institutions developed in the past (including the past century) and contemporary legal debates. This, according to the professor, involved taking an ahistorical approach. Such a 'TWAIL approach' was to be avoided in favour of 'proper' historical method. Yet the 'TWAIL' approach could equally be called a 'juridical approach' – TWAIL scholars, like legal scholars more generally, engage in the practice of developing arguments about contemporary political problems that draw on inherited concepts with a history of legal meaning attached to them. Thus a critical practice that had developed as an intervention in the conventional operations of legal method was dismissed because it was 'ahistorical'. Interdisciplinary work can often be enlivening, productive, and critically transformative and can open things up in a discipline that has become insular, but it can also do the opposite: it can be used to shut things down, to police, to constrain new work in a discipline, or make it harder to ask certain questions.[37] Here was inter-disciplinarity operating to shut down critical work rather than open it up.

As I began to argue in response, the consolidation of the turn to history as method was having a constraining effect on critical approaches to the field of international law.[38] The argument that international lawyers should not study the movement of concepts across time raises serious problems in relation to meaning and understanding in international law. The first problem it raises relates to delimiting the proper 'context' for a legal concept or indeed for understanding the meanings attributed to the work of a particular scholar. To take one example,[39] the overly simplistic idea that the only proper context for studying the effect of Vitoria on international law is the world of Salamanca in the sixteenth century ignores the multiple contexts *for the discipline of international law* of writers such as Vitoria. Attention to the 'context' in which Vitoria was reclaimed for modern (American) international law shows that early modern *ius gentium* was systematically and carefully reconstructed in the US at the dawn of the twentieth century to make sense of practices and institutions that were already re-shaping the world.[40] Vitoria's humanitarian critique of Spanish empire was invoked by ideological innovators such as James Brown Scott to provide a language for rationalizing the form of empire that would triumph in the twentieth century. Of course the political theorist Richard Tuck was right to say that the first generation of scholars who looked systematically at the early modern jurisprudence of war – that is, the scholars funded by Carnegie and working under the influence of James Brown Scott – 'left us with a very misleading picture of the pre-Grotian ideas about the laws of war and peace'.[41] As Tuck comments of Scott and his colleagues: 'Like many older historians of a particular discipline, they assumed that the subject of "international law" was gradually uncovered and understood in increasingly less primitive terms by writers from the Middle Ages onwards'.[42]

And yet international lawyers, as the heirs of both Vitoria *and* Scott, cannot ignore the fact that Scott and his generation did successfully weave Vitoria, Gentili, Grotius, Vattel and many others into a universal history with a cosmopolitan purpose. In so doing, they and their colleagues and fellow travellers re-made the world in their image. Unless we remember that history of the twentieth century, we cannot fully understand the rhetorical and ideological force of international law doctrines, concepts or programmes of action today. Thus for international lawyers, the need to think about context beyond that which is contemporaneous with the lifetime of the author, both in terms of what an author was trying to do in writing a text and in terms of the reception of that text in later historical situations, is pressing.

Second, the dogmatic argument that international lawyers must work according to historical protocols when it comes to studying concepts and ideas ignores the way that international law operates. It is not plausible to instruct a lawyer to think about a concept purely in the present tense. Lawyers work by invoking the history of meaning that has accrued to legal concepts, principles and doctrines over time. The legal operation of relating past and present will continue whether or not critical scholars engage with it. One goal of legal education is to teach new lawyers how to assimilate the complex set of political debates and logical moves that are condensed into particular legal concepts or fictions.[43] The end result is often that over time, such concepts are worn smooth. They cease, at least for lawyers who have grown accustomed to them, to be politically volatile. Critical work in law tries to recover that process and reanimate the political potential embedded in all legal fictions.[44] The attack on anachronism will not shut down the movement of law, but it threatens to shut down the ways in which critical legal scholarship seeks to challenge that movement when it produces authoritarian or exploitative effects.[45]

In his subsequent historiographical work, Koskenniemi has written that he was inspired by my work on the limits of contextualism and defence of anachronism to think again about whether conventional historical methodology is sufficient for critical thinking about international law.[46] Yet his continued adherence to history as genre and indeed as method still does not fully address the analytical and political stakes of the turn to history. I want to suggest that those stakes are more significant than he makes them appear, and that the turn to history as method has a constraining effect on the ability of critical legal scholars to engage with the law in new and politically productive ways. Some sense of why that might be the case emerges from a consideration of the effects of the history of the disciplines project more generally.

11.3   The Potential and Limits of the History of the Disciplines

The history of the disciplines is a project that gained institutional ground, particularly in the US and France, during the 1980s and 1990s. It was inspired partly by work on the role of intellectuals and the sociology of the professions informed by sociology, history, and science studies, and revolutionized by the publication of Michel Foucault's work on the emergence of the disciplines in late-eighteenth-century Europe.[47] In the US, the sociology of knowledge had been established as a major genre of critical thinking about the relation of science and society due to the influence of scholars such as Robert K Merton, Talcott Parsons and Thomas Kuhn.[48] Work on the sociology of science had begun to inspire scholars working not only in the physical sciences but also the human sciences. Much of that sociological study of the physical and social sciences was initially undertaken by disciplinary insiders interested in the operation of their discipline and its shifting relation to other fields of knowledge or forms of power in the new conditions that shaped the Cold War academy. A second centre of gravity for the sociology of the professions could be found in France. The reflexive sociology of Pierre Bourdieu and his collaborators offered rich insights into fields of professional practice, analysing how fields were constituted, how fields managed to acquire relative autonomy and status, the relationship of a field to other centres of power such as the state, and the way in which key agents acted as entrepreneurs building the status of the field and its forms of knowledge.[49]

Michel Foucault's work was revolutionary in that it focussed attention away from the occupational grouping of the 'profession' and its self-understanding, and served to defamiliarize the way that professionals understood themselves and the history of their role.[50] Rather than start with the sociological model of the 'profession', Foucault worked with the 'discipline' as his object of study. His early work offered studies of how certain practices had been deployed upon the poor, the homeless, the mad and the indigent to produce new forms of knowledge and new forms of control. Often the people administering those new disciplinary practices did in fact overlap with the 'professionals' studied by sociologists, such as physicians, psychiatrists, criminologists, architects or economists. Foucault was not however primarily interested in studying those professional men and their internal struggles for status and power, but rather in redescribing the attributes of their practices as seen from the perspective of those upon whose bodies discipline was administered. He was thus interested in tracing the emergence of disciplinary practices and their relationship to other forms of bureaucratic and police powers. The language of 'discipline' evoked both power-wielding techniques and bodies of knowledge, as developed by emerging fields that aspired to be, but were not quite, sciences.[51] Foucault's work was overtly opposed to the ways in which the social and human sciences had been deployed to control populations. He sought to show that the apparently benign disciplines of psychiatry or indeed medicine more generally were built upon social practices of internment and segregation.[52]

These rich streams of intellectual work informed the flourishing of varied studies published during the last decades of the twentieth century that sought to trace the invention, professionalization and conditions of possibility of numerous fields. Scholars engaged in these projects moved between external histories of the disciplines that took a more oppositional view of the violence of powerful disciplines and a sceptical view of their claims to expertise, and internal histories that sought to challenge the more congratulatory narratives that practitioners told themselves and yet still work with disciplinary concepts rather than treating them as facts to be taken as given. As most, if not all, academic disciplines are organized around invented traditions, in which historical figures, texts and narratives are invoked to situate current disciplinary practices within a longer progressive narrative, these counter-histories were political interventions. Such histories stressed the contingency of the ideas and individuals that came to dominate the field, the precariousness of the truth-claims of the discipline being studied, its social and institutional bases, its collusions with power and acts of exclusion, and the political economy of struggles over authority and influence. In many cases the writing of these histories was also 'a humanistic reaction to the movement of the social sciences toward quantification: telling their histories as constructed ones allowed some means of reminding hard-core economists, for example, that much of what they were championing as "scientific" was in fact the product of struggles with other disciplines, of the need to define the world in a particular way, of attempts to claim power over others'.[53]

In many ways these revisionist disciplinary histories were and remain a major critical resource. They provide a counter to monumentalist or teleological narratives of disciplinary progress in their more flamboyant guises. Scholars inspired by this aspect of Foucault's work developed highly critical accounts of the emergence and consolidation of powerful 'normalizing' disciplines such as psychiatry and criminology. Many such histories offered important insights beyond 'confirmational narratives offered from within the respective disciplines'.[54] Yet at the same time, as this form of scholarship developed into a more recognizable subdiscipline of historical work, it became increasingly conventional in terms of historical method. In order to boost their *own* status and influence, the truth-claims of disciplinary histories were often premised on being able to provide a more 'professional' form of history writing than was offered by the self-mythologizing histories produced by those seeking to establish disciplinary myths of origin. In performing these 'more or less confident acts of historicization', these 'critical' histories ironically shored up the status of history as a master discipline dedicated to producing the objective truth about the past. Even as these histories revealed the constructed nature of the disciplines they were critiquing, they reaffirmed 'the power of history as a disciplinary practice'.[55] As noted above, a similar trend in international law followed the publication of *The Gentle Civilizer*.

This matters for two reasons. First, the effect of the turn to history as method is to displace the conventional methods that govern work in the field being historicized. The effect is to create a separate field of 'disciplinary history', which operates in hermetic isolation from the practice of the field itself. This is also the point made by Suzanne Marchand about disciplinary histories more generally. She comments that many of the histories of the disciplines produced during the 1980s and 1990s 'were written not by insiders, but by professional historians, writing from outside the discipline, and never intending to practice it themselves'.[56] The result was that '[f]ew of those who wrote disciplinary histories ...

had much to offer those seeking a less repressive and more honest future for, say, classical archaeology, or physical anthropology'.[57] Indeed as we have seen, it was vital to those advocating the adoption of historical method that those studying the past of a discipline should have nothing to say about its contemporary practice. To link past and present would be to commit the sin of anachronism. Similarly for reflexive sociologists working in the tradition of Bourdieu, it was key to the integrity of their project that they not seek to understand the internal logics of disciplinary reasoning. For Bourdieu, the nature of the knowledge constituted by intellectuals in a field was placed outside the investigation of the field's emergence. It was taken as given that a field must have a knowledge base, but it was not considered relevant or indeed desirable to study the nature of that knowledge. Thus for sociologists studying the legal field, it was essential to avoid being 'situated too close to the orthodoxy of law', as to engage with the disciplinary understanding of lawyers would run 'the risk of being trapped by this logic of domination and, thus, becoming legally biased'.[58]

Second, the external orientation of much work in the history of the disciplines, and the cynicism it manifests towards 'expertise' and the professions, seems also to be increasingly out of touch with the changing political situation in which that critique takes effect. In the contemporary world of managed and globally ranked organizations, few professionals are still able to maintain autonomy and control over their own work. The production and dissemination of knowledge is not the sole province of intellectuals working within ivory towers, but is part of 'a vast industrial complex' involving corporate research and development, military research, university research and a range of communications media.[59] The autonomy of professionals, particularly those funded publicly, is increasingly challenged, popular scepticism towards expertise and government is expanding, and many professionals are unable to maintain 'occupational control' in the face of other institutional and market-driven demands.[60] The drama of revealing that the history of the disciplines was about people with projects who were out to further their own individual dreams of power, realize their own fantasies, and from time to time join with others who could help them achieve those ambitions, provided a powerful weapon when turned against those experts who were able to make their own visions of the future appear natural, inevitable and uncontested. Yet the relentlessly negative operation of that critique offers less purchase today on a neo-liberal political culture that depends upon cynical reason for its consolidation and expansion, and in which taxpayers are already encouraged to be sceptical about the stability, legitimacy and value of science and other forms of expert knowledge.[61]

Perhaps then the history of the disciplines has, in the words of Suzanne Marchand, 'had its day', particularly when it ceases to attend to the politics of its methods and the situation in which it operates. Yet as Koskenniemi overtly declared, his history of the profession was directly engaged with the present and the aims of his project were intensely political. In closing, I want to return to consider what *The Gentle Civilizer* itself might suggest about the possibility of developing forms of interdisciplinary work in international law that take responsibility for engaging with the practice of the discipline and for its present politics.

11.4   The Situation of Critique

I have argued to date that the effects of *The Gentle Civilizer* on the field have been both critical and conservative. The critical effect has been to unsettle celebratory histories of international law as a profession self-evidently working collectively in the interests of a common humanity and universal values, and to challenge the notion that the tradition of international law can be traced back to a period before the late nineteenth century. It offered an extremely powerful alternative to the idea that international law operates as science or rules that determine outcomes. It has inspired rich and evocative new studies of the profession in the nineteenth and twentieth centuries, opened up new conversations about the overlapping histories of international law, international relations, and economics, and paved the way for critical accounts of sub-fields including human rights law, international trade law and international investment law. Yet as discussed above, the conservative effect is a result of the way that *The Gentle Civilizer* has been taken up by those exhorting a turn to historical method in international law scholarship – including, for a period, Koskenniemi himself.

It is therefore timely to reconsider what the historicizing of international law as a critical gesture might mean for the field going forward. As discussed above, some scholars responded to the publication of *The Gentle Civilizer* and the broader 'turn to history' in international law by calling for a more professional form of history writing and a clearer delimitation of the fields of international law and history of international law. In my view this is the wrong direction for the field to take from a critical perspective. In order to think about future directions for historical work in relation to international law, it is vital to articulate what that history is *for*. As Constantin Fasolt has shown, it is important to remember that history in its heyday *was* theory – a theory of the relation between the past and the present that was designed to undermine a present form of political authority. The practice of history and the inherent theory of history were harnessed to attacking Papal authority and its reliance upon revealed forms of knowledge, and to securing the independence of present rulers from past obligations.[62] The loss of that self-understanding of the meaning and purpose of history has led to a division between a historical practice that is growing in speed and becoming every more specialized, and a theory that is unable to find any meaning in that practice.[63] Similarly, the adoption of a very objective and externalist approach to writing the history of the disciplines risks forgetting that historical work is itself a politics. As a result, the vital sense of the inherent interrelationship between the history, theory and practice of the discipline is lost. The result is that work in each sphere – history, theory and practice – can proliferate endlessly, with an increasing number of technical studies being produced but with a decreasing sense of their meaning and relevance for political engagement in the world. Academic work becomes less critical and less responsible, even as the language of critical thinking and responsibility is heard more and more regularly.

The separation of history, philosophy and practice has marked the 'professionalization' of many fields during the twentieth century. We might think, for instance, of the failed attempts in the US to create a philosophy of science that would be in active collaboration with scientists and the practice of science after World War 2,[64] the abandonment by mainstream economic thinking of a commitment to reflecting critically upon the relation between its history, concepts and practice,[65] the movement in international law towards an abstract measuring of law against external ideals rather than maintaining a critical comprehension of its scientific methods as value-laden,[66] or indeed the inability of historians to comprehend the historically contingent and deeply political nature of the myths and methods at the heart of their practice.[67] The effect of such scholarly delimitation is to produce a division between history, theory and practice, in which practice is measured against transcendental or absolute values understood to be upheld by external disciplines such as philosophy, rather than as a source of values that must be comprehended and addressed as such.[68] Once the history and philosophy of a discipline are abstracted and treated as distinct from its practice, a politically engaged vision of that practice is much harder to realize.

In the case of international law, historians seek to import the conviction that historical methods provide the only form of interpretive practice that can produce an adequate knowledge of the past, not only for historians but also for international lawyers. The effect of the argument that historical method should replace legal method as the means of engaging with the past of international law means that critical practitioners lose the capacity to intervene in development of the law. As a result, international lawyers who have been trained in the techniques and languages of international law are asked to give up their responsibility for creating a less repressive future for the field.

Yet is it not inevitable that the embrace of interdisciplinary work by international law scholars must lead to the displacement of engagement with the concepts, methods and practices of the discipline itself. It remains possible to link the insights made by historians of disciplines to the practice of those disciplines – for example, to respond to insights about the role of science in constructing nature and its relationship to imperialism and industrial technology as scientists rather than as historians, philosophers or external critics of science, or to respond to insights about the imperial legacy of legal concepts as international lawyers, albeit lawyers with a critical orientation, rather than historians of international law.[69] However, this requires an allegiance to the integration of history, philosophy and practice, rather than the institutional fragmentation of those approaches into distinct fields of specialist expertise.

And this was, after all, the initial ambition of The Gentle Civilizer. As I noted in opening, Koskenniemi referred to that book as an experiment. It is here that the enduring contribution of his work becomes visible. Across his scholarly projects, Koskenniemi has attempted to integrate critical engagement with the substance of international legal doctrines, the history and sociology of the profession, and the political situation of the international lawyer. Koskenniemi has studied the profession of international law not only from a sociological perspective, but also as an insider deeply concerned to preserve the internal formalist culture that he sees as the legacy of 'the profession in its best days'.[70] His aim in The Gentle Civilizer was to say something about 'international law's heroic period' in order to provide 'a historical contrast to the state of the discipline today'.[71] He challenged his readers to remember that the discipline of international law had started out in the nineteenth century with a clear political project, but by the dawn of the twenty-first century had become a faded version of its earlier self, committed only to 'worn-out internationalist causes' and at the whim of 'academic and political instrumentalization'.[72] In writing histories of international law, Koskenniemi has sought to remind international lawyers of the ways that our discipline has been transformed in the past, so that we might take responsibility for its transformation in the future.

Notes

1. M. Koskenniemi, *The Gentle Civilizer of Nations: The Rise and Fall of International Law 1870–1960* (Cambridge: Cambridge University Press, 2001).
2. See e.g. G. R. B. Galindo, 'Martti Koskenniemi and the Historiographical Turn in International Law', *European Journal of International Law* 16 (2005): 539–59; A. Becker Lorca, 'Eurocentrism in the History of International Law', in B. Fassbender and A. Peters (eds), *The Oxford Handbook of the History of International Law* (Oxford: Oxford University Press, 2012), 1055 (describing the publication of *The Gentle Civilizer* as 'a turning point in the writing of history by legal scholars').
3. Koskenniemi, *Gentle Civilizer*, 5–6, 9.
4. M. Koskenniemi, 'Histories of International Law: Dealing with Eurocentrism', *Rechtsgeschichte* 19 (2011): 152–72; M. Koskenniemi, 'A History of International Law Histories', in Fassbender and Peters, *Oxford Handbook*, 943.
5. The classic text is A. Anghie, *Imperialism, Sovereignty and the Making of International Law* (Cambridge: Cambridge University Press, 2007), arguing that if 'the colonial encounter, with all its exclusions and subordinations, shaped the very foundations of international law, then grave questions must arise as to whether and how it is possible for the post-colonial world to construct a new international law that is liberated from these colonial origins' (8).
6. J. T. Gathii, 'Neoliberalism, Colonialism and International Governance: Decentering the International Law of Governmental Legitimacy', *Michigan Law Review* 98 (2000): 2020.
7. See e.g. N. Berman, '"But the Alternative Is Despair": European Nationalism and the Modernist Renewal of International Law', *Harvard Law Review* 106 (1993): 1792–903; N. Berman, 'Between "Alliance" and "Localization": Nationalism and the New Oscillationism', *NYU Journal of International Law and Politics* 26 (1994): 449–92; D. Kennedy, 'International Law and the Nineteenth Century: History of an Illusion', *Quinnipiac Law Review* 17 (1997): 99–136; J. von Bernstorff, *Der Glaube an das universale Recht: Zur Völkerrechtstheorie Hans Kelsens und seiner Schüler* (Baden-Baden, Germany: Nomos, 2001); A. Anghie, 'Colonialism and the Birth of International Institutions: Sovereignty, Economy, and the Mandate System of the League of Nations', *NYU Journal of International Law and Politics* 34 (2002): 513–633; L. Obregón, 'Completing Civilization: Nineteenth Century Criollo Interventions in International Law' (PhD diss., Harvard Law School, 2002).
8. Koskenniemi, *Gentle Civilizer*, 7. See also M. Koskenniemi, *From Apology to Utopia*, reissue with new epilogue (Cambridge: Cambridge University Press, 2005), 569 (arguing that 'law is what lawyers think about it and how they go about using it in their work').
9. Koskenniemi, *Gentle Civilizer*, 5.
10. Ibid., 6–7.
11. Ibid., 8.

12. Ibid., 10.
13. Ibid.
14. See the discussion recorded in D. Schmalz, 'On Kitsch, Zombies and True Love – an Interview with Martti Koskenniemi', *Völkerrechtsblog*, 21 May 2014, where Koskenniemi reflected that '[p]ublic international law arose as a gentle civilizing set of institutions and practices at the end of the nineteenth century but had expended much of its inspirational and political force by the 1960s. I sometimes think that some of its institutions are today like zombies – dead, but not knowing that they are dead, they simply do not lay down and disappear ... It would not matter much for anybody if they simply stopped their endless meetings. I suppose this is just another description for fragmentation, the sense that the center has collapsed'. While the zombie reference may merely be colourful for some, for those of us who are aficionados of the Walking Dead, it conjures up a very disconcerting image.
15. Koskenniemi, *Gentle Civilizer*, 2. He subsequently pointed to the Cambridge school as a model for work in the history of ideas; see M. Koskenniemi, 'Why History of International Law Today?', *Rechtsgeschichte* 4 (2004): 61–66.
16. Koskenniemi, *Gentle Civilizer*, 9.
17. Ibid., 7.
18. On the role of invented traditions in legitimizing contemporary practices and institutions more generally, see E. Hobsbawm and T. Ranger (eds), *The Invention of Tradition* (Cambridge: Cambridge University Press, 1983).
19. A. Orford, 'The Past as Law or History? The Relevance of Imperialism for Modern International Law', in M. Toufayan, E. Tourme-Jouannet and H. Ruiz Fabri (eds), *International Law and New Approaches to the Third World: between Repetition and Renewal* (Paris: Société de Législation Comparée, 2013), 97, first published as *NYU Institute for International Law and Justice Working Paper 2012/2*.
20. I. Hunter, 'The Figure of Man and the Territorialisation of Justice in "Enlightenment" Natural Law: Pufendorf and Vattel', *Intellectual History Review* 23 (2013): 289–307. See also I. Hunter, 'Global Justice and Regional Metaphysics: on the Critical History of the Law of Nature and Nations', in S. Dorsett and I. Hunter (eds), *Law and Politics in British Colonial Thought: Transpositions of Empire* (New York: Palgrave Macmillan, 2010), 11.
21. G. Cavaller, 'Vitoria, Grotius, Pufendorf, Wolff and Vattel: Accomplices of European Colonialism and Exploitation or True Cosmopolitans?', *Journal of the History of International Law* 10 (2008): 207–9.
22. P. Zapatero, 'Legal Imagination in Vitoria: the Power of Ideas', *Journal of the History of International Law* 11 (2009): 268, 271.
23. R. Lesaffer, 'International Law and Its History: the Story of an Unrequited Love', in M. Craven, M. Fitzmaurice and M. Vogiatzi (eds), *Time, History and International Law* (Leiden, Netherlands: Martinus Nijhoff, 2007), 34–35. See also, however, R. Lesaffer, 'Law and History: Law between Past and Present', in B. van Klink and S. Taekema (eds), *Law and Method: Interdisciplinary Research into Law* (Tübingen, Germany: Mohr Siebeck, 2011), 133. Lesaffer there distinguished between 'true historical study of past law' and 'historical jurisprudence', accepting that not all studies of the relation between the past and the present should be considered as 'legal history'. His argument in that later piece is much closer to the one I make here – that it is important for lawyers to engage with the context of past texts or utterances, but that it is also appropriate for historical jurisprudence or those

attempting to understand current law to trace the evolution or transformation of concepts across time.

24. See particularly Q. Skinner, 'Meaning and Understanding in the History of Ideas', *History and Theory* 8 (1969): 3–53.

25. Ibid. See also Q. Skinner, 'Interpretation and the Understanding of Speech Acts', in *Visions of Politics*, vol. 1, *Regarding Method* (Cambridge: Cambridge University Press, 2002), 103.

26. Skinner, 'Meaning and Understanding', 48

27. Ibid., 49.

28. A. Orford, 'On International Legal Method', *London Review of International Law* 1 (2013): 166–97.

29. Ibid.

30. Koskenniemi, 'Histories of International Law', 166.

31. Ibid., 170.

32. Koskenniemi, 'A History of International Law Histories', 969.

33. Ibid.

34. Ibid.

35. M. Koskenniemi, 'Empire and International Law: the Real Spanish Contribution', *University of Toronto Law Journal* 61 (2011): 10–11.

36. To be fair, it may be that Anghie was one of the unnamed colleagues Koskenniemi had in mind when he commented that, '[w]hile it is understandable that public international lawyers and historians have traditionally focused on the public activities of sovereigns and on the formal imperial relationships that may be embodied in international law rules and institutions, these are only a small part of imperial relations ... In this essay, I will join colleagues who have worked to analyse relations of private ordering within such aspects of public international law as the laws of war and intervention, post-conflict governance, arbitration, trade and investment, and so on'. Ibid., 2.

37. See further my comments in A. Kemmerer, '"We Do Not Need to Always Look to Westphalia": a Conversation with Martti Koskenniemi and Anne Orford', *Journal of the History of International Law* 17 (2015): 4.

38. Orford, 'Past as Law or History?'; Orford, 'On International Legal Method'.

39. This example is explored in greater detail in Orford, 'Past as Law or History?'

40. Ibid.

41. R. Tuck, *The Rights of War and Peace: Political Thought and the International Order from Grotius to Kant* (Oxford: Oxford University Press, 2001), 11.

42. Ibid., 11–12.

43. A. Riles, 'Is the Law Hopeful?', *Cornell Law Faculty Working Paper* 68 (2011), http://scholarship.law.cornell.edu/clsops_papers/68, 18–20.

44. A. Orford, 'Food Security, Free Trade, and the Battle for the State', *Journal of International Law and International Relations* 11 (2015): 1–23.

45. See further A. Orford, 'Theorizing Free Trade', in A. Orford and F. Hoffmann (eds), *The Oxford Handbook of the Theory of International Law* (Oxford: Oxford University Press, 2016), 701.

46. M. Koskenniemi, 'Histories of International Law: Significance and Problems for a Critical View', *Temple International and Comparative Law Journal* 27 (2013): 215–40; M. Koskenniemi, 'Vitoria and Us: Thoughts on Critical Histories of International Law', *Rechtsgeschichte* 22 (2014): 119–38.

47. Of particular relevance are M. Foucault, *Folie et déraison: Historie de la folie à l'âge classique* (Paris: Libraire Plon, 1961), initially published in English in an abridged form as *Madness and Civilization: a History of Insanity in the Age of Reason*, R. Howard (trans.) (New York: Pantheon, 1965); M. Foucault, *Naissance de la Clinique: Une Archéologie du regard medical* (Paris: Presses Universitaires de France, 1963), published in English as *The Birth of the Clinic: an Archeology of Medical Perception*, A. M. Sheridan Smith (trans.) (New York: Vintage, 1975); M. Foucault, *Surveiller et punir: Naissance de la prison* (Paris: Éditions Gallimard, 1975), published in English as *Discipline and Punish: the Birth of the Prison*, A. Sheridan (trans.) (New York: Vintage, 1977).

48. S. Marchand, 'Has the History of the Disciplines Had Its Day?', in D. M. McMahon and S. Moyn (eds), *Rethinking Modern European Intellectual History* (Oxford: Oxford University Press, 2014), 131.

49. P. Baert and J. Isaac, 'Intellectuals and Society: Sociological and Historical Perspectives', in G. Delanty and S. P. Turner (eds), *Routledge International Handbook of Contemporary Social and Political Theory* (Oxon, UK: Routledge, 2011), 200.

50. J. Goldstein, 'Foucault among the Sociologists: the "Disciplines" and the History of the Professions', *History and Theory* 23 (1984): 170–92.

51. Ibid., 178.

52. This is captured well in Georges Canguilhem's description of Foucault as a 'denouncer of the normality of anonymous norms'; see G. Canguilhem, 'On *Histoire de la folie* as an Event', in A. I. Davidson (ed.), *Foucault and His Interlocutors* (Chicago: University of Chicago Press, 1997), 28, 29.

53. Marchand, 'History of the Disciplines', 136.

54. W. Breckman, 'Intellectual History and the Interdisciplinary Ideal', in McMahon and Moyn, *Rethinking Modern European Intellectual History*, 281.

55. Ibid.

56. Marchand, 'History of the Disciplines', 139.

57. Ibid., 145.

58. Y. Dezalay and M. Rask Madsen, 'The Force of Law and Lawyers: Pierre Bourdieu and the Reflexive Sociology of Law', *Annual Review of Law and Social Science* 8 (2012): 436.

59. R. Martin, *Under New Management: Universities, Administrative Labor, and the Professional Turn* (Philadelphia: Temple University Press, 2012), 2.

60. Ibid., 4–5, 203.

61. For a more detailed analysis of the emergence of this form of critique in the US, and its relation to the rise of public choice theory, see A. Orford, 'Law, Economics, and the History of Free Trade: a Response', *Journal of International Law and International Relations* 11 (2015): 155–80.

62. C. Fasolt, *The Limits of History* (Chicago: University of Chicago Press, 2004).

63. C. Fasolt, '*The Limits of History* in Brief', *Historically Speaking* 6 (2005): 7–8.

64. G. A. Reisch, *How the Cold War Transformed Philosophy of Science: to the Icy Slopes of Logic* (Cambridge: Cambridge University Press, 2005).

65. See further the arguments in K. Tribe, *Land, Labour and Economic Discourse* (London: Routledge and Kegan Paul, 1978); G. M. Hodgson, *How Economics Forgot History: the Problem of Historical Specificity in Social Science* (London: Routledge, 2001); L. Magnusson, *The Tradition of Free Trade* (London: Routledge, 2004).

66. See further A. Orford, 'Scientific Reason and the Discipline of International Law', *European Journal of International Law* 25 (2014): 369–85.
67. Fasolt, *Limits of History*.
68. Reisch, *How the Cold War Transformed Philosophy of Science*, 376–79.
69. See further Orford, 'Food Security, Free Trade, and the Battle for the State'. The question of who can properly occupy the position of the international trade lawyer is the basis of the exchange I engage in with Michael Trebilcock; see further M. Trebilcock, 'A Sceptical Reaction to both Diagnosis and Prescription', *Journal of International Law and International Relations* 11 (2015): 142–46; Orford, 'Law, Economics, and the History of Free Trade', 177–78.
70. Koskenniemi, *Gentle Civilizer*, 4.
71. Ibid., 5, 511.
72. Ibid., 5.

Bibliography

Anghie, Antony. 'Colonialism and the Birth of International Institutions: Sovereignty, Economy, and the Mandate System of the League of Nations'. *NYU Journal of International Law and Politics* 34 (2002): 513–633.

Imperialism, Sovereignty and the Making of International Law (Cambridge: Cambridge University Press, 2007).

Baert, Patrick, and Joel Isaac. 'Intellectuals and Society: Sociological and Historical Perspectives'. In Gerard Delanty and Stephen P. Turner (eds), *Routledge International Handbook of Contemporary Social and Political Theory* (Oxon, UK: Routledge, 2011).

Becker Lorca, Arnulf. 'Eurocentrism in the History of International Law'. In Bardo Fassbender and Anne Peters (eds), *The Oxford Handbook of the History of International Law* (Oxford: Oxford University Press, 2012).

Berman, Nathaniel. 'Between Alliance and Localization: Nationalism and the New Oscillationism'. *NYU Journal of International Law and Policy* 26 (1994): 449–92.

'"But the Alternative Is Despair": European Nationalism and the Modernist Renewal of International Law'. *Harvard Law Review* 106 (1993): 1792–903.

Breckmann, Warren. 'Intellectual History and the Interdisciplinary Ideal'. In Darrin M. McMahon and Samuel Moyn (eds), *Rethinking Modern European Intellectual History* (Oxford: Oxford University Press, 2014).

Canguilhem, Georges. 'On Histoire De La Folie as an Event'. In Arnold I. Davidson (ed.), *Foucault and His Interlocutors* (Chicago: University of Chicago Press, 1997).

Cavallar, Georg. 'Vitoria, Grotius, Pufendorf, Wolff and Vattel: Accomplices of European Colonialism and Exploitation or True Cosmopolitans?' *Journal of the History of International Law* 10 (2008): 181–209.

Dezalay, Yves, and Mikael R. Madsen. 'The Force of Law and Lawyers: Pierre Bourdieu and the Reflexive Sociology of Law'. *Annual Review of Law and Social Science* 8 (2012): 433–52.

Fasolt, Constantin. *The Limits of History* (Chicago: University of Chicago Press, 2004).

'The Limits of History in Brief'. *Historically Speaking* 6 (2005): 5–10.

Foucault, Michel. *Folie Et Déraison: Histoire De La Folie À L'âge Classique* (Paris: Libraire Plon, 1961).

Naissance De La Clinique. Une Archéologie Du Regard Médical (Paris: Presses Universitaires de France, 1963).

Surveiller Et Punir: Naissance De La Prison (Paris: Éditions Gallimard, 1975).

Galindo, George R. B. 'Martti Koskenniemi and the Historiographical Turn in International Law'. *European Journal of International Law* 16 (2005): 539–59.

Gathii, James T. 'Neoliberalism, Colonialism and International Governance: Decentering the International Law of Governmental Legitimacy'. *Michigan Law Review* 98 (2000): 1996–2055.

Goldstein, Jan. 'Foucault among the Sociologists: the "Disciplines" and the History of the Professions'. *History and Theory* 23 (1984): 170–92.

Hobsbawm, Eric, and Terence Ranger. *The Invention of Tradition* (Cambridge: Cambridge University Press, 1983).

Hodgson, Geoffrey M. *How Economics Forgot History: the Problem of Historical Specificity in Social Science* (London: Routledge, 2001).

Hunter, Ian. 'The Figure of Man and the Territorialisation of Justice in "Enlightenment" Natural Law: Pufendorf and Vattel'. *Intellectual History Review* 23 (2013): 289–307.

'Global Justice and Regional Metaphysics: on the Critical History of the Law of Nature and Nations'. In Shaunnagh Dorsett and Ian Hunter (eds), *Law and Politics in British Colonial Thought: Transpositions of Empire* (New York: Palgrave Macmillan, 2010).

Kemmerer, Alexandra. '"We Do Not Need to Always Look to Westphalia": a Conversation with Martti Koskenniemi and Anne Orford'. *Journal of the History of International Law* 17 (2015): 1–14.

Kennedy, David. 'International Law and the Nineteenth Century: History of an Illusion'. *Quinnipiac Law Review* 17 (1997): 99–136.

Koskenniemi, Martti. 'Empire and International Law: the Real Spanish Contribution'. *University of Toronto Law Journal* 61 (2011): 1–36.

From Apology to Utopia: the Structure of International Legal Argument, reissue with a new epilogue (Cambridge: Cambridge University Press, 2006).

The Gentle Civilizer of Nations: the Rise and Fall of International Law 1870–1960 (Cambridge: Cambridge University Press, 2001).

'Histories of International Law: Dealing with Eurocentrism'. *Rechtsgeschichte* 19 (2011): 152–77.

'Histories of International Law: Significance and Problems for a Critical View'. *Temple International and Comparative Law Journal* 27 (2013): 215–40.

'A History of International Law Histories'. In Bardo Fassbender and Anne Peters (eds), *The Oxford Handbook of the History of International Law* (Oxford: Oxford University Press, 2012).

'Vitoria and Us: Thoughts on Critical Histories of International Law'. *Rechtsgeschichte* 22 (2014): 119–38.

'Why History of International Law Today'. *Rechtsgeschichte* 4 (2004): 61–66.

Lesaffer, Randall. 'International Law and Its History: the Story of an Unrequited Love'. In Matthew Craven, Malgosia Fitzmaurice and Maria Vogiatzi (eds), *Time, History and International Law* (Leiden, Netherlands: Martinus Nijhoff, 2007).

'Law and History: Law between Past and Present'. In Bart van Klink and Sanne Taekema (eds), *Law and Method: Interdisciplinary Research into Law* (Tübingen, Germany: Mohr Siebeck, 2011).

Magnusson, Lars. *The Tradition of Free Trade* (London: Routledge, 2004).

Marchand, Suzanne. 'Rethinking Modern European Intellectual History'. In Darrin M. McMahon and Samuel Moyn (eds), *Rethinking Modern European Intellectual History* (Oxford: Oxford University Press, 2014).

Martin, Randy. *Under New Management: Universities, Administrative Labor, and the Professional Turn* (Philadelphia: Temple University Press, 2011).

Obregón, Liliana. 'Completing Civilization: Nineteenth Century Criollo Interventions in International Law' (PhD diss., Harvard Law School, 2002).

Orford, Anne. 'Food Security, Free Trade, and the Battle for the State'. *Journal of International Law and International Relations* 11 (2015): 1–23.

'Law, Economics, and the History of Free Trade: a Response'. *Journal of International Law and International Relations*, 11 (2015): 155–80.

'On International Legal Method'. *London Review of International Law* 1 (2013): 166–97.

'The Past as Law or History? The Relevance of Imperialism for Modern International Law'. In Mark Toufayan, Emmanuelle Tourme-Jouannet and Helene Ruiz Fabri (eds), *International Law and New Approaches to the Third World: between Repetition and Renewal* (Paris: Société de Législation Comparée, 2013).

'Scientific Reason and the Discipline of International Law'. *European Journal of International Law* 25 (2014): 369–85.

'Theorizing Free Trade'. In Anne Orford and Florian Hoffmann (eds), *The Oxford Handbook of the Theory of International Law* (Oxford: Oxford University Press, 2016).

Reisch, George A. *How the Cold War Transformed Philosophy of Science: to the Icy Slopes of Logic* (Cambridge: Cambridge University Press, 2005).

Riles, Annelise. 'Is the Law Hopeful?' *Cornell Law Faculty Working Paper* 68 (2010).

Skinner, Quentin. 'Meaning and Understanding in the History of Ideas'. *History and Theory* 8 (1969): 3–53.

 Visions of Politics, vol. 1, *Regarding Method* (Cambridge: Cambridge University Press, 2002).

Trebilcock, Michael. 'A Sceptical Reaction to Both Diagnosis and Prescription'. *Journal of International Law and International Relations* 11 (2015): 142–46.

Tribe, Keith. *Land, Labour and Economic Discourse* (London: Routledge, 1978).

Tuck, Richard. *The Rights of War and Peace: Political Thought and the International Order from Grotius to Kant* (Oxford: Oxford University Press, 2001).

von Bernstorff, Jochen. *Der Glaube an Das Universale Recht: Zur Völkerrechtstheorie Hans Kelsens Und Seiner Schüler* (Baden-Baden, Germany: Nomos, 2001).

Zapatero, Pablo. 'Legal Imagination in Vitoria: the Power of Ideas'. *Journal of the History of International Law* 11 (2009): 221–71.

Even the Dead Will Not Be Safe

International Law and the Struggle over Tradition

ANDREW LANG AND SUSAN MARKS

How and why might we come to know the past? According to Walter Benjamin, 'the past can be seized only as an image that flashes up at the instant when it can be recognized and is never seen again.'[1] Benjamin continues: 'To articulate the past historically does not mean to recognize it "the way it really was"'. Rather, it 'means to seize hold of a memory as it flashes up at a moment of danger'.[2] What kind of danger? Writing in 1933, Benjamin had a very particular and dreadful peril in mind, but he characterizes the moment of danger in general terms as 'a conformism that is about to overpower tradition'. 'In every era', he writes, 'the attempt must be made anew to wrest tradition away from a conformism that is about to overpower it'.[3]

Benjamin is presenting here a distinctive vision of history-writing that ties it, on the one hand, to the idea of an arresting 'flash' that lights up in an instant and is gone, and on the other hand, to the idea of tradition that is always on the verge of lapsing into conformism. We come to know the past (he seems to be suggesting) not, or not primarily, by means of rational explication or interpretation, but through an embodied and even perhaps in some sense magical process that enables us to recognize and seize the there-and-then in the here-and-now. And we do this – we take hold of memories as they flash before us – in order to reclaim the tradition to which those memories belong from the forces that would otherwise overpower it. For Benjamin, '[o]nly that historian will have the gift for fanning the spark of hope in the past who is firmly convinced that *even the dead* will not be safe from the enemy if he [the enemy] wins'.[4]

Viewed in this light, history-writing – the 'articulation of the past historically', in Benjamin's formulation – is a terrain of struggle over tradition. Conversely, the struggle over tradition reveals history-writing as an effort to rescue the dead not just from obscurity, but from misappropriation, understood by Benjamin as appropriation in the service of the ruling order. The English word 'tradition', from the Latin *tradere* (to hand over or hand down), refers both to an action and to the object of that action. We do certain things at certain times 'by tradition'. We also appeal to 'tradition' as a reason for doing things. 'Traditions' are our inheritance from earlier generations. Theologically speaking, there is divine authority not only in the scriptures, but also in oral 'tradition'. Aesthetically speaking, it is of interest when someone follows 'in the tradition' of another. In one early and now obsolete usage, 'tradition' denoted as well the act of giving up, surrender or – most intriguingly, considering what Benjamin writes – betrayal.

International law is a tradition in the sense, and to the extent, that it is made up of beliefs, practices, habits and unwritten rules which are handed down and carried forward within the community of international lawyers. What is at stake in the struggle over this tradition? What forms of conformism currently threaten to overpower it? Can historical research 'fan the spark of hope in the past' of international law by challenging those forms? What would it mean to seize hold of international legal history through acts of recognition and apperception, themselves occasioned by momentary instances of what Benjamin calls elsewhere 'profane illumination'?[5] Our chapter takes up these questions. But they are big questions, and we will only be able to address them here in a small and suggestive way. In doing so, we turn to the manifestly illuminating work of Martti Koskenniemi, which is also profane in Benjamin's sense that its author penetrates the mysteries of the world as a 'reader' and 'thinker', rather than as a 'dreamer' or an 'ecstatic'.[6]

We will begin by revisiting Martti's marvellous study of the history of international law, *The Gentle Civilizer of Nations*.[7] Before *The Gentle Civilizer* was published, Martti presented parts of the study in a series of lectures at the University of Cambridge, and we will also refer to those. Both in the preliminary lectures and in the book, he made very clear the conformist threat to international legal tradition that most troubled him: managerialism – the eclipse of ethical engagement and political responsibility by a form of professional practice in which international lawyers experience and represent themselves as the 'diplomat's [and international business executive's] best helper'.[8] We propose in what follows that Martti's history of international law can be read as an attempt to counter this threat by recovering a practice of responsible moral agency which he takes to have been lost, or badly weakened, in contemporary times. How does he go about this? After all, agency is not given, but made.[9]

In the succeeding parts of our chapter, we highlight three aspects of his method (if that is the right word). One invokes the power of similarity, setting up exemplars or role models from the past. Another puts us into contact with the past, such that it becomes an active force in the present. A third involves the production of artefacts for use in these ways. Similarity and contact recall the phenomenon of 'sympathetic magic' which anthropologists once saw as a feature of pre-modern cultural life. Thus, there was the idea that an effect could be produced simply by imitating it. And there was the idea that things or people that had been in contact would continue interacting even after contact had been severed. In Benjamin's hands, sympathetic magic becomes the 'mimetic faculty', the human 'gift of producing similarities ... [and] of recognizing them'.[10] Benjamin thought the mimetic faculty was at its strongest in pre-modern societies, but he did not doubt that it also persisted in modernity in multifarious forms. As we shall see, the 'flash' that was his way of expressing historical comprehension may be one such form.

12.1   Two Lectures and a Meeting

In late 1997 Martti Koskenniemi delivered the Hersch Lauterpacht Memorial Lectures at the University of Cambridge. The lecture series was inaugurated in 1983 to commemorate the contribution to international law of Sir Hersch Lauterpacht, Whewell Professor of International Law at that university from 1938 to 1955. Martti began his first lecture by evoking another lecture, delivered in the same city almost sixty years earlier by Hersch Lauterpacht himself.[11] The occasion was a meeting of the Cambridge University League of Nations Union that took place very shortly after Lauterpacht's arrival to take up his chair, in November 1938. At this moment of impending war, Lauterpacht stood before the assembled enthusiasts for the League of Nations to discuss the failure of international law and institutions to keep the peace. As Martti recounts the story, Lauterpacht spoke in a 'rhetorical, anxious tone',[12] appealing directly to his audience: '[W]hat have we to do?'

> Ought we to abandon the League ... ? Ought we to maintain it and adapt it to the needs of a retrogressive period? Ought we to [reform it] so as to make acceptable for everyone? Ought we to admit that if peace cannot be achieved by collective effort, there are other good things than can be achieved through it?[13]

The answers were clear to Lauterpacht. There must be no giving up on the project of liberal internationalism. Equally, however, there could be no denying that the 'we' to whom he appealed had become thoroughly 'estranged from the course of inter-war politics – the politics of national over common interests, ... the reign of "short-sighted benefits" over stable and balanced growth, and the rise of dictatorships "on a scale unprecedented in history"'.[14] How were he and his audience to deal with this estrangement? The strategy they needed to adopt appears to have been no less clear to Lauterpacht. Just as, centuries earlier, the man whom he regarded as the 'father' of international law, Hugo Grotius, had '[sought] authority from the customs of the Romans', so Lauterpacht would invite his audience to '[turn] to the past'.[15] He and they would retain their relevance, hold onto their principles and fight back in the name of their community, their tradition, by recovering the memory of 'better peoples and better times'.[16] Thus, Martti reports:

> To find a place for law in a dangerous time, Lauterpacht looked back to the middle of nineteenth century, hoping to resuscitate its liberal rationalism and its ideal of the rule of law, its belief in progress, its certainty about the sense and direction of history.[17]

Martti writes of the 'tone of unmitigated Victorian nostalgia' that inflected Lauterpacht's lecture as he spoke of the 'heyday of the bourgeois century' and lamented the decline of progressive outlooks, initiatives and institutions since that time.[18] In Lauterpacht's words, 'How immeasurably far backwards do we seem to have travelled from those days of unbounded optimism?'[19] As is indicated also in the passage quoted above, Lauterpacht regarded the inter-war years as a period of 'retrogression'. In Martti's gloss, this was a 'retrogression from the cosmopolitanism that inspired Wilson in Paris in 1918–19, but which owes its origin to the high liberalism of a century earlier'.[20] Yet if Lauterpacht 'never gave up' the liberal ideals of the nineteenth century,[21] Martti observes that he also belonged firmly in the 'modernist camp' of the twentieth century.[22] Believing that '[l]aw is how it is interpreted', he hewed to a sophisticated modern interpretivism that stressed the 'primacy of interpretation over substance, [and] process over rule'. This led him into 'an institutional pragmatism that', Martti notes, 'is ours too'.[23]

As Martti presents him, then, Lauterpacht 'bridges the gap between the liberal rationalism of the nineteenth century and the functional pragmatism of the late twentieth century'. His commitment to Victorian ideals of progress and the 'harmony of interests' combines with a modern 'hermeneutics of judging' to give his work both a 'historical and con-temporary feel'. Martti concludes: 'Close and distant at the same time, [Lauterpacht] is uniquely placed to provide an understanding of why it is that we stand now where we do'.[24] So where *do* we stand now (or where did we stand in 1997, when Martti delivered his lecture)? In the discussion that followed this evocation of Lauterpacht's 1938 address to the Cambridge University League of Nations Union, as well as in Martti's other speeches and texts, it emerged that his interest in Lauterpacht was occasioned at least in part by a belief that the later twentieth century too was a period of decline and fall for international law. For Martti, this fall consisted of a descent into precisely that functional pragmatism which Lauterpacht had anticipated. By the end of the twentieth century, functional pragmatism had become pervasive 'managerialism'.

In Martti's telling, the 'managerial' mind-set sees international law as functionally responsive to the objectives, values and interests of states, and assesses it by reference to its effectiveness in facilitating the achievement of those objectives, values and interests.[25] Managerial international lawyers tend to lose sight of the gap between law as an instrument and law as a 'surface over which we carry out our projects and ... criticize those of others'.[26] At the same time, managerial international lawyers are disposed to treat the law's purposes as given, asking only questions about how those purposes should be implemented, rather than 'engaging the point of international law' as an object of contestation.[27] As they imagine and undertake it, the role of the international lawyer is to be 'counsel for the functional power-holder'; there is no, or only very limited, space for acting as a 'moral politician' who uses 'critical reason [to] measure today's state of affairs from the perspective of an ideal of universality'.[28] At its worst, managerialism obscures 'the way power works and [makes] particular intellectual or social hierarchies appear as natural aspects of our lives'.[29]

Martti writes that, like Lauterpacht, 'we too are historically situated in a project that is not only an abstract exercise in ideas but a contin-uum of political, moral and professional choices'.[30] If managerialism inclines us to forget this, then for Martti international legal renewal depends on recovering the memory. In practical terms, the challenge is to locate resources that could engender a sense of responsible moral agency in the professional practice and self-image of the international lawyer. Following his forebear, Martti finds these resources by turning to the past. *The Gentle Civilizer of Nations* famously traces the origins of modern international law to the 'men of 1873': a group of European lawyers, diplomats and politicians who met in Ghent in September 1873 to inaugurate the *Institut de droit international*. As he depicts them, these men were people with projects: not 'philosopher-lawyers', but men of action; practical, engaged men, who were convinced that the role of the lawyer was to contribute to social progress, rather than observe it from a scholarly distance.[31] Domestically, their causes were character-istic of mid-century Victorian liberalism: penal reform, electoral reform and enfranchisement, child labour, universal education.[32] Internationally, their instincts were cosmopolitan.

Despite the economic depression of the 1870s, these men were advo-cates for freedom of commerce and the protection of property rights, taking such measures to be integral to any strategy for assuring peace among nations. Disturbed by the conduct of the Franco-Prussian War in 1870–71, they looked to humanitarian law to make hostilities less savage. They urged arbitration as a means of international dispute settlement, and encouraged efforts to promote mutual understanding between nations, in the interests of securing peace and preventing unnecessary war. Above all, they adhered to a vision of law which conceived it not as sovereign command, but as the emanation of a 'popular consciousness', itself best understood as 'popular conscience'. To them, the jurist's task was to act as the mouthpiece of that popular consciousness/conscience, discerning its content through scientific reason, philosophical reflection and historical enquiry.[33] Against that backdrop, Martti shows how the men of 1873 came to understand their role in highly moralized terms, and to represent their new profession (now notoriously) as the 'legal conscience of the civilized world'.[34] It is this moralized sensibility which, in Martti's telling, most clearly sets these inaugural international legal professionals apart from the managerialists of today.

We have given, we hope, a fair account of Martti's diagnosis and pre-scription. But how is the recovery to occur? Historical investigation can put before us a moralized, as distinct from managerialist, sensibility, but how is it to make that image impinge on lived reality? It is a striking part of Martti's wager that 'connection' is the real battle in the strug-gle over international legal tradition. Through Martti, we connect with Lauterpacht and, beyond him, with the men of 1873. Through Martti's connection with Lauterpacht, we also connect with the earlier nineteenth century 'classical liberals', and still further back, with Grotius. At one level, this multi-generational story spanning centuries simply signals that there exists a shared disciplinary tradition to which all international lawyers belong. It situates us on a common historical trajectory. In doing so, it emphasizes the importance of individuals and their projects, and invites us to consider the specific conditions under which those individuals became as they were and acted as they did, along with the specific contexts in which their projects arose, took shape and were (more or less conflictually) pursued. At another level, however, Martti's multi-generational account clearly invites us to consider as well what those individuals and their projects might mean to *us*.

Lauterpacht and the men of 1873 appear as, in some way, role models. While Martti comments on Lauterpacht's tone of unmitigated nostalgia, he is certainly aware that his own writing has a tone of nostalgia too. That is part of the sense in which Lauterpacht is a role model. The original meaning of nostalgia was homesickness. First discussed in the seventeenth century, it was an illness diagnosed in Swiss mercenaries fighting in the lowlands of northern France and Italy who became sick from longing for the mountains of home. Nostalgia comes, as we know, from feelings of loss and estrangement. Of course, Martti's admiration for Lauterpacht and the men of 1873 is by no means uncritical. It is plain that the world in which they lived is not one to which he would seek to return. Nonetheless, the thrust of his narrative is that there was something valuable in the work of Lauterpacht and the men of 1873 which has been lost, and that that loss is our loss. The estrangement from some form of moralized sensibility, Martti seems to suggest, has estranged us from our tradition and thus also from ourselves. In putting this across, Martti asks us to notice Lauterpacht's *feel*, which is both antiquated or 'historical' and 'contemporary'. Holding up to our eyes his shifting telescope, he leads us to *see* that Lauterpacht is at once 'distant' and 'close'. Like Martti himself, Lauterpacht becomes a 'bridge' which *connects* us to the past – and does so not just in a symbolic way, but also through the senses.

As foreshadowed in our introductory remarks, our own wager is that this phenomenon of 'connection' has something to do with the exercise of what Benjamin called the mimetic faculty. To explore this further, we need now to make a short theoretical side-trip to (re)familiarize ourselves with the main, relevant contours of the concept to which Benjamin himself appeals: mimesis.

12.2 On Mimesis and Sympathetic Magic

Mimesis is a concept with a tangled and fascinating history.[35] An ancient Greek term, it is most commonly translated into English as 'imitation', but also sometimes translated as, or associated with, a variety of other terms, including: correspondence, emulation, resemblance, mimicry, verisimilitude, representation, depiction, realism, repetition, simulation and duplication. The word comes from the root *mimos*, meaning a person who imitates, as well as a particular theatrical or perhaps dance genre of the time that revolved around imitation. Although he did not invent the term, Plato appears to have set the initial, and in some respects enduring, frame of reference for thinking about the concept of mimesis. He used the term to theorize representation and what he took to be its dangers. Representation posed for Plato the question of the relation between images and reality. Inasmuch as that is a relation of similarity, but necessarily also of difference, the thrust of his analysis was that representation opens the way to distortion, deception and manipulation. Mimesis encourages us to think we are confronted with reality when in fact we are confronted with biased and falsifying images. Plato's student, Aristotle, was famously more positive in his assessment of aesthetic representation. To him, mimesis might not be without dangers, but it is also a matter of great skill and has the capacity to promote virtue and understanding.

Accounts of mimesis indicate that, from Roman times until the eighteenth century, the term was most commonly rendered as the Latin *imitatio*. Whereas for Plato and Aristotle, the focus was on the imitative relationship between images and reality or between art and life, for thinkers of these later times a primary concern was the imitative relationship between a master and his (or, much more rarely, her) disciples. Thus, mimesis came to refer to the emulation of exemplary forerunners. Importantly, a distinction appears to have been drawn between emulation and 'mere' copying. Aspiring artists and writers were taught to use skill and judgement in learning from role models and deploying old forms in new ways. Beginning around the seventeenth century, however, this way of approaching artistic activity and knowledge production began very evidently to lose ground. Descartes articulated a philosophical 'method' that involved searching 'for no knowledge other than what can be found within myself.'[36] Later philosophers and artists likewise emphasized contemplation and originality – the individual genius, rather than the fertile tradition – as the basis of scholarly insight and artistic achievement.

But if modernity became principally preoccupied with liberation from tradition, modern (and postmodern) theorists went on to use the concept of mimesis to highlight and investigate a huge array of ways in which 'the doctrine of the similar'[37] nonetheless remained pivotal. Their work spans literary theory,[38] psychoanalytic theory,[39] critical social theory,[40] historiographical theory,[41] anthropology,[42] post-colonial theory,[43] and art and architectural theory,[44] among other bodies of thought. In very general terms, it seems that at least two themes run through this literature. One is the idea that what we may imagine as 'autonomous' often has an imitative aspect. This may be unconscious, as with Freud's theory of identification with others as the basis of selfhood. Or it may be conscious, as with literary accounts of convention, influence and the confidence or anxiety associated with it. But either way, mimesis points to the difference that lies at the core of identity, the succession without which there can be no initiative. The second theme concerns the ambiguities of imitation. Is it a compliment to the one imitated or an insult? Scholars remind us that satire and parody work by producing resemblances, and so too does mimicry. In an important contribution to post-colonial theory, Homi Bhabha postulates a concept of 'colonial mimicry'.[45] From the perspective of the colonizer, the colonized must be sufficiently similar to be 'civilizable', but sufficiently different to justify domination. Yet this condition of being 'almost the same, but not quite' is also unsettling, inasmuch as colonial authority is threatened by a mimetic relation that is inevitably 'at once resemblance and menace'.[46]

The conjunction of resemblance and menace is one way in which the ambiguities of mimesis may be felt, but it is not the only one. To bring out another, it is helpful to return for a moment to Renaissance *imitatio*. In his study of mimesis, Matthew Potolsky recalls the account given in 1336 by the Italian poet Petrarch of his ascent of Mount Ventoux in southern France.[47] Petrarch explains that he wanted to make the climb because of a passage he had read in Livy. Livy recounts in this passage how Philip of Macedon had climbed Mount Haemus in Thrace because he believed that he would be able to see from the summit as far as Italy in the west and the Danube in the north, and this would help him as he contemplated war with Rome. Potolsky observes that 'Petrarch's desire is imitative'; he wants to climb a mountain in order to gain an expansive view, just as the ancient king Philip of Macedon had done. Yet 'this imitation is complicated by ambivalence'.[48] For it was part of the point of Livy's retelling that Philip never got to see the anticipated panorama: the summit of Mount Haemus was shrouded in mist when he reached it, so his journey was futile and he only succeeded in exhausting his troops.[49] As Potolsky reads it, the 'example of Philip suggests that, although the ancients remain a source of inspiration for the present, their path is fatally flawed'. Petrarch plainly finds something inspiring in Livy's story of Philip. He seeks to 'retain the idea of classical imitation [but] without necessarily endorsing all the ideals of the classical world'.[50]

So far we have seen that mimesis confronts us with the role of imitation in human and social affairs. It also confronts us with the ambiguities of imitation, whether because there is mocking menace as well as resemblance, or, more benignly, because what is involved is inspiration rather than endorsement in all respects. Insofar as imitation is a token of admiration, the concept of mimesis delivers a reminder that that admiration is rarely unmixed or without some reservation or disquiet, and that a heightened awareness of imperfections may be among the by-products of enthusiastic copying. Our focus to this point has been on mimesis in the relation between images and reality (art and life, narrative and experience, representation and truth) and in the relation between people or groups of people (master and disciple, self and other, colonizer and colonized). However, mimesis does not arise only in those relations, and before concluding this brief survey of ideas associated with the concept of mimesis, we should note an influential strand in the study of mimesis that goes back to the work in the late nineteenth century of the Scottish anthropologist and scholar of comparative religion, James Frazer.

Frazer's monumental work *The Golden Bough* (first published in 1890) is commonly credited with being the first systematic study of the practices and principles of 'magic'.[51] The study was based mostly on information about the non-European world related to Frazer by other anthropologists and by travellers, but it also included discussion of European practices, both pre-Christian and, controversially, within Christianity. Frazer argued that magic revolved around two general principles.[52] One, which he called the 'Law of Similarity', was that 'like produces like, or that an effect resembles its cause'. Thus the 'magician infers that he can produce any effect he desires merely by imitating it'. The second, which Frazer called 'the Law of Contact', was that 'things which have once been in contact with each other continue to act on each other at a distance after the physical contact has been severed'. Here the magician 'infers that whatever he does to a material object will affect equally the person with whom the object was once in contact'. Frazer proposed that both these 'laws' could be 'comprehended under the general name of Sympathetic Magic' – 'sympathetic', because 'both assume that things act on each other at a distance through a secret sympathy'.[53]

Frazer's idea of sympathetic magic extends the discussion of mimesis so that it encompasses not only the relation between images and reality and between people or groups of people, but also the relation between people and objects. Indeed, his idea extends mimesis so that it encompasses the entire animate and inanimate worlds in their complex interrelation.

As Potolsky puts it, *The Golden Bough* describes a 'sympathetic network [that] binds humans, animals and objects in a kind of mimetic network of reciprocal influence'.[54] Frazer discusses examples of imitative magic that include the burning of effigies of people to whom harm is desired to be done, and the display of images or totems of fish, birds and other animals to encourage food supply. He also discusses examples that show how contact activates the mimetic magic in a special way. Body parts, clothing and footprints are treated as though they maintained a connection to the person to whom they belonged long after any physical connection to that person has been broken. In one practice, a woman digs up earth from a man's footprint, puts it in a pot, and plants a flower in it so as to cause love to blossom between them.[55]

As these examples also illustrate, sympathetic magic involves the production of artefacts – effigies, totems, flower-pots – and their use to take advantage of correspondences between the animate and inanimate. On the one hand, the artefact may work by imitation or representation – an effigy that resembles a person, a totem that mimics the swimming of a fish. On the other hand, it may trade on contiguity or on the power of what Frazer terms 'contagion' – a flower that acts on the 'owner' of a footprint out of the soil of which it was grown. In both cases, the artefact brings what is distant into active relation with those near at hand. The anthropologist Michael Taussig has drawn on Frazer's work to explore the phenomenon of mimesis in capitalist modernity.[56] Taussig is particularly interested in this artefactual aspect. He highlights 'the notion emerging from Frazer's discussion of imitative magic as power that the copy extracts from the original'.[57] To Taussig, copies do not merely reflect their original; they interact with their original in a way that renders the latter susceptible of appropriation and influence. In his words, '[t]he wonder of mimesis lies in the copy drawing on the character and power of the original, to the point whereby the representation may even assume that character and that power'.[58]

12.3 Fanning the Spark of Hope in the Past

Our side-trip has taken us across many branches of thought and many, widely disparate historical epochs. For all that this concept is concerned with similarity and contact, it is a feature of accounts of mimesis that they have a decidedly dizzying quality, and we recognize that ours may be no exception. Steadying ourselves now, we can begin to discern some elements that bear on the issues we raised earlier. You will recall that our interest was in the tradition of international law, and that we found in Martti Koskenniemi's work the argument that managerialism is the 'conformism' that currently threatens this tradition. We followed something of Martti's attempt to wrest the tradition of international law away from its managerialist orthodoxy by recovering a moralized sensibility and commitment to responsible agency that existed in former times.[59] This took him back to Hersch Lauterpacht in the 1930s and earlier still, to the founders of the *Institut de droit international* in 1873, with their sense of being the 'legal conscience of the civilized world'. What unfolded was a multi-generational story in which Lauterpacht served as a bridge, connecting us to the past.

What is to be gleaned from our discussion of mimesis? In the first place, *similarity* is plainly central to Martti's method. As already suggested, Lauterpacht and the men of 1873 are presented as, in some way, role models. The logic of Martti's story is that these men incarnate the kind of sensibility we need to recover. From the perspective of his critique of managerialism in international law, they are our exemplary forerunners, the ancestors on whom we should model ourselves. Just as a crowd might seek to produce harm to a person by burning him in effigy or a community might seek to produce an abundance of fish by scattering fish-shaped totems in the sea, so Martti seeks to produce a new generation of morally charged international lawyers by prompting the imitation of earlier generations of them. Importantly, however, the principle of similarity is not the principle of sameness. Needless to say, Martti is not seeking to encourage the revival of a professional self-identity as the 'legal conscience of the civilized world'. Nor is Lauterpacht's 'liberal rationalism, ideal of the rule of law, belief in progress and certainty about the sense and direction of history' a helpful outlook for the project Martti envisages. Like Petrarch following in the footsteps of Philip of Macedon – or rather, like Livy narrating the story of Philip – Martti offers his history as a source of *inspiration*, inviting us to imitate these international lawyers from the past but without necessarily endorsing all the ideals they espoused.

Second, Martti's method also involves *contact*. Like the law of similarity, the law of contact presupposes that things act on each other at a distance. That distance may be spatial – a distant location – but, as we have just seen, it may also be temporal – a distant time or distant times. There is no soil to dig up from the footprints of those who lived long ago, and nor are there generally any body parts left or items of clothing. But the metonymic principle of contiguity still finds forms of expression that are distinct from those associated with the metaphorical principle of resemblance. Martti reports that Lauterpacht is reputed to have kept an engraving of Grotius on the wall of his study.[60] If true, Grotius died in 1645 and Martti does not say when the engraving was made and, in particular, whether it was made before 1645. But this surely does not matter. Whether or not the engraving had ever had – or could ever have had – any direct physical contact with Grotius, it seems reasonable to suppose that Lauterpacht hoped to produce by it a kind of *contagion* through which Grotius would act on his (Lauterpacht's) thoughts and on his writing, and would guide him in his work. We have seen that Martti hopes to produce a kind of contagion too. He wants to bring Lauterpacht himself into our world, and to make us 'see' and 'feel' him as a presence who might act on us.

A third aspect of Martti's method concerns the production of *artefacts*. It is, for the most part, *things* that do the work of activating mimetic connection. These things may be fabricated objects, like effigies, totems, flower-pots or engravings. They may also be intellectual products like texts. Petrarch only knew about Philip of Macedon's ascent of Mount Haemus because he read about it in Livy's *History of Rome*. And reading about it there, he was evidently struck by something in Livy's telling of the story. But it seems that what really inspired Petrarch was the classical idea of imitation – Roman *imitatio* – itself. He set out to recapture it and give it fresh life in post-classical times. Livy's text was able to inspire Petrarch to imitate Philip because it was a point of contact with this idea. Might we think of Martti's various texts in a similar way? If so, they can be understood to perform something of the function of the flower-pot in the south Slavic practice we mentioned earlier. Just as the flower-pot serves to put the woman into contact with the distant owner of the footprint, so the text would serve to put us into contact with earlier generations of international lawyers. And just as the flower-pot is made out of the footprint but does not resemble the footprint or its owner, so the relation between the text and those earlier generations would not be a relation of fidelity. It would need to be rooted in or 'made out of' the historical evidence, but it would depend less on faithful accuracy – on presenting the past 'the way it really was' (to recall Benjamin's phrase) – than on correspondence.

Texts are one thing, but as described in earlier sections of this chapter, Martti has not only written about our connection to Lauterpacht and the men of 1873. With his Hersch Lauterpacht Memorial lecture and its evocation of Lauterpacht's own lecture in the same city almost sixty years earlier, he has also *performed* it. As recalled earlier, the word 'mimesis' was originally associated with a particular kind of performance, though

apparently little is known about the genre. Whilst performance is among
the simplest kinds of mimetic artefact, it may involve forms of imitation,
impersonation or simulation that are quite subtle. Martti tells of how
Lauterpacht confessed at the outset of his 1938 lecture to the Cambridge
University League of Nations Union that his subject was one 'about which
he felt so strongly that he was unable to trust the "freely spoken word"';
he would 'read from a manuscript in order to maintain restraint and
deliberation'.[61] But in fact, Martti recounts, Lauterpacht did not did not
always maintain his usual high standard of restraint and deliberation in
this lecture. Lapsing into 'informality and engagement', he 'switched to
the first personal plural' and posed the questions we quoted earlier on
('[W]hat have we to do?' etc.).[62] Martti's own complex interweaving of
biography and autobiography, historical narrative and apparent personal
disclosure[63] replicates this, closing the gap between the 'first persons' of
the past and present by bringing them together in the body of the speaker
and the circumstances of the performance.

We have spoken a lot in this chapter about Martti Koskenniemi's work
on the history of international law because we find it inspiring and con-
tagious and truly inimitable. But we are also intrigued by the possibilities
of the mimetic faculty for historical scholarship in the international legal
field more generally. We noted earlier Benjamin's characterization of the
mimetic faculty as the 'human gift of producing similarities ... [and]
of recognising them'. In a similar vein, Taussig writes of the mimetic
'sixth sense'.[64] It seems likely to us that this gift or sixth sense is itself
socio-historically produced. The history of mimesis is presumably also
the history of the mimetic faculty. Leaving that vast terrain of enquiry to
one side, what fascinates us is the way, with mimesis, *the copy becomes the
thing*. As Taussig puts it in a passage we quoted earlier, the copy '[draws]
on the character and power of the original, to the point whereby the representation may even assume that character and that power'. Of course,
others have theorized this phenomenon in many different ways.[65] But here
we want to follow Taussig in stressing its artefactual dimensions. Mimesis
is, above all, about making things – not (for the most part) things to be
exchanged, but things to be used, and not things for instrumental use,
but things for 'magical' use, things for use in establishing sympathetic
connection across space and time.

The anthropologist Marilyn Strathern has written of a way of thinking
about history in the Melanesian societies that she has studied in which
the focus is less on interpretation than on 'improvisation'.[66] In this way of
thinking, history is seen not as material to be synthesized, contextualized

and decoded, but as a basis for improvised 'performances'. These performances are, in turn, seen as significant for their 'effects': they are for use 'the way [one] may use a knife'; one should create things with them 'the way [one] may create a mask'.[67] What kind of use? Create things to do what? Strathern reports that, in the practices she has studied, one aspect is to show 'how people act as though they had power when confronted with the untoward'.[68] We have been concerned in this chapter with the untoward, in the shape of Benjamin's 'conformism that is about to overpower tradition'. How can people act as though they retained power when their tradition is on the verge of being overpowered? The move we have discussed is to turn to the past. On this premise, it is in the earlier generations that the 'spark of hope' is to be found. The past may be a foreign country, yet those not residing there can be enabled to 'go-between'.[69] We *can* seize the past and bring it into active relation to the present. But if Benjamin is right, we can only seize it as an 'image that flashes up at the instant when it can be recognized' and then is gone. The 'flash' of recognition reveals history not simply as a set of facts to be known, but as a force to be felt, a secret sympathy to be sensed, and an occasion to be grasped for producing new artefacts that might be used to activate new connections.

Notes

1. W. Benjamin, 'Thesis V on the Philosophy of History', in *Illuminations*, H. Zorn (trans.) (London: Pimlico, 1999), 255.
2. W. Benjamin, 'Thesis VI on the Philosophy of History', ibid., 255.
3. Ibid.
4. Ibid., emphasis original.
5. W. Benjamin, *One Way Street and Other Writings*, E. Jephcott and K. Shorter (trans.) (London: Verso, 1997), 237.
6. Ibid.
7. M. Koskenniemi, *The Gentle Civilizer of Nations: The Rise and Fall of International Law 1870–1960* (Cambridge: Cambridge University Press, 2001).
8. M. Koskenniemi, 'Letter to the Editors of the Symposium', *American Journal of International Law* 93 (1999): 352.
9. Timothy Mitchell makes this point in the context of a fascinating account of the fabrication of 'agencies, connections, interactions and forms of violence' in modern Egypt. See T. Mitchell, *Rule of Experts: Egypt, Techno-Politics, Modernity* (Berkeley: University of California Press, 2002), 52.
10. W. Benjamin, 'On the Mimetic Faculty', in *Reflections: Essays, Aphorisms, Autobiographical Writings*, E. Jephcott (trans.) (New York: Schocken, 1978), 333.
11. The story is retold in Koskenniemi, *Gentle Civilizer of Nations*, 353–55, and M. Koskenniemi, 'Lauterpacht: the Victorian Tradition in International Law', *European Journal of International Law* 8 (1997): 215–17.

12. Koskenniemi, 'Lauterpacht', 216.
13. Ibid., 215–16.
14. Ibid., 216.
15. Ibid.
16. Ibid. See S. C. Neff (ed.), *Hugo Grotius: on the Law of War and Peace* (Cambridge: Cambridge University Press, 2012), 15: 'History in relation to our subject is useful in two ways: it supplies both illustrations and judgements. The illustrations have greater weight in proportion as they are taken from better times and better peoples; thus we have preferred ancient examples, Greek and Roman, to the rest'.
17. Koskenniemi, 'Lauterpacht'.
18. Ibid., 217.
19. Ibid., 216.
20. Ibid., 217.
21. Ibid.
22. Ibid., 218.
23. Ibid., 219.
24. Ibid., 221.
25. M. Koskenniemi, 'What Use for Sovereignty Today?', *Asian Journal of International Law* 1 (2011): 66; M. Koskenniemi, 'Miserable Comforters: International Relations as a New Natural Law', *European Journal of International Relations* 15 (2009): 406ff.
26. Koskenniemi, 'Miserable Comforters', 412.
27. M. Koskenniemi, 'The Politics of International Law – 20 Years Later', *European Journal of International Law* 20 (2009): 18.
28. Koskenniemi, 'Miserable Comforters', 401, 411, 414, 415.
29. Ibid., 16.
30. Koskenniemi, 'Lauterpacht', 211, 215.
31. Koskenniemi, *Gentle Civilizer of Nations*, 57–58.
32. See e.g. ibid., 18.
33. Ibid., 51–54.
34. Ibid., 41.
35. Most of what follows is drawn from M. Potolsky, *Mimesis* (New York: Routledge, 2006), an exemplary survey of the concept to which we are heavily indebted. See also A. Melberg, *Theories of Mimesis* (Cambridge: Cambridge University Press, 1995), and G. Gebauer and C. Wulf, *Mimesis: Culture, Art, Society*, D. Reneau (trans.) (Berkeley: University of California Press, 1996).
36. R. Descartes, *Discourse on Method*, D. A. Cress (trans.) (Indianapolis, IN: Hackett, 1998), 5.
37. See W. Benjamin, 'Doctrine of the Similar (1933)', K. Tarnowski (trans.), reprinted in *New German Critique* 17 (1979): 65–69.
38. Perhaps the best known work on mimesis is Erich Auerbach's study of the 'representation of reality in Western Literature', first published in 1946. See E. Auberbach, *Mimesis: the Representation of Reality in Western Literature*, W. R. Trask (trans.) (Princeton, NJ: Princeton University Press, 2003). Regarding the extraordinary conditions under which this text was composed, see A. Krystal, 'The Book of Books', *The New Yorker*, 9 December 2013.
39. See e.g. S. Freud, *The Joke and Its Relation to the Unconscious*, J. Crick (trans.) (London: Penguin, 2002). The concept is also held to be latent in much of Freud's other work, e.g. on the theory of identification.

40. See e.g. T. Adorno and M Horkheimer, *Dialectic of Enlightenment*, J. Cumming (trans.) (New York: Continuum, 1993), 180–86.
41. See e.g. H. White, *Figural Realism: Studies in the Mimesis Effect* (Baltimore: Johns Hopkins University Press, 2000).
42. See e.g. M. T. Taussig, *Mimesis and Alterity: a Particular History of the Senses* (London: Routledge, 1993).
43. See e.g. H. K. Bhabha, *The Location of Culture* (London: Routledge, 1994).
44. See e.g. T. Adorno, *Aesthetic Theory*, R. Hullot-Kentor (trans.) (New York: Continuum, 2002), and, in architectural theory, N. Leach, *Camouflage* (Cambridge, MA: MIT Press, 2006).
45. H. Bhabha, *Location of Culture*, 121–31.
46. Ibid., 86, emphasis omitted.
47. Potolsky, *Mimesis*, 62–63. See F. Petrarch, *Selections from the Canzoniere and Other Works*, M. Musa (trans.) (Oxford: Oxford University Press, 1985), 11.
48. Potolsky, *Mimesis*, 62.
49. Livy writes, 'When they came down they said nothing to contradict the general notion – not because the different seas, mountains and rivers could in fact be seen from one place, but to prevent their futile expedition from providing material for mirth'. See T. Livy, *Rome and the Mediterranean: Books XXXI–XLV*, H. Bettenson (trans.) (London: Penguin, 1976), XL: 22, 462.
50. Potolsky, *Mimesis*, 63.
51. J. Frazer, *The Golden Bough: a Study in Magic and Religion* (Ware, UK: Wordsworth, 1993).
52. See ibid., 11–47.
53. Ibid., 12.
54. Potolsky, *Mimesis*, 138.
55. For these examples, see Frazer, *Golden Bough*, 12–13, 17–19, 38–41, 43–44.
56. Taussig, *Mimesis and Alterity*.
57. Ibid., 59.
58. Ibid., xiii.
59. For the purpose of this chapter, we take at face value Martti's claim that a 'moralised sensibility' is the (sole or primary) alternative to managerialism and a suitable way of overcoming its hegemony. However, we question this claim in A. Lang and S. Marks, 'People with Projects: Writing the Lives of International Lawyers', *Temple International and Comparative Law Journal* 27 (2013): 437–53.
60. He apparently also had photographs of Hans Kelsen and Arnold McNair. See Koskenniemi, 'Lauterpacht', 215, 217–18.
61. Ibid., 215.
62. Ibid.
63. We discuss this in some detail in Lang and Marks, 'People with Projects'.
64. See Taussig, *Mimesis and Alterity*, 213.
65. See e.g. Jean Baudrillard's work on the simulacrum and hyperreality. Among many other works, J. Baudrillard, *Simulacra and Simulation*, S. G. Glaser (trans.) (Ann Arbor: University of Michigan Press, 1994).
66. M. Strathern, 'Artifacts of History: Events and the Interpretation of Images', in J. Siikala (ed.), *Culture and History in the Pacific* (Helsinki: Transactions of the Finnish Anthropological Society, 1990), reprinted in M. Strathern, *Learning to See in Melanesia: Lectures Given in the Department of Social Anthropology, Cambridge*

ANDREW LANG AND SUSAN MARKS

University, 1993–2008, vol. 2 (Manchester, UK: HAU Masterclass Series, 2013), 157–78.
67. Ibid., 174.
68. Ibid. Strathern gives this phenomenon a rather different inflection to the one we give it here.
69. See L. P. Hartley, *The Go-Between* (1953; repr., London: Penguin, 1997), 1 ('the past is a foreign country: they do things differently there').

Bibliography

Adorno, Theodor W. *Aesthetic Theory*, Robert Hullot-Kentor (trans.) (New York: Continuum, 1997).

Auerbach, Erich. *Mimesis: The Representation of Reality in Western Literature*, Willard R. Trask (trans.) (Princeton, NJ: Princeton University Press, 2003).

Baudrillard, Jean. *Simulacra and Simulation*, Sheila Faria Glaser (trans.) (Ann Arbor: University of Michigan Press, 1994).

Benjamin, Walter. 'Doctrine of the Similar (1933)'. *New German Critique* 17 (1979): 65–69.

One-Way Street and Other Writings, Edmund Jephcott and Kingsley Shorter (trans.) (London: Verso, 1997).

'On the Mimetic Faculty'. In *Reflections: Essays, Aphorisms, Autobiographical Writings* (New York: Schocken, 1978).

'Thesis V on the Philosophy of History'. In *Illuminations* (London: Pimlico, 1999).

'Thesis VI on the Philosophy of History'. In *Illuminations* (London: Pimlico, 1999).

Bhabha, Homi K. *The Location of Culture* (London: Routledge, 1994).

Descartes, René. *Discourse on Method*, Donald A. Cress (trans.) (Indianapolis, IN: Hackett, 1998).

Frazer, James G. *The Golden Bough a Study in Magic and Religion* (Ware, UK: Wordsworth, 1993).

Freud, Sigmund. *The Joke and Its Relation to the Unconscious*, Joyce Crick (trans.) (London: Penguin, 2002).

Gebauer, Günter, and Christoph Wulf. *Mimesis: Culture, Art, Society*, Don Reneau (trans.) (Berkeley: University of California Press, 1995).

Hartley, Leslie P. *The Go-Between* (1953; repr., London: Penguin, 1997).

Horkheimer, Max, and Theodor W. Adorno. *Dialectic of Enlightenment*, John Cumming (trans.) (New York: Continuum, 1993).

Koskenniemi, Martti. *The Gentle Civilizer of Nations: The Rise and Fall of International Law 1870–1960* (Cambridge: Cambridge University Press, 2001).

'Lauterpacht: the Victorian Tradition in International Law'. *European Journal of International Law* 8 (1997): 215–63.

'Letter to the Editors of the Symposium'. *American Journal of International Law* 93 (1999): 351–61.

'Miserable Comforters: International Relations as New Natural Law'. *European Journal of International Relations* 15 (2009): 395–422.

'The Politics of International Law – 20 Years Later'. *European Journal of International Law* 20 (2009): 7–19.

'What Use for Sovereignty Today?' *Asian Journal of International Law* 1 (2011): 61–70.

Lang, Andrew, and Susan Marks. 'People with Projects: Writing the Lives of International Lawyers'. *Temple International and Comparative Law Journal* 27 (2013): 437–53.

Leach, Neil. *Camouflage* (Cambridge, MA: MIT Press, 2006).

Livy, Titus. *Rome and the Mediterranean: Books XXXI–XLV*, Henry Bettenson (trans.) (London: Penguin, 1976).

Melberg, Arne. *Theories of Mimesis* (Cambridge: Cambridge University Press, 1995).

Mitchell, Timothy. *Rule of Experts: Egypt, Techno-Politics, Modernity* (Berkeley: University of California Press, 2002).

Neff, Stephen C. (ed.). *Hugo Grotius: on the Law of War and Peace* (Cambridge: Cambridge University Press, 2012).

Petrarch, Francesco. *Selections from the Canzoniere and Other Works*, Mark Musa (trans.) (Oxford: Oxford University Press, 1985).

Potolsky, Matthew. *Mimesis* (New York: Routledge, 2006).

Strathern, Marilyn. 'Artifacts of History: Events and the Interpretation of Images'. In Jukka Siikala (ed.), *Culture and History in the Pacific* (Helsinki: Transactions of the Finnish Anthropological Society, 1990).

'Artifacts of History: Events and the Interpretation of Images'. In *Learning to See in Melanesia: Lectures Given in the Department of Social Anthropology, Cambridge University, 1993–2008*, vol. 2 (Manchester, UK: HAU Masterclass Series, 2013).

Taussig, Michael T. *Mimesis and Alterity: a Particular History of the Senses* (London: Routledge, 1993).

White, Hayden V. *Figural Realism: Studies in the Mimesis Effect* (Baltimore: Johns Hopkins University Press, 1999).

Martti Koskenniemi and the Historiography of International Law in the Age of the War on Terror

SAMUEL MOYN

The appearance of Martti Koskenniemi's *The Gentle Civilizer of Nations* coincided with an extraordinary spike of scholarly attention to the history of international law that shows no signs of abating.[1] This essay assesses some features of that convergence between book and moment, with an emphasis on the scene in the US, and tries to distinguish what has been powerful from what has been implausible in the results. In particular, I want to explore the worry that, in many of its versions, the new historiography that shared the same era and overlapped with the reception of *The Gentle Civilizer* has been a proxy for a burning political debate in recent American and (more broadly) global life: how to assess the promise and perils of international law, in the novel circumstance of the nation's 'war on terror'.

In virtue of its timing and not just its insight, Koskenniemi's work was received into this debate, and has accompanied it in interesting ways. And if Koskenniemi renovated the history of international law, his own rationale for undertaking it, against the backdrop of the historiography of the war on terror, may have proven sharply limited. A product of 'critical legal studies', Koskenniemi's historiography, to put it bluntly, has been received in ways that have proven uncritical towards the politics of international law. I hasten to add that if the era of Koskenniemi's centrality suffered from historiographical shortcomings, it is entirely understandable given the initial impress of events. But it also means that some other approach to and retrieval of the history of international law than has occurred in the era of Koskenniemi's reception needs to be emphasized in response.

Having written recently about the contributions and defects of Koskenniemi's story of post-war American international law very specifically, I now would like to broaden my optic in order to offer a parallel assessment of this great scholar's contribution to the historiography of international law more generally.[2] And I would like to draw the larger implications of my earlier claim that his neo-formalism proved historiographically, as well as politically, misleading. Mainly, it is because his version of historiography failed to situate international law within a larger set of actual and possible modes of politics. While breaking with the doctrinalism of traditional writing on the subject, *The Gentle Civilizer of Nations* did not break with its internalism: the commitment to study the politics of the guild of international lawyers centrally as a problem of textual reconstruction rather than contextual interpretation. And this fact arguably had decisive consequences. Especially when it concluded in neo-formalism, the book's internalism made difficult the evaluation of the political uses of – and especially the political alternatives to – international law, especially for progressive causes.

A central difficulty of the post-9/11 world, however, is how much hope ought to be reposed in international law as a tool of achieving justice or even of chastening power – and what alternative tools there are if international law proves accommodating or counterproductive. In focussing on that difficulty, this essay doubles as a critical overview of recent historiography and an assessment of Koskenniemi's influence on it. Clearly, Koskenniemi could not have intended it. But it turns out the much of the new historiography about the pre-9/11 past is really the post-9/11 political debate in reflected form. And its single most significant feature is a romance of international law as a saving grace in the face of otherwise unconstrained power, rather than a weak tool against or an ideological accomplice of it.

13.1   The Political Context of Liberal Historiography

After the Cold War, and with special intensity after 2001, a scholarly fascination with – even romance of – international law set in. Within and outside the US, liberals turned to international law as a source of political leverage, lacking more powerful tools at a moment of national unity or fearing to use them – finding in international law one that would offer a less divisive mode of opposition, still compatible with necessary patriotism. (Torture is un-American, as the saying went.) Many outside the country, on a wider spectrum of opinion, mobilized similarly. Somehow it had become culturally meaningful and strategically opportune to oppose America's global war on terror not as *imprudent* or *immoral* but as *illegal* – especially by the standards of international law. This is the political context that has had a massive impact on the writing of the history of international law, and Martti Koskenniemi's own impact – with his perfect timing – interacted with the scene in complex ways that I explore in what follows. For surprisingly, Koskenniemi designed his own intervention to conclude with a call for a 'culture of formalism' that proved both attractive and diversionary in response to this circumstance.

The central historiographical move has taken a predictable and transparent form. International law was represented as a pristine source of humanity that Americans now trampled, and the strategy worked better if historians claimed that Americans themselves had at some prior time signed on to international law as a humanistic agent of improvement. Take your choice when this was: the American Founding, the early-twentieth-century formation of the American Society of International Law, the Nuremberg trials, the human rights revolution and so on. Correspondingly, those who disdained international law before the (newly?) ugly Americans joined their unholy tradition were, inevitably, exceptional Germans, Isabel Hull has now demonstrated.[3] From Theobald von Bethmann-Hollweg to George W. Bush: no one wants to be on their side of history.

Consider a couple of examples of this literature. It became very popular to insist that, as an Enlightenment nation or a new one seeking legitimacy, the fledgling US hewed to the civilized rules of humanity and insisted on their universal validity – not to mention domestic application.[4] To read the liberal arguments in the famous litigation concerning the Alien Tort Statute of 1789 is to be presented with claims, including ones backed by professional historians, to the effect that Americans entered the world attempting to set up a human rights regime from the start.[5] Centuries later, and far more plausibly, the US was similarly credited for enacting the international legal regime, and especially the human rights regime. For example, Elizabeth Borgwardt tried to show that Nuremberg and related innovations in the 1940s (including global macroeconomic governance) that she creatively ranged under the heading 'America's vision for human rights' stemmed from a legal moment of bipartisan understanding of the need for multilateral engagement with the world.[6]

This strategy joined history to a more popular and journalistic narrative in which it was simply outrageous for America to shirk international law after 9/11, especially when the country had done so much to create the regime in the first place. America, *New Yorker* journalist Jane Mayer wrote, 'had done more than any nation on earth to abolish torture and other violations of human rights' – which made its betrayal of these 'American ideals' that much more appalling. Philippe Sands showed how Donald

Rumsfeld, secretary of defence at the time of the Iraq war, 'betrayed America's values' – and the country's prior inestimable contributions to the international legal regime – by sanctioning torture. Sands's example, and similar claims by many others, shows that this liberal strategy of appealing to international law to constrain the hegemon proved equally appealing abroad.[7]

It would be false to say that this dominant mode of engagement with the history of international law went entirely uncontested. In his famous study of Francis Lieber, the Civil War era professor responsible for the first written modern codification of the rules of war, John Fabian Witt insisted that there were in fact contending aspects of the American spirit, the humanistic and militaristic, rooted equally deep and in a dramatic long-term struggle through the present.[8] Witt played J. W. von Goethe to America's Faust ('Two souls, alas, are dwelling in my breast'): international law was America's gift to the world, but also and equally its congenitally shirked burden. Historicizing those for and against international law after 9/11 – George W. Bush and his liberal critics – showed they merely reflected moments in a self-divided soul. If so, then the historiography of international law, Witt contended, should not pick sides simplemindedly but present the age-old struggle within American identity now taking the form of the standoff of conservative and liberal foreign policy opinion about the war on terror. If humanitarianism was as American as apple pie, militarism was too; and breaking international law was certainly not something Germans do alone, compared to Anglos who supposedly prefer to make it (Francis Lieber was a German-American who embodied a more general paradox – and a wider view might have shown there was nothing particularly American, let alone uniquely German, about the syndrome).[9] Where some historians wanted America simply to (re)join the law-abiding angels of history, others acknowledged that power, and especially great power, has required the repeated Faustian pact with the devil. (If torture is un-American, national weakness, losing wars, and subordinating independent judgement to foreign or 'cosmopolitan' opinion are too.)

Yet there was another view – but the truth is that it remained less visible than the simple liberal romance of international law or the more subtle attempt to reveal that liberalism and its conservative adversary have been the entwined helixes of America's genetic destiny. This third view said that international law was never some priceless means of salvation, but only another tool of power. Who could believe otherwise? If war is politics by other means, as Carl von Clausewitz noted, or politics war by other means, as Michel Foucault added, wasn't international law always just another version of both? According to Carl Schmitt's dictum that Koskenniemi famously stigmatized (though he wasn't later above adopting it himself), whoever adopts humanity's mantle is (probably) lying.[10] 'Humanity's law' was not a snow-white alternative to pitch black horror, nor even the superego's ethics to the id's passions within a divided self. At least in most cases, international law was simply another version of ongoing power relations, not least since the modern state embraced it with alacrity. Unsurprisingly, then, international law worked compatibly with the interstate politics of potent sovereigns and even superpowers – with few exceptions. In Koskenniemi's own terms, it was always much closer to, when it was not identical with, apology, rather than utopia; and compared to other modern utopias, its undoubted progressivism was slight indeed. Even mobilizations 'from below' appealing against governments to international law and later international human rights were, from a historical perspective, just one sort of politics, and a weak form for that matter. (Post-9/11 torture consciousness stopped obscene practices, to be sure, but this success tweaked the ongoing war on terror that itself did not end, and may even have helped launder hygienic war.)

On this final view, it followed that liberals and conservatives in the American context were not good versus evil or symptoms of deep internal division but two faces of mostly harmonious identity, with international law simply playing a different role in how each side talked and operated. To tell tales about America's contributions to international law until it unaccountably destroyed its own creation after 9/11 is not only or so much to strike a blow for good or the American superego: it is also to collude in a recent strategic choice about how to organize liberal-conservative debate in American politics, one that forestalls other perspectives – most notably, that liberals and conservatives in the US cyclically share power and overlap in their views about the country's role in the world, differing on the margins. Koskenniemi did not mean to contribute this syndrome, I am sure, but the reception of his work abetted it, and failed to provide tools to undermine it.

13.2   From Bethmann-Hollweg to Bush

For that marginal last alternative about how to understand international law only peeks out from Koskenniemi's history, in spite of his own origins in critical legal studies, because of his resounding call for a 'culture of formalism' at the end of his book. The more general and crucial fact about *The Gentle Civilizer of Nations* is that it was received by professional historians not as a proposed step in the evolution of critical legal studies, and a sequel and complement to Koskenniemi's classic earlier work.[11] Rather, and not unsurprisingly, it was viewed as a reclamation of the history of international law that historians had disdained in their treatments of modern history before. Koskenniemi's origins story was read as respectful of his protagonists. And the fact that Koskenniemi ended *The Gentle Civilizer* indicting America specifically and its international relations apologists for Cold War violence provided grist for the mill of the simpleminded belief that international law provided a panacea in a continuing age of American power and war. That is, Koskenniemi's deceptively simple call for the virtues of formalism in an age of American hyper-power – made already before 9/11 showed the colossus running further amok – fit best with the first popular and idealizing approach to the historiography of international law, not the second and ambivalent version of it, let alone the final and sceptical approach.

In his own intention and the details of his argument, I gather, Koskenniemi's 'culture of formalism' was intended as a step within, rather than a surrender of, critical legal studies. Indeed, he was particularly anxious to refute the possibility that neo-formalism would repeat the paleo-formalist naiveté of the past. Rather, Koskenniemi understood it as a *response* to scepticism about form that may once have seemed alluring to the left but, he insisted, had been central to American Cold War rejection of international law. Neo-formalism, therefore, now beckoned those anxious about American 'hegemony'. But the sophistication of his proposal ultimately came too close to a naïve romance of international law as bulwark of civilization against state barbarity to escape the gravitational pull of its post-9/11 liberal historiographical uses.

To consider how, it is useful to examine Hull's *A Scrap of Paper* a bit more closely, since it so wonderfully epitomizes the liberal historiographical revival of international law and cites Koskenniemi repeatedly as an ally. (The favour was returned in his fulsomely positive endorsement, to the effect that her history offers 'the most powerful defense of the role of law in international crisis that I have read, and as such is of obvious contemporary relevance'.)[12]

In World War I, Hull reports, there was a villain, the exceptional Germans, who in her account treat with blithe disregard the central bulwark of civilization against barbarism: international law. The Germans' strategic vision, the famous Schlieffen Plan, required them to wheel through Belgium on the way to northern France, to avoid exposing themselves to massive risk. When it executed the plan as the guns of August sounded, Germany became the only nation occupying large swaths of territory in an age when most of the laws of war covered such matters. Hull's discussions of Germany's widely decried violation of Belgian neutrality and the atrocities that followed make for chilling reading. (The book's title comes from a famous remark by the German chancellor, Bethmann-Hollweg, who said that the treaty guaranteeing Belgian neutrality was merely a 'scrap of paper'.) Historians are now sure that German depredations in Belgium, once treated as propaganda, were real and violent: massacres, executions, deportations, arson and pillaging. In each chapter, Hull provides a useful explanation of what the consensual and contested points in the law of war were in 1914, and then proceeds to show how Germans went far beyond anyone else in their cavalier treatment of its standards. As the book goes on, she considers Germany's attitudes to new weapons like zeppelins, poison gas and flamethrowers, as well as its famous tactic of unrestricted submarine warfare. In most cases, the pattern that began in 1914 continued through the entirety of the conflict, with Germans coming up short compared with the British, who tended to take the constraints of legality much more seriously.

All good: but as a Sonderweg history, Hull's book wants to set up Germany as an outlier compared to British (and secondarily French) obeisance to an international law she treats with great admiration. Britain, that is, comes out the hero of the book because of its culture of formalism. It was a historiographical strategy that forsook any critical perspective on international law itself, as if what mainly mattered were its uses in liberal politics to indict American warfare after 9/11. ('I have been deeply dismayed by the lawlessness of my own country in its pursuit of the "war on terror"', Hull writes in the beginning of her book.)[13] Screened out was that Britain was a modern state, not to mention a modern empire, and its attitude to international law was that of a great power. And perhaps Britain could treat international law as more sacrosanct because it wasn't in position to break it and, given its strategic position, did not need to do so. That Germany broke the law first does not necessarily mean that its attitude to law was different; it only means that its strategy compelled its forces to make the first move. Moreover, just because Britain didn't trample existing legal standards hardly means that its own strategies were not deadly to civilians – sometimes more deadly than Germany's. For this reason, the most difficult matter for Hull's case is the British blockade, which caused hundreds of thousands of Germans to die, including many women and children. In part because so little was settled about the law of war at sea, Britain had less need to violate it. Britain's hegemony as a naval power made it unsurprisingly averse before 1914 to tying its hands. Giving Britain high marks, as Hull does, for a punctilious attitude towards international law masks the fact that Britain could commit horrendous acts that undoubtedly cost more civilian life than German legal infractions but without breaking the law – as if law matters more than morality. Should the Brits really get that much credit for setting up the world (and a fortiori international law) in their image, which saved them the trouble of violating it later?

Hull claims that the reason people (or is it just Americans?) have weakened their commitment to international law and stopped taking World War I as an object lesson of what goes wrong when it is treated cavalierly is that German 'revisionists' succeeded in obfuscating their memory. That is, she agrees entirely with Koskenniemi's story of Carl Schmitt's influence on American international relations theorists who disdained morality (except that she views Schmitt as a garden-variety German nationalist).[14] She powerfully argues that this campaign, with its twentieth-century legacies, obliterated not merely how much legal standards mattered to policy but also how central Germany's violation of international law had been to sparking the conflict in the first place. Lost in this view, however convincing, is any possibility that international law generally serves and not merely subverts great power. It also screens out the corresponding reality that fundamental checks on authority (especially in war) have normally come in political, rather than merely legal, form.

If all this is correct, a brilliant liberal history of international law like Hull's may retrieve the past selectively, because of the heat of a post-9/11 situation in which international law beckoned as a counter-hegemonic restraint. Her history in effect burnishes the credentials of international law as a response to power, but at the high price of screening out its origins and its uses as a tool of the powerful, treating its universal form as salvation, and ignoring the salience of non-legal modes of opposition – reducing political struggles around the scourge of war to legal and often judicial ones. The truly valuable legacy from the past that might have been challenging after 9/11, however, was that international law had long been marginal as a framework for political debates because other possibilities were live.

13.3 Koskenniemi's Intervention: Three Debates

The agenda Koskenniemi set for the field was broad rather than narrow – and yet ultimately it did harmonize with and contribute to its historiographical moment. Perhaps the greatest weakness of the *Gentle Civilizer* is that it opened up debate on many topics in the history of international law, but not about the historical conditions for the possibility of the post-9/11 liberal historiography of international law in the first place. Clearly both the millennial dreams of the 1990s and then the disruption of 9/11 – and the shocking reversal in which George W. Bush did not behave with the same beliefs about humanity's law that either progressive hopes entertained or certain theories like liberal internationalism predicted – were the real sources of scholarly absorption in various chapters of the past. But *The Gentle Civilizer*, in part in virtue of appearing and monopolizing the field at the right time, determined the shape of the interest in the annals of international law in a few key respects.

One – in my view the most valuable – was to focus on lawyers as a prism on law, which allowed trained historians to take the subject seriously for the first time, at least in recent memory. Unlike the typically doctrinal focus of work done by trained lawyers – 'law office history' even when written in the academy – Koskenniemi adopted the assumption more common to card-carrying historians that professionalization and institutionalization mattered most. Legal ideas were relevant, but less as doctrines working themselves pure than as ideology, even if only in the crude sense of justifications for status seeking or even as apologetics for state interest and power. And yet even here there was a risk. The very focus on lawyers that Koskenniemi pioneered deflected attention from the states they served and attempted to 'civilize', and from the agendas that were realized through international law, with its classic indenturement to sovereignty that Koskenniemi himself emphasized.[15]

Further, because of the contingencies of its framing, Koskenniemi's book stoked three key debates that, for all their contributions, now appear of declining importance. One concerns origins. It is characteristic that by far the most influential part of *Gentle Civilizers* has been its account of the beginnings of professionalization.[16] And not surprisingly, there has since been the widespread revival interest in the deeper origins, with much new literature on Alberico Gentili, Hugo Grotius and other early modern classics.[17] Koskenniemi himself has moved backwards to the early modern age, in an imminently forthcoming major study. Yet especially if one concludes that the turn to history is properly motivated by the desire to put the present in perspective and achieve critical purchase on it, the 'origins' debate simply doesn't get very far, whether it comes to early modern origins or mid-nineteenth-century origins (or, I will argue later, early-twentieth-century origins or mid-twentieth-century origins).

A second debate concerns international law and nineteenth-century imperialism. Some scholars have taken up the broader imperial context of international law (or more accurately made sure to add law to ongoing accounts of empire).[18] And clearly Koskenniemi's intervention was catalytic here in making the formation of professional international law in the age of empire a central object of attention. But others have disputed Koskenniemi's emphasis on how closely aligned founding international lawyers were with imperial projects, since more harboured the unsurprising doubts that a nineteenth-century liberal might about the civilizing mission than Koskenniemi's research let on.[19] Yet this debate, for all its fruitful results, seems unconnected to explaining the rise of international law in our time whether for a broad public or even for politicians or academics (including lawyers themselves). And if the imperial lineages of international law are relevant to current politics, as I believe they are, it would not go without saying but would require an intricate and indirect case.[20]

A third concerns the rise of international relations as a wayward and ultimately parricidal child of international law – another undoubtedly interesting set of considerations that have rightly been taken up by scholars after Koskenniemi in large numbers. But it is this focus, in spite of its obviously salutary contributions, that not only obscured other potential topics in the history of international law since World War II – notably the true conditions of possibility of the new historiography of international law itself after 9/11. When joined to Koskenniemi's closing neo-formalism, it overlapped with and did not provide grounds for repudiation of the liberal historiographical reclamation of international law after 9/11. It abetted, rather than forestalled, the study of the past of international law for the sake of restraining American power – a project that that seemed so politically attractive after 9/11 and the 'forever war' against terrorism.

13.4   A Late-Twentieth-Century History

It is important to see how Koskenniemi's intervention in these regards powered and limited the larger historiography. And the first crucial fact is an absence: there is little good historiography of international law after World War II – when international law came to matter, especially in public debate (if it does). When it comes to *how international law became important for ourselves*, historians have so far had essentially nothing to say. Arguably, the answer to this question is not Hugo Grotius, Francis Lieber, Koskenniemi's 'men of 1873', or the founders of the League of

Nations or the United Nations, at least not proximately. Obsessed by origins, it is as if historians had trained their sights on everywhere except *their own origins*. It is a massive failure of self-reference.[21]

To be sure, recent concerns, projected into other times and climes, have led to a huge amount of worthwhile scholarship. After a long Cold War phase of marginality, the centrality of international law to debates concerning global politics in our time made allegedly comparable prior eras (like the inter-war years, and perhaps the immediate aftermath of World War II) interesting again or in a new way. Indeed, the historiography of the inter-war and immediate post-1945 moment has been transformed by concern with legally inflected internationalism, rightly or wrongly.[22] More sober analysts see such histories championing supposed past breakthroughs as sentimental fictions – in fact reflecting our own era's hopes for international law, rather than any live possibility at the time.

Once derided as a legalist utopia that failed, and then presented as a tragically short-lived triumph of the *esprit d'internationalité*, it has turned out that the League of Nations was founded on the rejection of legalism.[23] To say the 'grand days' of inter-war Geneva are not uninteresting now – hardly a major claim in any case – is not to say they were massively relevant in the scheme of things then.[24] In truth, international law had little if any opening in the moment after World War II, which featured a great power settlement with a few fine words in the mix. In spite of the restoration of the importance of international law in the past, one thus sometimes wonders whether, however absorbing to us now, it really cries out for more centrality to historiography than it has achieved so far – or whether the truth is that it has anachronistically achieved too much centrality already.

Worse, when it comes the era straddling the end of the Cold War – that is to say, when the need for historiographical attention is most plain – the literature falls silent. And in the cold light of reflection, Koskenniemi's own intervention in the period after 1945 turns out to be misleading and unhelpful. It may be flawed on its own terms, if Hans Morgenthau wasn't a realist in the first place.[25] Either way, Koskenniemi's story is one of international law's *fall* rather than its *rise* – the opposite of what, in the end, actually occurred and needs to be explained. It may be true that eminent Victorians were sanctimonious true believers in various things (God, chastity, international law), but that is not to say that those among them who signed on to belief in international law were terribly significant in their time. Conversely, who after Auschwitz can naively sign on to the 'civilization versus barbarism' framing on which hope in international law still depends? Yet it could be that a half-believed international law at some point in our era acquired simply unprecedented salience – even relative to its alleged Victorian heyday. How unconvincing it is, then, that Koskenniemi chose to conclude his account with the narrow (whether or not correct) claim that Americans wrecked international law by allowing international relations to rise! Even more fatefully, he closed it too early: in particular, before the human rights revolution, and the end of the Cold War that transformed out of all recognition the geopolitical conditions in which international law could seem plausible. Could this be even half the story?[26]

So there is a lot more to do. In his magisterial integrative account of the long-term trajectory of 'internationalism', Mark Mazower incorporates Koskenniemi's international relations story.[27] But he hardly consents to Koskenniemi's neo-formalist moral. Unlike Koskenniemi, Mazower refuses to truncate the narrative in the middle of the Cold War, so reaches human rights and liberal internationalism from the 1970s through the present: a very different endpoint that properly changes the meaning of the tale. As a synthetic or 'bird's eye' account, of course, much of the landscape passes by in Mazower's account in a blurry whiz. One cannot synthesize literature that doesn't exist, so his account also leaps from the later Cold War with chapters on development, third world revolt, and neo-liberalism to 'humanity's law' in our time, even though the latter did not come out of nowhere.[28] The ground with its intricate details beckons as a topic for scholars willing to descend to it.

Only one feature of this necessary research is provincially American of course (though it is the geographical area that matters most – with European émigrés once again, as in Lieber's time, playing the critical role). Europe itself after World War II, not to mention the decolonized world, cries out for some of the attention historians have chosen to lavish on its prior epochs when, in spite of trying, no one has succeeded in finding a terribly significant role for international law. In Western Europe, the basic tale is one of a junior partner in the Cold War, liberated from its traditional security tasks by this fact (and, more important, from colonial governance by decolonization), with new space to construct a novel self-image. The true European internationalists were arguably the ones not from Victoria but from Venus (in Robert Kagan's notorious expression), freed by the American Mars to make a moral turn.[29] In the global south, the basic tale is a newly extant and empowered cadre of lawyers who explored international law as a potential tool of gaming a still intolerable world order – but a weak tool that they have exploited in mostly weak ways after their more activist plans in the age of third world revolt badly failed.

In all-important America, the story is very much one of a cadre of European-trained (or at least -born) lawyers, but who made very different moves as the Cold War era waned than they or their predecessors had in its early years. Above all, they prepared options – human rights law, as I tried to show in a preliminary way, as well as the project of 'the humanization of humanitarian law' (actually, reconceiving the law of armed conflict in a humanitarian spirit in the first place) – that then stood ready to come into their own after the Cold War surprisingly ended.[30] The scene shifted in unexpected ways that rescued their agendas from lawyerly obscurity and unimportance. (Plans for an international criminal court focussed on atrocity, suddenly activated after the Cold War, are an excellent example here.) A first crucial period was one after Vietnam when the country needed to 'reclaim virtue', and for a small group of people international law was central to this task.[31] A second and even more pivotal moment occurred after 1989: international law suddenly became central to liberal hopes. It was only on this immediately prior basis that, after 9/11, the current liberal historiography of betrayal could arise – and which Koskenniemi's history did not help see beyond given his own neo-formalist jurisprudential commitments.

Never mind that those hopes even before the war on terror sullied them were, essentially, of a new peace sponsored by one country, with no economic justice except that brought by markets. Never mind that modern history had offered the prospect of many political alternatives to that model, or that many other options are still hypothetically possible. But instead of reviving or inventing those alternatives, historians turned to seek the lineages of the newly consecrated utopia of international law. After 9/11, they had little on which to fall back except for the memory of the international law they once dreamed would provide utopia but that America agonizingly ditched at the first sign of trouble. A highly impressive but instrumentally questionable historiography followed. Koskenniemi did not provide the tools to disrupt this historiography. Even if he had never intended merely to burnish international law's credentials for the sake of indicting America's fecklessness, this was because he had set out before 9/11 occurred to revive formalism for the left rather than a version of the critical legal studies more sceptical about form and more open to its political uses. (It was just such a version that that provided the context for his own historiography; but then Koskenniemi's histories are also guilty of paying attention to a diverse range of contexts in the annals of international legal thought, except the recent ones that produced his own historical inquiry and in particular his neo-formalist agenda.)

As a result of this conjuncture, we now know a lot about the history of international law. But not when it counts: it mostly diverts from understanding the real ideological path we have recently travelled, which led to our historiography in the first place. As for off roads to that path, we do not yet seem set on exploring them, whether for the sake of their importance in the past or for their relevance to the future.

13.5 Conclusion

Perhaps the greatest difficulty raised by the new historiography, one Koskenniemi with his otherwise revealing internalist approach to the history of international lawyers did not confront, is how to judge the relative importance of international law to politics overall from time to time and place to place. The relatively ancient chronology of recent writing, skirting the recent spike in salience of international law, implies a great risk not only of a redemptive attitude towards the topic but also of a promotional one: insisting that whatever the promise of international law to bring order and morality to the world, our ancestors understood that promise with the same level of enthusiasm as our contemporaries have, and therefore organized their disputes around it as we have.

I have been suggesting, in response, that the greatest error of recent writing is the common assumption that international law was somehow central to political thought and political debate all along, and debate ensued only about how it figured. The task – undoubtedly a crucial one – was to reclaim law from the lawyers in order to rethink its role in the history of international affairs. Yet it is possible that recent historians colluded with lawyers, with whose foreshortened version of intellectualism they otherwise rightly saw the need to break, in assuming that international law mattered much in the first place, for good or ill. It is part of the lawyer's self-imposed professional task to publicize international law's otherwise discreet role.[32] And historians concurred in that promotional attitude: the topic had to be *important*. They routinely professed themselves surprised to find that no one had ever written on international law in various places and phases (it was entirely neglected in the historiography of the Civil War or World War I, to take two above cases). But they believed that this insight should justify their own attention to it, rather than cause them ponder the possibility that international law was marginal to the conduct of politics (including war) until recently.[33]

But what if the presence of international law was never much of a phenomenon of note, especially for the broad public, for whom its (alleged) significance never seriously registered? The weakest point in Hull's excellent book is that, apart from the much decried violation of Belgian neutrality, she never thinks to prove that publics truly cared about the disasters of war in legal terms, as opposed to moral ones. And even if – in what I believe was a genuinely major development – international law did become an increasingly important causal and constitutive factor in government policymaking over time as opposed to a perfunctory rationalization of it, and especially in the last forty years, was the post-9/11 recourse to a historiography of international law ultimately misleading about how much it had mattered along the way, inside and especially outside government?

This argument is worth considering, not just in order to debate the comparative salience of international law for different audiences in different eras, but to recall what historians themselves used to care about in writing history – and enacting politics. Why, after all, was international law a marginal topic before Koskenniemi intervened? Is the answer that, prior to our age, there were independent moral and political resources for engaging in contemporary affairs that people (including historians among them) once placed first as they thought about their own times, and that sometimes functioned more powerfully than law has in our time to articulate hopes for a better world? What have we lost as historians in focussing on international law – and for what gains? What was lacking after 9/11 – popular understanding of international law forsaken along the way or never achieved, or popular understanding of how to improve the world politically, for which international law (and a fortiori debates about its history) is a poor substitute?

Ultimately, then, I am worrying that our interest in international law is our interest, not something it is legitimate or helpful to project too far or at least too exactly on diverse episodes of the past. At a minimum, if this is right, Koskenniemi's historiographical influence testifies not only to his own considerable intellectual power. It is also raises the puzzle of the reception of a project like the one he offered, which suddenly made the history of international law a source of fascination rather than a scholastic backwater, and for historically specific reasons. A tour through the contemporary historiography of international law – as I would very idiosyncratically lead it – thus ends in the place it began, known for the first time. It is a place in which we are interested in international law unlike our ancestors, but in which we are not better but potentially worse off than them, because international law is our most attractive option for thinking about a better world (even though it has most frequently served and serves power), with superior and more transformative alternatives unavailable for the time being. International law is our fate as scholars – and citizens too – in the absence of more believable and pronounced hopes. As if law were not merely a necessary feature and servant of good politics, and more frequently the accomplice of bad politics, the historiography of international law in the age of Koskenniemi's brilliant contributions is in part a symptom of the loss of better politics – for the moment, at least.

Notes

1. M. Koskenniemi, *The Gentle Civilizer of Nations: The Rise and Fall of International Law, 1860–1960* (Cambridge: Cambridge University Press, 2002); see also Koskenniemi, 'Histories of International Law: Significance and Problems for a Critical View', *Temple International and Comparative Law Journal* 23 (2013): 215–40. An early and different version of this essay was prepared for a Columbia University conference on the recent historiography of international law, and I am grateful to the organizers and participants on that occasion for their observations.
2. S. Moyn, 'The International Law That Is America: Reflections on the Last Chapter of *The Gentle Civilizer of Nations*', *Temple International and Comparative Law Journal* 23 (2013): 399–415.
3. I. V. Hull, *A Scrap of Paper: Making and Breaking International Law during the Great War* (Ithaca, NY: Cornell University Press, 2014).
4. See e.g. D. M. Golove and D. J. Hulsebosch, 'A Civilized Nation: the Early American Constitution, the Law of Nations, and the Pursuit of International Recognition', *New York University Law Review* 85 (2010): 932–1066.
5. *Kiobel v. Royal Dutch Shell Petroleum*, Brief of Amici Curiae Professors of Legal History, available at http://harvardhumanrights.files.wordpress.com/2012/06/supplementalkiobelbrieflegalhistoriansl.pdf (last accessed 7 March 2016).
6. E. Borgwardt, *A New Deal for the World: America's Vision for Human Rights* (Cambridge, MA: Harvard University Press, 2006).
7. J. Mayer, *The Dark Side: the Inside Story of How the War on Terror Turned into a War on American Ideals* (New York: Doubleday, 2008), 9; P. Sands, *Torture Team: Rumsfeld's Memo and the Betrayal of American Values* (New York: Palgrave Macmillan, 2010).
8. J. F. Witt, *Lincoln's Code: the Laws of War in American History* (New York: Simon and Schuster, 2012).
9. Cf. R. Giladi, 'A Different Sense of Humanity: Occupation in Francis Lieber's Code', *International Review of the Red Cross* 94 (2012): 81–116.
10. Cf. Koskenniemi, *Gentle Civilizer*, 432, with Koskenniemi, review of R. Teitel, *Humanity's Law, Ethics and International Affairs* 26 (2012): 395–98.
11. Koskenniemi, *From Apology to Utopia: The Structure of International Legal Argument*, reissue with a new epilogue (Cambridge: Cambridge University Press, 2006).
12. The following tracks some passages in my 'Bulwark against Barbarism', *Wall Street Journal*, 5 June 2014. Koskenniemi's full endorsement is as follows: 'Isabel V. Hull's

passionate narrative of the role of international law in the decision-making processes in Berlin and London during the First World War opens a strikingly original perspective on the consciousness of the wartime actors. This was a war waged also by legal arguments. In the end, the inability and unwillingness of Imperial Germany to defend its case in legal terms crucially undermined its war effort. This is not only superb history, but also the most powerful defense of the role of law in international crisis that I have read, and as such is of obvious contemporary relevance'.

13. Hull, *A Scrap of Paper*, x.

14. Cf. Koskenniemi, *Gentle Civilizer*, 353–412, with Isabel V. Hull, 'Zwischen Konservatismus und Revolution: Carl Schmitt's völkerrechtliche Schriften', in P. U. Hohendahl and E. Schütz (eds), *Perspektiven konservativen Denkens: Deutschland und die Vereinigten Staaten nach 1945* (Bern, Switzerland: Peter Lang, 2012).

15. Koskenniemi, *Gentle Civilizer*, 98–178.

16. See B. Coates, *Legalist Empire: International Law, Civilization, and U.S. Foreign Relations in the Early Twentieth Century* (Oxford: Oxford University Press, 2016), or M. Mazower, *Governing the World: the Rise and Fall of an Idea* (New York: Penguin, 2012), esp. 65–93, powerfully influenced by Koskenniemi's account of professional origins.

17. B. Kingsbury and B. Straumann (eds), *The Roman Foundations of the Law of Nations: Alberico Gentili and the Justice of Empire* (New York: Oxford University Press, 2011).

18. L. Benton, *A Search for Sovereignty: Law and Geography in European Empires, 1400–1900* (Cambridge: Cambridge University Press, 2009).

19. See notably Andrew Fitzmaurice's exemplary article and the larger *American Historical Review* forum of which it is a part: A. Fitzmaurice, 'Liberalism and Empire in Nineteenth-Century International Law', *American Historical Review* 117 (2012): 122–40.

20. A. Anghie, *Imperialism, Sovereignty, and the Making of International Law* (Cambridge: Cambridge University Press, 2007); S. Pahuja, *Decolonising International Law: Development, Economic Growth, and the Politics of Universality* (Cambridge: Cambridge University Press, 2011).

21. A similar remark applies to the otherwise epoch-making B. Fassbender and A. Peters (eds), *Oxford Handbook of the History of International Law* (New York: Oxford University Press, 2012).

22. See D. Gorman, *The Emergence of International Society in the 1920s* (Cambridge: Cambridge University Press, 2012); A. Prost and J. M. Winter, *René Cassin and Human Rights: from the Great War to the Universal Declaration* (Cambridge: Cambridge University Press, 2013); B. Cabanes, *The Great War and the Origins of Humanitarianism, 1918–1924* (Cambridge: Cambridge University Press, 2014); and so on – and more interestingly and critically, M. Lewis, *The Birth of the New Justice: the Internationalization of Crime and Punishment, 1919–1950* (New York: Oxford University Press, 2014), and N. Wheatley, 'The History of International Society, Remembered and Forgotten', H-Diplo (2013), www.h-net.org/reviews/showrev.php?id=37488 (last accessed 7 March 2016).

23. S. Wertheim, 'The League That Wasn't: American Designs for a Legalist-Sanctionist League of Nations and the Intellectual Origins of International Organization, 1914–1920', *Diplomatic History* 35 (2011): 797–836; Wertheim, 'The League of Nations: a Retreat from International Law?', *Journal of Global History* 7 (2012): 210–32.

24. F. Moorhouse, *Grand Days* (Sydney: Macmillan, 1993).

25. W. Scheuerman, *Morgenthau: Realism and Beyond* (Malden, MA: Polity, 2009).
26. For exploration of this line of criticism, see my 'The International Law That Is America'.
27. Mazower, *Governing the World*, 214–43. As I mentioned earlier, Hull also includes it, moralistically but challengingly, as the belated victory of interwar German 'revisionism' – but one wonders, if so-called realism was simply German nationalism *sub specie aeternitatis*, how was anybody fooled? Hull, *A Scrap of Paper*, 1–15.
28. Mazower, *Governing the World*, 244–405.
29. R. Kagan, *Of Paradise and Power: America and Europe in the New World Order* (New York: A. A. Knopf, 2003), 1.
30. S. Moyn, *The Last Utopia: Human Rights in History* (Cambridge, MA: Harvard University Press, 2010), 176–211.
31. B. J. Keys, *Reclaiming American Virtue: the Human Rights Revolution of the 1970s* (Cambridge, MA: Harvard University Press, 2014). On the law of war, see my 'From Antiwar Politics to Antitorture Politics', in A. Sarat et al. (eds), *Law and War* (Stanford, CA: Stanford University Press, 2013), and, in more popular form, 'The Promise World War I Couldn't Keep', *CNN*, 8 August 2014, www.cnn.com/2014/08/08/opinion/moyn-world-war-i/.
32. 'If you look at the very first words that were ever published in the *American Journal of International Law*, it was a short piece by Elihu Root called "The Need of Popular Understanding of International Law"', Lori Damrosch recently noted. 'Now, 108 years later, there's still the need for popular understanding of international law. If anything, the need is even greater … But people in general are even less aware of how important international law is in their daily lives'. Cited in 'Lori Fisler Damrosch Appointed President of American Society of International Law', Columbia Law School Public Affairs, 15 April 2014, www.law.columbia.edu/media_inquiries/news_events/2014/april2014/damrosch-asil.
33. For the contrasting argument that war was only truly legalized in living memory, together with a related but overly rough distinction between a 'political' approach to law that obtained before and a 'legalistic' approach now, see J. L. Goldsmith, *The Terror Presidency: Law and Judgment inside the Bush Administration* (New York: W. W. Norton, 2007).

33. Bibliography

Anghie, Antony. *Imperialism, Sovereignty and the Making of International Law* (Cambridge: Cambridge University Press, 2007).

Benton, Lauren. *A Search for Sovereignty: Law and Geography in European Empires, 1400–1900* (Cambridge: Cambridge University Press, 2009).

Borgwardt, Elizabeth. *A New Deal for the World: America's Vision for Human Rights* (Cambridge, MA: Harvard University Press, 2007).

Coates, Benjamin. *Legalist Empire: International Law, Civilization, and U.S. Foreign Relations in the Early Twentieth Century* (Oxford: Oxford University Press, 2016).

Fassbender, Bardo, and Anne Peters. *The Oxford Handbook of the History of International Law* (Oxford: Oxford University Press, 2012).

Fitzmaurice, Andrew. 'Liberalism and Empire in Nineteenth-Century International Law'. *The American Historical Review* 117 (2012): 122–40.

Giladi, Rotem. 'A Different Sense of Humanity: Occupation in Francis Lieber's Code'. *International Review of the Red Cross* 94 (2012): 81–116.

Goldsmith, Jack L. *The Terror Presidency: Law and Judgment inside the Bush Administration* (New York: W. W. Norton, 2007).

Golove, David M., and Daniel J. Hulsebosch. 'A Civilized Nation: the Early American Constitution, the Law of Nations, and the Pursuit of International Recognition'. *New York University Law Review* 85 (2010): 932–1066.

Gorman, Daniel. *The Emergence of International Society in the 1920s* (Cambridge: Cambridge University Press, 2012).

Hull, Isabel, V. *A Scrap of Paper: Breaking and Making International Law during the Great War* (Ithaca, NY: Cornell University Press, 2014).

'Zwischen Konservatismus Und Revolution: Carl Schmitt's Völkerrechtliche Schriften'. In Peter Uwe Hohendahl, Peter Uwe and Erhard H. Schütz (eds), *Perspektiven Konservativen Denkens: Deutschland Und Die Vereinigten Staaten Nach 1945* (Bern, Switzerland: Peter Lang, 2012), 105.

Kagan, Robert. *Of Paradise and Power: America and Europe in the New World Order* (New York: A. A. Knopf, 2003).

Keys, Barbara J. *Reclaiming American Virtue: the Human Rights Revolution of the 1970s* (Cambridge, MA: Harvard University Press, 2014).

Kingsbury, Benedict, and Benjamin Straumann (eds). *The Roman Foundations of the Law of Nations: Alberico Gentili and the Justice of Empire* (New York: Oxford University Press, 2010).

Koskenniemi, Martti. *From Apology to Utopia: The Structure of International Legal Argument*, reissue with a new epilogue (Cambridge: Cambridge University Press, 2006).

The Gentle Civilizer of Nations: The Rise and Fall of International Law 1870–1960 (Cambridge: Cambridge University Press, 2001).

'Histories of International Law: Significance and Problems for a Critical View'. *Temple International and Comparative Law Journal* 27 (2013): 215–40.

'Review of Ruti Teitel, *Humanity's Law*'. *Ethics and International Affairs* 26 (2012): 395–98.

Lewis, Mark. *The Birth of the New Justice: The Internationalization of Crime and Punishment, 1919–1950* (Oxford: Oxford University Press, 2014).

Mayer, Jane. *The Dark Side: the Inside Story of How the War on Terror Turned into a War on American Ideals* (New York: Doubleday, 2008).

Mazower, Mark. *Governing the World: the History of an Idea, 1815 to the Present* (New York: Penguin, 2012).

Moorhouse, Frank. *Grand Days* (Sydney: Macmillan, 1993).

Moyn, Samuel. 'Bulwark against Barbarism'. *Wall Street Journal*, 5 June 2014.

'The International Law That Is America: Reflections on the Last Chapter of *The Gentle Civilizer of Nations*'. *Temple International and Comparative Law Journal* 27 (2013): 399–415.

'From Antiwar Politics to Antitorture Politics'. In Austin Sarat, Lawrence Douglas and Marta M. Umphrey (eds), *Law and War* (Stanford, CA: Stanford University Press, 2011).

The Last Utopia: Human Rights in History (Cambridge, MA: Harvard University Press, 2010).

Pahuja, Sundhya. *Decolonising International Law: Development, Economic Growth and the Politics of Universality* (Cambridge: Cambridge University Press, 2011).

Prost, Antoine, and Jay Winter. *René Cassin and Human Rights: from the Great War to the Universal Declaration* (Cambridge: Cambridge University Press, 2013).

Sands, Philippe. *Torture Team: Rumsfeld's Memo and the Betrayal of American Values* (New York: Palgrave Macmillan, 2010).

Scheuerman, William E. *Morgenthau: Realism and Beyond* (Malden, MA: Polity, 2009).

Wertheim, Stephen. 'The League of Nations: a Retreat from International Law?' *Journal of Global History* 7 (2012): 210–32.

'The League That Wasn't: American Designs for a Legalist-Sanctionist League of Nations and the Intellectual Origins of International Organization, 1914–1920'. *Diplomatic History* 35 (2011): 797–836.

Wheatley, Natasha. 'The History of International Society, Remembered and Forgotten'. *H-Diplo* (2013), www.h-net.org/reviews/showrev.php?id=37488 (last accessed 7 March 2016).

Witt, John F. *Lincoln's Code: the Laws of War in American History* (New York: Simon and Schuster, 2012).

14

Martti Koskenniemi's Critique of Eurocentrism in International Law

LILIANA OBREGÓN

14.1 A Koskenniemi Fan Confesses

I must start with a disclaimer: I am a Martti Koskenniemi fan. I became a fan when I first read *From Apology to Utopia* as an LLM student in David Kennedy's International Law course at Harvard. Coming from a mainstream human rights practitioner world, I had insufficient conceptual tools to fully understand this very extensive and difficult work, but I was hooked by Koskenniemi's monumental effort to critically engage with classic narratives of international law and his unique writing style.

My fanship increased when at the end of my first doctoral student presentation at an ASIL meeting, he encouraged me to continue studying the nineteenth- and early-twentieth-century Latin American internationalists (he was writing the *Gentle Civilizer* at that time). Since then, I have had the fortune and privilege to engage with Koskenniemi, the scholar, and Martti the person, at crucial moments of my academic career. From his generous observations on my dissertation to the University of Helsinki research fellowship (2009–12) I participated in under his direction, Koskenniemi's incisive and interdisciplinary analysis has more-often-than-not made me stop to think and re-evaluate my own work, shift in direction, or accept a particularly helpful insight. But more profoundly, I have learned, grown and felt inspired and supported by Martti, who, as others who have worked closely with him would know, is as insightful as a friend and mentor as he is as a scholar. Maybe his incisiveness comes from that unnerving Finnish ability to let you know in very few words what you need to hear: an honest, verbal slap in the face that does not feel judgemental or condescending while at the same time supports your intellectual instincts and academic interests.

360

Being a Koskenniemi fan, however, does not mean that I follow his work *fanatically* but rather that I find that his thorough research, engaging writing style and profound grasp of theory, history and law brings a refreshing way of rethinking classical doctrines, events, authors, and narratives of international law that may be cited and celebrated by both the critics and the mainstream. As a non-European scholar, however, I was intrigued but not too sure what Koskenniemi's perspective was on Eurocentrism in international law until his 2012 article directly dealing with this topic that made his understanding and position explicit despite his approaches to the issue in previous texts. For this chapter, I wish to contribute with a further exploration of Koskenniemi's critique of Eurocentrism in international law by first, presenting an overview of what was distinctive about 'European International Law' (EIL) according to several authors, including Koskenniemi; second, distinguishing the different reactions to the idea that EIL was sufficiently universal in theory to be adapted to other regions; third, revisit Koskenniemi's views on Eurocentrism in key pieces of his work and finally, transcribe an interview to him done in Finland in 2013.[1]

14.2   European International Law (EIL)

Koskenniemi is certainly not the first to highlight the problem of Eurocentrism in international law, but before presenting an overview of some of these critiques, the uses or descriptions a 'European International Law' (EIL) should be briefly addressed.[2] After the colonization of the Americas in the sixteenth-century, some European scholars distinguished differences in principles, origins or application of natural law or of *jus gentium* on non-European peoples, though a universalist assumption prevailed. By the eighteenth-century, as colonialism expanded, jurists gradually shifted from the universalist *jus gentium* to a law of nations used by diplomats and applicable among European States. In 1732 Johann Jacob Moser (1701–85) argued that the 'European Customary Law of Nations' was 'European' because this law did not apply to trade relations with Asian sovereigns or in the occupation of foreign lands. Shortly after, L'Abbé de Mably wrote *Le droit public de l'Europe fondé sur les traités*.

Other authors such as Christian Baron de Wolff, Emeric de Vattel, Cornelius Van Bynkershoek, Baron de Montesquieu, Thomas Rutherforth, Jean Jacques Burlamaqui, used 'European' in their titles and contents of their books directed at the effort to improve and spread treaty practice among European diplomats.[3]

Though Cobald Toze (1715–89) also referred to a European law of nations in a title, in 1780 he made a significant distinction when he argued that 'the existence of a European Law of Nations is undoubtable' and distinguishable from barbarian peoples because of the 'many usages and customs that the Nations of Europe observe among them, both in times of peace and war'.[4] For Toze, the distinct characteristic of a European law of nations was its changeability, progressive potential, and acceptance by the Christian people of Europe through war and peace, treaties and other agreements. 'Other peoples' (Turks, Tartars, Asians, Africans, Savages) were seen by Toze as unmoveable, who treated their prisoners of war as slaves 'or ate them' and thus were part of an 'Asian, African or American law of nations' that was radically different from that of the nations of 'Christian Europe'.[5]

Georg Friederich von Martens (1756–1821) emphasized the change-able character of a European positive law of nations because of the many treaties made among European states and the shared mores of Christian Europeans. By compiling European treaties into a publication that was first of its kind, well received and imitated, Martens sought to distin-guish European nations from others that did not have written agreements among them.[6]

Robert Ward (1765–1846) is an example of another author making an effort to distinguish European difference in an eighteenth-century treatise. Ward was the first post–French Revolution publicist to describe the European nature of the law of nations from a historical account. In his 1795 *Enquiry into the Foundation and History of the Law of Nations in Europe from the Time of the Greeks and Romans, to the Age of Grotius* Ward described Europe's unity and use of the law of nations as supported by a shared system of mores based on a belief in Christianity. Like Toze and other contemporaries, Ward believed there were different law of nations applied to different peoples that were binding 'only upon particular Sets or Classes of Nations, as they fall into different divisions of it, observing different Religions and pursuing different systems of Morality'.[7]

Jeremy Bentham (1748–1832), the British legal philosopher known for founding the theory of modern utilitarianism, coined the term 'interna-tional law' as a side thought in a footnote of his 'Introduction to Principles of Morals and Legislation'. In later texts Bentham discussed the meaning of international law further and asked 'if a citizen of the world had to prepare a universal international code, what would he propose to him-self as his object?' His answer: 'the common and equal utility and … the greatest happiness of all nations taken together.' For Bentham, 'all nations' meant European powers for which he proposed a 'Plan for an Universal and Perpetual Pleace'.[8]

Parallel to Bentham's coining of the term 'international law' and his proposal, Immanuel Kant (1724–1804) was also thinking of how to solve conflict among European nations. Though Kant and Bentham had radically different approaches to a proposal for perpetual peace and a common law among nations, both wrote as philosophers with ideas accepted as universal but informed by an image of Europe as the centre of the world and as imperial. Nonetheless, both Kant and Bentham, like several other figures of the late eighteenth-century, doubted the universal application of a European law of nations and questioned the benefits of expanding colonial projects.[9] Bentham wrote the anti-imperialist *Emancipate your Colonies* and *Rid Yourselves of Ultra María* while Kant criticized the treatment of non-European peoples and commercial domination in *Towards Perpetual Peace* and *A Metaphysics of Morals*.[10] In the nineteenth-century, authors continued to distinguish the particular European character of international law as coming from its 'cultural, ethnographic, psychological and sociological characteristics' and the positivist practice of custom and treaties.[11]

14.3 EIL Challenged from the Americas

The independence of the North and South American colonies provoked varied responses to the understanding of the law of nations or international law as European. US lawyers initially accepted EIL and promoted its benefits.[12] Chief Justice John Marshall (1755–1835), argued that the European character of the law of nations made the US a successor nation of Great Britain's right of 'discovery' with the power of 'ultimate dominion' over occupied lands against all other European governments 'notwithstanding the occupancy of the natives, who were heathens'.[13] Henry Wheaton (1785–1848), praised the US adoption of a political system based on the Westphalian European law of Nations because it gave new strength to positive law and had 'grown up with the progress of Christianity and civilization, commerce and colonization, the multiplication of alliances and extension of diplomatic relations, the establishment of the balance of power, finally all those causes which have jointly contributed to form that great society of nations now existing in Europe'.[14]

Spanish American creole elites who had thought about issues of difference and identity and used exceptionalism as a discourse of response to external domination for several centuries, were less amicable to an unquestioned adherence to EIL.[15] They would have shared Koskenniemi's argument that the European origins and heritage of the law of nations was an unavoidable fact, but at the same time the creoles struggled for a creative role and an identity position based on an argued regional uniqueness. Creoles knew that they had to participate in a European discourse that claimed universality but felt entitled to be co-creators in the construction of knowledge.[16] This exception/inclusion idea was not unique to the regional international law promoted by Spanish Americans: it also provided the framework for a continuous reconstruction of 'American' and/or 'Latin American' identities that set forth (successful and failed) economic, educational, cultural and artistic projects of the most varied political and social trends. Even today, the idea that there are unifying regional commonalities continues to provide traction for all types of collective efforts.

Independence leader, Simón Bolívar, was the first to propose a confederation of American States to defend against the Holy Alliance and its interest in recolonizing the newly independent states. Bolívar's integration proposals were discussed as early as his *Cartagena Manifest* (1812), *Letter from Jamaica* (1815), and Angostura Congress (1819). But it was in the 1826 Bolivarian 'Congress of Panamá' where he organized these ideals in a common proposal which he believed was 'destined to form the widest, most extraordinary or strongest league ever appeared to this day on earth ... The relations of political societies will receive a code of public law that will rule universal behaviour ... the New World will be constituted by independent nations, bound together by a common law defined by their external relations'. Indeed, the first proposal for an 'American International Law' was made at the Panama Congress, though at that moment it failed to be much more than a grand ambition.[17] Though in creative imitation of European institutions such as the Greek amphyctionic leagues of antiquity, as said so by Bolívar himself[18], or the Congress of Vienna of 1815, the integration effort held at Panama could be called a first challenge to a law of nations assumed as only created by, or applicable to, Christian European states. Bolívar's purpose was not to ignore European law of nations, or marginalize the new states, but to participate as equals in what he believed to be a universal and necessary law.[19] The 1826 Treaty of Union, League and Confederation signed at Panama contained in its articles principles that were later hailed as the origins of a 'Latin American International Law' such as collective defence against foreign intervention (Arts 2, 21, 22) political independence (Art. 3) continental solidarity (Art. 3) and equality of states (Art. 5) among others.[20]

In 1832, four years after the Congress of Panama, the Venezuelan-Chilean, Andrés Bello (1781–1865) published the first international law treatise in the Americas purposefully written with an 'American perspective' as part of his region building agenda which sought to demonstrate that the new American states would be able to complete the deficient civilization left by their Spanish forefathers but were in no way inferior to Europe or could be considered as primitive as Africa.[21] Like Bolívar's Congress, Bello's Americanism was non-threatening to EIL. Bello viewed the new American states as entitled to participate in the international community as equals because of the region's burgeoning civilization and its European inheritance. International law was the appropriate legal tool and language which Bello claimed would be effective in the defence of recently acquired independence.[22]

By the mid nineteenth-century, however, the utopian ideal of neighbourly relations with the US and brotherhood with Europeans had diminished as both Europeans and US military interventions increased in the region. Thus the creole elites began to appropriate the concept of a *'Latin America'* originally derived from the idea of *Pan Latinism* promoted by the French economist Michel Chevalier (1806–79) and Ernest Renan (1823–92).[23] The argentine publicist, Carlos Calvo (1824–1906) was the first to begin using the term *'Latin* America' (with emphasis on the *Latin*) in a title of a treatise and as a term to advocate defence of sovereignty and independence, and recognition from European nations.[24] Simultaneously, however, Calvo was an advocate of bringing European immigrants to help 'civilize' South America and he played an active role in the Berlin Conference on West Africa of 1884–85 in which colonial titles over African territories were partitioned among European powers.[25] Calvo was remembered as the lawyer who defended Portugal's rights over African territories *vis a vis* the rights of more powerful European nations.[26] He regarded the 'right of civilization' (*droit de civilization*) as the right civilized peoples have to manage savages whether they are in their own countries (i.e. the US, Mexico and the nations of South America) or in other regions (such as West Africa).[27] Calvo saw no contradiction between supporting the European scramble for Africa and his doctrine of non-intervention in protection of sovereignty for the Americas. For Calvo, African peoples were as uncivilized (or more) than the indigenous peoples of the Americas and did not understood as having an equal status to the independent states of Latin America that had acquired sovereignty and had been recognized as participants of the international community for almost a century.

After Bolívar's Congress and many other proposals, treaties, projects and conferences seeking the region's legal and political defence and integration, the Chilean lawyer, Alejandro Álvarez (1868–1960), theorized these nineteenth-century events as a 'Latin American International Law' (LAIL) and promoted them for half a century.[28] Like Bello, Calvo and others before him, Álvarez's challenged Eurocentrism by arguing that the region's particularities (of history, culture, geography, climate, peoples) made for *sui generis* international legal problems which required different solutions than those of old Europe. Álvarez wrote that the American nations have a 'liberal and democratic spirit' based on solidarity, equality and universal suffrage while Europe represented the 'unstable and dangerous' concepts of 'individualism, the balance of power, alliances and armed peace'.[29] The birth of the Organization of American States (OAS) in 1948 epitomized the highest development of LAIL, while for others it was the beginning of its end due to the gradual fragmentation of international law into specialized problem solving areas, the death of Álvarez, its main promoter, and the Cold War polarization that followed. More recently, however, LAIL history has been revisited as well as innovative approaches of grassroots organizations that looks at international law 'from below'.[30]

14.4 Soviet Critiques of Eurocentrism

LAIL promoters challenged Eurocentrism in order to be equal participants under international law with regional differences recognized but they were not in opposition to the economic (capitalism) and religious (Christianity) tenants structuring EIL. Soviet approaches to international law (SAIL), on the other hand, perceived Eurocentrism as the centrality of capitalism, colonialism, and class struggle to the discipline's theory and practice.

Soviet lawyers presented the 1917 Russian revolution as marking the shift from the "old colonial laws of war to the new laws of peace and socialist values; from a false universality to legal pluralism; from a bourgeois EIL that benefitted a few powers, to, ultimately, the paradoxical utopia of the elimination of international law because the future would be 'nation-less and class-less'. In essence, SAIL scholars challenged what they considered as the 'bourgeois underpinnings of international law'[31] as they incorporated the views of Marx, Engels and Lenin into their perspective. SAIL promoted the end of Europe as the centre of power because it was 'decadent liberal, and colonialist' while Russia's past was 'unique, superior and separate'.[32] The ultimate objective of SAIL, however, was the gradual disappearance of international law through 'a provisional inter-class law which aims to further the interests of organized national labouring classes in their common struggle for proletarian world supremacy'.[33]

Soviet lawyers, like the Latin Americans, were not homogenous in their approach and differed in the particularities they highlighted. Evgeni Korovin (1891–1963), inspired in Alejandro Álvarez's LAIL proposals, advocated a 'socialist international law or international law of the transitory period as one of the special systems of international law'.[34] Evgeny Pashukanis (1891–1937) denounced international law as the structure in which the capitalist bourgeoisie hide behind their particular class interests behind a technical and legal language while they fight over world domination of their colonies and the proletariat.[35] Sergeï Krylov (1888–1958), the first soviet-socialist judge on the International Court of Justice, argued that by introducing the Soviet State's socialist principles international law's democratic tendencies would open.[36] Fyodor Kozhevnikov (1893–1998) wrote on the Russian State (1947) and the Soviet State (1948) in International Law and emphasized that Russia's (or the USSR's) socialist victory in 1917 initiated Russian interests over Europe's.[37]

Grigory Ivanovich Tunkin (1906–93) was a well-known SAIL jurist who proposed the principle of 'proletariat internationalism' described as 'fraternal friendship ... close cooperation, and mutual assistance of the working classes of various countries in the struggle for their liberation'.[38] Tunkin was more conciliatory than Pashukanis, Korovin, or Kozhevnikov because he did not advocate for an end of international law but rather regarded Soviet doctrines and the Russian revolution as making international law truly 'universal' by not allowing it to belong exclusively to the 'civilized', Christian, colonialist or stronger states.[39]

14.5   African Regionalism after Decolonization

LAIL lawyers often identified with the colonizers as their forefather's and did not disregard their Spanish imperial heritage of law and culture, though they rejected European claims of superiority and permanently fought for recognition as equal participants and contributors to the development of international law. During and after the decolonization period in the 1960s, however, African scholars presented international law's European origins and character in a negative light in relation to its imperial history.

African international lawyers argued that unequal treatment was given to their new states in practices such as the principle of automatic succession of (unfavourable) treaties, or in the status of their states as United Nations 'trust territories' because they were presumed incapable of bearing sovereignty.[40] The first book with an African approach to international law was published by the Nigerian lawyer, Felix Chuks Okoye (1940–83) as 'International law and The New African States' where he discussed the legal personality, decolonization, state succession and the concept of regionalism.[41] Okoye did not promote an 'African International Law' because he did not want European and US scholars to marginalize the region based on ideas of cultural or religious difference. Okoye's position is similar to Latin American lawyers such as Carlos Calvo, who did not want to advocate a LAIL because they felt it would marginalize them further from the Eurocentric international law. But differently from Okoye, the Latin American lawyers who opposed a LAIL position, did not see it as a marginalization based on culture or religion because they thought themselves Europe an descendents. Rather, the LAIL critics understood regionalism as a way of being kept out of the production and application of international law occurring in the centres of power. Okoye's position was to embrace a Third World perspective on inequality based on the African states post-colonial character, a shared identity with Asian and Latin American States struggles in nation-building and the economic issues that came from their underdevelopment.[42] As such, African regionalism not only surged from an obvious need for unity among the newly decolonized states, but also from critiques of anti-colonial and anti-Eurocentric positions, as well as from the proposal for a New International Economic Order.

African scholars approached international law in the 1970s with more optimism as it supported their independence and the United Nations General Assembly agreed on Resolutions 3201 on 'Declaration of the Establishment of a New International Economic Order' and 3281 on 'The Charter of Economic Rights and Duties of States'. The British educated Nigerian lawyer, Taslim Olawale Elias (1914–91) and ICJ judge, initially promoted an integration of West African customary law with English common law but by the 1970s he had become more radicalized by advocating an African contribution to international law and highlighting the shared African experience in face of their differences with the European colonizers.[43] Elias argued that Europe's creation of a Third World was based on inequality and imperialism.[44]

The 1980s, however, brought the debt crisis that came with the excessive accumulation of interest and a devastating impact on the new African states. The politics of the International Monetary Fund's restructuring program as well as the rise of conservative governments in the US and the UK obscured everyday African claims for global justice and domestic equity and allowed for corrupt African leaders to enter the scene.[45] The beginning of the 1980s also brought a structured idea of the global economy. The Algerian diplomat and international lawyer, Mohammed Bedjaoui (1929–) wrote the book 'Towards a New International Economic Order' which was published in 1979 as a first in a UNESCO series on 'New Challenges to International Law'. The book came out the same year in French, English and Spanish giving it a broad distribution and impact. Its anti-Eurocentrism, like Okoye's, was not based on African regionalism, but rather on the idea of Third World versus the West, or North versus South. Bedjaoui also described European international law as an 'exclusive club of States' conceived only for the benefit of those who called themselves 'civilized'.[46]

In the late 1990s a new group of African and Asian scholars that lived the impact of the 1980s debt crisis, began to publish critical work which revisited the anti-colonialist literature of the 1960s and 1970s. James Gathii, a Kenyan, Harvard educated law professor wrote in 1998 on Third World Approaches to International Law (TWAIL) scholarship. Gathii argued that TWAIL included a strong and weak strand. The strong strand did not see Eurocentrism as problematic in itself, but rather that it originated in industrial capitalism. Strong TWAIL claims, Gathii describes, vowed for self-determination, promoted solidarity on the role of economic, political, social and cultural discourses and revisited the relationship of colonized and colonizing countries.[47] The strong strand criticized the weak strand for being more apologetic than critical in the post-decolonization era and for repressing the record of imperial actions over their own parts of the world.[48] The weak strand, as described by Gathii, critiqued Eurocentrism for its geographic origins, claimed integrationism through self-determination, uncritically endorsed the UN human rights and development agendas; failed to examine the structures of colonialism; assimilated politically, legally and culturally into the structures of the global system; paid no attention to questions of power, hierarchy and ideology; used history to 'spiritually rehabilitate' Africa by connecting the commercial and social relations pre-colonial kingdoms had with European societies; argued that Eurocentric international law can be reformed and improved;

believed that human rights can alleviate inequality; proposed that civilizational pluralism, cultural diversity, cooperation, economic openness,
participation in international institutions, and focussing on interdepen-
dence are a better way of addressing the inequalities of international law
than a radical or fundamental challenge to the status quo. Ultimately, the
weak strand was also criticized for failing to acknowledge the historical
role of racism and contemporary inequalities in any fundamental way.[49]

Other well-known scholars of the second TWAIL generation, like
Makau Mutua and Antony Anghie, took stronger strand positions. In
addition to the general critiques of Eurocentrism, Mutua noted that there
is also racism within Africa, such as that of the Arab Muslims who enslaved
and allowed for the enslavement of millions of black Africans for many
years.[50] Anghie has demonstrated that European colonialism and empire
is essential to the international legal structure and initiates with the 1648
Treaty of Westphalia's classical concept of sovereign equality which considered Non-European nations as lacking and allowed for the colonization
of Asia, Africa and the Americas.[51]

14.6 Asian Critiques of Eurocentrism

In the 1960s Ram Prakash Anand (1933–2011) initiated an Asian perspective by revisiting the history of international law in order to challenge the
'newness' posited by States that were recently independent.[52] Anand, an
Indian born lawyer, with graduate studies from Yale university, published
more than twenty books and one hundred articles, many of which were
subtitled an 'Asian perspective' in order to promote the role of the new
Asian-African states in the international order.

By the 1980s, Anand incorporated his view of Eurocentrism in a book
titled *Origin and Development of Law of the Sea: History of International
Law Revisited* (1983). In this book Anand rejected the Eurocentric narrative of the history of international law and emphasized the inequality
between nations and the colonial past. Anand argued that international
law 'consists of a series of doctrines and principles that were developed in
Europe, that emerged out of European history and experience, and that
were extended in time to the non-European world which existed outside
the realm of European international law.'[53] International law, according
to Anand, was told as the history that developed during the last three centuries as a product of 'European or Western Christian civilization' and of
the 'European mind' and 'European beliefs' to which Asian and African
countries had made little or no contribution. Anand was adamant in

promoting the contribution argument that Ghatti would later label as the weak strand of TWAIL. He questioned the European history by re-reading canonical works and demonstrating that Grotius theory was not original because he borrowed from Asian maritime practices in the High Seas. This argument led to the conclusion that Asian states were not 'new' but 'old' and had contributed to the foundation of international law. Though Anand began writing with an Asian perspective, his work became more broadly accepted when he proposed that international law that does not benefit the interest of Third World peoples and States should be contested, the history of international law cannot exclude the Third World, and international law regimes can be reformed to serve Third World peoples and States.

Anand's oeuvre had a major impact on Asian and African international law scholars. By 1987, Frederick E. Snyder and Surakiart Sathiratathai gathered many TWAIL authors (including Anand) in the book *Third World Attitudes toward International Law: an Introduction* to present the particular problems of the new states in the frame of the post-decolonization period. Though Gathii compared the first TWAIL to the LAIL project[54] a closer look shows that Latin American regionalism was based on quite the opposite reasons than the TWAIL approach. Anand argued that Indonesia, Malaysia, the Philippines, Singapore and Thailand, members of the Association of Southeast Asian Nations (ASEAN) were joined by the sea and that 'despite all differences in languages, religions, customs and legal systems, . . . [they were] – bound together by common bonds of geography, pre-colonial history and similar aspirations for the future'.[55] Though LAIL regionalism was also based on a common pre-colonial history, their main argument for regional unity was the sharing of a continent, the Spanish language, Catholic religion, customs and legal systems inherited from the Spanish colonizers. LAIL advocates of the first half of the twentieth-century disregarded unity based on the millions of native indigenous, peoples of African descent, or any other of the mixed population that constituted the majority of the continent's inhabitants.

Japan's insertion into Eurocentric international law began with the unequal imposition of treaties in the mid nineteenth-century, the consequent 1865 translation of Henry Wheaton's 1835 *Elements of International Law*, the first international law course in 1870 at the University of Tokyo taught by foreign scholars until 1883, the founding of the Japanese Society of International Law in 1897 and the Japanese Journal of International Law in 1902.[56] Pre–World War I scholars Sakuye Takahashi (1865–1920) and Nagao Ariga (1860–1921) published books focussed on the wars between

Japan and Russia, and China. As the Japanese government got involved in international conflicts, especially in East Asia, diplomatic theory and history became a more important area of study in Japan. However, Japan's perspective in the region has been seen as distinct from an Asian perspective of international law. When Anand described the region as connecting Indonesia, Malaysia, the Philippines, Singapore and Thailand he left out Japan. Japan has been thought of by Asian scholars as 'in-between' the European world of the colonizer and its outside world of the colonized during the inter-war period.[57]

Soon after international law was introduced in Japan, the Japanese Imperial Government enthusiastically supported the idea of the Versailles system of the 1920s, but when Japan invaded Manchuria in 1931 and consequently withdrew from the League of Nations in 1933, Japanese scholars assumed their country as a major power and as a 'semi-European' state.[58] Some liberal Kelsenian cosmopolitan idealist scholars (Kamikawa, Osawa, Royama) used this turn of events to promote either East Asian regionalism[59] or isolationism in order to survive the inter-war period.[60] Kaoru Yasui, a leading Japanese international scholar at that time and an ideologist of the Japanese war effort, relied inter alia on the Japanese translations of Schmitt, Korovin and Pashukanis in order to argue that classical international law was not universal, but particular and European-imperialist.

Eurocentrism continued to be a challenge for the Japanese government as it built a new regional order the Greater East Asia Co-Prosperity Sphere (*Dai Tôa Kyôei Ken*).[61] 'The Greater Asia' argued that their union was based on European colonial rule and their need to claim emancipation from European international society.[62] Other scholars argued for a regional unity around the rejection of a Schmittean Völkerrecht or a universalized European international law while proposing an alternative international order supported by foreign policy.[63] The problem for Japan was that its policy towards East Asia was not coherent[64] but 'pro Greater-Asia scholars, such as Kaoro Yasui (1907–) and Shigejiro Tabata (1911–2001) wrote a "Greater East Asian International Law" *(Daitoua Kokusai-hou)* based on Schmitt's theory of the *Grossraum* in which he argued that the Greater Asia was a 'new order' emancipated from the European world and its rules. Schmitt's theory was also used by other Japanese imperialists to posit a regional legal system in which Japan would head the new order apart from Europe.[65] Tabata viewed the entry into international law as Japan's acceptance of rules for dealing with European states but not as the 'Europeanization' of those states nor that international law had become 'universalized'.[66] For Tabata, regionalism was a European, Kelsenian single and integrated theory of international law, while Schmitt's framework was based on a world order of blocs and on sovereign inequality.[67] Hardly a critique of Eurocentrism in the TWAIL way, Japanese scholars viewed the need to shift the centre of power in their region to Japan as natural leaders. Therefore, what Tabata and other Japanese internationalists did was transfer, in theory and in practice, Eurocentrism to 'Japan-centrism'.

14.7   Eurocentrism Viewed from the Second Generation of TWAIL

The second generation of TWAIL scholars (or TWAIL II) made the critique of international law's Eurocentrism more visible and updated. In a 2012 article in which Balakrishnan Rajagopal distinguishes between TWAIL I and II he argued that the 'most important critique of modern international law has been the charge that it is a Eurocentric regime, which has helped to erect and defend a world of deep injustice characterized by violence, exploitation, and inequality'.[68] Rajagopal places the beginnings of Eurocentric critiques in the early twentieth-century with TWAIL I understood as the Latin American 'Calvo and Drago doctrines of non-intervention; the rise of Japan; the establishment of administration of colonies under international control instead of under colonial powers; the call for a new welfarist function for international law; and a rethinking of international law as administration; and decolonization'.[69] In this characterization of the first TWAIL generation, authors such as Bedjaoui, Anand and Elias, viewed the solution to international law's Eurocentrism as the need to make it 'truly universal'. Rajagopal presents TWAIL II as more radical and less compliant because it sees the world system as inherently exploitative and protest and revolt as the only chance for the poor.[70] TWAIL II scholars such as Abdullahi An-Na'im, Richard Falk, V. S. Mani, Judge Weeramantry, Upendra Baxi, B. S. Chimni, Issa Shivji, often see international law as 'part of the problem' and an instrument of injustice rather than the need to apply or reform international law to adapt to third world necessities. Rajagopal states that despite TWAIL II's commitment to a more democratic and just global system its proponents have abandoned the faith of TWAIL I. They view the historical and structural conditions of changing economic, political, and cultural power more deeply and are critical of the transformation of international law's main institutions.[71] Rajagopal concludes that today's problem is not Eurocentrism but rather the 'model of economic development and globalization which has played out as overproduction, ceaseless accumulation, consumption, and destruction of resources as well as a crisis of the normative and institutional foundations of global order'.[72]

In sum, international law's Eurocentrism was challenged beginning with the independence of Haiti and the Spanish American nations in the eighteenth and nineteenth centuries and continuing well into the twentieth-century with African, Soviet, Third World and Asian approaches to international law. This brief overview took into account that critiques of international law's Eurocentrism are not limited to challenging the geographical origins of the discipline, but rather to the impact of Europe's colonial history on the economic, political, racial, or religious structural underpinnings of international law which still result in injustice and inequality for the most impoverished states and peoples around the world. Eurocentric assumptions in which justice, power or resistance are understood to be operating have been challenged from different approaches, the most conservative as reformist and contributionist, the most radical as the complete elimination or revolt against the sources and institutions of international law.

Appendix

Overview of Koskenniemi's Take on Eurocentrism in International Law

Before presenting the Lake Saimaa interview, I will highlight Koskenniemi's written views on Eurocentrism from a few of his most relevant texts.

The Absence of a Critique of Eurocentrism in From Apology to Utopia

Koskenniemi's acknowledgement of international law's European origins is not new. In his doctoral dissertation published by Cambridge University Press as *From Apology to Utopia: The Structure of International Legal Argument* (1988) Koskenniemi does not argue in favour or against the 'truistic claim of international law's Western heritage' as an identity issue, but rather acknowledges it as a set of 'pluralistic or individualistic ideas ... associated with the liberal doctrine of politics'. In this sense, anyone who relies on the classical law of sovereign equality, Koskenniemi argues, has to simultaneously accept the liberal doctrine of politics. Thus Koskenniemi presents us with the paradox of the authors who 'deplore Western intellectual heritage are most anxious to universalize it under a rigid international system of sovereign equality' while undermining 'the intellectual principles of their own culture'.[73] The example used by Koskenniemi is a reference to one of the TWAIL I scholars, the Indian lawyer R.P. Anand (1933–2011) who published *New States in International Law* in 1973. Anand claims that a complex system of international ideas and social organization existed before Europeans destroyed it and therefore the newly decolonized States must participate in their rebuilding. Koskenniemi's point is to demonstrate that origins claims are not critical, but rather agree with liberal politics and strengthen the mainstream status quo of international legal thought. He supports implied critique of inequality in international relations by non-Western lawyers but proves that its argumentative structure is flawed.

In *Apology to Utopia*, Koskenniemi is not interested in the non-European discourses on international law for their political, economic or social value. His objective was to get to the core understanding of the structure of international legal thought. In his first book, Koskenniemi never uses the term 'Eurocentrism' and his references to 'civilization' or 'colonialism' are in passing. He makes it clear that if 'even if the semantic or evaluative indeterminacies were cleared, the international legal system as a whole would still remain indeterminate and lack the capacity of providing coherent justification because indeterminacy follows as a structural property of the international legal language itself and is not an externally introduced distortion'.[74]

In *Apology to Utopia*, Koskenniemi does not view the world in terms of Europe and its former colonies. He does make a slight distinction between 'Western liberal internationalism' and its 'influence' or rejection by developing or socialist nations. In this description, non-Western lawyers do not make claims aimed at discussing 'morality, common interests or the nature of international law or relations' but rather prefer to focus on protecting 'self-determination, national identity and the pursuance of domestic policies'.[75]

Eurocentrism Uncovered in The Gentle Civilizer

As all readers of Koskenniemi's work know, and as he explains in the introduction, his bestselling *The Gentle Civilizer of Nations: The Rise and Fall of International Law 1870–1960* published more than a decade later, is a very different book. While in *Apology to Utopia*, Koskenniemi gave the problem of Eurocentrism very little thought, in the Gentle Civilizer, he says that 'one of the most remarkable feats in the discipline's self-construction is its overwhelming Eurocentrism'.[76] This book takes into account critical legal studies approaches and recent work that linked European international law to its colonial past. By the time of the *Gentle Civilizer*'s publication, Koskenniemi acknowledges the work of Antony Anghie, Nathaniel Berman, Anthony Carty, David Kennedy, Karen Knop and Annelise Riles among a few others that wrote new historical approaches to international law's past and places himself as one of its contributors. In the second chapter on 'International lawyers and imperialism 1870–1914' he makes a disclaimer on why all his protagonists are 'white men' because his purpose is to tell 'the narrative of the mainstream as a story about its cosmopolitan sensibilities and political projects'.[77] At the same time, he makes a call for the need for more histories coming from or about women and 'non-Europeans' in international law. Koskenniemi is very conscious of where his major contribution will be and sticks to that role of meticulously (and respectfully) deconstructing the mainstream while inviting others to present histories from places and people that are not from the European centre of production of international legal thought.

Koskenniemi's chapter on imperialism discusses the works of several writers and argues that though there was no *necessary* relationship between the 'Comparative Method, pedigree history, and racism' because the results were practically inevitable as were generalizations about the 'lack of the concept of a State by the Orient, the stagnation of non-European societies, ... the East as voiceless, irrational feminine, and the West as male, ... democratic and forward looking'.[78] Koskenniemi is careful to describe how the European discourse on colonialism and civilization was far from being a homogenous one, but only briefly begins to unravel the problem of Eurocentrism.

Eurocentrism as a Topic

Fast forward a decade later, Koskenniemi gave a series of lectures and wrote an article specifically on the topic of Eurocentrism in the histories of international law.[79] In the article on 'Dealing with Eurocentrism' he argues that until the late nineteenth-century, histories of international law were unthinkingly Eurocentric. Europe served as the 'origin, engine and telos of historical knowledge'.[80] Histories of international law of the twentieth-century, on the other hand, 'turn away from Eurocentrism to universal institutions designed to carry out the technical and functional tasks called for by the management of a globally interdependent world'.[81] Koskenniemi praises the twenty-first century efforts by contemporary scholars in different locations, to finally begin to engage with the 'elephant in the room'. He finds it compelling and necessary for new histories to recognize the role of Europeans and non-Europeans, center and periphery, colonial and anti-colonial subjects in the construction of a history, discourse and practice of international law.

Lake Saimaa Interview

The interview transcribed below resulted from Koskenniemi's informal and unprepared responses to a few questions I posed to him on Eurocentrism. Though I did my best to be 'critical' in this interview, it became evident that Koskenniemi is his own fiercest critic: he is in constant self-reflection on many topics which he has explored and developed in his work or has acted on in his professional practice, from which he takes a stand when convinced of them, or departs from them when they are confronted by further research or by the evidence in reality, or when they become stale or useless. In any case, I hope the previous overview of critiques of Eurocentrism by Koskenniemi and other authors provided a background in which to understand what may be missing from the interview that took place at Lake Saimaa, Finland in 2013.

I have several questions from the perspective of 'the Eurocentrism of Koskenniemi's Eurocentrism'. The first question is: when did you first encounter Eurocentrism as a problem in your work?

I suppose this was when I started reading critical literature in the 1980s, and for the first time began to think what resonance that might have in international law – and of course what kind of a profile I should have as a scholar in the field. At that time, one could not avoid the topos of Eurocentrism – but it was unclear to me what it would involve in terms of international law. I think the debate itself has developed quite a bit from the 1980s. Even though a decade earlier I was a political conservative, I had a leftish perspective to the problem of Europe's omnipresence and Europe's historical legacy as well as the extremely boring character of everything European. But it was not obvious how this would reflect in finding an appropriate orientation in legal science.

How would you define Eurocentrism and why have you only recently written about it?

There are several meanings of Eurocentrism. First, one can approach it as a problem among others, like social injustice or the position of women in society. But at some point the nature of Eurocentrism changed, so it did not seem to be quite like those other problems that you can deal with through social instruments, technologies and thought. Eurocentrism was more like the *Alien* that had entered inside you, it was part of the very vocabularies that enabled you to think about those other problems. The question was, then, whether it was at all possible to exorcise it, to get rid of it. I realized that I was completely Eurocentric in the sense that my vocabulary, my experience, my education, my view of the world had Europe as their focus. But I was never too obsessed about this. I suppose this was because it was always relatively easy for me to have an ironic distance to my own views of the world, my own vocabularies and experiences. So I thought I could deal with it with a little self-analysis, remembering that everything I had to say about all those other problems, social injustice, gender problems, problems in education and so on, were articulated through a vocabulary that, even though Eurocentric, was still capable of expressing many different ideas and experiences.

So that would lead to the obvious question: can you detach from your own Eurocentrism? And I don't mean Martti Koskenniemi's Eurocentrism, I mean anyone who practices, writes or thinks about international law (or international legal history) has to have a Eurocentric position because of the roots of international law. I remember the first time we met, when I presented my first paper on the Latin Americans at a panel at ASIL and you were writing your 'Gentle Civilizer' and at the time of the talk you came to me and you said: 'You need to keep on writing about this because I am writing the European story but yours is the part that is not known'. It was only much later that I came to realize that the Latin Americans were as Eurocentric as their European colleagues. Though they were arguing regionalist exceptionalism they were trying to position themselves through a Eurocentric discourse and tools, and they didn't want to be marginal. They wanted to be at the centre. And to do that they had to use French, the language of European international law, and they had to speak from Paris or Geneva. Their strategy wasn't to be left out, it was actually to be at the centres of production of knowledge. So, in that sense they were as Eurocentric as the Europeans. It was very interesting for me after understanding this, to see TWAIL people presenting the Latin Americans as initiators of a Third World perspective, but then, when they understood (from my own work) that these guys were as Eurocentric as the Europeans, then they had a strange feeling (rejection) towards the Latin Americans. So, is it possible to NOT be Eurocentric, without being completely marginalized from the field?

In post-colonial studies, that is a big problem: is it possible to participate in the debate about Eurocentrism and not adopt a standpoint that commits you to speak in Eurocentric language? I suppose there is a way in which one can say that when one is working in a technological or economic idiom, or perhaps simply working in academia – the very idea of academia is a European idea – then one is committed to Eurocentrism. That is an aspect of the fact that Europe has ruled the world for a long time. Its influence cannot be escaped. We cannot wish it would disappear overnight. Nor am I sure we should. 'Eurocentrism' is a really blurred concept; so many different things are expressed by it. This means that one also ought to deal with it in differing ways. One might, for example, think of Eurocentrism as just a natural aspect of human situatedness – the way in which all of us speak from *some* point of view. Having a point of view – even a 'European' point of view (whatever that might mean) is then not a problem as long as one can be analytical, or self-critical about it. I often think like this. One should also remember like Eurocentrism, 'Europe' stands for many ideas, practices or experiences. It is not a solid identity to embrace or not to embrace. That something originates in or associates with Europe is not a sufficient reason to reject it. The Eurozone crisis is a good reminder that 'Europe' is often invoked for opposite agendas and policies, alternative forms of domination.

But there are also other ways. In anthropology and the social sciences, even in law, we have come to think in terms of hybrids. I see the attraction of hybridity as coming to terms with a kind of schizophrenia; one is always speaking from a place but is nevertheless never quite at that place. One is speaking a Eurocentric language, but at the same time the fly on the wall, observing one's speaking. True, when one thinks in those terms one is still kind of captured within the iron cage of Eurocentrism. The *Alien* persists, but one is conscious of and seeks to deal with it. There is also a further reaction, and I find myself suggesting this to students in class increasingly often. At some point Europeans just need to stop talking and begin to listen, without yielding to the impulse of responding by way of some solution, blueprint or technology. It is extremely hard for Europeans to do this. It is hard for me. I mean, just to stop talking and to admit that our speech – whatever its content – lacks legitimacy not because of what it suggests but because of who is speaking. This is not a Eurocentric idea: it is a very non-enlightenment idea, and as I see it written down, it seems frankly weird. But I find myself thinking in those terms with more frequency, and I just put it out for you. I do not have a further defence of it.

Ok, so that would be one way to deal with Eurocentrism. In your writings you look for or challenge Eurocentric positions, or you deconstruct the objects that you study. Those are also ways to destabilize Eurocentrism. Would you say that the other way that you, have tried to challenge Eurocentrism is through the academic milieu that you have formed through colleagues, students and institutions outside of Europe?

Well, I hope one could do more of that. But there are many practical problems. For example, we organize events at the university in Helsinki and receive at our summer course many applications from outside Europe, perhaps one-third of them from Africa. Unfortunately, we know already that either these people, won't get a visa or if they do get a visa we will never see them. They will disappear in some other place in Europe, once they receive the Schengen visa. That, of course, is a fact of the way the world is organized. What can one do about it, I mean practically? So we continue admitting non-European applicants, and we write to Finnish visa authorities, and hope that the situation will improve. This is somewhat frustrating. There are clear limits to what one can do inside the (European) academy. Of course, there are many senior scholars – like you – who work at European and American universities and contribute greatly to putting our inherited Eurocentrism into question. That is very important. But often these more senior scholars turn out to be educated in American universities or in Paris, or at SOAS in London, and continue to pursue their careers in the West. For reasons that are of course understandable. It's hard to create a more mass-oriented contribution. No doubt, more could be done. But let me add that it is disappointing that most of the cooperation between European academy and the world outside is with China, and not with other parts of the global South.

What you were just talking about speaks directly to a type of Eurocentrism ... And now we could talk about the twenty-first century as the non-European century yet we see a lot of the same language of the past. Is this century being led by China, India and other non-western emerging powers? Are we still talking about Eurocentrism here or is this something else? Is Eurocentrism another name for modernity? If that is going on elsewhere, what are the strategies, then, to deal with this?

Eurocentrism is precisely about the process whereby a European vocabulary becomes a universal vocabulary; the entire world becomes 'Europe' in the sense that the languages that rule us, (languages of economy, technology, democratic party politics, statehood, nation State, etc.) lead us to European ways of thought and domination. Can we then say that we are all 'Europeans'; that the *Alien* has come inside all of us? I suppose yes, we can. Interacting with a Chinese, Japanese or, say, Indian colleagues these days is pretty easy. It is easy not because I know much about China or

Japan or India, but because they speak English and they are international lawyers, and they have an experience from academic and political institutions that are familiar to us – institutions whose history and curriculum is Eurocentric. But I suppose Europe may also often act as a vessel – the empty signifier – through which anything can be expressed. At that point it will no longer be useful to be obsessed about its pedigree. Of course, one must be wary about the hidden structures: black faces, white masks as Fanon would have put it. But there must come a point where our politics of conscience should be directed against something else than the possibly 'Eurocentric' character of our vocabularies and technologies.

But it could be that instead of being really Eurocentric, it was something else – it was modernity.

Yes, that is what Europeans always thought. They never thought that this was something specifically European.

What is being obvious here is not the Eurocentric element but maybe another thing. Maybe it is not that we should stop worrying but rather that we should develop other kind of strategies? I don't know. Is that a valid question? Maybe we don't even need to talk about Eurocentrism anymore in terms of the critical languages or the critical tools that we use as produced in Europe as Eurocentrism, because is a place of deduction of knowledge possible as well? I mean, it is sometimes confusing because, is there something like 'good' Eurocentrism and 'bad' Eurocentrism?

I suppose there is 'good' and 'bad' Eurocentrism. The languages and knowledges that rule us are mostly produced in Europe or in the US (understood as an extension of Europe). For most of the time the expansion of these languages and technologies has been regarded as equivalent to modernization, globalization and the world becoming united. That world unity is brought about by languages of European origin has not always been regarded as a problem. It is only through decolonization and post-colonial theory that the *topos* of Eurocentrism has enabled us to make the critical point that what you think is a universal language actually is a European language presenting it as universal, but in fact embodying very specific preferences. Now, that point can be read either as a historical description, a datum of sociology of knowledge – or it can be taken as a criticism of a specific type of knowledge. It's not clear always which one it is and my own uses of Eurocentrism do move between historical description and critique without myself always being clear as to which side I am on.

What about biology for example? Biology was invented in the seventeenth to eighteenth -century at certain European institutions. One can perhaps then say 'biology is Eurocentric'. Is that is a critique of biology? I doubt that. But there is again a final, a complex point, which I have to bring out although I don't have the means to analyse it really. The further question to ask is: 'who is it that uses that language' (of biology)? Whom does it empower and whom does it disempower? These questions do open the door for criticisms of the various uses – above all racist uses – in which the vocabularies of biology have been put. Again, this is to break down the universalism into the particular agendas that loom behind it. As is my intuition that when, a moment ago, you asked the question, legitimately, as to what happened when we use that language, I was immediately struck by your use of the 'we'. What do you mean by 'we'? We Europeans have this linguistic tendency of using the first person plural as indicating everybody in the world, especially when 'we' are enthusiastic about something. That is surely a dubious tendency. This does not mean it is always wrong. And yet, it does involve a capture of other peoples' voice – this 'we'. Europeans should be particularly careful when using it.

But wouldn't that lead you to 'strategic essentialism'?

Well of course, I notice that I move within 'strategic essentialism' often. But I don't like the way Spivak puts this notion forward. I find the term 'strategic essentialism' alienating as a kind of a stopgap, whereas it could also be an opening that doesn't have such a bad faith connotation that Spivak's term has. Perhaps if you work on it more you will get beyond the idea that it is merely strategic.

I see a lot of examples in the alliance between anthropology and law, especially when indigenous communities are seeking to claim legal benefits. Are those the kind of practices badly described as strategic essentialism?

Am I entitled to say that I don't know? I don't have an opinion on the benefits of that strategy. I suppose that as a strategic choice, it cannot or should not be assessed in the abstract. Everything depends on what a group wants to do with it in a particular situation.

This is quite pertinent to the debate in Latin America, there is a lot of identity politics.

I was thinking what happened to me in a recent conference. They asked me to talk (again) about regionalism through the Latin America story, and I told my critical version but the person who was supposed to comment on my paper (one of the Latin American judges at the ICJ) instead gave a counter presentation in order to correct what I said and present the '"correct" and "classical" contribution of Latin Americans to international law' argument. So he corrected my mistaken interpretation of the 'truth'. This is not rare, however, because the other version understands my work as promoting Latin American particularity in international law despite my critique of its imperialist consequences in the region. But in general, as an elite that had a project I wouldn't look at their efforts as critical or as an opening for a broader inclusion of protections for people in Latin America. It was the project of a small elite that wanted to be at the centre of the production of knowledge. So, would this be an example of the reverse effect in terms of letting 'them' (non-Europeans) speak? Because, though they are not from Europe, at the same time they may have a very authoritarian position that from a critical perspective one would not agree with.

One thing we have learned in the course of these years is that criticism does not stop, cannot stop at Europe's boundaries. So, even if one realizes that Eurocentrism is a big problem, one also realizes that what exists outside of Europe isn't made any better by a mere restatement of well-known critiques of European history, ideas or practices. Things that come from outside Europe must be met with an equally critical attitude. I really have a hard time with the kind of nostalgic attitudes otherwise critical lawyers from the global South sometimes have towards structures of rule antedating the consolidation of European rule, just to give an example.

That leads me to another experience from a recent conference of the European Society of International Law, where you were not present. In that conference, your name came up in almost every panel that I went to, including the inaugural lectures, so rather than being a marginal, critical voice, all of a sudden, you had blossomed into the mainstream. By using your work, it was now legitimate to safely say things that before would sound too radical. And I kept thinking, 'is this a good thing or a bad thing'? Are they using it because his work has been so good he has been able to make them think about these issues or are they using it as necessary cause and effect but they don't really understand the critique you have there? So, when does the critic become the mainstream and manage to change something? Or, when is the critic's work used by the mainstream to continue the status quo?

It is true that it is very easy for the European (or US) mainstream to appropriate aspects of my work. In part I think this is because I am just saying something that everybody has known all along; I may have been able to give expression to some of this silent knowledge. I have no problem with that. To the contrary, I am delighted that I have been able to catch the attention of practising (mainstream) lawyers. I hope that this may have prompted some self-critical reflection as well. But then I also see some parts – especially the 'indeterminacy thesis' – being used by reactionary jurists for purposes I do not share. Of course I find this problematic, and I think of those moments as invitations for further thinking on my part. But nobody is a master of the uses (or indeed of the meanings) of what they say or write, so I try to take this calmly.

Notes

1. I have edited the interview for easier reading, but it has been left as faithful to the original as possible. I thank Maria Angélica Prada's assistance in transcribing the interview filmed on Lake Saimaa, Finland, 12 June 2013.
2. See A. Becker-Lorca, 'Eurocentrism in the History of International Law', in B. Fassbender and A. Peters (eds), *The Oxford Handbook of the History of International Law* (Oxford: Oxford University Press, 2012), 1053–56.
3. M. Vec, 'Universalization, Particularization, and Discrimination: European Perspectives on a Cultural History of 19th Century International Law', *InterDisciplines* 2 (2012): 85. In note 7, Vec lists nearly twenty German law books with 'European' in the title.
4. E. Toze, *La liberté de la navigation et du commerce des nations neutres pendant la guerre, considerée selon le droit des gens universel, celui de l'europe, et les traités* (London: Thomson Gale, 1780), 9.
5. Ibid.
6. E. Jouannet, *The Liberal-Welfarist Law of Nations: a History of International Law* (Cambridge: Cambridge University Press, 2012), 137.
7. R. Ward, *An Enquiry into the Foundation and History of the Law of Nations in Europe from the Time of the Greeks and Romans, to the Age of Grotius*, 2 vols. (Dublin: P. Wogan, P. Byrne, W. Jones and J. Rice, 1795), 24.
8. M. W. Janis, 'Jeremy Bentham and the Fashioning of International Law', *The American Journal of International Law* 78 (1984): notes 52 and 53.
9. J. Pitts, 'Empire and Legal Universalisms in the Eighteenth-Century', *The American Historical Review* 117 (2012): 195.
10. P. Kleingeld, 'Kant's Second Thoughts on Colonialism', in K. Flikschuh and L. Ypi (eds), *Kant and Colonialism: Historical and Critical Perspectives* (Oxford: Oxford University Press, 2014), 43.
11. A. Orakhelashvili, 'The Idea of European International Law', *European Journal of International Law* 17 (2006): 315–47.
12. J. E. Hall, 'Tracts on the Constitutional Law of the United States', *The American Law Journal* 6 (1817): 583.
13. B. M Ziegler, *The International Law of John Marshall* (Chapel Hill: University of North Carolina Press, 1939), 46.
14. H. Wheaton, *History of the Law of Nations in Europe and America: from the Earliest Times to the Treaty of Washington* (New York: Gould, 1845), 327.
15. E. Dussel, 'Philosophy in Latin America in the Twentieth Century: Problems and Currents', in E. Mendieta (ed.), *Latin American Philosophy Currents, Issues, Debates* (Bloomington: Indiana University Press, 2003), 15.
16. J. Lund, 'Barbarian Theorizing and the Limits of Latin American Exceptionalism', *Cultural Critique* 47 (2001): 76.

17. G. A. De La Reza, 'América en la hora del Congreso Anfictiónico de Panamá', *Documentos sobre el Congreso Anfictiónico de Panamá* (Caracas: Fundación Biblioteca Ayacucho, 2010).

18. 'How beautiful it would be if the Isthmus of Panamá could be for us what the Isthmus of Corinth was for the Greeks! Pray to God that someday we may have the good fortune to convene there an august assembly of representatives of republics, kingdoms, and empires to deliberate upon the high interests of peace and war with the nations of the other three-quarters of the globe'. In reply of a South American to a gentleman of this Island (Jamaica). See S. Bolivar, *Selected Writings of Bolivar*, Lewis Bertrand (trans.) (New York: Colonial Press, 1951).

19. I. González Niño, *Simón Bolívar, precursor del derecho internacional americano* (Bogotá: Instituto Colombiano de Estudios Latinoamericanos y del Caribe, 1985).

20. M. Mackenzie, *Los ideales de Bolívar en el derecho internacional americano* (Bogotá: Biblioteca del Ministerio de Gobierno, 1955).

21. See I. Jaksic, *Andrés Bello: la pasión por el orden* (Santiago de Chile: Editorial Universitaria, 2001), 323; L. Obregón, 'Construyendo la región americana: Andrés Bello y el derecho internacional', in B. González Stephan and J. Poblete (eds), *Andrés Bello y los estudios Latinoamericanos* (Pittsburgh, PA: Instituto Internacional de Literatura Iberoamericana, 2009), 189.

22. A. Bello, *Principios de derecho de jentes* (Santiago de Chile: Imprenta de la Opinión, 1832).

23. See J. L. Phelan, *El origen de la idea de América* (México: Universidad Nacional Autónoma de México, 1979).

24. C. Calvo, *Annales historiques de la revolution de l'amerique latine: accompagnees de documents a l'appui: de l'annee 1808 jusqu'a la reconnaissance par les etats europeens de l'independance de ce vaste continent* (Paris: A. Durand, 1864).

25. For a further analysis of the Berlin conference and its role in colonial management of Africa, see A. Anghie, *Imperialism, Sovereignty and the Making of International Law* (Cambridge: Cambridge University Press, 2007), 65–99.

26. J. Y. Limantour, *Memoria sobre la Vida y la Obra de D. Carlos Calvo* (Paris: Librería de la Vda. de C. Bouret, 1909), 16.

27. C. Calvo, *Le droit international théorique et pratique précédé d'un exposé historique des progrès de la science du droit des gens* (Paris: Librairie Nouvelle de Droit et de Jurisprudence, 1896), 383–412.

28. A. Álvarez, 'Origen y desarrollo del derecho internacional americano', in *Tercer Congreso Científico Latino Americano* (Rio de Janeiro, 1905). The essay was later modified and published as 'Le droit international américain, son origine et son évolution', in *Revue générale de droit international public* (Paris: A. Pedone, 1907), XIV:253. In the revised edition, the geography was broadened to include the US, and 'Latin America' was changed to 'America' so as to include the entire continent. In this early period he also published *American Problems in International Law* (New York: Baker, 1909), and *Le droit international américain: son fondement, sa nature: d'après l'histoire diplomatique des états du nouveau monde et leur vie politique et économique* (Paris: A. Pedone, 1910).

29. Álvarez, 'Origen y desarrollo del derecho internacional americano', 14–79.

30. A. Becker-Lorca, 'International Law in Latin America or Latin American International Law? Rise, Fall, and Retrieval of a Tradition of Legal Thinking and Political Imagination', *Harvard International Law Journal* 47 (2006): 283–305; J. L. Esquirol,

'Latin America', in A. Peters and B. Fassbender (eds), *Oxford Handbook on the History of Public International Law* (London: Oxford University Press, 2012), 553; O. Guardiola-Rivera, *What If Latin America Ruled the World? How the South Will Take the North through the 21st Century* (New York: Bloomsbury, 2010); L. Obregón, 'Latin American International Law', in J. D. Armstrong and J. Brunée (eds), *Routledge Handbook of International Law* (New York: Routledge, 2009), 154; C. Rodriguez-Garavito (ed.), *El derecho en América Latina: un mapa para el pensamiento jurídico del siglo XXI* (Bogotá: Siglo XXI Editores, 2011); J. M. Barreto, 'A Universal History of Infamy: Human Rights, Eurocentrism, and Modernity as Crisis', in *Critical International Law: Postrealism, Postcolonialism, and Transnationalism* (Oxford: Oxford University Press, 2014), 143; K. Sikkink, 'Latin Americans Countries as Norm Protagonists of the Idea of International Human Rights', *Global Governance* 20 (2014): 389–404.

31. J. T. Gathii. 'International Law and Eurocentricity', *European Journal of International Law* 9 (1998): 184–239.
32. L. Mälksoo, 'The History of International Legal Theory in Russia: a Civilizational Dialogue with Europe', *European Journal of International Law* 9 (2008): 211–32.
33. T. A. Taracouzio, *The Soviet Union and International Law: a Study Based on the Legislation, Treaties and Foreign Relations of the Union of Socialist Soviet Republics* (New York: Macmillan, 1935), xvi, 530.
34. E. A. Korovin, *Mezhdunarodnoye pravo perekhodnovo vremeni* [International law in the transition period] (Moscow: Izd. Kommunisticheskoi akademii, 1923).
35. E. B. Pashukanis, 'International Law', in P. Beirne and R. Sharlet (eds), *Selected Writings on Marxism and Law* (New York: Academic Press, 1980), 168–85.
36. S. B. Krylov, 'Les Nations Principales du Droit des Gens: (La doctrine soviétique du droit international)', *Recueil des Cours* 70 (1947): 415–22.
37. F. Kozhevnikov, 'Iz zapisok diplomata', in A. N. Vylegzhanin and Y. M. Kolosov (eds), *Rossia i mezhdunarodnoe pravo. Materialy mezhdunarodnoi konferentsii, posvyashtshennoi 100-letiu F.I. Kozhevnikova* (Moscow: MGIMO-Universitet, 2006), 27, 30. As cited in Mälksoo, 'History of International Legal Theory in Russia'.
38. G. I. Tunkin, *A Theory of International Law* (Cambridge, MA: Harvard University Press, 1974).
39. Mälksoo, 'History of International Legal Theory in Russia', 211–32.
40. See E. E. Seaton, *Tanzania Treaty Practice* (Oxford: Oxford University Press, 1973), cited by Gathii, 'International Law and Eurocentricity', 188.
41. F. C. Okoye, *International Law and the New African States* (London: Sweet and Maxwell, 1972).
42. Ibid., 211.
43. C. Landauer, 'Regionalism, Geography and the Institutional Legal Imagination', *Chicago Journal of International Law* 11 (2011): 557–95.
44. M. Bedjaoui, *Towards a New International Economic Order* (New York: Holmes and Meier, 1979), 110, cited by Gathii, 'International Law and Eurocentricity', 188.
45. A. Orford, 'Locating the International: Military and Monetary Interventions after the Cold War', *Harvard International Law Journal* 38 (1997): 443–85; Gathii, 'International Law and Eurocentricity', 208.
46. M. Bedjaoui, 'General Introduction', in *International Law: Achievements and Prospects* (Boston: Martinus Nijhoff, 1991), 7.

47. Ibid., 187.
48. Ibid., 189; F. Fanon, *The Wretched of the Earth* (1963; repr., New York: Grove Press, 2005), 119–99, describes how African elites undermined the political and economic goals of their own countries for selfish gain.
49. Gathii, 'International Law and Eurocentricity'.
50. M. W. Mutua, 'Limitations on Religious Rights: Problematizing Religious Freedom in the African Context', in J. D. van der Vyver and J. Witte (eds), *Religious Human Rights in Global Perspective* (Boston: Martinus Nijhoff, 1996), 417.
51. Anghie, *Imperialism*, 32–114.
52. Gatthi, 'International Law and Eurocentricity', 186n7.
53. R. P. Anand, *Origin and Development of Law of the Sea: History of International Law Revisited* (Leiden, Netherlands: Martinus Nijhoff, 1983).
54. Gathii, 'International Law and Eurocentricity', 186n7.
55. Anand, *Origin and Development of Law of the Sea*, 7–8.
56. T. Kamino, 'The Twenty Years' Crisis, 1919–1939: an Introduction of the Study of International Relations', in K. Shimizu, J. Ikeda, T. Kamino and S. Sato (eds), *Is There a Japanese IR? Seeking an Academic Bridge through Japan's History of International Relations* (Shiga, Japan: Afrasian Centre for Peace and Development Studies, Ryukoku University, 2008), 32.
57. Ibid., 22.
58. Ibid.
59. See J. Ikeda, 'Japanese Vision of International Society: an Historical Exploration', in Shimuzo et al., *Is There a Japanese IR?*, 26, esp. T. Sakai, *Kindai Nihon no Kokusai Chitsujo Ron* [The political discourse of international order in modern Japan] (Tokyo: Iwanami Shoten, 2007).
60. Kamino, 'Twenty Years' Crisis', 30.
61. Ibid.
62. Kaoru Yasui published five volumes on the Greater East Asia International Law. See, *inter alia*, K. Yasui, *Oushu Kouiki Kokusai-hou no Riron* [Theory of European regional international law] (Tokyo: Yuhikaku, 1942), and *Ōsyū Kōiki Kokusai Hō no Kiso Rinen* [Basic concepts on the European regional international law] (Tokyo: Yuhikaku, 1942).
63. S. Tabata, 'Kokusai-hou Chitsujo no Tagen-teki Kousei' [The pluralist structure of international legal order], *Kyoto Journal of Law and Politics* 47 (1942–43): 383–402 (Part 1), as cited in Kamino, 'Twenty Years' Crisis', 22; U. M. Zachmann, 'Race and International Law in Japan's New Order in East Asia (1938–1945)', in R. Kowner and W. Demel (eds), *Race and Racism in Modern East Asia: Western and Eastern Constructions* (Leiden, Netherlands: Brill, 2012), 469.
64. S. Hatano, 'Sumio Kokka Byoudou ron wo Koete – Daitoua Kyouei-ken no Kokusai-hou Chitsujo wo Meguru Katto' [Beyond the theory of sovereign equality – on international legal order of the greater East Asian co-propensity area], in T. Asano and T. Matduda (eds), *Shokuminchi Teikoku Nihon no Houteki Tenkai* [The legal development of imperial Japan] (Tokyo: Shinzansha, 2004), as cited in Shimizu et al., *Is There a Japanese IR?*.
65. J. Ikeda, 'Japanese Vision of International Society a Historical Exploration', 18.
66. See Kamino, 'Twenty Years' Crisis'.
67. Ikeda, 'Japanese Vision of International Society a Historical Exploration'.

68. B. Rajagopal, 'International Law and Its Discontents: Rethinking the Global South', *Proceedings of the Annual Meeting of the American Society of International Law* 106 (2012): 176–81.
69. Ibid.
70. Examples of such revolts are the Haitian revolution, the nineteenth-century labour movement, the women's movement and the anti-colonial revolutions of post–World War II.
71. Rajagopal, 'International Law and Its Discontents'.
72. Ibid., 181–82.
73. Koskenniemi, *From Apology to Utopia*, 156–57.
74. Ibid., 62.
75. Ibid., 480.
76. M. Koskenniemi, *The Gentle Civilizer of Nations: The Rise and Fall of International Law, 1870–1960* (Cambridge: Cambridge University Press, 2002), 9.
77. Ibid.
78. Ibid., 102.
79. M. Koskenniemi, 'Histories of International Law: Dealing with Eurocentrism', *Rechtsgeschichte* 19 (2011): 152–77.
80. Ibid., 158.
81. Ibid., 159.

Bibliography

Álvarez, Alejandro. *American Problems in International Law* (New York: Baker, 1909).

   Le droit international Américain. Son fondement, sa nature, d'après Álvarez, Alejandro l'histoire diplomatique des états du nouveau monde et leur vie politique et économique (Paris: A. Pedone, 1910).

   'Le droit international Américain – son origine et son évolution'. *Revue Générale De Droit International Public* 14 (1907): 253–404.

   'Origen y desarrollo del derecho internacional Americano'. In *Tercer Congreso Científico Latino Americano* (Rio de Janeiro, 1905).

Anand, Ram P. *Origin and Development of the Law of the Sea: History of International Law Revisited* (Leiden, Netherlands: Martinus Nijhoff, 1983).

Anghie, Antony. *Imperialism, Sovereignty and the Making of International Law* (Cambridge: Cambridge University Press, 2007).

Barreto, José-Manuel. 'A Universal History of Infamy: Human Rights, Eurocentrism, and Modernity as Crisis'. In Prabhakar Sing and Benoit Mayer (eds), *Critical International Law: Postrealism, Postcolonialism, and Transnationalism* (Oxford: Oxford University Press, 2014).

Becker-Lorca, Arnulf. 'International Law in Latin America or Latin American International Law? Rise, Fall, and Retrieval of a Tradition of Legal Thinking and Political Imagination'. *Harvard International Law Journal* 47 (2006): 283–305.

Bedjaoui, Mohammed. 'General Introduction'. In Mohammed Bedjaoui (ed.), *International Law: Achievements and Prospects* (Boston: Martinus Nijhoff, 1991).

Bello, Andrés. *Principios de derecho de jentes* (Santiago de Chile: Imprenta de la Opinión, 1832).

Bolívar, Simón. *Selected Writings of Bolívar*, Lewis Bertrand (trans.) (New York: Colonial Press, 1951).

Calvo, Carlos. *Annales historiques de la révolution de l'amérique latine: Accompagnées de documents à l'appui: De l'année 1808 jusqu'à la reconnaissance par les états Européens de l'indépendance de ce vaste continent* (Paris: A. Durand, 1864).

Le droit international théorique et practique précédé d'un exposé historique des progrès de la science du droit des gens (Paris: Librairie Nouvelle de Droit et de Jurisprudence, 1896).

Carty, Anthony. 'Convergences and Divergences in European International Law Traditions'. *European Journal of International Law* 11 (2000): 713–32.

de la Reza, Germán A. 'América en la hora del Congreso Anfictiónico de Panamá'. In *Documentos sobre el Congreso Anfictiónico De Panamá* (Caracas: Fundación Biblioteca Ayacucho, 2010).

Dussel, Enrique. 'Philosophy in Latin America in the Twentieth Century: Problems and Currents'. In Eduardo Mendieta (ed.), *Latin American Philosophy Currents, Issues, Debates* (Bloomington: Indiana University Press, 2003).

Esquirol, Jorge L. 'Latin America'. In Bardo Fassbender and Anne Peters (eds), *The Oxford Handbook of the History of International Law* (Oxford: Oxford University Press, 2012).

Fanon, Frantz. *The Wretched of the Earth* (1965; repr., New York: Grove Press, 2005).

Gathii, James T. 'International Law and Eurocentricity'. *European Journal of International Law* 9 (1998): 184–211.

Gonzalez Niño, Ivonne. *Simón Bolívar, Precursor Del Derecho Internacional Americano* (Bogotá: Instituto Colombiano de Estudios Latinoamericanos y del Caribe, 1985).

Guardiola-Rivera, Oscar. *What If Latin America Ruled the World? How the South Will Take the North through the 21st Century* (New York: Bloomsbury, 2010).

Hall, John E. 'Tracts on the Constitutional Law of the United States'. *American Law Journal* 6 (1817): 583.

Ikeda, Josuke. 'Japanese Vision of International Society: a Historical Exploration'. In Kosuke Shimizu, Jousuke Ikeda, Tomoya Kamino and Shiro Sat (eds), *Is There a Japanese IR? Seeking an Academic Bridge through Japan's History of International Relations* (Shiga, Japan: Afrasian Centre for Peace and Development Studies, Ryukoku University, 2008).

Jaksic, Iván. *Andrés Bello: La pasión por el orden* (Santiago de Chile: Editorial Universitaria, 2001).

Janis, Mark W. 'Jeremy Bentham and the Fashioning of "International Law"'. *American Journal of International Law* 78 (1984): 405–18.

Jouannet, Emmanuelle. *The Liberal-Welfarist Law of Nations: a History of International Law* (Cambridge: Cambridge University Press, 2012).

Kamino, Tomoya. 'The Twenty Years' Crisis, 1919–1939: an Introduction of the Study of International Relations in Japan'. In Kosuke Shimizu, Jousuke Ikeda, Tomoya Kamino and Shiro Sat (eds), *Is There a Japanese IR? Seeking an Academic Bridge through Japan's History of International Relations* (Shiga, Japan: Afrasian Centre for Peace and Development Studies, Ryukoku University, 2008).

Kleingeld, Pauline. 'Kant's Second Thoughts on Colonialism'. In Katrin Flikschuh and Lea Ypi (eds), *Kant and Colonialism: Historical and Critical Perspectives* (Oxford: Oxford University Press, 2014).

Korovin, Evgenij A. *Mezdunarodnoe Pravo Perechodnogo Vremeni* (Moscow: Izd. Kommunisticheskoi akademii, 1971).

Koskenniemi, Martti. *From Apology to Utopia: the Structure of International Legal Argument*, reissue with a new epilogue (Cambridge: Cambridge University Press, 2005).

The Gentle Civilizer of Nations: the Rise and Fall of International Law 1870–1960 (Cambridge: Cambridge University Press, 2001).

'Histories of International Law: Dealing with Eurocentrism'. *Rechtsgeschichte* 19 (2011): 152–77.

Krylov, Sergeï; B. 'Les notions principales du droit des gens: (La Doctrine Soviétique Du Droit International)'. *Recueil des Cours* 70 (1947): 407–76.

Landauer, Carl. 'Regionalism, Geography, and the Institutional Legal Imagination'. *Chicago Journal of International Law* 11 (2010): 557–95.

Limantour, José Yves. *Memoria sobre la vida y la obra de D. Carlos Calvo* (Paris: Libreria de la Vda de C. Bouret, 1909).

Lund, Joshua. 'Barbarian Theorizing and the Limits of Latin American Exceptionalism'. *Cultural Critique* 47 (2001): 54–90.

Mälksoo, Lauri. 'The History of International Legal Theory in Russia: a Civilizational Dialogue with Europe'. *European Journal of International Law* 19 (2008): 211–32.

McKenzie, Mauricio. *Los ideales de Bolívar en el derecho internacional Americano* (Bogotá: Biblioteca del Ministerio de Gobierno, 1955).

Mutua, Makau wa. 'Limitations on Religious Rights: Problematizing Religious Freedom in the African Context'. In Johan D. van der Vyver and John Witte (eds), *Religious Human Rights in Global Perspective* (Boston: Martinus Nijhoff, 1996).

Obregón, Liliana. 'Latin American International Law'. In David Armstrong and Jutta Brunnée (eds), *Routledge Handbook of International Law* (New York: Routledge, 2009).

Obregón Tarazona, Liliana. 'Construyendo la región Americana: Andrés Bello y el derecho internacional'. In Beatriz Stephan González and Juan Poblete (eds), *Andrés Bello y los Estudios Latinoamericanos* (Pittsburgh, PA: Instituto Internacional de Literatura Iberoamericana, 2009).

Okoye, Felix C. *International Law and the New African States* (London: Sweet and Maxwell, 1972).

Orakhelashvili, Alexander. 'The Idea of European International Law'. *European Journal of International Law* 17 (2006): 315–47.

Orford, Anne. 'Locating the International: Military and Monetary Interventions after the Cold War'. *Harvard International Law Journal* 38 (1997): 443–85.

Pashukanis, Evgeny B. 'International Law'. In Piers Beirne and Robert Sharlet (eds), *Selected Writings on Marxism and Law* (New York: Academic Press, 1980).

Phelan, John L. *El origen de la idea de América* (Mexico: Universidad Nacional Autónoma de México, 1979).

Pitts, Jennifer. 'Empire and Legal Universalisms in the Eighteenth Century'. *The American Historical Review* 117 (2012): 92–121.

Rajagopal, Balakrishman. 'International Law and Its Discontents: Rethinking the Global South'. *Proceedings of the Annual Meeting of the American Society of International Law* 106 (2012): 176–81.

Riles, Annelise. 'Aspiration and Control: International Legal Rhetoric and the Essentialization of Culture'. *Harvard Law Review* 106 (1993): 723–40.

Rodríguez-Garavito, César. *El derecho en América Latina: un mapa para el pensamiento jurídico del siglo XXI* (Bogotá: Siglo XXI Editores, 2011).

Sikkink, Kathryn. 'Latin American Countries as Norm Protagonists of the Idea of International Human Rights'. *Global Governance* 20 (2014): 389–404.

Taracouzio, Timothy A. *The Soviet Union and International Law: a Study Based on the Legislation, Treaties and Foreign Relations of the Union of Socialist Soviet Republics* (New York: Macmillan, 1935).

Toze, Eobald. *La liberté de la navigation et du commerce des nations neutres pendant la guerre: consideree selon le droit des gens universel, celui de l'europe, et les traites* (London: Thomson Gale, 1780).

Tunkin, Grigoriï; I. *Theory of International Law* (Cambridge, MA: Harvard University Press, 1974).

Vec, Miloš. 'Universalization, Particularization, and Discrimination. European Perspectives on a Cultural History of Nineteenth Century International Law'. *InterDisciplines* 3 (2012): 79–102.

Ward, Robert P. *An Enquiry into the Foundation and History of the Law of Nations in Europe: from the Time of the Greeks and Romans, to the Age of Grotius* (Dublin: P. Wogan, P. Byrne, W. Jones and J. Rice, 1795).

Wheaton, Henry. *History of the Law of Nations in Europe and America: from the Earliest Times to the Treaty of Washington* (New York: Gould, 1845).

Yasui, Kaoru. *Kokusai Hō No Kiso Rinen* [Basic concepts on the European regional international law] (Tokyo: Yuhikaku, 1942).

Oushu Kouiki Kokusai-Hou No Riron [Theory of European regional international law] (Tokyo: Yuhikaku, 1942).

Zachmann, Urs M. 'Race and International Law in Japan's New Order in East Asia: 1938–1945'. In Rotem Kowner and Walter Demel (eds), *Race and Racism in Modern East Asia: Western and Eastern Constructions* (Leiden, Netherlands: Brill, 2013).

Ziegler, Benjamin M. *The International Law of John Marshall* (Chapel Hill: University of North Carolina Press, 1939).

Epilogue

To Enable and Enchant – on the Power of Law

MARTTI KOSKENNIEMI

What a variety of themes, standpoints and arguments – history and method, formalism, indeterminacy and critique, relations between theory and practice, and the nature of international law as 'work'. Because there is no reason to expect critical resolution of the many questions raised, let me instead try to think with the contributors about two themes that unavoidably lie at the centre of many of the essays – the themes of language and power. As the editors observe, much of my own work has been about those themes, about the power of the idiom of international law. This may be conveniently divided into two types. One is the *enabling power* law possesses, transforming the raw exercise of influence into (lawful) authority, making power appear acceptable, legitimate. But law also enables challenging authority, showing the limits to rulership. To speak law is an act of power, and lawyers, as native language-speakers of law, are powerful men and women. As language, law also has another kind of power. I call this its *enchanting power*. Law makes us believe things to be right or wrong, true or false. This power is also exercised by lawyers when they speak law; they are the guardians of the legal right and true. But it is also exercised by law on lawyers themselves, trained to say 'this must be done because it is what the law says'. The fact that a lawyer *chooses* to read the law in this way (for example, in the way their colleagues *usually* read it) is made invisible. The appearance is created that 'law' itself decides what is authoritative and what is not, how social hierarchies should be organized and scarce resources distributed. Many of the above essays enquire about law's enabling and enchanting power. Through methodological or jurisprudential analysis, they flag the importance of sociology, theology or international relations for a better understanding of how (international) law operates in the world: what does it stand for, and what against? This throws a welcome light on law's power and the extent to which my texts may have illuminated it. In this brief epilogue I am interested in the contribution they make into *critical analysis* over the effects law has as

393

an enabling and enchanting devise in a profoundly unjust international world.

For that purpose, I will link the essays to an ongoing legal-political theme that raises issues of relevance for the practice of international law and for thinking about how we are governed and what kind of a world law helps to build. I mean the construction of a global investment regime in ongoing international negotiations about the Transpacific and Transatlantic 'Partnership' Treaties (TPP and TTIP), an emerging network of international instruments inspired by the view that expansion of free trade and investment would, to quote freely from the website of the European Union, be likely to intensify economic activity across the globe and thus spread employment, generate welfare and contribute to the spread of liberal values. The rule of law is also flagged, especially with respect to the planned investor-state 'dispute settlement system' (ISDS). Some even regard an arbitration system a *sine qua non* because only this (and not for example domestic courts, assumed to be biased in favour of their states) can guarantee the impartial implementation of the regime (as if bias for the "international" were not a bias at all).

The above essays do not mention these treaties. Their focus was – that was their brief, too – to concentrate on the general, methodological aspects of international law through my oeuvre. But I would think it worrying if nothing could be derived from them for thinking about a global investment regime under construction. And of course they do imply a number of things from the problematization of the idea of the 'rule of law' to the details of a legitimate negotiating regime, from the role of ethics and argument in the arbitration process to whether attention to the *longue durée* might help us better understand the project's significance. Issues of formalism and instrumentalism abound. Is a 'shared understanding' being formed in the process as discussed by Brunnée and Toope as well as Nigel White? Will the outcome be efficient? – A concern flagged by Posner. What about the relations of investment law to the environment and development, the topic of Jaye Ellis? Have lawyers turned into 'policy-wonks' or is the debate just a (Schmittean) antagonism, concerns voiced by Kratochwil and Dyzenhaus? The essays by Marks and Lang and Singh query about moral agency or the very 'subjectivity' manifested on the different sides while Moyn, Orford and Obregón invite us to think about the historical frame to understand investment law's political implications. Rajkovic poses the question about the worth of the legal and international relations idioms through which to assess an phenomenon such as investment law as well as reactions to it, while Mégret and Noll shift the reader's attention to the value of the sociology of knowledge and Catholic theology for our understanding of the depth of the protagonists' feelings.

Law's power to enable and to enchant is visible everywhere in the debates on investment law. Like law in general, it is a place for contrasting understandings of the world, different values and priorities. Many actors are no doubt served while others feel their values threatened. If critical thinking has a contribution to make, it is above all to making the speakers of law aware of the commitments this entails. Some of them are freely chosen, others come as part of operating in the legal idiom, as part of law's enchanting effect. The above essays distinguish between the 'inside' and the 'outside' – the uses of legal language and the way we occasionally reflect on such uses. The idioms of participation and analysis are different but influence each other, and many of the above essays examine just how they do this. I am delighted that international law has become a place for critical reflection on 'practice' and 'theory'. We know today that it does not stand automatically for a blueprint of a just society. Instead, it is a platform for conflicting purposes, part of the struggles of the world. A critical study of law is an examination of how its enabling and enchanting effects influence that struggle and what kind of a world it helps to build around us.

1

Many of the essays take up the role of international law as a symbolic order facilitating the work of international governance. On the one hand, as Nigel White, Jaye Ellis as well as Jutta Brunnée and Stephen Toope stress, international law enables communication between actors pursuing different and sometimes outright opposite agendas. This is the enabling face of the international legal idiom, easy to point out as an account of the service it offers for those not joined by immediate solidarity. Enabling hides enchantment. To what extent does communication create or sustain a 'shared understanding'? Critical analysis would suggest that a bargain may appear 'shared' because the agents have learned to respect each other's preferences or because the weaker party no longer has resources to challenge it; 'consensus' at an international conference means that a weak party simply has to yield. Or perhaps it marks a moment when parties draw a breath in order to challenge the hegemonic view as soon as they feel strong enough. I agree with the 'interactional' theory that following (Fullerian) 'practices of legality' may sometimes lead into 'genuinely' shared understandings. They are valuable as criteria for a just process even when they hide incomprehension, bad faith or contrasting substantive understandings. But psychological access to whether something is 'genuinely' shared is not open to observers and the hermeneutics of suspicion that inspires critical analysis reminds us that a variety of 'subjective' and 'objective' techniques will ensure the endless possibility of interpretative discord. In the end whether an understanding will be challenged is a function of time, resources and the intensity of participant perception of their interests. What critical analysis would add to the interactional view is a reminder that a hegemonic understanding builds on a history of conflict its participants will remember when they finally come to choose its implications for policy.

No doubt, the proposed investor-state dispute settlement may embody practices of legality – the public debate has focussed on transparency, consistency, coherence and other matters important for the interactional theory. Through the accumulation of cases of investment arbitration a certain 'culture of legality' may emerge that might indeed socialize participants in certain preferences so as to 'create[] a continuing possibility of a Rule of Law'. This is how proponents of investment arbitration, too, argue. If disputes between host states and investors were not decided by 'impartial' arbitrators, 'politics' would overtake the process (and 'politics' is bad). The power of enchantment is at play. Recourse to the technical vocabulary of investment law neutralizes the jurisdictional politics of shifting power to elite insiders in the ICSID system under the World Bank where conflict is translated into expert calculations about commensurate 'welfare gains'. The rule of law means many things and the choice to imagine it as 'balancing' between corporate interests and domestic priorities (as imagined by outsiders) is hardly 'neutral'. Even the meticulous proceduralism of investment arbitration fails to explain how the interests of domestic constituencies can be translated into 'legitimate regulatory interest' without assuming the presence of a global language of 'legitimacy' whose authoritative speakers would be just those actors whose power it is designed to justify and consolidate.

Dyzenhaus worries over a purely strategic notion of (critical) law that appears to make no distinction between power and authority and gives no good reason to believe in anything being 'shared'. For him, indeterminacy appears both political and threatening, or threatening *because* political. But I certainly do not think that, as he suggests, if there is no 'objectively verifiable' legal control, then there is no law. Dyzenhaus writes that if, during the Iraq war, neither France nor the US had 'the force of the better argument', then 'in the result it was politics of force that resolved and had to resolve the disagreement'. This is both true and false. It is true in the trivial sense that in the end, force won, Americans attacked and there still is no end in sight to the disaster that ensued. But it is wrong in the assumption – that few international lawyers would share – that there has to be one standpoint, preferably a court, that would determine, for all concerned, where the force of the better argument lay. There almost never is such. International lawyers argue towards a variety of audiences that take different views on questions such as the Iraq war. The goodness of arguments depended and continues to depend on the audience or the institution, operating as any institution does, by reference to its embedded bias. This kind of perspectivism in no way denies the distinction between power and authority. On the contrary, it relies on some arguments being better than other arguments while focussing on the process that make institutions decide one way or another: what does it 'take' for an institution to believe the Iraq war either 'lawful' or 'illegal'? But it denies the aspect of enchantment: that authority would exist like medieval political theology's 'invisible crown' that proved the genuineness of the material crown on the king's head for all concerned.[1] Power is 'authority' by reference to some systemic set of propositions, as institutionally understood in some context, for the moment. I become a closet Schmittean for Dyzenhaus because of the two-value logic of his analytical toolkit: either it *is* law or then it is *not*. But just as light can be both waves and particles, depending on how you look at it, and the theory of relativity suggests that things may be both identical and non-identical with themselves, a deep critique not only deconstructs purportedly shared understandings but also decentres the critics' own preferences, creating awareness of the way symbolic orders tend to fix identities (such as 'lawyer' or 'good legal argument') for the purposes of other people's agendas. Against a political theory that thinks abstractly about the value of normative arguments, seeking coherence and logical fit, critical analysis in no way denies the value of legal normativity but situates it as an element of institutional decision making, a social practice where loyalty to one's political intuitions is constantly negotiated as against the biases of the institutions where one is called upon to work.

2

The theme of the 'culture of formalism' is unsurprisingly flagged in many of the essays. How does it link with the critique of 'indeterminacy'? Does it, as Rajkovic suggests, embody a 'descent into a Pantheon mentality' enabling elite jurists to employ false classical metaphors for the defence of their jurisdictional privileges? Of course nothing can intrinsically prevent that. When in January 2015, a group of British law firms and connected actors set up the 'European Federation for Investment Law and Arbitration, EFILA', all speakers in its inaugurating conference spoke in the name of legalism and the rule of law. By moving investor-state claims from domestic institutions and diplomatic processes to arbitration between a handful of individuals that specialize in such cases, elite jurists are empowered, their practices are glorified as 'rule of law', a 'Pantheon mentality' does become visible. But when I came upon the notion of 'culture of formalism' in the *Gentle Civilizer*, the point was to give a name to an experience where enchanting expressions such as 'rule of law', 'impartiality', 'fairness' and even 'human rights' also appear as shallow disguises for power and privilege. I wanted to examine the possibility of a legal practice beyond the purely strategic, or one that even if it were described as 'strategic' (which is what the hermeneutic of suspicion does), was not necessarily committed to the hegemonic view but instead interested in a complex and plural understanding of the normative issue. I wanted to query why most people, when reading the account of the debate between the lawyers defending the US government intervening in the Dominican Republic in 1965 and Wolfgang Friedmann feel sympathy with the latter as he notices that his adversaries reconstruct the law in defence of US foreign policy goals. Does the sympathy merely arise from anti-American bias? What role plays Friedmann's background as a jurist forced to flee his native Germany in 1933? Both may have been significant but I think most of the sympathy was engendered by the assumption underlying his opponents' position that international law's point was to assist US foreign policy – as if that policy were self-evident and merely mentioning it would stop the conversation, as if law were but a wink and a nod among specialists playing a game to placate an audience but of no relevance for doing what 'a man's gotta do'. To the extent that readers felt sympathy with Friedmann, I wanted to characterize him as a representative of 'culture of formalism', but did not want to *define* that expression more closely (though, as many contributors noticed, ideals about 'fidelity' to the law's proceduralism played a part). As Wittgenstein suggested, it is often better not to define but to *show* what one means. Lang and Marks are right to argue that the point of such stories is about emulation, what they define as an effort to 'recover[] a moralised sensibility and commitment to responsible agency that existed in former times'. Although 'responsible agency' was surely the point of the example, I am wary of the suggestion that 'former times' are its privileged repository. That connotation bears a moralist conservatism that may have inspired Rajkovic to suggest that what he calls my 'counterdisciplinarity' project was actually a conservative move to defend entrenched privilege against all that is new and innovative in political science. I hope that is not the case. Like any professional sensibility, 'formalism' can have many uses – at least as many as 'anti-formalism'. I wanted to tell the story of Friedmann in 1965 for the same reason I now want to highlight investment arbitration: to avoid speaking in abstractions so as to keep the relations of legal language and power constantly in view.

My critique of the political science enterprise, referred to in many of the essays, has to do precisely with its preference for a theoretical language that *obscures* those relations. Who has not heard countless PhD students complain about their being instructed to write on such abstractions as 'liberalism', 'realism', 'constructivism' etc. – when what brought them to the field was interest in some real phenomenon, event or process in the international world. I wanted to attack the endless flow of 'IR' books from major academic publishers subordinating events or processes to mere evidence about the correctness *vel non* of some such 'ism'. The particular would be interesting only to the extent it can be made to lose its particularity and translated into an incident of methodological abstraction; the mastery of that abstraction, students are then told, will make them masters of that particular, too. The struggle between law and political science as expert vocabularies is about the power of language: what is made visible and what gets lost? Where Rajkovic suggests that international relations is 'orientalized' by critical legal thought, ruling boldly over the academic centre, this clever but wholly counter-intuitive suggestion can be sustained only because of the enchanting abstraction of his argument.

I am interested in the power of this language – and the status of its attendant 'knowledge'. Who produces it and who finances it? Which are its privileged research projects? Answers to these questions do not at all produce an image of the exotic but of the mundane and ubiquitous.[2] A better reference than Said's *Orientalism* might be his *Culture and Imperialism* that accounts for the way theoretical abstraction operates at the service of an ideological machinery for which anything particular is interesting only as raw material for some commensuration under a global calculus, such as investment arbitration. Twenty years ago, Said wrote of the US academy's service to US policy as follows: 'Policy-oriented intellectuals have internalized the norms of the state which, when it calls them to capital, in effect becomes their patron. The critical sense is then conveniently jettisoned'.[3]

Something like this was also Friedmann's concern. Today it is more appropriate to point to the intellectuals' service not to the US but to a wholly
global system of power and knowledge where Julian Benda's concern
over how 'vocation' loses out for the instant gratification of 'influence',
referenced by Said, remains pertinent. What we witness is 'the process
of regulation and force by which cultural hegemony reproduces itself,
pressing even poetry and spirit into administration and the commodity
form'.[4] Proclaiming himself interested in 'resisting the vast penetration of
neo-liberal thought across the humanities and social sciences' Rajkovic
surely has reason to feel orientalized, but not by the 'culture of formalism'.
Glancing over his shoulder at fellow travellers in 'IR', Rajkovic would find
men and women of methodological abstraction – modelling, rational
choice, efficiency calculation, busily measuring, interviewing, predicting
and classifying so as to enlist the power of scientific vocabularies to reach
the prince's ear. When Posner engages in 'empirical analysis' of the effect
of human rights treaties – and concludes that those treaties have no effect
because so few of their signatories have turned into liberal-democratic
states – the project and problem of 'social science analysis' becomes clear.
Whoever thought it was the point of human rights to support 'liberal
democracy'? Empirical studies invariably presume that norms are clear
(i.e. that they aim to bring about 'liberal democracy') and all that is
needed is a study of whether that outcome is being produced. To study
the effect, the 'cause' must be held stable. But norms – including human
rights norms – are open-ended, amenable to contrasting interpretations
and to the support of contradictory agendas. Nobody is ever 'empirically'
not complying – everyone will argue for an exception or an unorthodox
of manner of complying. Beneath its empirical jargon, positivist social
science imposes its unacknowledged values and choices on the world that
it seeks to rule in the name of what it thinks of as incontestably 'real'.

Busily reorganizing the intellectual deck chairs on the Titanic of a
wholly positivistic discipline Rajkovic may indeed feel that onlookers on
passing vessels are overly absorbed in 'the perennial sanctity of perceived
turf'. One feels sympathy for his wish to escape. If there is hope for shared
projects with a critical edge, this must begin by focussing on the powers of
enchantment offered by disciplinary mores and their relationship to the
structures of global governance that distribute research funding together
with political priorities. Critiques of legalism are invaluable in showing
law as a politically engaged enterprise. In Germany at the beginning of
the twentieth century, and then in Scandinavia and in the US, jurists
frustrated with the techniques of conceptual deduction in what Duncan

Kennedy instructed us to call 'classical legal thought' produced radical, sociologically and psychologically sensitive techniques for understanding the role of law and legal decision making. Although Posner is right to identify the culture of formalism as being born out of 'critique of social scientific methods', it is also deeply informed by those methods so that the question is never whether to occupy a perspective from social theory or political science but *what sort of social theory or political science one should practice?* The question is not only (though it is that too) about how to count the consequences of any action but what count as 'consequences' and for whom, how they should be evaluated and how to deal with incommensurate scales of evaluation. People experience regimes and institutions differently; whose experience counts and how they are measured is an aspect of political value and bias that must be examined by other vocabularies. Empirical studies on TTIP and TPP differ on whether welfare gains or welfare losses ought to be foreseen and which constituencies' experience should be taken as the point of reference. The difficulty is not so much choosing the right model but identifying the preferences with which 'welfare' is associated and then deciding between them. This requires democracy, of course, precisely the sort of public debate geared to local concerns and decision-processes that the global organization of investment and investment law seek to liberate themselves from. Empirical studies on welfare point in different directions owing to difficulties in interpreting the data underlying the models. That is not an objection to producing them, only to the belief that they would be policy-determining on their own right.

3

So I agree with Fred Mégret that there is need for a properly sociological understanding of international law and international relations in their different 'fields'. What are the biases and commitments of the idioms of trade and investment, for example, or of environment, security and human rights? Kratochwil's examination of professionalism and expertise as systems of knowledge with inherent preferences is an important opening – as he knows – to the study of fragmentation of international law as well. As has been pointed out in many places, fragmentation is not a technical problem but a deliberate consequence of struggle for authority. New legal idioms – such as 'investment law' – put forward new types of knowledge that then present themselves as the new cutting edge ready to be enlisted for policy. Take a group of investment lawyers and a group of environmental lawyers. Each possesses a highly professionalized vocabulary; each knows some things about the world (but fails to know, or at least believe other things), and with the strength of that knowledge buys its access into influential institutions. Indeed, it could not be otherwise. *Not* to share the knowledge *and* the project of the profession is not to be an 'expert' in the expected sense of seeking to make an impact – being a 'problem-solver' in a world where what count as 'problems' are externally given and conclusively determinative of what legitimate intellectual work should consist in.

A of sociology of knowledge that examines the effects of 'discipline' and expertise on the politics of international law is necessary to grasp the political meaning of 'globalization'. It may not even matter so much which types of substance get to be professionalized as long as the body from which powerful institutions draw their data is produced within accepted forms of professionalism speaks the day's jargon. Kratochwil suggests that when law is conceived as expertise and lawyers as 'policy-wonks', managerialism has already taken over; autonomy and legitimate political contestation, plus the sense of choice and responsibility have already collapsed. The struggle of incompatible values, Weber's iron cage of a modern world of struggle and compromise would be over, as would democracy as anything more than local 'regulation' of economic activity – the dystopian image projected in the debates on investment arbitration. Kratochwil and Rajkovic are both dubious about the possibility or resuscitating of a humanist professionalism where something like 'commitment' or 'vocation' (dare I write 'culture of formalism'?) could counter-balance managerialism. I wonder how 'interactional theory' might react to this predicament? Anyway, they are right that mere professional ethics is not the way out; it is fine to sympathize with Friedmann-like individuals lost in a world of 'policy-wonks'. But nothing in world changes by ethics-codes. Which large transnational corporation fails to have one? 'Arbitrator ethics' softens the iron hand of global governance but contributes to the ubiquitous translation of social problems into issues of individual consciences. It will then ignore the way those consciences are produced by historical and institutional structures, systems or knowledge and practice. To aim at those systems is to have learned the lessons of the best of critical sociology, indispensable in a serious examination of international law's enabling and enchanting roles.

The task is to try to see present legal professionalism in its context, to understand what the world that legal professionalism thrives in is like. There are many ways to think about this but here would one. Some time ago, a report was released by Oxfam according to which in 2014, the richest 1 per cent of human beings owned 48 per cent of global wealth, and by 2016 the richest 1 per cent would own more than the remaining 99 per cent. The trend is for the leading elite to become completely independent from anything outside its own magic realm.[5] The most important decisions about economy and society will then made by a class leading a wholly 'global life' that has no relationship – least of all a relationship of responsibility – to any really existing human community. This is the context in which projects such as the TTIP or TPP also become understandable. They are not just about the more than 300 cases of ISDS arbitration – did the arbitrators interpret the 'fair and equitable treatment' standard justly? Was the territorial state awarded sufficient room for legitimate policy-objectives (as if it were for a small group of jurists to determine this)? The right context in which to understand the law of international investment is the historical continuum where the complex of hierarchies and patterns called 'the economy' has striven to free itself from any local system of legislation or government, where it has sought to become the single standard through which all else is measured.[6]

Investment law, human rights law and environmental law – these are incompatible fields of expertise in constant competition for authority, for being able to say 'I am the law, I am the general regime'. The chapter by Jaye Ellis deals with such conflict – in her case, especially that of trade and health, as represented in the generic drugs problem by the TRIPS and WHO regimes. She agrees about the dangers of instrumentalization, that the preferences of the one or the other regime should be taken as given. With reference to the works by Teubner and Fischer-Lescano she suggests, however, that law's procedural turn might enable it to mediate between such systems, create a *modus vivendi* between them. As she notes, the problem is often (including in investment law) that participants invoke conflicting technical information. Might law have 'stop rules' that indicate where the potentially interminable argument should stop? Although I appreciate the search for the legal proprium in such procedural devises, I wonder about them in the international world. In the domestic context, courts do carry out mediating functions. But there are no courts 'of the sovereign' in the international world that could mediate, say, between health and environmental interests, the interests of investors and those of the state. The 'legal' is always already infected with the regime-rationale of which it is a part. Is it a human rights body or a trade institution? Has it been set up in the European Union or does it work for some global institution that is occupied with a substance? In the case of disputes between states and foreign investors, the forum is either a state court or an ISDS body. The relevant political choice is the choice of jurisdiction: who should decide? Once that is known, we already have a pretty good idea of what the decision will be. Occasionally, regimes are able to supersede their regime-rationale – a trade tribunal might use a human rights treaty, for instance. But I agree with Alston about the dangers of such 'merger and acquisition', the grasp of authority by trade experts to speak on human rights (or the other way around).[7] An investment arbitration tribunal may of course occasionally, perhaps even frequently, celebrate the state's 'right to regulate'. But in so doing it will raise itself as the authority on where the limits of such authority lie, and who should adjudicate instances of its use.

I am increasingly wary of the gesture of labelling as 'politics' all that cannot be accounted for by reference to rules or procedures of expert decision making and the connected strategy – familiar from much Left history in the academy – to call for 'openly political' decision making, typically by bodies by general representation. The gesture relies on the (positivist) idea that questions of value ('politics') and fact ('expert knowledge) are to be treated separately. Instead it seems necessary to me to re-describe professionalism and the various expert languages as *already political*. We see this in the way every discipline is always already divided against itself, between an orthodox mainstream and one or more forms of heterodox challenge. What becomes the hegemonic view is the result of complex disciplinary moves that are sure to lead to its becoming overcome sooner or later. One problem with disciplinary thinking lies in the presupposition of professionalism as closed or homogenous when, after little scratching on the surface it will reveal itself as open-ended and insecure, based on assumptions that are routinely contested within the profession itself. To believe otherwise is to suggest that professional men and women are not really responsible for their choices, but only 'doing their job' – a version of the jurisprudence of 'one right answer'. Investment law may be a complex form of expertise – but it is no less political for that reason.

4

Looking back at the last chapter of the *Gentle Civilizer*, I agree with Moyn that there never was any single American attitude to international law, neither after 1776, 1945 nor 2001. The view of the US as the bulwark of international legality is as much an ideological concoction as the view of the US as the great devil. Outsiders, perhaps especially Europeans, have been keen to portray themselves by reference to some straw man image about what the US 'really' stands for. So I do not think that the US 'betrayed' values it had earlier embraced after 9/11. Its *Realpolitik* tendencies had always been mixed with moral rhetoric, from Morgenthau to Obama. As many have shown, a full-bloodied 'Realism' is not only compatible with but may even require the backing of a an attitude of normative rigour. Moyn is right that we still lack a good post-World War II history of international law, and especially one that would avoid the illusion that the 1990s constituted an exceptional moment of liberal opportunity, betrayed by the war on Iraq and everything that ensued.

Have I really given the impression that if only it were rightly understood, international law might save us? According to Moyn, if all we have is international law, 'then we are worse off than our ancestors'. I am not sure if we are actually *worse* off (that depends on who he might think of as our 'ancestors') but I certainly do not think international law is somehow essentially superior to traditional moral or political vocabularies. The (Left) neo-formalism at the end of the *Gentle Civilizer* was not put forward to save the world but to offer to international lawyers a way to think about their professional practices and institutions in a more meaningful way than standard academic accounts allowed. If the public in Europe nowadays tends to turn to international lawyers instead of going to church, that is a real problem both for the lawyers and their interlocutors (as well as for the church) but it is not something that can be wished away. I certainly do not believe that international law is, or should be, as Moyn puts it 'somehow central to political thought'. International lawyers have also not been well equipped for the care of souls. But it *is* central to the practice of the men and women who work with it at domestic and international institutions, sometimes making important choices and in desperate need of some way to think about the power and limits of their professional commitments and the role of moral and political responsibility.

I agree with Moyn that while international law had long remained in the margins of intellectual or political debates, in the post-1989 period it suddenly came to seem of altogether inflated significance. I was puzzled by this. There was a reason for why the *Gentle Civiliser* ended with an account of a *fall*. It may have been a mistake to discuss only the 'American discipline' of international relations as its successor – but I thought that the preceding chapters had sufficiently clearly demonstrated the forms and consequences of Europeans' moral escapism. In any case, in an essay years ago I tried to make the point that behind the self-gratulatory effort by the UN General Assembly to label the 1990s as a 'decade of international law' there was nothing: the rhetoric was empty.[8]

In her essay Anne Orford returns to the theme of the collapse of law to history as a result of the recent upsurge of interest in international legal histories. She accuses me of having, in my post-Gentle Civilizer texts, put forward a conservative agenda by embracing conventional contextualism, and joining historians' indictment of the 'sin of anachronism'. I thereby isolate the past from the present and condemn the making of moral or political judgements on it. I do not recognize myself in this critique. In a recent essay on precisely this theme I wrote that

> contextualism ... tends to rely on a 'positivist' separation between the past and the present that encourages historical relativism and end up suppressing or undermining efforts to find patterns in history that might account for today's experiences of domination and injustice.[9]

I agree with Orford that law is not history – even if I think she exaggerates the difference. Let me make three points. First, I think that international law has officially rejected any such 'pure' contextualism. In the *Namibia* case (1971), the International Court of Justice needed to interpret the expression 'sacred trust of civilization' in Article 22 of the Covenant of the League of Nations to characterize the mandates under the Covenant. South West Africa had been allocated as a 'mandate' to South Africa as part of the process whereby the colonies of Germany and Turkey were allocated to the victors. What did the expression 'sacred trust' mean? The Court held that 'an international instrument has to be interpreted and applied within the framework of the entire legal system in force at the time of its interpretation'.[10] With this statement – one of the most famous in its entire history – the Court drew a definite line between the colonial past and the post-colonial present. The time of paternalism, of development 'in the interests of the natives' under the purportedly benevolent eye of the 'civilized' world, would be over. In this way, the Court corrected the damage done by its notorious 1966 judgement where it had rejected a claim by Liberia and Ethiopia over the same subject matter. With its 1970 opinion the Court decided to read the words 'sacred trust' in view of the UN's new post-colonial sensibility, thus not only facilitating Namibia's entry into independence but also affirming international law's continued relevance in the new period. Whatever the expression 'sacred trust' might have meant for the (almost exclusively European) drafters of the provision in 1919 was not decisive for how it should be understood in 1970. If this was 'political jurisprudence', it was no more so than the 1966 judgement.

But it was political jurisprudence in support of equal rights and self-determination to former colonies. This was the better politics.

Second, there is little reason to fear (limited) contextualism, and much reason to embrace it, as Orford concedes. The suggestion that seeking to examine the past 'through their eyes' leads into conservatism assumes that to understand is always to excuse. But surely this is so only if the examiner's standpoint is so weak or so prone to relativism that there would anyway be little reason to trust their judgement. By contrast, not trying to understand past actors 'through their eyes' is surely just as arrogant an imposition as would be to dismiss an indigenous group's self-understanding because the anthropologist knows better. I have no doubt that Orford agrees and therefore our divergence (if there is such) is about how to operate with the limits of historical understanding. Orford argues that I 'do[] not fully address the analytical and political stakes of the turn to history'. But, and this is my third point, I think her insistence on the distinction between 'history' and 'law' goes too far. It compels her to think of history in such a profoundly contextual way that few historians would agree. Full contextualism is impossible just like full positivism is. The choice and interpretation of the 'context' take place from the perspective of today's interests. The process of interpretation-production is only controlled by the discipline of history in which some methods may be hegemonic, but great pluralism reigns. Among those are also critical and post-colonial histories that insist on the need to acknowledge the present-day concerns that illuminate the past – just like the International Court of Justice stated in *Namibia* case. If 'history' approaches 'law', so does 'law' in many ways approach 'history'. Working as a legal advisor, I often felt the advisor's task was to be a historian of the office. For the political decision maker, every situation was new. The lawyer's task was to show what was done five, fifteen, fifty years ago in an analogous situation (to great relief of the political decision maker who would frequently decide to do 'what we did then'). As academic fields of enquiry, law and history are of course different, they have different histories, agendas and methods. But they are also united in that one aspect of both is an effort to offer a platform in which the past and the present can be brought together in some discussion that enhances the understanding of our historicity as well as the choices we face.

Few items in today's law and politics are more in need of critical histori-cization than investment law. Orthodox narratives of the field refer to the establishment of the ICSID in the 1960s, and show the growth and increasing sophistication of the relevant case-law. The choice of context is that of free trade and globalization. A wholly different view would be received by focussing instead on the movements of capital from the mid nineteenth century into foreign territories and the protection of foreign investments by military and legal interventions. This history would demonstrate the increasing internationalization and enforcement of Western standards of economic behaviour and compel the conclusion Adam Smith long ago drew from his study of the growth of civil government, namely that,

> so far as it is instituted for the security of property, [such internationaliza-tion] is in reality instituted for the defense of the rich against the poor, or of those who have some property against those who have none at all.[11]

I completely agree with Orford's discussion of the effects of disciplinary history. Like sociology of knowledge, its initial impulse and effect were no doubt critical, providing a vocabulary and an external standpoint from which the practitioners could reflect on the commitments and put to question assumptions that cannot be questioned in practice because they form the conditions of its very possibility. But as she points out, that external perspective may itself become a 'discipline' like the one it has studied – with the exception however, that it would lack the *engagement* with the world that the discipline possessed. As standardized 'disciplinary history' it would simply follow the tricks of that trade, operating, as she puts it, 'in hermetic isolation from practice itself', potentially reducing professional work to object of ironic commentary.

5

Sahib Singh attacks the many antinomies and paradoxes that underlie a text such as *From Apology to Utopia*. One obvious antinomy has to do with the relation between subject and structure, the complexity of which is often addressed but perhaps too easily disposed of in the language of 'co-constitution' (not used by Singh, to his credit). The sense of nervous movement between the two poles is part of the human situation, hence the situation of the lawyer, too, worth thinking about though not in the mode of problem-solution. The paradox of community and domination is only a little less familiar, though its glaring absence from the inter-national legal consciousness, genuine or not, is one of the latter's more disturbing aspects. By contrast, awareness of the dangers in the search for a 'perfect' communal institution – the hermeneutic of suspicion – is a defining aspect of critical legal sensitivity. Singh is right to ascribe to it an ironic dimension, one hard to reconcile with the cultural commitments in international legal work but, I think, inseparable from a 'formalism' that is aware of its own limits. The many antinomies of freedom are likewise well-known to the critic as an aspect of a philosophy of the subject which, like the 'liberalism' or 'super-liberalism' it is often accompanied by, is deeply problematic at the level of philosophical statement. These antinomies, Singh rightly notes, 'are not idle intellectual musings' but provide critical thought in the sense of constant movement, the impossibility to 'stop' at any single place. As *Apology to Utopia* was intent on demonstrating, this was an absolutely central aspect of the international legal situation, too, of the toolbox that lawyers use to construct and operate their world of normative commitments.

But there is something about the concentration on the subject and identity that now seems to me, well, part of a world of the 1980s. The linguistic aspects of professional practices such as law now seem pretty obvious as does the way they constitute the legal subject's relationship to the world – a *world* that I think now calls for more attention than the observing subject. There is a certain lightness in the provisional resolution of the subject/structure antinomy in *From Apology* (the myth it weaves) that can perhaps be used to thinking critically about of the linguistic construction of the world of international lawyers. Political struggle is increasingly about the description and re-description of aspects of the world. Phenomena addressed today under the themes of 'governance', 'fragmentation' and 'constitutionalism' have to do with technical vocabularies competing over which is able to produce the most powerful description of the world. Once a description will 'stick' – that is to say, as soon as we have become accustomed to thinking about the world's problems in a particular way (as problems of 'efficiency', 'security', 'environment' or 'investment', say) then those who are its masters will possess authority on the world it purports to describe. The implication of this operation – perfectly natural and legitimate in itself – lies in the way change of language is accompanied by new truths and hierarchies and a re-distribution of values to fit the new description. It is perhaps symptomatic that Singh makes no mention of any current description of the international world but concentrates on aspects that we might think of as purely internal and subjective, hence 'eighties'. But I now think it more important to get on with critical work in the 'field', to examine the way things such as 'investment' operate like armies in the field of global struggle clashing against the rival troops of 'environment', 'human rights' or 'democracy', each with the ambition of turning itself into a ruling description, with all that this entails in institutional politics and division of resources. Perhaps it is the case that the contingency and politics of the 'truth' that underlies international governance cannot be critically grasped without a live sense of the contingency of the place the subject occupies in the prevailing structure of opportunities. If so, then the distance between the 'eighties' and now is not that great and that temporal dislocation marks merely another fruitful antinomy to be employed at the service of critical work.

Which is what is also suggested by Gregor Noll's analysis of 'gaps and incoherences'. I have no doubt more work should be done to examine the effects of the legal language, the symbolic of law, in 'disciplining' lawyers to a specific professional consciousness. The descriptions and re-descriptions of the world offered by law's symbolic order are the sea where lawyers are the fish, breathing through it, being carried by it through their lives as professional men and women of authority. To seek to set aside that symbolic universe is not a critical contribution to law, any more than it would be to say to fish that they should learn to fly. I think it would be wrong to simply dispense with international law altogether as the product of a colonialist history, a hopeless legitimizer of an unequal world. This would be insensitive to the lesson of indeterminacy that teaches us that whatever law has been or has done, is not owing to its intrinsic, essential features. People have *used* it in such ways. If staying with law, indeterminate as it is, is still something to be considered, that can only be, as Noll suggests, by understanding that it has no intrinsic authority, that it is a vocabulary that can go this way, but equally that. The law won't save anybody – but it might be possible to use it for a good purpose. The law's unending oscillation – apology to utopia, community to domination, subject to structure – will not change. The progress we hope for is not *within* law but can be accomplished *through* law. That is why hope of progress cannot be fully articulated within the symbolic order itself; it is about transgression and otherness, if not strictly otherworldliness, at least 'a fleeting sensation of transcendent normativity' as Noll writes. Perhaps I should finish by returning to Adam Smith who once wrote about 'justice' not as a theory or a program but something like a 'fleeting sensation' about a wrong having been committed.[12] His theory of moral sentiments may have emerged from a specifically eighteenth-century Scottish intellectual world. But its continuing critical power lies in the suggestion that law's virtue is recognizable in individual instances and 'feelings' more than in the day's rational discourses. Although he tried, Smith never succeeded in articulating that intuition in a new critical jurisprudence. Instead, he produced the *Wealth of Nations* (1776) as an analysis of commercial society and an indictment of the 'mercantile spirit'. The point is well known:

But the mean rapacity, the monopolising spirit of merchants and manufac-
turers, who neither are, nor ought to be, the rulers of mankind, though it
cannot perhaps be corrected, may very easily be prevented from disturbing
the tranquillity of any body but themselves.[13]

For Smith, the symbolic order of political economy could not contain
in itself the principles of its critique. It is no wonder that the relationship between his two books has remained enigmatic for interpreters.
The conversation between those two works, the normative desire and the
vicissitudes of a commercial world (utopia and apology?) continues to the
present, including in the effort to think about investment protection. It
may be doubted whether the bourgeois sentiments of Smith's world could
discipline the dark sides of commercial modernity. Surely we should now
be better placed than Smith to think about alternative vocabularies. Perhaps one of them is spoken by Noll's example, the Jesuit Erich Przywara,
though I remain agnostic about that. But I agree that critique (unlike mere
'criticism') requires escape from the pure immanence offered by systems
of governance that are professional talk all the way down. Another way
to put this is to acknowledge that critical law is perhaps not reducible to
abstract discourses, methods or 'principles' but identified by a gut feeling
about the way the injustice of the world is a *product* of its ruling symbolic
order and therefore cannot be treated through it.

Notes

1. See E. Kantorowicz, *The King's Two Bodies: a Study of Medieval Political Theology*
   (1957; repr., Princeton, NJ: Princeton University Press, 1997), 336–42.
2. One relatively recent study concluded that there existed 'a remarkable and growing
   consensus within the US academy that a positivist epistemology should guide IR
   research' and that 'when we look at the research that is published by the major
   journals, 90% of articles in 2006 were positivist, up from 58% in 1980'. D. Maliniak,
   A. Oakes, S. Peterson and M. J. Tierney, 'International Relations in the US Academy',
   International Studies Quarterly 55 (2011): 454. The dominance of this US research
   is recorded a many places. A classic is Ole Waever, 'The Sociology of a Not So
   International Discipline: American and European Developments in International
   Relations', *International Organization* 52 (1998): 687–727. Above all, however, in
   the literature on 'interdisciplinarity', the contribution of 'international relations'
   is very predominantly expected to be of the quantitative, rationalist and positivist
   type – while even what international law's contribution in those debates might be is
   anybody's guess.
3. E. W. Said, *Culture and Imperialism* (New York: Vintage, 1994), 303.
4. Ibid., 304.
5. See e.g. D. Dorling, *Inequality and the 1%* (London: Verso, 2014).

6. See my 'It's not the Cases, it's the System' 18 *Journal of World Trade and Investment* (2017, forthcoming)
7. P. Alston, 'Resisting the Merger and Acquisition of Human Rights by Trade Law: a Reply to Petersmann', *European Journal of International Law* 13 (2002): 815–44.
8. M. Koskenniemi, 'Between Commitment and Cynicism: Outline for a Theory of International Law as Practice', in *The Politics of International Law* (Oxford: Hart, 2011), 276–84.
9. M. Koskenniemi, 'Vitoria and Us: Thoughts on Critical Histories of International Law', *Rechtsgeschichte* 22 (2014): 124. I also preface that essay with an epigraph from one of her texts where she makes precisely that point, ibid., 119.
10. ICJ, *Namibia* case, Reports 1971, para. 53.
11. A. Smith, *The Wealth of Nations*, Books IV–V (1776; repr., London: Penguin 1999), V.1 (302).
12. A. Smith, *The Theory of Moral Sentiments* (1759; repr., New York: Barnes and Noble, 1979), II II (109–21).
13. Smith, *Wealth of Nations*, IV 3 (72).

Bibliography

Alston, Philip. 'Resisting the Merger and Acquisition of Human Rights by Trade Law: a Reply to Petersmann'. *European Journal of International Law* 13 (2002): 815–44.

Dorling, Danny. *Inequality and the 1%* (London: Verso, 2014).

Kantorowicz, Ernst. *The King's Two Bodies: a Study in Medieval Political Theology* (1957; repr., Princeton, NJ: Princeton University Press, 1997).

Koskenniemi, Martti. 'Between Commitment and Cynicism: Outline for a Theory of International Law as Practice'. In *The Politics of International Law* (Oxford: Hart, 2011).

'Vitoria and Us: Thoughts on Critical Histories of International Law'. *Rechtsgeschichte* 22 (2014): 119–38.

Maliniak, Daniel, Amy Oakes, Susan Peterson and Michael J. Tierney, 'International Relations in the US Academy'. *International Studies Quarterly* 55 (2011): 437–64.

Said, Edward W. *Culture and Imperialism* (New York: Vintage, 1994).

Smith, Adam. *The Theory of Moral Sentiments* (1759; repr., New York: Barnes and Noble, 1979).

The Wealth of Nations. Books IV–V (1776; repr., London: Penguin, 1999).

Waever, Ole. 'The Sociology of a Not So International Discipline: American and European Developments in International Relations'. *International Organization* 52 (1998): 687–727.

INDEX

413

Hobbes, Thomas, 41, 42
homo economicus, 29
House of Commons, 40–41
House of Lords, 40–41
Hull, Isabel, 342, 345–47
human cognition, limits of, 23–25
human rights, 121–34
democracy and, 125–26
evidence, 124–27
frequency of mention in legal
articles, 131–32
institutionalization of, 122
internationalization of, 123
Koskenniemi's writings on,
121–34
lack of respect for, explanations,
127–31
oppressive, 128
outcomes, 126–27
rights hypertrophy and, 128
treaty regimes and, 121
human rights law, 403–04
indeterminacy of, 131
moral values and, 123
human rights treaties, 400
continued entrenchment of,
130
failure of, 127–31
number of, 125
rights hypertrophy and, 128
humanitarian intervention, 139–40,
152, 225
humanitarian organizations,
244–45
humanity's law, 225, 344, 348
Hungary, 70, 125
Hunter, Ian, 301
Husserl, Edmund, 22

ICC. *See* International Criminal Court
(ICC)
ICCPR. *See* International Covenant on
Civil and Political Rights
(ICCPR)
ICSID. *See* International Centre for
Settlement of Investment
Disputes (ICSID)
identity, 213–15

IMF. *See* International Monetary Fund
(IMF)
imitation, 329–30, 333
immanent determinism, 269
imperialism, 349
indeterminacy of international law,
4, 7
culture of formalism and,
10–13
human rights and, 122
legal positivism and, 43–46
structuralism and, 201
India, 61, 126, 150
Indonesia, 126, 371
inequality, extreme, 138
inquiry, 78
Institut de Droit International (IDI),
285, 326, 332
institutional formalism, 42
instrumentalism, 28
intellectual history, 301–02
intelligence, 228
interactional international law,
140–41
interactional theory, 395–96
interdisciplinarity, 178, 183–85,
186–87
internal realism, 46–52
International Centre for Settlement of
Investment Disputes (ICSID),
407–08
International Court of Justice, 407
diplomacy and, 77
as forum for disputes, 77
International Covenant on Civil and
Political Rights (ICCPR),
126–27
international crimes, 72
International Criminal Court (ICC),
124, 149–50
international environmental law
counter-culture and, 97–100
culture and, 97–100
culture of formalism and, 108–09
environmental problem complexity
and, 93
transboundary harm and, 98–100
international governance, 395